uttwell served in France as
1st/4th Royal Berkshire Regiment, and later as an Intelligence Officer at the War Office.

He was Principal of Hertford College, Oxford, from 1930 to 1939 and was formerly a Fellow of All Souls College, Oxford. He died in 1942.

C.R.M.F. Cruttwell

A History of the Great War
1914–1918

SECOND EDITION

A PALADIN BOOK

GRANADA
London Toronto Sydney New York

Published by Granada Publishing Limited in 1982

ISBN 0 586 08398 7

First published in Great Britain by
Oxford at the Clarendon Press 1934
Second Edition 1936

Granada Publishing Limited
Frogmore, St Albans, Herts AL2 2NF
and
36 Golden Square, London W1R 4AH
866 United Nations Plaza, New York, NY 10017, USA
117 York Street, Sydney, NSW 2000, Australia
100 Skyway Avenue, Rexdale, Ontario, M9W 3A6, Canada
61 Beach Road, Auckland, New Zealand

Printed and bound in Great Britain by
Richard Clay (The Chaucer Press) Ltd,
Bungay, Suffolk

To the Memory of
CHARLES FLETCHER

ὁ δὲ πόλεμος ὑφελὼν τὴν εὐπορίαν τοῦ καθ' ἡμέραν βίαιος διδάσκαλος καὶ πρὸς τὰ παρόντα τὰς ὀργὰς τῶν πολλῶν ὁμοιοῖ. THUCYDIDES III. 82, § 2

'*War, which takes away the comfortable provision of daily life, is a hard master and tends to assimilate men's characters to their conditions.*'

(JOWETT'S TRANSLATION)

'*Sine justitia quid sunt regna nisi magna latrocinia?*'

ST. AUGUSTINE

PREFACE

THIS book, as its title implies, is a history of the War: it deals neither with its causes remote or immediate, nor with the so-called settlement which followed. It aims at presenting the general reader with an accurate, intelligible, and interesting account of the greatest conflict between civilized states.

The War is indeed passing rapidly into history. To the younger generation now growing up it has become but the remotest and vaguest of memories; the majority of undergraduates who will be coming to the Universities this autumn were born in its third year.

Moreover, the materials now at the disposal of the historian are of such a character that he may feel reasonably confident of being able to establish the truth, if not in every detail, at least in the broad outlines of his work. A large proportion of the principal actors on either side, both political and military, have published accounts of their stewardship. These naturally have a very varying value of reliability and ingenuousness, but in almost every instance they are fortified by official memoranda and secret documents, which show the contemporary grounds on which decisions were taken. In the defeated countries (particularly in Germany) commissions of inquiry have thrown much important light on many points. Though the official histories (with the exception of that of the British navy) have not yet been completed, it is improbable that any new disclosures of serious importance remain to be made.

I have endeavoured to keep a just proportion between the military, diplomatic, and political aspects, as also between the different theatres of war, and to prevent the reader from being lost in a mass of detail. No tactical analysis of the battles has been attempted, except where it illustrates a general principle of high importance.

It has been necessary ruthlessly to omit much which it would have been interesting to include. To take a few instances, no account is given of the campaigns in Africa, of the civil war and foreign interventions in Russia after the treaty of Brest-Litovsk, or of the Irish rebellion, while the internal history of the belligerent countries is very summarily and imperfectly sketched. As I am writing for English readers, the great 'side-shows' have been perhaps given more prominence than their intrinsic importance deserves. But as the controversy between Easterner and Westerner, still raging unabated, is mainly of British origin, it is important to follow the attempts made to strike at Germany through her weaker allies, and to estimate whether any opportunities were neglected of bringing the War to an earlier conclusion.

I have not given a bibliography, partly because I am not sure that it would be useful to the general reader, but mainly because I have called attention by footnotes at the appropriate passages to nearly a hundred and fifty books. This will probably be sufficient to glut most appetites.

This book owes much to the late C. R. L. Fletcher, to whose memory I have ventured to dedicate it. He had read through it all, with the exception of the naval chapters, when he was seized by his last illness. He was both the most exacting and kindest of critics, who habitually devoted to the works of others an enthusiasm and a laborious accuracy which many authors will hardly expend on their own creations. I also owe much gratitude to Mr. C. T. Atkinson, Fellow of Exeter College, who has read the whole work in proof. His exact and profound knowledge has saved me from many mistakes. He must not, however, be held in any way responsible for my conclusions, with a number of which he is in hearty disagreement.

The index is due to the skill and diligence of Mr. Charles Ker, formerly a scholar of Hertford College, who has generously spent part of his leave from the Indian Civil Service in compiling it.

Finally, I must express my deep gratitude to the Clarendon Press, of which I have the honour to be a delegate; to its officials, and craftsmen.

C. R. M. F. C.

September 1934.

NOTE TO SECOND EDITION

I have inserted a number of corrections which I owe to the kindness and vigilance of critics, friends, and correspondents; and have added as an appendix a chronological table of the chief events of the War, military and political, on all fronts.

CONTENTS

LIST OF ILLUSTRATIONS

MAP. I. EUROPE IN 1914

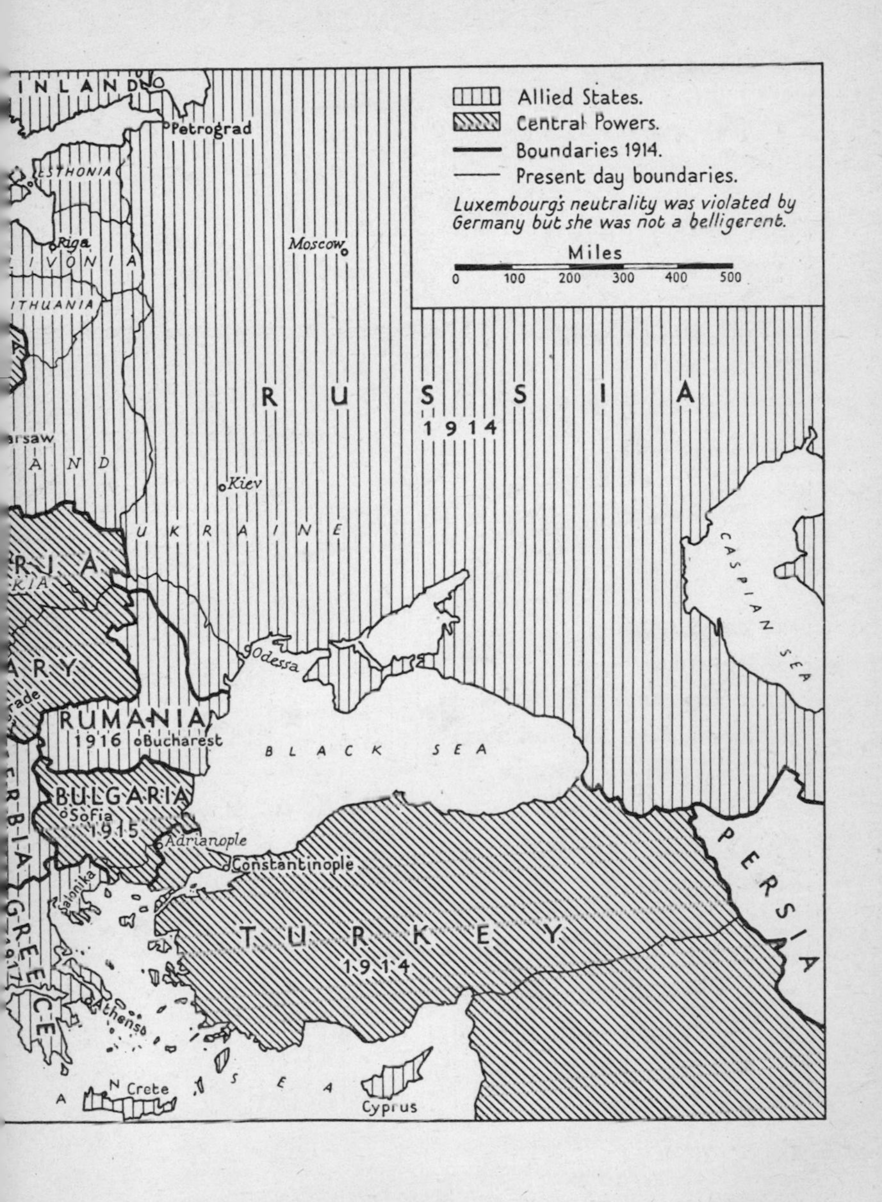

Allied States.
Central Powers.
Boundaries 1914.
Present day boundaries.
Luxembourg's neutrality was violated by Germany but she was not a belligerent.
Miles
0 100 200 300 400 500
Petrograd
ESTHONIA
Riga
LIVONIA
LITHUANIA
Moscow
RUSSIA
1914
Kiev
UKRAINE
CASPIAN SEA
Odessa
RUMANIA
1916
Bucharest
BLACK SEA
BULGARIA
Sofia
1915
Adrianople
Constantinople
PERSIA
TURKEY
1914
Salonika
Athens
Crete
SEA
Cyprus

LIST OF MAPS

I

ARMIES AND PLANS

I

THE great states of Europe had never been so powerfully prepared for war in human and material resources as in 1914. And this was a natural result of the policy which they had pursued. In spite of the lip-service rendered in theory and practice to international law, each had tended, partly subconsciously, to organize itself upon a basis of absolute power, and to worship its own collective image. The idea of European solidarity was no longer seen with even the deceptive clearness of a mirage. Thus the period has been well named by the author of a poignant book 'the international anarchy'. The motive which inspired this great and increasing military organization was not so much hatred of other states as a determination to be as strong as possible without regard to the effect which any accession of strength might have abroad. It would be wrong to ascribe this determination solely to a low and material ambition. The scramble for colonies can indeed be largely set down under this head of condemnation. Though in some cases the happiness of the subject populations may have been increased, no one will assert that this was the motive which prompted the conquest. Further, this sharing out of the world largely increased the points of envy and hostile contact between nations.

But the greatest of all problems which called for the intensive organization of national power was how to use man's ever-increasing command over nature in such a way as to provide greater happiness for an ever-increasing population. In democratic countries this was the direct result of the constitutional pressure of the multitude upon its governors, but even in a despotic state like Russia the fear of revolution exercised a certain intermittent influence.

Naturally the ordinary man was led insensibly to exalt the power of the state, and to demand that it should perform more and more tasks for his benefit, without adopting any such full-blooded theory as Treitschke elaborated for the Germans. Naturally also he believed that its strength was the only guarantee that he would be able to enjoy present and future benefits without interference from strong neighbours similarly organized. Moreover, the nineteenth century had identified the nation with the state to a degree hitherto unknown. Thus, on behalf of the state, the nation as a whole was prepared to make unprecedented sacrifices which were also in accordance with the democratic principle of equality. Where on the other hand the nation was not identified with the state, as in Austria-Hungary and Russia, the governing and best-organized nationalities within it had the sharpest incentive to impose no less thorough an organization, lest failure should mean disintegration. Moreover, when once the principle of universal service was firmly established on the Continent, there was little possibility of its relaxation. The ex-conscript was unwilling that younger men should escape his own burden, while to the youth itself the prospect was as natural and inevitable as going to school—in some countries more so. Thus it came about that the nineteenth century, and in particular its last three decades, intensified and universalized the principle of universal service. It is an amazing paradox that, in the very age when the working class were everywhere gaining power and increasing in comfort, when commercial competition was becoming keener and keener, they should have been ready, nay, often anxious, to impose upon themselves this tremendous servitude and potential risk. It is impossible to explain except on the principle that they believed more and more in the power of the state, and identified the state with themselves. To say that they were deceived by their rulers is to trifle with words: 'You cannot fool all the people all the time.'

Yet the object of these enormous armaments remained

obscure. The peoples of Europe did not certainly, in so far as they reflected upon them, believe that their aim was to provoke war at a favourable moment, yet because they felt continually insecure they did not shrink from the idea of war. It is true to say that the growth of insecurity corresponded with the growth of armaments. Therefore, while the peoples did not envisage war, they did not clearly embrace peace; their desire was rather for security, an impossible ideal, given the unrestricted sovereignty of the state-system. So, realizing something of the delicate poise and unstable equilibrium of Europe, they were content to hand over foreign affairs to the almost uncontrolled discretion of those in power, ready to accept the consequences which might flow from the secret search for security. Thus came about the terms of the great alliances, while the very atmosphere engendered by these 'hidden manœuvres for position' still further heightened the insecurity which it was intended to dissipate. Hence arose the ominous series of international crises in the last decade before 1914—more alarming and more frequent than those which had troubled the uneasy Continent since 1870. And the natural result of these crises was to intensify military preparation and to influence national hatreds. So the vicious circle went round.

My object is not to apportion war-guilt but to write a history of the war. But it is impossible to write about the war without trying to explain, however generally and inadequately, why the peoples of Europe, claiming to be more reasonable and more civilized than at any time in history, were prepared to make war on one another *à outrance* with all their strength. The only possible explanation seems to be this deep-rooted and ineradicable conviction of insecurity. Consequently it was both natural and inevitable that the war should be regarded everywhere, on its outbreak, with passionate sincerity, as a sacred duty to defend not merely the national honour but the national existence. Yet that it was so regarded is no proof that the peoples can be exonerated from blame.

Populus vult decipi, et decipiatur is a pregnant saying. The enthusiasm which almost everywhere greeted the advent of the greatest war in history is its own condemnation.

II

If war is rightly defined as 'the continuation of policy by other means', the soldiers of the Central Powers had no reason to thank the diplomatists when they received from the latter the instructions to organize decisive violence. The most favourable conditions under which they might expect to wage the great war were these: Germany, Austria-Hungary, and Italy, with Rumania as a subsidiary ally, were to oppose France and Russia with the probable subsidiary support of Serbia and Montenegro. Great Britain was expected to remain neutral for the opening at least of the campaign.

The reality in 1914 was far different. Germany and Austria-Hungary stood by themselves. Italy declared that she was not bound by the terms of the Triple Alliance which held good only for a defensive war. It is indeed improbable that the Central Powers expected any active assistance from her,[1] for she had been edging towards the Entente ever since 1902. In fact Conrad von Hotzendorf, the Chief of the Austrian Staff, who presented his master with a proposal for war every spring with the regularity of an almanac, had more than once suggested that a first experiment should be made on Italy. But the unconditional terms in which Italian neutrality was couched relieved the French of the necessity of watching their south-east frontier. Rumania was always torn by two rival ambitions, to obtain Bessarabia from Russia and Transylvania from Hungary, both of which she has accomplished since the war, probably without adding anything to the happiness of the transferred populations. In 1914 the

[1] Moltke's Memorandum of 1912 (December) states that it was already ascertained that under no circumstances would the Italians send the five corps and two cavalry divisions to Alsace which they had undertaken to do under the Military Conventions of the Triple Alliance.

cry of the Transylvanians sounded more enchantingly in her ears, and the old Hohenzollern King Carol was obliged with reluctant shame to tell Czernin, the Austrian ambassador, that his country could not fulfil her obligations. It is said that his death, which occurred soon afterwards, was hastened by the bitter sense of his humiliation. The importance of Rumania's neutrality is obvious: it not only deprived the Central Powers of a shaft at southern Russia, but left the Danubian plain open to a side thrust. It is true that both these consequences were mitigated by secret agreements with Turkey and Bulgaria, which, however, it was recognized would be contingent for their fulfilment on great and speedy successes by the Central Powers.

The participation of Belgium must obviously have entered into the calculations of both German diplomatists and soldiers as they had determined to invade the country. But they held the view, certainly shared by many Belgians, that any resistance would be in the formal nature of a protest to be speedily abandoned before the enormous superiority of the enemy. In any event they counted on encircling and destroying the Belgian field army before it could reach the refuge of the great entrenched camp of Antwerp.

The entry of Great Britain into the war affected the statesmen and commercial classes of Germany far more acutely than the military. Neither of the former really believed in the short war, irresistibly concluded by a swift series of overwhelming blows, in which the soldiers put their trust. The event which moved the Kaiser to write the most hysterical and yet the most prophetic of his minutes, which wrung from Bethmann-Hollweg the most penetrating of self-revelations, and threw Ballin the great shipowner into the profoundest dejection, was not considered as affecting in any vital way the plans of the General Staff. At the worst it would allow the unimpeded transfer of a small army-corps from Morocco and the use of French 'coloured' resources; it would free a certain number of French garrison troops from the necessity of protecting their northern ports, and would oblige the Germans to provide for the coast defences of Schleswig-Holstein and Pomerania. Finally, it would add perhaps 100,000 seasoned troops to the French left wing. To this last consideration little importance was attached, for it was believed that the blow in contemplation was of so overwhelming a nature that such a contingent, however excellent its quality, could not avert decisive defeat. The army therefore put no pressure upon the navy to interfere with the shipment of the British Expeditionary Force, for it naturally preferred that the latter should be involved in a common ruin rather than remain intact after a French *débâcle*.

III

The problem to be solved by all the countries at war except Great Britain was in its general lines the same: so to dispose of the armed and trained manhood with which mobilization provided them as to strike with the utmost speed a blow strong enough to destroy their opponents' will to resist. All the continental belligerents had therefore made plans for a short war in which victory should be decisively achieved by an offensive concentration. These plans, matured during peace, had to be carried out on mobilization; any improvisation, except in detail, was impossible, as it would have destroyed the elaborate schedule for rail and road transport and thereby created chaos. Every General Staff was therefore irrevocably committed to its own plan of campaign until the first great shock of armies brought its own inexorable changes.

Of all the Powers engaged Germany had the most compelling reasons for staking everything on a short war—she had to face both west and east. The enormous population of Russia, which exceeded that of both the Central Powers by nearly half, might be expected to provide an almost inexhaustible human reservoir. Germany's ally, Austria-Hungary, neither believed herself, nor was believed by others, to be capable of a long war, and was in any event likely to receive a stab in the back from Italy after any serious reverse. The control of the seas by Great Britain would restrict, and perhaps finally bar, the import of all those commodities by whose means alone modern war can be waged.

Now it was clear to the German Staff that the only hope of a speedy decision was by an attack upon France. The Russians had almost unlimited means of parrying a deadly blow by retreating and devastating wide areas which were always badly provided with communications, and the feeling of whose inhabitants, mainly Poles, Lithuanians, and Jews, they would not be likely to consider in the smallest degree. Moreover, it was very plausibly believed that Russian finances could not last if once France were knocked out. It had therefore been determined for many years to attack France and to stand on the defensive against Russia; then after crushing the former to turn rapidly on the latter and strike her down before she had been able to use her slowly gathering masses, whose capacity for mischief would meanwhile be limited by the opposition of nearly the whole of the Austro-Hungarian army.

This tremendous plan demanded unprecedented speed in achievement; for it was hoped that 'the battle without a morrow' would be concluded in the west within three weeks. It also demanded a thorough and devoted attention to detail, without which this great double transportation would be impossible. The Germans prided themselves justly on their superiority in this respect over any other nation. But it was considered impossible to pierce the powerful French line between Luxembourg and Switzerland within the required time-limit. The ground is naturally strong and had been more heavily fortified since 1870 than perhaps any other region in Europe. The Vosges, densely wooded, with a steep eastward escarpment falling into the Rhine Valley, protected the French right flank; three large rivers, Meurthe,

Moselle, and Meuse, ran at right angles to the German advance. Farther north on either side of Verdun the heights of the Meuse rising to 1,300 feet commanded the road from Metz. The great chain of concrete forts stretched from Verdun to Belfort with one intentional gap of thirty miles between Épinal and Toul, called the gap of Charmes. On the south the gap of Belfort was far too narrow for the deployment of modern armies and led to the fortified region of Langres. Finally, on the north the passage between Metz and Luxembourg led into the confused and densely wooded hills of the Argonne. Moreover, the common frontier between France and Germany was too short to allow the latter to use fully her superiority in numbers, and the strategy of envelopment long taught by the General Staff.

Schlieffen, the Chief-of-Staff from 1891 to 1906, a typically iron and secret soldier, had worked out the invasion of Belgium as the appropriate solution. He was so contemptuous of small nations that he included Holland in his plan of violation.[1] He proposed to pass through the so-called 'Maestricht appendix', which juts out south almost to Liége, in order to have more room for the deployment from Aix. His successor Moltke, a nephew of the great organizer of victory of 1870, struck this out, realizing that a mere military convenience would be too heavily purchased by the resistance of the Dutch, who could have thrust continually at an open flank from behind their water defences. Moreover, a neutral Holland would be invaluable to Germany for the importation of war material and commodities in the event of a prolonged war. As Moltke wrote, 'If we make Holland our enemy, we shall stop the last air-hole through which we can breathe'.[2] He made also another grave alteration, which many critics believe was responsible for the

[1] He hoped to force France into violating Belgian neutrality by mobilizing on that frontier, which he expected the French armies would then cross in self-defence. He had the odd optimism to believe that an amicable arrangement could be made with Holland.

[2] Memorandum of 1912 (December).

failure at the Marne. Schlieffen had staked everything upon the strength of his encircling right, and had been content to hold Alsace-Lorraine with a mere cordon; his last authentic words were apparently, 'Strengthen the right wing'. But his successor thought more seriously of a French offensive towards the Rhine—he very probably had information that it was intended; for political reasons also an invasion of southern Germany was particularly dreaded, as history showed that its consequences might be incalculable. He therefore made, as we shall see, a very large addition to the number of troops designed for the left wing. Schlieffen had intended to consummate victory entirely by the great sweep of his right to the west of Paris, driving the enemy eastward towards the Swiss frontier. Moltke apparently hoped by a subsidiary offensive through Lorraine to break through the Meuse line and isolate the French centre by a double envelopment.

The French knew well that they would have to face an immediate German attack in full strength. Accordingly their Staff had two kindred tasks. First, to parry it with their own forces; secondly, to ensure such immediate Russian action in the east as to diminish its violence. With regard to the former, they had two main difficulties. First, inferiority of numbers and a stationary population—in 1914 about 40 million Frenchmen faced 63 million Germans. This inferiority, as far as the initial striking force went, had been partly compensated in 1913, when three years' service with the colours was restored. Secondly, the uncertainty whether they would be able freely to engage the enemy on favourable ground; for if the German blow was delivered through Belgium, the gentle undulations of an open country sloping with the rivers towards Paris would help the invaders. The Germans had indeed made little secret of their probable intentions. Enormous detraining stations, great camps like that of Elsenborn, had been established on the Belgian frontier. Consequently the French Staff had taken up and rejected a number of plans before deciding upon the notorious No. 17, which was adopted in 1913 and put into operation in the succeeding year.[1] The earlier and discarded intention had been to delay the enemy's advance by strong advance-guards, but not to engage the full mass of manœuvre until his intentions were clear and his commitment complete. In the years immediately preceding the war, however, the generation which knew not 1870 was soaked in the doctrine of the immediate and brutal offensive, the efficacy of which was preached with almost mythical fervour. It appears to have been partly inspired by the philosophy of Bergson, then so popular in France, of which the effect was to exalt instinct and intuition above the intellectual process of reasoning. It was also supported by the more material and solid consideration that the French field-gun, the famous '75', was greatly superior both in rapidity and accuracy of fire to anything which the Germans could produce. Plan 17 therefore aimed at stopping the German attack dead by a great movement against its supposed centre, destined to paralyse the enemy communications in Lorraine. It aimed not at envelopment, but at a break-through, which would fling the two wings asunder. Its defects both in conception and execution will become clear when the French dispositions are considered in greater detail.

Russia on paper disposed of great masses far outnumbering any other belligerent, but her prime difficulty, as always, was to approach Western standards in organization and military communications. It had therefore always been admitted in conferences between the two Allied Staffs that the main Russian offensive could not synchronize with the main clash of arms in the west. The strategic railways in Poland had certainly been improved, by a large expenditure of French money, but their completion was not possible before 1916, by which time it was hoped that

[1] It was a deliberate rejection of that proposed by Gen. Michel in 1911, who had divined the German plan almost exactly, and had allotted the main bulk of the French armies to a line from Lille to Rethel to withstand the attack anticipated by him on both banks of the Meuse. See A. Percin, *Les Erreurs du haut commandement, 1914* (1920).

the Russian forces would also have completed their reorganization. But Russia engaged to have about 800,000 men ready to move against either East Prussia or Posen, the alternative to be decided according to the German defensive dispositions, by about the eighteenth day of mobilization. Such a number would enormously outweigh the German forces, and it was hoped that their unexpectedly rapid action would force the enemy to withdraw several corps from the West at the very moment of crisis. Russia, however, was determined also to attack Austria on a large scale. Galicia was an inviting prize. Apart from its important oil-wells, its possession would make impossible an Austrian attack on the south of the Polish salient, would threaten and perhaps secure the Hungarian passes, and finally might open a path to Berlin by way of Silesia. In 1914 these considerations were reinforced by the intense popular hatred of Austria, whose ultimatum to Serbia had been both a challenge to Russia and the direct cause of the war.

Great Britain stood in an entirely different position from the other great belligerents. In the first place she entered the war in defence of her treaty obligations towards Belgium and not under the terms of any general alliance.[1] Her small professional army, though acting as an independent force, must necessarily subordinate its strategy entirely to that dictated by circumstances for the French left wing. Nor had it been intended that France could rely upon any considerable British reinforcements, after the expeditionary force, of a maximum strength of 150,000 men, had come into line. The numbers of our regular army were in fact considered as the definite limit of our military commitments, in accordance with our traditional methods of waging continental war. It was believed that the British army, with its training and practical experience outweighing its smallness, might well turn the scale decisively in the comparative equipoise of the first great battle. Yet

[1] At the outbreak of war official circles in Great Britain had no knowledge of the terms of the Franco-Russian alliance or of Plan 17.

it was also clear that, in the event of a prolonged war, Great Britain alone would be free to improvise and to multiply her military strength; in short, to make of the length of the war an enormous asset, provided that her naval plans fulfilled expectations.

The essential tasks of the Navy were to protect our islands from invasion, to cover the safe passage of our army overseas, to ensure free communications over all the trade-routes of the world, and lastly to exercise at will a strangling grip upon the food and commerce of our enemies. But, as we shall see, this last weapon was neither fully used nor indeed fully understood until the static warfare of the winter took away every prospect of an immediate end.

II

DEFEAT AND VICTORY IN THE WEST

I

THE wheels of mobilization ran smoothly, accompanied on the Continent by a greater or less degree of martial law. No such preliminary break-down was anywhere experienced as threw the French army into chaos in July 1870. The figures for France show that between August 2nd and 18th 3,781,000 men were transported in 7,000 trains, which at some periods succeeded each other day and night every eight minutes. It is probably a true generalization that throughout the war the problems of concentration and supply were everywhere, except in Russia, more efficiently tackled than that of strategic direction. The Germans brought about 1,500,000 men into line against France, divided into seven armies. The deployment of the two southern armies was simple; they covered very large fronts, and were for the present to stand defensively upon the line from Metz to Switzerland. The remaining five were to take part in the great wheel through northern France and Belgium. A successful accomplishment of this task was difficult. The high, wooded country of the Ardennes and Eiffel does not favour rapid movement; though the violation of neutral Luxembourg (August 2) had provided an indispensable centre of roads and railways converging from the west. Moreover, the denser the formation, the narrower was the area allotted for concentration. Von Kluck's Ist army, 320,000 strong, on whose unimpeded march everything depended, had to pass first through the bottle-neck of Aix-la-Chapelle, then through a strip six miles wide between the Dutch frontier and Liége. The IInd army of von Bülow of 260,000 men had likewise to pass through, and immediately south of, Liége before extending its front more comfortably. It is therefore obvious that the possession of this city, with the adjacent crossings of the Meuse, was absolutely vital to the German plan. The fortress was considered exceedingly strong; it had been constructed some twenty years before by the famous engineer Brialmont. It consisted of twelve detached armoured forts in a ring round the city, each sup-

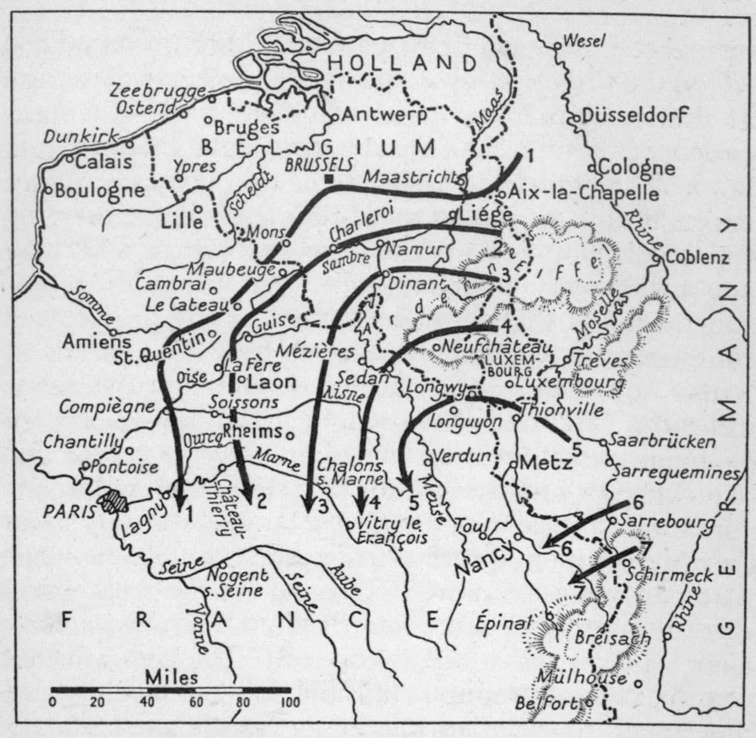

MAP 2. The Great German Wheel: the arrows show the general direction followed by the seven German armies.

porting the other with five heavy guns mounted in cupolas.[1]

It was decided to penetrate by a surprise night attack through the girdle of forts and to seize the city with the bridges over the Meuse. On the night of August 5th–6th this extremely hardy and dangerous enterprise was carried through. It would certainly have failed but for the pre-

[1] The German General Staff expected to find the fortress garrisoned by only 6,000 men, its peace strength: but the Belgians, who had started mobilization by August 1, had been able to complete it to the full strength of one division. The modern guns, however, ordered from Krupp's works had (probably of set purpose) not been delivered to Belgium when war broke out.

sence of Ludendorff, who was Chief-of-Staff to the army. It may almost be said that he took Liége by himself. The attacking brigades had lost their way and were held up in blind and violent fighting. Ludendorff himself took command of one, pushed forward to the heights immediately overlooking the city, planted field-guns upon them, seized the bridges, and on the morning of the 7th arrived at the citadel in a car to receive single-handed the surrender of its garrison. Heavy guns were speedily brought up to reduce the forts, amongst them the famous 17-inch Austrian howitzer from Skoda, the greatest and most effective surprise of the early days of war. The cupolas were smashed to pieces and the garrisons buried or poisoned by the fumes. Though the last fort held out till August 17th the passage to the west was clear for the Ist army by the 14th. As this army had not completed its concentration before the 12th and as it reached the line laid down in the mobilization-schedule on the 20th, it does not seem that the brave Belgian resistance, though unexpected, interfered with the German plans. It cost them heavy casualties, probably amounting to 40,000 men. German official accounts, however, show that the effect of the demolition of railway tunnels and bridges was much more serious than was believed at the time. This seriously hampered the transfer of troops to the right wing, and was an important factor in the victory of the Marne.

The great westward sweep therefore continued to fulfil its time-tables, though it failed to cut off the Belgians from their camp of refuge at Antwerp. On August 20th the Ist army triumphantly entered Brussels in all the magnificence and panoply of war. Its progress through Belgium had been disgraced by a savage and indiscriminate severity against the civil population. The Germans alleged, doubtless with some truth, that a guerrilla warfare was waged upon them; but even by their admissions the innocent perished with the guilty. The question of guilt is indeed wholly inapplicable to a frenzied population of peaceable folk defending their homes against a brutal attack in violation of treaties—treaties which Germany herself had signed. The real German object was to insure against the necessity of leaving strong forces to guard their communications by a policy of *Schrecklichkeit* which burned whole towns and massacred hundreds of inhabitants as at Louvain, Andenne, and Dinant.

Thus the first part of the German plan was complete. The Ist and IInd armies had reached their jumping-off ground in southern Belgium in enormously superior force. Two French offensives had been held and beaten without any change of disposition. A foolish dash into Alsace by weak detachments of the 1st French army took Mülhouse on August 8th, but the frontier was recrossed two days later under the pressure of superior enemy forces. A similar advance followed by a more disastrous retreat occurred a few days later. But the fighting in Alsace was a mere incident, its only military value being a permanent French occupation of the eastern foot-hills of the Vosges. Its main motive, which was political, had unfortunate results, as the wretched inhabitants who had welcomed the French[1] were naturally treated throughout the war with rigorous suspicion. General Joffre, the French Commander-in-Chief, had himself drawn up Plan 17, which he had now put into execution. It is difficult to associate such a wild and premature offensive[2] with this exceptionally calm, even unperturbable soldier, with his large beneficent face, who allowed nothing to interfere with his sleep, and who was affectionately known to the mass of Frenchmen as Le Père Joffre. Doubtless it reflected the ardent arrogant spirit of his ambitious young staff, whom the army had nicknamed 'les jeunes Turcs'. But Joffre was not a man to be led against his wish; jealous of authority and always able to command obedience, his control was always very firm. Foch said of him that though no

[1] This welcome was by no means universal. See Commandant Bréant, *De l'Alsace à la Somme* (1917), ch. i.

[2] 'Whatever the circumstances, it is the intention of the Commander-in-Chief to advance, with all forces united, to the attack of the German armies' (Plan 17: Directions for the Concentration).

originator he never hesitated in decision, and that 'he did not know where France would have been without him'.

His five armies were drawn up on a curved line from Belfort to the west of Mézières, with the intention of making a great attack on either side of Metz which would drive the Germans away from the fortress and dislocate their communications on the left bank of the Rhine. This concentration allowed for a German advance through Belgium south-east of the Meuse, but left all the frontier to the north-west practically undefended. The whole array of fortresses between Belgium and Paris, which had played so famous a part in former wars, had fallen into complete obsolescence and had, with the exception of Maubeuge, been deprived of their guns. General Lanrezac, commanding the 5th army round Mézières, was exceedingly and justly anxious. He alone divined the intended envelopment by the first two German armies before it became manifest about August 18th. But unfortunately this able and clear-sighted soldier was not able to make his views prevail. Even after a personal call at General Head-quarters his fears were dismissed as without foundation. The French Intelligence generally was very poor, partly no doubt owing to their inferiority in aeroplanes, which are said to have been outnumbered by ten to one, partly also because the French Staff had 'made a picture', as Napoleon used to say, of what they expected the enemy would do and ignored all contrary indications.[1] On the 15th, it is true, Lanrezac at last received permission to move his army north-west towards Givet, while the region between Maubeuge and the sea was watched by three territorial divisions. Inadequate as these dispositions proved, it seems certain that without them the French armies would have suffered irretrievable disaster.

[1] Galliéni, Lanrezac's predecessor in command of the 5th army, who retired in July 1914 by reason of age, had made many ineffectual representations before the war on the inadequacy of the forces on the north-east frontier and of the defences of Maubeuge. Lanrezac had called the attention of Joffre to the probability that the Germans' outflanking movement would extend west of the Meuse in an official letter as early as July 31.

The day before marked the opening of an immense battle called by the French that 'of the frontiers', which spread northwards and continued without intermission till the 25th.[1] The French were everywhere heavily defeated with enormous losses of about 300,000 men, or nearly 25 per cent. of the combatants—a rate of wastage never equalled in all the rest of the war—yet, in spite of this, they maintained cohesion and contact. They fought for the most part with extraordinary devotion—the action of the cadets from Saint-Cyr, who dressed in their conspicuous parade uniforms to receive their baptism of fire, was typical of the prevailing spirit—but the tactical training, particularly of the reservists who formed five-eighths of the active army, was very insufficient, as Joffre himself noted at the time.

This battle gave the first of many examples to prove the sovereign advantage of a resolute and well-organized defence against a precipitate attack.

The 1st and 2nd French armies advanced with delusive ease into Lorraine, and stood roughly on the line of the great railway from Strasbourg to Metz about Sarrebourg and Château-Salins. On the 16th the enemy met that ill-inspired thrust in prepared positions round the lakes of Dieuze and the thickly wooded hills of Morhange, counter-attacked and drove them on the 20th in great disorder[2] back to, and behind, the frontier with the loss of 20,000 prisoners and 150 guns. Foch commanded in this battle the famous 20th corps or Iron Corps, the peace-time garrison of Nancy, which fought much better than its neighbours; for the 15th corps in particular broke completely and was fired upon by its own artillery.

After Lorraine came Luxembourg. Here again the high, wooded hills of the Ardennes, rising to nearly 2,000 feet, intersected with valleys full of blind ground and cover, were far from favourable to the pell-mell offensive of the

[1] The most complete and intelligible account of these battles is to be found in Sewell Tyng, *The Campaign of the Marne* (1935).

[2] This applies rather to the 2nd army (Castelnau) than to the 1st (Dubail).

3rd and 4th armies, of which it was quite wrongly supposed that the enemy was in complete ignorance. According to French reports practically no reconnaissance had been made, particularly on the left, where each army corps was given a slice of ground and ordered to attack over it.[1] The tactical handling of machine-guns by the Germans, as throughout the war, was exceedingly dexterous and resolute. The French 75's, unequalled as were their achievements in open country, were unable to search all the nooks and corners of dead ground; the German superiority both in field and heavy howitzers was decisive. French military opinion was extraordinarily slow in recognizing the value of high-angle fire; for we shall find that even in 1917 its insufficiency was one of the many causes of the failure at the Chemin des Dames. Moreover, the telephonic liaison both between forward observing officers and between the infantry and the gunners was very inadequate, and co-operation was correspondingly ineffective. According to many French writers the artillery entered the war in a spirit of arrogant superiority over the infantry, and insisted on choosing its targets at will without reference to the latter.

The final climax of the French failure was Lanrezac's defeat at Charleroi, which left open the northern frontier and necessitated the great retreat which threw back the armies on the west of Verdun to a maximum distance of nearly 150 miles in twelve days. Charleroi and to a lesser extent Mons were encounter battles, where each enemy was searching for the other, and had not pinned him to the ground. Kluck, as we saw, had reached Brussels on the 20th, and as the march of his army regulated the whole German wheel, the southward movement into France was now ready to begin. The position of the two German armies on the map appeared hazardous. Kluck had to protect the right flank against a combined move

[1] Cf. C. L. J. Regnault, *La 3e division d'infanterie, août 1914* (1920). The 2nd corps commander gave no orders to his divisions except to put out two battalions as advanced guards. He then left in his car. Many other similar instances of gross carelessness are given.

of the British and Belgians from Antwerp and the adjacent coast. This he believed probable, as he obstinately maintained the hypothesis that the expeditionary force had landed between Calais and Ostend. Consequently his inclination was to extend towards the south-west. Such a movement if accentuated would be certain to leave a gap between him and Bülow's IInd army, advancing south with Namur on its left. Into this gap Lanrezac might thrust and drive the two armies north-west and north-east respectively. German Head-quarters were alive to this danger and had placed the Ist Army under Bülow's orders, much to the annoyance of the impetuous and self-willed Kluck. The fog of war was very thick at this time. The Allies had no idea of the strength of the Ist army and of the extent of its western encirclement. The Germans were entirely ignorant of the whereabouts of the B.E.F. and were in very vague general contact with the outposts of the 5th (Lanrezac's) army.

It was, however, certain that the key and pivot of the whole Allied position both for offence and defence was the great Belgian fortress of Namur in the angle of Sambre and Meuse, reputed almost impregnable—*The Times* described it at the moment as a tough nut which might be expected to take even Prussian jaws six months to crack. But Namur fell in two days before the blast of the great howitzers, and the enemy entered on the 23rd. Lanrezac, it is true, had already been defeated, but the smashing of this great corner-stone of the frontier destroyed all chance of a defensive stand and threw an unfettered initiative into the hands of the Germans, whence only their own subsequent errors wrested it at the Marne.

The British army had by now come upon the scene. Contrary to some French statements it appears to have been just in time to take its place in the Allied alignment, though neither its commander, Sir John French, nor the British Government had been acquainted with the French plan of campaign. Sir John's command was therefore in the words of Lord Kitchener 'an entirely independent one and . . . you will in no case come in any sense under the orders of any Allied General'. The expeditionary force of four infantry and one cavalry division, amounting to less than 90,000 men, had crossed in complete secrecy and security, often without visible escort, from August 11th to 17th, mainly between Southampton and Le Havre, and concentrated between Le Cateau and Maubeuge. Kluck, as we saw, was completely ignorant of its position, and even sceptical of its arrival in France until a cavalry skirmish on the 22nd at Castreau north of Mons. French's intention was still to take the offensive until late that evening news arrived that Lanrezac had been driven back from Charleroi. The British right was not yet uncovered, but an attack was clearly impracticable, and the greatest assistance possible to the French was to stand in position for another twenty-four hours. The 2nd corps (Sir H. Smith-Dorrien) was hastily entrenched on the line of the canal from Condé to Mons, with the 1st corps (Sir D. Haig) bent back to face south-east and protect its flank.

The battle next day was fought in thickly enclosed mining country, littered with slag heaps often too hot for the foot, cut up by the narrow winding alleys of a succession of drab towns. It was a small affair in the scale of the next three years; not more than 30,000 of our men were seriously engaged against nearly three times as many Germans. The casualties, 1,650, had been exceeded more than once in the Boer War. Yet apart from the interest involved in the first encounter of British troops with a continental enemy since the Crimea, it was in many respects characteristic. The resolute and repeated attacks in massed formation, and the great superiority both in number and weight of the enemy artillery; the astonishingly rapid and accurate fire of our infantry, which made the Germans state that we possessed twenty-eight machine-guns per battalion instead of two; the skilful tactical handling of small bodies especially in covering retirement—all became commonplaces of the campaign. Kluck was greatly impressed by the expeditionary force, and spoke of it to

British officers after the war in the most generous terms as 'an incomparable army'. Mons was neither a victory nor a defeat, but a delaying action which achieved its purpose. Though we had been drawn out of the salient formed by the canals' northward loop round Mons, the idea of a general retreat was not contemplated; on the contrary the two corps expected to stand next day on a straighter and freer line three miles in rear. But this was quite impossible, as the French 5th army was being attacked not only from the north but also from the east, and was hastily retiring. The general retirement, without hope of an immediate stand, was therefore begun by all the Allied forces west of Verdun.[1]

The troops facing Alsace-Lorraine would, it was hoped, roughly maintain their positions within the great fortified and hilly region.

German Head-quarters seem now to have been guilty of a serious error. Encouraged by his success in Lorraine, Prince Rupprecht of Bavaria was allowed to make a costly and unsuccessful attack upon the French defences round Nancy. In fact Moltke was modifying his plan; instead of staking everything upon the strength of the right wing, he regarded an attack in the south as promising an encirclement on either flank, according to the old classical doctrine of 1870. So confident was he of success that the Kaiser appeared before Nancy at the beginning of September to witness the expected break-through. It would probably have been possible to transfer a force of two or three corps to Kluck in time for a decisive blow. The rolling-stock kept in reserve in Lorraine was said to have been sufficient for the rapid transfer of most of the VIth and VIIth armies; while 60 per cent. of the Railway Construction and Operative Companies were working in rear of the Ist and IInd armies.[2]

[1] No preparations of any kind had been made, no trenches dug or barbed wire put up. It may be noted that by August 25 the B.E.F. had marched out of the ground covered by the maps originally issued to them.

[2] See, however, p. 15 for the effect of the demolitions in Belgium on the problem of transportation.

Meanwhile the retreat continued. At first the pressure was most severe against the British, whom Kluck was trying to thrust into Maubeuge. As the two British corps were separated by the great forest of Mormal, a gap of at least twelve miles existed between them on the morning of the 26th. On that day Smith-Dorrien, contrary to the original intention of Sir John French, fought the famous delaying action of Le Cateau. He believed that his troops were too tired to extricate themselves from an enemy so close upon them without standing and fighting it out on the ground. He showed wonderful courage in his decision, for he started the battle with both flanks in the air, against an enemy double in numbers and more than double in artillery. The long, low spur running south of the Cambrai—Le Cateau road had already been sited as part of a general line, and some feeble trenches dug by civilians, but it was in no sense a prepared system, and the British suffered severely from the overwhelming artillery fire to which no adequate answer was possible. Early in the afternoon the right was enveloped, but the three divisions as a whole escaped with losses of about 8,000 men and thirty-eight guns. The enemy were very hard hit and attempted no pursuit that evening.[1] This is a sufficient justification for this costly battle, the effects of which were still severely felt by the 2nd corps at the battles of the Marne and Aisne.

Unfortunately Sir J. French possessed that mercurial temperament commonly associated with Irishmen and cavalry-soldiers; his letters to Kitchener show vividly the extremes of confidence and depression which alternately possessed him. After Le Cateau he became convinced that the B.E.F. must be withdrawn from the line to refit. From his head-quarters far in rear he exaggerated the condition of the 2nd corps, which he described as 'shattered', and had entirely lost confidence in his Allies whose 'present tactics', he wrote to Kitchener, 'are practically to fall back

[1] The pursuit when undertaken was rendered ineffective by Kluck's obstinate belief that the B.E.F. was based on the ports between Ostend and Dunkirk, from which he was determined to cut them off.

right and left of me, usually without notice'.[1] Consequently by the 29th he had determined to withdraw behind the Seine west of Paris in order to retain 'complete independence of action and power to retire on my base when circumstances render it necessary'.[2] As the base had been changed from Le Havre to Saint-Nazaire at the mouth of the Loire on the 29th, it is clear that the Commander-in-Chief conceived that it might become necessary to abandon his French Allies altogether. Kitchener acted with the greatest energy—for he believed that such action would mean irreparable disaster. Crossing to France, in his field-marshal's uniform, he partly persuaded, partly overawed Sir John into maintaining immediate contact with the French. This was the more easy as the enemy was now barely in touch and our numbers were daily increased by parties of rejoined stragglers. The total casualties down to the end of the retreat amounted to less than 15,000 men.

Joffre on the other hand showed all the calm of greatness in face of his ruined hopes. He prepared steadfastly for a new great battle of manœuvre as soon as his armies could be extricated, regrouped, and aligned. The surrender of territory was of merely secondary importance as long as a swift victorious and decisive return was envisaged. It is true that he had hoped at first not to carry the retreat so far: his intention had been to fight on the lines of the rivers Somme and Aisne and Ailette, but the 6th army which he was creating on the left by transferring troops from Alsace could not be ready in time.

In spite of a real success by Lanrezac on the 29th when he threw back three of Bülow's corps behind the Oise near Guise, the time was not ripe; 'the smallest check', Joffre wrote afterwards, 'would have run the risk of being turned into a hopeless rout'. Lanrezac himself suffered the common fate of subordinates who have prophesied and pro-

[1] To Kitchener, August 31.

[2] To Kitchener, August 30. French, it is true, had been warned in Kitchener's instructions that he was 'to be very careful how he used his troops as he could not expect large reinforcements'. This consideration influenced his projected action.

tested without being believed. As soon as he had been proved right, he was dismissed.[1] By September 5th Paris, deserted by the Government and about 500,000 of its population, was commanded as a fortress by Galliéni, a splendid old soldier, whose first proclamation announced his determination to defend it 'jusqu'au bout'.[2] Maunoury's 6th army had already begun to harass the Germans' right flank; the British and the 5th French army were lying south-east of the capital, the former close to the outermost forts, in contact with the rest of the armies, which stretched in a shallow crescent to north of Verdun and thence southward along the frontier. The barrier of the fortresses had held splendidly. Prince Rupprecht in particular had for thirteen days been suffering a very bloody defeat before the Grand Couronné, the great fortified work which protected Nancy. On this day, September 5th, Joffre issued an order to the effect that the time for looking backward had passed, and that every effort was to be used in attacking and driving back the enemy.

It is now time to see what were the mistakes of his enemy which Joffre was able to turn to the profit of France at the Marne.

The capital error of German Head-quarters, from which almost all others flowed, was that of maintaining itself too far in the rear, and thereby losing ability to control, either by sufficient information or direction, the army commanders. Moltke, after moving from Coblenz to Luxembourg at the end of August, remained at this remote though central spot, using wireless as his method of communication, which was delayed by congestion at head-quarters and suffered serious interference from the French station in the Eiffel Tower. This deliberate aloofness was probably adopted with the belief that all information could

[1] It is fair to Joffre to say that Lanrezac seems to have lost his nerve by the end of August, and according to eyewitnesses recognized this himself, and showed great relief at his dismissal (Brig.-Gen. E. L. Spears, *Liaison 1914* (1930)).

[2] He has described the insufficiency of its armament, garrison, and provisionment in his *Memoirs* (1920), pp. 19–20, 24–8.

thus be more thoroughly collected and digested than in a more forward position, and that the co-ordination of the whole plan would therefore be more effective. The experience of 1870 had shown the difficulties and even dangers caused by the independence of an earlier generation of commanders. Moltke was a very intellectual and thoughtful soldier with plenty of moral courage, often shown in his attitude toward the Kaiser, but in wretched health, which further accentuated his normal lack of executive quickness and decision. Until September 11th neither Moltke nor the Chief of the Operations Staff nor the Quartermaster-General visited any of the armies. Actually the army commanders either did what they liked, as, notably, Kluck, or did what they thought best in the absence of information, like Hausen. The attack in Lorraine itself seems rather to have been permitted than ordered by Moltke, if we can believe the statement that 'Rupprecht raised objections to continuing his retirement when every one else was advancing. He, too, wanted to attack, and the Supreme Command allowed him to do so.'[1]

As early as August 25th the Chief-of-Staff fell into a curiously premature optimism, and believing that the decisive battle in the war had been won, prepared to send six corps to Russia, of which two were actually dispatched. They arrived as idle spectators of the overwhelming victory which Ludendorff had achieved without their aid. But they had been taken from the IInd and IIIrd[2] armies, where their presence would probably have turned the scale at the Marne; especially as three reserve corps had already been detached, two to observe the Belgian army in Antwerp, one to besiege Maubeuge. As the operations of the first three armies were so closely linked together with the immediate object of destroying Lanrezac and Sir J. French by complete envelopment, it would have been

[1] W. Förster, *Graf Schlieffen und der Weltkrieg, 1914–18* (1921).

[2] Moltke himself states that he meant to take them from the VIIth army, but its losses had been too great to permit further weakening. He adds: 'I admit that my action was a mistake, which revenged itself upon us at the Marne.'

desirable to give them unity of command in a single group, as was the constant practice later on.[1] Actually Hausen received very inadequate and tardy information both from Head-quarters and Bülow, and diverted forces in response to appeals from the IVth army towards his left. Worse still, on the 27th, Kluck was given complete independence of Bülow in which he proceeded to revel with headstrong obstinacy.

It is not indeed right to blame his action on the 30th, when he threw over his orders to continue marching to the west of Paris, with his left on the Oise. It was perfectly evident that the scope of the original wheel must be modified or an enormous gap would open between himself and the uneasy IInd army marching south. His move south-east that day to help Bülow, who had urgently asked for assistance after being so badly knocked about at Guise, was in accordance with the spirit of his instructions to act as flank-guard, and was accepted without demur by Moltke.

Schlieffen's plan had been completely jettisoned. Moltke's new ideas are by no means clear. But he seems now to have pinned his chief faith to a break-through in Lorraine. Rupprecht, who had failed completely to force the Trouée des Charmes, the gap between Épinal and Toul enticingly left open in the French fortified chain, turned against Nancy and began his great assault on September 4th. Moltke was getting some information about the 6th French army, which he placed on the lower Seine, and probably thought that the Lorraine front had been dangerously weakened. On the right wing his new aim (communicated to army commanders at midnight on September 2nd) was to drive the British and French away from Paris in a south-easterly direction. If success attended, the Allied armies would thus be cut into three fragments.

The role of the first two German armies was obviously dangerous. They were to drive obliquely across the front of the British and the French 5th army, both of which

[1] Curiously enough this had been done at the outset only in the Russian army, in most respects so backward in organization.

Moltke wrongly believed to be utterly defeated: the right flank and even the rear might be exposed to the garrison of Paris and Maunoury's army. Moltke naturally realized this danger and ordered the advance in echelon, Bülow leading, with Kluck as a great flank-guard on the right rear. Unfortunately Kluck, whose energy and power of squeezing the last drop out of his men were admirable, was already at least a day's march ahead of Bülow, and actually straddled across his path with his left corps. He had reached a line from Chantilly to Château-Thierry, at its nearest point little more than twenty miles from Paris, while Bülow was merely on the Aisne at Soissons. It might therefore have been expected that the Ist army would halt for at least thirty-six hours in order to be able to perform its flanking duty. But Kluck acted quite otherwise. He gauged the condition of the B.E.F. and the 5th army much more accurately than General Head-quarters, and estimated that unless the pursuit was vigorously continued they would reform so strongly that it would be impossible to drive them from Paris. On the other hand, he was almost entirely ignorant of the growing threat to his right flank, on which he apparently believed Joffre had collected only two or three territorial divisions and some cavalry. He therefore persuaded himself that he could best fulfil the intentions of the Supreme Command by continuing his south-easterly march with unabated vigour. His army was still to be the spear-head of the advance instead of acting as a flank-guard.

By the morning of the 4th even he began to be nervous. His two left corps (IX and III) were well south of the Marne, he was still twelve miles in advance of his colleague, and had a justified suspicion that all was not well on the battle-front as a whole. He voiced this uneasiness in a curiously insolent message to German Head-quarters asking to be informed 'of the situation of the other armies, whose reports of decisive victories have so far been frequently followed by appeals for support[1]. . . . Owing to

[1] Falkenhayn said two months later: 'The lies which these army

the ever-changing situation, it will not be possible for the Commander of the Ist army to make further important decisions unless he is kept continuously informed of the situation of the other armies, who apparently are not so far advanced.' He was quite right; the balance was now heavily weighted against the invaders. Moltke at last realized the danger though scarcely its urgency. His message of September 4th (7.45 p.m.)[1] emphasized the importance of the French forces gathering north of Paris. He abandoned his intention of driving the French south-east, and ordered the Ist and IInd armies to face south-west against the expected flank attack between the Oise and the Seine. He still clung to the hope of breaking the French right and centre with his remaining five armies.

Meanwhile Galliéni, full of confidence and fire, was urging immediate action by Joffre and Sir J. French.[2] On the 4th the 6th (Maunoury's) army which was under his orders had completed the concentration round Dammartin, twenty miles north-east of Paris, but was not yet in touch with enemy patrols.[3] Kluck had begun the exceedingly difficult task of changing fronts, relying on the assurance of Lieut.-Colonel Hentsch, an emissary of German General Head-quarters, who had just reached

commanders combine in telling are quite incredible' (J. von Stürgkh, *Im deutschen Grossen Hauptquartier* (1921)).

[1] Received by Ist and IInd armies about 6 a.m., September 5.

[2] The share of Galliéni in the Marne battle has been much disputed. His energetic action on Kluck's flank immediately he had received reliable air reports made it possible for Joffre to take his decision: the latter would have delayed it had not Galliéni insisted on the telephone at 8 p.m. on Sept. 4 that 'the launching of the attack should take place without any change in the conditions of time and place prescribed' (Commandant Muller, *Joffre et la Marne* (1931)). He seems to have overawed his old subordinate into immediate compliance. Galliéni has been reproached with developing the attack of the 6th army too early, but his justification seems valid. If it had been delayed, Kluck, who was still advancing energetically, might have driven a wedge between the B.E.F. and the 5th army. Joffre tried later unworthily to minimize Galliéni's role.

[3] Its fighting force consisted of six divisions at the commencement of the battle. The initiative for its formation seems to have come from M. Briand, who persuaded the Cabinet to insist that Galliéni should have sufficient forces to ensure a mobile defence of Paris.

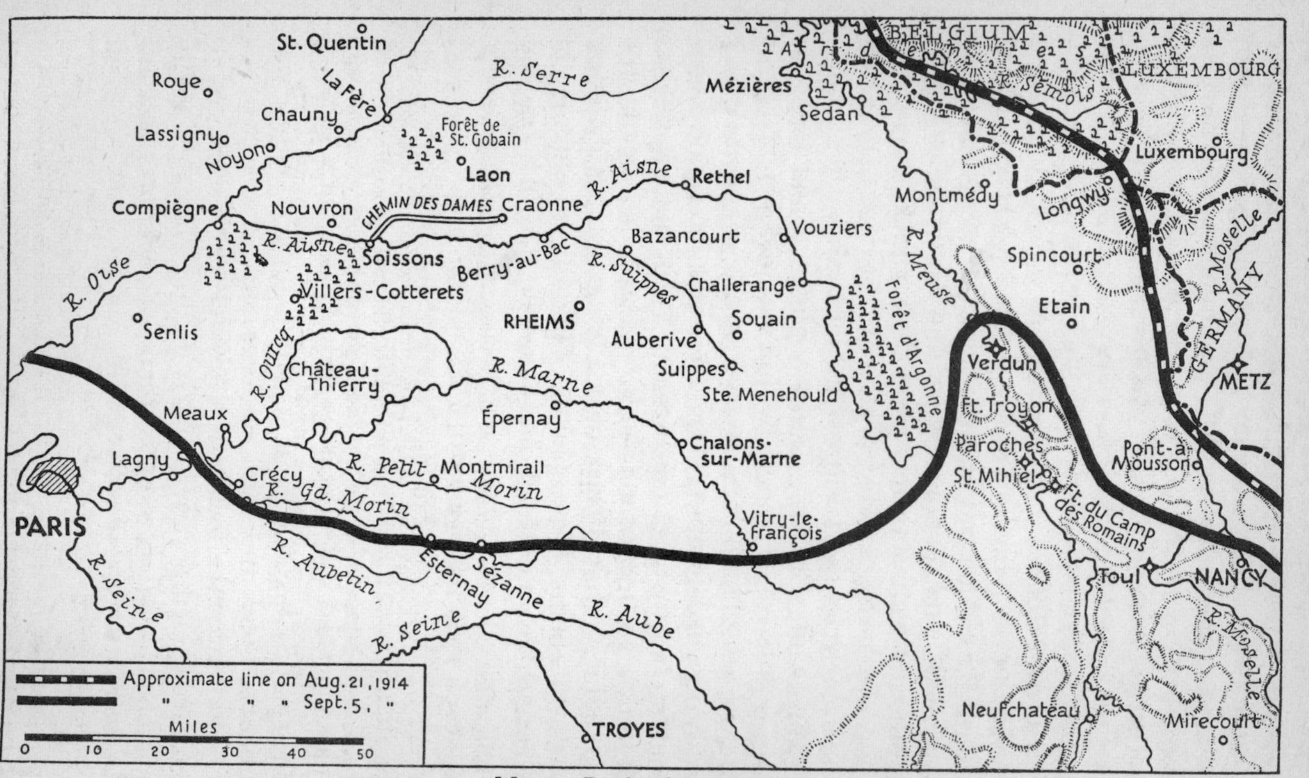

Map 3. Battle of the Marne.

him, that 'the movement could be made at leisure; no special haste was necessary'.

On the 5th the battle of the Ourcq, the prelude of the Marne, began with an encounter between the IVth German reserve corps which its commander, von Gronau, had boldly pushed forward to search out the enemy, and Maunoury's advanced forces. The Germans advanced a little during the day, and withdrew from their exposed positions under cover of darkness. Next day Maunoury resumed his attack in stronger force. The sting, however, had been partially drawn by the vigourous and unexpected initiative of the enemy.

II

Joffre had at last completed his dispositions. He had prepared his blow in complete secrecy. The enemy had been deceived by the continued retreat, and felt sure that it would continue beyond the Seine, as indeed had been contemplated on September 2nd. It was thought impossible that troops so apparently demoralized could turn and fight without at least several days' rest out of contact with the enemy. Down to the night of the 4th–5th the great columns had been seen from the air still retreating south by every available road. Moltke, it is true, no longer believed that the French had been overthrown beyond remedy, for he told Helfferich, the Foreign Secretary, on September 4th that 'we must not deceive ourselves. We have had successes but we have not yet had victory. . . . The hardest work is still to be done.' But he had not the smallest inkling that a general counter-offensive was about to break upon his footsore armies.

The Marne then was not a 'miracle' as it appeared to amazed contemporaries, but a brilliant advantage rapidly snatched from the enemy's errors. It is therefore necessary to see more exactly the dispositions of the combatants on September 6th.

The German armies were still in fairly good coherence. Kluck was strengthening his flank, but maintained contact with Bülow through the IIIrd and IXth corps, which were south of the Grand Morin between La Ferté-Gaucher and Esternay, some forty miles south-east of Paris. These were placed temporarily in Bülow's (the IInd) army, of which they formed an advanced right flank. On Bülow's left the IIIrd Saxon army was still advancing well up in line with its left on Vitry-le-François. Thence the Crown Prince's army curved sharply back through the Argonne to the north of Verdun. He and his colleagues were hammering bloodily at the great fortified area; while the enjeopardized German right was outnumbered by four to three, almost as if it formed a great bag, thinly stitched at the bottom.

Joffre's plan was to push in the west side of this bag and smash the bottom; isolate and destroy Kluck; strike Bülow in his right flank and rear, and thus open an enormous hole northwards. The danger to its success was the solid Saxon (the IIIrd) army of Hausen, which had neither marched so far, nor been so heavily engaged as its two right-hand neighbours. If it could break through the weak opposition, the tables would be turned upon Joffre. The right flank and rear of his offensive wing would lie open. Most fortunately the commander was Foch, the most intellectual, magnetic, and unshakable of French generals. Even when the extravagant legends about the next four days assiduously fostered by his staff have been discounted, he stoutly carried out his famous maxim: 'A battle lost is a battle which you think is lost.'

Between the 6th–8th the Allies could gain no decisive advantage. Kluck showed himself the incarnation of offensive energy. Not content with warding off Maunoury's thrust, he determined to smash him entirely by an outflanking movement from the north. He carried troops with extraordinary rapidity from his left to his right—apparently his favourite peace-time manœuvre.[1] One corps is said to have covered 108 kilometres in forty hours, an almost incredible feat. He left Bülow to fend for

[1] See Gén. C. J. Dupont, *Le Haut Commandement allemand en 1914* (1922), p. 66.

himself by withdrawing the IXth and IIIrd corps early on September 7th, filling the gap with a screen of von der Marwitz's cavalry and Jägers well supplied with machine-guns. By the evening of the 8th the IInd army was almost in extremity; but on the other hand Bülow and Hausen were still pushing desperately against the weary and shaken troops under the command of Foch and Franchet d'Espérey (now commanding the 5th army). At 8 p.m. the former is said to have sent that legendary telegram to Joffre: 'Mon centre cède; mon aile droite plie—Situation excellente. J'attaque demain.'[1] But deliverance was very near at hand. The gap between the Ist and IInd armies had increased by more than twenty miles. Until now the B.E.F. had not taken adequate advantage of the opportunity for penetration. This was partly due to a rearward march of some twelve miles on the 5th, which Joffre's instructions had not reached French in time to prevent. But the advance towards the Marne was not pushed with the utmost energy, and the use of the cavalry was weak. The ground was certainly difficult, affording plenty of cover to rearguards and intersected by the deep valleys of two unfordable rivers, the Grand and Petit Morin. The opposition, though weak, was skilfully handled, but the total British casualties during these three days scarcely exceeded 1,000. All accounts agree that the advance had put the men into the most eager and hearty spirits. It seems that greater resolution on the part of the higher command would have brought the B.E.F. to the Marne by the night of the 8th.[2]

[1] It now seems certain that the German attacks against the Allied left centre were not aiming at a break-through, but at extricating Bülow's IInd army and enabling it to wheel westwards to close the gap. See B. H. Liddell Hart, *Foch, the Man of Orleans* (1931), ch. ix, for an authoritative summary of the evidence.

[2] This criticism, which is generally and forcibly expressed by French military writers, especially Huguet, is considered baseless by Gen. Edmonds, from whose great authority I dissent with hesitation. But it seems that an earlier start was possible on the 7th, that the defence of the Grand Morin was very weak, and that air reports showed that the ground northward was almost clear by 7 a.m. for several miles. Lord Ernest Hamilton in his *First*

Still, the British advance was decisive in bringing about an uncontestable victory, for on the 9th the Ist and IInd German armies fell into a definite retreat. By the 8th the still-expected break-through in Lorraine had definitely failed: the endangered right wing could not therefore be thus indirectly succoured. Moltke then sent Lieut.-Colonel Hentsch, a Staff officer, to tour the head-quarters of the first five armies. His duty was not merely to report but to use if necessary full powers, verbally given, to arrange for a concerted retreat 'should rearward movements have already been initiated'. All seemed reasonably well until he reached Bülow's head-quarters in the evening (Sept. 8). The latter, who was very much cast down, considered retreat unavoidable, and definite orders were given next morning, when the aviators reported the long British columns streaming to the Marne. Kluck, still preoccupied with his own battle, was expecting to gain complete mastery over Maunoury with the aid of a brigade just arrived from Brussels which was fastening on his right rear. Hentsch did not see him, but instructed his Chief-of-Staff, Kuhl, to order a retreat at least as far as Soissons, for he realized that the British were on the rear of the Ist army. Whether or not a victory might have been expected over Maunoury had not the battle been broken off is impossible to answer. But the position and fighting strength of the IInd army seemed to Hentsch so poor that his duty was imperative. It is most probable that his action saved the German right wing, the concerted action of which was now better secured by placing the Ist army again under Bülow's orders.

Seven Divisions (1916) states most frankly, from information supplied by cavalry officers soon afterwards, that 'the advance was slow and cautious, which was perhaps excusable in a tired army to whom anything but retreat was a new experience'. The British cavalry showed no enterprise comparable to that of the French 5th division which almost captured Kluck in his head-quarters at La Ferté-Milon on the evening of the 8th; and the orders do not suggest any possibility of their breaking through the opposing screen into the enemy's communications, which could easily have been thrown into confusion, to judge from German accounts of the conditions in rear. The German cavalry by the 10th was absolutely exhausted. Foch criticized the

The retreat spread eastwards until on the 11th it reached the Crown Prince, who had been attacking violently west and south-west of Verdun, where Sarrail conducted a skilful defence outside the fortified perimeter. The German armies were now on a better alignment, though the gap between Kluck and Bülow had not been filled. They retreated stubbornly and in good order; there was no serious congestion, and no wholesale losses of material.[1]

III

By September 13th the Germans stood and faced their pursuers. They were upon the north of the Aisne on its whole course between Compiègne and Berry-au-Bac, north-west of Rheims. On retrospect, with a full knowledge of their dispositions, it is difficult to see how they could have been driven from this position, except by the demoralization of the defence, or a panic on the side of General Head-quarters,[2] or a wide turning movement from the west, for which the Allies had no forces available in time. The Aisne, particularly between Soissons and Berry-au-Bac has been truly described as the great natural bastion of northern France. It is flanked on the north-west by great forests, and on the south-east by the hills of Rheims, which in turn connect with the naked chalk *glacis* of the Champagne pouilleuse, itself joined on to the tumbled wooded heights of the Argonne. The hills on the north bank not only dominate the country southward, but throw out such a multitude of curving spurs and shoulders towards the river as to dislocate and throw out of direction

inaction of his cavalry on the same day most severely, declaring that they could not believe that the enemy was really beaten. This is doubtless the true explanation of the ineffectiveness of the whole pursuit. The diary of a British infantry officer published in the *Army Quarterly* for 1935 strongly confirms the view that the B.E.F., if called upon, would have been capable of much greater exertions. Duff Cooper in *Haig* (1935) reveals that Haig in his diary strongly criticized the slowness of the advance as due only to French's hesitation.

[1] The Germans lost no more than 14000, prisoners and about 40 guns.

[2] Which almost occurred on the 14th when permission was given to the first three German armies to fall back to the line La Fère–Laon–Rheims, if the Ist could not hold the Aisne position.

any general attack on the crest. This narrow, nearly level summit line, famous in the war by the name of the Chemin des Dames, from the road built by Louis XV for the diversion of his sisters, is only a stage, not a goal. Behind it lies the Ailette stream, with its own steep northward banks rising almost as high. Nine miles to the rear is the great dominating isolated keep of Laon.

Moreover, the enemy, now close to the excellent railway system of northern France, disposed of much larger forces to protect his right wing. The VIIth reserve corps after weary forced marches[1] arrived from the fall of Maubeuge just in time to fill finally the gap between Kluck and Bülow. Between the 14th and 16th two corps arrived from Belgium, where they had been engaged in repelling an important Belgian sortie from Antwerp, which unfortunately was broken off too early to be of serious strategic assistance. The defeated German left wing had at last been considerably weakened by transfers, and the formation of the VIIth army round La Fère gave the Germans a strategic reserve to maintain stabilization. Finally, the weather, which had been hot and brilliant, became consistently unfavourable to the attack. A strong and cold north wind drove rain and sometimes thick mist into the face of the Allies. The British share in this bloody, protracted[2] and almost stationary battle was both brilliant and tenacious. Great dash and ingenuity were shown in crossing the river under heavy fire on the 13th when all the bridges but one had been wholly or partially destroyed. The fighting is chiefly notable for the tactical handling and extreme bravery shown by small units. It has been truly described as a typical 'soldier's battle'. For that very reason no details will be given, for the scope of this work necessarily confines it to the larger issues.

The Aisne marks in many ways the end of a war epoch.

[1] Forty miles in the last twenty-four hours: it arrived on the 13th two hours before the British 1st corps.

[2] The battle continued almost without intermission on the British front from September 13 to 25, though its latter stages degenerated into local conflicts.

The Marne had put an end to German hopes of a quick 'knock-out' blow, for it is impossible to suppose that, had they taken the Channel ports in November, they could have obtained a decision in the bogs of Flanders at the approach of winter. The immediate dismissal of Moltke illustrates the enemy's disillusionment. On the other hand, the stabilization was a cruel disappointment to the Allies, where an optimism had arisen even in the highest military circles[1] which appears extravagant now, as it then did to Kitchener. Nearly one-tenth of France remained in the grip of the enemy, and that perhaps the richest part of her soil. This was not merely mortifying, but materially of enormous importance: 80 per cent. of French coal, almost the whole of the iron resources, together with the great factories of the north had been lost for the whole of the war. Without this aid it is most improbable that the Germans could have endured for more than four years. On the other hand, time was ensured for the British Empire to develop fully its enormous strength, and for Russia, before her final collapse, to deal the Central Powers many terrible blows. To use a financial metaphor, capital appreciation must be on the side of the Allies unless both statesmen and soldiers were criminally spendthrift.

From a military point of view the Aisne began the long period of stationary warfare over two-thirds of the front. From Compiègne to Belfort for three and a half years in spite of the most tremendous battles, sometimes thrice fought, as in Champagne, over the same country, the ebb and flow of advance never reached ten miles.

Trench-warfare it is true was in its merest infancy. A soldier of Vauban would have despised the deep, narrow, discontinuous holes and the improvised shelters in which the combatants lay over against each other in the everlasting posture of cramped gladiators. But the Germans were already reasonably well equipped with bombs, rifle-grenades, and illuminating flares, thus holding a great

[1] See, for example, the extracts from Sir Henry Wilson's diary given in Gen. Sir C. E. Callwell, *Life and Diaries of Sir Henry H. Wilson* (1927), vol. i.

advantage over the Allies. They also led the way in bringing up quantities of heavy howitzers, the immobility of which made their use impracticable in open warfare. The superiority of high-explosive over shrapnel for blasting a way through fortified positions was now becoming evident. Herein the British were extremely short of munitions as compared either with the Germans or the French. Another lesson of stationary warfare was being brought home alike to all the combatants. The enormous amount of ammunition daily required far exceeded all estimates in peace-time; and by the end of September the quantity and quality of the shells fired on either side was deteriorating. On the other hand the gunners, with unprecedented opportunities of finding the range at leisure—the process was called 'registration'—on all important tactical features developed an extreme accuracy. They were powerfully supported by the liaison of aeroplanes equipped with wireless. In this new tactical contrivance the British seem to have been pioneers.

The war already showed signs of developing that immense superiority of material over the individual which stamped it with its most ruthless and terrifying feature.

III

TANNENBERG AND LEMBERG

I

In March 1914 an article, generally attributed to Sukhomlinov, the War Minister, appeared in a Russian paper saying boastfully: 'The army is not only large but excellently equipped. Russia has always fought on foreign soil and has always been victorious. Russia is no longer on the defensive, Russia is ready.' In reality the army which went out to war was more curiously compounded of good and bad elements than even most human products.

Its Commander-in-Chief, the Grand Duke Nicholas, an uncle of the Tsar, was the austere, reserved and very capable general whose strategical capacity and iron determination have received many tributes of respect and even admiration from his enemies. His great hold over the army, which he maintained in comparatively strict discipline, made him unpopular in Court circles, especially with the jealous and neurotic Tsarina, who was constantly moving her husband's feeble mind against him. Among the higher command there were Russky and Alexeiev, who were among the most scientific soldiers in Europe, Brussilov and the Bulgarian Dmitriev, unsurpassed fighting leaders; there were others, of whom we shall see examples in the East Prussian campaign, of almost incredible inefficiency and carelessness. The Staffs seem on the whole to have been bad, partly because of the prevalence of social influence in planting unsuitable young aristocrats, partly because officers went to the Staff College too young and had little or no regimental experience.[1] The technical

[1] Practically all the higher commands down to and including that of a regiment were ear-marked for them. This discouraged regimental officers and increased their natural laziness. A good picture of the slackness and slovenly organization of the General Staff at Petrograd is given by Sir S. J. Hoare, *The Fourth Seal* (1930), pp. 49, 50. During May 1916 there were fifteen public holidays during which the office was completely closed. See also Gen. A. A. Brussilov, *A Soldier's Notebook, 1914–18* (1930), pp. 23–5.

equipment, as might be expected, was much behind western standards; the proportion of field-guns to infantry little more than half the German, and the amount of heavy artillery negligible. Reserves both of ammunition and rifles were exceedingly insufficient, and facilities for their manufacture very poor, especially after the German agents blew up the Putilov works at Petrograd in 1915. Finally, both the civil, and to a less degree the military, administration were ruined by the grossest corruption and by pro-German influences. Sukhomlinov, for example, was a shocking mixture of corruption and cynical inefficiency. Colonel Myasoyadov, a Staff officer of the 10th army, was hanged in April 1915 for systematically betraying all its secrets to the Germans.

Russia could not, therefore, reap the advantage of her immense population, which in 1914 was at least as great as that of France, Germany, and Austria-Hungary combined. For a long time the Western Allies pinned their faith to the inexhaustible supply of dumb, lazy, patient, fatalistically brave peasants, whose supposedly irresistible weight was popularly described as 'the Russian steam roller'. As they could not be brought into the field neither could they be led. It is supposed that two-thirds of the population of Russia were illiterate, and the N.C.O.s, 75 per cent. of whom were short-term conscripts, compared wretchedly with the magnificent long-service cadre of the Germans.

The enemy's secrets were soon revealed by the progress of mobilization. The whole weight of Germany was against France. In the east she left the minimum of forces which the Russian Staff had considered possible, namely, eleven infantry divisions and one cavalry.

The Russian plans, in the event of this occurrence, had not provided for any decisive concentration against either Germany or Austria; it was apparently proposed to conduct a leisurely offensive against both. But it was willingly recognized that something must be done as soon as possible to help France. It is perhaps a hard saying to suggest that casual and unbusinesslike persons are very ready with chivalrous gestures, just because they attach so little value to their own plans. Accordingly the offensive against Austria was to go on—as we have seen in the previous chapter, its abandonment would have been very difficult in face of the intense popular excitement about Serbia—while an improvised one was to be vamped up against Germany. The French wanted the attack to be made on Posen, the nearest point to Berlin. But this would have delayed its opening by requiring very extensive changes in concentration, and would have brought the Russians against a formidable area of permanent fortifications which they had no heavy guns to reduce. Consequently East Prussia was chosen as the objective. No important strategical result could be gained until the line of the Vistula should be forced,[1] but it was hoped to destroy the weak German forces before they could gain the security of that great stream. Moreover, the province was the home of the old Prussian aristocracy; the Kaiser himself had great estates there, and it was regarded with peculiar pride as an outpost of Teutonic culture, captured in medieval times from the heathen by the Knights of the Sword. The political consequences of a successful invasion might therefore be great. In fact the flow of refugees pouring westward from the invaded territory, many of whom reached Berlin, powerfully contributed to the determination of Moltke to reinforce the German troops in the east on August 25th. The country, as the Russians knew well, presented many most formidable military obstacles. In particular a chain of almost continuous lake and forest, known as the Masurian lake position, extending for fifty miles north and south, blocked more than half the route of invasion from the east. Between this barrier and the sea a flat and more open country, following the course of the Pregel, was suitable to operations. But the important

[1] Ludendorff, however, points out that, if the Germans had been forced to retire to that river, they would have been unable to help the Austrians in September. This might have caused the total collapse of the latter with fatal consequences for Germany.

naval fortress of Königsberg would menace the right flank of a force pushing forward towards the Vistula. The Russians were not, however, forced to rely solely on a frontal attack, as their position in the Polish salient made possible an advance from the south, which would take the

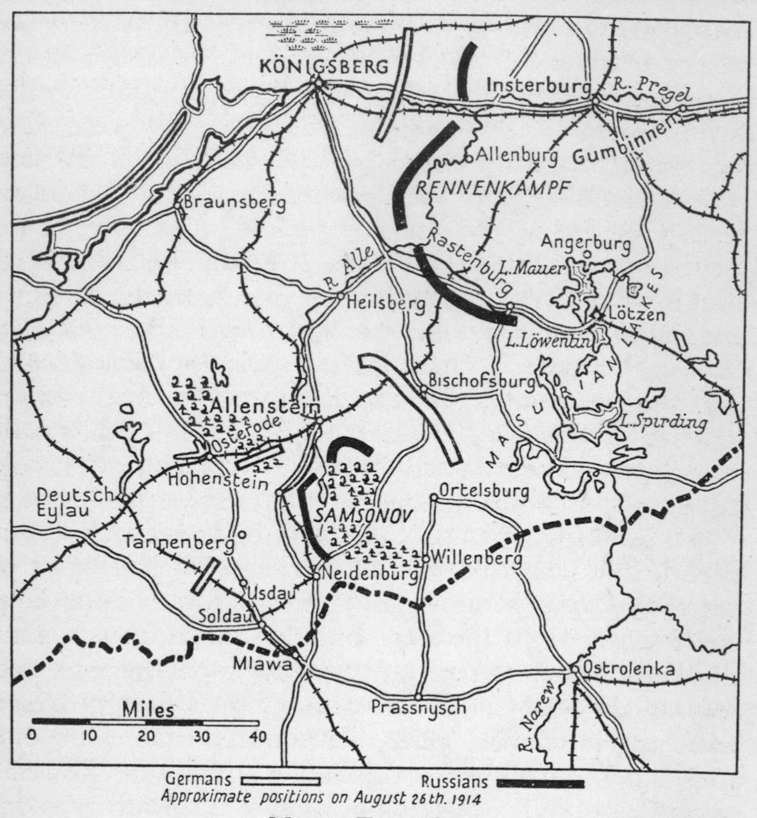

MAP 4. Tannenberg.

Masurian lakes in the rear and might hope to join hands with a successful invasion along the coast route. This concentric advance was adopted. It is obvious that success in war can only be expected if a careful time-table is drawn up, if transport and supplies are sufficient to enable it to be maintained, and if close touch is kept between two converging armies. None of these conditions were fulfilled in the East Prussian campaign.

The Russian advance began on the 17th. Rennenkampf, commanding the 1st army of three corps, marched westward in the direction of Königsberg. The commander of the German VIIIth army, von Prittwitz, opposed him with all his available forces except one corps, which watched the south, where it was believed that no enemy offensive would be possible for some days. Three of his corps were defeated on the 20th, though not heavily, at Gumbinnen, about ten miles within the frontier. The local situation was awkward, as the best line of defence (the River Angerapp) was too close to the battle-field to be securely held if the Russians pushed on quickly; but it was by no means desperate. Rennenkampf had been hard hit:[1] his left was entangled in a large forest, roads were few, and his movements from the 17th did not suggest any capacity for speed. But at the same time it was reported that Samsonov with the 2nd Russian army had almost reached the frontier 100 miles to the south-west; the available opposition amounted to one corps only. Prittwitz collapsed, and issued orders for a retreat behind the Vistula.

It is perfectly true that Schlieffen had constantly practised such a manœuvre in war-games with the object of preserving intact the small German forces until help could arrive from the west, and for that reason Ludendorff himself takes a curiously lenient view of the projected retirement. Yet the abandonment of a whole province by a retreat of more than one hundred miles after one partial defeat seems unjustified even on military grounds, apart from political. It seemed so to his Staff, who regarded their chief as panic-stricken.[2] Prittwitz's own report to Moltke expressing doubts whether he could hold the Vistula itself owing to the lowness of the water suggests that he had lost his head. His orders were not carried out and he was dismissed next day.

[1] Russian casualties on the 20th were 16,000.

[2] Max Hoffmann in *The War of Lost Opportunities* (1924) shows the military objections to such a course very clearly, and points out that the army while retreating would have been exposed to a deadly flank-blow from Samsonov.

II

Moltke now by his happiest inspiration called into their war-long partnership that famous pair, Hindenburg and Ludendorff. The perfect harmony of their collaboration is not less striking than their apparent contrast—Hindenburg, the most loyal, honourable, and unselfish of all Germany's great soldiers, was a veteran of noble birth, called out of retirement to rescue his native province, a shrewd fighting man with no pretence of intellectual distinction. Ludendorff, of middle-class origin, nearly twenty years his junior, harsh and overbearing in temper, considered nothing outside the province of his restless mind His power of work and mastery over detail can rarely have been equalled in history. He was the finest product in all its excellencies and defects of a staff whose technical training was unrivalled. All would have set down his temper as unshakable had it not broken suddenly on September 29th, 1918. The exact relation between the two men is not certain—Hindenburg himself compares it to a happy marriage—but the directing and creative mind was that of the young Chief-of-Staff. The two met at Hanover station for the first time in their lives.

On arrival at the head-quarters of the VIIIth army at Marienburg on the 23rd, Ludendorff, though received with the most distant chilliness, found conditions less black than they had been painted. The ingenious and profound Colonel Hoffmann, head of the Operations Department, who played one of the most interesting roles in the war, had already stopped the retreat and actually prepared a scheme which Ludendorff embodied almost without alteration in his orders and which secured the most spectacular victory of the war.

Samsonov commanded an army of five corps, or nearly 200,000 men, which had been hastily improvised and was rushed to the attack without any proper commissariat. Its marches over a sandy desert, unfed, in the burning heat, had already, by the 22nd,[1] demoralized its fighting

[1] The men had no field-kitchens. They seem—not unnaturally—to have

capacity. Samsonov paid no attention to the orders of the Commander-in-Chief of the north-west front, Jilinski, a fussy and incompetent man who owed his appointment to his assiduity at Court. But his own deviation is inexcusable, for instead of moving north with his right on the lakes in such a way as to gain touch with the 1st army between Insterburg and Königsberg, he kept extending his frontage to the west. This increased the distance between the two armies, especially as Rennenkampf halted for nearly three days after the 20th. Samsonov's miserable army, without reconnaissance, without information, crawled slowly forward towards Allenstein–Osterode, constantly extending its frontage as its wastage grew greater. On the 26th it spread over sixty miles, facing north-west, with its right thrust forward and isolated in the lake district, its left on the Russian frontier.

Ludendorff's dispositions appear bold to the point of rashness. He actually removed all his forces except a cavalry division from facing Rennenkampf, who had covered rather more than half the distance between Gumbinnen and Königsberg by the 26th, and prepared for the annihilation of Samsonov.

The Germans could obviously always shift troops far more quickly than their opponents, as they had the advantage of interior lines admirably served by their railways. But the Russian movements were known to their enemy almost completely: they used wireless *en clair*[1] with the utmost recklessness, and their cipher was also in German hands. Moreover, there is strong suspicion that Rennenkampf was a traitor. In itself no explanation so plausibly accounts for the transformation from the daring leader in the Russo-Japanese War to the supine, nay, paralysed incompetent of 1914. His German origin and his desertion of his army next year support this melancholy

committed many outrages in East Prussia, whereas the 1st army on hostile evidence maintained a very strict discipline.

[1] This practice, due to the inability of many staffs to decode ciphers, went on for more than a year.

conclusion. It is quite inconceivable that a commander, who had been himself a cavalry leader, who had five divisions of cavalry or five times the total force left to oppose him, should have allowed whole divisions to entrain within twenty miles of his main body unless he deliberately held up his own cavalry. It is true that Jilinski had particularly told him to deal with Königsberg, into which he incorrectly supposed that the bulk of the German forces had retired. It is also true that the role of the Russian cavalry in the war was most disappointing; their power of reconnaissance was extremely limited. But these considerations are wholly inadequate to explain his prolonged inaction. The only other possible solution is that given by Hoffmann, who believes that Rennenkampf deliberately refused to help Samsonov, because the two had been at bitter enmity since the Russo-Japanese War, when they had so far forgotten their dignity as to fight on Mukden station. If the former assumption is true, Ludendorff deserves no credit for his justified belief that the 1st army would remain immobile; but it does not minimize the glory of the splendid manœuvres against Samsonov. By thus uniting all his forces, he gained a superiority over the 2nd Russian army.[1]

The strategic railways of East Prussia allowed this concentration to be accomplished within three days. By the 26th Ludendorff was ready for battle. On that day the Russian right was routed and took no further part in the fighting. On the 27th it was the turn of the extreme left, which was bombarded out of a strong defensive position near Usdau, utterly disorganized and cut off from the main body. The centre itself fought better in spite of its famished condition; for Samsonov, who had not yet any idea of the great forces arrayed against him, was himself attacking. But the Germans poured through the gaping left flank. That famous fighter von François for the third time disobeyed, with the happiest results, the orders of his

[1] Of 23 battalions, 82 field- and 116 heavy guns. In cavalry the Germans were outnumbered by exactly two to one.

superiors. Instead of taking his XXth corps northward as directed, he thrust straight east in the enemy's rear along a good road beyond the forest fringe. By the 30th the German columns extended southward far beyond the possible line of their enemy's retreat. Two whole corps, enmeshed in the forest, where they were staggering in blind exhaustion, surrendered. Samsonov crept aside from his staff in the darkness and shot himself, to be buried in an unknown grave. Few victories in history have been so crushingly complete. The number of prisoners exceeded that taken at Sedan:[1] though owing to the difference in scale between the two wars, the earlier victory was far more momentous in consequences. Ludendorff named this masterpiece Tannenberg, to avenge the medieval overthrow of the Teutonic Knights by the Slavs. But he owed its annihilating completeness entirely to François.

Rennenkampf's foot-tied army still brooded over the north. The next task was to free German soil completely from the invader, with the aid of the two corps which Moltke had dispatched from the West. Rennenkampf occupied a strong defensive position from the sea to the northern edge of the Masurian lakes, covering Insterburg, his chief advanced base.[2] No double envelopment, therefore, could be practised against him. But his weak spot lay to the south. The Lötzen gap, no more than a mile wide, between the lakes was still in German hands, as the Russian lack of heavy artillery had prevented them from reducing the little fort which commanded it. This attack was in charge of François, whose ardent and resolute spirit had led him to be chosen for all the critical flanking movements in this campaign. He pushed on far to the east, but Rennenkampf escaped destruction. He hurriedly left on September 9th–10th his strongly fortified position, before which the German frontal attack had been repulsed

[1] Sedan about 85,000; Tannenberg about 120,000 including wounded.

[2] Russian rolling-stock could not be used on the East Prussian railways owing to the difference of gauge.

and which Ludendorff considers to have been impregnable with the forces at his disposal. The Russian 1st army fell into a confused rout, of which the German commander perhaps failed to take complete advantage. Rennenkampf himself left his troops and fled eighty miles to Kovno with his staff. 'News so improbable as to require verification', was Jilinski's comment. It was not a Tannenberg, but it was bad enough. The 1st army had lost 125,000 men; its moral was shattered.[1] The Germans pressed on as far as the lower Niemen and the great forest of Augustovo, the last home of the wild bison or Lithuanian aurochs which was almost exterminated during the war.

Other imperative calls were being made upon the German troops, for their Austrian allies were being critically defeated far to the south in Galicia.

III

The Austrian army had some good points. The regimental officers though often too old were as a whole hard-working and keen on their profession and on good terms with their men.[2] The heavy artillery was admirable. But the Staff work, as the Germans constantly complained, was loose and untrustworthy, and its members almost as completely out of touch with regimental officers as were the Russians. Its chief, Conrad von Hotzendorff, was a most accomplished strategist, a devoted worker, a grim disciplinarian, one of the most voluminous minute-writers of his generation, but an incurably political soldier. Yet the whole body was infected with a mortal disease

[1] The Russian losses during the first month in East Prussia amounted to over 300,000 and 650 guns, or about a quarter of their fighting troops then mobilized. These figures compare curiously with French losses in the battle of the Frontiers; but the Russians had little of the astonishing recuperative capacity of the French.

[2] They must have often had great difficulties in making themselves understood, as 75 per cent. of them are said to have been of German origin, while the German-speaking soldiers were only about 25 per cent. 'It often happened that a platoon-commander could not make himself intelligible to his motley collection of men' (*Austrian Official History*).

when faced with a war against Russia. For at least half[1] of the combatants were indifferent or actively hostile to the cause which they were nominally espousing. The Russians, it is true, had in their armies a considerable mass of subject peoples herded in their own regiments, but they were for the most part too unintelligent and illiterate to cause trouble, and were moreover united in their hatred and fear of the Germans. The Slavs of the Dual Empire were far better organized and expected their deliverance from a Russian victory, though by no means all regarded Russia as a liberator. The Poles of Galicia on the whole preferred Austria to Russia—Pilsudski, the dictator of Poland for many years after the war, had even organized a legion to fight the Tsar's armies when hostilities began—for Austria had treated her Poles with indulgence during recent years owing to the decisive position which their deputies held in the Reichsrath. The proclamation by the Grand Duke Nicholas promising a resurrection of the ancient kingdom, autonomously governed under the sceptre of the Tsar, was not unjustly suspected as an insincere snare. This cynical view was confirmed by the Russian occupation, which favoured the Orthodox Ruthenian against the Catholic Pole, and provided in a new Archbishop of Lemberg a most tactless, forcible missionary. The Poles therefore, though far from enthusiastic soldiers, caused the rulers of Austria-Hungary little serious uneasiness. It was far otherwise with the Czechs and Slovaks[2] and the southern Slavs. The former in particular were universally and secretly organized from abroad by such great patriots as Masaryk and Benes. Men of both these nationalities took every opportunity of deserting to the Russians, often being able by prearranged signals and songs to allow the latter to know of their presence in the line. That the Dual Monarchy finally shivered into fragments is no

[1] The *Austrian Official History* reckons the German-Magyar element at 48 per cent.

[2] The unreliability of these soldiers was proved in the first battles against Serbia, where the XXIst division allowed itself to be routed and dispersed.

marvel. The marvel is rather that it survived the death, in 1916, of the aged Francis Joseph who had gradually gathered to his person some of that shadowy and superstitious loyalty which clings to a permanent fetish, and that it endured four and a half years of a war, long considered hopeless by its more penetrating statesmen. It is no paradox to say that the army was partially rewelded by the fresh war which broke out in 1915, for the great majority of Slavs hated, feared, and despised the Italians.

It appears that, on the outbreak of war, the German Staff in justified mistrust would have preferred to see the Austrians stand defensively on the River San and allow the Russian waves to break against this natural barrier, reinforced by the two great fortresses of Jaroslav and Przemysl, until the German armies were in a position to lend substantial aid. For Moltke was quite unable to fulfil his pre-war promise of an immediate offensive on the Narew. The Austrians complained bitterly of this desertion by their ally, and not unreasonably. But even so it was almost impossible for them to agree to such a confession of weakness for many reasons. Time was presumably on the Russian side; her hordes, if allowed an unruffled concentration, might prove literally overwhelming. The evacuation of East Galicia would involve the abandonment of the oil-wells and of the great city of Lemberg, an important centre of communications, and it would endanger the eastern plain of Hungary. It would have the worst effect upon the doubtful and calculating attitude of Rumania and might jeopardize the agreement already signed with Turkey.

The Austrians employed an obvious but quite good strategy, provided that they were in a position to carry it through with relentless energy, which they were not.[1]

[1] This plan had been betrayed to the Russians before the war by an officer, Col. Redl, in the Austrian War Office who on discovery accepted the choice of suicide. Fifteen divisions besides the 'minimum Balkan force of eleven and a half' had been assigned to the southern front in the original mobilization against Serbia, thus seriously weakening the northern offensive. It was found impossible to transport most of these to Galicia in time to

They knew that the Russian concentration was mostly taking place to the east of Warsaw behind the screen of the Vistula. Consequently they hoped by an advance from north-east Galicia between Lublin and Cholm to cut the railways leading thence to Warsaw and Brest-Litovsk; and, in the event of a further success, to reach the main line between the last two places. The Vistula fortresses would be menaced both from north and east if the Austrians could maintain their positions until the expected German attack from the Narew. The danger lay in the possibility that they might be caught in the advance and so mauled as to compromise the security of the San, the vital barrier to Cracow, that double key whence open roads lead north and south through the Moravian gate to the hearts of Germany and Austria. And so it came about. The Austrian forces, organized in three armies of ten divisions each, made at first good if delusive progress to the north. Here their enemy was thinnest, being a flanking force designed to reach the San and intercept the expected retirement of the Austrians on Cracow under pressure from the main advance farther east. The Russians, whether by accident or design, had placed their best soldiers in charge of their southern armies. Ivanov, Russky, Dmitriev, and Brussilov were all men of power and energy. Brussilov drove back the Austrian right flank, outnumbered by nearly three to one, through the broken country of eastern Galicia, where river after river, running north and south into the Dniester, lay athwart his advance. Lemberg, the capital of Galicia, the fourth city of the Empire, a great centre of communications, where four railways meet, was encircled from north and east and fell on September 3rd. The Austrian left still thrust forward far into enemy territory when Auffenburg, its commander, who in ten days' strenuous battle had narrowly missed an enormous victory of encirclement, was finally hurried

take part in the battle of Lemberg, while the one corps which was allowed to remain behind with Potiorek was quite insufficient to prevent his defeat by the Serbs.

back. The counter-attack of Dankl, the most resolute of their generals, in the centre was unavailing. On September 10th the last buttress was broken by a Russian victory at Rava Russka thirty miles north-west of Lemberg, where the armies returning hastily from Poland in a last vain attempt to outflank the Russian masses were themselves almost pinched out of existence. The Austrian retreat did not stop until the San had been crossed and Russian forces appeared on the Wisloka, the next tributary of the Vistula. Of the two fortresses Jaroslav fell immediately, and Przemysl was invested. Its huge garrison of 150,000 men was to suffer many vicissitudes, including one temporary and partial deliverance, during the ensuing siege of six months. In the south Brussilov overran the Bukovina (which is, being interpreted, the 'country of the Beech-woods') and took its capital Czernovitz, which was destined to change masters fifteen times during the war. His advanced posts had reached the easternmost passes leading to Hungary through the wooded Carpathians.

The Austrian losses had been very severe, especially in younger officers and N.C.O.s, who were irreplaceable. The number of prisoners claimed on both sides in the east can seldom be trusted, but probably the Russians collected about 120,000, including many wholesale and calculated surrenders. Yet, though they had outflanked, they had by no means enveloped their enemies, who were able to reform during the last half of September behind the Wisloka, while the Russians were busily employed in broadening the gauge of the Galician railways.[1] It is obvious that more decisive results could have been obtained had a Russian army advanced up the Vistula with the aim of cutting the Austrians from Cracow, but apparently this was considered too dangerous a manœuvre. And so the five cavalry divisions in south-west Poland

[1] The difficulty of bringing up supplies was increased by the scarcity of railways in the Government of Lublin. This had been a deliberate policy in order to create a desert of communications—in case of invasion, for the Russians had intended to stand on the defensive in this region, as they knew the Austrian plan of attack.

seem to have frittered away their opportunities in aimless cavalcades during September, instead of seriously threatening the enemy's rear in West Galicia.

Meanwhile the Austrians, both by hatred and policy, felt themselves obliged to carry out the 'punitive expedition' against Serbia, which they had prepared before the general war had broken out. And they attempted this with barely half the force ear-marked for the purpose. Two reserve corps (little adapted to meet the primitive bravery of the skilful mountaineers among their native hills) had, by the end of August, after a number of confused combats, been thrown out of the north-west angle of Serbian territory, which they had so rashly invaded. At least 40,000 men had been squandered without any result. No further attempt was made against Serbian territory for three months.

Austria, everywhere defeated, was in sore straits.[1] For the first of many occasions she had to request the immediate support of her ally. The German Staff responded at once with that admirable promptitude and superior arrogance which made the senior partner such a trustworthy and unpleasant ally.

The VIIIth army was deprived of its best troops, which were sent to form a new offensive IXth army to be concentrated round Breslau in the second half of September. More important still, Hindenburg and Ludendorff also came south to take command. Risks had been taken and sacrifices were exacted, for the weakened forces on the Niemen could not stand against the Russians. But though the enemy appeared again in East Prussia in the first week of October, he was firmly held in the outermost nook of that province, eastward of the lake barrier. The renewed invasion was grievous to the inhabitants and galling to national pride, but it had no military importance. Therefore no attempt at expulsion was made until the whole eastern front was stabilized. When it came in February it

[1] The *Austrian Official History* admits the loss of 350,000 men in the battles against the Russians alone.

was a typically crushing blow. The forward march for the first great combined invasion of Poland began on September 28th. These operations, which form a connected whole, led to an almost continuous clash of armies until the end of the year.

IV

THE NAVAL SITUATION AT THE BEGINNING OF WAR

I

IT seems at first sight far easier to gauge the relative strength of fleets than of armies. As a satirical writer put it, each great Power claimed to have the best army in the world, but its navy was inexorably graded according to the number of capital ships and big guns which it possessed.

On such a comparison the strength of the Entente, after the adhesion of Japan and the neutrality of Italy, appeared absolutely overwhelming. The British fleet alone was considerably superior to that of the two Central Powers combined, while Austrian naval strength was inferior to that of France or Japan or even Russia.

Yet the sea is far larger than the land, and almost every part of it is a highway for ships. And while the conflict on land must be confined to comparatively small areas within which the defence could be concentrated almost as rapidly as the attack, the vital interests of the Entente were flung about and scattered over all the oceans. One error in strategy, perhaps even a grave tactical mistake, might expose all these interests to immediate and irretrievable ruin.

Moreover, the whole conditions of naval warfare seemed to be in the melting-pot of a wholly untested revolution. 'His (the admiral's) warfare is almost entirely novel. Scarcely any one had even had any experience of sea-fighting. All had to learn the strange, new, unmeasured and, in times of peace, largely immeasurable conditions.'[1]

Since Admiral Togo had annihilated the Russian fleet

[1] Quoted from an article by Winston Churchill in *London Magazine* (September 1916). The violent controversies since 1918 between eminent professional sailors as to the fundamentals of British war strategy confirm Churchill's view.

in the Straits of Tsushima in 1905, the change had been astounding. There can be no other decade in naval history in which technical development progressed with such giant strides.

The *Dreadnought* had at a stroke made all earlier warships obsolete. The all-big-gun battleship, with no secondary armament, helped by its flexible gun-mountings threw a weight of broadside which could utterly overwhelm any rival of a former design. In consequence vast new fleets had to be feverishly built, almost every unit of which was itself an experiment.[1] The range of the big gun itself increased at a no less revolutionary speed. While in 1904 its limit of effectiveness was placed at about 4,000 yards, the great ships in the war opened against one another at five times that distance. Such a change obviously demanded new tactics of gunnery and generally a higher standard of scientific fire control and direction.[2]

As the battleships towered in progressive majesty over their predecessors, so also their lesser enemies, who act by stealth and cunning, increased their power of inflicting a deadly wound to at least the same degree.

The destroyer steaming at 40 knots could carry five or six torpedoes capable of hitting a target at least five miles away with an explosive power which had been multiplied threefold in a few years.

The submarine had not indeed attained its full stature in 1914; but it was already able to cruise continuously for days over the whole extent of the North Sea, to lie submerged for many hours waiting to discharge a torpedo at point-blank range, and to sow unsuspected mines wherever it went.

To all these new factors must also be added the enormous power which wireless gave the Admiralty or the admiral of instantly informing, controlling, and concen-

[1] Tirpitz says in his *Memoirs*, with some exaggeration, 'Every ship became obsolete by the time it was finished'.

[2] An excellent description of fire control on a battle-cruiser, the *Derfflinger*, is given in G. von Hase, *Kiel and Jutland* (1921; 2nd ed., 1927).

trating scattered units; whilst airships and aeroplanes vastly enlarged the area of scouting. The value of a Zeppelin in clear weather was estimated by the British Commander-in-Chief to be equivalent to that of two light cruisers.

It is clear therefore that the sea presented far more unknown hazards than the land in the event of a great war—and the danger was greatest where the weight of responsibility was most heavily borne. For the conduct of the naval war depended absolutely upon Great Britain. If the British navy were decisively defeated, the fleets of the Entente would weigh but as straw in the balance against that of victorious Germany. Her siege would be raised, and she would regain liberty of action over all the seas, and carry on the land struggle with the confident assurance of continually replenishing her supplies and denying to her enemies all that they drew by sea. So for her continental allies the fleet of Britain was always an indispensable condition of victory, if their own unaided military effort failed to force an immediate decision. This they came very gradually to understand,[1] though many Germans had realized it from the beginning.

Even the most uninstructed civilian realized that the Navy was the one 'sure shield' of the British Empire and its parent island in the North Sea. As long as it was extended in unshaken defence the war could not merely be indefinitely prolonged, but nourished on the Continent in an ever greater degree with men, munitions, and money. One decisive defeat, however, would doom the alliance to almost certain ruin, and immediately destroy

[1] The following quotation from Sir H. Wilson's *Life*, vol. i, p. 122, shows the astonishing pre-war misconceptions about sea-power prevalent among generals of the Entente: 'My talk with Castelnau and Joffre was about Repington's recent articles in *The Times*, where he claims that our navy is worth 500,000 bayonets to the French at the decisive point. I had written to Fred Oliver that our Navy was not worth 500 bayonets. Castelnau and Joffre did not value it as one bayonet! Except from the moral point.' For a far-sighted German point of view, see Adm. A. von Tirpitz, *My Memories* (1919), vol. ii, App. 1: *Extracts from my War Letters*, *passim*.

the British Empire. As Churchill said with truth and point, the Commander-in-Chief of the British fleet was the only man 'who could lose the war in an afternoon'. The British Isles even without an invasion could be starved out in a few weeks, as soon as the enemy's ships had gained control of the trade routes which converge upon our ports. They would not even have been put to the trouble of capture, for not a merchantman would have moved out of harbour to face such a domination. The inevitable surrender would have been one of the most complete in history. Great Britain would have been instantly reduced to 'the conscript appendage of a stronger power'.[1] It is not within the scope of this work to sketch the intense Anglo-German naval rivalry of the pre-war decades. Both sides thought of this rivalry essentially in terms of capital ships. The British Admiralty therefore acted on three guiding principles in relation to these units. A superiority of at least 60 per cent. must be maintained over the total number possessed by Germany; ship for ship the British design must be (as far as practicable) swifter and more powerful; finally, the whole fleet must be capable of such a rapid concentration as to make its component parts secure against a surprise attack at the enemy's selected moment with his whole strength.

All these three desiderata were obtained at the outbreak of war, though the concentration upon great ships had left a comparatively small margin of superiority in light cruisers and destroyers, while the enemy had the advantage in the number and quality of his submarines.

The Grand Fleet included twenty dreadnoughts against the thirteen of Germany, or a proportion of 100 to 65.[2]

[1] The phrase is taken from a speech of Viscount Grey.

[2] If battle-cruisers are included the British margin is slightly diminished, as we had four to Germany's three (the battle-cruiser had a similar armament to that of the battleship but was swifter and less heavily armoured). The comparison in these figures is between the fleets in the North Sea only, the decisive point. Thirteen British ships were armed with 13·5 guns and the remainder with 12-inch. Nine German ships had 12-inch and the remainder 11-inch guns. In other areas we had four dreadnoughts against one German.

Each of these on paper appeared more formidable than her contemporary adversary; in fact, however, as will be shown, battle experience showed this assumption to be not altogether well founded, though it was entertained at the beginning by the enemy as well.

The safe passage to and concentration of the fleet in its war stations on the North Sea was assured by a providential coincidence. The British Admiralty had arranged as early as October 1913 that a test mobilization[1] should take the place of the normal manœuvres for the summer of 1914. All the most valuable ships had therefore assembled at Portland when the Austrian ultimatum to Serbia was announced. On Churchill's initiative the fleet was not dispersed when the allotted time had expired; and during the night of July 29th–30th it steamed secretly through the Straits of Dover without lights and next day was distributed in its allotted posts facing Germany.

II

Thus the fleet was in a position to carry out fully its prearranged strategical plan before the outbreak of war. It was now able to intercept and engage with its full force any enterprise by the German High Seas Fleet, and possessed a superiority which should be sufficient to inflict a decisive defeat upon the latter if it offered battle.

If, on the other hand, the enemy remained in harbour, our dispositions were well adapted to close the two exits from the North Sea to the Ocean (the Straits of Dover 21 miles wide, and, 500 miles to the north, the passage between the Shetlands and Norway 190 miles wide) to his merchantmen and raiders; to protect Great Britain

[1] The importance of this scheme lay in the fact that reservists, though not legally liable, had been invited to join these ships for the period of the mobilization. The numbers who responded proved to be very large, and the fleet was therefore fully manned on a war footing. There seems to be no reason to suppose that the mobilization had been arranged so far in advance from any fear of European complications—on the contrary the chief motive was economy (see Winston Churchill, *The World Crisis 1911–14* (1923), 189–90).

MAP 5. The North Sea.

against invasion; and to secure the passage of an army to France.

Though the map shows that geography greatly favoured the British strategical position on the North Sea as opposed to that of Germany, steps had not been taken to develop this asset. As our naval dispositions had been directed primarily against France for hundreds of years, the south coast contained an abundance of fortified and securely defended ports. On the east, however, no such advantages existed. The plans for the new concentration there had gone far ahead of the provisions for carrying them out safely. Only four naval bases were available along the whole coastline: Scapa Flow in the Orkneys, Cromarty, Rosyth on the Firth of Forth, and Harwich (this last being suitable for light craft only). None of these were submarine-proof; and Scapa and Cromarty were defended only by improvised detachments with light guns. Docking facilities, moreover, were wholly inadequate.

Although, therefore, the fleet had reached its destined havens, it was to be for several months, paradoxically enough, far more uneasy when resting in them than when cruising in open sea. Thus an added burden was placed upon the Commander-in-Chief, on whom descended automatically so immense a responsibility.

Sir John Jellicoe entered upon his command only at the outbreak of war, after opening a sealed letter which ordered him to supersede his own immediate superior Sir G. Callaghan, considered too old in years to bear the strain. Jellicoe was a man of the highest character, deeply religious, modest, and incapable of intrigue. His career had been that of a pattern officer, distinguished in every examination, deeply versed in every branch of the service. Of his last twelve years more than half had been spent in varied administrative posts, including that of Second Sea Lord.[1] He had a most orderly, exact, comprehensive mind with great mastery over detail. His natural caution was enhanced by the knowledge of the tremendous issues

[1] His duties are concerned with the personnel of the fleet.

always involved in his decisions. Such a personality, as may be imagined, entirely lacked that burning appeal, that irresistible magnetism, which since the days of Nelson had been traditionally expected of the ideal naval leader.

As Sir David Beatty, the commander of his battle-cruisers and his eventual successor, was in almost every particular the very reverse of his chief, it is natural that a most bitter controversy has since raged about their respective theories of war. It is alleged that Jellicoe became so much preoccupied with the problems of defence as to emasculate the offensive spirit. His conduct of the battle of Jutland, which will be later described, is adduced as the culmination of this fault. The spirit which refused to engage the enemy except under conditions of assured superiority is certainly neither romantic nor inspiring. Yet its success in maintaining and increasing British superiority is undeniable. Its correctness has received many sour tributes from the enemy, who was forced to admit that Jellicoe's inactivity provided for Great Britain almost all the essentials of 'a fleet in being'.[1]

If Beatty had been in supreme command in 1914 and had adopted a more daring policy he might have shortened the war by years through the destruction of the German fleet, or he might have ruined the British Empire by incurring a disaster. History has decreed that either hypothesis must remain unproved. The ultimate responsibility for the strategy pursued rests in any event with the Admiralty rather than with the Commander-in-Chief; for the latter was continued in office after he had frankly explained his policy early in the war to his political superiors.

In effect the Admiralty from its great wireless masts in Whitehall necessarily directed and controlled strategy far

[1] The exception was the continued German control of the Baltic, which (i) made it impossible for Prussia to be invaded from the sea; (ii) secured Germany the transport of iron ore from Sweden—both very important advantages.

more powerfully than in earlier wars. For it had unrivalled facilities for intercepting and decoding the messages of the enemy, and thus was able to piece his intentions together far more completely and quickly than Jellicoe's Staff could have done.

The disposition of the fleet in home waters was as follows. The Grand Fleet under Jellicoe's direct command consisted of all the dreadnought battleships and battle-cruisers. The former were based on the lonely Orkney harbour of Scapa Flow, and on Cromarty; as the most precious nucleus of indispensable strength they were placed as far to the northward as possible, always protected by a strong screen of destroyers. The swift battle-cruisers had their head-quarters at Rosyth. The east coast of England was guarded by flotillas of light craft, issuing from the main estuaries. Harwich provided the centre from which destroyers and submarines worked in the North Sea and against the German coast. The Channel was protected by the Second Fleet which was built up round the most powerful pre-dreadnought battleships, while a number of still more obsolete units were combined in a reserve Third Fleet.

The main weakness therefore inherent in the British position was the long line of coast to be defended,[1] and the scarcity of secure harbours; its main strength lay in its capacity to deal a swift converging blow from the two wings at an enemy emerging into the North Sea from his only exit. For the German fleet was compelled by geography to go out and come back by the same road, the comparatively narrow area bounded on the west by the Dutch frontier, and on the east by the Danish promontory. On the other hand, this restricted sea-space was obviously favourable for defence, and its great geographical advantages had been assiduously improved by art. The so-called 'wet-triangle' enclosed an elaborately fortified system.

[1] The constant westward trend of the coastline, however, made attacks upon it increasingly hazardous the more northerly the point against which they were directed, as a longer journey was necessary from the German bases.

Its apex was the island of Heligoland,[1] which had been transformed in the years preceding 1914 into a great fortress armed with long-range guns. Its other extremities were the island of Sylt off the Schleswig shore, where the channel was navigable only for light cruisers and destroyers, and the mouth of the Ems adjacent to Holland. The estuaries (Ems, Weser, Jade, and Elbe) within these confines contained the battle harbours of the High Seas Fleet. Lying within them, it enjoyed an almost absolute immunity. The approaches are screened by a multitude of islands; the channels themselves are so shallow as to make impossible the unperceived approach of submarines, while the whole triangle was quickly converted into a labyrinth of mines.

All the modern battleships were naturally stationed in the North Sea ports to guard against the British menace. Consequently the independent force which operated in the Baltic (under Prince Henry, the Kaiser's brother) was not able to exercise undisputed control of that sea over the Russians, whose ports curved all round its eastern half from Helsingfors in Finland through Kronstadt to Riga in Livonia, giving them many sally ports and harbours of refuge. The German Admiralty, however, had no need to be anxious lest powerful British forces should break unawares into the Baltic, even if Denmark were induced to join the Entente.[2] For since June 1914 the Kiel Canal, which joined the two seas, had been sufficiently deepened to allow the passage of the newest super-dreadnoughts, and Germany could effect a strategic transfer of any force likely to be necessary within a few hours.

[1] Heligoland was originally a Danish island seized by Great Britain in 1807 as a basis for smuggling goods into the north German rivers in order to evade Napoleon's continental system. It was exchanged in 1890 for Zanzibar. Its great value to Germany was not then in any way recognized by the British Admiralty. It is, however, highly improbable that any use could have been made of it had it remained in British hands in 1914.

[2] Unless this happened the passage was almost impossible, for Denmark had mined the Sound. On the other hand, this mine-field also prevented the German fleet from seeking refuge in the Baltic if hard pressed in the North Sea.

At the beginning of hostilities each side expected and prepared for the other to come out and offer battle speedily. This expectation on the part of the Germans was most natural. The British navy was superior. Its unrivalled prestige had been almost unbroken for centuries. Popular tradition at least credited it with the unvarying intention of seeking out and destroying the enemy's fleet. It had continually taken the lead in new inventions, and had compelled its rivals to imitate its designs. Every detail of construction was supposed to be undertaken regardless of cost. Above all, as many German writers have admitted, their sailors were involuntarily impressed by the air of effortless superiority so naturally assumed by the Englishman at sea. They had seen this immense armada safely ensconced in its war stations at a moment when the German fleet was hurrying home in a precarious and exposed return from Norwegian waters.

Under this impression, the enemy kept his battleships strictly in harbour, improving the defences of the Heligoland Bight. A minelayer was sent out on the night of August 4th–5th and sowed its burden off the Thames estuary before discovery and destruction.[1] Patrols penetrated fruitlessly into the northern part of the North Sea, and a flotilla of submarines had an unfortunate cruise, for no damage was inflicted and two boats were lost, one by the ram of the cruiser *Birmingham*.

This extreme caution surprised Jellicoe, who undertook several extensive sweeps with his whole fleet in the North Sea in the hope of finding the enemy. On August 16th our cruisers penetrated to the southward of the Horn Reef (off Jutland) without seeing any hostile vessel except one submarine.

Expert opinion in Germany was bitterly divided over the strategy adopted. Tirpitz, whose dogged perseverance and indomitable energy as Secretary of State for the

[1] This vessel the *Königin Luise* was the first ship destroyed in the war (morning of August 5); shortly afterwards the British light cruiser *Amphion* was blown up by one of her mines.

Navy since 1897 had given him the well-deserved title of 'Father of the German Navy', was still in office. He was, however, completely ignored by the Kaiser and the Chief-of-Staff, Pohl, and boiled with indignation at what he believed to be the criminal mishandling of his carefully forged weapon. The fleet he declared in his vigorous way was 'muzzled' and 'embalmed'. It is certainly true that the hands of the commander-in-chief were most vigorously tied. A man of stronger personality than Ingenohl, who held that post, would certainly have kicked against such restrictions, as his eventual successor, the gifted Scheer, did. Ingenohl, however, who was in bad health (like Moltke, the Chief of the Military General Staff), proved a willing instrument.

The motives underlying the Kaiser's decision appear to have been partly political, partly military. After the entry of England into the war William foreboded defeat.[1] Even if he could overthrow his enemies on land he did not expect victory at sea. He therefore attached the greatest importance to keeping his fleet intact until the end of the war. It would thus remain the surest safeguard that England's 'will for annihilation' could not be carried into effect; it would weary her of bolstering up the continental alliance, and would ensure at least a tolerable peace. Strategically it was hoped through the action of destroyers, submarines, and mines gradually to wear down the British supremacy in capital ships until equality had been obtained. After such a success it would be time to consider a change of strategy. Jellicoe himself has testified that this plan caused him great anxiety, and that the holding back

[1] See his famous minute written as early as July 28, 1914: 'My function is at an end. Wantonness and weakness are to engulf the world in the most terrible of wars, the ultimate aim of which is the ruin of Germany. For now I can no longer doubt that England, France, and Russia have conspired to fight together for our annihilation . . . and so the notorious encirclement of Germany is at last an accomplished fact. . . . England stands derisive, brilliantly successful in her long-meditated, purely anti-German policy—a superb achievement, stirring to admiration even him whom it will utterly destroy. The dead Edward is stronger than the living I.'

was correct as far as the German battleships were concerned. But the use made of the light forces, the natural weapon of the weaker power, was at first exceedingly unenterprising. The submarines indeed maintained a perpetual menace. Though no capital ship fell to their torpedoes, a spectacular success was obtained on September 22nd by Commander Weddigen of the U. 9, who destroyed three old armoured cruisers, *Hogue*, *Cressy*, and *Aboukir*, with the loss of 1,600 lives off the Dutch coast, where the Admiralty had foolishly kept them on a leisurely daily patrol. No other submarine throughout the war approached this simultaneous bag.

Three kinds of possible adventure, however, much dreaded by our Admiralty, were left unattempted.

With the exception of one liner, *Kaiser Wilhelm der Grosse*, which slunk through the blockade along the Norwegian coast on August 5th, no cruisers or armed merchantmen were dispatched from German ports on an errand of commerce-destruction.

The surprising failure to interfere in any way with the transport of the expeditionary force to France must be chiefly placed to the discredit of the military authorities. In Moltke's view the British army was so small that it would be convenient to have it all in France to be involved in the *débâcle* which he was preparing for its Allies. The German navy took this view thoroughly to heart, for it failed to gain any information about the date or the route of the shipment, and did not even get into contact with the covering forces spread out from Harwich to the Dutch coast.

Finally, no invasion was ever tried. The British Admiralty had always considered such a scheme practicable, and had refused to take responsibility for preventing the transit of 60,000 men across the North Sea. It was believed that a sufficient number of flat-bottomed boats could be secretly collected in the German ports and towed across without discovery on a moonless night.[1] By the

[1] A well-known novel, *The Riddle of the Sands*, by Erskine Childers was

end of August 1914 only one regular division was left in England. The Territorials were as yet a force of small fighting value, for most of the units had to take in 30 per cent. of recruits to bring their numbers up to war strength after mobilization. The infantry had not yet fired their musketry course; the gunners were armed with obsolete weapons of which they had little experience. The new armies were still unsupplied with rifles or even uniforms. The grave shortage of mines made it impossible adequately to defend the approaches to the coast.

No one can tell what would have been the effect of a landing at any point upon the moral of a population which was being encouraged with the motto 'Business as usual'. But there were three areas where a successful raid would have immediately obtained important military results. An attack on the mouth of the Tees would have secured the blast-furnaces of Middlesbrough and the Cleveland iron-mines. The capture of Hull and Immingham would have followed a descent on the Humber. A landing in the Essex estuaries of the Blackwater or Crouch would have immediately threatened London from the north-east, where nature has interposed no serious obstacle in the path of an invader.[1]

The enemy does not appear even to have seriously considered the execution of such a scheme, though our Admiralty still held it to be possible as late as December 1917, and large military forces were retained for home defence. German writers have been so reticent on the subject that it is uncertain whether the Naval Staff vetoed the attempt, or whether the soldiers consistently refused to risk the necessary three or four divisions. No doubt such a force must have been written off as an eventual total loss. Still, the hazard was a comparatively

published some years before the war (1903), giving minute details of such a hypothetical scheme.

[1] Elaborate defences were dug to defend London on this quarter, but were in a very rudimentary state until October 1914. Eventually there were three trench systems, the outermost running north of Chelmsford by Maldon and Danbury Hill, and the innermost by Ongar and Epping.

small one in comparison with the results to be expected from violating so vaunted and secular an immunity.

III

Apart from the great central stage of the North Sea, another and much swifter drama was immediately played in European waters. The plans of the Entente in the Mediterranean ended in a tragic farce. This result was partly due to the extraordinary uncertainty of the political situation, but mainly to the fumbling of the Admiralty and the indecision and timidity of the British commanders.

Germany had in the Mediterranean a squadron of two modern vessels, the *Goeben*, a battle-cruiser of great power and speed (ten 11-inch guns and a speed of 26 knots), and the *Breslau*, a light cruiser. The forces of which the Entente disposed were enormously superior. The French alone had one dreadnought and fifteen older battleships,[1] six armoured cruisers, and twenty-four destroyers. The British force, divided into two squadrons, consisted of three battle-cruisers, each more powerfully armed than the *Goeben* though slower (they had eight 12-inch guns and steamed at 23 knots) under the Commander-in-Chief, Sir Berkeley Milne, and four armoured cruisers, four light-cruisers, and sixteen destroyers under Rear Admiral Troubridge. Such an array might well be considered sufficient to hunt down two ships without fail.

The position, however, was far from simple. In the first place the preliminary dispositions of the Entente navies had to guard against hostile action both by Italy and Austria-Hungary, though in fact the former declared her neutrality on August 4th and the latter entered the war (Aug. 11) too late to influence the course of events directly.

Secondly, the French were involved two days before their ally. Consequently on August 3rd–4th the British commander suffered a double disadvantage. He could shadow the Germans but take no action, and he was entirely ignorant of the French dispositions.

[1] Six of these were of an immediate pre-dreadnought class.

Thirdly, these dispositions were in fact purely defensive, their aim being to ensure the immediate convoy of the Algerian army corps to France. This they were quite competent to do without British aid, though the *Goeben* made a lightning dash from her harbourage at Messina

MAP 6. The Mediterranean.

on August 3rd to bombard Bona and Philippeville. The German vessels returned next evening to Messina, having been sighted well within range by two British battle-cruisers, still precluded from taking action, since our ultimatum did not expire till midnight (August 4). There they remained coaling until the afternoon of the 6th. Milne's dispositions for intercepting their exit were strange. The Admiralty with an excess of unsolicited good nature had impressed upon him the primary duty of protecting the French transports. This order seems to have fixed in his mind the belief that the enemy would come out of the northern end of the Strait and turn west. Consequently he kept two battle-cruisers between Sardinia and the west coast of Sicily. One light cruiser only (the *Gloucester*) watched the southern exit, while the third battle-cruiser *Indomitable* was coaling at the Tunisian port of Bizerta. Admiral Souchon, the German commander, was intent only on escape. His secret orders indicated the Dardanelles as his refuge, for as is related elsewhere,[1] Turkey had already (August 1) committed herself to a German alliance. Yet, knowing what overwhelming forces the Entente could collect against him, he had little hope of a good deliverance when he steamed south from Messina on the afternoon of August 6th. Fortunate beyond expectation, he found no enemy to dispute his exit, only the little *Gloucester* shadowed him in the offing. She hung on throughout the night, reporting his false start northwards into the Adriatic and his subsequent turn south-eastward towards the Aegean.

Now Troubridge was lying with his four armoured cruisers off Cephalonia, to prevent a passage up the Adriatic to the Austrian war-harbour of Pola. He could not intercept the Germans during the hours of darkness, but could have forced an action early on the morning of August 7th. He had, however, received the order that he was not to engage a superior force. His gloss upon these instructions seems singularly poor-spirited, for he deemed the *Goeben* in daylight superior to his four armoured cruisers with their accompanying escort of eight destroyers. The *Goeben*, he maintained, could have kept out of range of his lighter armament and destroyed each of his units piecemeal. This would indeed, as Churchill writes, have been 'a prodigious feat' on the part of the battle-cruiser. Still, Troubridge was exonerated by the court martial for which he had asked, though he received no other command afloat.[2]

Very different was the conduct of the two brothers, Captains John and William Kelly, commanding the light cruisers *Dublin* and *Gloucester*. The former with two destroyers tried to attack the enemy in the night

[1] p. 131.

[2] He was subsequently employed in commanding the Danube flotilla and some British heavy guns on the Serbian front.

(August 6–7); the latter single-handed dogged his eastward voyage until the evening of August 7th, apparently escaping destruction only because Souchon thought such extreme daring must imply close support by the battle-cruisers. The latter, however, moved eastward much at leisure and far behind. There seemed indeed no need of haste, for the Admiralty had not passed on any information about the attitude of Turkey, and did not itself suspect Constantinople as a possible destination. Nor did the moderate party in the Turkish capital consent to so glaring a violation of neutrality without a further struggle. For three days Souchon had to prowl uneasily about the Archipelago, until the news reached him that the door of his refuge had been definitely unlocked by the Young Turks.

During this vigil his usual luck held good. He might well have been searched out and destroyed had not the Admiralty sent Milne on August 8th a false report that war had been declared against Austria. By prearranged orders this news implied a concentration at Malta, and the pursuit was abandoned until a countermanding telegram arrived too late. Thus at 5 p.m. on August 10th the *Goeben* and *Breslau* entered the Dardanelles unmolested, carrying with them graver destinies than any other vessel in modern history.[1]

IV

It is now time to cast a rapid and comprehensive eye over the great expanses of the world seas, where it was vital for Great Britain to maintain freedom of communication over the main trade routes.[2] At home during the first few days of war there was natural alarm at the shadow of so vast and uncertain a menace. Food hoarding began, and the rates of insurance, if obtainable at all, shot up.[3]

[1] The escape of the *Alabama* from Liverpool in 1863 is the nearest parallel. This commerce destroyer prolonged the American Civil War, and brought the north within measurable distance of war with England.

[2] In 1914 64 per cent. of her food supplies came from overseas.

[3] The Government on August 4 guaranteed 80 per cent. of war risks and fixed the premium of insurance.

Almost immediately, however, confidence was fully restored. Hardly a British merchantman was posted as missing, while scores of enemy vessels, helpless in port, fell into our hands. The harbour of New York was filled with German liners not daring to put to sea. Only one converted liner from the North Sea evaded our patrols, and four others escaped in time from neutral ports. The problem of the high seas therefore contained no surprises for the Admiralty. The number and approximate position of the scattered German cruisers was known. It remained only to hunt them down and to prevent the escape of any successors in order to allow commerce to run a practically normal course. For in these early months submarine warfare against merchantmen, most deadly and secret of weapons, had not yet begun. Obviously the task of rounding up the roaming units of the enemy would be much simplified if Germany could be deprived of all her naval bases overseas, and her warships forced to depend for fuel and provisions on ships chartered before war started, on supplies captured from her enemies, or on the precarious and fleeting hospitality of neutrals. Consequently the expeditions planned almost at once against the German colonies were then actuated rather by this motive than by a lust for conquest.[1] By the middle of August six expeditions had been put in train, four against the enemy's possessions in Africa (Togoland, Cameroons, South-West and East Africa) and two by Australia and New Zealand against Samoa and the scattered German islands of the Pacific. About the same time Japan, after entering the war, undertook to reduce the only German base in China, the strong fortified harbour of Tsingtau or Kiaochau. As

[1] Later on when the 'War-map' in Europe became so unfavourable to the Entente the acquisition of large African territories was regarded as a valuable make-weight, and a card to play in any peace discussions against claims for European territory by the Central Powers. One of these 'side-shows', the East African campaign, assumed vast proportions, and was not finally completed on November 11, 1918. It is said to have cost about £75,000,000. In the expeditionary force were included British Regulars, Indians, South Africans, both British and Boer, and natives from almost every part of Africa.

all German cables had been cut as soon as war started, the raiding cruisers had to rely entirely upon wireless, which they were chary in using for fear of disclosing their whereabouts to a pursuer.

The enemy himself set no exaggerated store on the results of cruiser warfare, which history suggested could exercise a decisive influence only after a successful fleet action. It would, it was hoped, lower British prestige among neutrals, cause panic and soaring prices at home, and force the British Admiralty to detach powerful vessels from the Grand Fleet, thus paving the way towards an equalization of strength in the North Sea.

In fact the German forces available were neither very numerous nor very formidable, for the ever-increasing Navy Budgets had not provided enough money to build cruisers on a scale commensurate with the new dreadnought fleet.

When war began the Germans had one powerful squadron on the China station, consisting of two armoured cruisers, *Scharnhorst* and *Gneisenau*, crack gunnery ships of the German navy, each armed with twelve 8·2 guns, together with three fast light cruisers, *Emden*, *Nürnberg*, and *Leipzig*. A similar light cruiser, *Königsberg*, was off East Africa, and two more, *Dresden* and *Karlsruhe*, were allotted to the West Indies.[1] None of these was immediately rounded up; all were to take part in varied Odysseys of achievement and ultimate disaster.

The task of hunting these raiders to death was very complicated. The vast Pacific in particular afforded unlimited cruising space and its islands innumerable lurking places. The shortage of fast cruisers made it difficult to seize the prey even if it were sighted. Moreover, the tasks of the British Admiralty were varied and exacting. Apart from the protection of trade routes, great troop movements had to be safeguarded by convoy. By the middle of October five regular divisions had been brought from India, and three territorial divisions sent to replace them; two more regular

[1] There were also a few gunboats and sloops of almost no military value.

divisions had been brought home from various outposts of the Empire; a division from Canada had been convoyed over the Atlantic, and an army corps was beginning to move from Australia to Egypt. More than seventy warships were employed in all these duties and in the search for eight enemy cruisers. In the circumstances it is surprising that the latter, boldly and skilfully handled as they were, did not work far greater execution. In all they destroyed less than fifty British merchantmen[1] (or little more than 1 per cent. of our mercantile marine) and five men-of-war, including two armoured cruisers (the *Good Hope* and *Monmouth*). By the end of the first week in December the tale of their own destruction was complete, except for one light cruiser, *Dresden*, which prolonged an innocuous existence till March 1915 by persistent disregard of the neutrality of remote Chilean possessions.[2] As sample of their fortunes we may take the *Emden*, most famous of single raiders, before describing the exploits of the China squadron.

The *Emden*'s resourceful and subtle captain Müller succeeded in decking out her exploits with a glow of romance attractive even to the enemy. He was detached to the Indian Ocean from the China squadron at his own request. His ship was a fast light cruiser of about 3,500 tons, armed with ten 4·2 guns, with a crew of 361. He hoped not merely to sink British vessels and to paralyse the Indian trade, but to stir up unrest among the natives, for which purpose he carried a store of propaganda. With a collier as consort he passed westwards through the Straits of Molucca on the night of August 22nd, coaled at Timor and rigged up a false fourth funnel before proceeding to the Bay of Bengal. Within this fruitful area the *Emden* cruised for a fortnight, and captured thirteen ships. Her appearance was an unsuspected thunderbolt, all shipping

[1] As against this loss, 133 German merchantmen were captured by the British within a few weeks of the outbreak of war.

[2] She was finally sunk by the cruiser *Kent* within a neutral Chilean harbour in the islands of Juan Fernandez.

was detained in port, and the Indian warehouses and quays were congested with goods heaped up for export. Before leaving the bay she bombarded the great oil-tanks near Madras, setting two on fire with a conflagration which destroyed 500,000 gallons. Müller refrained from firing either on Madras or Pondicherry as being undefended towns, and took his leave of the bay, sailing south of Ceylon to the comparatively narrow channel between the Maldive and Lakadive islands. Here he hoped for a good hunting-ground against steamers moving on the Aden–Colombo route, and captured three, including a collier with 4,300 tons of the best Welsh steam-coal, a real godsend. Learning by wireless of the concentration which was being planned against him, he ran south 1,000 miles to the remote island of Diego Garcia. Here the simple British subjects who had not yet heard of the outbreak of war (October 4) received him gladly and gave him every facility for coaling and for cleaning his ship. Thence he daringly returned to his former lair by the Maldives, and had a good haul of seven large ships, including another collier, before the scent got too hot (October 20). Thence passing south of Colombo he took a long course eastwards, and was next heard of on October 28th. Very early that morning he ran quite unsuspected into the harbour of Penang in the Malay States. Within it lay the Russian light cruiser *Zemtchug*, a French gunboat, and two destroyers. The Russian captain in spite of the counsels of the British harbour master had consistently refused to take any precautions.[1] His ship was twice torpedoed at point-blank range and disappeared in explosion and flame. The *Emden* while emerging stopped to take a merchant-prize and immediately afterwards saw the French destroyer *Mousquet*, who had been on patrol, coming towards the harbour mouth. She was speedily shot to pieces, and a number of her crew rescued. They were afterwards dismissed on parole by Müller in one of

[1] He was afterwards cashiered by court martial and sentenced to a term of imprisonment.

the vessels which he kept from time to time to take off the crews of other sunken merchantmen. The *Emden* now ran right down the west side of Sumatra, and started upon her last errand to destroy the wireless station and important cable junction at Cocos Island, about 500 miles south-west of Java. Here she arrived early on November 9th, steaming in with her false funnel as usual up. The operators had, however, been warned of her activities and noticing that the funnel was a poorly constructed dummy, sent out the message 'Strange ship off entrance' before the *Emden* could jam it. She then sent a landing party to destroy the installations and cables, and waited for a collier which had been given rendezvous at his spot. Now all unknown to Müller the great Anzac convoy was steaming westward only fifty-five miles away. The *Sydney*, an Australian light cruiser, was instantly detached on receipt of the message. When Müller saw the smoke upon the horizon he took it for that of the expected collier, but it was a warship for which the *Emden* was no match. The *Sydney* was 2,000 tons heavier, three knots faster, and had eight 6-inch guns. The *Emden* fought a good fight, shooting at first much more accurately than her opponent; but was overwhelmed and driven by her captain a blazing wreck upon the reef.

The success of the *Emden* in her long cruise was partly due to luck. Twice she passed the armoured cruiser *Hampshire* so close that in clear weather the two ships must have seen each other; and had she not chanced upon the two colliers her life could not have lasted so long. But Müller was very skilful in piecing together the wireless messages which he took in from India and from British ships, in the choice of the areas visited, and in the arrangements which he made for coaling and for meeting his supply ships. In dealing with his prizes he scrupulously regarded international law and invariably treated the captured crews with politeness and consideration. By order of the Admiralty he and his officers were allowed to retain their swords as prisoners.

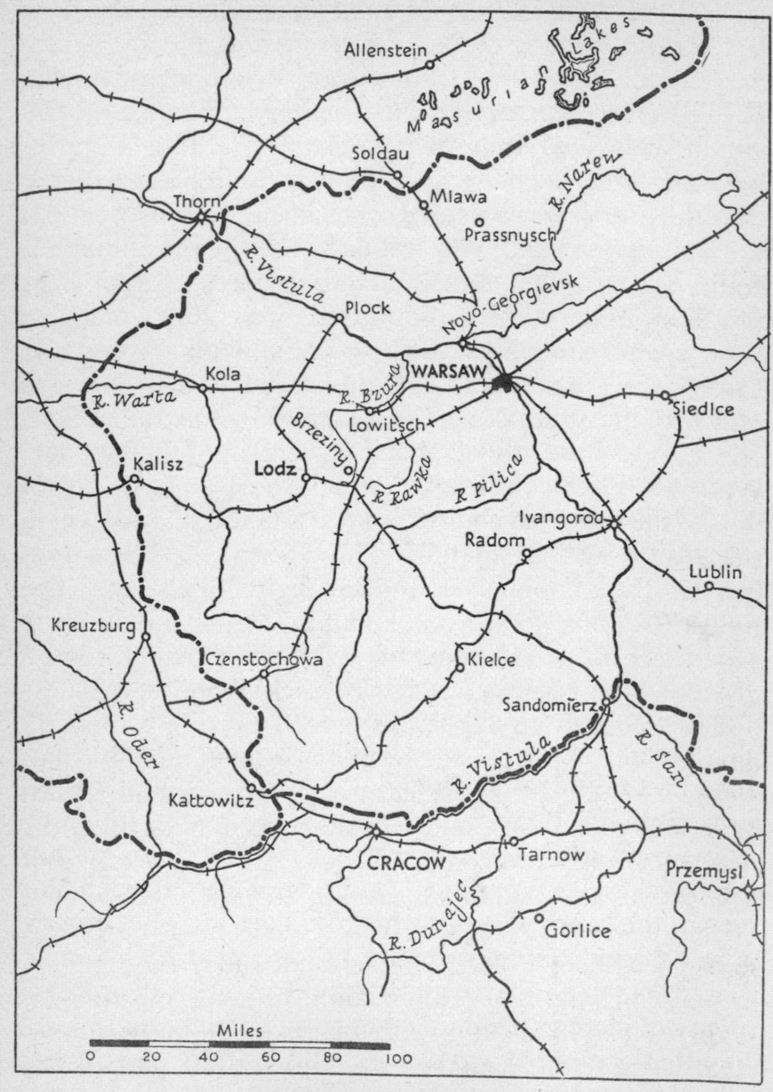

MAP 7. The Polish Salient.

V

THE CAMPAIGN IN POLAND, 1914

I

HINDENBURG's first attack on Warsaw gave the Eastern Front a freedom and wideness of manœuvre which had so far been curiously lacking. The battle had been joined in the extreme north and in the extreme south, while the great projecting salient of Russian Poland, west of the Vistula, had been merely the scene of some desultory cavalry skirmishes.

Both Austrians and Russians were lumped together in a confined and cramped space between the Vistula and the Carpathians. The Austrians had indeed suffered such enormous losses that they could fit in without much overcrowding, but the Russians were far too thick on the ground and had continual commissariat difficulties. Moreover, this unnecessary concentration had left the Vistula unguarded, and therefore menaced the security of their occupation of Galicia.

When Hindenburg began to advance on a large front on September 28th between Cracow and Czenstochowa, he found at first no opposition before him. The Russians had abandoned the whole of western Poland. The Grand Duke had taken his decision to draw no less than twelve corps from the Galician army, and to transport them behind the Vistula. He expected to be in position in time to meet the German forces before they could reach the river in the rainy autumn which had set in. The Grand Duke's magnificent manœuvre has received high praise from his opponents. He aimed by his vast transference of troops not merely at foiling his enemy, but at obtaining an absolute decision by enveloping Hindenburg's left flank with immense forces collected in the angle of the Vistula between Novo-Georgievsk and Warsaw. The transference was effected with greater speed and secrecy than was usual in Russian operations, though the troops endured miseries on their march along the few wretched roads of the Government of Lublin, and the 5th army is said to have been without bread for six days. The Germans, too, had to contend with the Polish mud, which Ludendorff tells us was knee deep even on the great main road from Cracow to Warsaw.[1] But large numbers of pioneers repaired their communications as they advanced.

Meanwhile the Austrian advance had begun in Galicia. This had been discounted by the Grand Duke, who was perfectly contented to fall back on the San provided that Dmitriev could set bounds to the retreat on that line.

On October 9th Jaroslav had been taken and Przemysl relieved, but the Austrians could get no farther. This arrest was a great blow to the whole strategical conception of the battle, for it meant that the Russian left flank was secure.

It was about this time that an order and a map giving the whole of the Russian dispositions were captured on the body of an officer;[2] down to that day the concentration behind the Vistula had been only partially known through the wireless messages of various Russian corps giving their situation. This revealed the danger impending over the left of the German IXth army. But there was as yet no intention of retreat. Mackensen, who commanded it, had already been deflected to the north, and was within seven miles of Warsaw on the 12th. Farther south the Germans had just won the race to the Vistula, and had thrown back all the Russian forces which had crossed, with one exception: this was north of Ivangorod where the Caucasian corps bravely maintained a bridge-head against incessant attacks in the swamps. Ludendorff singles out these battles for their peculiar ferocity and horror.

It was clearly impossible for Mackensen's dwindling

[1] The road between Lublin and Krasnik was quite impassable; carts covered 300 yards of plough-land on either side, while the infantry plodded along still farther outside. Compare Napoleon's saying of Poland, 'Dieu, outre l'eau, l'air, la terre, et le feu, a créé un cinquième élément, la boue'.

[2] October 9 according to Ludendorff; October 11 according to Hoffmann, who gives more circumstantial details than Hindenburg.

force to stand any chance unless it could be reinforced. Moreover, the reinforcements must arrive with speed, or they would be unavailing. The nearest troops available were Dankl's Ist army, which was behind Hindenburg's right flank in South Poland. Here a grave difficulty arose. By order of the Austrian Supreme Command they could only be employed south of the Pilica. Even personal representations from the Kaiser to Francis Joseph were unavailing. This wretchedly short-sighted policy was presumably dictated by the determination to avoid further invasion of Austrian territory at all costs. Yet the best security for the country was the defeat of the Grand Duke's armies. This was not the only occasion during the campaign on which the Germans had reason to complain of the uncomradely attitude of their allies.[1]

Hindenburg was obliged to accept the alternative offered by Conrad of the relief of the German troops round Ivangorod by the Ist army. This had a double disadvantage: it would require longer time for its completion, and it was doubtful whether the Austrians would hold the positions in face of the splendid fighting qualities revealed by the Caucasian troops. Conrad with light-hearted optimism affirmed that if the Russians came out of Ivangorod they would be beaten. The boot was on the other leg, as Ludendorff feared, for the Austrians were heavily defeated, in spite of the amount of work which they had put into entrenching their positions to the astonishment of the Russians.

Mackensen maintained himself uneasily just west of Warsaw until the 16th, when he swung back about thirty

[1] Hoffmann gives a very characteristic instance. A German signal-corporal intercepted an Austrian message stating that the Ist Austrian army was to retire immediately from the region round Ivangorod, but that the German Guard reserve corps on its left was not to be informed till five hours later. This corps was actually at the moment under orders to make a relief attack to support the Austrian left (October 27). Conrad's feelings towards the Germans are described in J. von Stürgkh, *Im deutschen Grossen Hauptquartier* (1921): 'He regarded any limitation of his powers in his own theatre of war as a mortification of his pride and self-respect. That his allies gave him help in abundance caused no warmer feeling for them to arise in his breast.'

miles. But there was no possibility that any forces would be withdrawn from the great cloud of strength on his left. On the contrary the Central Powers were faring badly everywhere to the southward; for, in Galicia as well, the line of the San was forced on the 18th, and a retreat began which this time halted only under the shelter of the Cracow forts.

By the 27th the decision was taken to break off the battle, which had been raging for the last few days, and to withdraw the IXth army out of the reach of the Russians, who might otherwise have cut it off completely from the German frontier. It was confidently reckoned that no pursuit could be maintained by the enemy at a greater distance than 120 kilometres from his railways. Thus it was believed that the German forces would be able to stand in complete security well within the borders of Russian Poland.

Ludendorff's methodical mind had worked out beforehand all the details of the necessary destructions, though he had to abandon a larger quantity of food and warlike stores than he had foreseen. The Germans claim, not without justice, that their operations constituted a model 'strategic retreat' on a large scale. The railways, roads, and bridges were thoroughly demolished. But the villages were left intact and there was little plundering.[1] There were none of those spiteful and vindictive actions without military value which were the shame of the withdrawal to the Hindenburg line in France in March 1917. Here in Poland the Germans were no doubt partly actuated by policy: they had no desire to arouse bitter hostility in an area which they hoped again shortly to traverse, and not improbably to annex at the conclusion of the war.

The forecast of Ludendorff was singularly accurate, for the Russians were obliged to halt on the very line which he had anticipated. Their menacing attempts to penetrate again into East Prussia from the south were foiled.

[1] See, for example, the testimony of Gen. Knox and Sir Bernard Pares, both of whom traversed parts of the line of retreat immediately afterwards.

II

On November 1st Hindenburg was appointed Commander-in-Chief of all the German forces in the east, handing over the IXth army to Mackensen. He instantly started preparations for a new and powerful offensive in North Poland.

Hindenburg and his staff were at grave variance with Falkenhayn, the new Chief-of-Staff, as to the objects and scope of the new offensive. Hindenburg was convinced that a decisive blow was possible, which would knock Russia out of the war. Both would have agreed that this in itself would not bring the war to an end. It was firmly held in all military and political circles in Germany that France was too much in the power of Great Britain to be forced into peace by the failure of her eastern Ally. The question at issue therefore was simply this: was it possible to destroy the Russian strength before the winter, and then transfer enough troops to France, in order to inflict a crushing blow before the new British levies had been sufficiently trained to enter the battle line? Hindenburg based his view on the following considerations. It would be possible at once to break off the Yser battle and to stand on the defensive in the West, for the Allies were far too much exhausted to attempt any serious counterstroke. This would free for the East a large proportion of the new formations amounting to about three corps, composed of volunteers which, as we shall see,[1] were mainly in the field round Ypres. It was perfectly true that apart from their magnificent bravery they lacked experience and tactical skill; the men were too young and the officers too old. But this was a potent reason for employing them in the East rather than the West. It had already been proved that the Landwehr were perfectly capable of standing against the Russians in the open field; all the eastern fortresses had been depleted of their Landwehr garrisons, who had fought with the utmost confidence.

Moreover, a campaign in the east could move with

[1] See p. 98–99.

greater swiftness and certainty. It was no gamble in the dark against an unknown enemy; for the Russian wireless continued to broadcast the most valuable information with undiminished prodigality day by day. Again, November was not a bad period for a Polish campaign; the frost set in towards the middle of the month, dried the roads, and made it impossible for the enemy to entrench himself, while no heavy falls of snow were to be expected until later.[1]

Falkenhayn, however, was inexorable. He was determined to finish the Yser battle. His decision was doubtless influenced by political as well as merely military considerations. The capture of the Channel ports was from both points of view a greater prize than could, in his judgement, be won in the East. He would be perfectly satisfied if the threat to Cracow and Silesia was finally stopped, and a winter-line securely held in Poland at a sufficient distance from the German frontier. Consequently he refused any considerable reinforcements to Hindenburg until the beginning of December, when the lines in France and Belgium had been fruitlessly stabilized. By the time of their arrival the second attack on Warsaw had lost all the advantage of surprise.

It has often been stated that Falkenhayn was partly actuated by jealousy of Hindenburg. The old field-marshal was already being celebrated in Germany with almost divine honours, and his name was on the lips of all classes as the only possible saviour.[2] But there is no need to introduce any such unworthy motive. Hindenburg himself has frankly confessed that he may not have viewed the situation in its full proportion, and that he never understood the situation in the West until his visits in the autumn of 1916, when he had become Chief

[1] This was certainly true of November 1914 (see the careful weather notes kept by Gen. Knox), although during the later years enforced stabilization seems to have begun early in November. But it must be remembered that the quality of the troops was by then definitely inferior.

[2] See, for example, Adm. A. von Tirpitz, *My Memories* (1919), vol. ii, *passim*.

of the General Staff. The campaign of 1915 shows that Falkenhayn's views were perfectly just. The Russians showed great skill in timing and carrying out their retreats; it was a type of strategy traditional to an ill-equipped army with infinite elbow-room. They still had comparatively good supplies of rifle and gun ammunition, drawn it is true from almost exhausted reserves, but sufficient for a short winter campaign. If another 100,000 troops had been sacrificed in Poland by Germany without a decision, it might have been impossible to last out the next year. Falkenhayn knew well, what Head-quarters in the East probably did not consider, that the Central Powers had to expect new enemies in 1915. Finally, he doubtless took a more accurate measure of the Tsar's loyalty to the alliance, which would certainly not have been impaired, even in the improbable event of the destruction of his armies in Poland.

III

Hindenburg had therefore to start his attack with the forces already at his disposal. The plan was one of Ludendorff's best, strong and simple, with risks calculated and taken in order to gain a superiority at the critical point.

It was assumed that the Russians, who were now spread out over practically the whole of Poland, would not be able to advance against Silesia in strength for a considerable period, owing to the devastations, which extended for seventy miles in their rear.[1] Most of the IXth army[2] was consequently transported northwards to the district south

[1] According to Russian wireless orders it had been intended to pursue the attack against Silesia on November 14, leaving North Poland very weakly guarded. General Knox thinks that Mackensen would have been able to cut them off entirely from Warsaw, and therefore from their supplies, if he had been held back a week or two longer.

[2] It was not found possible to move it all, as the Austrians already considered it necessary to have a stiffening of German troops. On the other hand, the VIIIth army in East Prussia was also stripped of two corps. Mackensen had a strength of about three and a half corps and five cavalry divisions.

of Thorn. Such a great troop movement, for which more than 800 trains were used, could not have passed undetected but for the hopeless inferiority of the enemy in the air.

By November 11th everything was ready for the advance. Mackensen was to keep his left on the Vistula, and move south-east against the Russian flank. The railways and roads in the north, though both were scarce, had not suffered, as they had been outside the range of the October retreat.

The strategy of this campaign has always been considered as of peculiar interest by military writers. It also brought the Russian supply of ammunition to a degree of exhaustion, probably not realized fully by their enemies. The fighting was almost continuous and of a most determined character, for many of their best troops were engaged, as for instance two corps from Siberia. The daily expenditure of shells by the Russians is said to have been considerably in excess of their monthly production (45,000 against 35,000). The guns of each infantry division had already been reduced from forty-eight to thirty-six.

The Russian intelligence was badly at fault, and Mackensen got at least two days' start before measures were taken to deal with a situation already seriously compromised. Rennenkampf's 1st army was mainly north of the Vistula facing East Prussia. The solitary corps on the south bank was speedily smashed by Mackensen, who moved about fifty miles in four days, a fine performance considering the roads and the fighting. Touch was completely broken between the 1st and 2nd Russian armies. The latter hurriedly faced north-east with the object of covering Lodz and of deflecting Mackensen in a southerly direction, by threatening his flank if he moved directly on Warsaw. Mackensen caught it while the movement was in progress; after a furious battle, in which the Russians lost about 25,000 prisoners, the 2nd army was thrust back on Lodz in a confused and jumbled condition, with a different corps on every side of the town except the south. Now began the strangest of all the battles of the war, in which either combatant in turn was within an ace of suffering a capital disaster. The Grand Duke was naturally anxious to save Lodz, a city of 500,000 inhabitants, a valuable winter-billeting area, and the centre of the cotton industry. But he was far more concerned with the rescue of his threatened 2nd army. Its position seemed desperate. It was hemmed in on three sides and isolated to the south, where its neighbour, the 5th army, was still pursuing its march westward. Plehve, its commander, a little wizened man, broken in health but full of moral and intellectual energy, instantly recalled his troops by forced marches to close up the open flank.[1] Several corps of Rennenkampf's army were hurriedly assembled at Lowitsch about fifty miles north-east of Lodz. Meanwhile the Germans, having intercepted a wireless message from the Grand Duke ordering the evacuation of Lodz, believed that a general retreat was in progress and thrust two infantry and one cavalry corps far to the eastward. The battle between November 18th–25th was exceedingly confused, bloody, and terrible. Snow and bitter frost held the country so that the wounded were frozen to death in thousands, and motor transport was impeded by the freezing of the radiators. The Russians held firmly to Lodz: their 5th army thrust itself up from the south; the Lowitsch detachment advanced from the east. Instead of being enveloped themselves, with whole corps cramped and twisted, with batteries firing from advanced positions both north and south, they turned the tables on their enemy. The wound in the front through which the German spear had pierced was closed; it seemed as if the head must be broken clean off. At least 50,000 Germans were fighting in a trap more than twenty miles from their comrades. The Russian wireless, naïvely premature, announced the dispatch of special trains to carry away the prisoners; an official message was sent to the army lying before Cracow that 26,000 had been

[1] Two corps actually marched seventy miles over the winter roads in forty-eight hours, and joined battle within a few hours.

taken. But two things prevented this spectacular victory, the anticipation of which kept all the belligerent peoples in the utmost suspense of joy or agony for two days. The wretched Rennenkampf was late in completely closing the enemy's only way of salvation by the north. The German commander, von Scheffer, was master of his emergency. He broke the resistance of a Siberian division and drew out his forces in true fighting order, bringing proudly with them 10,000 prisoners and sixty guns. It is noteworthy that the chief credit for this splendid feat of arms belongs to a reserve formation (XXVth reserve corps) formed since war broke out.

The remainder of the campaign seems an anti-climax to this dramatic struggle. The fighting did not die down for a month, but it could not maintain the same pitch of furious intensity. The best troops on both sides had been engaged without intermission and had suffered cruelly. The Russians began to feel bitterly their lack of munitions, that continual thorn in the flesh, never to be extracted until, as irony would have it, their hearts broke just when their stores had been refilled in 1917. Fortunately for them, the reinforcements from the west reached Hindenburg tardily and in driblets at the beginning of December. Their arrival ensured at length the fall of Lodz (December 6) and an advance of some thirty miles to the lines of the Rivers Rawka and Bzura. Here the Russians had strongly entrenched themselves—it is said that their first supplies of barbed wire were used for this fortification—about thirty-five miles west of Warsaw. Against this barrier Hindenburg hammered in vain for a miserable fortnight of alternate thaw and frost. It was not to be broken until July 1915. Ludendorff tells us that his soldiers in the east showed the greatest dislike for trench warfare, and could only be induced to dig by the continual pressure of their superiors. In France on the contrary the Germans had set the example, and were already developing the art with a laborious and unrivalled ingenuity. This is the best example among many of the profound difference in psychology produced by the two 'theatres of war'.

IV

While these great events had been passing in Poland, the Austrians were essaying their desired task of clearing Galicia, now that the best Russian troops had been attracted to the Germans. In this aim they were far from successful. The Austrian army was suffering from a miserable sense of inferiority and expected to be beaten before it was engaged. Conrad, as the Germans often complained, had very good ideas but was never able to bring them to fruition. By the end of November Russian cavalry detachments were within fifteen miles of Cracow, and Dmitriev's Staff spoke optimistically of its investment within a week. Conrad launched an attack against the Russian left and hoped, by issuing from Hungary, to drive Brussilov from the Carpathian passes, to relieve Przemysl, and then, striking into the main Russian communications in central Galicia, to force their armies northwards towards the Vistula. He won indeed some qualified successes, and even had, with the help of a German division, the advantage in the pitched battle of Limanova. Three of the passes fell temporarily into his hands, but his strategic success was confined to the safeguarding of Cracow. The Russian front was stabilized along the line of the Dunajec, some thirty-five miles from the fortress, and thence curved southward just below the crest of the mountains. For three months the operations were buried in frost and snow.

Thus by the first war-Christmas the vital ways of entering into Silesia had been firmly closed, yet it was certain that with the first approach of spring the Russian armies would make a determined effort to force their way into the Hungarian plain; this was the most important granary of the Central Powers, whose position in Europe was already threatening to become that of a gigantic besieged population within a ring of enemies.

V

The second attempt of Austria to destroy her hated enemy in the south resulted in a more resounding defeat than even the first. On both military and political grounds the annihilation of Serbia was urgent. To extinguish this beacon of hostility in the Balkans was of still greater importance after the adherence of Turkey to the Central Powers (November 1). The Danube frontier would be secure; an Austrian occupation of Serbia might ensure the neutrality of Rumania, and possibly of Italy; it would surely bring in Bulgaria as an ally and thus open direct communications with Turkey and the great expanse of Asia. Greece, too, with her Hohenzollern queen, might be won over and access to the Aegean secured at Salonika.

Accordingly a force was collected at the end of October which appeared adequate for a conquest as opposed to a mere punitive expedition. More than 200,000 good troops crossed the frontiers well equipped with artillery. The Serbs were in extreme straits for munitions; this was their third war within two years; they had only one arsenal of an inferior character, and without an outlet to the sea they could not be supplied from their normal sources in France. Their capital, Belgrade, so dangerously exposed on the frontier-edge at the junction of Save and Danube, was soon in the enemy's hands. This did not matter, for the mean little town was in no way the heart of the country, as are the capitals of more civilized peoples.[1] The main Austrian plan was, however, very dangerous. It was a great semicircular invasion from the north and west where the land is comparatively low, with the object of smashing through the Serbian resistance, and gaining Nish, the nodal point of all communications, where the great railway to Constantinople runs through the Morava Valley.

[1] According to J. Andrassy, *Diplomacy and the War* (1921), the capture of Belgrade was due to Potiorek's desire to present it to the Emperor on his birthday (December 2), and the division of forces which it entailed was the chief cause of the subsequent disaster.

The whole transport-system of the country would thus be cleft in two; the Serbs, cut off from their arsenal, Kragujevatz, which lies westward of the railway, would be scattered abroad among the mountains to starve or freeze in

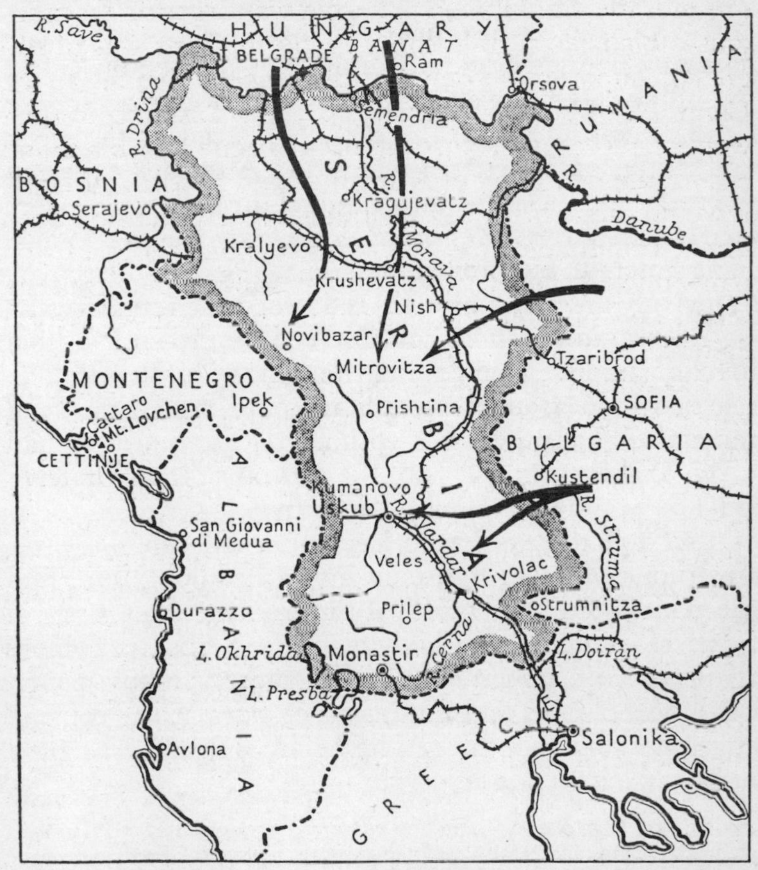

MAP 8. Serbia. The direction of the arrows refers to the third attack in conjunction with Bulgaria. September 1915, see Chap. XIV.

the hard Balkan winter. General Potiorek in command of the invaders had a strong personal incentive for revenge, as he had been military Governor of Bosnia in June 1914, and therefore chiefly responsible for the safety of Franz Ferdinand, whom he accompanied to his death at Sarajevo on the 28th of that month. The Austrian Staff, however, found the Serbian campaigns very difficult of comprehension. They advanced with a foolhardy ease without any great battle, as far as the ridge which guards the watershed of the Morava. They seem to have believed that the Serbian army had dispersed into guerrilla bands, and so Conrad recalled nearly half the troops to the Carpathians. He had originally protested vehemently against the numbers employed, but had been overruled by the Government for political reasons. Instead of the weak and dispirited opposition which the Austrians expected to brush finally aside as they climbed the slopes, they were faced by the supreme effort of a desperate counter-attack. King Peter 'an old broken man on the edge of the grave', as he truly described himself, redeemed the repulsive circumstances in which he had received the crown.[1] With a touching and inspired courage he told the soldiers that he released them from their military oath, but bade them remember that other oath without release that they had taken to their country, with the assurance that whatever befel he would remain with the army.

After a three-days' battle, December 3rd–6th, the whole Austrian army was shattered into a headlong rout, and the remnant which recrossed the frontier was a body of fugitives rather than soldiers. The Serbs took more than 40,000 prisoners, and, a far more valuable booty, quantities of guns and munitions of war. Their country enjoyed a nine-months' respite before Bulgaria was lured in to make its conquest certain.

[1] In 1903 King Alexander and his consort Draga were murdered in their palace by army officers with peculiar cruelty. Peter, the Pretender of the rival Karageorgevich dynasty, was almost certainly an accessory before the fact. On ascending the throne he promoted and rewarded the principal murderers.

VI

THE FIRST BATTLE OF YPRES

I

NEITHER side in the west had yet cast away the hope of a speedy decision. There was yet time to improvise new plans; and room for fresh manœuvre-battles. The incompetent had been ruthlessly jettisoned. Joffre had offered up during the retreat an unexampled sacrifice of defeated generals. Moltke, whose nerves appear to have been completely shattered, was secretly replaced by Erich von Falkenhayn,[1] the Minister for War. The new Chief of the General Staff was only fifty-three years of age and junior in rank to all the army commanders. But he possessed tact and attractiveness as well as confidence and firmness. His tall, handsome figure with his exceptionally clear eye and grey curly hair was in pleasant contrast with the lumbering awkwardness of his predecessor. His account of his stewardship, though incomplete and inaccurate, is a model of stately and tranquil dignity.[2]

Generally speaking, both the French and German Staffs during the next two months tried to regain the initiative in the same way, by repeated attempts to outflank one another in the open and mainly level country between the Oise and the sea. The Crown Prince, it is true, again assaulted that pivot and inexpugnable bastion of the whole French line, the fortress of Verdun. On the west he succeeded in pushing a little farther into the Argonne forest, and captured Varennes, where the flight of Louis XVI had been arrested in 1791. On the south a German detachment, meeting with singularly feeble resistance,[3] broke through the fortified barrier on the Meuse and reached the western bank with a solitary

[1] The greatest pains were taken to conceal this admission of defeat, which was not publicly notified for two months.

[2] *General Headquarters and its Critical Decisions 1914–1916.*

[3] Its total casualties amounted only to 100.

bridge-head; but the Saint-Mihiel salient, thus created, remained a finger pointing in impotent threat to Paris, until it was cut off by the Americans in September 1918.[1]

At present the German position was the more uncomfortable and even dangerous. They could not move forward without being continually reminded of an actual and potential threat to their rear. The whole of the Belgian field-army, still amounting to at least 65,000 men, was snugly ensconced within the immense perimeter of the fortress of Antwerp.[2] Moreover, an English landing might be expected on the Belgian coast. The advent of 2,000 marines at Ostend early in September had already greatly alarmed German Head-quarters. It was, indeed, well known that we had not more than one regular division available for such a diversion; but the possibility that several territorial divisions might be so employed could not be neglected. Nothing, however, could be accomplished against such a landing, except by naval action, which was not forthcoming. Yet an immediate attack against Antwerp was not only feasible but necessary. Von Beseler, an experienced engineer, was given this task. Falkenhayn very properly economized to the utmost with men, for the besieging force consisted of no more than five divisions of inferior quality.[3] But the artillery was extremely powerful,[4] entirely outclassing and outranging the armament of the fortress. Strictly speaking there was no 'siege' of Antwerp, for it was obviously impossible for Beseler's forces to surround a perimeter of more than sixty miles. The German plan was to smash a hole in the defences with shells, and pour the infantry through. The sector of assault was to the south-east of the city. After a bombardment of three days, to which the Belgian batteries, outranged and firing with

[1] By cutting the Paris–Nancy railway, however, it hampered any French concentration in Lorraine. See the plan of Saint-Mihiel (September 1918), p. 558.

[2] Which had also its own garrison of about 80,000 second-line troops.

[3] The equivalent of another division had to guard his communications and took no part in the siege.

[4] 173 heavy guns, of which thirteen ranged from 16- to 12-inch.

black powder, were unable to reply with any effect, the ruined forts and the trenches between them were occupied on October 1st. The city, still beyond the range of bombardment, possessed two further lines of defence, the encircling Néthe, an unfordable river, and its own main *enceinte*. But the position was bad. The Belgian Government had no intention of leaving the field-army within the fortress until it might be in danger of capitulating, or of being driven over the Dutch frontier, if the enemy, by an advance across the Scheldt, should threaten its retreat towards France. But it was well known that the garrison thus abandoned by the field-army would have neither the heart nor power to resist unless supported by strong bodies of the Allies, of whose tardiness they were already complaining. It seems strange that the latter had taken no thought to succour Antwerp until it was stricken almost to death. Their own preoccupations and an obstinate belief in its invulnerability[1] must be their excuse. Now, however, they acted with the disconcerted energy of despair. Winston Churchill, the First Lord of the Admiralty, had urged Sir Edward Grey as early as September 7th to put pressure upon the Dutch to open the Scheldt, both banks of which they controlled, as far as Antwerp, but it was thought impossible to request Holland thus to compromise its neutrality. Help therefore could not come directly up the river. But the Belgian Government was promised that Franco-British forces amounting in all to 53,000 men should be immediately dispatched. Churchill himself on October 3rd arrived and by the strong persuasion of his confident personality confirmed the King in his resolve to postpone the departure of the Government and field-army. The aid thus offered through the cumbrous machinery of a coalition came too late, as so often in the later years. Barely 12,000 British troops were added to the defence, two-thirds of whom had little fighting value.[2] This was not

[1] See the curious leading article in *The Times*, October 1, 1914.

[2] One marine brigade of royal marines, who were fairly good troops: two naval brigades recruited since the war began, imperfectly trained in drill

the aid to put permanent heart into the Belgians, resisting dismally behind bushes, or in shallow water-logged trenches, which gave little protection against the incessant hail of a superior artillery. The Néthe was lost on the 6th, and the field-army began to leave. Antwerp became a spectacle of pity and terror. About a quarter of a million people were flying by way of the sea, into Holland, or towards France. The bombardment opened on the night of the 7th upon a city without electric light, gas, or water supplies. Throughout the next day many conflagrations raged under a canopy of dense, black smoke emitted by the oil-tanks which the retreating Belgians had fired. Thirty-eight great steamers lay in the Scheldt with their machinery hopelessly damaged. Meanwhile the resistance in the perimeter of the main forts had entirely collapsed. A capitulation was signed on the 9th. The Belgian army escaped safely to the west to win immortal glory upon the Yser. Owing to confusion and inexperience 1,000 of the naval brigade were captured, and 1,500 suffered internment in Holland. This small force, more by moral than material aid,[1] had delayed the fall of the fortress by perhaps five days.[2] The great influence of this reprieve on the whole Allied plan will shortly become manifest.

II

The strategy of the next two months has become familiarly known as 'the race to the sea'. This popular title is only partially accurate. Certainly a flank which rests on salt water can no longer be turned from the land. But the

and the use of the rifle, and badly equipped. Most of them went into Antwerp without water bottles, haversacks, or bandoliers, and had to carry their ammunition in their pockets and their bayonets in their garters.

[1] Its battle casualties amounted to less than 200.

[2] Gen. É. J. Galet (*Albert, King of the Belgians, in the Great War* (1931)) shows conclusively that Deguise, the fortress commander, made no attempt to carry out the instructions given him of resistance to the end. All the north-eastern forts, which had been neither bombarded nor attacked, were tamely surrendered. Had Beseler been forced to reduce them piecemeal the shifting of his siege-train and infantry would alone have taken several days.

security of his northern flank was not the prime object of either antagonist. Each in turn extended his line until it touched the coast, because he had been unable to envelop and roll up his adversary. The protection of the water was welcomed only when the destruction of the opposing army by manœuvre was proved impossible. Time after time during those fifty days of continual fighting every blow was parried, sometimes at the last possible moment, until stabilization set in with the commencement of winter in the middle of November. First, Castelnau commanding the 2nd French army failed to turn the German flank between the wooded hills of Lassigny and the chalk slopes around Bapaume. Northward round Arras in the first days of October Maud'huy, after the bitterest fighting, just foiled Falkenhayn's new plan of pinching out the northern French forces by a simultaneous attack there and at Roye with the VIth German army under Prince Rupprecht. Yet farther north great masses of cavalry under von der Marwitz were directed towards the lower Somme between Amiens and Abbeville with extremely ambitious plans of destroying the French communications. But they accomplished nothing worthy of mention, and by October 9th were being driven back from the neighbourhood of Hazebrouck, their farthest point of penetration.

Meanwhile the British were beginning to appear in two new directions. The army on the Aisne, now augmented to six divisions, was awkwardly wedged in between the French forces, whereas its natural place both for ease of communications and for general strategy was obviously on the extreme left. Joffre agreed that it should be shifted north, though the move inevitably hampered his own concentrations and had to be carried through piecemeal. This transference was decided by French without instructions from his government and was of priceless service to the Allied cause. In spite of difficulties the 2nd corps was detrained near Abbeville by October 9th in immediate readiness to move upon Béthune. On the same day the 7th division, composed of well-seasoned troops, mainly collected from various garrisons within the Empire, was lying at Ostend with the 3rd cavalry division. This force destined to relieve Antwerp had been put under the independent command of Sir H. Rawlinson, much to the annoyance of the Commander-in-Chief. But on this same day, its first object having been frustrated, it became part of the B.E.F.[1] and was charged with the duty of protecting the retirement of the Belgian army. After various adventures with the German cavalry, which as we saw had been scouring the country far to its right rear, it occupied a line covering Ypres, while the Belgians began to fortify the Yser. By October 14th, therefore, a torn and weary force was in position to guard the coastwise route to Calais. But a great gap still existed between Ypres and La Bassée thinly sprinkled with French cavalry and territorials until the transfer of the B.E.F. was completed.

The fall of Antwerp was a great and well-deserved advantage to the Germans. They could now use all their heavy artillery for offence in the field, and push forward without regard to their rear. Napoleon once said, 'I can give you anything but time'; this imperious need of haste seems to have determined Falkenhayn's decision. He had now five reserve corps available, but he resisted the importunity of Hindenburg for their employment in the East. They were to win the war in Flanders. They alone were available for instant action; and were to break through to Calais between Menin and the sea. Falkenhayn apparently thought that the Franco-British concentration farther south was more advanced than it really was, for he kept his VIth army, unreinforced, partly on the defensive. He realized that these new formations were largely composed of untrained men with indifferent officers.[2] But the

[1] Henceforward it was known as the 4th corps, a 3rd corps had already been formed under Pulteney.

[2] The proportion of fully trained men is given by the *German Official History* (*Der Weltkrieg 1914 bis 1918*) as 39 per cent. 'The men were too young and the officers too old.' The Allied Intelligence at first rated them below their actual value; hence the attack east of Ypres was maintained even after it was known that two of them had arrived.

spirit and devotion of the young volunteers might be accounted a compensation for their lack of technical knowledge; and indeed their ecstatic bravery, like that of our own new armies, was the admiration of their enemies.

Moreover, they would have behind them an unusually powerful artillery, the Antwerp siege-train; and the meagre resistance put up by the Belgian army in the fortress augured an easier victory in the open field. The German Staff has conclusively shown that these formations could not have been used anywhere so rapidly as in the extreme north. Falkenhayn knew that Indian troops might soon be expected in France; he could not be certain that some of the British territorial divisions were not already battle-worthy. Even if complete envelopment were denied him, he was perfectly correct in thinking that the possession of Dunkirk, Calais, and Boulogne would be of infinitely greater value than any other territory in northern France. Hence his decision seems right, even though it ended in failure after a long agony for the Allies.

The battle now about to be joined between Arras and the sea lasted for about a month[1] and was most furious and desperate. At the outset the offensive was divided, for whereas the Germans attacked on the coast, and between Arras and the La Bassée Canal, the Allies were themselves thrusting forward between Givenchy and Ypres. But by October 21st the enemy had everywhere gained the initiative, and spent the next three weeks in continuous efforts to impose his will with a growing superiority in men and artillery.

Down to October 20th the Allies had won fair tactical successes. The miry and blind Flemish plain, so thickly enclosed and studded with farms and cottages in the intervals between large villages, was ideal for defence. Nevertheless the enemy had been pushed beyond those insignificant hillocks looking down into Ypres from the east, for the possession of which at least 500,000 men were

[1] Approximately from October 12 to November 11, when the last attack of the Prussian Guard on Ypres was defeated.

to die during the war; the Lys had been crossed, Armentières secured, and a line held thence to Givenchy on another tiny ridge covering Lille.[1] The defensive flanks remained substantially intact. Falkenhayn was now ready for a general attack. He has been criticized for extending it over so large an area; but he had obtained a superiority at the two points meant to be decisive and by his activities elsewhere made any transfer of troops by his enemy impossible.

The assault upon the Belgians had begun on the 18th. They were entrenched in a flat, naked, and oozy country where the roads and railways are carried on embankments six to ten feet high. The Yser, merely the largest of the numerous intersecting dikes, is surely the most insignificant stream that is assured of an immortality in history. It flows in a shallow curve from Dixmude to Nieuport, the two bastion-bridge-heads on the right bank. The attack on the latter was hampered by the unwearying fire of British monitors and old battleships, which scourged the flanks of the columns advancing through the sand dunes. The former was gloriously held by Admiral Ron'arch's 6,000 Breton sailors until November 10th. During the last week in October the sluices were opened and the sea-water slowly flooded all the area between the Yser and the railway embankment, which runs in a straight line between the two towns. An inundated zone two miles wide and three or four feet deep gave rest to the exhausted army,[2] and allowed King Albert to retain throughout the war a tiny fraction of his kingdom. Falkenhayn's last hope of manœuvring freely round an open flank had been finally foiled.

Before the battle in the centre reached its full intensity

[1] We were driven off this Aubers ridge two days later.

[2] The Belgian casualties amounted to about 20,000 men or 35 per cent. of their strength. From October 23 they were supported by one French division besides the marines. Their unswerving resistance is the more remarkable, as on the evidence of their own historian (Gen. Galet, op. cit.) the army was a mere disorganized mob immediately after the retreat from Antwerp.

yet another furious German assault was made upon Arras, where Maud'huy's defeat might have isolated the whole Allied left wing. The enemy had brought up his heavy guns, including 11-inch mortars, but was foiled, after five days' conflict, mainly through the devotion of the Alpine division. Its historian says that even in the last days of the war the old soldiers would recall the intensity of the struggle round Saint-Laurent; 'c'était rudement dure'.[1] The city with all its exquisite survivals of the old Spanish sovereignty was laid waste, thus following Rheims in the long list of historic ruins.

By October 20th the offensive strategy of the Allies was doomed, though their leaders did not realize it. The optimism which still prevailed was partly due to defective intelligence, but mainly to the characters of the two principal commanders. French was now as sanguine as he had been disconsolate during the retreat. He had already launched Rawlinson on a fruitless advance towards Menin, and now confidently expected to use the 1st corps, which was just coming up, as a spear-head to thrust right through the enemy into Ghent. This confidence was by no means shared by Haig, whose handling of the corps throughout was a model of cautious resolution. Foch, whose present mission was to co-ordinate the action of the armies of the three nations, was, as ever, ardent and unshakable in the doctrine of attack, whether with the hope of a break-through or as the most powerful weapon of defence. While it is true that the persistence in large-scale attacks down to the 29th used up so many men that the line was in the utmost extremity of exhaustion when the German wave broke, it is also true that these repeated onslaughts deceived the enemy as to the forces arrayed against him. Time after time successes were followed up with a perplexed hesitation, from fear of hidden reserves available for a crushing counter-attack. In fact, until long after the war, German historians asserted that their troops had been outnumbered throughout the battle. At the

[1] A. Humbert, *La Division Barbot* (1919).

time they probably believed that a large proportion of our fourteen territorial divisions were available near at hand as reserves.

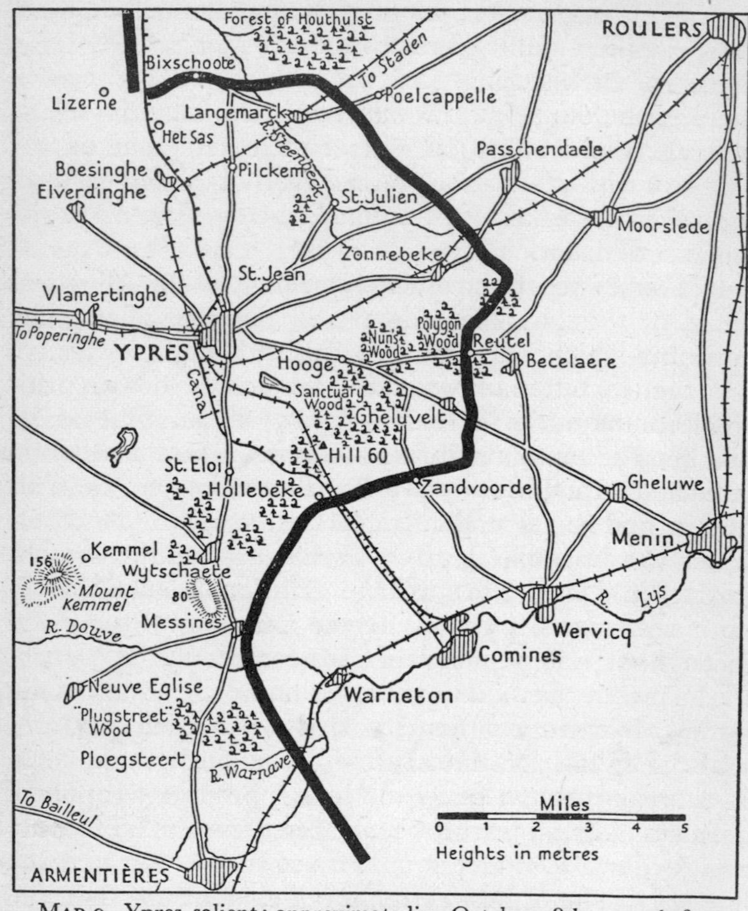

MAP 9. Ypres salient: approximate line October 28th, 1914, before the loss of Messines ridge.

The 21st, therefore, found the British standing defensively from Givenchy to Ypres,[1] and attacking farther north in conjunction with the French. The great encounter battle which started on that day lasted without intermission until the 29th with little result except great

[1] 2nd corps Givenchy–Fromelles; 3rd to 'Plugstreet' Wood; and, in succession northwards, Allenby's cavalry corps and 7th division.

losses on either side. It was a curious mixture of open and trench warfare. The fighting swayed backwards and forwards over the same ground, and allowed little time to dig, much less to build the elaborate breastworks of sandbags required in a soil where the water wells up within a foot of the surface. The landscape, in later years a featureless desert of tormented mud, was still very close. The leaves were still on the hedges and the frequent woods, so that battalions, and sometimes even companies, fought it out without knowledge of what was happening on their flanks. Hence arose the odd curves, angles, and salient projections within the great curve of the famous salient itself.

Throughout these days French remained exceedingly confident. On the 22nd he sent a message to Kitchener that 'the Germans were vigorously playing their last card', and another on the 26th forecasting that they 'were quite incapable of making any strong and sustained attack', and maintained their positions only by the support of their very powerful artillery. Even on the night of the 28th he had so little knowledge of the culminating storm which was to fall upon him that he was issuing orders for the renewal of the joint offensive for the morrow.

Meanwhile the Germans were preparing with a secret rapidity to concentrate such a force on the south-eastern angle of the salient as to ensure a superiority of at least three to one at the selected point.[1] Five new divisions were brought up under the command of von Fabek, whose army-order of October 29th proclaimed that 'The break-through will be of decisive importance. We must and will therefore conquer . . . end the war and strike the decisive blow against our most detested enemy.'

No progress in any way worthy of these great expectations was made on October 29th–30th. The enemy

[1] Between Gheluvelt and Messines the superiority was about six to one in all arms. See Sir J. E. Edmonds, *Military Operations: France and Belgium*, vol. ii (1925), p. 284. Fabek's five new divisions were, however, partly new reserve formations.

hesitated and fumbled and clearly was unaware of the weakness and weariness of his opponents, who by choice of ground and controlled rapidity of fire used every art of concealing their position. The cavalry, it is true, were thrown back for one and a half miles near Hollebeke, where the southern extremity of the curve straightened out along the Wytschaete–Messines ridge, and most of the French reserves were ungrudgingly sent by General D'Urbal behind the threatened spot. But no serious alarm was felt. Yet the 31st was to prove one of the very few days of universally recognized crisis which are possible in a war fought on such an immense scale. None of the required elements was wanting, the paralysis of the Staffs most immediately effected, the rupture of a fluid line in a vital spot, no reserves, and no prepared rearward line. The presence of the Kaiser himself in the battle area had specially been made known to the attacking troops.

Shortly before noon the line of the 1st division was broken at Gheluvelt. This village is on the high road from Menin to Ypres, nearly five miles south-east of the latter, towards which the ridge slopes at a very gentle gradient. Its possession was, therefore, of great tactical importance. But Gheluvelt was not in itself necessary for the defence of Ypres, for the salient stood fast long after it was taken. Yet if at that moment the great German reinforcements available close at hand had been thrust through the gap and had spread out fanwise, they would have taken the defenders on either flank in the rear, and broken the cohesion of the British army to pieces. Already limbers and guns were streaming back towards Ypres. The impulse of retreat began to be felt. General FitzClarence commanding the 1st brigade, one of those supremely ardent and inspiring spirits who seem destined to fall before war has given the full reward to their qualities, got hold of the 2nd Worcestershires, part of the reserve of the 2nd division on the north, and ordered them to counter-attack immediately. This movement was scarcely in train when a shell burst in Hooge Château, where the Staff of both divisions had assembled for a conference, and practically destroyed them. But the Worcestershires—a tiny force of eight officers and 360 men—swept all before them. They fell upon the Bavarians, dispersed and relaxed after victory, and drove them back in confusion from the village. The line was re-established. This was the climax of the battle, though many moments of desperate anxiety were yet to follow. On November 1st we were driven off the hill of Messines, where the London Scottish, the first territorial infantry battalion to be engaged, received a hard baptism of fire. Next day with Wytschaete went the whole of the high ground on the south of the salient. By now a certain inadequate degree of reinforcement had become possible. The 2nd corps came up from La Bassée, where the Indians had arrived to face a wholly strange war in the depressing advent of winter. The French had thrown in every available man, and disposed of larger forces than their ally between Messines and the sea. The defence of Ypres is the most perfect example of real comradely co-operation in the west. The troops of the two nations were intermingled even in small detachments, as hard necessity demanded. Foch, never failing in confidence, loyalty and tact, exercised a very powerful influence over French, often by suggestion rather than by direct advice, and won the hearty affection of all those who were brought into contact with him. The defence of Ypres wiped out all those feelings of mutual distrust which had been so prevalent in the first month of the war.

The battle itself died down like a great storm, with spasmodic threatenings of general renewal and one tremendous clearing shower. On November 11th twelve and a half picked German divisions, including the Guard, attacked in dense formation on a front of nine miles from Messines to north of the Menin road, in pouring rain and wind. Failing completely after great sacrifices in other sectors, they thrust forward about 1,000 yards on either side of the road. Here they were met by an improvised resistance of all the last scraps of men who could be collected, sappers, cooks, servants, and transport-drivers, and were driven back through the tangled undergrowth of the Nun's Wood by the Oxfordshire Light Infantry. The winter set in immediately afterwards with snow and foul weather, and fighting ceased, except for insignificant local enterprises.

The defence of Ypres is the chief glory of our old army, which in its performance practically ceased to exist. More than 50,000 British soldiers fell; many battalions were completely annihilated and the strength of divisions was reduced by more than half.[1] The inviolate city became the symbol of its invincibility, and its abandonment would have been felt as an indelible moral disgrace. From the strictly practical view of military convenience, this was unfortunate. Ypres itself was not a centre of communications but a bottle-neck, and every movement in the low ground could be observed by the enemy, whose commanding semicircular position enabled him to direct fire into the flanks and rear of the British positions. Within the salient bullets and shells flew from all quarters, and the daily casualties were probably more than twice as heavy as in any other sector occupied by the British. In short, had not sentiment forbidden, the natural line to hold would have been that of the canal just west of the city.

The war had now assumed its unique character; for the flanks had ceased to exist. Trench lines, practically continuous, stretched from the sea to Switzerland. There was as yet no such bewildering maze of elaborate and even comfortable field fortifications, as the industry of years was to scrawl across the face of the ravaged country. A narrow, irregular ditch, with holes cut in the sides for shelter, represented the front line; two or three hundred yards farther back the supports were similarly housed. The only rearward organization would probably consist of villages organized for defence, with isolated strong

[1] The 7th division arrived at Zeebrugge on October 6 with 17,948 men. It was withdrawn from the line on November 5 with 8,711 men; and less than a third of its infantry.

points in houses or woods. Rations would be brought up and reliefs carried out over the open—but only at night. For the most part the trenches had not been deliberately sited; they were more often an elaboration of the holes into which the combatants had dug themselves when unable to advance. As any yielding of ground was foolishly supposed by the higher commands to be bad for moral, these positions might possess a good field of fire, or practically none; they might be thirty or eight hundred yards from each other. Close proximity to the enemy meant immunity from artillery fire, but a constant bickering with grenades, mortars, and all the paraphernalia of siege-warfare, in which the Germans possessed for many months an unchallenged supremacy. At night no-man's-land, a hive of wiring activity, was lit up intermittently with flares[1] shot from a pistol carried by the officer on duty in each company. Co-operation between the infantry and artillery changed its character, becoming more formal and stereotyped. In the earlier fighting the guns had been mobile, sections or single guns had been constantly brought close up to the infantry to deal point-blank with local obstacles. Now they were dug in and fixed two thousand yards at least in rear, restricted to certain targets, carefully registered. The character of the ammunition required also changed. Against troops in the open a well-directed burst of shrapnel is an unequalled killer, but against trenches, or even a mass of barbed wire, it is practically impotent. Hence arose the ever-increasing demand for heavier guns, with high-angle fire, to drop high-explosive shell in the trenches.

Stationary warfare inevitably breeds a sense of isolation and of disproportionate risk between the troops in the line and the staffs. The army and corps commanders became empty and unreal figures living ten or fifteen miles behind

[1] The first five Verey pistols were issued to the B.E.F. at the close of the battle of Ypres. Here also the Germans throughout 1915 surpassed the Allies both in the quantity and quality available, of lights, 'star-shells' and searchlights.

in luxurious and unmolested *châteaux*;[1] even the divisional and brigade staffs lost much of their intimate significance, and were often regarded as fussy amateurs when they visited the trenches. The higher staffs studied the map, but seldom the ground itself.

In the summer, it is true, life in a quiet sector was very popular with the troops, who often got far more rest and sleep than when in reserve, where they were constantly employed in night-digging. But darkness, cold, and mud —particularly the last named—were invincible enemies. While diseases like typhoid, the scourge of all earlier campaigns, had been entirely conquered by medical science, new ailments arose, whose very names 'trench-fever', 'trench-foot', testified that they owed their origin to the new conditions. After the first winter these dangers were largely averted, partly by remedies and palliatives, but mainly because the construction of large dug-outs and the greater number of troops available, enabled hours of duty to be much shorter and less exhausting.[2]

From the first French and British methods of trench warfare differed widely. The former held their trenches with few men, relying at need on their incomparable 75's, which seem never to have run short of ammunition. Moreover, in almost all sectors, unless an attack was arranged or expected, they encouraged an inactive forbearance, with the object of avoiding casualties. Whereas the British were very thick on the ground, and the troops were enjoined to harass the enemy by every possible pin-prick, such as fighting patrols, and bursts of fire on his nightly working parties. Yet it was the British and not the French soldiers who were the actors in the curious 'Christmas truce' of 1914, when fraternizing between the

[1] 'Head-quarters (except during a battle) are unsuitable targets' (instructions to R.A.F., February 16, 1918). This immunity from attack seems to have been generally conceded to each other by the higher staffs of the respective belligerents throughout the war.

[2] During the winter of 1915–16 it was rare for any man to spend more than forty-eight consecutive hours in the firing-line, and fairly adequate supplies of thigh-boots were available.

lines, even games of football and mutual trench visits were common, and in some sectors lasted for nearly a week.

The Germans being on the defensive naturally conformed more or less exactly to the tactics of their respective enemies. Hence the importance of the role played at any time by the British armies cannot be judged by the length of line held,[1] but by the number of German divisions which faced them. Few things aroused more ill feeling between the Allies than the persistence of French politicians and some soldiers in repeating the false comparison for purposes of propaganda.

The Germans were always able to economize men more than the Allies, for until 1918 they mainly stood on the defensive, had a peculiar gift for machine-gun tactics, which remained unequalled to the end of the war, and occupied a hostile country. They were thus able to use its material and physical resources without stint or consideration for the inhabitants. The elaboration and completeness of their fortifications were a revelation to their enemies when they were first deeply indented at the Somme. Finally, they possessed complete unity of communications; and on the whole a better network of railways, especially in the north, where they occupied a level and thickly populated industrial area.

It is appropriate at this point to give some description of the line, which until March 1917 never varied by as much as ten miles in either direction. The Belgians remained in charge of the sector from the coast to Dixmude, where the floods prevented any serious infantry fighting. A small French enclave followed to about four miles north of Ypres; this is said to have been kept for political reasons, in order that the defence of Dunkirk should not be wholly in foreign hands. The Flemish plain as far as Givenchy was defended by the British, who had well behind them the high hills stretching westward from the wooded hump of Kemmel to town-crowned Cassel

[1] In November 1914 the French held about 430 miles, the British 21, and the Belgians 15; a year later the British share had been increased to about 50.

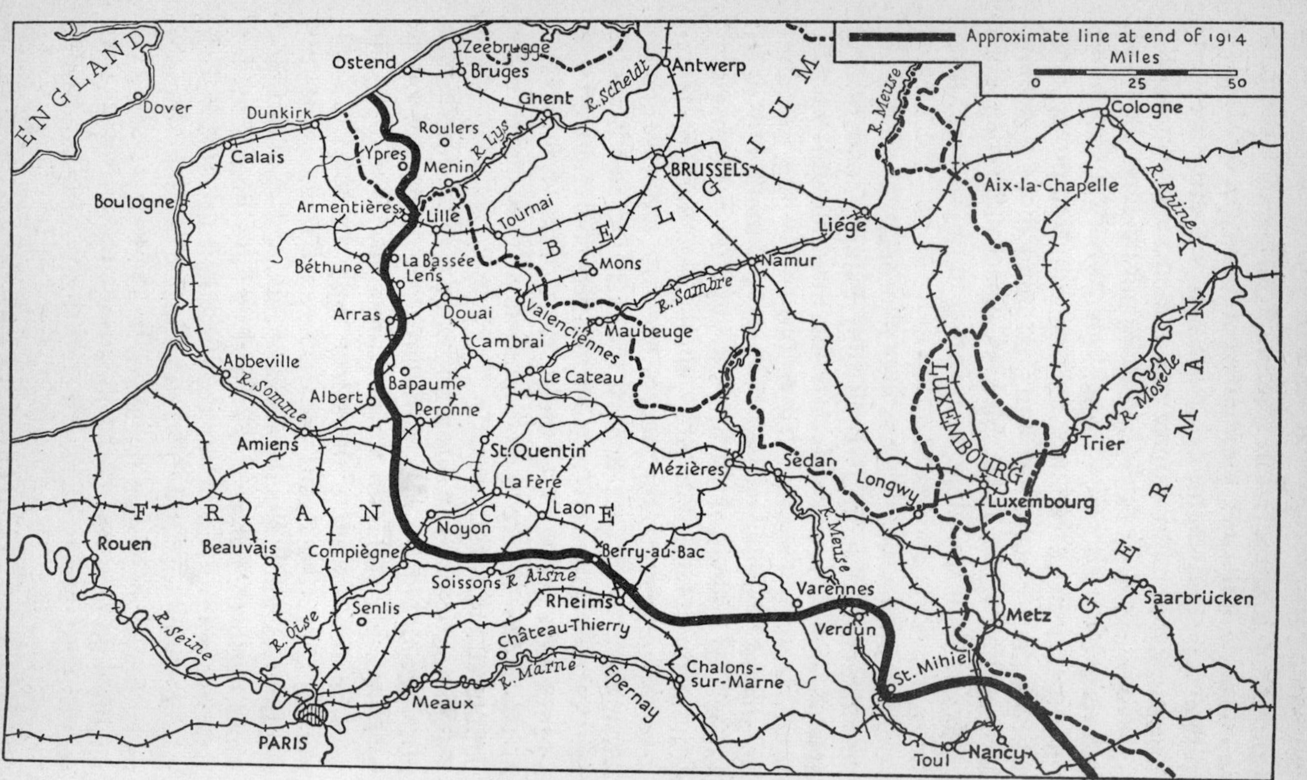

MAP 10. The Western Front.

(about 500 feet high), but were tactically overlooked both north and south of Armentières by the ridges of Messines and Aubers. Armentières itself, an industrial town of about 25,000 inhabitants, was the social centre of the fighting troops. Though two miles only behind the front, it was seldom shelled in 1915; shops, cafés, and hotels remained open, plays and variety entertainments were given in the theatre. The enemy was more snugly ensconced in the great city of Lille. About Givenchy the coal-mines begin, and except for Lens, just within the German lines, there are no large towns but a number of drab villages studded in an undulating country. To these succeed the chalk uplands of Artois, where the villages, closely grouped round wells, appear as little woods on the landscape, with their ringed orchards of cider-apples. Here, a few miles north of Arras, the Germans had maintained a firm grasp of the long plateau of Vimy, which guarded and shrouded from view their vital communications in the plain of Douai. From Arras the line ran south for about fifty miles through the same type of country on both sides of the Somme, with its wide marshy loops. Here again the enemy possessed the pick of the ground, and was to make a great fortress of the hills between the Ancre and the Somme. Towards Lassigny the country becomes more wooded and diversified. Here the trenches came nearest to Paris. Every day Clemenceau's paper *L'Homme enchaîné* had printed in thick type at the top of the front page—*LES ALLEMANDS SONT À NOYON.* For Noyon is only sixty miles from the capital. Here also came an abrupt change of direction from south to east. For about forty miles the French held the north bank of the Aisne among the beautiful wooded hills, earlier described. East of Soissons they maintained a precarious hold on the river heights, the crest of which they were not to conquer for another three years. At Berry-au-Bac a southward curve found the Germans in possession of the fortified heights which dominate Rheims from the north. Thence succeeded the naked and almost waterless chalk region of the

Champagne pouilleuse; here the French were overlooked by a line of downs reaching nearly 1,000 feet in height, which they assailed in at least four great battles. Any serious loss of ground here would jeopardize the very foundations of the invaders' security, for it would uncover the communications of Belgium with Germany and leave the whole of the right wing in the air. The Argonne forest was cut in two by the trenches; it was a notoriously dangerous area, of almost constant and bloody fighting. Verdun formed a salient similar to that of Ypres, but Sarrail had thrust the French defences about nine miles beyond the fortress, and held all the highest crests of the abrupt and tangled hills which stand 800 feet above the right bank of the Meuse; he had even retained a footing in that level plain, called the Woevre, which stretches to Metz barely twenty miles away. From Verdun to the Swiss frontier is very nearly half the whole length of the line, but owing to the difficulties of communication in the broken country, most of it was always held by each side with a mere fraction of its strength. The French tried more than once in the spring of 1915 to bite off the Saint-Mihiel salient, which was strongly garrisoned and was full of dead ground. They also built up immensely strong fortifications some twelve miles east of Nancy to guard against another attempt to break through over the Moselle between Toul and Épinal. But southward both sides settled down to desultory mountain warfare in the Vosges, where many of the summits exceed 4,000 feet. Here no continuous trenches were ever constructed, but lines of outposts faced each other, generally held by old reservists or dismounted cavalry, with an occasional stiffening of Alpine troops. No larger operations were recorded during the remainder of the war than desperate local struggles for commanding tactical features, such as the Hartmannweilerkopf, or as the French called it 'Le Vieil Armand', which changed hands repeatedly. South of the Donon the French never relaxed their grip on the minute portion of Alsace which they had conquered during August 1914.

They nowhere succeeded in getting right down to the plain, but blocked the eastern passes at a distance of from six to eight miles from the crest. Though lacking in military importance this occupation had some political interest, as after the Russians were driven out of Memel and Tilsit in April 1915 it remained until the end of the war the only piece of German territory in Europe in the hands of the Allies. The enemy, on the other hand, possessed nearly a tenth of France, including the great industrial area of Lille, Roubaix, and Tourcoing, four-fifths of her coal and nine-tenths of her iron resources, as well as a rich agricultural district, especially devoted to the cultivation of beet-sugar, and a number of large forests. All these, combined with the exploitation of Belgium and Luxembourg, were of capital importance for counteracting the strangling effects of the blockade.

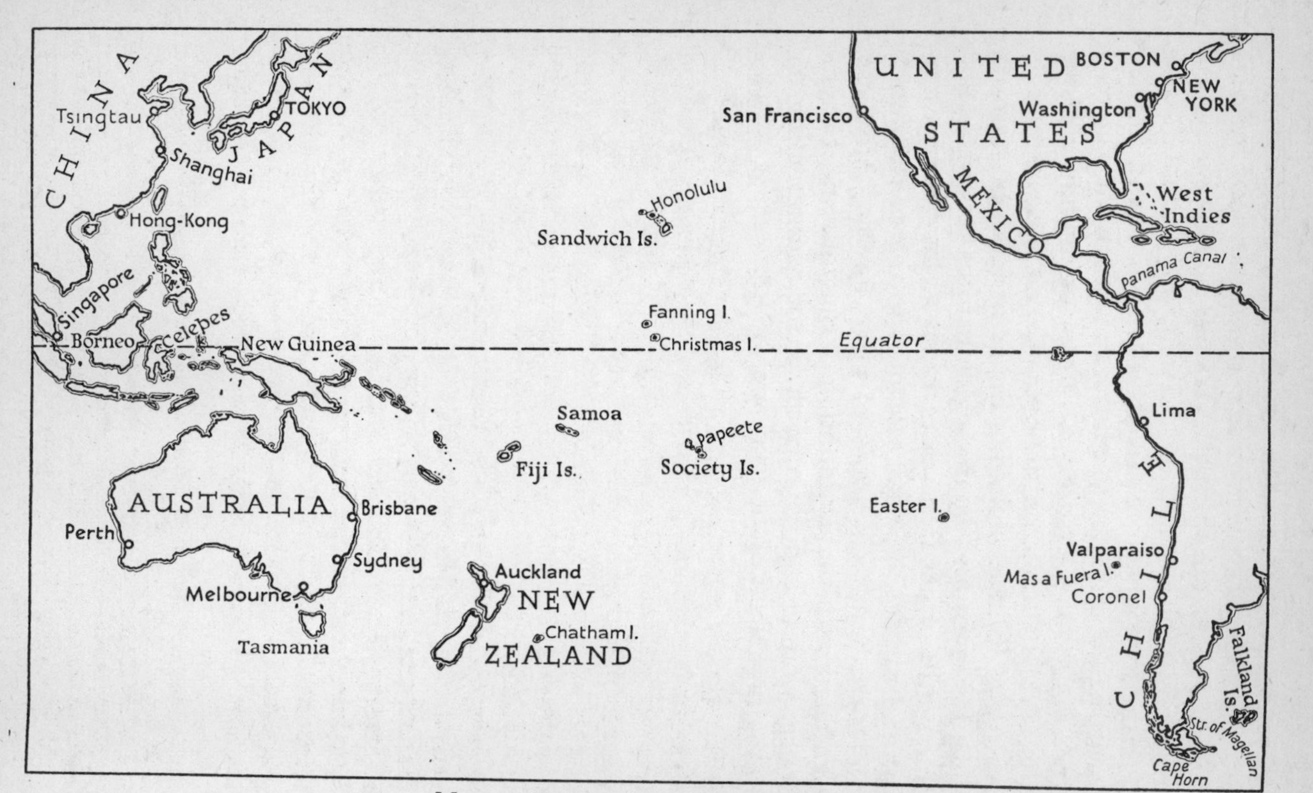

Map 11. The Pacific and South America.

VII

THE FORTUNES OF ADMIRAL VON SPEE

I

THE commander of the German squadron on the China station, Count von Spee, was a fine inspiring sailor whose example encouraged his crews in high devotion and efficiency. He found himself at the outbreak of war in the open sea,[1] having left his base at Tsingtau before the period of strained relations began. He was well supplied with colliers, and able to take advantage of the free hand given him by his Admiralty to choose his strategical direction as he thought best. He lay about islands of the Western Pacific until the news of the Japanese declaration of war (August 21) determined his course. He then decided to make for the western coast of South America, where he thought it improbable that Japan would follow him from fear of political complications with the United States. This voyage would also take him out of reach of the battle-cruiser *Australia*, stationed in the South Seas, which was capable by its speed and 12-inch armament of destroying the whole of his squadron single-handed. It could also be accomplished by easy and secret stages, for the maze of remote islands offered a series of secluded harbourages. Except for a fruitless visit to Samoa, already occupied by a strong New Zealand garrison (September 14), a bombardment of the French establishments at Papeete (September 22), and the destruction of the British cable station at Fanning Island, the voyage was quite uneventful.[2] At Easter Island the squadron remained a week (October

[1] He had with him at this time the armoured cruisers *Scharnhorst* and *Gneisenau*, the light cruisers *Nürnberg* and *Emden* (shortly to be detached into the Indian Ocean), with a fleet of colliers.

[2] There is something almost ludicrous in the care with which the Admiral swept up the tiny public till in any small British or French possession at which he touched. He records a haul of £720 2*s.* 6*d.* from Fanning Island; Hakapeki yielded 9,862 fr. 20 centimes, and Atuona (Marquesas Islands) 12,000 fr.

12–18), being joined by the light cruisers *Dresden* from the West Indies and *Leipzig* from the Californian coast. News of the war had not penetrated to this wild outpost of Chile, and ironically enough it was an English overseer who arranged for the supply of fresh meat so badly needed by the squadron. On October 26th Spee anchored off the island of Mas a Fuera some 500 miles west of Valparaiso, having thus practically completed in safety a voyage of more than 10,000 miles across the Pacific. Fresh colliers had been chartered by telegram from Honolulu, and the *Dresden* and *Leipzig* had arranged for a news service from the wireless of German steamers interned in Chilean ports.

The British Admiralty had long suspected Spee's probable destination. As early as September 14th Admiral Cradock, commanding the South American station, had been warned to expect his approach, and ordered, as soon as he had a superior force, to 'search the Magellan Straits, being ready to return and cover the River Plate, or according to information, search north as far as Valparaiso, break up the German trade and destroy the German cruisers'.[1] On October 5th he was given a still more definite order to concentrate on the west coast in order 'to search and protect trade'. Accordingly Cradock collected his squadron at the Falkland Islands, with the object of preventing the enemy from slipping round the Horn and attacking the Argentine trade route, so vital for the war-services of the Entente.[2]

By October 22nd Cradock had under his command an old battleship *Canopus*, armed with 12-inch guns but limited to a speed of 15 knots; a large armoured cruiser *Good Hope*, his flagship with two 9·2 guns; an armoured cruiser *Monmouth*, with no larger armament than fourteen 6-inch guns; and a light cruiser *Glasgow*.

He was placed in the following dilemma. If he kept the *Canopus* with him, his squadron would be safe but confined

[1] Admiralty telegram sent via British Minister at Rio, September 14, 1914.

[2] The export of horses, mules, meat, and maize was of extreme military importance.

to the defensive. In that case the enemy's superior speed might enable him to round the Horn unobserved, and to pass into the Atlantic where Admiral Stoddart's squadron off the east coast of South America was barely strong enough to deal effectively with the enemy, especially as Stoddart was distracted by another elusive raider, *Karlsruhe*, working off that coast. If, on the other hand, his mission was offensive, 'to search', it would be made of no avail if he kept the slow *Canopus* in company; and if he left her behind, his strength would be inferior to that of his enemy.[1]

His instructions were in fact contradictory. He was told to keep his entire squadron concentrated, but the previous orders to search, thrice reiterated, had not been cancelled. The real intention of the Admiralty appears to have been that the *Glasgow*, which was swifter than any of Spee's vessels, should locate them and draw them down to the combined British squadron.[2]

The choice of the *Canopus* was most unfortunate. It is clear that a battle-cruiser should have been sent. If Jellicoe's extreme reluctance to part with any of his capital ships was held to be an insuperable bar against temporarily weakening the Grand Fleet, the *Australia* might well have been brought from her home waters as soon as Spee's destination was reasonably certain (i.e. after September 14), and could have arrived in time to ensure his swift destruction. The retention of this vessel round Perth was no doubt determined by Australian public opinion.

In any event Cradock, after requesting the Admiralty for an armoured cruiser from Stoddart's squadron, started

[1] The broadside of either the *Scharnhorst* and *Gneisenau* exceeded in weight that of the *Good Hope* by 25 per cent. and that of the *Monmouth* by more than 100 per cent. Moreover, Cradock's two ships had been manned by reservists at the beginning of war and had had little opportunity of gunnery instruction and practice.

[2] See Winston Churchill, *The World Crisis 1911–14* (1923), pp. 414 sqq. If Spee went north his movements would cause much less anxiety, as a Japanese battleship with two attendant cruisers would be more than a match for him.

to cruise up the west coast with his existing cruiser strength, leaving the *Canopus* behind to convoy colliers (October 22). Thus apparently he conceived himself to be following most fully the spirit of the Admiralty instructions.[1]

II

The two squadrons were now daily drawing closer to each other. Spee moved from Mas a Fuera on October 27th towards Valparaiso, where he hoped to find his new colliers waiting. Disappointed in this, he began to cruise west of that port, keeping fairly close to the land and picking up at intervals wireless signals from the three British cruisers. On October 31st the *Glasgow* put into Coronel and Spee moved south to cut her off. At the same time Cradock, who had taken in very loud signals from the *Leipzig*, was sweeping north to catch and destroy her in supposed isolation. Thus though both were eagerly seeking battle, the actual encounter off Coronel on November 1st was a surprise to either adversary.

When the smoke of the opposing squadrons (about 17 miles apart) became visible on the horizon at 4.17 p.m., Cradock might almost certainly have avoided an action and retired on the *Canopus* 300 miles to the south.[2] This, however, was far from his intention; he turned towards his enemy. His motive can only be guessed. He can have had little doubt that he was going to destruction, but presumably hoped before the end so to damage the German ships as to cripple their freedom of action. Thus with their stings drawn they would have fallen an easy prey to his avenger.

[1] See his last message October 26: 'With reference to orders contained in Admiralty telegram received October 7 to search for enemy, and our great desire for early success, consider it impracticable, on account of *Canopus*'s slow speed, to find and destroy enemy squadron. Consequently have ordered *Defence* to join me. . . . *Canopus* will be employed on necessary convoying of colliers.'

[2] He could have done so easily had he abandoned his auxiliary steamer *Otranto* which was limited to about 15 knots. Spee's squadron when sighted was only steaming 14 knots, and its maximum combined speed was 20. There were just under three hours of daylight left.

It was 'thick and wicked weather',[1] with rain squalls, a strong wind and heavy seas, as the squadrons manœuvred for position. Both were steering a course roughly south. Cradock, being farther from the land, kept the rays of the declining sun striking from behind him into the eyes of his enemy, and sought to force an action as soon as possible. Spee on the contrary aimed both at preventing the British from seeking the shelter of the neutral coast, and at delaying battle until after sundown when the British cruisers would be silhouetted against the flaming horizon, and his own practically invisible. In this object he was successful. His gunners did not belie their reputation; in less than an hour the *Good Hope* had been sunk and the *Monmouth* driven burning into the darkness, where by ill luck the *Nürnberg* found her. Helpless but grimly determined she refused surrender and was destroyed. Not a man was saved from these two ships, as the high seas and the fear lest other British forces might approach deterred the Germans from any attempt at rescue.[2]

The *Glasgow* escaped without serious injury from the very article of doom.

The losses as generally in modern naval battles were enormously disproportionate, for the German ships were practically undamaged and only two of their crews were wounded.

III

The defeat of Coronel, in itself a heavy strategical stroke, came at an evil moment in the fortunes of the Entente. Turkey had just declared war. The first battle of Ypres was on the last throes of its protracted crisis. The great battleship *Audacious*, one of the most modern super-dreadnoughts, had just been sunk by a mine off the north coast of Ireland, as is related elsewhere.[3]

If Spee moved immediately he might do incalculable harm. His comparative liberty of choice brooded like an

[1] This expressive phrase is that of the British Consul at Valparaiso who sent the British Admiralty the first news of the battle.

[2] 1,440 men perished.

[3] See p. 307.

uncertain thunder-cloud over our scattered and inadequate dispositions. It was not probable that he would recross the Pacific, or that he would go north up the Californian coast. His most likely alternatives, however, were the most alarming. A passage through the newly opened Panama Canal would bring him swiftly[1] before the West Indies. But in this event he must at once reveal the secret of his presence. Most probably therefore he would round the Horn. The Atlantic would offer him first the choice of a dash against Africa, where his presence would imperil the impending invasion of German South-West Africa, and might rekindle the sparks of the Boer rebellion scarcely quenched. Or he might fall upon the La Plata route, with the risk of a doubtful battle with Stoddart's squadron, if met in its full strength. Or finally he might venture north-eastwards to break through the blockade and return to German waters.

It so happened that a few days before Coronel, the First Sea Lord, Prince Louis of Battenberg, groundlessly and cruelly suspected by public opinion for his German origin, had resigned. His successor was the aged Lord Fisher, still the most volcanic and furious spirit of his generation, who gloried in the ruthlessness and remorselessness of conduct demanded by war. Fascinating, repellent, and terrible, he exacted from his subordinates an intuitive obedience to his despotic decisions, often charged with an uncanny insight. At this time, though not for long, Churchill and he acted like two twin thunderbolts of war in the vastness and rapidity of their remedial measures.

Thirty armoured ships in all[2] were collected at the threatened points, to ensure that wherever Spee went he should find a superior adversary. Three battle-cruisers were taken from the Grand Fleet, one the *Princess Royal* to guard the West Indies, two, the *Invincible* and *Inflexible*,

[1] It could be swiftly accomplished because three warships were allowed by American regulations to enter the canal together, and three more could wait at the entrance.

[2] Twenty-one of these were British, the remainder Japanese and French.

to bar the passage round the Horn. They were to be the spear-head of Admiral Sir Doveton Sturdee, sent to assume the widest command ever entrusted to a British admiral. Commander-in-Chief of the Pacific and the South Atlantic, he was to bring any commander in the latter ocean under his flag if he moved north out of his station.

While all these preparations were being made with the utmost secrecy and dispatch, the German admiral was consuming precious time in inactivity. After spending a night in Valparaiso, where he put aside the natural vauntings of the German colony in a mingled spirit of high modesty and melancholy foreboding, he led his squadron back to Mas a Fuera, and thence into the St. Quentin bay farther south. It was not until November 26th that he resumed his voyage. Instructions from the German Admiralty had directed him, if possible, to break back home, and he apparently believed that one if not several battle-cruisers from the High Seas Fleet had evaded the blockade and would meet him in mid-Atlantic. His immediate task was therefore to get safely into that ocean. Victory had redoubled his desire to inflict another direct military blow. War on trade, so German accounts tell us, he despised as being beneath the honour of his squadron.

So he decided upon an enterprise against the Falkland Islands, so important as a defended base, coaling-station, and centre of communications. We do not know what, if any, men-of-war he expected to find within the harbour, though he was probably aware that the *Canopus* was moored there as a floating fort.[1] Spee's intention failed to win the approval of the majority of his captains at a conference held on the flagship.[2] It was indeed to take an

[1] The available evidence is given in *Der Krieg zur See 1914–1918*: Kreuzer-Krieg, Band 1, pp. 242 sqq.

[2] The chief-of-staff and the captain of the *Nürnberg* were in favour. The other three captains opposed. Spee's last recorded signal during the battle to the captain of the *Gneisenau* was 'Sie haben doch recht gehabt', 'You were quite right'. Sir J. S. Corbett, *Naval Operations*, vol. i (1920), p. 414, is in error in stating that the captain of the *Gneisenau* persuaded Spee against his own better judgement.

unnecessary risk. The ships might be damaged, much of their remaining ammunition would probably be shot away, and any chance of a return home seriously jeopardized.

Most fortunately for Sturdee, the enemy dawdled in his oncoming, spending three days in discharging the coal of a prize into his own colliers.

In the Falkland Islands there was anxiety and eager preparation. The *Canopus* was berthed in the mud of the inner harbour, ready for indirect fire over the little hill which shielded her from sea-view. The outer entrance was closed with extemporized mines.

Suddenly Sturdee brought in his great squadron on December 7th. Besides the battle-cruisers he had one large armoured cruiser *Carnarvon*, two smaller ones, *Cornwall* and *Kent*, and two light cruisers, *Glasgow* and *Bristol*.

Next morning at 7.50, while coaling was in progress and parties of officers were going off for a day's shooting, the enemy's smoke was seen in the offing. It was the *Gneisenau* and *Nürnberg*, advance-guards of the squadron. These ships soon noticed the great clouds of smoke pouring out of the harbour, but at first took them for coal and oil dumps set alight to escape capture. It was not until about 9.30 after they had avoided the fire of the *Canopus* and were seeking to cut off the British guardship *Kent* that the distinctive tripod masts of the battle-cruisers were clearly seen in the harbour. The sight was equivalent to a sentence of certain death. They returned instantly to the main squadron which fled to the south-east. Within less than half an hour Sturdee was bringing his pursuing vessels through the outer entrance. The day was favourable to chase and battle, with calm seas and a brilliant visibility. Sturdee was in no hurry: he got his squadron together and ordered the crews to have their dinner before beginning the action. Spee, being hampered in movement by the lagging *Leipzig*, which was encircled by salvoes from the battle-cruisers before fighting became general, signalled to his three light cruisers to fall out of line and scatter at 1.20 p.m. Thus he hoped to save them to do future harm, while turning with his two big ships to a fight of forlorn sacrifice. He received an inadequate reward for his noble resolve; for, while his own agony was cruelly drawn out, two of his three small consorts were run down. The destruction of the *Scharnhorst* took three hours, that of the *Gneisenau* nearly five. This long delay was partly due to the blinding black smoke emitted by the battle-cruisers, which interfered with accurate spotting, and partly to the faulty design of the armour-piercing shells, which burst practically on impact.[1] But even so the end would have come sooner had not Sturdee taken the utmost precaution to protect his precious ships against serious damage, so that they might be speedily returned intact to the Grand Fleet. Consequently he fought at long range and avoided all attempts of the enemy to close and bring his powerful secondary armament to bear.

The *Nürnberg*, chased by the *Kent* with such ardour that the latter exceeded her hitherto maximum speed, was sunk at 7.30; the *Leipzig* fell an unequal victim to the *Cornwall* and *Glasgow* at 9 p.m. The *Dresden*, as already related, made her solitary escape.

The Germans had fought with the same fury and defiance as Cradock's men, flying their colours proudly to the last, while on the *Gneisenau* the remnants of the ship's company were assembled to give three cheers for the Kaiser as the vessel foundered under them. Spee perished with both his sons and with 1,800 men, only about 200 being saved. As before the victors were almost unscathed, and suffered in all some thirty casualties. The honours in so ill-matched a contest must go to the defeated;[2] Sturdee was the

[1] This defect will be noticed later on both at Dogger Bank and Jutland. It meant the expenditure of a very large amount of ammunition to sink an enemy, but caused heavy casualties to personnel, e.g. in this engagement both battle-cruisers practically used up all their 12-inch shells, while the *Gneisenau* before sinking lost three-quarters of her personnel.

[2] The superiority of the broadside of the two battle-cruisers with the *Carnarvon* over the two Germans was 370 per cent. It is a serious reflection on our gunnery that it took $1\frac{1}{2}$ hours for all three ships combined to sink the *Gneisenau*, already seriously damaged in the earlier part of the action.

fortunate instrument of the great designer at Whitehall who had so quickly and cunningly forged his plan of annihilation.

The high seas were again in the sovereign grasp of the British navy.[1]

[1] The *Königsberg* had been blockaded since October in the Rufigi delta in East Africa; the *Karlsruhe* (unknown to us) had blown up at sea off the West Indies (November 4)—next to the *Emden* she had been the most successful raider, accounting for sixteen ships with a value of £1,500,000.

VIII

THE FIRST EFFECTS OF THE WAR ON BELLIGERENTS AND NEUTRALS

THE outbreak of war revealed everywhere an astonishing unanimity of enthusiasm. All the continental nations believed it to be just and necessary; the Fatherland was threatened, and defence was the most sacred of duties. Hence instead of accentuating party animosities, it appeased and for the time destroyed them. That often-repeated threat of the International Socialists, the General Strike, proved the thinnest of phantoms. Only two members of the German Reichstag voted against the war-credits; and the Kaiser said with thrilling effect: 'Henceforward I know no parties, I know only Germans.' In France the great Socialist leader Jaurès had been murdered by a diseased young fanatic, but the Socialist groups joined the other parties in promoting the 'Union Sacrée'. The strikes and riots which had been seething in Petrograd during July instantly ceased. There was not the slightest need for any organized repression except in the creaking Empire of Austria-Hungary among the Czechs and southern Slavs.

The division of opinion within Great Britain, so keenly reflected to the last moment within the bosom of the Cabinet, had been instantly healed by the invasion of Belgium. August 4th was the first day on which the country could have entered the war with a united heart. For there were millions within the well-guarded island who, unable to see in the war any clear call to fight for self-defence, or for allies, were profoundly moved by a spirit of religious idealism to fight for the sanctity of a treaty which had protected a small inoffensive nation for more than two generations. It was mainly this indignation on behalf of the weak which quenched on the moment the impending civil war in Ireland, and led John Redmond, the leader of the Nationalist party, to promise on behalf of his people that every English soldier could be removed from the island.

The war created on the Continent a profound transformation of life. Not only were all men of military age called to the colours, but vast districts under the threat or experience of invasion were largely withdrawn from the process and safeguards of ordinary law. The Russian autocracy took the opportunity to prohibit the sale of vodka, an example praised but not elsewhere followed.

The position of the British people was very different. Probably not half a million men had been automatically taken from civil life by the proclamation of mobilization. Though Lord Kitchener, who had been made Secretary of State for War, called for an immediate addition of 500,000 men to the regular army,[1] though volunteers poured in faster than they could be armed, clothed, or fed, it was still believed—and the belief was most plausibly supported by history—that the main British contribution to the Allied cause, apart from the Navy, would be made in money and labour. Hence the popularity of the catchword 'Business as usual'. This was intended primarily to restore a commercial confidence, shattered by the unparalleled demoralization of the money and stock-markets, but was sometimes interpreted to mean that life should seek as far as possible to pursue its normal habits. It is curious to remember that the county cricket matches were played with little curtailment until the end of August.

Though this great war of nations only gradually assumed its unique character of grinding and inexorable remorselessness, though many of its later developments would have been everywhere repudiated in the first months, it assumed from the first a grim and impersonal character unlike its predecessors. Earlier historians, French as well as British, had united in condemning the action of Napoleon when in 1803 he detained as prisoners all male British subjects found in France. This notorious

[1] He is said to have added with his own hand another cipher to the 50,000 proposed by his staff at the War Office.

exception was now to be applied as an almost universal rule, until there were few enemy aliens in any country—with the possible exception of Austria-Hungary—who were not under a restraint involving considerable discomfort and almost complete lack of privacy.

The measures thus taken do not admit of any rational defence. The numbers involved were far too small to make any appreciable difference to the fighting strength of any of the armies; in combination, they would have been a mere fraction of the casualties incurred in a week of the great opening battles. Nor could it be claimed that the dangers of espionage or sabotage demanded such a step. The few professional spies resident at the beginning of the war were, in practically every country, well known to the police; and in any event the ordinary resident alien is neither inclined nor adapted to a work so technical and dangerous as espionage. The remarkable absence of sabotage at the very moment when its commission would have been comparatively easy, and its effects on mobilization deadly, might have suggested the harmlessness of the alien population in belligerent countries. But in fact the treatment meted out to them was the result of the intense nervous stress imposed by modern war, which made the ordinary man half unconsciously find it unbearable to see the face or hear the name or speech of enemies about him. In order to justify this hatred to himself he accepted the inventions of the press, which set itself to prove how real and imminent was the danger. To take an instance from our own country: it was confidently believed that hard tennis courts and other concrete constructions belonging to Germans resident near London had been prepared before the war as gun emplacements to bombard the city. The power of the press is always greater in war than in peace, for in war-time a newspaper lives more on sensation, is more influenced and indeed controlled by the Government, and supplies information which is less susceptible of independent check. Brandès, the Danish Socialist, made the terrible comment that 'the war means the assassination of truth'. Consequently in every country, while the press did much to preserve cheerfulness and even constancy, it did more to intensify the spirit of unreasonable and often petty hatred. Non-combatants were naturally the more readily infected with this virus, which is spread by feelings of inactivity and helplessness. Lissauer's famous *Hymn of Hate* was far more popular with civilians than with German soldiers. Later on the increasing privations, miseries, and dangers created still further embitterment. But in the early months danger was almost non-existent outside the zones of the armies and the invaded regions. Except for a few insignificant bombs dropped on Paris at the beginning of September, no organized attempt to break civilian moral by threat of death was made until the Zeppelins crossed the North Sea for the first time in February 1915 to attack the eastern counties, while a reluctant permission to bomb the industrial quarters of London was not extracted from the Kaiser until the ensuing summer. Neither was there any shortage of food or of the other necessaries of life. On the contrary, it is probable that the standard of living was in most countries raised during the first year of war. The vast armies were well—often abundantly—fed; almost every factory could be adapted to produce materials of national importance; the amazing consumption of munitions, in particular, created an inexhaustible demand, while the imperious necessity for speedy delivery ensured high prices and wages. The consumption of food, and above all of meat, tended to increase. The Germans when in the pinch of the 'hunger blockade' bitterly repented their wholesale slaughter of young pigs and calves in the first winter.

The fate of the inhabitants of invaded territory was, indeed, from the first most wretched. They were faced with the miserable alternative of remaining under the military rule of enemies or of abandoning their homes and possessions to seek an uncertain refuge. Hundreds of thousands of Belgians fled to Holland and England to receive a welcome, the warmth of which tended to diminish as the struggle was indefinitely prolonged. The inhabitants of ten French departments were scattered all over the country. Many Alsatians who had followed the retreat of the unsuccessful French invasion received in return for their devotion the suspicion which their German accent and halting speech made natural in remote parts of the interior.

Very few in authority in any country believed that a long war was probable or even possible. Kitchener, with his wonderful power of brooding intuition, stood almost alone in significantly enlisting his new recruits 'for three years or the duration of the war', and in so framing his far-reaching plans that the British army should reach its maximum strength in the third summer. Statesmen and economists held that such a dislocation of national life, such a destruction of wealth, could not last for more than a few months. Soldiers, as we have seen, had pinned their faith to the quick 'knock-out blow'. Though trench-warfare had been remarkably developed in the Manchurian War, where the battle of Mukden lasted for nearly a month, no soldier had prophesied a Chinese Wall of fortification which presented no brighter prospect than an interminable flankless battle.

Hence the need for new allies became keener, as soon as the hopes of a speedy end had faded.

Montenegro had instantly thrown in her lot with Serbia. The Japanese had fulfilled their obligations to our alliance by demanding on August 15th the restoration of Tsingtau in an ultimatum textually recalling the words of the German note which had forced them to give up Port Arthur in 1895. But no help was expected or desired from them in the European theatre of war. On September 3rd, 1914, the three great Entente Powers were united by treaty in a common cause, undertaking not to conclude peace except in common.[1]

[1] Until that date Great Britain was not technically in alliance with France or Russia, both of whom had naturally acted from the start under the terms of their Dual Alliance.

It was not, however, until the end of October that the existing balance of forces was disturbed by the coming of a new belligerent. Turkey now joined the Central Powers, and it is easy to see why she believed this step to be dictated by her interests. Great Britain had long since lost her traditional role of staunch protector, and had in fact, in 1906, threatened the Porte with war over an Egyptian boundary dispute, while the Russian entente in the following year marked the definite reversal of our policy consistently pursued for nearly a century. For it was perfectly clear that Russia, in accepting British friendship, had not the smallest intention of modifying her ancient hostility towards Turkey. On the contrary the Balkan League of 1912, a 'veritable instrument of war', as Poincaré called it, had been forged by Russia. The collapse of the Ottoman armies in 1912 had been a bitter disappointment to the restless Young Turks, whose unscrupulous leader, Enver Bey, was athirst for revenge. William II had constantly expressed his flamboyant sympathy with Mohammedan ideals, and the spade work of patient diplomacy had been performed at Constantinople by Marschall von Bieberstein, who gained there, during his fifteen years' service (1895–1910), an ascendancy almost comparable with that of the great Englishman, Stratford de Redcliffe, half a century before.

The advantages of Turkey as an ally to the Central Powers were staring. Russia and Great Britain would be compelled to divert large forces for the defence of Caucasia and Egypt. Restlessness, and perhaps open rebellion, might be expected from the divided allegiance of the vast quantities of Mohammedans subject to the Entente. The military action of India in particular might be paralysed. It might be hoped that the eyes of the wavering Balkan States would be decisively turned from the Entente. Moreover, Germany cherished vaster ambitions, of which her financing of the Baghdad railway had been the chief pre-war manifestation. If Bulgaria could also be drawn into her net, an unbroken line of railway would connect

Berlin with the Persian Gulf and provide central Europe with an outlet to the east. Friederich Naumann in an exceedingly interesting and able book *Mittel Europa* explained how this great area, united into an economic federation under Teutonic supremacy, would provide Germany with a counterpart to the empires of Great Britain and Russia.

The treaty which provided for the entry of Turkey was signed secretly by three members of the Turkish Cabinet as early as August 1st, when the *casus foederis*, war between Germany and Russia,[1] was already accomplished. The Turks took little trouble to keep it secret, and it was in fact known to the French Government within a week. By an unfortunate coincidence the mind of the ordinary citizen was inflamed against Great Britain by our appropriation of two Turkish battleships building in English yards, which had been paid for by public subscription. In any event the spectacular entry of the *Goeben* and *Breslau* into the Bosporus, already described, and their fictitious sale to Turkey, left little doubt as to the intended course. The Entente made little effort to change its direction. There were indeed many influential moderates who would gladly have done an advantageous deal on the basis of firm neutrality or even perhaps alliance. But without very definite encouragement they would not risk opposition to the ruthless young men who controlled Turkish policy.[2] Though the British ambassador at the Porte believed that the Marne had given pause to this forward party, he was speedily undeceived. On October 28th Enver, who considered his preparations to be complete, suddenly, without a declaration of war, made a naval attack on Odessa.[3] Liman von Sanders, the German

[1] The clause in question reads: 'If Russia intervenes and takes active military measures, and the necessity arises for Germany to carry out her pledges to Austria-Hungary, Turkey is under obligation in such case to carry out her pledges to Germany.'

[2] See A. Emin, *Turkey in the World War* (1930), pp. 69–75.

[3] It seems impossible that the German Admiral Souchon could have acted thus on his own initiative, as the Turks alleged, without secret orders from Enver, the most ardent of the war-party.

military adviser, had prepared plans for an invasion in the same area, to be followed by an advance into the Ukraine, where it was expected that the numerous German inhabitants would rise at its approach. Enver, however, was set upon a campaign through Armenia to the Caucasus. His ill-equipped armies failed miserably in the high, barren, and bitter country, but not before their onset had so much alarmed the Russians that they made an official request to the British Government for a diversion. This was, as we shall see, the germ of the Dardanelles expedition.

The remaining Balkan States were not yet ready to take the plunge into either stream of war. Public opinion in Rumania was so strong against Austria that the aged King Carol had, as we saw, no alternative at the outset but to inform the Austrian ambassador that his country would not perform the terms of the secret treaty of alliance. After his death in October the chances of intervention were brighter for the Entente, but fear of an attack from Bulgaria and Turkey, an intention of acting in concert with Italy, and a deep-rooted suspicion of Russia both in power and policy, put off the deliberate choice of the most favourable opportunity for nearly two years. Ferdinand, the evil and cunning Coburg who ruled Bulgaria, had as yet received no such encouragement from Austrian action in Serbia to suppose that his adherence to the Central Powers would bring him the coveted Macedonia, and continued to negotiate tortuously with both sides. Until the Dardanelles expedition there could be no inducement to Greece to depart from her nervous neutrality.

Italy alone of the great European Powers remained outside the struggle. It is difficult for any great Power to stand undisturbed during a general war unless, as seldom happens, it is perfectly secure that its position cannot be adversely affected by any changes which ensue in the balance of power. Italy was far from being in this position. Whichever side were to be victorious, her absence from a peace conference at which the map of Europe would probably be reconstructed would have been insupportable. Her territorial aspirations, which she had cherished incessantly since 1870, though with a postponed hope, might be thrown away for ever. The Italian policy therefore of preparing for war under cover of immediate neutrality was perfectly natural. Salandra expressed this idea in a repellent and naked form when he spoke of his country's *sacro egoismo*. Yet in fact it represents much the same point of view as the words with which Viviani answered the German ultimatum: 'France will consult her own interests.'

However, the transition from peace to war required time and calculation. For, while Italy was still nominally a member of the Triple Alliance, it was impossible after her initial refusal that she should ever intervene on that side. Italian sympathies were generally with the Entente Powers; few indeed would have been satisfied to attack them for a contingent bribe of Savoy, Nice, Malta, and perhaps Albania. She had indeed always stipulated in the Triple Alliance that she should never take the field against England, to whose naval supremacy her long coast-line was so nakedly exposed. Moreover, her army was thoroughly unprepared. Its spirit had been impaired by anti-military propaganda, and its equipment was most defective.

Now, both strategic security and nationality urgently demanded that the screw should be put upon Austria. From Lake Garda to the Piave the Austrian frontier hovered on the edge of the plain, a continuous military threat to Italian independence. Moreover, in the Trentino and in Istria nearly half a million Italians fixed their eyes more or less ardently beyond the existing frontier. Two great and coveted ports, Trieste and Pola, at the head of the Adriatic, came within Italian views and coloured their hopes.

If diplomacy could get what was wanted without war so much the better. Italian subtlety had already extracted much from the compliance of Austria during the Triple Alliance. This instrument itself gave a legal peg on which to hang demands for compensation. For one article of it, notoriously and designedly left obscure, had given Italy the right to compensation in the event of Austria's altering the balance of power in the Balkans by a permanent or temporary occupation of territory.

Haggling went on for months between the two foreign offices of Rome and Vienna with ever-increasing acrimony as Italian preparations advanced, and Austrian misfortunes were monotonously multiplied. Berchthold at first denied that any compensation was due, as no intention existed of diminishing Serbian territory. Driven from this point he obstinately refused to admit under any circumstances that it could come from Austrian territory. He was dismissed in January and a new start was made under the urgent pressure of Germany, who sent the famous ex-Chancellor Prince Bülow on a special mission to Rome, where his own seductive manners were reinforced by the popularity of his Italian wife. Burian, who succeeded at Vienna, was a better diplomatist than his irresponsible predecessor, but he had a hopeless task, as he asserts in his own interesting *Memoirs*. His antagonist Sonnino, a patient implacable old realist,[1] held all the cards. It will be convenient by forestalling our chronology to trace these negotiations to their conclusion.

The military position seemed to grow progressively worse for Austria during the early spring of 1915. The Russians stood at the gates of Hungary on a wide Carpathian front; Przemysl, the great Galician fortress in their rear, fell in March. German pressure in favour of wide concessions was urgent, for it was feared that if Italy declared war, Rumania and Bulgaria would follow suit and break the cause of the Central Powers to fragments. Burian's own offer did not go beyond part of south Tyrol, which was not to be handed to Italy until the conclusion of hostilities. He was, however, forced by Germany to the humiliating necessity of considering much wider demands, when the pressure of the Entente prevailed. Napoleon

[1] He was of mixed Italian, Jewish, and Scottish descent, ingredients which should make a perfect recipe for the 'old diplomacy'.

III once said of Bismarck: 'he offered me all sorts of things which did not belong to him', and the Allies were even more lavish in their proffers of enemy territory. The Treaty of London, signed on April 26th, 1915, not only promised the present Brenner frontier on the north (with 300,000 Germans) and Istria, but also the larger part of Dalmatia[1] with many other advantages.

The Italians had chosen their date most carefully, but they had chosen it wrong. They do not indeed merit the bitter French gibe that their sole object was 'courir au secours du vainqueur'. For, after all, the struggle was as yet quite undecided, although the omens for the spring campaign in April seemed very favourable. Yet within that very month which was allowed by the treaty to lapse before a declaration of war[2] fortune, as we shall see, turned cruelly against the Entente. Russia had been routed on the Dunajec; the attacks in Artois had failed; and stalemate had set in at Gallipoli. Such are the difficulties of a calculation in war. Giolitti, the champion of neutrality, made a spirited effort to avert the plunge. Relying on his unrivalled influence over the Chamber, where he controlled 300 members, he manipulated the resignation of Salandra. But the voice of the country was stormily decisive; the eloquence of Gabriele d'Annunzio, the erotic poet now turned patriot warrior, produced amazing enthusiasm. Giolitti's manœuvre was brought to naught by a decisive vote of the Chamber on May 20th. The Rumanians, who had been within an ace of a similar committal, managed to back out in time, though they were no more fortunate in their final choice of August 1916.

The Entente statesmen have been severely blamed for the terms of this secret treaty. It is indeed a purely realist

[1] Where the Italian population was probably not more than 2 per cent.; the area, however, had been for centuries part of the Venetian Empire, and historically owed much to Italian culture, especially in the coastal region.

[2] The Treaty of London was technically violated as soon as it was implemented. Italy had engaged to declare war on all the enemies of the Entente within a month. Actually the declaration against Germany was postponed for more than a year, principally for financial reasons.

document, and fits in ill with the respect for small nationalities which they had been so fond of sonorously chanting. It is therefore to be defended only on grounds of expediency, as has been realized by Lord Grey in his book *Twenty-five Years*. He asserts that the aid of Italy was necessary for the triumph of the Entente, and that she would not come in on any less favourable terms. Whether this is correct or no, we have not at present sufficient evidence to judge. The comparative moderation of the latest demands addressed to Austria in April by the Italians had as their price neutrality, not adherence to the Central Powers. However, if Italian armed support was really judged to be essential by the Entente, it is not certain that its statesmen could have made a better bargain. In any event it must be remembered that the policy of the Entente at that time aimed at preserving Austria as a great Power, though partially emasculated. Consequently the security which Italy intended to obtain on the Brenner frontier was much more justifiable than it appears to-day, when forty millions face an impoverished seven.

IX

THE STRATEGICAL PREPARATIONS FOR 1915

WINTER had come with the stabilization of the fronts to impose some months of comparative inactivity upon the armies. Statesmen and soldiers had now to consider their plans for the campaign of 1915. All were determined so to overcome or circumvent the continuous and ever-growing lines of opposing fortifications as to gain an absolute decision before the favourable season ended. To the hopes and fears of the opposed counsels only one new factor presented itself as certain, namely, the great increase in the fighting strength of the British armies. A saying was current among the soldiers that Kitchener, in reply to a question as to when the war would end, replied that he did not know but that it would begin in May. It is true that the maximum weight of British effort would not be available until the middle of 1916. But it could be anticipated with reasonable certainty that the fourteen first-line divisions of the Territorial force would be ready for battle a year earlier. Except for a few isolated battalions who, brigaded with regulars, had won high praise from French during the battle of Ypres, this force of 250,000 men was still intact. Although armed with a semi-obsolete field artillery and a somewhat inferior rifle, these troops had a very high spirit and often a higher level of intelligence and general education than the old regulars. The enlistment of the new regulars, or 'K's army', as they were familiarly called, had, during the early weeks of the war, far exceeded the capacity of the War Office for armament or even uniforms. They had drilled in their own clothing with sticks to represent rifles. But it was anticipated that at least ten divisions could be armed and trained in time to be sent overseas to take part in the campaign of 1915.[1]

[1] Actually twenty-one had been sent abroad before the end of that

The 'First Hundred Thousand'[1] were the most splendid material that ever went out to fight from this country. Of the officers some six or seven in each battalion were regulars, the remainder being composed of professional men, and above all of the undergraduates and schoolboys from the Officers' Training Corps, without which, as Lord Haldane had most providently foreseen, it would have been impossible to build up this great force. The men drawn from every rank of life, mainly young and very ardent, created an intense democracy of equal comradeship. Finally, an army corps from Canada and another from Australia and New Zealand were already in the later stages of preparation. These men in physical fitness and strength excelled all the troops of any of the European armies. In their ruthless self-confidence, their individual initiative, their impatience of form, ceremony, and tradition, they bore upon themselves the unmistakable mark of the new nations. They had also the defects of their qualities, inasmuch as they (the Australians in particular) had the greater difficulty in reconciling their independent personalities to that machine-like subordination of self which modern war in so many aspects demands.

Thus an addition of at least five hundred thousand men to the British fighting forces during the year 1915 might be confidently anticipated. But their probable value in the day of battle was very differently estimated. In England the proud belief in this great voluntary army felt by the people was generally shared by the higher command, though there were not lacking soldiers like Sir Henry Wilson who sneered at the scheme 'as a crazy idea of Kitchener's'. Both French and German experts doubted whether it was possible to improvise an army of serious solidity and technique during a war. The experience of 1870 had shown how little value attached to Gambetta's

year. Eleven took part in serious fighting and about six more held their own trench-front.

[1] The story of this title, by Ian Hay (1915), gives a brilliant description of the training and spirit of one of these divisions (the 9th Scottish).

improvised levies. It is true that no real parallel could be drawn, as most of these, badly directed, were thrown into the furnace with less than three months' experience under the shadow of overwhelming defeat. But the continental theorists held that at least eighteen months' training under experienced officers and N.C.O.s was now necessary to create an efficient soldier; and the increasing technicality of warfare during the last generation seemed powerfully to reinforce their thesis.

However, the surest way to increase the efficiency of the new soldiers was obviously to allow them a gradual and easy apprenticeship in war. Falkenhayn saw this clearly, and desired to forestall the new campaign with a great blow in France. Two reasons, a military and a diplomatic, prevented him from doing this. The importunity of Hindenburg and Ludendorff, backed by the immense influence which their victorious prestige had gained with the Kaiser, forced Falkenhayn to disgorge on January 20th four of the six corps which he had laboriously built up into a General Reserve. Reinforced by them the German Xth army in East Prussia performed prodigies of endurance and courage in clearing the Russians out of that province. The 'Winter battle of Masuria', as the Germans call it, was fought in a continuous blizzard; their troops marching chest-deep in snow captured nearly 100,000 Russians and drove them back to the Niemen. This was a brilliant success, tactically and sentimentally, but in a broad sense it was wasted effort. For the Russians, in spite of German-aided attacks in the south, relaxed no whit of their grip upon Galicia; they were still at the mouths of the Carpathian passes, and on March 22nd captured the fortress of Przemysl with 120,000 men of the enormous garrison which had been so long fruitlessly shut up in it.

Falkenhayn still hoped to deliver his blow in the west. He was ingeniously creating another reserve by withdrawing three battalions from each division in France, which was brought up to the equivalent of its former strength by drafts from the depots and by extra machine-guns. By the beginning of April he had at his disposal a substantial force of fourteen divisions, and was working out a great plan for rolling up the British line against the sea by a break-through on its extreme right flank.

The position of his allies, however, was now so desperate that a dramatic stroke against Russia appeared to be the only hope of salvation. Turkey, whose ambitious attacks against the Caucasus and Egypt had been brought to naught,[1] was threatened with a combined attack on Constantinople from north and south, the success of which would almost certainly prove fatal. Rumania and even Bulgaria were swaying ominously towards the Entente's side of their precarious fences. Worst of all the Italians, as we have seen, were squeezing Austria with a relentlessly increasing pressure. The hatred inspired in Vienna by the 'blackmail' of the despised ex-ally was so intense that it was actually proposed to conclude a separate peace with Russia at the price of Galicia, rather than agree to put Trieste and Pola into Italian hands. It may well be doubted whether the Austrian Government would have fulfilled its threat. A separate peace would have doomed Germany to utter defeat, and a broken Germany would have involved the Hapsburgs in far greater losses than Galicia, if not in the ruin of their dynasty.

Germany, a faithful, if rough and overbearing ally, recognized the extremity. Falkenhayn's reserves flowed eastwards, and within three weeks the two staffs hatched that great overthrow of the Russian armies on the Dunajec, which is known as the break-through of Gorlice (May 2). This decision is one of the great turning-points of the war. If the new troops had been sent to France, the effects of a great spring attack, supported by gas, against the British army, tired and short of men, crippled by the acutest crisis of the munitions shortage, would have been disastrous.

Meanwhile in the West the French and British statesmen and soldiers were revolving their plans. French strategy,

[1] See ch. xx.

as always through the war, was determined by a mixture of sentiment and logic, or perhaps rather sentiment logically expounded. France's passionate desire was for 'the liberation of the national territory', the recovery of the lost provinces, and the advance to the Rhine. This end, then, must be achieved by attacking the principal army of the principal adversary. The more constantly he was attacked the more necessary it would be for him to expend his reserves until finally he had none left to avert a decisive blow. The French therefore believed that 1915 would see the great day of deliverance prepared through a preliminary series of partial attacks, each one of which would diminish the resisting power of the enemy. This was the meaning then attached to the phrase *la guerre d'usure*.[1]

Of all the great Powers at war except Austria, France was the most parochially minded. To her the struggle was essentially the last and most terrible round of the secular contest between herself and Germany. The land forces of Great Britain were regarded as those of her most powerful auxiliary.[2]

The weakness of the French thesis was that it proposed to solve a new problem by an intensive application of the old methods. Granted that a frontal attack on field fortifications is the most arduous and costly operation in war, yet it was argued that difficulties can be overcome by an unprecedented accumulation of men and guns. But such an accumulation itself makes surprise almost impossible; and without surprise the power of the defence, even in the forward areas, is so great as to prevent a break-through in the first critical twenty-four hours before reinforcements

[1] One of the favourite phrases attributed to Joffre was 'Je les grignote', 'I keep nibbling at them'.

[2] The opposite opinion of Gen. de Castelnau must, however, be cited. He said to Gen. Seely, January 1, 1915, that the new armies ought not to be employed in France but at 'Salonica Drama Dedeagatch. . . . The inevitable result of an attack of magnitude in that region will be the instant co-operation of the Greeks and the detachment first of Bulgaria, then Turkey, and finally Austria. Then Germany is doomed. But it is a race with time.' J. E. B. Seely, *Adventure* (1930), p. 215.

are available to the enemy. To gain a strategic success it was necessary to capture the whole of a trench system together with the gun-positions, that is to say, to make a uniform advance of at least four thousand yards on a front of at least ten miles. All the accumulated brains and efforts of all the armies in the west were unable to achieve this during the next three years.

It is easy in retrospect to condemn this strategy, or rather lack of strategy, for in reality it consisted merely of the simplest and most brutal massed tactics, reinforced by an unprecedented amount of metal. Yet these views were equally shared by most British generals; in fact Sir William Robertson, when he became Chief of the Imperial General Staff in 1916, was to be the protagonist of the most deadly and lumbering doctrine of the 'war of attrition'.

Every country had the General Staff which it deserved. Senior officers schooled in many years of hierarchical obedience are lacking in alertness, very unimaginative and very conservative. A witty French minister said with cynical discernment: 'Modern war is too serious a business to be entrusted to soldiers.'

It was impossible that the French view of the war should commend itself instinctively to the statesmen of the uninvaded island, whose military traditions were so sharply opposed to those of continental warfare. At the close of 1914 the British army in France was already at least six times as numerous as any contingent previously sent by Great Britain to a continental theatre of war. And it was still fed by voluntary enlistment, which could not be expected ceaselessly to replace increasing casualties. The command of the sea, the enormous amount of disposable transport, as yet undiminished by submarine depredation, afforded wide prospects of great liberty of action.

It was certain therefore that, before any irretrievable commitment, the British Cabinet would ask itself two questions. First, whether it was possible under existing conditions to break the German line in France. Secondly, whether any other project afforded a more alluring hope of victoriously concluding the war within the year.

The name of Winston Churchill is most prominently associated with both these questions and their suggested answers—he and Lloyd George were the most vivid, plastic, and persuasively eloquent members of the Cabinet. But Churchill, unlike his colleague, had real experience of modern war, and had thought and even written at some length about the subject. He was already becoming convinced that the rupture of the western labyrinth needed for its success not merely the unlimited output of existing weapons, but the employment of new engines of war and new methods of protection for the attackers. Without these he believed any further offensive in France to be waste of blood. He had already fruitlessly pushed upon the attention of the War Office an early model of the tank, which, rejected by its own proper father, was undertaken by the Naval Construction Department in March. But it was obvious that, during the current year, no such revolution in warfare could bear fruit. The utmost possible was to develop and perfect those ancient tactical aids to fortress warfare, the hand-grenade and trench-mortar. Kitchener in his heart agreed with this view;[1] and as his voice in all military matters was, on the authority of his colleagues themselves, absolute and unchallenged,[2] it is certain that, if he had insisted upon restricting the British forces in France to defensive action, he would have carried the Cabinet with him. But he was torn from a firm resolve by his age, by his old love for France (which had led him, as a cadet at Woolwich, to join her defeated armies in 1870),

[1] See his letter to French, January 2, 1915, quoted in *Military Operations*, vol. iii, p. 61: 'I suppose we must now recognize that the French army cannot make a sufficient break-through the German lines to bring about the retreat of the German forces from northern Belgium. If that is so, then the German lines in France may be looked on as a fortress that cannot be carried by assault, and also that cannot be completely invested; with the result that the lines may be held by an investing force whilst operations proceed elsewhere.' (Cf. also Gen. Sir Ian Hamilton, *Gallipoli Diary*, vol. i (1920), p. 4.

[2] See Winston Churchill, *The World Crisis 1915* (1923), pp. 172, 173.

and by the optimism of the two Commanders-in-Chief and of most of the eminent soldiers. He had never closely studied the technique of modern warfare between continental armies; and could only oppose intuition against dogmatism based on experience. Finally, with a clear insight into Falkenhayn's frustrated intention, he believed until May that the Germans, after a short blow at Russia, would return with all their power against France. In that event would all the forces of both the Western Allies be more than would be required to avert utter disaster?

From such an oracle proceeded, as may be supposed, no certain voice. Kitchener never in council advocated the deposition of France from its position as the primary seat of war. To have done so might have broken the alliance to pieces. But the decision finally reached in the spring of 1915 shows neither clear thinking nor foresighted calculation of chances. The Dardanelles Expedition which emerged is one of the most striking examples in history of willing the end without willing the means. If the campaign in France was to come first, then definite calculations ought to have been first made of its needs, on the assumption that it was to be either offensive or defensive. It ought to have been clearly worked out what proportion of troops could be spared elsewhere before the campaign in France opened and during its assumed course, and, further, what number of trained troops it would be necessary to keep at home to resist a possible invasion. War cannot be waged without risks, and risks on exact calculation are less dangerous than those incurred through haphazard improvisation. If no men were available immediately for the Dardanelles, what could be done by naval action alone? If unaided naval action failed, would troops then be available? if so, could the numbers then available be usefully employed in concert with the fleet? to what extent would subsequent reinforcements be possible? All great captains have emphasized and illustrated by their actions the supreme importance of time in war. Nothing is such a time-saver as an exact balance of ways and means before action. It will be seen, when the Dardanelles expedition is described, that the questions here asked were either not put or were evaded.

The Dardanelles project was unquestionably the most fruitful and feasible of all those which flitted through the brains of the War Office and the War Council Sub-Committee[1] as they passed possibilities in review. The various schemes trumpeted by Lord Fisher for combined action on the north German coast (aiming at landings either at Borkum or in Schleswig-Holstein), or, still more ambitious, for forcing an entrance to, and commanding the Baltic, so as to threaten Berlin by putting masses of Russians in Pomerania, appear exceedingly hazardous, complicated, and speculative. An attack on cracking and divided Austria was also tempting; yet if this were to be delivered up the Adriatic, a base had first to be conquered in an area where the Dalmatian shores afford about the snuggest lairs in Europe for submarines and small craft incessantly to prey on communications. If delivered through Salonika on the assumption (probably justified under these conditions) that Greece would be an ally, it would have to climb over the wall of the Balkans right across Serbia with the aid of only one line (Salonika–Nish–Belgrade) before it came into touch with the enemy. A descent on Asiatic Turkey, as, for example, on Alexandretta or Beyrout, would almost certainly have succeeded in view of the miserable character of Turkish communications. But it could have effected nothing more than a showy diversion.

The attack on the Dardanelles alone offered reasonable conditions for an amphibious expedition; for a close and continuous co-operation between fleet and army. This great advantage was doubled at the moment. The Army, as we shall see, was desperately short of guns and shells,

[1] Appointed January 8 with Messrs. Lloyd George, Churchill, Balfour, and the Chief of the Imperial General Staff (Lt.-Gen. Sir J. Wolfe Murray) as members. It had no executive powers but prepared and reported upon plans to the Cabinet.

but the Navy was comparatively affluent, and could in many ways make good the deficiency for the sister service.

It is hardly doubtful, in the light of subsequent enemy testimony, that a combined expedition at the beginning of March with a minimum force of three corps could have seized Gallipoli, opened the Dardanelles, and occupied Constantinople. Turkey, if she had continued the war at all, would have been condemned to a hopeless resistance in Anatolia without means of replenishing her munitions. Greece, Rumania, and Bulgaria would instantly have entered the Entente fold. Austria, with Russia clawing at her northern flank, would have been overwhelmed from the rear, and the collapse of the Central Powers would have been speedy and certain. The conception was indeed so fertile and obvious that its achievement was likely to depend upon a rapid and well-organized surprise. As this was not secured, the British Cabinet was faced during 1915 with the hard task of carrying on two offensives, one in France, one in Gallipoli, with undefined liabilities which enabled, or even entitled, either Commander-in-Chief to urge insistently his own paramount needs.

It is not my contention that the force at Gallipoli frustrated the campaign in France, as in my view the attacks made in the West were not justified on military grounds,[1] as being without hope of strategic success, even if undertaken with larger forces. As it was the French, the protagonists of both great offensives in the West, could throw in there their maximum force with the exception of two weak divisions at Helles. But if better reinforcements had been sent earlier in rather greater numbers to Hamilton, it is probable that within three months of the landing a victory could have been won of very high importance, though not the shattering decision which might have been attainable in March.

[1] It is possible though not probable that Russia might have made a separate peace with the Central Powers, if all her requests for action in the West had been refused during 1915; and if Turkey had not been paralysed.

X

THE CAMPAIGN IN FRANCE AND FLANDERS, 1915

I

No unity of command or direction existed for the French and British armies. Consequently the plan of campaign had to be worked out through agreement between the two Staffs. In practice, each army carried out, as was natural and proper, minor operations independently. With regard to more important schemes, the object of which was strategical success, it may be generally said that the British did not undertake anything to which the French strongly objected, and agreed to everything which they strongly advocated. This again, though by no means always desirable, was inevitable as the scene of battle was French soil, and the French army throughout this year at least was four times as great as the British.

The clash of interest had already manifested itself before the great lines of action for the year had been discussed. In January Sir John French proposed an advance along the coast towards Ostend, which had long been in his mind and that of the Admiralty. Churchill, its ardent champion, promised 'an absolutely devastating support' from the sea, and believed that a descent upon Zeebrugge could be successfully synchronized. Though the submarines had not yet begun their campaign against merchantmen, and had sunk no warship of great consequence except the *Formidable* (January 1), the shadow of their menace was already cast, and a provident desire was felt to deny them the use of those Belgian nests from which in future years they issued so disastrously. The French, however, for this very reason saw in the proposed operation a predominantly British interest; any such advance, they pointed out, would be in an excentric strategical direction, which could not influence the western theatre as a whole, and if successful would involve a longer trench line. The British

Government was the more disposed to fall in with these objections, as the War Council was then engaged in studying the possibilities of a campaign elsewhere.[1]

Joffre meanwhile had committed himself to two great preliminary local attacks, both of which were complete failures, and through their costliness appreciably weakened the offensive strength of his army. In eastern Champagne, though the German IIIrd army occupied a dominating position on the long range of bleak and naked chalk-hills, their local communications were unsatisfactory. They depended for their supplies upon a single-line local railway (from Challerange to Bazancourt) some five miles behind their front. If this could be reached, the whole line between Rheims and Verdun might be forced to retreat. Great quantities of shells had been collected for the French attack. The Germans, far inferior in numbers, experienced for the first time the so-called 'drum-fire' (*Trommel-feuer*) or continuous rain of shells of every calibre upon the trenches which it was believed would blast away all opposition. The battle raged almost continuously between February 16th and March 30th. But the 4th French army won no more than a few hamlets and trenches on the forward slope of the hills at a cost, estimated by their own writers, of 240,000 men. This was the first of five great battles fought for the command of this grisly region, where an examination of the map shows that an advance of fifty miles to Mézières would have cut the great lateral railway from Thionville to Valenciennes, on which the communications of the German centre mainly depended.

The second spring failure was at Saint-Mihiel. This curious loop, apparently the most indefensible contortion on the whole western line, was particularly obnoxious to

[1] See Memorandum of the War Council, January 9, 1915, quoted in Visc. French, *1914* (1919), pp. 313–14. The War Council was a Committee of the Cabinet instituted in Nov. 1914. Its regular members were the Prime Minister, Secretary of State for War, and First Lord of the Admiralty with the technical advisers of both services. Other ministers (especially Sir E. Grey and Mr. Lloyd George) attended intermittently. For the French view, see Sir G. C. A. Arthur, *Life of Lord Kitchener* (1920), vol. iii, p. 898.

the French, who feared that an enlargement of the enemy territory on the left bank of the Meuse would outflank their hold upon Verdun. The Germans beat off all attacks in a tangled country of woods, ravines, and hills, which favoured the defence. The salient, however, proved too narrow to be of use for any offensive thrust—it even remained in quiescence through all the throes of the battle of Verdun—and hardly figured in the *communiqués* until the French directed the successful American blow in September 1918.[1]

This was not a propitious overture, particularly if contrasted with the one local attack undertaken by the enemy, which had proved a model of limited completeness. On January 14th when the Aisne was in flood, and some of the bridges had been carried away, General von Lochow stormed the French positions on the north bank near Soissons and captured 5,000 men with thirty-five guns.

British Head-quarters had not embarked upon any enterprise since the bloody and futile scramble in the mud before the German trenches near Messines in December, which it had been hoped would plant us upon the ridge. This fiasco did nothing to improve the low estimate which the French Staff had formed of the attacking capacity of the British army. It was probably a desire to correct this impression which led Sir John to undertake the battle of Neuve-Chapelle (March 10–13).[2] The attack had been planned as part of a combined operation. The British were to seize the Aubers ridge and threaten Lille, while Foch took the heights of Vimy, north of Arras, dominating the plain of Douai. A converging exploitation of victory was intended so to mangle the enemy's communications as to force him to retire from Noyon, his blunt spear-head pointed at Paris.

The French commitments in Champagne naturally made it impossible for them to adhere to their side of the arrangement. Yet Sir John French decided to proceed

[1] See pp. 557 seqq. [2] See Sir J. E. Edmonds, *Military Operations: France and Belgium*, vol. iii (1927), p. 73.

independently. Such a decision could be justified by nothing but success. Though neither G.H.Q. nor the Cabinet yet realized how cruelly the shortage of ammunition would cripple the main British attacks in May, it was recognized that stringent economy was necessary. It was short-sighted extravagance to fire away 100,000 rounds, or nearly a sixth of the total amount available for the entire B.E.F., in a gamble. The operation can hardly be otherwise described. It aimed at breaking the enemy's line on a very narrow frontage (initially 2,000 yards) at a point close to Lille, his principal railway junction, by independent action practically unsupported by diversions and with inadequate reserves.[1]

The actual arrangements by Sir D. Haig and the Staff of the 1st army[2] were admirably businesslike and thorough. In fact the main interest of the battle lies in the fact that it provided the army with a kind of preliminary grammar of offensive trench-war, which, though enormously expanded, was never in its principles superseded. Aerial photographs were taken of the enemy's defences, models laid out in the back areas, where the assaulting troops rehearsed the details of the attack. The familiar large-scale trench-maps (on a scale of 1 in 5,000) were issued for the first time to all officers. Every battery received its timetable and target for the battle. The first British attack was also the last to obtain a real surprise through secrecy of preparation until the break-through of the tanks at Cambrai two and a half years later.

When March 10th arrived, after thirty-five minutes of hurricane bombardment, fourteen battalions moved forward to assault three. High hopes were entertained that when the Aubers ridge had been secured

[1] The only infantry reserve was the 46th (N. Midland territorial division, which had arrived in France a week previously). The cavalry corps and Indian cavalry corps would obviously be of value only if a rupture allowed open warfare to develop.

[2] The B.E.F. had now been divided into two armies; the first on the right under Haig, the second on the left under Smith-Dorrien, the point of junction between them being some four miles south of Armentières.

the cavalry could move forward to raid Lille. The course of the battle, however, deceived expectation and in this respect also it proved the too faithful forerunner of many weary attacks. The initial success was speedily held up, every subsequent attempt at exploitation gained less or no ground at the cost of progressively increasing losses. Practically all the ground won in the three-days' battle was won in the first three hours. Even without a close examination of tactical details the main causes of failure can be plainly pointed out. In the face of brave and very skilful defenders, however few in number, it was impossible to make uniform progress, as some strong points and wire were certain to have escaped annihilation by the artillery. The mishaps of local commanders, thus held up, caused unnecessary delay in a general advance. This was increased by the difficulty of assembling troops quickly, after gaining one line, for the assault of a second. Moreover, lateral communication across an unknown debris of trenches was bad, communication with the rear was hindered by the inevitable destruction of telephone lines. This meant that the guns could not be switched quickly on to the unidentified targets which were delaying the infantry, and that reinforcements could not be directed at will to the required positions. The enemy's artillery, on the other hand, none of which had been captured, knew every inch of the ground which he had momentarily lost. Consequently every hour's delay lessened the disparity between the opposing forces, and helped towards an equilibrium. All these problems, inherent in every trench-attack, are admirably illustrated in miniature by Neuve-Chapelle.

The British remained in possession of the village with 1,600 prisoners. They had lost about 13,000 men, but had inflicted nearly equal casualties, a balancing of accounts not attained again until Messines (June 7th, 1917).

II

The preliminaries were now over and the first main act of 1915 was to begin. French Head-quarters re-staged a plan almost exactly identical with that of which Neuve-Chapelle was to have been the British contribution, to open in the beginning of May. The enemy, however, with that forestalling enterprise which was to stand him in good stead on many later occasions in the war, robbed it of much of its sting by the gas attack, started on April 22nd, which developed into the five-week-long struggle known as the second battle of Ypres.

Smith-Dorrien's 2nd army had extended its line north-east of that city during the middle of the month to release French troops for the attack farther south, but there were still two French divisions between it and the Belgians holding the northern edge of the salient from near Poelcapelle to the Yser Canal. Its southern extremity had been disturbed since April 16th, where ferocious local fighting had developed out of our seizure of Hill 60, a mound of earth thrown up from a railway cutting. But no one had the slightest idea that an attack was imminent. Ypres, by no means yet its later proverbial scene of desolation, was still an animated centre; a band played in the Grande Place where the civilians maintained a market for the troops. The surprise, however, of April 22nd was unjustified, as being due to the neglect of circumstantial warnings. The western staffs did not, it is true, know that this violation of the conventions of civilized warfare had already been practised against the Russians in January. Possibly the latter did not recognize the experiment, and took it for a protective smoke cloud,[1] as German reports state that the extreme cold made the results of the emission unsatisfactory. More probably, with their habitual unbusiness-like carelessness, the Russians failed to report it to their Allies. Still the accounts given by a prisoner captured by the French on April 14th were most circumstantial: he gave details of the cylinders prepared on the Langemarck

[1] Our own gas attack at the third battle of Gaza was similarly so innocuous that Turkish reports from the field expressed doubt whether gas had been used. Lord Cavan reported that the Austrian gas shells on the Asiago plateau (June 15, 1918) were almost inconceivably feeble.

front, and, most significant fact of all, had actually had a respirator in his possession.[1] This was followed on the 17th by a lying German accusation that the British had employed asphyxiating gases in their shells, the object of which might have been guessed, in conjunction with the other evidence—namely, to prepare public opinion for the German action as being merely retaliatory.

The introduction of gas warfare was received with an indignation which, though fanned by the newspapers, was deep and abiding among soldiers. Lord Kitchener was moved from his usual restraint to a passion of anger. When, however, he wrote to French that it was 'contrary to the rules and usages of war', his statement was too sweeping It was certainly contrary to 'usage', but it was not explicitly condemned, as has often been stated, by the wording of the Hague Convention of 1899. The passage referred to forbids 'the use of projectiles the sole object of which is the diffusion of asphyxiating gases'. This prohibition may have been intended inferentially to condemn the emission of cloud-gas, but it certainly does not say so. The action may well be held to be contrary to the spirit, but a legal document must be interpreted according to the grammatical meaning of the text. The effects of chlorine in those early days when no protection was available were certainly very cruel, yet perhaps less repulsive than the burning alive of men by liquid fire, another innovation apparently first used by the French.[2] In fact there is little to choose in horror and pain between the injuries inflicted by modern war. The extent to which a human body can be mangled by the splinters of a bomb or shell, without being deprived of consciousness, must be seen to be believed. The real explanation of the fury felt by the soldiers, which invested the war with a more savage character, is to be sought elsewhere. In the face of gas, without protection,

[1] For further details, see Sir J. E. Edmonds, *Military Operations: France and Belgium*, vol. iii (1927), pp. 163, 164.

[2] General Dubail states with complaisance that his 1st army was the first to experiment with this weapon in the autumn of 1914 in the Argonne.

individuality was annihilated; the soldier in the trench became a mere passive recipient of torture and death. A final stage seemed to be reached in the whole tendency of modern scientific warfare to depress and make of no effect individual bravery, enterprise, and skill. Again, nearly every soldier is or becomes a fatalist on active service; it quietens his nerves to believe that his chance will be favourable or the reverse. But his fatalism depends upon the belief that he has a chance. If the very air which he breathes is poison, his chance is gone: he is merely a destined victim for the slaughter.[1] Later on, when gas-masks became increasingly efficient, this type of warfare was regarded merely as an unpleasant incident, for suffering became contingent on carelessness or surprise.

It has often been contended that the Germans threw away an unrivalled opportunity of victory through their premature and local use of the new weapon. It is true that the military mind always moves slowly and tentatively towards novelties (as witness the tanks), and the protagonist of gas warfare has related the suspicion, scepticism, and dislike of the commanders with whom he had to deal. But if its use had been postponed till the next year (for the campaign on Russia made any great attack in France impossible in 1915), it is most improbable that the secrecy necessary for unremedied surprise could have been preserved. Again cloud-gas, which alone was available in large quantities for the next fifteen months, depends entirely for its efficacy upon the direction of the wind. Owing to the irregularities of the trench-line it would probably have been impossible to stage an attack on any long front which could have been continuously supported by cylinders. Finally, winds from between north and east are neither very common nor regular in northern France, and the chances of victory might be further impaired by successive postponements.[2]

[1] The writer was in the trenches south of Ypres in April 1915, where a gas attack was constantly expected though not experienced. He therefore had opportunities of judging of the men's feelings.

[2] The original attack was in fact so postponed from April 15 to April

In the long run it is probable that the introduction of gas warfare was disadvantageous to the Germans, as the blockade tightened and the whole chemical resources of the world were available against their ever-straitening supplies.

On April 22nd, a brilliant spring morning, shells of an unprecedented calibre began to fall upon Ypres; they weighed a ton, and came from the celebrated 17-inch howitzers, which had destroyed the great fortresses at the beginning of the war. At 5.30 in the evening the cylinders which had been placed in the German trenches, some thirty yards apart, began to emit dense greenish-yellow clouds of chlorine against the two French divisions in line between Langemarck and the Yser Canal. The French broke in panic: the Zouaves in particular fled for many miles. British troops resting near Poperinghe received the first information that something was amiss from seeing the Africans still running, who pointed at their throats and cried out incoherently 'gaz asphyxiant'.[1] By nightfall the remnants of the French were lining the west bank of the Yser Canal, leaving Ypres unprotected with a gap of four and a half miles between them and the 1st Canadian division holding the extreme left of the British line. Most fortunately German Head-quarters had formed no plans whatever for immediately exploiting this very promising tactical success. The attacking IVth army had to rely entirely upon its local reserves.[2] The German troops also were naturally nervous about the effects of the chlorine, and were disposed to hang behind the cloud as it rolled along. They had got within 2,500 yards of the city and there was nothing in front of them. The confused and cruel fighting which followed can be divided into three

22 and would have allowed a week's counter-preparation had the Entente Staffs accepted the warning offered to them.

[1] Information received from an officer of a battalion of the Duke of Cornwall's Light Infantry then at Poperinghe.

[2] Four corps were heavily and two slightly engaged in the battle. The British engaged seven infantry and three cavalry divisions, and the French five infantry divisions.

phases: (i) the joint Franco-British attempt to restore the positions; for the salient now resembled an apple with a great piece bitten out of its side, and seemed to be utterly untenable (April 22–28); (ii) the preparations for the evacuation of the outer rim (April 28–May 3); (iii) the struggle to maintain the new positions, which were still open to encircling attacks on three sides (May 4–24).

(i) During the night of the 22nd–3rd the Canadians, who so far had not suffered severely, threw back and prolonged their left flank so as to form a string of posts in touch with the French. The improvised line was very thin, and had hardly any artillery support, as eight French batteries covering that area had been captured. The salient had always been a congested and dangerous region, as all traffic had on its way forward to cross the canal, pass through the city and emerge from the ramparts by the Menin Gate. The enemy had compensated for his comparative weakness in infantry by a very powerful concentration of artillery which completely dominated the Allies. The defile could be swept by the fire even of field-guns from both north and south. Troops marching through the streets were already losing heavily: one company had eighty casualties during the night from falling masonry. A retreat would obviously become necessary if the French could not in conjunction with the British left push forward from the canal. But the enemy was already solidly established on the western bank between Het Sas and Lizerne. The ground lost had in itself no value at all; in fact to preserve the salient meant dooming those who held it to suffer continually heavier proportional losses than in any other part of the line. To give up anything, however, ran contrary to the self-respect of the chiefs, who alleged that any tactical retreat impaired the moral of the troops. This was often quite untrue, as was proved in 1917 when the German soldiers fought, if anything, better after the great withdrawal to the Hindenburg line. Smith-Dorrien understood this. When he saw that the continual appeals of Foch (commanding the northern group of French armies) to attack merely resulted in fruitless and unsupported attempts by his army—the Canadians in their first battle lost more than a third of their infantry—he wished to withdraw to the ramparts of Ypres. Sir John French, who had always disliked him, at once sent him home.

(ii) The cautious, methodical, and imperturbable Plumer took over the 2nd army. He was the most uniformly successful of all the British army-commanders. He chose his staff admirably, never moved without careful preparation, and knew the limit of the possible better than any of his colleagues. His most spectacular success (Messines 1917) achieved its superb completeness just because it had been elaborated for more than a year. He was almost an ideal general for siege-warfare. In his characteristic way he executed perfectly a half-measure which satisfied Foch and French and provided a tenable if unpleasant position two or three miles east of the city.

(iii) The temptation to carry on a trench-battle beyond the limits of the profitable is always very strong. When the enemy has been driven out of his strongest lines, when prisoners and trophies have been collected, it is always difficult to believe that the impetus of the attack is really more exhausted than the determination of the defence. It always seems as if one more effort must produce the decision. The deadly fascination of butting perpetually against the wall selected for attack seemed to conquer every commander, even one like Nivelle, who, as we shall see, had declaimed most powerfully against it.

The Germans continued for the next three weeks to lavish their gas, artillery, and infantry assaults, but gained nothing of serious importance. The salient remained substantially as Plumer had traced it, until Gough's army broke out of it on the sinister 31st July 1917. Still the enemy could show a good balance sheet, having inflicted losses nearly double those which he had suffered,[1] having

[1] In round numbers the casualties were British 60,000, French 10,000, Germans 35,000 (these last, however, are not complete).

reduced the British artillery reserve to its lowest limits, and emasculated our offensive of May 9th.

III

For the French the new attack on May 9th opened with a transient and deceptive brilliance; for the British it had failed completely within an hour of its launch.[1] In the one army the artillery preparation was overwhelming; in the other ludicrously inadequate. The French threw against the enemy positions 700,000 shells from 1,200 guns,[2] almost all high-explosive, and it was calculated that every yard of the front line would receive eighteen. At that time the British had in France only seventy-one guns of a larger calibre than 5-inch; all the remainder, that is to say, threw a shell of less than 40 lb. weight. Further, the proportion of high-explosive was exceedingly low. Consequently on May 9th our bombardment lasted for only forty-six minutes and 92 per cent. was shrapnel. Shrapnel is indeed an unrivalled man-killer against troops advancing in extended order: it is also capable, if used in enormous quantities, of destroying barbed wire. It has also one great advantage over the high-explosive shell, as it does not cut up and pit the ground.[3] But it is absolutely incapable of destroying field-fortifications. Hence the defenders remained safely in their trenches. They were able to man the parapets instantly, without the delay inseparable from an emergence from deep dug-outs. Their machine-guns remained intact in their emplacements. Thus they mowed down without difficulty the heavily loaded waves of brave men lumbering towards them. In Artois, on the other hand, the 33rd French corps, commanded by Pétain, that calm, tenacious soldier who defended Verdun, and who as Commander-in-Chief was to rescue the army from the slough

[1] The British called this battle Festubert and the French Souchez, being the names of villages round which the fighting centred.

[2] Six-sevenths of the total number possessed by the whole British army in France.

[3] This was altered in 1917, when a new fuse (No. 106) had been perfected which burst on graze.

of mutiny and despond in May 1917, broke right through. In ninety minutes they covered three miles. The soldiers looked down on the plain of Douai. They were passing over green spring country almost untouched by war; they picked flowers and put them in their caps as a symbol of the open warfare which they believed was beginning. Then the same old difficulties occurred once more, the breach was in the centre, but two-thirds of the attack had been partially or completely foiled. The enemy had equipped his communication trenches with fire-step and parapet, and was able to use them immediately for organized defence. At each turn he had placed machine-gun posts, which, in the infancy of the bombing art, were exceedingly difficult to reduce. This in itself might not have been fatal, as the thrust of the 33rd corps had produced grave disorganization. But the French reserves were eight miles in rear. It was desired to preserve them intact against gun-fire, and also to keep them in a central position, for the very reason that unequal progress was expected on the front of attack (about six miles). So they could not be brought up in time to fulfil the strategical dream of every attack, to spread out fanwise over open country in rear of the adjacent trench system. On the contrary the enemy got there first. The cork was put into the hole. The fighting degenerated into drawn-out and piecemeal struggles for fortified villages and strong points. The reverberations of the storm lasted on until the end of June. But the long level crest of Vimy still barred all observation eastward at the close of the battle. Even had it been won it would have made no difference, except a tactical improvement of the French position. It was to be proved over and over again that a resolute army, well backed by artillery, can defend itself in almost any position good or bad, if only it digs hard enough. The French losses were gigantic, apparently about 400,000 men.

May 9th had other than military consequences, for it also overthrew the British Cabinet. It was indeed tottering to its fall, when Fisher so petulantly resigned from the

Admiralty, but it was French's hand which actually thrust it over the brink. In its place arose the first Coalition Ministry in which Liberals and Conservatives enjoyed an equal share of office under the premiership of Asquith, and representatives of Labour joined the Government. French gave full details of the shell-shortage, and of its effects upon the battle of Festubert, to Colonel Repington, the military correspondent of *The Times*, in which paper it was immediately published. He also sent emissaries to London to stir up public opinion, particularly among Conservative members of Parliament. The shortage was indeed inevitable, given the immense expansion of our army as compared with that of the other belligerents. Even in France and Germany, where scientific warfare on a large scale had been so minutely studied, the voracity of modern battles far exceeded all calculation. But its calamitous consequences had been increased by the scepticism displayed in the War Office as to the usefulness of high-explosive against entrenchments, and by the failure in certain factories loyally to increase output to the maximum of capacity.[1] As so often happens in war the penalty was exacted after large remedial measures had already been taken. For the vast improvement already accomplished by September 1915 the army had to thank the War Office.[2] The consuming zeal and imagination shown by Mr. Lloyd George, first at the Committee of Munitions (April 8), then at the Ministry (June 9), bore its fruit in the later stages of the Somme battles in 1916.

The formation of a Coalition Ministry (May 26) made little or no difference in the position of Sir John French, or in the policy directed towards the Western Front. The bill already being presented for Gallipoli made it certain that some at least of the new divisions would have to go

[1] The deficiency between contract-numbers and numbers delivered in 18-pounder shells between January and May 1915 amounted to 960,000 or rather more than 50 per cent. See Sir W. Robertson, *Soldiers and Statesmen 1914–18* (1926), vol. i, p. 61.

[2] In October 1915, the last month which represented entirely War Office orders, production reached 1,200,000 rounds.

there. Kitchener's suspicious attitude towards great attacks in France had naturally not been diminished by the object-lessons already presented to him. During this period (June–July) he and Sir John were in much closer accord than previously, for the latter had been staggered by the sacrifice of Festubert. But Joffre kept asking for more. And if political considerations had called for the offensive earlier in the year, their appeal was now far more strident. The enormous and apparently endless misfortunes of the Russians, and the entry of Italy into the conflict, were very cogent reasons for further hammering in the West.[1]

In view of the situation of the Alliance as a whole a 'passive defence' was entirely 'out of the question' (report of Conference of Franco-British Staff, Chantilly, June 24). But it seems doubtful whether a constant show of threatening activity, with bombardments, gas-attacks,[2] and raids would not equally have achieved the result of pinning the existing German forces to France, and thereby preventing any alteration of the balance elsewhere.

By the beginning of July the B.E.F. had increased to twenty-one divisions, and a 3rd army under Monro took over some fifteen miles between Arras and the Somme, being separated from its comrades by the 10th French army before Arras. These dispositions remained practically unchanged to the end of the year.

IV

The French plans this time aimed at a grandiose combination of their former tentative models. Down till this time they had tried to force the abandonment of the great Noyon salient by smashing in one of its sides. The autumn campaign was to burst it by a simultaneous blow at either flank. A great door was to be opened to the Meuse and Belgium. The Germans were so heavily committed in Russia, where their victorious armies throughout August were constantly pursuing an elusive decision in the farthest

[1] See Sir W. Robertson, op. cit., vol. i, pp. 66–7.

[2] The Allies had gas at their disposal in the field by September, but not earlier.

corners of Poland, that no quick transfer of troops would be possible. On the whole Western Front they were outnumbered by about three to two, and it would obviously be possible to secure a far greater local preponderance for the attack.

The optimism of Joffre remained as ever unruffled, but he found unexpected difficulty in imposing his will upon Sir John French, who was disposed to limit the British share to artillery demonstrations unsupported by infantry attacks. Soon, however, the disasters and disappointments of August, Warsaw, Suvla, and the Isonzo convinced Kitchener that the common cause demanded an unrestricted co-operation with the French, 'even though by so doing we may suffer very heavy losses'.

The plan was entirely French: an immense effort was to be made in the plain of Champagne. A subsidiary but powerful combined attack was to be delivered in Artois, and Foch was again to assault the heights of Vimy. With that brutal lack of consideration for his ally, who was cast for a subordinate role, which Joffre frequently displayed, he intimated that the British were to prolong the attacking line northward from Lens to the La Bassée Canal.

Haig, who was entrusted with the operation, vainly protested that the ground, a mining area full of villages,[1] pits, and slag-heaps, heavily fortified, was exceedingly unsuitable. The Commander-in-Chief shared his views, but soon allowed himself to be overpowered by Joffre, to whom he had been placed in a position of general subordination by the British Cabinet.

Meanwhile the enemy employed his two months of respite in ceaselessly strengthening his defences, largely with the aid of forced civilian labour. The attack was indeed no secret; it was a common topic of both military and political discussion for a month beforehand. More-

[1] One of the main considerations which influenced the French choice of Champagne was precisely the absence of villages, as they had found in Artois that such fortified localities as Carency, Ablain, and Souchez had proved the most formidable obstacles. See Gen. P. L. Palat, *La Grande Guerre sur le front occidental* (1917–27), vol. ix, p. 407.

over, the preparations, particularly in the bare chalk fields of Champagne, were patent. The front of attack extended over more than fifteen miles. Thirty-five divisions, perhaps 500,000 men, were assembled to take part in it. The great fortresses, like Verdun, had been stripped of their siege guns. New assaulting trenches were dug, vast communication trenches three miles in length were opened

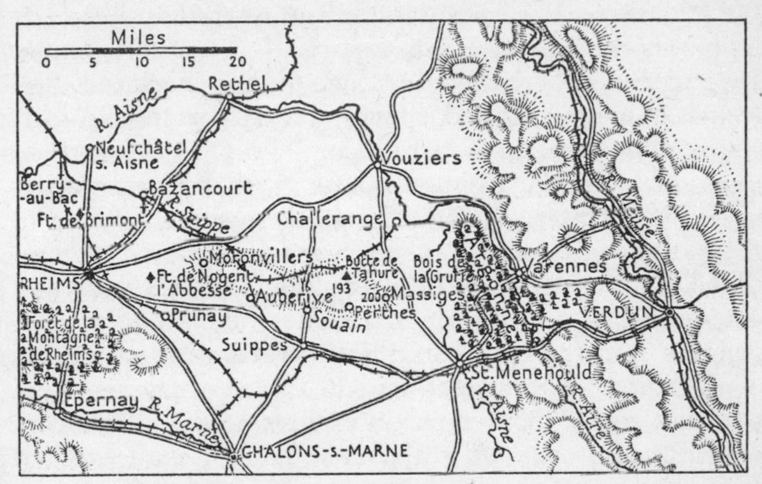

MAP 12. Champagne.

up to the rear. From their observation-posts on the high downs the Germans could note every indication of the devouring activity engaged against them.

The bombardment lasted three days (September 22–4). Nothing had yet approached this concentrated force of 900 heavy and 1,600 field-guns: 'This whirlwind of fire and steel let loose', as Joffre described it in his proclamation to the troops. This document (which, by the way, fell into the enemy's hands) aroused tremendous hopes: 'Votre élan sera irrésistible. Il vous portera d'un premier effort jusqu'aux batteries de l'adversaire au delà des lignes fortifiées qu'il nous oppose. Vous ne lui laisserez ni trêve ni repos jusqu'à l'achèvement de la victoire.' Ten divisions of cavalry were held in readiness to exploit the expected rout.

As generally happened when the Allies attacked, the morning of September 25th dawned in pouring rain. The assaulting troops, packed all night in soaking trenches, were covered with chalky mud. Nevertheless accounts of eyewitnesses agree that ardour and expectation were great. The advance began on the whole front at 9.15 a.m., the *Marseillaise* was played, the drums and fifes kept pace with the attackers. The enemy was outnumbered at the outset by nearly three to one. His organization was very strong. He had everywhere the advantage of higher ground. His trench system was linked up with five elaborate field-fortresses, nodal centres of resistance. The French hoped to mask them in the assault, isolate them by penetration between the intervals, and by rapidly pushing forward to the battery positions, to make their fall certain. General de Castelnau in the cheerful confidence of the rear had prophesied that the guns had done their work so thoroughly that the men could go forward with their rifles at the slope. The French and British infantrymen were to suffer many more such deceptions at the moment of ordeal in the next two years. The Higher Staffs studied maps and not the ground; they could not believe, sitting in their studies and workshops, that the means of destruction which they had assembled would prove less annihilating in practice than in theory.

As usual, a grim unco-ordinated series of local struggles ensued. Its progress showed characteristically that rhythm which came to be inseparably associated with the great trench battles. First a frantic intensity during the first twelve hours, never afterwards attained. During this phase the French bit deeply, though unevenly, into the enemy's centre. The next ten days were consumed in gnawing actions, costing much blood, at all the blobs of resistance still left within the conquered area. Finally, a jumping-off ground of some eight miles in length was consolidated for attacking the main second position. This had been cunningly sited on the reverse slope of the downs. The French gunners had little direct observation: the required angle of descent was too steep for anything but howitzers, of which the supply was quite insufficient. Many of the assaulting troops had already been through the furnace; the fresh formations arrived in an atmosphere of anticipated failure. The Germans husbanded their reserves with usurious carefulness, 'milking', as the phrase went, quiet sectors of regiments and even of battalions, and throwing them piecemeal into the danger spots at the last moment. The second line stood substantially intact, though two French cavalry divisions had been desperately launched at a momentary gap.

Strategically nothing had been achieved. Tactically the French had 'squeezed up' the higher ground with their enemy still on the top, both east and west. The trophies collected were considerable, 25,000 prisoners with 150 guns. The trumpeting forth of these figures in the *communiqués* partially hid the realization of defeat from the Allied peoples. The losses, which were kept rigorously secret, were about 145,000 men. The Germans in proportion to the numbers engaged lost quite as heavily.

The results in Artois were even more unfortunate. The British in particular, at enormous cost, succeeded only in worsening their local situation by the conquest of a narrow salient, from which the usual considerations of *amour propre* forbade the Higher Command to withdraw. It proved only less costly to hold than its notorious counterpart at Ypres. Though Foch commanded the French, a comradely spirit of co-operation was absent. Each side suspected the other, not without reason, of desiring to thrust off the heavier burden on to the shoulders of its ally.

Haig resolutely refused to launch a serious attack without the support of gas (its use by the Entente being one of the earlier stages in that competition of 'frightfulness' which was to descend to such horrible depths). His decision had to be deferred to the last moment, owing to uncertainty as to the wind's direction. It was not until 5.15 on the morning of the 25th that the line waveringly taken by the smoke of a cigarette determined Haig to give the order for its employment; and, as the event proved, he was mistaken. In Artois Foch, for his part, refused to conform to the British hour of attack (6.45 a.m.), as he wished to have some hours of daylight for his final artillery preparation. As, moreover, Sir John French kept his reserves under his own hand, sixteen miles from the scene of action, probably out of jealousy of his lieutenant (who had protested strongly against such retention and had been supported by Foch), the chances of success were slight. Nevertheless at the moment of assault the British were in a sevenfold superiority,[1] for no serious attack was expected by the Germans north of Lens, as the bombardment had been comparatively insignificant, about 250,000 shells only having been expended.

On the right the London Territorials (47th division), and Scottish New Army (15th), emerging suddenly from the dense clouds of gas and smoke, overran the large mining village of Loos, from which the battle is named. The Highlanders pushed on beyond the face of the low hill fronting them, and reached the north-western suburbs of Lens, a maze of drab, mean dwellings, housing a population of 40,000 in time of peace. This intricate area had been omitted from the plan of frontal assault of either army but was to be pinched out by flank thrusts. The alarm of the Germans in Lens at midday was great; for, though Foch had not yet launched his assault, the gun-fire had risen to a fury which rightly suggested its imminence. The bugle sounded the 'Fall in' in the streets, and the office details, even the sick, were hurried on parade. In reality there was little danger. Haig's forebodings had been amply justified. No reserves would be available for many hours. The Highlanders whose ardour had carried them beyond the crest were a mere handful; they had bent their line to the south, and with their right unsecured were soon obliterated by a counter-attack.[2] In the centre much patchy

[1] The whole of our 1st division when assaulting was opposed by some 600 Germans of the brave 157th regiment.

[2] The infantry of this division lost about 60 per cent. of their effectives.

success was obtained; on the left, on either side of La Bassée, failure had been complete. Sir John French lost the battle in the first few hours. Though the cavalry had been massed in villages so close behind the front as to be visible to the enemy, whose *communiqué* derided this futile parade, not an infantry reserve was available throughout the day. It is true that the subsidiary attacks farther north had completely failed to divert German troops, and that Foch's attack south of Lens upon the heights of Vimy proved a mere disaster. Still, about noon the German local commanders were at their wits' ends: their second and last line had been reached in three separate places, they were still outnumbered by four to one, and the arrival of 20,000 fresh adversaries might have smashed through their trench organization and led to such confusion as to make necessary a withdrawal on a wide front. Their transport for miles in rear was ready to move.[1] 'If there had been even one division in reserve close up we could have walked right through' was Haig's comment to a friend afterwards. The contemporary opinions expressed by Prince Rupprecht support this view. Sir John's whole conduct of the battle is inexplicable. He selected for his head-quarters a place where he was not in telephonic connexion with Haig. He did not release his three divisions till 1.20 p.m.: two of them (the third being the Guards) were completely untried units of the new army,[2] only just landed in France. The congestion in the rear, intensified by the inexperience of the improvised staffs, was such that their approach-march, accompanied by unnecessary discomforts, took twice the scheduled time.

[1] For evidence of the German preparations for retreat, see J. E. Edmonds, *Military Operations: France and Belgium*, vol. iv (1928), p. 304, note.

[2] One infantry brigade contained only one officer who had previously been under fire. The choice of these divisions was deliberate, not imposed by necessity. Regular divisions were used for the subsidiary attacks, others held quiet sectors on the Somme front. Various territorial divisions, e.g. North and South Midland and Highland had had four to six months' efficient service in France. These two in question (21st, 24th) on the contrary had received their rifles only in July 1915.

Consequently they had to march through the night (25th–26th) in pouring rain, across all the debris of the two trench systems, in great confusion to their assaulting-ground.

It is not surprising that their ill-directed attack next day on the German centre, though in many cases bravely pushed against enfilade fire from both flanks, ended in a disorganized retirement.

The battle should now have been stopped dead. Nothing, however, in warfare demands more moral courage on the part of a commander than cutting his losses. Time after time British, French, and German generals fell, through lack of will to stop, into the protracted futility of a wasting struggle.

Sir John might have been less anxious to continue had he known that Joffre was secretly instructing Foch to put on the brake while 'taking care to avoid giving the British the impression that we are leaving them to attack alone'. The attack of the 10th French army had been thoroughly foreseen by the enemy. Placards had been posted in the German trenches proclaiming: 'Terrain à vendre mais à prix cher'; and Souchez brook had been dammed into an impassable quagmire. The concentration of heavy German artillery actually surpassed that of the French, so Joffre's early discouragement was very natural. And, although the unneighbourly prohibition was not fully obeyed by Foch, on the last two days of concentrated fighting (October 13–14), the Allied defeat sustained was rendered more complete by the inaction of the French. It was obvious to the fighting troops that in the piecemeal trench struggle, into which the battle inevitably degenerated after the 25th, the enemy had every advantage. He knew every nook of his own labyrinth. His bombs and mortars were more numerous and of better quality. He still possessed, and was long to keep, a great superiority in machine-gun tactics. His batteries had been increased by 55 per cent. since September 25th. The Germans in fact were better organizers, better prepared. In Artois they inflicted losses almost double those which they suffered.[1] 'La guerre d'usure se fait contre nous.' This assertion by a French politician, M. Abel Ferry, sums up in a sentence the campaign of 1915. Loos proved fatal to Sir John French. In his dispatch he tried to conceal his responsibility by misdating the hour at which he transferred the reserves into Haig's hands.[2] His relations with his senior army commander had thus become quite impossible. After a decent interval he was relieved of his command (December 17) and Haig reigned in his stead.

The new Commander-in-Chief was also unfortunately a cavalryman; but this was his only resemblance to his predecessor. Haig had always been a model officer, whether regimental or staff. Even at Sandhurst his instructors had foreseen for him the highest prizes. Clear-headed, thorough, and obstinate, with an iron contempt for anything showy, vague, or insincere, he intensely disliked politicians, among whom he believed intrigue was almost universal. Haldane was perhaps the only one who obtained his real confidence and affection. Reserved and almost grotesquely inarticulate, he wrote excellently. His order to the troops in April 1918 is a perfect example of appealing soldierly eloquence. Religious to the depth of his Lowland soul, he gradually acquired an almost Cromwellian conviction that God had marked him out as an instrument for the triumph of the Allies. If adversity as Bacon says is the blessing of the New Testament, Haig grew with disappointment and disaster, until he stood out in the last four months of the war as a very great general.

[1] 98,500 (about equally divided between British and French) as against 56,000.

[2] See Brig.-Gen. J. Charteris, *Field Marshal Earl Haig* (1929), pp. 173–4; and Duff Cooper, *Haig* (1935), p. 276. The latter reveals that Haig wrote to Kitchener on September 29 commenting severely on the disastrous effect of French's generalship upon the course of the battle. 'I think it right that you should know how the lessons which have been learnt in the war at such cost have been neglected. We *were* in a position to make this the turning point in the war, and I still hope we may do so, but naturally I feel annoyed at the lost opportunity.'

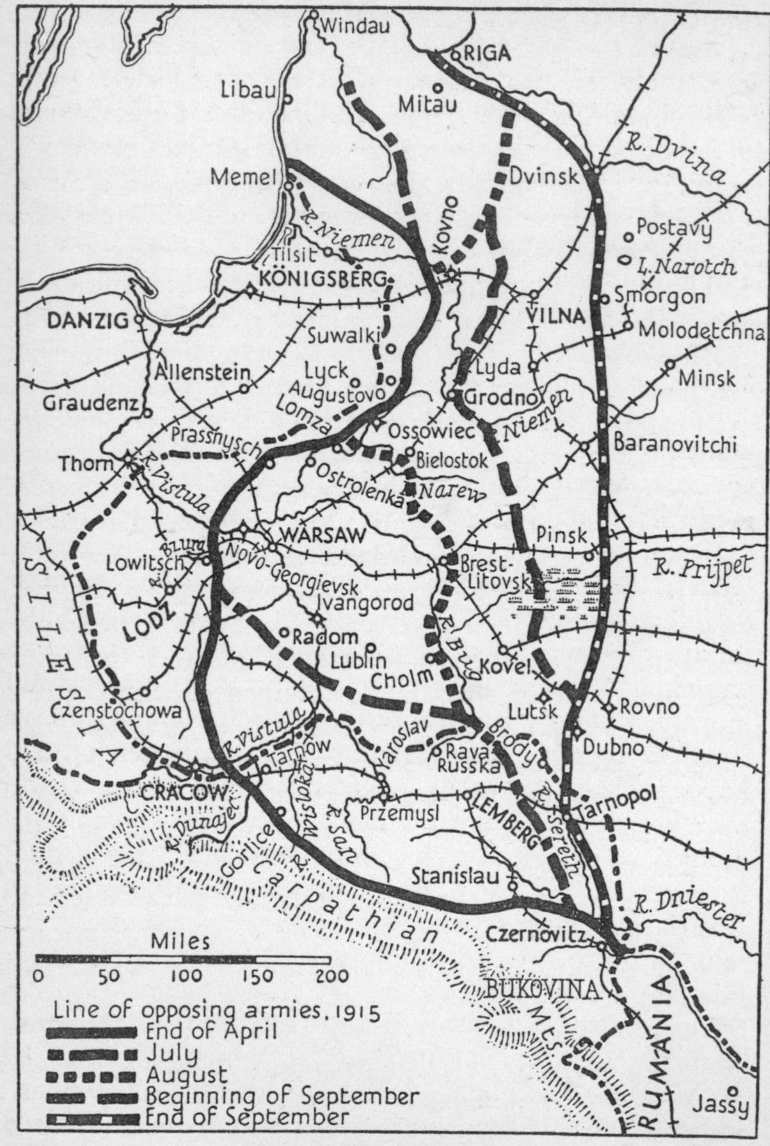

Map 13. The Eastern Front.

XI

THE RETREAT OF RUSSIA, 1915

By the beginning of 1915 Russia was in a pitiable state for waging modern war. Of the great horde of 6,250,000 men nominally with the colours at least a third could not be supplied with rifles. Of the remainder many were armed with Japanese, Mexican, or captured Austrian weapons, the diversity of which seriously complicated the supply of ammunition. The number of guns per battery had been reduced by a quarter, but even so shells were ludicrously insufficient. Commanders were threatened with court martial if they used more than three shells per day per gun. Nor could the situation be remedied for many months. The careless, sloppy, if not corrupt, methods in vogue, both with Staff officers and in government departments, could not be eradicated. The common way of dealing with an unpleasant fact was to deny its existence. General Knox, the British attaché, found all his requests for information met by evasion or lies. It was really unfortunate that their Austrian enemies were themselves so wretchedly dejected and demoralized. Had they appeared more formidable, the Russian armies might possibly have stood on a general defensive during this critical year, and have avoided great evils. Even a purely defensive task would have been hard enough, for they had to guard 800 miles, in many parts of which no continuous defences had been dug.

As we have already shown, it was only the plight of Austria-Hungary which compelled Falkenhayn most reluctantly to turn his reinforcements east. Even after Hindenburg had gained so signal a success in the Masurian 'Winter battle', which cost the Russians 200,000 men and, what was worse, 300 of their precious guns; even after the Grand Duke had made a last desperate attempt to smash his way into Silesia in February, Falkenhayn still hoped to bring back to France sufficient troops to break up the English by one great blow.

But on March 18th, 1915, the Grand Duke Nicholas gave a definite order that all offensive operations should henceforth be confined to the south. The battle for the Carpathians broke out again in full blast. The Russians stood at the head of the principal passes. After a month's continual battering they had forced their way about a fifth of the distance to the plains at immense sacrifice.

The political consequences of a break-through here might indeed prove decisive. Even if a descent into Hungary did not force the Dual Monarchy to instant peace, the itching neutrals would rush *au secours du vainqueur*. Nor was Austria under any delusions. Neither the mission of Prince Bülow at Rome, nor the £30,000 paid monthly in subsidies to Italian newspapers, could prevent her late ally from advancing remorselessly her demands and her military preparations. It was impossible for Germany to resist the supplication of her partner, backed as it was with the threat of a separate peace with Russia.

Help must therefore be given on a scale which would make any great undertaking in the west impossible. The two Supreme Commands had now to settle a plan of campaign against Russia, and its strategic aim. Hindenburg and Ludendorff passionately urged that she could be ruined in one campaign, and all forces united against the West next year. Conrad, with an optimism curious in the chief of a constantly defeated army cankered with treason, agreed. Fertile as usual in vast strategical paper-schemes, he favoured an immense envelopment from north and south to catch the whole Warsaw salient in a net, and bring off the greatest 'Cannae' of history. Falkenhayn, however, always the statesman-soldier, stood firm against these allurements. He did not believe in the possibility of timing and carrying through successfully two great wheels, which would have to start 600 miles apart. In any event it was an unwarrantable risk to plunge deeply into Russia with indefinite commitments of men and time. Under no circumstances would he thin the West beyond the margin of safety. He was also exceedingly anxious about Turkey, where the Gallipoli landing was weekly expected, and he was determined to finish with Serbia before the end of the year. It was therefore essential that the blow at Russia should be so limited that it would be possible to break off operations at will, and transfer large bodies of troops elsewhere. He stated frankly that in his opinion the annihilation of Russia was not a practical aim, but he hoped to achieve 'the crippling of her strength for an indefinite period'. As nothing could be done without German aid, Falkenhayn had his way, but the great eastern twin-generals never forgave him.

It now remained to fix a spot where the local blow would have the most far-reaching strategical consequences. Here the two Chiefs-of-Staff fell independently into accord. They agreed upon the area north of the Carpathians between the Vistula and the San, where the enemy front came nearest to Cracow. A break-through here, exploited in an easterly direction, might be expected at least to force a dangerous retirement on all the Russian armies enmeshed in the wooded defiles of the mountains. Falkenhayn even suggested that the defenders there should retire to the southern slopes, in order that their enemy, enticed forward, might lose all possibility of extricating himself in time. Such a step, however, was vetoed as too dangerous for the moral of both soldiers and civilians.

The great blow was to be delivered by a German army (the XIth) of eight divisions brought from France. Mackensen was its commander. His name is specially associated with enterprises demanding surprise and speed, like those against Serbia and Rumania. He seems to have had the secret, so rare in leaders under modern conditions, of inspiring his troops to their highest achievements. His singularly handsome and graceful figure, his winning tact, delighted the impressionable Austrians, who detested the rude and arrogant Ludendorff. His Chief-of-Staff, Colonel Seeckt, one of the ablest of those veiled personalities who in their secluded offices directed the fate of battle, has since gained wide recognition as the creator of the German post-war army.

German efficiency, Austrian self-respect, and the need for unity were happily blended in the method of command. Mackensen was to be over all the troops of both Powers in

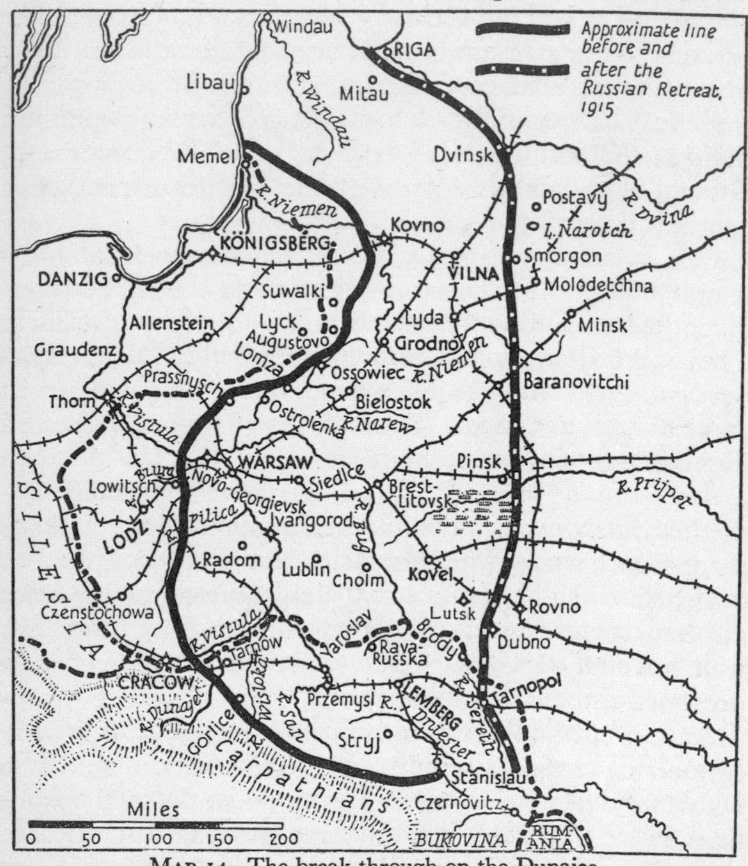

MAP 14. The break-through on the Dunajec.

the sphere of attack, was to receive his instructions from Austrian G.H.Q., which in turn undertook to communicate with Falkenhayn before any important decision. Falkenhayn in fact always had the last word.

The transfer of troops from the West began after the middle of April. So great a multitude passing through Germany could not be kept secret. The population crowded the stations with an enthusiasm rivalling that of the earliest war-days; to the Austrians their arrival came as a surprise almost beyond hope. It was feared that this triumphal transit might be reported to the enemy through his spies. But no suspicions were aroused, or at least none percolated to responsible quarters. The Staff, the earliest arrivals, were dressed in Austrian uniforms when they came to inspect the positions.

It was not until the detrainment was complete, and the Austrians relieved on April 27th, that the presence of Germans was identified, though not their number. The country in which they found themselves was a long, humpy plateau sinking on the north towards the central Galician rivers; rising, at points behind the Russian front, to about 2,000 feet. Unlike the wooded Carpathians, it was fairly open and thickly studded with large villages. Observation was excellent, and the artillery need waste little time in picking up their targets. The lines themselves seemed very odd to western experience. A vast no-man's-land of 3,000 or 4,000 yards separated the sentries, and within this area the inhabitants were living and pasturing their cattle with the mutual consent of both armies. (They were immediately removed, though even this measure does not appear to have alarmed the Russians.) The area was well fortified according to low Russian standards, as it possessed three lines of defences, the front line being continuous, and the second and third consisting in mutually supporting tactical points, such as hills and villages. The whole formed a belt some ten miles deep. Even the front line, however, must not be conceived as an intricate system of siege-defences after the western model, but rather as a shallow girdle of trenches with splinter-proof shelters. The weight of artillery therefore necessary for the work of sudden destruction was not estimated at anything approaching the concentration at Verdun next year. Mackensen disposed of about 700 guns, or one for every fifty-seven yards,[1] together with a great quantity

[1] At Verdun the total proportion for the front of attack was about three

of trench-mortars of every calibre. This proved to be ample.

May 1st was a day of brilliant cloudless sunshine. The visibility was perfect. 'Our God was again gracious to us', to quote from the official monograph a phrase which sounds strange to us in a publication of the General Staff. The gunners spent the day methodically in registering on their new targets. During the night the enemy was restrained by frequent bursts of harassing fire, while the German infantry crept forward and established themselves in their assaulting positions within easy reach of the opposing trenches. The bombardment proper began at 6 a.m. and lasted four hours. All German witnesses agree to its shattering effect. The enemy scarcely attempted any reply. For the first time in the war German aircraft, also almost unopposed, made a massed attack on billets and communications.

In many instances the infantry had no sooner entered the trenches than they received the surrender of the garrison, sometimes masses of ragged, demented figures ran out to meet them with uplifted arms, their faces distorted into the horrible staring vacuity of shell-shock. Radko Dmitriev, the Bulgar who commanded this sector, was reputed a fine fighting general who kept his men well in spirit, but so crushing a surprise would have overwhelmed any troops.

The great preoccupation of the Higher Command had been to keep the battle moving after the first breakthrough. The attack had been organized in great depth, so that detachments in difficulties would everywhere find local reinforcements at hand. The infantry were instructed to follow up everywhere with the greatest swiftness the effects of the artillery, so as to allow the enemy no time to repair his defences. The minutest liaison was enjoined between divisions and corps. General lines of advance were laid down for each day, but 'any progress beyond

times that at Gorlice, for heavy guns five times; and the preliminary bombardment was one of nine hours instead of four.

them will be thankfully received', provided that touch was maintained between units. Actually the Russians, as was natural in retreating troops with little confidence in their leaders and none in their artillery, were so nervous about their flanks as generally to give way on the least threat of envelopment.

The advance maintained its momentum splendidly. After the third day the Germans were in open country; in a fortnight they had covered ninety-five miles, pivoting continually on their right. The whole front in Galicia collapsed. In Dmitriev's army, divisions were reduced to 1,000 men, the size of battalions. The invaders of the Carpathians succeeded indeed in avoiding encirclement, but at the cost of a painful, scrambling retreat.[1] The task of reinforcement was difficult. A strong diversion had been launched in the extreme north, where German cavalry and landwehr had been sweeping through Courland towards the Dvina, a particularly sensitive spot, as it contained the main railway-line to Petrograd, while Riga was the centre of the Russian steel-industry. Troops had been hurried hither to parry it. Moreover, much delay was caused at the Galician frontier, where all troops on arrival had to detrain on account of the different width of the Russian and Austrian railway-gauges. But the Odessa corps had been brought up from the Black Sea, thereby freeing the Turks from the danger-cloud hanging over Constantinople from the north.

Towards the end of May the Russians had found a temporary refuge behind the San and Dniester, for river lines formed by far the most effective barrier in the generally featureless country of the eastern theatre. The Austrians, on the other hand, were obliged to reinforce the Italian front, where war had broken out on May 23rd; and the Allied attacks in Artois made any considerable fresh transfer from the west impossible. Still, June saw Galicia cleared of the Russians. Its capital Lemberg had been retaken on the 22nd. The inhabitants were glad at

[1] Mackensen's army alone took in May 153,000 prisoners and 128 guns.

their departing, for the retreating soldiery had committed wild excesses. Moreover, the proselytizing of the Orthodox archbishop among a population mainly Roman Catholic or Jewish by faith had been very unfortunate. His activities, according to a Russian general, were 'worth four army corps to the enemy'. The Warsaw salient now presented a most alarming appearance on the map. It was obvious that its evacuation could be only a matter of time. Would it be possible to deny that time to the enemy by new attacks? Falkenhayn now determined to strike due north, from the Galician front towards Lublin and Cholm, where the Austrian armies had crashed so disastrously in their first counter-battles. Any further penetration east had been ruled out on account of the legendary reputation of the great Prijpet marshes, where whole armies, it was believed, might be bogged.[1] Mackensen was still to be the spear-head of the new thrust. But a hot contention arose between Falkenhayn and the eastern commanders when they met, under the presidency of the Kaiser at G.H.Q. in the vast feudal castle of Pless, to determine the direction of the northern prong of the pincers to catch the Warsaw salient. The two easterners returned eagerly to their far northern designs. If the army already on the Memel were reinforced, it could cut Warsaw's connexion with Petrograd by a blow at Vilna. Here alone, they protested, was a strategic decision possible. It is true that the Russians, partly for political reasons, were very nervous of such an advance, and that preliminary measures were already being taken for the evacuation of Petrograd. But it had no appeal to Falkenhayn. It was a long, uncertain way round; if Hindenburg once had his way the demand for reinforcements would be insatiable, the time spent in the operations indefinite. It was known now that great Entente attacks might be expected after the middle of

[1] Ludendorff tells us that when the Germans arrived there later, the difficulties were found to be greatly exaggerated, as, except for water-courses, the marshes had been drained. The summer of 1915 was also abnormally dry.

September. That, too, was the moment when it was anticipated that Bulgaria, her harvest gathered, would throw off the mask and attack Serbia. But she would do so only if important German forces were available on the Danube to take part.

Falkenhayn therefore, supported by Kaiser Wilhelm, felt constrained to take the shortest and most direct way. The army of the Narew (von Gallwitz) was to strike south-east from its positions beyond the southern frontier of East Prussia, so as to arrive right behind the bend of the Vistula on which Warsaw stood.

While these great events were impending, an attempt was made, on Falkenhayn's initiative, to induce the Russians to conclude a separate peace. It was intimated that the Central Powers would demand no cession of territory. The Tsar rejected this bait and refused with indignation to desert his Allies, becoming more embittered and determined against his enemies than before.

Yet the Russians were now in the very depth of affliction. Their young recruits were sent to the front after four weeks' training, generally without having seen a rifle. The German *communiqués* reported that prisoners were being captured armed only with oaken clubs. The reserves waited behind unarmed till they could snatch a rifle from the dead or wounded. The native carelessness of the Russians was indeed partly to blame for this dreadful shortage: they generally failed to collect the precious weapons after a battle; in one case General Knox saw head-cover in the trenches constructed out of rifles. Yet in spite of all things, they put up, as a whole, an admirable resistance, which cheated the enemy of his larger strategic hopes.

The Grand Duke was now retreating towards shorter and better railway communications. Though there was much confusion and incompetence behind his lines, he could move troops about faster than his enemies. He buttressed up his flanks in the salient manfully, keeping only a screen standing directly before Warsaw. Mackensen progressed at a very different rate from his May advance through Galicia. When he took Lublin and Cholm on July 31st he had advanced only twenty-five miles in seventeen days.

Gallwitz began brilliantly by breaking through the whole fortified zone round Prassnysch, but was held up for a fortnight by the River Narew. For this delay Falkenhayn holds eastern head-quarters largely responsible, as in his opinion another six divisions could have been spared from other sections of the front.

Warsaw fell on August 4th. The capture of the Polish capital seemed to fire the German imagination, for even in the west the trenches were placarded with boards bearing the legend 'WARSCHAU GEFALLEN'. The inhabitants were so much accustomed to rumours of the enemy's approach that they showed no disposition to leave until the last days. It is recorded that the life of nightly gaiety for which the city was famous went on almost unabated to the end.

For the next three weeks the Russians multiplied their speed in retreat, for they were determined as soon as possible to present a comparatively straight front running north and south against the invaders. Contrary to his usual principle, the Grand Duke actually left a great garrison of 90,000 elderly reservists in the fortress of Novo-Georgievsk, which commands a crossing of the Vistula north-west of Warsaw, to delay the pursuers. It was the only point of the whole river-line to offer resistance, but it was of little avail. The aged conqueror of Antwerp, von Beseler, took Novo-Georgievsk within three weeks. Its vast stores of tinned provisions proved very serviceable to the captors, though in other respects the garrison had effected a thorough destruction, and had carefully killed all their horses.

A far heavier blow to the Russian plans was the simultaneous fall of Kovno,[1] far to the north on the road to Vilna. This might at the eleventh hour open the way for

[1] Now Kaunas, capital of Lithuania.

the realization of the Eastern Command's long-cherished hopes. This fortress, attacked by small forces with a contemptible siege-train, was lost through the ignominious cowardice of its commander Gregoriev. After immuring himself in the only concrete emplacement, he abandoned the place the day before capitulation, and drove to Vilna. He was deservedly arrested and sentenced to a long term of imprisonment.

Meanwhile an enormous exodus of the population with all their belongings accompanied and impeded the retreating army. Russian writers state that they fled in fear of the German cruelties. But it appears that any who remained were accused of sympathy with the enemy, and that their subsistence was made impossible by the requisitioning of their cattle, horses, bacon, tea, and sugar.[1] It is said that along all the main roads mounds and crosses every hundred yards mark the stages of that hopeless and goalless exile.

By the end of August the Russians had been thrown out of the burning ruins of Brest-Litovsk, the fortress which protected a great railway junction where five lines met, and so their lateral communications with the north had been cut. They were already 125 miles east of Warsaw, and had more than that distance still to go before the line could be cleared of embarrassing salients and brought to a halt. But Falkenhayn had already (August 14) told Hindenburg in the most definite terms that the victory which he had expected had been won. His desire was now to stabilize the front as soon as possible, whilst time remained to construct winter-quarters before the weather broke.

Already at the beginning of September he gave an outward sign of his new intentions. One of Mackensen's German divisions was moved to the uttermost extremity of Hungary, to Orsova on the Danube beyond the Iron Gates, a symbol of menace to Rumania, and of encouragement to the Bulgars. On September 6th the latter

[1] See Maj.-Gen. Sir A. Knox, *With the Russian Army 1914–17* (1921), vol. i, pp. 305 and 322.

signed a military convention with the Central Powers, and within three weeks Mackensen and a German army were standing over against Belgrade.

On September 5th the Tsar took a step which is generally considered as an important one in the downfall of his dynasty. Dismissing the Grand Duke, who was relegated to the distant viceroyalty of the Caucasus, he assumed personal command of the armies. He doubtless persuaded himself that he was acting from the purest motives of patriotism and duty. 'We shall fulfil our sacred duty to defend our country to the last. We will not dishonour the Russian land.'

The Duma when it met on August 1st had shown a burning spirit of self-sacrificing devotion, as expressed in the speech of their President Rodzianko who said, 'our duty—sparing neither strength nor time, nor means—is to set to work without delay. Let each of us give our labour into the treasury of popular might. The Army and Navy have set each of us an example of duty dauntlessly fulfilled. They have done all that man can do; our turn has come.' This spirit, it may be noted, was ill requited, for as soon as the Assembly passed to criticism of the administration, it was ruthlessly prorogued. Yet undoubtedly its manifestation encouraged the Tsar to take up his residence at 'Stavka'.[1] The moment was also thought opportune in that no further great reverses might be expected to tarnish the personal responsibility of the autocrat. Mingled, however, with all these motives was a skein of court intrigue. The letters of the Tsarina show that she was jealous of the power and popularity of the Grand Duke and was determined to make an end of him. In this resolve she was strengthened by the sinister influence of the monk Rasputin. Partly by a hypnotic power of sensual attraction for women of high rank, partly by the soothing effect which he exercised on her poor miserable son the Tsarevitch, who suffered from haemophilia,[2] he had

[1] The Russian name for General Head-quarters.

[2] A disease prevalent among European royalties in which the blood is

gained an incredible ascendancy over the Tsarina and the Imperial Household. The Grand Duke viewed Rasputin with contempt and loathing, and is said to have promised to hang him if he visited the front. The Tsar's action was therefore popularly regarded as putting the whole conduct of the war under the control of the most superstitious and degraded court-circles. Far from reassuring the patriotic elements in Russia, the effect was the contrary; for the Tsarina was regarded as a strong pro-German.

The new Chief-of-Staff, Alexeiev, a silent and scholarly man of humble birth was, it is true, an entire stranger to all such intrigues. He had gained, before the war, a great reputation as a scientific soldier, and had commanded the central group of armies before his promotion. But he was not a powerful personality. Many complaints were raised of his indecision and prolixity on paper. He had little idea how to delegate work, troubling himself with the smallest details to the great detriment of his health.

The campaign then seemed to be dying down to its natural autumnal conclusion; but Hindenburg, with his single-minded obstinacy in persisting upon what he believed to be right, returned once more to his darling northern project. The Austrians, too, always nervous for Lemberg, their great artery, wished for more elbow-room beyond north-east Galicia. They hoped to take the 'Volhynian Triangle', the three fortresses of Lutsk, Dubno, and Rovno which guarded the entrance to the Ukraine. Thus the battle was stirred up again on the two wings. Falkenhayn disliked this recrudescence, but since he regarded the operations, from which he expected little, as of local importance he raised no objection. On two matters he was as firm as a rock—the moment at which he would require his reserves for Serbia and for the West, and their number. The Austrians certainly accomplished nothing of moment except the capture of Lutsk, and suffered so severely in

incapable of clotting. Consequently a small cut, or even a scratch or bruise, has very serious if not fatal results.

counter-attacks that two German divisions had to be sent to stiffen a failing resistance. The Russians remained firmly fixed in that strip of eastern Galicia confined by the Sereth, and in eastern Bukovina. Here they were to stand undisturbed in enemy territory until the final collapse of their military strength in August 1917.

Hindenburg, who still believed that, if he could bring off a successful engagement, he could break Falkenhayn's will and retain the divisions which the latter had earmarked for dispatch elsewhere, staged an enormous attack. It extended from the Baltic to below Kovno. On the extreme north he hoped to force the enemy behind the great River Dvina, and to take Riga and Dvinsk. But his main ambition was centred, as always, on the break-through at Vilna, where a deep thrust might get right behind the communications of the two northern Russian armies and lead to their destruction. The Russians held on to Vilna until the last moment (September 18). A great mass of 30,000 German cavalry had already swooped from the north far to their rear, and was swarming over and round the vital railways, and at the same time collecting booty, particularly in cattle. This was by far the most notable exploit of this arm during the war, until it was easily eclipsed by Allenby's converging drive on the Jordan fords in September 1918, which destroyed the Turkish army. Feebly opposed by Cossacks, they had swept forward more than 100 miles, reaching the junction of Molodetchna on September 15th. If they could have held this point till their infantry arrived, the Russian 10th army from Vilna would have had no railway, and, it is said, only one metalled road open for retreat to Minsk. This, however, was quite beyond the powers of the cavalry. The Russians, as we have seen, were always very sensitive to this area. They drove the cavalry back fifty miles to the advancing mainguard in an utterly exhausted condition, with the loss of most of their horses. Vilna and a few score thousand prisoners were the only results of the last act. Riga, Dvinsk, and the river barrier in the north still remained unshaken. Hindenburg had finally to recognize that the enemy had eluded a decision, and behind his rivers, lakes, forests, and marshes would be able to rest for the long winter, and then to renew the fighting with a less overwhelming inferiority of material. He vented his disappointment upon Falkenhayn in a ponderous, dogged memorandum, impeaching the whole conduct of the campaign, with the request that his views should be placed before the Kaiser. Falkenhayn seized the opportunity to speak out plainly. 'Whether Your Excellency agrees with the view of G.H.Q. does not matter, once a decision has been made by His Majesty. In this case every portion of our forces has to adapt itself unconditionally.' He reiterated in the clearest words his fundamental view of the limits of possibility in the East.

'One cannot hope to strike a comprehensive and deadly blow, by means of an encircling movement, at an enemy who is numerically stronger, who will stick at no sacrifices of territory and population, and in addition has the expanse of Russia and good railways behind him. . . . But it is indeed possible to inflict quite enough damage . . . for our purposes by keeping up contact with him along all the front and thus preventing him from shifting his troops; then to take him really by surprise in a well chosen spot, and with comparatively weak but strongly concentrated forces, to thrust deep into his lines.'

This great campaign had been a triumph not of the 'big battalions—for the Central Powers were outnumbered by about 450,000 men[1]—but of superior organization. The Russian losses were probably over two million, half consisting of prisoners whose strong, patient labour proved an invaluable adjunct to the man-power of the enemy.

The loss of territory was in itself insignificant when compared with the enormous expanse of Russia. But Poland was a very valuable political pawn. Governing circles in Russia attached the greatest importance to this hated and hating alien territory, as its window to the West. And yet

[1] The figures given by Falkenhayn for the end of April 1915 are in round numbers, Germans and Austrians 650,000 each, Russians 1,750,000.

the Central Powers had themselves proved too harsh task-masters to win the confidence of the Poles or to induce them to fight their battles by the belated grant of muzzled autonomy next year. Germany also was too stubbornly bound by pride of conquest to Alsace-Lorraine to agree in 1917 that its cession to France should be compensated by her annexation of the old Russian 'Kingdom of Poland' with Galicia, Austria's despairing offer, added thereto.

It will be clear, when the events of 1916 are narrated, that Falkenhayn had not, as he believed, brought about 'the indefinite crippling of Russia's offensive strength'. The actual results achieved were in fact accurately summed up by the Kaiser's flamboyant telegram to his sister Queen Sophie of Greece, 'My victorious sword has crushed the Russians. They will not be able to recover for six months. Woe to them that yet draw the sword against me!'

It was indeed by the Germans alone that the Russians felt themselves to be defeated. More than that, they felt themselves powerless before German industry, skill, and organization. They were fascinated before a collective higher intelligence, employed with such ruthless efficiency. Knox related that in the autumn of 1915 he heard officers constantly repeating that 'the Germans can do anything'. Next year whenever they attacked parts of the German line they had no manner of success, and wherever the Germans arrived to stiffen their crumbling allies, the tide of their victories was stayed.

XII

THE BRITISH BLOCKADE AND THE FIRST GERMAN SUBMARINE CAMPAIGN

I

THE Napoleonic struggle had familiarized the world with a war against trade rivalling and sometimes even transcending in importance the purely military happenings. A century later the duel was refought by Great Britain against another continental antagonist, who used even more ruthless weapons in reply to the slowly growing pressure of an economic strangulation ever more scientifically employed.

It is difficult to over-value the importance of this long-drawn secret conflict, which knit the war so inextricably into the fabric of national life. For, without the blockade, it is at least doubtful whether the Allies could have forced Germany to a military defeat. On the other hand, the final reluctant assent of the German Government to use its submarines without limit or pity rendered that defeat inevitable. For, though the war on commerce in 1917 brought Great Britain within measurable sight of capitulation, it also raised up a fresh and unconquerable adversary in America to sustain the weariness of the Allies.

It is obvious that naval, in comparison with land warfare, gives almost unlimited opportunities for interference with a belligerent's trade with neutrals and consequently for the seizure of private property. As Great Britain had been the dominant naval power for at least two hundred years, it was inevitable that her conception of the law at sea should have been generally imposed in time of war both upon belligerents and neutrals, who for their part seldom ceased to complain of the maritime rights thus asserted. And the result in the Great War proved to be the same.

In fact there existed no comprehensive code of international law at sea, comparable with the Hague Conventions to regulate warfare on land. Great Britain had indeed generally objected to the discussion of such questions at peace conferences. The need for such a code had, however, been recently recognized, and a committee of jurists had agreed upon the Declaration of London a few years before the war. But as this instrument had not been ratified by any of the belligerents it clearly had no binding force, and Lord Grey has frankly admitted that its rules 'played little part in the war'. Still, the provisions of the Declaration of Paris (1856) had never been abrogated, and remained binding upon its signatories.[1] By this instrument privateering was abolished,[2] and it was laid down that a blockade to be legal must be effective, and that the neutral flag covered enemy goods except contraband of war.

Conditions, however, had changed so vastly since then that the terms employed had become quite obsolete. An 'effective' blockade in 1856 meant a line of ships stationed outside the enemy's ports to stop ingress and egress. When such a cordon was maintained, any ship of any nation attempting to pass it was liable to seizure and confiscation. But in 1914 such a close blockade was made utterly impossible by mines, torpedoes, and long-range guns. That being so, it was obviously unreasonable to suppose that a power commanding the sea would refrain from all systematic interference with trade to and from the enemy, because of a physical incapacity to conform with an obsolete provision. Further, the strategic deployment of the British fleet, covering as it did the northern and southern exits of the North sea, automatically provided for a distant blockade of the German ports almost as effective as its earlier prototype.[3] Now it would clearly

[1] All the European Powers engaged in August 1914 were signatories except Belgium.

[2] Something analogous with privateering was reintroduced by the Hague Conference in 1907, when it permitted the use of armed merchantmen as auxiliary cruisers.

[3] In 1915 3,098 ships were intercepted on the northern route and only 19 evaded the patrols. It is believed that not a single ship passed the Straits of Dover unnoticed.

have been an act of unconscionable tyranny to have barred the North Sea to all vessels, since within its area lay Holland and the three Scandinavian neutrals. Consequently in technical accuracy there never was a blockade, but merely a system of control and examination based on force. The resort to force was seldom necessary, for the traffic was almost entirely neutral. Though neutral ships might resent the interference, they were not disposed in their own interest to evade it, since the North Sea became more and more like one vast mine-field; while neither the vessel, nor, as a rule, the cargo was confiscated in the event of contraband being discovered.[1]

At the beginning of the war the British Government, though desirous of striking as hard a blow at German economic life as possible, had no intention of preventing all kinds of commodities from reaching the enemy. Such an attitude would have been desperately foolish, since it would have roused the United States, the all-important neutral, if not to actual hostility at least to retaliatory measures, which might well have proved fatal to the Allied cause. 'The object of diplomacy was to secure the maximum of blockade that could be enforced without a rupture with the United States.'[2] The avoidance of such a rupture was mainly due to the extraordinarily intimate and harmonious association between Grey and the American ambassador Walter Page. Both men were patterns of frankness and open dealing, and understood one another instinctively. Page was described as 'the best friend whom England ever had'. He was devoted from the beginning to the Allied cause, and angered and embarrassed his cold President by his espousal of it in private letters. He took infinite pains to smooth down the rough edges of the harsh dispatches which the State Department at Washington continually sent him for communication to our Foreign

[1] The usual procedure was to purchase the cargo and return the ship. See B. J. Hendrick, *Life and Letters of W. H. Page* (1922), vol. i, p. 380; ii, p. 63.

[2] See Visc. Grey of Fallodon, *Twenty-five Years, 1892–1916* (1928), vol. ii, pp. 103 sqq.

Office. He literally wore himself out by his four years of intense labour, for he returned home in November 1918 only to die of exhaustion a few weeks later, having just lived to see the Allied triumph.

The controversies of the first few months centred in the definition of contraband, and the measures necessary in order to prevent contraband goods from reaching the enemy through neutral channels.

America repeatedly urged the Allies to accept the list of contraband articles given in the Declaration of London, as Germany at once agreed to do. It was obviously in Germany's interest that the list should be as short as possible, while the aim of the Allies was the exact opposite. Now the list given in the Declaration was absurdly inadequate. Oil, copper, rubber, and cotton, four of the most potent auxiliaries of modern warfare, were omitted altogether. Aeroplanes were designated only as conditional contraband, that is to say, they were liable to seizure only if destined for the belligerent government or for the use of its fighting forces.

The British Government therefore, which was the invariable spokesman for the Entente in all these matters, insisted upon drawing up its own list. In deference, however, to the immense American interests involved, cotton was excluded for a year.[1] It was feared that without this concession the United States would convoy its merchantmen with warships, which would have meant surrender or war; or at least put an embargo upon the export of munitions, which would have placed the Allied armies in the most cruel straits during 1915.

The second problem was that of preventing contraband, absolute and conditional, from reaching the enemy, if directed to neutral ports and to neutral firms. The old doctrine of 'continuous voyage', used so freely by the Northern States during the American Civil War, was extended to

[1] After August 1915 when cotton was placed on the list, the British Government guaranteed a minimum price for it, and so enormous was the Allied consumption that the price kept on rising.

apply to conditional as well as to absolute contraband. This meant that if the ultimate destination of the goods in question could be established as an enemy one, their ostensible neutral address could not save them from seizure.

Under American pressure, however, conditional contraband was practically excepted from this rule in October 1914. Consequently foodstuffs, which came under this heading, were for some months imported into Germany with considerable freedom through neutral ports. It is therefore important to remember that the first German submarine campaign which started in February 1915 was not a retaliation for the 'hunger blockade', as was alleged by the German proclamation at the time.[1] On the contrary the beginning of the real blockade of Germany in March 1915 was a retaliation for the submarine campaign. It was then only that an Order in Council abolished all effective distinction between free goods, conditional and absolute contraband, and expressed the intention of 'detaining and taking into port ships carrying goods of presumed enemy destination, ownership and origin'.

To carry it out effectively meant an immense interference with neutral trade, though it involved no danger to neutral lives or ships from the Allies. There is a good deal of truth in Colonel House's remark that 'the British have gone as far as they possibly could in violating neutral rights, though they have done it in the most courteous way'.

It is, however, very far from true to affirm that Germany was deprived of imports by the Order in Council. On the contrary, during the years 1915–16 Holland and the Scandinavian neutrals supplied her with immense quantities of goods of every description from explosives to food-

[1] The best proof of this is the fact that the German Government refused an American proposal that the submarine campaign should be given up if England would give up the food blockade. Grey seems to have regarded such a proposal favourably. See *The Intimate Papers of Col. E. M. House* (1926), vol. i, pp. 376, 396. It is true that at the beginning of the war foodstuffs had been declared to be absolute contraband on a false report that the German Government had taken over the entire stock. This in fact was not done till January 25, 1915.

stuffs,[1] the vast majority of which were allowed to pass our blockade.

It was only very gradually that our pressure became effective. A system of rationing was set up for neutrals in 1916 which was carried through by a central trading association in each country which dealt direct with the British Department of War Trade. The German taunt that the neutrals allowed Great Britain to control their own internal trade was not unjustified.[2]

The postal control and censorship established by Great Britain in conjunction with the blockade gave an immense amount of information about the character of neutral firms. Compliance with the regulations was enforced by the publication of a 'black list', containing the names of those neutrals who were known to trade with the enemy. Such firms were debarred from trading with Great Britain, their cargoes forbidden to British vessels, and any neutral ship which carried them was refused bunker coal at British ports.

It was not, however, possible hermetically to seal up Germany until the great American neutral became an ally in 1917. Then indeed the United States as a belligerent pursued relentlessly all those methods against which as a neutral they had so often protested. When Balfour was on his mission at Washington in 1917, Polk, Counsellor of the State Department, said to him: 'Mr. Balfour, it took Great Britain three years to reach a point where it was prepared to violate all the laws of blockade. You will find

[1] See Rear-Adm. M. W. W. P. Consett and Capt. O. H. Daniel, *The Triumph of Unarmed Forces 1914–18* (1923), *passim.* The first-named author was Scandinavian naval attaché during the war and gives a most interesting analysis of the trade of these countries with Germany, illustrated by numerous statistics. During 1916 the exports of food to Germany from Scandinavian countries (together with Holland) was 25 per cent. larger than during 1913. It should be added that at least during 1915 a large portion of such neutral trade with Germany was in goods of British origin. 'Trading with the enemy' went on briskly and seems to have been winked at by the Board of Trade.

[2] For a description of these various associations see K. Helfferich, *Der Weltkrieg* (1919), pp. 245–6; C. E. Fayle, *Seaborne Trade*, vol. ii (1923).

that it will take us only two months to become as great criminals as you are.'[1]

'The Allied Powers in conjunction with the United States now possessed an almost complete control of many of the principal commodities, and the combined pressure they exerted was so tremendous that the goods never got as far as the sea, and the blockade was practically transformed into an embargo.

'The final cutting edge of the blockade in 1917 and 1918 was enforced not at sea but on the custom house quays at Boston, Liverpool, and New York. The Downs and Kirkwall languished and the control services were transferred to Halifax, Jamaica, and Sierra Leone.'[2]

The needs of the blockade, so intimately connected with the ever-increasing war against submarines and mines, was one of the principal causes for the unprecedented expansion of the Navy. Already at the close of 1915 the fleet, still destined to yet greater growth, numbered more than 3,000 vessels. Every kind of craft was pressed into its all-embracing service. Trawlers, drifters, and motor-boats formed a great part of its heterogeneous array. The price of the command of the sea was indeed eternal vigilance.

While by far the larger share of the work fell to the Southern Patrol in the Straits of Dover, the task of the 10th Cruiser Squadron in the north was beyond comparison more arduous. The armed liners to whom it was entrusted had to keep perpetual watch in the bitter and furious waters between Iceland and the north of Scotland;[3] they had to ensure the safety of the vessels which they stopped and in many cases directed to Kirkwall for examination. Although the patrol had been pressed back from the shorter line between the Shetlands and Norway by the imminent dangers of submarine and mine, these scourges followed them on their more northern beat. In 1915 alone four ships of the squadron were sunk in these waters.

[1] See B. J. Hendrick, *Life and Letters of W. H. Page* (1922), vol. ii, p. 265.

[2] Quoted from article 'Blockade' by Capt. A. C. Dewar, R.N., in *Encyclopaedia Britannica*, 12th ed., vol. xxx (1922).

[3] The cordon was sometimes drawn between Iceland, the Faroes, and the Shetlands, sometimes between Iceland and the Hebrides.

It is undeniable that the blockade was a harsh and indeed ruthless weapon. It applied the analogy of a besieged city to the inhabitants of a whole country with a degree of completeness never yet approached in warfare. Though the enemy by periodic extension of his conquests mitigated its effects both upon industry and sustenance, the suffering of the civil population for at least the last eighteen months of the war were intense. The weakest fell inevitably the easiest victims. The object of the 'hunger blockade' was not to kill old people, women, and children, but to break the war-will of the German people. But while it is impossible accurately to assess how many non-combatants succumbed to its indirect effects, through under-nourishment and its attendant diseases such as tuberculosis, the number was undoubtedly very considerable.[1]

II

The intention of the German Government in launching its submarine campaign was precisely the same as that of the British, namely, to compel peace by paralysing the far more vulnerable economic life of its adversary.[2] The difference in method, however, was enormous. The British blockade caused great inconvenience and delay to neutral trade, but it did not in any way endanger the lives of non-combatants, either enemy or neutral, upon the seas. The essence of the German plan, on the contrary, was to arrest all shipping by the immediate threat of death.

[1] The figure commonly given by German writers is 750,000. The civilian death-rate in 1917 was about three times that of 1913; though, of course, an accurate comparison between the two years is almost impossible.

[2] To take a comparison of foodstuffs alone. In 1913 Germany imported less than a quarter, and even during the war did not depend wholly upon sea-borne imports for the deficiency. It must be remembered, however, that (during the war) German soil was practically cut off from fertilizers, of which there had been an enormous peace-time import. It therefore became far less productive. Holland always had an exportable surplus of her own, and later on Rumania, Ukraine, and NE. Italy could be drawn upon. In 1913 Great Britain imported about 64 per cent. of foodstuffs, every ounce of which had to be sea-borne.

This plan was not indeed put into complete and unreserved application until 1917, in spite of the urgent and repeated pressure of both naval and military authorities. The Chancellor, Bethmann-Hollweg, was firm until then in insisting upon such modifications as would prevent, though only by a hair's breadth, the United States from joining the enemies of Germany. It is therefore true, as Scheer complains, that the development of the U-boat campaign was almost entirely a matter of politics. From the first, however, it was fertile in the destruction of non-combatant lives, both enemy and neutral.

At the beginning of war Germany observed its laws much better on sea than on land. Except for the mining of open waters in the North Sea,[1] and for a few decisions straining the law of contraband, her cruiser war against trade had been correctly and humanely waged.

But this power of interference practically ceased with the destruction of Spee's squadron. It was exceedingly galling for the enemy to watch his own trade being strangled with no method of reply, except the spasmodic and uncertain scattering of mines round the eastern and northern approaches to the British Isles. The position was the more serious since the failure of the first battle of Ypres made it clear that no swift end to the war could be expected, and so far little had been done to organize industry for a prolonged struggle.

It was almost inevitable that the German Admiralty should throw longing eyes at the submarine as a commerce-destroyer. Both sides, as the event proved, had over-estimated its danger to modern warships. Older and slower types had indeed fallen its victims and continued to do so throughout the war, but it was becoming increasingly clear that the desired process of equalizing the two

[1] This was contrary to the Hague Convention, which allowed mines to be laid only in territorial waters, e.g. within a three-mile limit of the coast. The practice was soon followed by Great Britain, who declared the southern part of the North Sea a War Area in November 1914. All shipping was warned that navigation here was perilous.

fleets was not likely to be brought about by its attacks.[1] On the other hand, it had unique advantages as a commerce-destroyer. It could move secretly to its selected point; it could wait patiently in invisibility; it betrayed its presence at the moment of attack only by an inconspicuous periscope, and could then instantly re-submerge into the depths.

Yet it was equally clear that such a method of warfare could not possibly be waged under the existing rules. No men could be spared to take over a prize crew. Every ship therefore would have to be sunk, instead of being seized. Again, a submarine on the surface is a helpless creature: one shell from a small gun is capable of sinking it; in the populous waters where it would naturally operate the time required for stopping and examining the papers of a suspected steamer would be exceedingly dangerous. The commander therefore would be under the strongest temptation to sink the ship unexamined. If so, how could he be sure that he had sunk an enemy and not a neutral, especially as British merchantmen often hoisted neutral colours? How could he ensure that the sinking ship would have time to lower her boats, or that if lowered they would convey the crew to safety? For all these reasons of mingled humanity and policy the British Admiralty had rejected the possibility of such a method of attack, when Fisher with his usual prescience in 1913[2] had forecasted its employment by the Germans. Consequently no measures of precaution had been devised against it.

The German proclamation of February 4th, 1915, did not declare a state of blockade. It followed the analogy of the 'War Zone' established by us in the North Sea in November 1914, and announced that all the approaches to the British islands constituted a similar region.[3] It

[1] Actually no British or German dreadnought was sunk throughout the war by a submarine, though three or four were damaged.

[2] See Winston Churchill, *World Crisis 1915* (1923), pp. 279–80.

[3] The analogy is obviously imperfect for (i) the North Sea was actually the scene of operations for the rival fleets; (ii) its danger was caused by minefields, which had been started by the Germans themselves; (iii) no threat

stated that Germany would combat hostile shipping in those parts with every weapon at her disposal.

'For this purpose . . . she will seek to destroy every hostile merchant ship which enters the War Zone and it will not always be possible to obviate the dangers with which the persons and goods on board will be threatened. Neutrals are therefore warned not to risk crews, passengers, and goods on such ships. Further their attention is drawn to the fact that it is highly desirable that their own ships should avoid entering this zone. For although the German Navy has orders to avoid acts of violence against neutral ships, so far as they are recognizable, yet in view of the misuse of neutral flags employed by the British Government, it may not always be possible to prevent them from falling a victim to an attack directed against an enemy ship.'

In reality the danger to neutrals was even greater than thus suggested. For the secret instructions to submarine commanders laid down that:

'The first consideration is the safety of the U-boat. Consequently rising to the surface in order to examine a ship must be avoided for the sake of the boat's safety, because, apart from the danger of a possible surprise attack by enemy ships, there is no guarantee that one is not dealing with an enemy ship, even if it bears the distinguishing marks of a neutral. The fact that a steamer flies a neutral flag, and even carries the distinguishing marks of a neutral, is no guarantee that it is actually a neutral ship. Its destruction will therefore be justifiable unless other attendant circumstances indicate its neutrality.'

Finally, commanders were informed that they would not be held answerable for their mistakes.

Yet the results of this onslaught were so small as to constitute almost a complete failure, and this for a variety of reasons. The enemy fell into the error, so common in the war, of trying an experiment without waiting for the means to make it effective. The sinister secret was given away too early. It was impossible to create a real terror over so large an area. According to Scheer there were only twenty-four

was made to sink merchantmen within that area. It was merely pointed out that it was actually dangerous for shipping.

U-boats available, which meant that not more than six or seven could cruise simultaneously. Tirpitz, the most ardent apostle of the method, had foreseen this difficulty and had in vain pleaded for a blockade of the Thames estuary only. Moreover, though some U-boat commanders appeared to relish the destruction of non-combatants, the large majority did not attack without warning.[1] This leniency not only allowed the crew to escape, but obviously endangered the submarine itself and restricted her activities. Moreover, counter-measures were multiplied with fertile ingenuity. More and more merchantmen were armed, until by the end of 1916 the numbers thus protected exceeded 1,400. They were encouraged to ram the submarine and rewards were offered for its destruction.[2] Decoy ships were fitted out by the Admiralty which behind the guise of a defenceless battered tramp concealed gun-fittings. The crew when attacked by a submarine apparently all left the ship in panic. The gun-layers waited until the enemy had come close up and was engaged in sinking its quarry with gun-fire.[3] Then at the last moment, often when the ship was on fire, and casualties were reducing its scanty occupants, the screens would fall, and the secret gun fire at point-blank range.

The Straits of Dover were closed by a double barrier of mine and net. So formidable was the obstacle that from May 1915 onwards all submarines destined for the Channel were ordered to reach it by the long roundabout

[1] See Adm. Visc. Jellicoe, *Crisis of the Naval War* (1920), p. 37: 'Prior to the month of January 1917, it was the usual practice of the enemy submarine . . . to give some warning before delivering her attack . . . in the years 1915 and 1916 only 21 and 29 per cent. respectively of the British merchant ships sunk by enemy submarines were destroyed without warning.'

[2] Such a posture on the part of the merchantman obviously made it unlikely that the submarine would give warning before attack. Early in 1916 the United States endeavoured to effect a compromise by which Great Britain would agree to give up arming merchantmen and Germany to give up attacks without warning. By now, however, Great Britain was too distrustful of the good faith of her enemy to agree.

[3] As many ships as possible were sunk by this method or by bombs. Only a limited number of torpedoes could be carried; if therefore they were extravagantly expended the submarine's tour would be unduly curtailed.

voyage north of Scotland. Trawlers assiduously worked all suspected areas with explosive sweeps. After U. 21 had daringly made the passage through the Straits of Gibraltar in May following hard in the wake of a British transport, the Mediterranean became the scene of increasing activities. Here the submarines fell also upon their legitimate prey, working havoc among the old battleships off the Gallipoli peninsula, and scoring rare successes against the transports. In home waters the war against commerce languished more and more, and was practically at a standstill by the close of 1915. During the whole of that year the submarines scarcely sank more tonnage than in one terrible month of 1917.

The British reply had been on the whole effective, though grievously handicapped by a lack of sufficient destroyers for patrol work. So many of these were permanently required for the protection of the Grand Fleet that the devoted service of the overworked residue fell far short of requirements. During the year the enemy lost only nineteen submarines and added fifty-four; he had in fact more than doubled the available number.

It is clear, therefore, that the relaxed strain was not primarily due to British effort. It was in fact due to the determination of the German Government not to break with the United States.

III

President Wilson is reported to have said in 1915 that the American people demanded energetic words, but would not endure energetic action. They were above all things anxious that their immense trade with the Allies in munitions and every kind of war-material should continue unabated. It was rapidly turning the United States from a debtor nation into the world's greatest creditor. But while a majority—probably a large majority—was in sympathy with the Allied cause, at least 90 per cent. of the whole eagerly desired to keep out of the war.[1] And

[1] This estimate may be accepted as approximately accurate as it is given

indeed at this time this mighty nation was wholly unprepared for war. The regular army numbered less than 100,000 men, a large proportion of whom were awaiting trouble on the Mexican frontier. Until the autumn of 1915, when a great scheme was put into operation, no additions had been made to the pre-war navy.

The President always hoped that a time might come when he would be able peacefully to impose his mediation upon the belligerents, and to induce them to agree to his conception of a just settlement. 'If we come into the war,' he said more than once to the German ambassador Bernstorff, 'there will be no one to help you out.' But he knew from the beginning that if America entered the war at all it must be on the Allied side. And he was determined to take no such decisive action without the whole-hearted support of the people of the United States. In retrospect it is clear that Wilson steered an extremely clever, if unattractive and humiliating, course through the tortuous waters of negotiation. His notes and phrases were at the time generally regarded as the self-righteous devices of a hypocritical puritan to conceal his own impotence and nakedness. The enemy and Allied press, particularly the comic papers, vied with each other in shooting shafts of derision at his pharisaical posturing. The famous defence of his attitude after the sinking of the *Lusitania*, 'There is such a thing as being too proud to fight', was long remembered against him.

Yet it is undeniable that he finally extorted from Germany without war the desired recognition of American rights, and as its sequel the crippling of the submarine campaign for eighteen months. From the beginning he refused to discuss the question of these rights with Germany; he merely stated what they were. Nor would he allow that they could legitimately be endangered in retaliation for breaches of international law by the British, against which he himself continued to protest.

independently by House, by Spring Rice the British Ambassador, and by Bernstorff the German ambassador at Washington.

In February 1915 he declared that Germany would be held to a strict accountability for the acts of her navy. On May 1st the first American ship, the *Gulflight*, was attacked and her master drowned. Five days later the great British liner *Lusitania*, homeward bound from New York, and crowded with passengers, was torpedoed without warning off the west coast of Ireland. There were 1,198 victims, including about 100 Americans. This tremendous outrage was a deliberate act of policy for which the German Government was directly responsible. It had disseminated warnings beforehand in the shipping offices of New York, and actually allowed a medal to be struck in commemoration. It was true, as alleged by the enemy, that the *Lusitania* carried some small-arm ammunition in her hold. This fact might justify seizure, but not destruction without warning. The object of Germany was patent, to paralyse all American trade with the Allies by an unexampled act of inhuman intimidation.

Both Page and House, the President's unofficial confidant then in London, thought war to be immediate and certain. Many believed that Germany was deliberately provoking it to stop the westward flow of munitions, which presumably the United States would retain for their own requirements as belligerents. This, however, was not so. Germany was under the impression that 'these idiotic Yankees'[1] would stand anything, and that Wilson's notes, which though firm in tone avoided any suggestion of an ultimatum, need not be taken seriously. It required the sinking of another liner, the *Arabic*[2] (August 19), with two American victims, to convince Bernstorff that a rupture was really imminent. On September 1st Wilson secured his first success with the assurance that 'liners will not be sunk without warning and without safety of the lives of non-combatants, provided the liners do not try to escape

[1] This is a phrase of Dr. Dumba, the Austrian minister at Washington, taken from a private letter stolen by a British spy. Dumba was sent home by Wilson at the end of 1915 for various unneutral activities.

[2] This ship was western bound and therefore incapable of carrying contraband.

or offer resistance'. By degrees he extracted a grudging apology and promise of compensation for the lives lost in the *Lusitania*.

Yet another crisis had to be faced in the spring of 1916. The German Admiralty, without the knowledge of the Chancellor and contrary to his instructions, authorized the torpedoing of the *Sussex*, a cross-Channel steamer, with eighty casualties among the passengers. This time Wilson was sufficiently roused to send an ultimatum without a time-limit declaring that unless the present methods of submarine warfare against passengers and freight-carrying ships were immediately abandoned, he had no choice 'but to sever diplomatic relations with the German Empire altogether'.

This display of vigour produced an undertaking from Germany 'to do its utmost to confine the operations of war for the rest of its duration to the fighting forces of the belligerents'. A definite promise was made that no more merchantmen would be sunk without warning and without saving human lives. An ominous proviso, however, stated that if the United States could not induce all nations to follow the laws of humanity, 'the German Government would then be facing a new situation in which it must reserve itself complete liberty of decision'. This liberty, as we shall see, was resumed in February 1917 to the final exhaustion of American patience.

Wilson might well write to House in the throes of the earlier controversy: 'My chief puzzle is to determine when patience ceases to be a virtue.'[1] Though so hesitating, he certainly acted neither from weakness nor in ignorance of the American character. The old saying that every nation has the government which it deserves is well illustrated by the events of 1915. Wilson undoubtedly owed his narrow re-election as President in November 1916 to the conviction that he was 'the man who has kept us out of the war'.

[1] To House, September 15, 1915 (*Intimate Papers of Col. E. M. House* 1926)).

Yet it remains amazing to Europeans that a nation so touchy, so brave, and so determined as the Americans should so long have put up with the sinking of its ships, the murder of its citizens, and the organization within its borders of strikes and outrages against munition works by aliens.[1]

[1] The German naval and military attachés at Washington, Boy-ed and von Papen, the Vice-Chancellor of the German Reich 1933–4, devoted themselves to these latter activities, and were sent home at the end of 1915. They had an unofficial ally in a German naval officer Rintelin who developed an ingenious plan of putting bombs in the bunkers of merchantmen, which exploded in mid-Atlantic, causing the loss of these vessels by fire.

XIII

THE DARDANELLES

I

TURKEY on the map resembled[1] in a general way a great Asiatic lying prone, with his head in Europe, his body in Asia Minor, his right leg in Mesopotamia, and his left in the Sinai Peninsula. Anatolia is indeed the true heart of this unwieldy giant, being practically impregnable and supplying his life-blood in the shape of its sturdy peasants, unsurpassed for a dumb enduring courage. Both the legs required to be secured lest they should give dangerous kicks. The Turk in the Persian Gulf might interfere with the pipe-line of the Anglo-Persian Oil Company, on which the oil-driven ships of the Navy depended for their supply. But a kick from the left leg would be even more dangerous; nay, possibly fatal. The Suez Canal was aptly called by our enemies the 'Jugular vein of the British Empire' through which flowed all the vital traffic between East and West. Even a temporary interruption of this stream would be very serious. Further, it was quite impossible to predict the repercussions upon our Eastern Empire of the presence of the Turk in Egypt.

In the far north-east of Asia Minor the frontiers of the Turkish and Russian Empires met in a tender spot among the great mountains of the Caucasus. Here the Russian was likely to prove the more dangerous invader, for in the line of his advance was placed the province of Armenia, whose Christian inhabitants had been maltreated, tormented, and massacred for generations by their Moslem rulers. In 1915 the most savage and wholesale of all these butcheries was perpetrated, in which it is reckoned that more than a million Armenians perished.

Finally, the head, Constantinople, though subtly protected by nature against a direct blow, was joined to the body by the frailest of connexions, a bridge across the water.

[1] For the map of Turkey see p. 350.

Thus if the bridge were broken the three great powers of the Entente would not merely be engaged in a common cause but would be able to use their resources in common.

Now although this sprawling giant had received many battering blows in the Italian and Balkan wars immediately preceding 1914 he was still tough and resolute enough. But his nerves and muscles, the communications available for war, were dangerously weak and exposed. Turkey had no common frontier with the Central Powers, who were powerless to send reinforcements. Even the dispatch of munitions and stores, so desperately needed, was dependent upon the precarious goodwill of Rumania, whose amenities of transport were entirely determined by the swing of the pendulum towards victory. Constantinople itself was not connected by rail with the Asiatic shore. No continuous line linked up Asia Minor with either Mesopotamia or Palestine; for the necessary tunnelling had not yet been completed to carry it through either of the great obstacles which close the south-eastern corner of Asia Minor, the mountains of Taurus and Amanus. From the junction at Aleppo in northern Syria ran two lines, one east, one south. The former was feeling its way across the desert to Baghdad. A gap of some 500 miles separated it from the Mesopotamian limb, which was being slowly extended up the Tigris. One branch of the latter ended at Nablus, in Palestine north of Jerusalem; the other crawled precariously as a single line down the deserts of Arabia to the holy places of Medina and Mecca.

It is quite evident that Turkey was scarcely knit together at all in a modern sense. No abundance of good roads compensated for the absence of railways; no abundance of motor vehicles was available for such roads as did exist. One of the principal theatres of war, the Caucasus, was actually 500 miles from Konia, its nearest rail-head.

Four campaigns were in progress against the Turk in 1915; one of the Russians in the Caucasus, three of the British in Egypt, Mesopotamia, and Gallipoli. The first three of these were to continue with varying intensity until the end of the war; the last, the most dramatic and potentially decisive, was alone complete from beginning to end within the year. It will therefore be first taken into consideration here.

II

The Dardanelles campaign, as we have seen, developed out of a request by the Russians that we should help their hard-beset forces in the Caucasus by a diversion (January 2, 1915). At that very moment the need had passed, for the widely scattered Turkish forces were being overthrown in the snowy mountains at Sari Kamish. Yet out of this grain of mustard seed developed a tall tree. As the British Ministers could not make up their minds whether they would or would not have troops available, it was decided to try what could be effected by naval action alone. The inducement was twofold. First the Admiralty had at its disposal a large number of battleships and cruisers of ten years of age and upwards. These had been rendered obsolete for service with the Grand Fleet since the construction of the dreadnoughts, and were ill suited for patrol purposes in the Channel or North Sea, as in submarine-infested waters their comparatively low speed made them an easy prey. But the number of guns available, from a calibre of 12-inch downwards, made a very powerful armament which it was believed could be successfully employed against the Dardanelles forts. This belief had been seriously strengthened by the results of a preliminary bombardment of the outer forts on November 3rd, which was an attempt by the Admiralty, unauthorized by the Cabinet, to discover the range of the fortress-artillery. Within twenty minutes the fort at Sedd-el-Bahr had been put out of action and all the guns dismounted. The question now to be decided was whether this bombardment was merely to be repeated, perhaps more than once, on a far larger scale as a demonstration. Such action might perhaps lead to the reinforcement of the Gallipoli garrison by two or three divisions but could not exercise any very serious effect on the campaigns either in the Caucasus or Egypt; far less could it leave its mark on the strategy of the war as a whole. But to do this very thing, to find a decisive way round the flankless fortified lines, was the most ardent desire of Churchill and Lloyd George. Desire provided hope. But hope required to be strengthened by expert knowledge. Accordingly Vice-Admiral Carden, commanding at the Dardanelles, was asked whether he considered 'the forcing of the Dardanelles by ships alone a practical operation'. His reply was: 'I do not consider Dardanelles can be rushed. They might be forced by extended operations with large numbers of ships.' The detailed plan which followed made two general assumptions of a vital character: (1) that the forts could be destroyed by indirect, followed by direct fire; (2) that minesweepers would be able to clear a passage for the fleet right up to the Sea of Marmara. Acting on these, the admiral anticipated that the operation could be completed in four stages in about a month. The Admiralty concurred in these views.[1] The floating and moving gun-platform of the warship was considered to be a match for the fixed fort; and the low trajectory of the high-velocity naval gun competent to effect its destruction. On questions of general policy experts may be often—the great Lord Salisbury said always—wrong, but as technical advisers in their own craft every government must either trust them or find new advisers. The enterprise was therefore quite properly blessed and taken in hand (January 28).

Yet the statesmen who ordered it do not appear to have thought out the consequences either of success or failure. The instructions given to the Admiralty were odd to the point of grotesqueness if a purely naval expedition was envisaged. 'To bombard and take the Gallipoli peninsula with Constantinople as its objective' is obviously an

[1] Lord Fisher afterwards stated that he had been against the expedition from the start. This can only mean that he disapproved of its strategic direction, as opposed to his own plan for operations in Schleswig-Holstein. He certainly raised no objection to the technical method proposed.

impossible task for a fleet acting by itself. Even if the meaning of this badly drafted sentence was that the fleet should proceed to Constantinople after subduing the forts on the peninsula, the effect of its appearance there was doubtful. It is uncertain whether the wavering neutrals would have been ready to attack Turkey unless an Allied army appeared on the scene. It is improbable that the mere presence of the warships before the enemy's capital would have constrained Turkey to make peace even had a revolution broken out there; or that the British Government would have been prepared to lay Constantinople in ashes to break their enemy's will.[1] Finally, in the opinion of Liman von Sanders no supplies could have been obtained as long as both sides of the straits remained in Turkish hands. If this reasoning be correct, a military force must in the long run have proved to be necessary. But the War Office was not consulted at all in the matter. Kitchener in his majestic and secretive way had constantly neglected his General Staff, which in fact consisted of inferior men hastily scraped together when the original personnel had followed the expeditionary force to France.

What, on the other hand, was to be done in the event of failure? One supposed advantage of the proposed expedition was that it could at any stage be broken off at will. But at what stage was it to be considered a definitive failure? Carden had been already told that 'importance of result would justify severe loss'. Nothing is more difficult in war than to know when to cut losses. Could an attempt which aroused such high expectation, which involved so deeply the prestige of the assailants, actually be broken off after one failure, however disheartening? If not, it had to be considered whether the same method could be repeated or whether recourse must be had to a combined expedition. In fact as early as January 19th

[1] This is on the assumption that the Turkish army would have retired and left Constantinople without defence. If so, it would have come under the category of undefended towns, against whose bombardment the British Government had raised the most energetic protests.

the Cabinet was deeply committed by Churchill's official letter to the Grand Duke Nicholas, in which he wrote: 'It is our intention to press the matter to a conclusion.'[1]

During February the War Council gradually got accustomed to the idea that troops after all were available. The French Cabinet, against the will of Joffre, was prepared to ear-mark two divisions for the Mediterranean; the Commander-in-Chief in France was reluctantly squeezed into an admission that he could do without two of the four divisions hitherto ear-marked for his own front. The failure of the Turkish attack on Egypt made it possible to cast envious eyes on the great accumulation of partially trained troops there. No definite decision was yet reached to employ a large military force with the fleet. On the contrary the alternative preferred was to strengthen the Serbs, if possible with the co-operation of Greece. It was generally agreed, therefore, to concentrate all available spare men somewhere in the Mediterranean and use them somehow! Meanwhile naval operations were in course. But by March 9th Carden, who had in three weeks merely reduced the outer forts with the puissant aid of the 15-inch guns of the new super-dreadnought *Queen Elizabeth*, declared himself to be held up by lack of sea-planes.

Even the preliminaries had so excited the Balkans that Greece, whose General Staff had carefully studied a Gallipoli landing in 1912, spontaneously offered three divisions (March 1). Whereupon Russia, who had already obtained from the Allies the potential gift of Constantinople, absolutely vetoed any such co-operation with the Greeks; nor was she able to lift a finger to aid this great enterprise which had been begun mainly to remedy her own grievous necessities. History in its long record of the short-sighted selfishness shown by individual members of coalitions, devoted in lip-service to a common cause, can hardly provide a more fatal example.

1 *World Crisis 1915* (1923), p. 119; see also Kitchener's view, p. 183: 'The effect of a defeat in the Orient would be very serious. There could be no going back.'

On March 10th Kitchener released the 29th division, the veteran regulars from India, for service in the East. He had kept this unit, which must be the spear-head of any force composed of new levies, within his fingers for nearly a month. Two days later Sir Ian Hamilton was made Commander-in-Chief of the Mediterranean Force. A considerable army was now to be used against Constantinople. But as yet there was no plan, no staff, and only the vaguest instructions. Hamilton had been Kitchener's favourite subordinate in South Africa, and he was being sent out to improvise a campaign against the strongest fortified area in Turkey, just as he had been sent out to improvise the rounding up of a small party of guerrillas.[1] He was to have about 75,000 men, to be employed only when all had been assembled. Military operations on a large scale were contemplated only 'in the event of the Fleet failing to get through after every effort has been exhausted'. Thus the naval attack still held the field. The chief duty of the Army presumably would be to occupy and defend Constantinople. Hamilton arrived without his army at the Dardanelles at the most dramatic moment. He was able to witness the great assault of March 18th upon the Narrows. On that day Admiral de Robeck, whom the illness of Carden had just placed in command, brought into action an Allied fleet of eighteen battleships —for the French had also put a squadron under his orders. A German flying officer described the spectacle of the fleet steaming in from Tenedos at daybreak as the most magnificent he had ever witnessed. The Straits had been thoroughly swept and were believed to be clear of mines within 8,000 yards of the Narrows. Within that area therefore it was proposed to confine the action of the battleships.

[1] See Gen. Sir Ian Hamilton, *Gallipoli Diary* (1920), vol. i, pp. 1–3. The only reasoned warning of the dangers involved in this blind plunge is the remarkable paper of Sir Maurice Hankey, the Secretary to the War Council, quoted in Brig.-Gen. C. Aspinall-Oglander's *Military Operations: Gallipoli* vol. i (1929), pp. 101–2. Hankey's immense services, not merely to the British Cabinet, but to the whole Allied cause, are only gradually becoming known; much of the advice which he gave is still hidden in secret documents.

The Turks, or rather their German instructor, Admiral von Usedom, had greatly improved their defences since the outbreak of war. The vital forts at the Narrows had received more modern guns, which were served by a brave and experienced German personnel. All along either rugged and broken shore towards the entrance mobile batteries were placed to annoy the ships as they passed up the Straits. Our enemies placed their main confidence in the mine-field as a shield. They were exceedingly short of ammunition, and believed that, if our ships could overcome the water-defences, nothing could prevent us from reaching the Marmara. And indeed at the end of the day they had fired away more than half their munitions; in some of the forts there were only about eight shells available for each gun; and there was a reserve of only twenty mines. But a small number of the latter, undiscovered by the sweepers, proved a decisive obstacle.

For about three hours the operations proceeded according to plan. The four most heavily armed battleships, with sea-planes 'spotting' for them, bombarded the Narrows at a range of 14,000 yards, causing explosions in several of the principal forts. Meanwhile the French squadron steamed up farther into the Straits, to engage them more closely. The mobile batteries on the banks shot well, and made a number of hits, but the armour of the warships protected them against serious damage. About 2 p.m. the French battleship *Bouvet* suddenly blew up with nearly all her crew. This was the first disaster, but it was attributed to a shell, and the relieving British squadron continued to fire with little molestation for two hours. It now seemed as if the forts were finally silenced, that the sweepers could run up the Narrows, and prepare the way for a triumphal entry into the Marmara on the morrow. At this very moment two British ships, *Inflexible* and *Irresistible*, struck mines, and a little later a third, *Ocean*, while engaged in rescue work, met the same fate. Thus a third of the attacking force had been put out of action.[1] These mines

[1] The *Inflexible* was beached and saved.

had been laid near the Asiatic coast by a Turkish steamer ten days before. The line had escaped notice mainly because, instead of running across the Straits, it ran parallel to the shore, on the course followed by the right of the advancing squadron. This became known only after the war. At the time it was believed that the mines were floated down by the Turks with the current from above. The danger was therefore believed to be far more incalculable and irremediable than it was in reality.

De Robeck at first expressed himself as ready to renew the attempt, as the enemy anxiously expected. But apparently the presence of a general at his elbow, the knowledge that a military force would shortly be available, weakened a resolution which might have remained constant had the Navy been the only instrument of salvation. On March 22nd he formally told Hamilton that 'he was now quite clear he could not get through without the help of all my troops'.[1] And so the position envisaged in London was reversed. The Army had now to land on and take Gallipoli in order to open the way for the Navy, whereas its original role was not to begin until the Straits were cleared.

Hamilton has poignantly depicted with his sensitive and imaginative pen the difficulties which beset his path. He had gradually to squeeze an adequate staff out of Kitchener. He was told at one moment that the enterprise must be pushed through at all costs, at another that France must come first in everything, and in particular that the 29th division must be regarded as a short-dated loan. Worst of all, the base chosen for him, in which 12,000 troops were already collected, the great harbour of Mudros in the island of Lemnos,[2] proved quite unsuit-

[1] See *Gallipoli Diary*, vol. i, p. 41. Hamilton had expressed the same view immediately after witnessing the attack. 'The Army's share will not be a case of landing parties for the destruction of forts etc., but rather a case of a deliberate and progressive military operation, carried out in force, in order to make good the passage of the Navy.'

[2] The Entente were using this island by an amicable arrangement with Greece. The loan might perhaps be considered to lie within the letter of neutrality, as Turkey had not acknowledged Greek sovereignty over the

able. Further, the stores sent from England had been so packed in the transports that most of them had to be re-shipped before they could be used for a debarkation on enemy territory.[1] It was only through intense co-operative labour between the two services that the landing was actually effected within forty days of Hamilton's departure from London.

Unfortunately this short respite was of vital value to the enemy. The base at Alexandria was a bustling centre of intrigue from which enemy agents sent out exact details of the preparations for a destination which was in the common mouth of every soldier. The Turkish Staff could not, it is true, be certain of the point of danger until a landing was actually attempted; combined expeditions having command of the sea obviously have great liberty of action, and can feint down to the last moment. So the hostile forces guarding the Straits were increased nearly fivefold between the end of February and April 25th.[2] After March 16th Liman von Sanders was given supreme command of all the troops; for, though the Turks did not like the Germans, they recognized and trusted an organizing ability which far exceeded their own. Liman found his command dotted about in little blobs, wherever a landing seemed possible, a dissipation of forces without any adequate reserve which would have played into the enemy's hands. The divisions were at once concentrated; the defensive positions constructed on any likely beaches, well-wired down to, and sometimes even below, the water's edge. Thus it was hoped to delay the invaders with snugly ensconced outpost troops, until local reserves could come up. Fortunately for the defence the cliffs fall sheer into the

island, which was taken from her in the war of 1912–13. The disadvantage of Alexandria, in itself an admirable base, was that it remained throughout under the orders and control of the Commander-in-Chief in Egypt, Sir J. Maxwell.

[1] See Brig.-Gen. C. Aspinall-Oglander, *Military Operations: Gallipoli*, vol. i (1929), p. 117; P. G. Elgood, *Egypt and the Army* (1924), p. 168.

[2] They amounted to six divisions, with a ration strength of about 100,000 and a fighting strength of 62,000.

sea on most of the Gallipoli coast; the beaches are few and generally quite narrow. Liman divided his forces into three main groups of approximately equal strength. Two divisions guarded the Asiatic shore; two the southern half

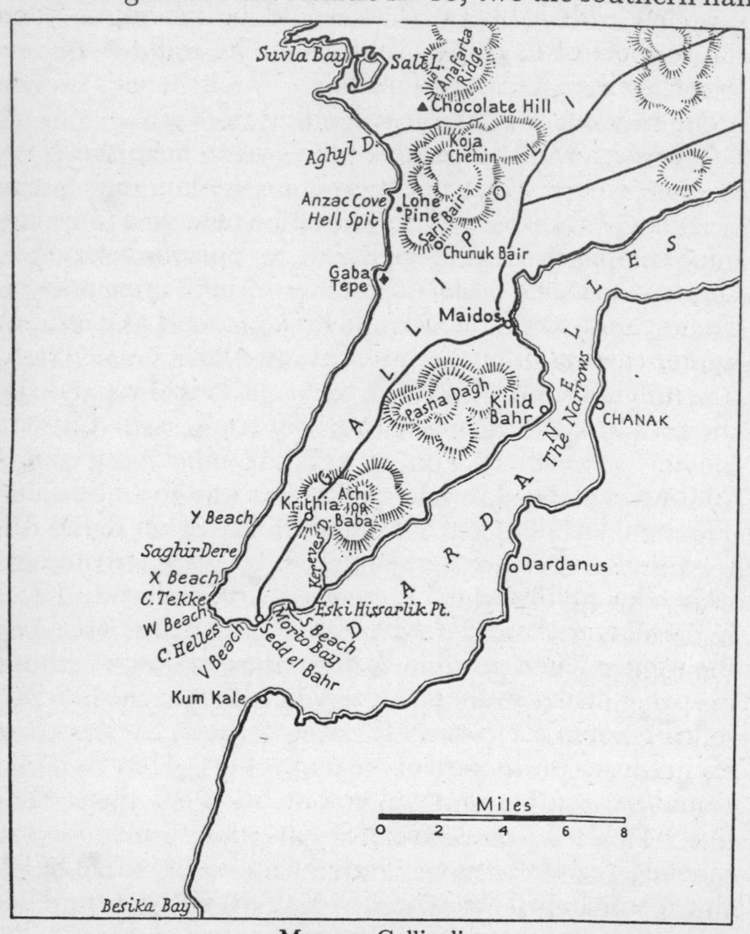

Map 15. Gallipoli.

of the peninsula, roughly from Suvla Bay to Maidos; the remainder being concentrated on either side of the lines of Bulair, where the neck of the isthmus protrudes from Thrace. The plan was good, for it provided the opportunity of speedy concentration on any one of the danger-points, which would remain in uncertainty until the actual moment of landing. His anxiety about Asia was not, it is true, justified by the event. He probably exaggerated the menace of an attack *en revers* upon the eastern defences of the Narrows by an expedition, which was in fact poorly supplied with artillery, that would be moving beyond the support of its ships. In any case he could not know that Hamilton had been forbidden by Kitchener's express order to make a permanent landing in Asia.

The essence of the British plan was to keep the Navy in close co-operation not merely at the landing, but as long as possible throughout the campaign, and to economize troops. A landing at Bulair, so obvious a target to amateur strategists, was unsuitable for both these reasons. To have advanced through Thrace towards Constantinople, leaving Gallipoli unsubdued, would have been rashness amounting to frenzy. A movement southward down the peninsula would have turned its back on the Capital, left an open flank in Thrace, and given the Navy merely the opportunity of a limited support on the right flank. The best and most extensive beaches were on the south-west shore, opposite the Narrows; but these advantages were not less obvious to the enemy, whose elaborate defensive preparations could be plainly seen from the sea. As the wide expanse of Suvla Bay was deemed impracticable in spring owing to the size of its salt lagoon, the extreme south point of the peninsula was indicated, by process of exclusion, as the theatre of the main effort. Here its flanks would be secure and naval co-operation complete. The five beaches selected were all exceedingly narrow and pinched, distant from each other from one to three miles. But it was hoped that the first day's landing would see a continuous line drawn across the toe, enclosing the dominating hill of Achi Baba whence the Turks got all their observation over the south of the peninsula.

Such a plan was only likely to succeed if the enemy's concentration was foiled by a flank attack and by diversions. The Australians were to land in force some ten miles farther north at Gaba Tepe, and form, by their possession of the central ridge, at least a threatening wedge against reinforcements moving south. The French were to effect a temporary landing at Kum Kale in Asia and to demonstrate in Besika Bay. And finally a naval feint was to be directed at Bulair.

Such a division of forces was inevitable given the narrowness and paucity of available beaches, but it was also desirable. It increased the number of men who could be put on shore simultaneously, and it bewildered the enemy, who has recorded the consternation at his head-quarters as message after message described different landings.

On the other hand, Hamilton found it impossible from the sea to control and shape the tactical destinies of these isolated forces into a harmonious strategical whole. April 25th is the most dramatic day of the whole World War. The doubtful battle ebbed and flowed in a historic setting, amidst all the sombre magnificence which a fleet lends to modern war. The diary of the British Commander-in-Chief has preserved with a vivid brilliance the transient emotions, generally concealed or distorted, of the principal actors.

The first landing at the point of dawn was that of the Anzacs,[1] who came for the first time under fire in this most hazardous venture. The tows which carried the covering force in open boats were pushed a mile north of their intended destination by the set of the current. However, they struck a serviceable beach free from obstacles, and scattered the handful of surprised defenders. In three hours 8,000 men were ashore with as yet no opposition beyond 500 snipers, but though our numbers were doubled by the close of the day, the all-important ridge dominating Maidos and the Narrows was very far from won. The mistaken landing-place was primarily responsible for this comparative failure. The invaders were faced with ground unstudied on the map, and every movement had to be improvised. Three successive ridges barred their path, precipitous, scarred, and tangled with dense scrub. Lack of

[1] The initial letters of Australian and New Zealand Army Corps.

planes had prevented aerial reconnaissance, while the wretched old maps provided scarcely marked any 'under-feature'. In this blind fighting scramble they were further impeded by their own loaded bodies (each man carried a weight of 88 lb.), and the lack of cohesion inevitable among confident individualists fighting their first battle. Their own dearth of artillery was by no means compensated by the fire of the warships, which, on this first of many occasions, was to prove very limited in aid against scattered troops in broken cover. Yet in spite of all Chunuk Bair, the citadel of these hills, might have been won but for Mustapha Kemal. The present [1934] dictator of Turkey then commanded the 19th division, collected as a general reserve north of Maidos. By a personal reconnaissance he saw the invaders on the left flank about 9.30 a.m. already slipping up the main ridge where it is joined directly to the sea-cliffs by a narrow neck. He instantly launched against them, on his own responsibility, a whole regiment, one-third of his total force, and not only held the flank all day but created a danger-point for his enemy. The Turks might well be proud of their stubborn and subtle fight, for they were never outnumbered by less than three to one.

Meanwhile all the south tip of the peninsula was being kindled. It is a commonplace of military history that battles are generally decided by a right use of the reserve. Sir John French at Loos kept it under his own hand so long that, when at last he grudgingly unclutched it, the opportunity had gone. Hamilton, with a more chivalrous liberality, had bestowed it before the battle upon Hunter-Weston, the local commander of the whole southern battle. As the latter also commanded the veteran 29th division, destined to make the decisive landing at Helles, it was probable that he would stake all on a rigid execution of the programme already arranged. And so it proved; for an unopposed landing elsewhere with its decisive possibilities was left entirely without reinforcements by General Hunter-Weston, whereas the 29th division suffered such cruel losses in disembarking, particularly among its senior officers,[1] as to be incapable of effort during the remainder of the day. The two warships which harboured Hamilton and Hunter-Weston[2] were constantly intent on their own tactical duties, consequently the two generals could neither communicate easily with each other, nor visit and view in correct perspective the scattered battles.

Y beach was occupied at dawn quite peacefully by two battalions, for there was not a Turk within a mile. Hamilton had himself insisted upon this flanking thrust, for he saw correctly that, if pushed forward to Krithia and beyond, it would jeopardize if not destroy the whole Turkish scheme of defence at Helles. The Staff, however, had entirely neglected it; no proper orders had been given and the colonels of the two battalions employed had been left uncertain which of them commanded the detachment. Hunter-Weston seems to have ignored Hamilton's suggestion that more troops should be diverted to exploit this unopposed entry. The men were allowed to sit on the cliffs and do nothing, as they vainly waited for an advance from Helles to join them. They had barely scratched some trenches when they were attacked at night by an inferior number of Turks. After losing a third of their numbers they were taken off next morning in unnecessary haste and confusion. It was a most pitiable episode. Similarly a small infantry force easily landed at S beach and feebly opposed, was allowed to remain without instructions or reinforcements at a point where a march of two miles westward over level country would have taken in rear the castle of Sedd-el-Bahr, whose brave handful of defenders prevented any forward movement from the beach all day.

On either side of Cape Helles there was epic fighting. The Turks, as we now know, were incredibly few on the ground, for during the whole of the day they had only 2,000 men engaged in the whole southern sector. Man for man they

[1] All the brigadiers were killed or wounded, with two brigade-majors and more than half the battalion commanders.

[2] The *Queen Elizabeth* and *Euryalus*: the former spent most of the day bombarding V beach, the latter lay off Helles.

were certainly not braver or better trained than the picked division which assaulted them. But such was their tenacity, fire-discipline, and use of cover that British Headquarters reported the garrison of Sedd-el-Bahr alone as consisting of the greater part of a division, when its true strength was a single company. The extreme deadliness of modern weapons fired from a trench against men nakedly advancing in the open had been already proved many times in France. Here the targets huddled in open boats, or stumbling through wired water were even more passively offered to the slaughter. Under such conditions the bare success of landing and clinging to the beaches was an extraordinary achievement, which indeed paralysed and exhausted even those tough fighters for the rest of the day.

At Sedd-el-Bahr (V beach) a striking stage was set. The shallow half-moon of the cove was crowned with low, steep cliffs. On the right, to one approaching from the sea, rose the solid masonry of the old castle; behind and to the left huddled the gaping village; trenches along and above the cliff prolonged the Turkish defences round the curve to another fort. The effect of the naval guns had been little more than sound and fury, when the expedition moved against the shore in broad daylight. About 3,000 men were approaching in tows and on the *River Clyde*, a converted collier in whose sides sally ports had been cut. The Turks, with that deliberate patience only possible in the best soldiers, reserved all fire until the boats had almost touched shore, and then blasted whole boat-loads of the Dublin Fusiliers out of existence. The same hail met the Munsters as they rushed out of the stranded collier over a bridge of lighters most heroically improvised by seamen under point-blank fire.[1]

The utmost effort of the survivors carried them to the beach, where a sunken bank under the cliff afforded them cover. The enemy prevented any further lodgement that day, and half the 2,000 men in the collier's hold remained

[1] This work was directed by Com. Unwin, R.N., who gained the V.C.

undischarged. Any attempt at movement instantly drew a devastating fire.

In spite of the complete success of the demonstrations, which had pinned every Turk at Bulair[1] on the Asiatic shore to his ground, expectation had been grievously deceived. No continuous line existed, no dominating ground, no depth to give shelter from shell-fire had been won. But for Hamilton's resolution the largest gain would have been abandoned. The Anzacs fell into great confusion and despondency at night, expecting an irresistible counter-attack. Even Birdwood, their cheerful and stout-hearted commander, was induced to favour immediate evacuation. Hamilton's reply bears the inspiring stamp of the true commander, and produced exactly the effect required on the frayed nerves of brave men. Next day Sedd-el-Bahr was stormed and the Allied line drawn across the tip of the peninsula. A general attack on April 28th failed owing to the arrival of strong Turkish reinforcements who broke the French on the right wing and foiled the British advance.

But the pent-up positions of the two separate detachments vitiated the whole plan of campaign for the next three months. They were squeezed into a trench-warfare, in which the enemy, now disposing freely of his large reinforcements, had every advantage. Hamilton had no respite; he had to break out of his prison. And his continual attacks, always foreseen, always uphill, with his reserves always shelled before they could be used, were, as the event was to prove, the forlornest of hopes. It is not within the province of this work to describe all the bitter struggles in the olive-yards before Krithia, or on the aromatic cliffs round 'Anzac Cove'.[2] The sufferings of the force were increased by the coming of summer and the withdrawal of the battleships. The heat of the sun was made less endur-

[1] Here Lt.-Com. Freyberg of the Naval division gained a D.S.O.: he swam ashore by night and lit flares along a mile of coast to simulate a landing. He had an amazing career as a fighter, and rose to the command of a brigade in France, where he won the V.C.

[2] By May 31 the British casualties alone exceeded 38,000.

able by lack of water; the plague of flies was such that food was blackened by them as it was raised to the mouth; rations were exceedingly monotonous, for fresh meat was hardly ever seen. Troops had no billets, no proper rest, since they were incessantly employed on fatigue duties and remained always under shell-fire except on the very rare occasions when they were transported to Lemnos or Imbros. In consequence dysentery was so prevalent that by July the major part of the force was more or less seriously affected.

The co-operation of the Navy in all questions of administration and supply remained throughout the occupation exceedingly efficient and harmonious.[1] But tactical support had largely to be withdrawn when German submarines appeared in the Mediterranean in May. The Army was terribly short of guns and munitions even on the humble scale to which France was then confined. The flat trajectory of the naval guns could not effectively search trenches and ravines, although it is true that the powerful weight of metal always available at least kept down the fire of the enemy's batteries, denied him freedom of movement, and hampered concentration in his back areas. Two exploits of the *Queen Elizabeth* were specially remembered. With one shrapnel-burst she practically destroyed a half-battalion advancing to the attack. With her third shot, firing directly over the Isthmus into the Straits, she sank a loaded Turkish transport at 16,000 yards.

She was sent home at once when the hostile submarines arrived (May 12) and after several old battleships had been sunk the fleet was normally retained in Mudros harbour, though brought out as far as was practicable to help Hamilton whenever he attacked. The Turks, realizing the improbability of any naval enterprise against the Straits, gradually stripped the fortresses of much of their artillery, which went to enhance the preponderance of their field-army. On the other hand, they were seriously

[1] Hamilton picturesquely wrote 'the Navy has been our father and our mother'.

annoyed by the exploits of the Allied submarines, which penetrated constantly into the Sea of Marmara, two actually cruising there for nearly three weeks during May.[1] The supply of hostile munitions, provisions, and even of troops was thus heavily impeded; for, owing to the lack of roads on the peninsula, transport by sea was much the quicker. This activity of our submarines was never wholly subdued, though made excessively dangerous by Turkish counter-measures, in particular by the stretching of a great net right across the Straits at Nagara.[2]

The naval situation was restored to our advantage at the end of July by the arrival of a number of monitors armed with 14-inch guns, and cruisers with bulged sides to protect them against torpedoes.

It was obviously quite impossible to cut losses at Gallipoli during the summer. No evacuation could have had a chance of success during the short nights. To remain merely on the defensive without the dispatch of reinforcements was almost equally impossible. For the Turks were steadily increasing their numbers, and a small advance anywhere must spell disaster to the cramped expeditionary force. Moreover, neither military nor public opinion would yet have dreamed of such an acquiescence in stalemate.

Great reinforcements were on their way to Hamilton; by the middle of August five new divisions would be at his disposal. Their dispatch three weeks earlier (which had been practicable) would have heightened the chances of success, for they could have been used immediately after the bloody failure of repeated Turkish attacks in early July.

Sir Ian's new plan was admirable and achieved com-

[1] E 14 under Com. Boyle, who sank a transport with 6,000 troops, and E 11 under Com. Nasmyth, who penetrated the harbour of Constantinople and sank a transport lying off the arsenal.

[2] Of 13 submarines, which made or attempted the passage, 8 were destroyed. They sank in all 1 battleship, 1 destroyer, 5 gun-boats, 11 transports, 44 steamers, and 148 sailing-ships. Figures quoted from Winston Churchill, *World Crisis 1915* (1923), pp. 421–2.

plete surprise at its most vital point. Some three miles to the north of Anzac was the deeply indented horseshoe bay of Suvla, where almost uninterrupted sandy beaches afforded easy landing-ground for a large force. This area appeared to be unfortified and practically unoccupied. After the landing had been effected the fresh divisions, in conjunction with the Australians at Anzac, were to converge on the great hills of the Anafarta range, thus turning the whole Turkish right and dominating the Narrows. Meanwhile a strong holding attack at Helles was to pin the enemy to his ground, and perhaps attract reserves; while the fleet demonstrated in the Gulf of Enos against that most sensitive spot Bulair. Secrecy of objective was excellently maintained. The organization for landing had been perfected after the lessons of April 25th. The big covered barges known as 'beetles', with their own engines, each holding 500 men, quadrupled the rate at which troops could be set on shore. Arrangements for water and ammunition supply had been greatly improved.

On August 6th[1] when the battle started Hamilton had about 110,000 effectives;[2] the enemy perhaps 10,000 less. The margin by which a decision was missed was very narrow. The principal cause of the failure lay outside Hamilton's control—it lay in the quality of the commanders, whom he had neither chosen nor desired.

A cynic might plausibly maintain that if Sir Bryan Mahon had not been such a senior soldier, success would have been won. For Mahon, who commanded the 10th division, was a very senior Lieutenant-General. Kitchener, with the traditional pedantry of military trade-unionism, rejected Hamilton's application for a young, energetic corps commander, such as Byng, and produced Stopford, an elderly and decaying general who had never

[1] The date was chosen because the moon on that night rose two hours after midnight, the landing therefore would be shrouded in darkness but the advance would be illuminated.

[2] Of the five new divisions, three belonging to the New Army had arrived and were used on the 6th. The remaining two (territorials) would be available after August 10.

commanded troops in war. To this man was entrusted the decisive landing on an unknown shore by night with raw troops.

Hamilton's orders were as usual based on an excessive optimism, partly psychological, partly due to his ignorance of the ground. The Anzacs were expected to break out to the north of their existing line and to seize the dominating heights during the first night. Between them stretched a 'mad-looking country', a tangled mass of ravines, spurs, and precipices. Most of the men were suffering from dysentery, and the task was for many units almost a physical impossibility. Tremendous struggles raged during the next four days for the possession of the heights, which were never completely in British possession.[1] To Mustapha Kemal fell the honour of personally leading the successful counter-attack on Chunuk which swept the last decisive vantage-point from our precarious grasp. The most cherished scene of all this fighting was the capture of the famous 'Lone Pine trench' by the 1st Australian brigade. The pine-log roofing of this work were torn away by the attackers, who then leapt down and engaged in a grisly bayonet struggle along the dark galleries. Seven Victoria Crosses were awarded for this episode alone.

The Turks just held fast at Anzac. But it would have availed them nothing if the landing at Suvla had not been submerged under the timidity and apathy of its leaders. At daybreak on the 7th our superiority was already nearly six to one, by sunset nearly fifteen. The wretched Stopford had lost confidence in the plan before it was launched. During the critical hours immediately following the landing he slept on the vessel, where he remained for two more days. The only recorded glimpse of his activity ashore was the superintendence of a splinter-proof shelter for his head-quarters on the beach. Naturally this same spirit sapped his senile subordinates. Counter-orders succeeded

[1] The leadership here is open to severe criticism. The attacks on Chanak were not co-ordinated. Godley who was in command of the Anzacs spent most of his time on a destroyer.

one another; the commanders evaded responsibility by delay, the brigadiers quarrelled. Numbers of intact troops lay along the shore bivouacking or bathing. Forty-eight hours elapsed without any appreciable addition to the enemy's strength; for Liman, solicitous as ever for the safety of Bulair, had retained two divisions there until the British plan had been made fully manifest. Hamilton, always generous in the discretion which he allowed to subordinates, did not emerge from Imbros until the afternoon of the 8th. The goad finally applied to the sluggish Hammersley commanding the 11th division came too late. The Turks just won the race for the heights, and the disorganized, dispirited army was pent into the plain, never to emerge. Many excuses were advanced to justify the failure. The shortage of guns and ammunition was of secondary importance in an attack on scattered posts, barely entrenched. The thick scrub doubtless concealed snipers and impeded progress, but afforded no insuperable difficulty to resolute men. The lack of water was partly due to mismanagement by the Navy, but was aggravated by the indiscipline of individuals who cut the hose-pipes with knives, and could have been overcome by an advance into the hills, where wells were abundant. 'Young troops and old generals', as Hamilton afterwards said, would not combine. If the Suvla force had been stiffened by the 29th division, though by now weakened by its losses, and directed by Hunter-Weston, whose bulldog tenacity rejected even palpable defeat, it could scarcely have failed. Success, as our enemies admit, would have forced the evacuation of the spine of the peninsula, and brought us to the Narrows. The Turkish forces, except any portion which might have escaped to the Asiatic shore, would have been cooped in the toe, and must have surrendered, unless reinforcements from Thrace had been able to smash the barrier. The political consequences in the Balkan States might well have forced Turkey out of the war.

The expedition was now doomed, for the autumn offensive in France devoured all available men; but it had a long agony. The spirit of the troops was low: they believed that they had been uselessly sacrificed; the Anzacs complained that they had been let down by the British. Almost all were distressed by chronic dysentery;[1] their rations were dully monotonous, and scarcely any canteen supplies, so plentiful in France, were available. Parcels from home often arrived with their contents ground to an unrecognizable powder; mails were erratic.

By the middle of September the Russian armies had been reduced to impotence, and Falkenhayn was planning the destruction of Serbia. Bulgaria was mobilizing, and the imminent threat could not be ignored by the Entente. On September 25th the decision was taken to send an army to Salonika. The French had always disliked the Dardanelles expedition, largely because it was under British command. The Government had already appointed Sarrail to a non-existent army of the East. This intriguer, styled 'the only Republican General', had been dismissed by Joffre in July; but, as he commanded 100 Radical-Socialist votes in the Chamber, he could not be jettisoned. Hence the opening for him in Salonika was greedily grasped. Evacuation was now in the air. Hamilton, who had stigmatized it as 'unthinkable', was recalled on October 16th. A fortnight later Monro, the solid, cautious commander of an army in France, arrived. His orderly mind was horrified at the confusion and congestion of the defences. Within twenty-four hours he sent home an adverse report—of which Churchill said in a cruelly brilliant phrase, 'He came, he saw, he capitulated'. This extreme haste was, however, due to Kitchener's peremptory order. The latter had at first repudiated Monro with indignation, but a visit to the peninsula swung him reluctantly round to the same opinion. The Cabinet had by now lost all faith in Gallipoli; they would not break with the French by abandoning the great camp springing up at Salonika, though this was already too late to save the encircled Serbs; they would not

[1] Of seven battalions of Anzacs examined in September, 5 per cent. had weak hearts, 78 per cent. dysentery, and 64 per cent. sores on the skin.

sanction the plan drawn up by the ardent and chivalrous Commodore Keyes for forcing a sudden entry into the Marmara, even when it received the approval of the new naval commander Wemyss (December 10). A final decision was overdue, for a frightful blizzard at the end of November had laid 15,000 men low with frost-bite; and winter storms might be expected to interfere increasingly with sea-borne communications at the very time when a direct passage for German munitions had been opened to Constantinople by the conquest of Serbia.

That evacuation must cost enormous losses was the almost universal view; even Monro had estimated it at 30 per cent. of the garrison, or 40,000 men. The Turks, however, were themselves nearly worn out and were completely deceived by the cunning co-operation of the two arms. The unmolested escape of the Helles force, three weeks after Suvla and Anzac had been cleared, seemed so inexplicable that rumours freely circulated of bribes taken by the Turks. Though enormous stores were abandoned, almost all the guns were removed and scarcely a casualty was incurred. The scheme was a masterpiece of ingenuity, and its details are fascinating.[1] The news was received in England and by the army in France with intense relief and even enthusiasm, being acclaimed like a victory.

[1] See Brig.-Gen. C. Aspinall-Oglander, *Military Operations: Gallipoli*, vol. i (1929), ch. xxxi.

XIV

THE COLLAPSE OF THE ENTENTE PLANS IN THE BALKANS IN 1915

FALKENHAYN, as we have seen, had long determined to destroy Serbia in the autumn of 1915. Until the route to Constantinople should be under German control, the capacity of Turkey to remain in the Alliance was doubtful. In spite of the Russian defeat, Rumania was allowing only a niggardly ration of ammunition to pass over her railways. Shells for the heavy howitzers, it is related, were sometimes smuggled in beer-barrels. Conrad was no less anxious for a final reckoning, for the Austrians had to avenge the lamentable loss of prestige incurred by two complete defeats. Moreover, since Italy had become an enemy, the threat to Bosnia had a greater strategic significance. If the Italians should succeed in breaking through towards Klagenfürt, the pressure of the Serbs on the eastern flanks might be highly dangerous.

But obviously the attack on Serbia required the co-operation of Bulgaria. All through this year she had been persistently wooed and cajoled by both sides. It is highly improbable that anything would have induced her to join the Entente except the capture of Constantinople. Her people burned with indignation against the Serbs, who had deprived them in 1913 of that part of Macedonia which they regarded as their just recompense for their sacrifices in the Turkish war. Their King Ferdinand, a Coburg by birth, one of the wickedest and most astute of European diplomatists, cherished an intense hatred against Russia, whom he regarded as responsible for the disaster of 1913. He is reported to have said to Alfonso of Spain at their meeting in Vienna in December 1913: 'I will avenge myself upon Russia, and my vengeance will be terrible.' In any case the Entente was quite unable to induce Serbia and Greece to make such territorial sacrifices as might alone pave the way to Balkan unity. The

Russian Foreign Office, better informed on Balkan questions, had no illusions about the intentions of Ferdinand such as Grey cherished down to the very last moment; but it could do nothing to combat them. The thrifty Bulgars would not look at promises of Turkish territory contingent on a victory, which faded every week into a more blurred improbability.

The Central Powers, on the other hand, were in a position to deliver the goods. On September 6th a military convention was concluded, by which Bulgaria received at once a strip of Thracian territory on the Maritza from Turkey, and was given a free hand in Macedonia in return for her undertaking to declare war on Serbia. A cautious proviso was inserted by which her entry was to take place four days later than the combined Austro-German attack on that country from the north.

The Serbian Government soon got wind of this decision, and begged the Entente to permit an attack upon the Bulgarians while in the act of mobilization. This, however, was refused on grounds of political prudence. This inhibition has been severely criticized, but it is very doubtful whether permission would have benefited Serbia, whose army now consisted of barely 200,000 men, or less by a quarter than the Bulgarian strength. It is practically impossible that the latter should have been decisively defeated in time to allow a shifting of strength against Mackensen's array upon the Danube. In any event such an anticipation of Bulgaria's action would have made it impossible for Serbia to invoke the defensive treaty concluded with Greece in 1913 which was held by Venizelos (the Greek Prime Minister) and the Entente to have now come into force.

The Staffs of the three attacking armies had to plaster a good many cracks in their co-operation. Conrad most tactlessly showed that in his view the Bulgars were auxiliaries rather than equal allies. Jekoff, their Chief-of-Staff, curtly refused to serve under Austrian direction, and made it clear that his country had confidence only in German efficiency. This suited Falkenhayn well. He had already strengthened his position by boldly making up a deficiency in the Austrian quota of troops with divisions withdrawn from the West, even while the great September battles were impending. Finally, he got his way on the essential points. Mackensen was placed in command of all the invading troops except the Bulgarian southern army and the Austrian contingent in Bosnia, both of which were to act independently. The supreme strategical direction was in effect, though not formally, conceded to the German Staff.

This time the weight of Teutonic invasion was to be directed from the north across the two great rivers, Save and Danube. Such was the parting advice of the unfortunate Potiorek, whose two earlier efforts from Bosnia had died away among the central mountains before reaching Serbia's spinal cord, the Morava Valley. 'Next time', he said, 'go by Belgrade.' The Bulgars were to move west in two armies against the railway, the former striking at Nish, and the latter at Uskub, the southern key to the kingdom, where the two lines from the north met on the upper Vardar. Thus the Serbian army, if not already destroyed, would be cut off from an asylum in Greece, and driven into the inhospitable savagery of the Albanian mountains.

If Venizelos had had his way the door to the south might have remained open. The Greek army had been mobilized for months and was ready. But as soon as he had given permission for an Anglo-French landing at Salonika, and declared that Greece accepted the obligations of the Serbian treaty, he was dismissed by King Constantine. The disembarkation of troops had been arranged with Venizelos, in fulfilment of an Allied promise to send 150,000 men to buttress the Greco-Serbian alliance. A formal protest had been made to safeguard Greek sovereign rights, and to deceive the Central Powers, but every facility had been given by the authorities.

The attitude of Constantine was very natural. The

majority of the population at that time certainly did not wish to be dragged into a general war. His earlier offer of military aid to force the Dardanelles had been selfishly refused by Russia. The obligation towards Serbia was disputed by lawyers, who asserted that its validity was confined to a purely Balkan struggle, while Serbia was quite unable to fulfil one of the terms, which bound her to maintain 150,000 troops in southern Macedonia. He regarded Venizelos with jealousy as a dictator, with suspicion as the creature of the Entente, and distrusted his excitable and enthusiastic temperament. Finally, he believed in the triumph of Germany, and was confirmed in these views by his wife, the Kaiser's sister. Yet to have come out in open hostility to the Entente was quite impossible, as the British navy could have speedily reduced Greece to starvation by a blockade. He aimed therefore at preserving a neutrality just benevolent enough to avoid serious trouble with France and England, while protesting to Germany that his actions were dictated by *force majeure*. The action of the Entente has often been compared in Germany to the violation of Belgian neutrality, especially as England, France, and Russia were the guarantors of Greek independence. It is obvious, however, that the original landing arranged with the Greek Premier, to enable his country to fulfil its treaty engagements, is in a quite different category. It is doubtless true that the Allied troops would not have been withdrawn after the fall of Venizelos, even if Constantine had made a formal demand.[1] Actually he did nothing of the sort, and for some time allowed the co-operation of Greek officials with those of the Entente. But the later developments of Allied policy, ranging from the seizure of Corfu (declared perpetually neutral in 1863) as a recuperating base for the Serbian army, to the bombardment of Athens and

[1] It has been held that the clause in the constitution of the Kingdom of Greece (1830), by which no one of the protecting Powers was to land troops without the consent of the other two, gave a right to such landing (if all were agreed) without the consent of Greece. The three protecting Powers were Great Britain, France, and Russia.

deposition of Constantine, have no defence in international law. They are simply acts of state dictated solely by the presumed interests of their authors under the same maxim invoked by Bethmann-Hollweg on August 4th, 1914: 'Necessity knows no law.'

The Allies could be in no position to bring effective succour to Serbia unless a decision had been instantly taken, to evacuate Gallipoli in the latter half of September. The two divisions which disembarked at Salonika had a combined strength of only 13,000. The British contingent had been rushed from the peninsula in its summer equipment, and faced the rigours of a Balkan autumn in khaki shorts. Their presence had no influence upon the course of the campaign, which was rigorously pushed to its inevitable conclusion.

The German-Austrian crossing of the rivers was begun on October 7th. For many months Colonel Hentsch, of Marne notoriety, had made an elaborate survey of landing-places, assembly-points, and battery-positions, into which Mackensen's preparations fitted with extreme precision. The Danube being connected by canal with the principal German rivers, it was easy to collect a vast quantity of steamers, barges, and lighters for the passage of the army. The fire of massed artillery drove Admiral Troubridge's launches off the river, where they had been for long a continual thorn, and overpowered the defenders on the southern bank, who were weakly strung out and uncertain as to the points of crossing. Belgrade fell two days later, and 250,000 men were soon on Serbian soil on wide fronts on either side of the capital. Bridging operations were hindered by the storm-wind called Kossovo, which blew incessantly, so that only two had been completed by October 21st. Yet the position of the Serbians was quite hopeless. They had been obliged to divide their forces and were outnumbered by two to one by both the invading armies. While their northern forces were being driven into the centre of the country, the Bulgars were easily able to close the Vardar Valley. Mackensen had hoped to force them to a battle of annihilation, as even German thoroughness found the difficulties of transport over the mountains almost insurmountable. A half-company of infantry had sometimes to be harnessed to a gun, when the native oxen were not obtainable.

By the middle of November the remnants of the Serbian army were in full flight towards the mountains of Albania, dragging with them 25,000 unhappy Austrians, the prisoners of their earlier victory. In their train followed a great concourse of the population, escaping from the savagery of the Bulgars and Austrians. The words 'Pray that your flight be not in the winter' can never have been more appropriate. The first snow fell heavily on November 17th. Mackensen desisted from his pursuit of the dwindling remnant, but the Bulgars pressed on implacably. Harried by Albanian brigands, frozen and decimated by typhus, less than 100,000 fighting men reached the Albanian coast, whence the British and Italian navies conveyed them to Corfu, an island which had been commandeered by the Entente for their recuperation. A party of British nurses organized by the Women's Suffrage Society shared all the horrors of the retreat.

The weak Franco-British forces which had advanced up the Vardar were driven back behind the Greek frontier, the crossing of which by the Bulgars was vetoed by Germany. The Greeks would certainly have opposed their entry, and the Entente would have seen their desire fulfilled. Conrad, it is true, vehemently urged an attack on Salonika, and on Falkenhayn's refusal reproached him with betraying the Alliance. A complete breach between the two followed, until Conrad was induced to write a letter of qualified apology. Falkenhayn insisted that not a single German soldier should be left 'to die of hunger and typhus in this inhospitable land' unless a real strategical advantage could be obtained, and he wholly denied that it was possible. The Bulgars could never be induced to fight on other fronts, whereas the Franco-British force could be pinned down, marooned one might almost say, and unable to affect the decision in the Western Front. For this reason German satirists derisively nicknamed Salonika 'the greatest Allied internment camp'. Such also was the view of the British General Staff, which constantly urged evacuation upon the Government. The French, however, under the inspiration of Briand, always powerfully attracted by the Balkans, treated the question as a test of the solidarity of the Alliance. Joffre, whose command had just been extended to this area, actually threatened his resignation if the British persisted in withdrawal. Far from being diminished, the new expedition was immensely swollen during the winter. Within the great entrenched camp, where the army remained until the summer of 1916, Sarrail, the unpopular Commander-in-Chief,[1] issued orders to the contingents of five different nations: French, British, Italian, Serbian, and Russian. Greek sovereignty inevitably sank to an ever lower ebb in the occupied area. Dangerous friction could be avoided only by complete submission to the will of the Allies.

In the light of the Bulgarian collapse in September 1918, German military writers often express the view that Conrad was right in demanding an immediate assault in December while the zone was practically unfortified and its garrison scarcely exceeded 50,000. This could have been delivered only by the Bulgars—as Mackensen's troops would have taken weeks to concentrate—and if it should be opposed by the Greeks, as was probable, would have been a rash gamble. Later on, as the experienced von Seeckt conclusively showed, an offensive would have required several months intensive preparation for siege-warfare, on a scale quite beyond the resources of the Central Powers without endangering their most vital interests elsewhere.

The Salonika expedition had two constant disadvantages. The Vardar and Struma valleys, through which the

[1] He was not officially recognized as such, except for the defence of the entrenched camp, until July 1916.

advanced lines ran, were exceedingly unhealthy in summer. Malaria and paratyphoid were endemic, and the proportion of sickness was higher than in any other theatre of war except Gallipoli. Secondly, the strain on British shipping involved in its maintenance grew steadily more serious. Enemy submarines were now particularly active in the Mediterranean. Not only were losses heavy, but much time was consumed in the circuitous voyages to circumvent the menace. It is amazing that the British navy was able to guarantee, and the merchant service to provide for, four overseas forces,[1] numbering in all more than a million men, besides the B.E.F., at the very peak of shipping destruction in the spring of 1917, without inflicting cruel hardship on the population at home.

Though Salonika was unassailable the Austrians reaped a modest success by subduing Montenegro. This little mountain nest above the Adriatic had a population of merely 250,000, but every man was a fighter from youth to age. King Nicholas, the descendant of the Prince-Bishops who had always defied the Turk, was a picturesquely appropriate head. He was a poet as well as a crowned brigand and a subterranean diplomatist, who had married one daughter to the King of Italy, and two more to Russian Grand Dukes. He had set the first match to the Balkan War of 1912 by declaring war on Turkey before any of his greater partners. Hitherto he had ardently supported Serbia. But he now clearly thought that the game was up. The impregnable mountain fortress of Lovchen, which overlooks the Bocche di Cattaro, one of the Austrian flotilla-bases on the Dalmatian coast, was surrendered after a mere show of resistance. Nicholas fled to France protesting his loyalty to the Allies, and left his son Danilo to make his peace with the Austrians. The old king lived in France for several years after the war on a small pension. His daughters for some time worked as dressmakers in Paris. The fate of the Montenegrins after the war was hard. Their individuality was merged in

[1] Salonika, Egypt, Mesopotamia, and East Africa.

Yugoslavia. They kicked against the pricks, and were repressed by the overmastering Serbs with extreme cruelty.

After the subjection of Montenegro, the Austrians pushed into the middle of Albania in order to circumvent the Italian ambition to control this most turbulent and warlike of European nations. The ports of Avlona and Durazzo were already in Italian hands to ensure control over the mouth of the Adriatic. A little mountain war of no significance continued until the Armistice. The Austrians there, under their genial old general Pflanzer-Balltin, cut off from authentic news, will go down to history as the last army of the ancient empire. A fortnight after the whole fabric had dissolved, the commander celebrated the birthday of the Emperor Karl with a ceremonial parade, the last act of the old order.

XV

VERDUN

THE past year had been one of harsh disappointment for the Entente: they had enjoyed good success in none of their undertakings great or small. Unity of command was impossible; as Lloyd George said in March 1918, any government which had proposed at an earlier date that its troops should be commanded by foreigners would have fallen instantly. Unity of direction, hitherto so sadly lacking, offered no such impossibility of principle. The difficulty was to unite in a common agreement three great Powers so widely differing in needs, aims, capacities, and government, and geographically prevented from combining forces at will. The democratic governments of England and France had to secure the support of Parliament, and were sensitive to the supposed breath of public opinion. The Russian autocracy was riddled with intrigue and corruption. Italy at present was allowed to wage her own war, without either let or help; and until she declared war against Germany her influence on major strategy must be feeble.

Again, even if unity of direction were nominally achieved, would its purpose in action be loyally maintained against the urgent push of so many private temptations assailing each member of the Alliance?

Broadly speaking, the Allied Governments accepted the principles laid down at the Chantilly Military Conference in December 1915. The 'principal fronts' were defined as those where the enemy maintained the largest part of his forces: Eastern (Russia), Western (France), Southern (Italy). Co-ordinated offensives on these three were to seek a decision with the available maximum of men and material. Only the minimum of effectives were to be retained in subsidiary theatres. The expedition to Salonika was to preserve its existing strength, and Egypt was to be adequately defended. This scheme was powerfully supported in England by the new Chief of the Imperial General Staff, Sir W. Robertson, a massive and dogged North Countryman who had risen from the ranks. He both stood up to and worked harmoniously with Kitchener, who had treated his predecessors as little more than exalted clerks.[1] Haig was also in cordial agreement with them, and as a result the influence of the Cabinet over military policy in 1916 was probably weaker than at any other period of the war. It was obvious, however, that this grandiose scheme could not be put into operation for many months. The equipment of the Russian armies could only be gradually effected by the devious route of the White Sea. Archangel was the only European port connected by rail with Petrograd, though a line was crawling painfully towards Murmansk, the building of which through the marshes cost the lives of at least 40,000 prisoners of war, inhumanly slave-driven.

Kitchener was also determined that the British effort this year should not be immaturely squandered, and July was the earliest date which he would allow for its employment. Voluntary recruiting was drying up, and it was recognized that compulsion must be adopted, if the existing formations were to be kept up to strength. No important results from conscription, which was voted in March 1916, could be expected till the late summer.

These considerations were not fully known to the Central Powers. But Falkenhayn, whose influence in directing their combined strategy was far greater than that of any single man in the Entente, knew how vital time was against an enemy in the West who was drawing freely on the immeasurable material resources of the United States.

The position of our enemies was, indeed, momentarily and superficially brilliant. All its members were geo-

[1] He obtained from Kitchener the very important concession that the C.I.G.S. should sign all strategical orders sent to the commanders of armies abroad. Subject to the authority of the Cabinet, he thus practically secured the strategical direction of the war, as waged by Great Britain.

graphically connected as soon as Serbia had been ground to powder. Great tracts of fertile territory in northern France and Poland were available for foodstuffs, nearly two million Russian prisoners eased the increasing strain on man-power. The malevolent neutrality of Rumania had been changed by fear into a complaisance which resulted in a favourable agreement for the export of grain and oil, without which Falkenhayn thought it doubtful whether Germany could have lasted throughout 1916. The British blockade, though always increasing in rigidity, had not prevented enormous imports of cotton, and the leakage through neutrals, in particular Holland, remained gratifyingly large.

To await the combined attack of the Entente was too dangerous. Even if all its assaults were shattered, Falkenhayn did not believe that 'the enormous hold' which England had over her allies would be destroyed, 'For she is obviously staking everything on a war of exhaustion'; and exhaustion must come first to the Central Powers. The only means by which he thought that England might be brought directly to her knees, unrestricted submarine warfare, was refused him on political grounds. Now, an attack on the British armies in France could not be begun early enough in the year, and would require the unattainable figure of thirty divisions.[1] England therefore must be struck through France, 'her best sword', as speedily as possible; if France went, Russia, already crippled and almost ripe for revolution, must follow and England would be left alone amidst incalculable hazards.

Falkenhayn had increased his forces in the West since the September battles by 400,000 men, and could count on a reserve of 25½ divisions. Though still outnumbered by three to two, he believed himself strong enough to

[1] Prince Rupprecht, however, expressed the opinion that a breakthrough against the British had much better chances of success than against the French at Verdun. See *Mein Kriegstagebuch*, vol. i, p. 420. For it he demanded 'at least 12 Army Corps'. South of Arras all three positions could be bombarded effectively without the necessity of moving the artillery forward; consequently he desired an attack in that area.

attack, given his superiority in numbers of heavy guns, and in the technique of their disposition and handling.

A narrow front was to be chosen against an objective 'to retain which the French General Staff would be compelled to throw in every man they have'. A break-through was not necessary; if the battle were kept alive with limited resources, the French forces would bleed to death.[1] He hoped also that the 'defeatist' movement in France, of

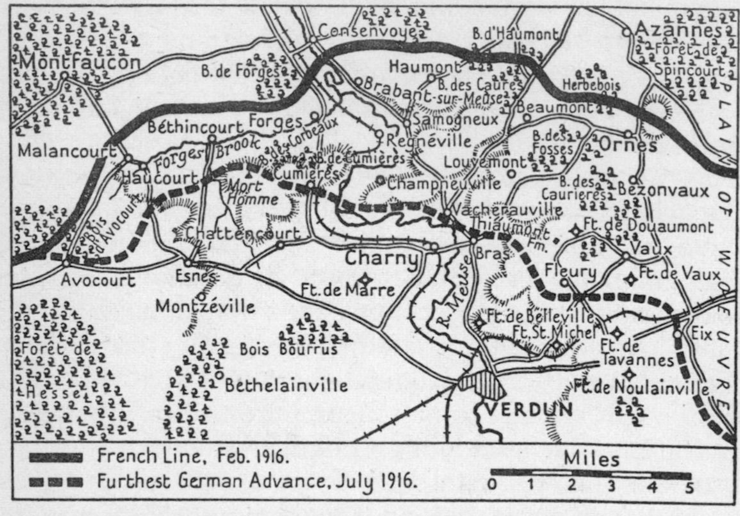

MAP 16. Verdun.

whose existence he was well aware, would meanwhile gather strength to sap the national spirit; and that the British armies might waste a raw strength in premature relief-attacks. For this experiment he selected Verdun. The famous fortress was already half encircled by the German lines, their communications were excellent, and those of the French were wretched. Success would add prestige to the name of the Crown Prince, within whose command the battle was to be fought. Verdun was incon-

[1] The account given by Falkenhayn in his book (*General Head-quarters 1914–16* (1919)) has been confirmed by the German General Staff, which proves that his aim was not a strategic break-through. It has been frequently affirmed, in particular by French writers (e.g. Pétain), that he untruthfully minimized his intentions to excuse his failure.

veniently near the vital railway-centre of Metz, and the great Briey–Thionville iron basin, the principal source of German shell production; and, although Falkenhayn did not regard extensive conquest of territory as his main object, he naturally hoped to thrust the enemy right off the Côtes de Meuse on to an improvised line between Saint-Mihiel and the Argonne.

He was right in believing that Verdun, quite apart from its military value, would become like Ypres a mystical symbol of life for the whole French people.[1] But he did not see that for this very reason it would become increasingly impossible to break off or limit the battle without inflicting a moral wound, hardly less deep, on his own country. The Crown Prince was therefore unquestionably correct when he vainly demanded that the initial operation should be launched simultaneously on both flanks of the Meuse with the object of pinching out the fortress by a rapid and irresistible encirclement. In the light of French unpreparedness this would almost certainly have succeeded. But Falkenhayn would not release more than six divisions, and his blow fell upon the right bank only.

We must now turn our eyes to the defenders of the threatened fortress. It had been constructed after 1870 by de Rivière as the most important link in the whole great chain defending the Meuse and Moselle. It had been almost surrounded, though not directly attacked, in September 1914. Though the enemy still clung round it in a great arc from north-west to south-east, the defending trenches had been thrust out far beyond the forts about eight miles from the city. It was therefore in practice held like any other salient in the West. But until August 1915 it remained technically a fortress, which meant that its commander was directly responsible to the Generalissimo, and that the armament and supplies for each fort were

[1] Its fall on September 1, 1792, had aroused the keenest alarm in revolutionary Paris and had led directly to the September massacre. It was on this occasion that Danton roused his countrymen to such a pitch of ardour with the famous words: 'De l'audace, encore de l'audace, toujours de l'audace, et la France est sauvée.'

maintained at full strength. After that date the French fortresses were degraded by decree,[1] on the ground that they had proved mere traps and might be written off as fallen, if invested. Moreover, French production of heavy guns was still insufficient; and a very large number could be transferred from the forts to the field-army.[2] Verdun, however, was still recognized as a point of exceptional importance, and retained a special commander for the so-called 'Fortified Region'. His position was one of complicated semi-dependence, first on the southern, then on the central, group of French armies. The change to the latter, though corresponding to the strategical situation, was effected only three weeks before the German attack, and the new head-quarters were almost ignorant of the local conditions.

The defences of the region had been gravely neglected during 1915, when an almost uninterrupted calm prevailed there. In December Colonel Driant, a local deputy who commanded a regiment near Verdun, informed the Army Commission, of which he was a member, of this neglect. They verified his information and brought it before the Government. Galliéni, Joffre's old superior in Madagascar, now Minister of War, demanded an explanation. The Commander-in-Chief replied in his harshest and most crushing style that the arrangements were satisfactory, and that if complaints were laid against him on information supplied by subordinate officers he would at once resign. Though ministers were rapidly losing confidence in him, they were quite unprepared for the effect of such an action on France and the Entente. His assurances were accepted, but Castelnau, perhaps the most subtle, charming, and tactful of French generals, was made Chief-of-Staff to control him as far as possible (which proved indeed to be very little).

[1] This was illegal, as constitutionally a law was required. The procedure adopted was doubtless in order to secure secrecy.

[2] More than 4,000 guns were taken from the forts, of which 2,300 were heavy, nearly all of old pattern dating from the 80's and 90's.

As usually happens when a misleading answer has been given by one in authority, steps were taken, too late, to make it true. Joffre certainly believed that Verdun was impregnable. 'I ask only one thing,' he said on January 16th, 'that the Germans should attack and should do so at Verdun. Tell the Government so.'

This arrogant confidence was, however, far from shared by the local general, Herr, an artilleryman with a good record, who took command some six months before the battle. He complained that his troops were too few and often of inferior quality, and that he was not given enough engineering material to complete the defences. Castelnau, who inspected them in January, found many weak points, but was comparatively well satisfied with those on the right bank. Herr had expected an attack since December, for increasing activity was observed on the enemy's railways, roads, and billeting centres, but G.Q.G.[1] preferred to believe that if an offensive was really intended its theatre would be Champagne, where exactly the same symptoms were being reported. Consequently Herr received no reinforcements except two territorial divisions, who were intended to dig rather than to fight. Mercifully for France, the attack was postponed for a week owing to bad weather. During this respite the bridges over the Meuse were increased, and the road from Bar-le-Duc to Verdun repaired and reserved for exclusive and continuous military motor traffic. This was actually completed by noon on February 22nd. Without it Verdun would have been doomed. For the French railway system here consisted of only one narrow-gauge line, the great line to Paris being under continuous fire in the Argonne. The enemy concentration on the right bank was on the contrary abundantly supplied by fourteen lines. Fortunately Verdun and its bridges were entirely shielded from German observation (except, of course, from the air). On the right bank the gaunt hills rise steeply 500 or 600 feet, forming a plateau five miles wide, deeply scarred by ravines. The

[1] Grand-Quartier-Général. The official name for French Head-quarters.

squat, grey concrete forts marked all the key-features within five miles of the citadel. The front line was about eight miles away along a broken and wooded line of transverse heights, descending sharply east and south-east of the city into the wide Woevre plain towards the Moselle. On the left bank the trough through which the Meuse runs in long, shallow loops is confined by no cliff-like wall. The hills are lower and take rather the form of successive spurs from the Argonne, thrusting towards the stream at right angles. Verdun was barred on the north-west by three successive promontories before the outposts were reached on the wooded slopes beyond the marshy banks of the Forges brook. The German preparations could not be entirely hidden, though the Staff took every conceivable precaution for secrecy, and French aerial observation was hindered by the dense woods, the winter weather, and the advent of the 'Fokkers', which soon gained superiority in the air. But when the attack broke, they were still believed to be incomplete, as the enemy had dug few extra communication trenches, and no assaulting trenches in advance of his old lines, though in some cases his infantry would have to traverse a no-man's-land of 1,000 yards. The German plans, however, did not aim at the unloosing of dense waves of troops. A solution seemed to have been reached for the vital problem of conquering the ground by the artillery and then occupying it with infantry. The Entente generals had erred by making their bombardments too long and not methodical enough. A bombardment of eight hours, plentifully interspersed with gas and lachrymatory shells, should give time to shatter the hostile artillery, and completely to obliterate the local garrison, and yet not allow time for reinforcements to arrive within the threatened zone. The Crown Prince disposed of 1,400 guns for a front of attack barely eight miles wide; half of these were heavy, and included the famous Austrian 15-inch Skoda howitzer. Massed in the forests, often wheel to wheel, their numbers astonished the French, whose aviators found it impossible to count the continuous flashes. On

February 20th, after a week's continuous snow-storm, the wind veered north with a binding frost. Next morning at 4.30 the enemy threw one symbolic 15-inch shell into the citadel, and three hours later the hurricane bombardment began. It far exceeded in tempestuous violence anything yet seen in the world, and two million shells were expended before the infantry began to creep forward in the fading light. Patrols of fifteen to fifty men led by an officer first emerged, testing any elements of resistance still left alive; if all was found well, dense lines followed with pioneers in their train to occupy and consolidate the deserted trenches. If necessary, the guns were signalled to complete their work. Thus it was hoped methodically to win ground with the minimum of loss. To French observers this steady advance through the darkness, heralded by salvoes of parti-coloured flares, suggested an irresistible power. The French resistance was uneven, and depended largely on the spirit of the local leaders. Colonel Driant's chasseurs under his splendid inspiration fought like lions, and lost nine-tenths of their effectives. Until the evening of February 23rd the Germans had small reason for boasting. They had advanced little more than two miles, and taken only 3,000 prisoners, in spite of a sevenfold superiority in guns and threefold in men. Next day the second main French position, the only continuous line left, was broken through. The local command thought the evacuation of the whole right bank unavoidable, but was deterred by an express order from Joffre, who threatened any general giving the order to retreat with a council of war. Castelnau proceeded to Verdun during that night and found Herr's head-quarters greatly cast down and confused. He at once sent for Pétain to take command. This officer, a colonel at the beginning of the war, had already risen to command an army. With all the firmness and calm of Joffre, he had none of his unapproachableness and love of publicity. He was a true soldier of France, absolutely unspotted by politics, always giving his real opinion bluntly without respect of persons, with a wonderful understanding of the *poilu* in all his moods; probably no one else would have lifted him out of the deep waters of mutiny in 1917.

While he was yet on his way, the Germans triumphantly published to the world a resounding new success, the fall of 'the great armoured-fort of Douaumont, the north-eastern pillar of the defences of Verdun'.

One of Herr's last orders had been to organize a defence *à outrance* on the line of the outer forts. The circulation of this order had been delayed both by the general confusion and by the pedantry of a staff officer who insisted on accompanying it with a sketch-map. The troops had constantly been warned that the forts were death-traps; they had seen them dismantled; they noticed that they attracted the hottest bombardment, and kept well away from them. Yet as a matter of fact, they showed an astonishing resistance to the heaviest shells;[1] their casemates remained the surest asylum, even the two remaining gun-turrets in Douaumont had not been put out of action. After the catastrophe they were rearmed, permanently garrisoned, and became, as they should always have been, the nodal points of the defence. During the afternoon of the 25th an Algerian division defending the steep slopes of the ravine which Douaumont crowns, broke hopelessly before a massed German attack. A certain Lieutenant Brandis, of the 3rd Brandenburg regiment, saw the great bulk of the fort looming in the twilight above him. Pushing forward a patrol through the driving snow, he found it, to his amazement, apparently deserted with the drawbridge lowered. It proved to contain only a few elderly artillerymen with a caretaker. Other lost German soldiers trickled

[1] See the remarkable evidence supplied by Pétain, *La Bataille de Verdun: annexe*, pp. 143 sqq. and Gén. P. L. Palat, *La Grande Guerre sur le front occidental*, vol. x (1925), pp. 460–2. Douaumont received 120,000 shells but the subterranean works were intact. A visit to these forts, which are maintained in the same conditions as during the war, leaves a feeling of astonishment that they should ever have been evacuated; especially when the defensive value of an ordinary village with its cellars was a commonplace of trench-warfare.

in, until about 300 men had gathered inside. In so casual a fashion was won this towering position, which, as seen from the left bank, dominates the whole field of battle. The way to Verdun was open for a few hours. The French reserves had been held up to the last moment by G.Q.G., as the Operations Department, in which Joffre reposed particular confidence, had never believed the preparations on the Meuse to be more than a blind. Falkenhayn, however, had been almost equally niggardly. His resources had been preciously husbanded, and he would not allow the Crown Prince to draw upon them at discretion. He was, moreover, confidently expecting a British relief-offensive in the north. And on this very day, in answer to an urgent appeal from Joffre, Haig started to relieve the French 10th army on the Arras section, and extended his own front by about fifteen miles.

Thus ended the first and most critical stage of the battle. Pétain worked wonders both with the organization and the spirit of the troops. They justified to the letter his first simple message: 'Tenez ferme. J'ai confiance en vous.'

The transport problem had been solved with amazing success by the transformation of the road from Bar-le-Duc into a *route gardée* reserved solely for an endless chain of lorries mounting and descending, the route being 'disciplined' as exactly as is a military rail-road. 'L'automobile', it was justly said, 'a sauvé Verdun'. *La Voie sacrée* to-day is flanked by special kilometre-stones adorned with the laurel of victory. Day and night at intervals of fourteen seconds the lorries kept up their continuous labour, regular stations being arranged for the discharge of men and materials, regular crossings for the passage of troops; in the case of a break-down every lorry which could not be towed was thrown into the ditch. Vast bands of territorials and civilians were continuously engaged in road-repair with materials from local quarries.

A comparative pause of ten days ensued, while the Germans painfully moved their artillery forward over the slushy and disintegrated crater-field. Meanwhile, as the

Crown Prince had foreseen, the French artillery, massed with astonishing speed on the left bank, galled them incessantly with enfilade fire.

Before renewing the attack Falkenhayn considered seriously whether it should be broken off. He decided that it would take too long to stage another offensive, as for example against the British in their lengthened lines round Arras. The German losses had not as yet been severe, and the hope of crippling the French remained reasonably good. The Crown Prince agreed, on the understanding that the next phase should be transferred to the left bank. This move had been foreseen and feared by Pétain, who asked the reporting officer every morning 'What news of the left bank?' The renewal took place under conditions far more unfavourable for the enemy. The defenders were no longer outnumbered; they were inspired with the most devoted spirit of sacrifice, and believed in their commander. No surprise except of a local tactical nature was possible. From March 6th to April 10th the fighting beat in alternate pulses on either wing. On the left the French maintained a desperate hold on the long ridge, world-famous under its sinister name of *Mort Homme*, three miles south of their advanced positions. On the right the fort of Vaux, on its commanding spur overlooking the whole Woevre plain, prevented any serious progress towards the second line of forts, the last refuge of the defenders. The Germans could no longer economize men; they had to attack in dense waves which were met by constant counter-attacks. Their losses in this phase were probably not inferior to the French; 'the Hell of Verdun' became a by-word among the rank and file. On April 10th Pétain published an order to the troops which, after admitting that the enemy would doubtless attack again, concluded with the famous words 'Courage! On les aura!' Falkenhayn was again in a cruel dilemma. If he sought to break off, he feared that the French forces now 550,000 strong might themselves take the offensive, a course already being constantly urged by the optimistic Joffre. If, on the other hand, he continued, who could guarantee that the last stage might not leave him with a confessed and patent failure. The Crown Prince maintained that 'the fate of the French army would be decided at Verdun', and its offensive power broken by the exhaustion of its reserves, if Falkenhayn would provide sufficient troops for attacks on the great scale. This, however, was refused, although Falkenhayn insisted that the piecemeal battles should continue. The Crown Prince, unsupported by his own Chief-of-Staff, von Knobelsdorf, had to give way. It was known that the French divisions were relieved much more rapidly than the Germans and consequently their losses were exaggerated. Falkenhayn insisted that a division should be kept in the line, until absolutely exhausted, whereas Pétain found that moral was best maintained by a rapid interchange of units on the battle-front.[1]

Finally, better results were expected by the Germans from the new phosgene gas-shells which would be available in great quantities during May. On the other hand, all their 17- and 15-inch batteries had been destroyed, or put out of action, by the first week in April, ironically enough by French siege-guns, more than twenty years old.

Meanwhile the French, as they alternately boasted and complained, were fighting Germany single-handed. For the relief-attack, to which half-trained Russian masses were driven during March by Lake Narotch,[2] was utterly mown down, and two German divisions were actually transferred to the West.

Just before the next phase opened Pétain was transferred to the command of the Central Group of Armies. Joffre had become increasingly impatient of his demands for men, and believed him to have lost all sense of proportion. Nivelle took his place. His rise had been as rapid as that of his predecessor. His achievements at Verdun,

[1] By the end of April 42 French divisions had been engaged at Verdun with the losses of 133,000 men. The reserve to be employed on the Somme having fallen that time from 40 to 30. The corresponding number of German divisions was 30, of which several had been engaged three or four times.

[2] See Chapter xvii, p. 283.

both in defence and attack, during the next eight months, brought him amidst the highest expectation to the Supreme Command. His fall was swift and complete beyond that of any other great commander. Tall and handsome, young for his years (he was 58), winning in manner, and lucid and concise in exposition, daring and swift to seize an occasion, rivalling Foch as an apostle of the mystical moral power of the offensive, he gradually drew all eyes as the lucky general, the predestined liberator of the national territory. Throughout May an almost uninterrupted succession of ferocious local actions left the combatants practically on their original positions. Both sides, by economizing on the quiet sectors, had collected gigantic masses of guns and ammunition. One of the German bombardments on the Mort Homme covered the ridge with a dense cloud of smoke and gases which reached the astonishing height of 2,500 feet. The unfortunate French assault on Douaumont (May 23) was preceded by a preparation which cast 1,000 tons per day for a week on a patch of 150 acres. The number and strength of French counter-attacks increased, as Joffre had intended, under the more impetuous leadership of Nivelle. Though seldom successful, they discouraged the Crown Prince yet more, who appealed again fruitlessly to Falkenhayn to cut his losses.

Yet the fifth month, while the shadow of the Somme was lengthening before the enemy's eyes, and Brussilov was shattering the Austrian front, was to try the defenders more hardly than any period since the first February crisis. After repeated assaults lasting for a week the Germans succeeded in taking Fort Vaux (June 7). It was heroically defended by a battalion under Major Raynal, whom the Crown Prince received with honour as a captive, restoring his sword. For four days he held the vaults, while the enemy swarmed over its superstructure. They fired through the crevices, squirted gas and liquid flame, and let down baskets of bombs. The defenders could communicate only by pigeons. Their water, already putrid, failed entirely for the last forty-eight hours; some were actually reduced to drinking their urine. Their story has been written in true epic style by Henri Bordeaux, in *Les Derniers Jours du Fort de Vaux*.

The tenacity of the French troops showed signs of crumbling. Many of the young reinforcements, especially from the south, were already becoming infected with the defeatist propaganda, directed by the journalist Almereyda in the *Bonnet rouge*, which was to inflict an almost fatal injury on the war-will of France next year.

June 23rd was a day of great crisis. The enemy thrust forward with a great weight of men, gas, and guns to the slopes of the last ridge on the right bank surmounted by the forts of Froideterre and Souville. If they gained a footing thereon, Verdun would be untenable, for all the bridges over the Meuse would be under direct observation. All the arrangements for evacuation had been made; and Pétain, on whom as commander of the Army Group the ultimate responsibility lay, now sought permission to begin the transfer, which could not be completed under four days. But Joffre, knowing that the Somme bombardment was to start that day, gave the order to hold fast. On being informed that in the event of a further reverse, it might be necessary to abandon 600 guns and a vast material, he took the responsibility upon himself saying with that air of cheerful serenity, wherein his greatness lay: 'I have taken many others.'

Joffre was justified, for the danger was past, though the battle died very hard. It was not until the failure of a last attack on Souville (July 11) that the Crown Prince received a definite order henceforth to stand solely on the defensive.

The French, however, were not prepared to remain indefinitely quiescent within their confined lines. On October 24th and December 15th Nivelle launched two attacks, which were considered as classic models of the limited offensive. The German position as a defensive one was very bad, having at its rear a crater-zone some eight miles deep,[1] indescribably glutinous and wretched under the autumn rains. The troops, as Ludendorff discovered on his first visit, were sadly dejected. Both attacks were executed by Mangin, a most vehement warrior, the incarnation of battle, who had built up the black army in Africa. He was reputed careless of human life and nicknamed 'the Butcher'. Yet in both these attacks, especially the latter, the French casualties were low. In the first they took Douaumont, evacuated by a garrison semi-suffocated through the fumes of an explosion, and Vaux with 6,000 prisoners. By the second their lines were extended nearly two miles farther north; 11,000 prisoners and 115 guns fell into their hands. The French artillery technique had reached a brilliant pitch, for their gunners had learnt both from their adversaries and from the long schooling of the Somme battles.

The French could not fail to be familiar with the salient points in the trench system which had been so long in their hands, and every detail had been studied through aerial photographs. The heavy artillery played principally upon the dug-outs, whilst a so-called *tir d'interdiction* smothered the trench exits and the whole ground behind them, thereby preventing either the retirement of the garrison or the arrival of reinforcements. Finally, the infantry were protected by a creeping barrage, behind which they advanced at the rate of 100 metres every four minutes. No large attack had yet exploited so successfully the minute cooperation between the two arms.

By the end of the year the losses of the two armies before Verdun showed small discrepancy, being both in the neighbourhood of 350,000. In the main battle the French certainly suffered the more severely, probably in the proportion of four to three. Falkenhayn was justified in claiming that their offensive power had been enormously reduced,

[1] It has been calculated that about 23 million shells were fired by the two sides between February 21 and July 15. An extraordinary photograph of the crater-field round Thiaumont is reproduced in Gen. H. von Zwehl's *Maubeuge, Aisne–Verdun* (1921).

for they were able to place on the Somme on July 1st only twelve instead of forty divisions. It has often been argued that the events of that terrible day would have been very different, if this great mass had made the principal thrust south of the river. But neither September 1915 nor April 1917 give confidence in the French capacity to co-ordinate attacks on a great offensive front. Moreover, Falkenhayn would on this supposition have retained his own reserve intact to meet the menace.

On a balance then, Falkenhayn's strategical decision seems to have been correct. A campaign of annihilation against the Russians in 1916 would have been a blow wasted, for the seeds of revolution were already thickly sown. Conrad's scheme for an encirclement of the Italian armies by a double attack, from Tyrol and on the Isonzo, has received the qualified approval of a very able German military critic, General von Kuhl. If successful it would certainly have destroyed the Italian army far more effectually than did the blow at Caporetto; and might have forced Italy into a separate peace. But it would have been a dangerous gamble, even if sufficient troops had been available, which Falkenhayn denied. The Italian army still retained much fighting spirit; it endured seven more offensives on the Isonzo before its collapse. The weather, as Falkenhayn points out, would not have allowed operations in the high Trentino mountains to begin until May. The Austrian lines in Volhynia might have been so weakened that Brussilov would have driven an irremediable wedge through them. Finally, it is exceedingly doubtful whether even the annihilation of Italy would have had any decisive effect upon the Entente.

On the assumption therefore that the Central Powers had the highest inducement to seize the initiative in 1916 (the year of decision as both sides confidently believed), Falkenhayn had no alternative left but to attack in the West as he did.

But he made two great errors. Like other directors of the German Supreme Command, he dictated too minutely to those immediately responsible for carrying out his orders. The Crown Prince was forced, against his better judgement, to start the isolated operation on the right bank of the Meuse, which seems even at the time to have been condemned by German military opinion in the West.[1] Even so a more liberal allowance of reserves would have ensured the fall of Verdun after that of Fort Douaumont. Secondly, he under-estimated the capacity of the French to maintain a long defensive battle. This was indeed a most natural error, probably shared by all students of French psychology, who have been far too apt to judge Paris as if it typified the temper of provincial France; yet the whole course of French military history seemed to prove that the strength of their armies lay in the offensive, and that repeated hammer-blows would cause demoralization. The amazing toughness and self-sacrifice of the French resistance before Verdun is perhaps the most wonderful of 'toutes les gloires de la France',[2] just because it ran so counter to the ordinary stream of national temperament.

[1] e.g. see Prince Rupprecht of Bavaria, vol. i, pp. 429, 435.

[2] The inscription on the Palace of Versailles is À TOUTES LES GLOIRES DE LA FRANCE.

XVI

THE SOMME

THE military chiefs in France were given an exceedingly free hand for the campaign of 1916. Haig had the confidence of the Cabinet in much fuller measure than his predecessor, and worked hand in hand with Robertson the protagonist of the supreme importance of the Western Front; while the relations of both with Kitchener were harmonious. The instructions which the new Commander-in-Chief received on his appointment made it clear that 'the closest co-operation between the French and British as a united army must be the governing policy'. The independence of his command was vaguely but materially qualified by a statement that he would 'in no case come under the orders of any Allied General further than the necessary co-operation with our Allies above referred to'.

This in effect meant a further extension of the powers of Joffre, who, with the support of the French Premier Briand, had just weathered a formidable internal crisis. An order for close co-operation does not necessarily involve cordial relationships. Haig, indeed, in the course of his command, had many serious and well-founded causes of complaint which are believed to be the principal theme of his hitherto unpublished memoirs. But the many differences of opinion which arose in the first half of 1916 were solved without arousing any such bitterness of feeling as was to be created later.

Even before Verdun it had been settled that a great Franco-British finale of attack should be staged about July 1st; the Russians and Italians, it was hoped, would burst into activity about a fortnight earlier. Mounted on a front of more than thirty miles, this finale was to be predominantly French (forty divisions against twenty-five British). But the gay belief in the easy and complete breakthrough had fled from the minds of the French leaders.

Not even Foch, Poincaré noted in his *Memoirs*, still kept that faith. Joffre then envisaged a long wearying battle of exhaustion, and held that even this grim type of struggle would offer good prospects only if the British engaged previously in important preliminary attacks to grind down the effectives and spirit of the enemy. It was their turn, he urged, to undertake this forbidding task. It was undeniable that, by the end of 1915, the French casualties had been about four times as large as those of their Ally,[1] though their population was smaller. They still held four-fifths of the total trench line (this fact, so admirable for propaganda when nakedly stated, was of course fallacious, for the British sector, being such a vital one, compelled a dense concentration and attracted nearly a third of the enemy's strength). Haig had no intention of blunting the bright spear of his new armies in this way, and by adroit temporizing contrived that his strength was kept intact for July. Besides, it must be noted that his rearward preparations took longer than those of the French. He had no territorials or gangs of civilians to work in the back areas; for the Labour corps, which subsequently embraced hordes of Chinese and other Orientals, had scarcely come into existence. The railways within this area were still run by Frenchmen. The British could not direct or command, but only request.

Even now it is by no means clear why the Somme area was chosen as the theatre of attack. Probably the decisive inducement was simply the crude fact that the two armies could here advance shoulder to shoulder. Haig had expressed a strong preference for the Flemish area, where an advance of twenty miles might have rolled a German army up against the sea and Dutch territory; such an attack was, if possible, to be combined with a naval landing. He did actually prepare an offensive here, to which he intended to divert his weight if the Somme should prove a complete failure.

The Somme offered no such strategical advantage as

[1] Roughly 2,000,000 as against 500,000.

Belgium. Joffre's 'directive' on the subject is mere verbiage of technical jargon. Robertson, indeed, saw an advantage in the fact that the line here approached nearest to Busigny, one of the most important junctions on the enemy's lateral system of communications. As, however, this point was sixty miles away, it seems a poor reason for a siege assault upon one of the mightiest opposing bastions. So indeed the German positions must be described, and so indeed was Haig later to describe them in his dispatch, dwelling so naïvely upon their manifold and labyrinthine subtleties as to provoke the simplest reader to ask, 'If they were known to be so strong, why did you attack them?'

There had been no serious fighting of any kind here since 1914; another desirable reason, according to Joffre, for the choice made. But the Germans had taken masterful advantage of the quiescence. They dug better and harder than their opponents and they kept on digging. The chalk soil was peculiarly favourable for the excavation of elaborate dug-outs, some of which were thirty or even forty feet deep, were furnished with electric light and washing apparatus, and would maintain a whole company in perfect security during the heaviest bombardment. The Allied soldiers were astonished when they entered these enormous subterranean strongholds.

The Somme running alternately north to Péronne and then west towards Amiens, meanders in many loops and streams through a wide valley of rushes and low willows, above which chalky uplands rise to a maximum of 300 feet in successive undulations. The country is of a type familiar to southern England. The downs are less imposing, there are very few steep escarpments (the bluff at Thiepval, round which the Ancre flows, is an almost solitary example of these); the villages are more concentrated and are generally shrouded by an orchard-ring of the communal cider-apple trees. Many large beech-woods relieve the monotony of the bare, cultivated slopes; in fact the Hampshire hills north and east of Winchester show a

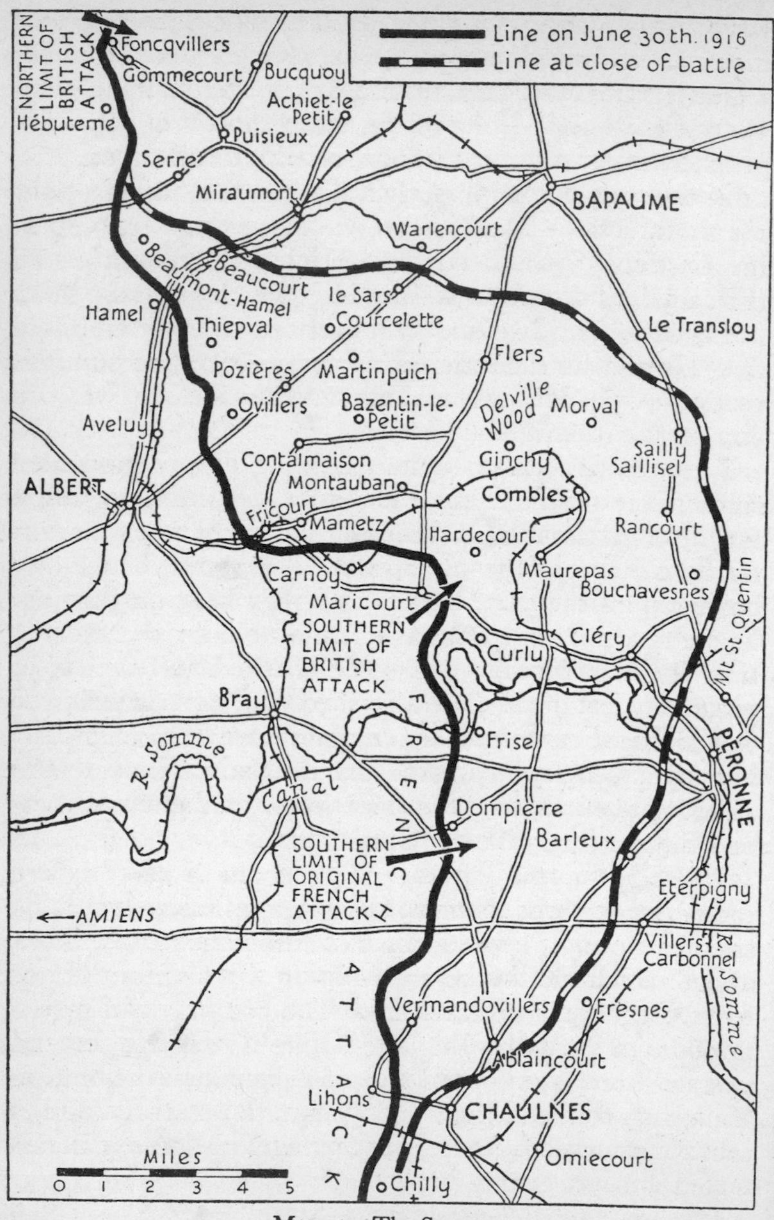

MAP 17. The Somme.

very similar English landscape. The woods and villages formed the hard knots of the system, for their defences were secret, whereas the trench lines on the open hill-sides were clearly writ in chalk. Observation was generally good; from many points, even in first-line trenches, the view ranged over 4,000 or 5,000 yards. The great advantage of the defenders was that their works rose tier upon tier along the ridges, up which the attack must laboriously crawl with a more limited horizon as each new stage was gained.

The front of the attack was finally fixed at about twenty-five miles, of which the French share, so great had been the ravages of Verdun, was less than a third. It extended from just north of the wooded fortress of Gommecourt to a point some five miles south of the Somme. The preparations seemed so obvious to those who took part in them that it was difficult to suppose that the enemy had not been certain of our intentions for months beforehand. The Allies, however, had obtained by May a strong mastery in the air, and German reconnaissance was largely blinded.[1] Von Below, the exceedingly able commander of the IInd army, tells us indeed that as early as February the building of additional hutments was noticed behind the front, but it was not until the middle of June that indications became so numerous and precise as to leave no doubt. Prince Rupprecht jotted down in his diary the evidence as it came in. It includes reports from The Hague and Madrid, where our military attachés seem to have spoken unguardedly, and the report of a speech by a Cabinet Minister, Henderson, to munition workers explaining (or rather, refusing to explain) why the Whitsuntide holidays were being postponed until the end of July. The French participation was guessed when their distinctive steel helmets were seen in the trenches on either side of the Somme, and regarded as certain when the famous 'Iron' corps, the 20th, was identified in the line.

[1] The Fokker by this date had been out-classed by the French Nieuport and the British De Haviland Scout machines. At the commencement of the battle the Germans were outnumbered in the air by two to one.

The plan of attack presented no important tactical novelty. It aimed at putting greater force and greater efficiency into the methods pursued in 1915, which the unimaginative minds at G.H.Q. still believed to be sound. The vastness of the material and mechanical power available in modern war seemed to produce a kind of dull megalomania in which the ingenuity of execution was sacrificed to the immensity and elaboration of the preparation. The task divided itself under three great overlapping heads: the organization of the rear as an offensive theatre; the accumulation of masses of guns and ammunitions; and the co-operation between the three great arms, infantry, artillery, and air force.

Three broad-gauge railways were built, roads were created, widened, and improved (though, owing to the expectation of a rapid advance, no supplies of road-metal had been included in the railway-programme, and in consequence of this omission the surface was entirely destroyed after the first fortnight of the battle). The water supply had to be largely augmented, for the chalk is very barren of springs and wells. Hutments, stables, engineering-dumps, field-hospitals had to be provided for a military population of 400,000 men and 100,000 horses. The civil population remained as a rule undisturbed within two or three miles of the trenches, and reaped an enormous harvest, every other house in any village setting up as a shop or estaminet.

The artillery concentration seemed enormous to the British troops, who saw, each time they came back from the trenches to rest, new emplacements in every orchard, copse and hollow way, already camouflaged by protective colouring, canvas screens, and garnished netting. Great howitzers were noted in increasing quantities, the 9·2 became common, pieces of 12- and even 15-inch were reported. Yet, formidable and terrible as this array appeared, it was far less weighty than the French concentration. On his eight miles of attack Foch disposed of 850 heavy guns and was able to lend the British 40. Even so,

Sir Henry Rawlinson had only 460 to cover more than twice the same frontage. The number of shells collected completely fulfilled the requirements of the Staff, except for the howitzers of the highest calibre. 1,738,000 were fired off in the preliminary bombardment. But during the latter stages of the battle, stocks were very seriously diminished, for the expenditure had not been calculated on the basis of a four-months' siege battle. The new trench-artillery proved a very valuable auxiliary. The old trench-mortars of 1915 had been wretched improvisations, and the unfortunate officer in charge had often had the greatest difficulty in finding a commanding officer who would allow them to be used in his sector. But the new Stokes mortar, which threw a high-explosive shell with great speed and accuracy, was welcomed by the infantry for its powers of concentrated trench-destruction.

In the early days of the war the Air Force played more or less a lone hand. But by now (and generally speaking these remarks apply to all the combatants) it was multiplying its tentacles of liaison. The indiscriminate bombardment of great cities for the express purpose of killing non-combatants was still in its infancy, though all the belligerents soon took it up with a horrible gusto. But the organization of great raids on centres of communication and dumps had grown greatly in efficiency, and sometimes produced sensational results.[1]

The development of aerial photography enabled the artillery to see exactly the nature of the strong points which they were required to demolish. It also marked out clearly tracks invisible from the ground, so that a hidden battery was often located by the recognition in a photograph of a beaten path leading to it. The improvement in wireless made it possible for the observer to 'spot' more accurately for the battery whose fire he was directing.

[1] e.g. the destruction of 9,000 tons of high-explosive shell at Andruicq (July 20) by a German bomb. It is generally supposed that this occurrence finally determined the postponement of the Messines attack until 1917. The great explosion at Spincourt near Verdun in May of 450,000 heavy German shells is believed to have been caused, not by a bomb, but by gun-fire.

The infantry were helped in two ways. The photographs, when pieced together, provided a bird's-eye view of the ground to be attacked. They were eagerly studied by officers, and often it was possible to construct a replica in the back-areas, and to rehearse the attack beforehand.[1] Such experiments were intensely disliked by the French peasants, whose land was thus requisitioned. Their Government, moreover, charged the British army with rent and compensation for damage in all cases where trenches were not actually required for defensive purposes. The Germans, who had obviously no occasion to consider the susceptibilities of the civil population, employed these rehearsals on a large scale—for instance, before the opening of the assault on Verdun. Secondly, a number of 'contact' aeroplanes were employed in battle to keep in close touch with the infantry, to locate and report their progress, and to carry their requests to the guns. They flew low and indicated their presence by Klaxon horns, while the infantry signalled to them by flares and shutters, which reproduced the Morse code. The direct method of attacking hostile infantry, particularly when marching in fours, by swooping upon them with bursts of machine-gun fire had not yet come into fashion, though the writer recollects an unsuccessful attempt to enfilade his trench by a hostile machine early in 1916.

The understanding between artillery and infantry was still far from perfect. The programme for the Somme was of an exceedingly rigid nature; the local commanders had no power to switch guns on to particular targets even in such a plain question of life and death as wire-cutting. The orders for July 1st were that the advance was to take place everywhere, whether the wire was reported as destroyed or not. During the attack the guns lifted according to a prearranged time-table from one line of hostile trenches to another, often getting far ahead of the infantry, who were

[1] Gen. Edmonds relates that a German aeroplane flew right over the troops who were practising the ill-fated Gommecourt attack a few days beforehand.

mown down by the unmolested fire of machine-guns. The best friend of infantry in attack, the creeping barrage, had as yet been merely sketched by the enterprising staffs of one or two corps. In its perfected form it meant a tremendous curtain of fire, composed of every kind of shell, moving slowly forwards about fifty yards in advance of the infantry at a rate previously agreed upon. It is, indeed, a most delicate operation, for it demands three essential conditions: that the infantry should be able to maintain a uniform rate of progress, that the gunners should shoot with extreme precision, and that the shells should burst exactly as intended. These conditions could not possibly have been fulfilled by July 1st. It takes longer to improvise a scientific gunner than an efficient foot-soldier; the quality of the shells which the Ministry of Munitions was turning out so feverishly was not good, and that of the large American supplies was even worse. Premature bursts not unfrequently destroyed the gun and its crew, many shells bursting short caused casualties and demoralization among the infantry, and still more failed to explode at all. The French encouraged a greater elasticity of programme, and assaults were often postponed until the trench garrison was satisfied that the opposing obstacle had been destroyed.

The character and conduct of the attack of July 1st provided a keen controversy between Haig and the 4th army commander, Rawlinson, who was entrusted with its execution. The latter, a very clever and ambitious general, desired a limited operation, methodically carried out, stage by stage. No such advance, he thought, should exceed in depth the belt of about a mile which his guns could make uninhabitable. Haig, however, oddly enough, became more optimistic as the Germans stuck more and more before Verdun. He may have thought that the long trial was demoralizing their army, although his chief ground for confidence seems to have been an exaggerated belief in the destructive powers of his artillery at long range. The British, it must be remembered, had never experienced a large-scale intensive bombardment covering the second line and the back-areas, and consequently expected too much from it.

A study of the map shows that their attack was to start on Gommecourt and extend as far as Maricourt; at this point the French took over, with a battle-front astride the Somme. Southward from the Ancre a long ridge, the dominating feature of the landscape, formed the German battle-zone. Haig insisted that the objective for the first day should include an advance of some 4,000 yards, including the German second line, on the whole centre of attack. A defensive flank was to be formed north of the Ancre on Serre ridge, in case the 3rd army failed in a subsidiary assault on Gommecourt. Having thus bitten into the second position, he hoped, in liaison with the French, to squeeze out the remainder and break through the last and incomplete trench system which covered Bapaume. The larger vision then opened of massed cavalry in open country, and the main British strength wheeling north towards Douai to take the enemy in the rear or compel his instant retreat.[1]

The advantages of so considerable an initial advance are indeed obvious. If ten miles of the second line had fallen within twelve hours, the Germans would have lost practically all their field-artillery within that area; and if confronted by fresh reserves would probably have fallen back on a wide front. Yet all analogy with later battles forbids the belief that open warfare would have resulted. An impressive total of prisoners and booty would have been collected, but the line would have been re-established in the familiar bulge.

Still, even such a result would have been a resounding success and would have strained German man-power cruelly, for the new line would have been at least twice the length of the old. Was it feasible? Rawlinson confided

[1] These expectations were not shared by the Intelligence Section at G.H.Q. Its head, Brig.-Gen. Charteris, who enjoyed Haig's closest confidence, expressed a very definite belief in a long, wearing battle: see his book *At G.H.Q.*, which consists apparently of genuine contemporary jottings.

his doubts to his diary and described it as 'a gamble'. So it undoubtedly was. It asked too much of the gunners, whose most delicate work of wire-cutting was thus doubled.[1] The assurance of a satisfactory result was impossible at such a distance. It was asking too much of the infantry, who were expected to conquer and consolidate, not two separate trenches, but two elaborate systems of which the defenders could dispute every yard with machine-gun and bomb. It is true that a hopeful presumption assumed that practically all the defenders in the first line would have been put out of action, but no one supposed that similar havoc could be wrought in the second.

However, the tactical methods employed by Rawlinson and his commanders effectively destroyed any existing possibility of success. Let us turn to the scene on July 1st. The seven-days' bombardment had reached its final climax. The infantry had watched it with exultation; many of them, waiting behind, went out in the evenings to the high ground to see the enemy positions pricked out with countless points of fire. Few were aware that repeated raids had proved his resistance to be still active and strong.

The great successes of the Russians in Galicia quickened the confidence that the final time of decision was at hand. It was the supreme day of the new armies of Great Britain and Ireland, the Newfoundlanders being the only overseas troops who shared in it. Their epitaph has been written by Churchill in noble and poignant words.[2]

The assaulting hour was fixed at 7.30 a.m., Foch having insisted upon several hours' daylight for observing the final effects of the bombardment. A blazing sun was high in the heavens. At this moment the guns lifted from the front enemy trench to prevent reinforcement of the garrison. Eleven mines were exploded. The officers blew their whistles and the crowded trenches began to empty. In

[1] The wire was very formidable both in quantity and quality. The belts were at least 20–30 yards deep, the barbs often as thick as a man's thumb, and the posts of iron.

[2] See Winston Churchill, *The World Crisis 1916–18*, part i (1927), pp. 195–6.

some places concealed by clouds of smoke, but more often in broad view they filed through the prepared gaps in the wire, and straightened out into long lines advancing shoulder to shoulder. But the advance was painfully slow, for the men were laden like beasts of burden. Each staggered under a weight of 66 lb., more than was borne in full marching order. They carried 220 rounds of ammunition, two bombs, and two sand-bags; a proportion were further encumbered with picks and shovels, boxes containing carrier-pigeons and telephone apparatus. In some places where no-man's-land was wide, four of these lines were out together in the open, stumbling over the shell-pocked ground. Thus it has been said with some justification that 'the battle was lost by three minutes', for such a saving in speed would have allowed the machine-gunners no time to man their weapons before their enemy was among them. This statement, however, cannot be fully accepted. We know from German accounts that their fire was sometimes deliberately kept back until the advancing wave was within 100 yards. Before Beaumont-Hamel the relieving troops buried long lines of corpses immediately in front of the British wire, which proved the readiness of the enemy at the very moment of zero. At La Boiselle also, where a telephone message had been overheard, which indicated the time of attack, all the machine-guns were in full blast immediately after the guns lifted. Here, too, and farther north by Hébuterne the enemy's batteries, unsubdued and in unsuspected force, made access over no-man's-land almost impossible throughout the day.

The slowness and denseness of the advance certainly contributed to the failure. Haig himself favoured an initial exploration by patrols of active men, taking advantage of natural features, as the Germans had done at Verdun, and as Foch's troops also did on July 1st. But the main causes appear to the writer to be: first the comparative failure of the bombardment, owing largely to the wretched quality of the ammunition, for only round Montauban were the great dug-outs found to be smashed; and the inability to use gas-shells—not yet manufactured by the Allies—which partially blind an enemy and make his movements slow and clumsy. Secondly, the hour of assault, forced on the British who had strongly favoured the misty dawn. Thirdly, the simultaneity of the attack in practically equal strength on the whole front. It seems, in retrospect, as if a series of punches at chosen sectors, not all delivered at the same moment, with the strong reserves, which would then have been available, in readiness for exploitation, would have been a more hopeful method. The French attributed their own complete success south of the river largely to the fact that their attack took place two hours later than on the other bank. The Germans had, in consequence, relaxed their vigilance and were overrun with ease.

Colonel Boraston, in his unpleasing book *Sir D. Haig's Command*, has suggested that the principal cause of failure was the inexperience of the troops themselves. It is true, as the *Official History* points out, that the Staff had given little pains to producing any useful manual of detailed tactical instruction. (This omission, it is fair to say, was remedied shortly afterwards, when well-written and thoroughly practical hints on trench-warfare became freely available.) It is also true that, here and there, notably in the ardent advance of the heroic Ulster division at Thiepval, the 'mopping up', or clearing the conquered ground of lurking enemies, was imperfectly done, so that the attackers were taken in the rear. Experience was to prove that the capacious dug-outs had to be treated with large explosive charges and incendiary phosphorus bombs, in order to ensure that no living beings were waiting an opportunity to emerge. The German accounts, while extolling the bravery of their adversaries, also constantly criticize them as unhandy in the more specialized technique of trench-warfare, compared with the French. The proportion of fully trained regular officers and N.C.O.s in the German ranks was still very much higher than in our own.

But the *Official History* proves to demonstration that the methods prescribed by the directing staff made any considerable success impossible.

By the evening the British had been utterly repulsed from Gommecourt to the great Bapaume road; a perfect chain of inter-connecting machine-guns, often secretly sited in armoured emplacements, had swept them away like chaff. On the other hand, on either side of Montauban, the projecting spurs of the ridge had been bitten off according to plan, and the whole French attack had met with almost complete success. The British losses were stupendous, and never approached on any other single day of the war. They amounted to nearly 60,000, or 60 per cent. of the officers and 40 per cent. of the men engaged, probably the highest proportion in any great battle recorded in history.[1] They were increased both by the extraordinary bravery and obstinacy of the troops and by the persistence with which the Higher Command renewed useless assaults. Telephonic communication had broken down, air reconnaissance proved almost useless for accurate and detailed information. In consequence of this, all favourable reports, however misleading, seem to have been passed back, whilst the others were suppressed or minimized.[2]

The situation was depressing. There was evidently no possibility of employing Gough's ambitiously named 'army of pursuit' with its masses of cavalry, who had waited all day, a few miles behind, in hollow lanes and farm buildings.

Rawlinson with a kind of dull fatalism proposed to renew the attack immediately all along the front. The 48th division was actually assembled that night to advance on Thiepval, which loomed before them like a dark

[1] Fourteen divisions were engaged, or about 140,000 infantry; the losses of other arms were not heavy. The Germans employed four and a half divisions—including the seven-days' bombardment they may have lost 20,000–25,000; the exact figures are not ascertainable.

[2] See Brig.-Gen. Sir J. E. Edmonds, *Military Operations: France and Belgium*, vol. v (1932), pp. 478–81.

cloud flickering with lights. Haig took a prompt decision. He vetoed Rawlinson's proposal, in spite of Joffre's strong remonstrance. But he did not adopt the alternative which had been in his mind (in the event of complete failure on the Somme), to move all his power northwards against Messines; and, indeed, the French success would have made such action practically impossible. Therefore he determined to limit the battle to the area where the German defences had been rudely dislocated. It had been calculated by the Intelligence, with great accuracy as the event proved, that for the next six days no formidable array of enemy reserves need be expected.[1] Falkenhayn persisted in believing that Prince Rupprecht farther north would have to face the main attack; and therefore important forces were kept behind the German VIth army, in spite of the protests of its chief-of-staff that he did not want them. No serious results could be expected from continuing the attack south of the Somme, where the river, soon reached, formed an almost impassable dike against further progress. Therefore the area for further penetration was little more than six miles wide, and the intention was to creep up the plateau from the south, so as to take Thiepval, that mighty hinge,[2] in the rear.

So the battle pursued its deadly way. The Germans now began to suffer more heavily, as by the express orders of Falkenhayn not a yard of ground was to be voluntarily ceded. Their defence of every village and wood was of unsurpassed doggedness. A Guards battalion, called the Cockchafers from their crest, surrounded in La Boiselle, held out in the ruins for nearly a week. It is said that arms were presented to them when they finally emerged as starving prisoners. A great wood like Delville (obviously nicknamed Devil's Wood) was for weeks a cauldron of

[1] Thirty-four battalions were in line on July 1, and fifty-four more had arrived by July 6.

[2] The extraordinary value, in trench-warfare, of such a hinge in cramping the attack and keeping the bulge of penetration narrow, will be illustrated again in the defence of Givenchy by the 55th division against all German attacks in April 1918.

contest. Its capture devoured six divisions; and it enshrines to-day the memorial of the South Africans. On July 14th Rawlinson attempted a bold stroke which almost produced a great success. It was one of the very few large night attacks of the war. The preliminary advance through the darkness of 1,400 yards, marked out by white tapes, went perfectly. The second German line (their last completed system) was overrun for five miles, where it ran through the twin Bazentins. In the late afternoon the 7th division passed through High Wood to the eastern edge of the plateau. On the farther side a squadron of cavalry rode among the ripening corn, spearing or cutting down stray fugitives. Eyewitnesses cherished memories of the broad evening view over unviolated country, of transport guns and limbers being driven to the rear. But the sight of that promised land was short, for counter-attacks next day regained a mile of that vital territory. Two months were to pass before it came into indisputed British possession. During that time nothing more than a little elbow-room on both flanks was clawed piecemeal out of the enemy's tenacious clutch.

On September 15th the Germans were confronted with a surprise, which was finally to have a far more decisive influence on the war than their own secret weapons, the great howitzers and poison gas. For the tanks, which now made their first appearance, were to be universally named after the Armistice, not without good reason, as 'Deutschlands Tod' ('Germany's Death').

The idea which lay behind their construction was a fairly obvious one, bound to occur as it did to many minds independently. Thirteen years before, Wells in a short story had imagined a fleet of irresistible land-ships spreading terror and devastation. The tank is not really the descendant of the ancient scythed chariot, for the latter's object was to cut lanes through masses in the open. Rather it has inherited the virtue of the battering ram and the Roman *testudo* in destroying fortifications which defied the assault of other devices. The armoured car, very valuable on roads and in open warfare, had become quite obsolete on the Western Front.

The first problem, therefore, was to create a mechanically propelled vehicle which could go practically anywhere, and, itself immune against machine-guns, could destroy them together with trench-obstacles. The second was to determine how these engines, once created, could be used to the best tactical advantage.

Major-General Sir E. S. Swinton, a Royal Engineer, who had shown remarkable imaginative distinction in his pre-war writings, was the first to suggest the imitation of the existing American caterpillar tractor. The War Office, whose single eye was long directed towards guns and shells, shelved the idea, which received its gestation in the womb of the Admiralty. Churchill, on his own authority, illegally diverted £75,000 to D'Eyncourt, the Director of Naval Construction, to experiment in the creation of a model. The first 'land-ship' therefore was designed by the Navy. The cruel failure at Loos induced G.H.Q. to nibble cautiously, when they saw the performances of the completed machine in January 1916. They went so far as to order forty.[1] Manufactured and exercised in secret during that year, they survived even an exhibition for the benefit of members of Parliament without the disclosure of their existence to the enemy. Tanks they were christened, because they were labelled as such and, it was hoped, looked as such when travelling by rail; and 'tanks' they remained. This homely nickname contrasts as characteristically with the romantic sounding French 'char-d'assaut' as with the ponderously accurate German 'Sturm-panzerkraftwagen'.

The original weighed about 27 tons, had a speed of three miles per hour, and could surmount a trench 8½ feet wide and 5 feet high. The design was of two types, named 'male' and 'female', each sex manned by a crew of seven, but whereas the former carried two 6-pounder guns, the latter was restricted to four heavy machine-guns.

[1] This number was increased to 100 by the War Office.

By the end of August sixty machines were ready, complete with crews. A great tactical controversy arose—were these precious virgins to be handed over to the tender mercies of G.H.Q. to be employed as it thought fit, or were they to be maintained intact as a nucleus of a great multitude? Swinton, with penetrating insight, had laid down in a memorandum the lines for a massed surprise-attack later on, such as that actually followed in minute detail in the famous battle of Cambrai, which will be described later. In this he was supported by Asquith and Lloyd George, now Minister of War.[1] However, Haig had his way and the machines were shipped to France.

It is easy to be wise after the event and to deplore this premature disclosure. But it must be remembered that the Germans did not retaliate by counter-building until the great surprise had actually been launched, with complete success, fourteen months later, and that they had not even at the close of the war discovered any efficient remedy against tanks. Secondly, manœuvres, however realistic and arduous, can never take the place of ordeal by battle, and the Staff not unnaturally refused to give *carte blanche* for the use of an untried arm. By using them in small groups, it was hoped to protect and hearten as many of the sorely tried infantry as possible. The correct tactical use of a new weapon is difficult to determine without experience. The French in 1870 largely neutralized the effect of their new *mitrailleuse* by turning it into a kind of subordinate artillery. Finally, at this moment the Germans were believed to be (and we now know were) in very hard straits. It seemed logical to bring up instantly against them any invention which might help to break a will strained to the utmost by the entry of Rumania into the field against them.

In fact the events of September 15th showed that the tanks were still in a very experimental stage, for out of the

[1] The French Government was of the same opinion, and received a promise from the British that they should be used only *en masse*. It is said that the liaison officer at G.H.Q. released his government from this promise.

forty-nine used, fifteen failed to reach the place of assembly, and only eighteen in all did any service in the field. The crews were unable to steer the machines through the intricate and gaping crater-field, of which they had no experience. A few, however, enjoyed spectacular successes, which were hymned to the world by the practised pens of the correspondents, writing to order. One took a village practically single-handed; another wiped up a whole trench with more than 300 prisoners. While they did not sow among the enemy the terror with which their successors were regarded in the latest months of the war, they afforded another proof of the inexhaustible superiority of the Entente in the *Materialienschlacht*, as the Somme battle was generally named.

This attack, and its sequel ten days later, caused the greatest anxiety to the German Command. Both were delivered on wide fronts of 15,000 yards, by seven divisions; the co-ordination between infantry and artillery had ripened greatly in efficiency, and each time an advance of about one and a half miles was made. This was the most dangerous crisis through which the Germans passed before August 1918. Their fortified zone was growing very thin; only by incessant mole-like operations was it possible just to keep pace with the successive losses of territory. Several divisions had been diverted to the east to stem the Rumanians, who were pouring into Transylvania. At one moment the total number of reserves in the west was diminished to five divisions, a low record never again reached till October 1918.

Such was the position which faced Hindenburg and Ludendorff after the dismissal of Falkenhayn on August 28th.[1] The famous pair had fought many battles with their late superior, whom they both accused of having neglected the opportunity of forcing a decision against Russia in 1915. But they have both frankly acknowledged that they had no conception of the state of their armies in the West. In the East the German soldier was justly proud of an

[1] See p. 289.

efficiency which raised him almost as much above his allies as above his enemies. His superiority in every kind of technique and weapon more than compensated for his great inferiority in numbers. But in France the new chiefs found great and general despondency. The resources of the whole world were being remorselessly poured out against them.[1] The harrowed infantry felt that they were deserted by the other arms. They hated their air force for allowing the sky to be perpetually filled with enemy planes, and often actually cheered when one of their own machines was shot down.

Ludendorff, who was a supreme organizer, did what was possible to alleviate the lot of the troops. In particular he modified the iron rule by which divisions were kept in the line to the point of utter exhaustion. In future the continuous spell was never to exceed fourteen days. Again he no longer insisted upon the retention of all ground, even if of no tactical importance, for he saw that nothing sapped the moral of his men more than continual little counter-attacks, hastily improvised, and quickly broken up.

By the end of September he believed correctly that the situation was just in hand. The Allies had by now at last won the whole of the tortured ridge, for the redoubtable Thiepval, so stoutly held by its Württemberg garrison, had fallen on the 27th. But he calculated that they would not be able to advance over the intervening valley quickly enough to seize the last ridge, guarding Bapaume, three miles away, before winter set in. Nor was it likely that the French, who had been continually increasing the area of battle south of the river in the level plain of Santerre, famous for its corn, could jeopardize the general strategical position. In spite of many half-successes they had nowhere crossed the river, and had reached it only on the short stretch before Péronne, the little walled city of ancient memories, which they were being forced gradually to lay in ruins.

[1] Nothing is more striking in German accounts of the Somme than the monotonous reiteration of the word *Überlegenheit*, 'superiority'.

October is generally the wettest month of the year in northern France, though 1915 had been abnormally dry. Consequently the Allies could not complain of bad luck (though of course they did so complain) when the rain became incessant. The mud of the Somme was not to be compared with the mud of Ypres next year, but it was bad enough. The vast area of devastation, six miles deep, could not possibly be 'organized' to allow any more great attacks. The battle degenerated into a series of desperate nibbles at a medley of shell-holes hastily strung together and called a trench. Yet, before the stagnation of winter finally settled down upon the great waste, one more set piece was staged. On either side of the Ancre the ground was still passable; an advance there would broaden and make more comfortable the great salient now thrust into the German lines. And so the struggle, begun under the blazing heat of the July sun, finished in fog and snow. Except on the left, where the sinister ruins of Serre still defied all attacks, the operation was completely successful, more than 7,000 prisoners being taken. During the capture of Grandcourt by the Royal Naval Division, Colonel Freyberg, the famous swimmer of Bulair, one of the legendary fighting men of the war, was wounded eight times before he relinquished the command of his battalion. This victory came as a mortifying surprise to the enemy; Ludendorff frankly admits that he had not thought it possible, the season being so advanced. It had been planned by Haig's especial favourite Gough, by far the youngest army commander (he was only 44 years old), another cavalryman, long esteemed a lucky general, dashing and supremely self-confident, but bearing the reputation, shared by his staff, of being inexact in detail and slipshod in method.

Thus the Somme ended, and it is necessary to make an estimate of its results. The actual gain of territory was not in itself important; a strip some thirty miles long with a maximum depth of seven miles had been conquered, which yet threatened no important artery. But the new enemy line was longer and much weaker than the old, and would require to be held by more troops at greater sacrifice. The retreat of the Germans next spring showed that they felt unable to face the abundant risk.

Again, the total of captures, amounting to about 75,000 men and 300 guns, does not look very impressive in relation to the vast numerical scales of the war. And these must be weighed against the total losses incurred by both sides. The Entente had to pay the enormous price of 600,000 casualties (roughly, British 410,000, French 190,000). It is not easy to assess accurately the German figures, over which an acute controversy has raged, notably between Churchill and his critics. The latest reasoned estimate in the *Official History* suggests that they were very little less than those of the Allies.[1] The round figure generally adopted in German histories is half a million. But whatever may be the exact numbers, it is undeniable that in the later stages of the battle the German losses kept mounting, while those of the Allies diminished. This was an ominous sign, and told its tale in declining moral. For the first time a steady trickle of deserters came across the lines. Voluntary surrenders, almost unknown before except under the pressure of absolute necessity, became comparatively common. The number collected by the French in their December attack at Verdun far exceeded their expectations.[2] By November two-thirds of the German divisions in the west had passed through the 'blood-bath'. Man for man the German soldier remained the equal of any in the world, but he was now experiencing the same conviction, which he had so long and so sternly taught the Russians, that whatever he might do he would never meet with a fair field of battle. The German army, perhaps more than any

[1] See Brig.-Gen. Sir J. E. Edmonds, *Military Operations: France and Belgium*, vol. v (1932), note ii, pp. 496–7. The difficulty in computing German figures mainly arises from the double method of assessment; the lists published during the war excluded all the lightly wounded remaining in the corps area.

[2] The officer-prisoners complained to Gen. Mangin of their cramped quarters. He gave the characteristic answer: 'I beg your pardon, gentlemen, but we did not expect so many of you!'

other, relied upon the skill and experience of its officers and N.C.O.s. Their military writers agree that the enormous vacancies caused in their ranks by Verdun and the Somme were absolutely irreplaceable. Prince Rupprecht, in an interesting note written before the Somme, observed that British prisoners always spoke enthusiastically of their officers as 'real gentlemen', even if they admitted that they did not know much. But the Germans, he said, are prone to envy and carp at the privileges of their officers, in particular their better food; already the men's rations were inferior, both in quality and variety, to those of the Entente, the daily allowance of meat in particular being about half. Moreover, these could not be really supplemented from home, for the 'hunger blockade' was already creating a scarcity which made the soldier anxious, lest a wife, child, or dependant should be suffering from hunger.

In short, it is impossible to deny that the German army had seriously deteriorated. Ludendorff actually says that at the end of the year it was 'absolutely exhausted'. His testimony may not be accepted as trustworthy, for he certainly had a motive in painting as black a picture as possible of the legacy of his predecessor, whose strategy he had so strongly combated. Also, when he wrote his book, as an exile in Sweden in 1919, he was in the grip of extreme nervous and physical exhaustion, from which he has never recovered. But regimental histories, memoirs, and novels all write of the Somme as having imprinted upon its actors a frightful and ineffaceable impression, though we may allow that German writers generally show more sensibility and less reticence than our own.

The Somme, therefore, in spite of the grave tactical mistakes which opened it, rendered, unlike the offensive of 1915, a serious service to the Allies. In spite of the slaughter, the British army gained experience rather than discouragement, as the attack before Arras was to show in the coming spring. It is astonishing that the supply of suitable officers was on the whole so well maintained, if it is realized that during 1916 the British suffered at least three times the officer casualties which they inflicted.[1] The maintenance of so high a standard in an improvised army was due to two causes. First, to the cadet-corps in the Public Schools and Universities, fostered by Lord Haldane, whom Haig described as 'the greatest War Minister that England had ever possessed'. This tribute was paid in the dedication of a copy of his dispatches, which with a beautiful thoughtfulness he brought himself to the house of his neglected and maligned old chief on the night that the Treaty of Versailles was signed. Secondly, to the Officer-Cadet-Battalions, which were first established in the spring of 1916; these were gradually expanded to receive, for a period of three months' training, practically all candidates for commissions except permanent ones in the regular army. The instructors, officers, and sergeants were as a rule carefully chosen from those who had seen service abroad. The overseas contingents had such belief in their efficiency that they sent their own candidates to be trained side by side with the British.

The French had every reason to be proud of the exploits of their army in 1916, but by the close of the year it was, taken as a whole, more fought out and infected by war-weariness than its opponent. It had lost nearly another million. Its reserves were very low; without encroachment on the last capital of youth, barely 700,000 remained. It was freely stated both by soldiers and civilians that next spring would see 'the last army of France' in the field, and that if it should not be successful, peace would become a necessity. The defeatists, headed by the fertile and unscrupulous Caillaux, were coming out into the open.

The moment therefore called either for a more ruthless vigour and decision, or for the frank recognition of a

[1] The figures given in *Statistics of the Military Effort of the British Empire during the Great War, 1914–1920* (1922) are British 27,482, Germans 6,152. A proportion of say 25 per cent. should be added to the latter for lightly wounded not reported.

peace of compromise. So it was not surprising that the same month, which saw the rejection by the Entente of the peace notes both of Germany and the United States, saw also a change of government and a change of supreme command.

XVII

EVENTS IN THE EAST IN 1916

I

THE winter lull lasted for more than five months (October 1915–March 1916) unbroken except for a futile Russian attack at Czernowitz in the Bukovina, where it was perhaps hoped that a success might incline the wavering Rumanian balance. In both camps it was a time of intense preparations. The Russians had pledged themselves at the Chantilly Conference (December 1915) to attack with all their strength not later than June 15th. Their position had in almost every respect improved and was still improving. In spite of their gigantic losses they had as yet mobilized a smaller proportion of their manhood than any of the great Powers at war, with the exception of Great Britain.[1] They would be able to open the new campaign with a reserve of at least a million men, who now received the reasonable amount of three months' training before being drafted to the front. Even the great rifle shortage had been overcome, mainly by importations, but their own factories had risen to an output of 100,000 per month. Though still undergunned and undershelled, they could look forward with reasonable confidence to a supply sufficient for the summer offensive, provided that they passed quickly from trench to open warfare. Regiments were now supplied with two or three times as many machine-guns as had figured in their pre-war establishment. The situation in the air alone remained thoroughly unsatisfactory. Their machines were very few and inferior in quality compared with those of the enemy. Throughout 1916 the system of spotting for artillery, which was being developed to an exact science in the West, was in an embryonic stage in the East. Their defence against the air was absurdly inadequate. As late as August 1916 Knox tells

[1] The Russian proportion was 10 per cent. against the French 14 per cent., the highest of all the combatants.

us that there was only one anti-aircraft battery in Russia, which was generally employed to protect Tsarskoe Selo, the Imperial residence near Petrograd, but was allowed for a few weeks to practise at the front. In view of the long agony of the preceding year, the spirit of the patient, enduring peasant remained wonderfully constant, though here and there an increase in desertion was noticed. At one point in the northern group of armies 300 absentees were collected in one canteen. The new class of officer consisted mainly of village schoolmasters who were well suited to instruct the moujik with sympathy and understanding. Yet already signs were multiplying of the political reaction which had been prophesied as a consequence of the Tsar's assumption of the Supreme Command. Stürmer, a mean intriguer of German extraction, a creature of the Court, was exalted to the premiership in February. A sinister result of his methods was seen in the dismissal of Polivanov (March 1916), the only efficient Minister of War Russia had during the whole war, for the reason that he was too closely connected with Liberal associations. His successor was a typical general of the old school who said: 'I know nothing about the work, but my devotion to the Emperor is such that if the door were to open and His Majesty was to come into the room and ask me to throw myself out of the window, I would do so at once.'[1]

The Central Powers under-estimated the power of recovery inherent in the Russians. Falkenhayn, it is true, was careful to retain the minimum defensive force which the Eastern Command thought necessary, though he took away much heavy artillery for his concentration at Verdun. Conrad for his part was obsessed with hatred for Italy. Years before the war he had pressed upon his master schemes for a preventive war against the ally of whose faithlessness he was convinced long before it was proved. He now poured into Falkenhayn's unsympathetic ear the

[1] Maj.-Gen. Sir A. Knox, *With the Russian Army 1914–17* (1921), vol. ii, p. 416.

proposal for a great set-piece in the Trentino, for which he hoped to obtain the loan of nine German divisions. On meeting with a refusal, he still determined to go his own way. With his own resources he could scarcely expect to deal a decisive blow, but prepared the so-called *Strafe-expedition*, or 'punishment-campaign', which made large demands on his reserves in Galicia and Volhynia. Though he undertook that his front should not be unduly weakened, he did not keep his promise. As a result his country most narrowly escaped complete collapse in June. Nor were conditions at, and behind, large parts of his front such as to justify the expectation of any intense or sustained effort. Treasonable propaganda was growing daily. Among the Czechs in particular it was organized with the greatest skill by the powerful exiles Masaryk and Benes. Regiments were instructed when in the line to whistle tunes which would be recognized by the Russians. Whole formations awaited only the opportunity, which occurred in the summer, to give themselves up. In some of the Staffs a light-hearted frivolity reigned which took all the pleasures traditionally associated with armies in winter-quarters. Nowak tells us that the head-quarters of the Archduke Joseph Ferdinand at Lutsk were the scene of incessant revelries, relieved only by shooting expeditions. Such habits were borrowed from the life of the capital. Czernin relates that a neutral observer, contrasting Vienna with the other war capitals, said to him: 'C'est une ville sans âme.'

Life in the conquered area of German occupation was strangely different. Under the iron organizing hand of Ludendorff every kind of problem, military, administrative, economic, and political, was being tackled with true German seriousness and efficiency. Only the British army could compare with the German in the care spent on the comfort of the troops in back-areas. We specialized in provision of sport and amusements, the Germans in educational and library facilities.

The German Command in the East had within its power

a great heterogeneous collection of discordant nationalities, embracing in all perhaps 15,000,000 souls: Poles, Letts, Lithuanians, Baltic Germans, White Russians, and Jews. Within the cage of the exact and minute regulations that enclosed them all, they were treated with different degrees of favour for political reasons. The Lithuanians were encouraged at the expense of the Poles; the German landowners in the Duchy of Courland were confirmed in the supremacy which they had long exercised, for it was hoped that this district at least might be permanently added to the Reich; but pains were also taken to conciliate the Letts, who had been seething with unrest against their Russian masters ever since the revolution of 1905. The Jews were everywhere both submissive and useful, as they knew German and were able to act as intermediaries between the occupying authority and the local population. Ludendorff in his interesting account prides himself on the extreme justice of the administration. But he admits that (as indeed was inevitable under the increasing rigour of the blockade) these countries were ransacked and exploited for German needs. The levies of cattle and horses pressed most hardly upon the farmers and peasants, although Ludendorff claims that their contributions in taxes were made lower than before the war. Otherwise the great forests, particularly in Lithuania, proved the most valuable asset; for, though seed was distributed to the peasants, the land proved unproductive and the harvest of 1916 was very disappointing.

Order seems to have been maintained with little difficulty, except for the presence of armed bandits in the forests and marshes. Later on Austria's own province of Galicia became almost masterless through the activities of far more formidable gangs, whose number in 1918 was estimated at 40,000, mainly deserters.

II

The winter calm was broken by the battle of Lake Narotch in the middle of March. The Russian High

Command showed its usual extraordinary complaisance towards the requests of the Allies for relief-offensives. This time the call was to relieve Verdun. The Russian reply was quixotic rather than chivalrous. Ill conceived and ill conducted, it did no good to France, and much harm to the Russian army. Subordinate officers loudly complained of the useless sacrifice. The choice was apparently determined by the fascination which the Vilna district exercised over the Staffs of both sides. But nothing could excuse the choice at a moment when the thaw might be normally expected. The thaw came and the attack was smothered, as the Germans said, 'in mud and blood'. As the battle was concluding the frost reappeared, and swallowed up whole companies in the stiffened swamps. The Russians are believed to have lost 120,000 and to have attracted nothing but the enemy's local reserves. One symptom disquieted Ludendorff: the weight of fire employed, particularly in heavy guns. Such an artillery effort had not yet been experienced from the Russians. It was on this occasion also that a German gunner-officer, Lieutenant-Colonel Bruchmüller, first came into prominence. In March 1918 he was to organize the whole artillery programme against the British front, and was well named 'Durch-bruch Müller' (Break-through Müller).

Russian head-quarters resumed its preparations for the main summer blow. Faithful to its original intention, the Vilna sector was again selected for the principal effort, whilst subsidiary attacks were to be launched by the northern and southern groups of armies on very extended fronts. The Germans knew well what was being staged against them both by observation and through spies.

Such were the intentions of the Russians when in the middle of May Conrad unloosed his forces in the Trentino. The Italians had come to believe that they would never be attacked. Now they saw with dismay Austrian armies making rapid progress towards the Lombard plain, thus threatening to place themselves in the rear of the main Italian forces which were battering at the Isonzo. A tremendous disaster was possible, and Italy set up an exceeding bitter cry. The appeal went naturally to Russia, for the weight of Austrian men and guns in the mountains was such that important transfers must obviously have taken place from Galicia. The King of Italy personally invoked the Tsar by a telegram. Now the Russian offensive, as we have seen, had been fixed for June 15th. Evert, who commanded the central army group, was quite clear that the date for his operation against Vilna, in the success of which he seems anyhow to have had little confidence, could not be advanced. But matters were different on the south-western front, where Brussilov was in charge. This general had supreme energy and self-confidence. He knew the ground thoroughly, for he had fought over areas of it in 1915 as an army commander, and had visited the front assiduously since he had been promoted to that army group. Unlike so many Russians, he realized the value of minute organization, and saw to it that his orders were actually carried out. He knew that his advancement was due to merit, for he was disliked by the Court. His memoirs show that he despised the Tsar and detested his wife; and that his own disposition was hot-tempered, sensitive, and jealous. His adherence to the Bolsheviks after the Revolution was ascribed by many to his resentment at the lack of support which he received during the campaign of 1916. He certainly believed that the Tsarina had done her best to ruin Russia.

Brussilov had got everything ready by May 23rd; and, when questioned by Alexeiev, the new Chief of the General Staff, emphatically declared that the sooner he moved the better. For he was confident that by his unorthodox methods he had gained the secret of surprise. He had prepared for an advance all along the 300-mile front of his four armies. Assaulting trenches had been dug everywhere. He had not been reinforced, and in numbers was almost exactly equal to his enemy; but he made no attempt to create a special concentration at any one point. He had indeed settled in his own mind the two areas where he hoped for a deep penetration, at Lutsk, to threaten Lemberg, and in Bukovina, on the flanks of Rumania, whose oscillation towards the Entente was now growing more pronounced. But his first task is best described in a metaphor much quoted at the time: 'He is like a man tapping on a wall to find out what part of it is solid stone and what is only lath and plaster.'

Alexeiev deeply distrusted this method, and did not finally sanction it till June 3rd, the evening before the appointed date, when he broke off a telephonic conversation by saying: 'Well, God be with you. Have it your own way.'

The bombardment next day produced surprising results, if it be remembered that the shells had simply been accumulated out of the daily ration for the normal amount of artillery. It is certain, however, that the resistance of German troops would not have been so lightly overcome. The majority of Austrians had little stomach for so unsuspected an onslaught. The taps inflicted by this immense reconnaissance indicated the soundness of Brussilov's judgement, for the wall fell down most completely on the two fronts which he had previously indicated as vital. The Austrian collapse in the direction of Lutsk was most startling. Von Cramon, the German representative, has vividly described the consternation at Head-quarters. The Archduke Joseph Ferdinand reaped the just reward of his frivolity. But he was dismissed only after the storm had burst. Curiously enough he was celebrating his birthday on the very day that his front was broken through. His conqueror, Kaledin, advanced forty miles with little opposition, and devoted his energies to widening the great bulge already created. Kovel was within twenty-five miles; if it fell into his hands, the railway northwards to Brest-Litovsk would be cut, and German help must be long delayed. Ludendorff was already putting into the task of relief all his tremendous energy, and sending every unit to the threatened spot as soon as it could be scraped together.

Meanwhile, on the extreme southern wing, the Russian 7th army was bursting through Bukovina, and before the month was out was among the wooded Carpathians, thereby covering a considerable stretch of the Rumanian frontier. The centre alone remained firm where Count Bothmer, the staunch Bavarian, maintained his positions near Tarnopol, with only one German division to stiffen his nine Austrian. Without his steadfastness there would have been a complete rout. As it was the Russians had captured more than 200,000 prisoners in the first three weeks.

No one at Russian Head-quarters had dreamed of such a success. It was in some ways a serious embarrassment. It was so promising that it must be exploited, but it could not be exploited without large reinforcements of men and munitions. These could come only from the central army group, where they had been accumulated for the main attack; yet it was obviously possible that, while they were in transit, the Volhynian hole might be permanently plugged. Hoffmann, Ludendorff's deputy, has expressed his opinion that the Russians made a grievous error in not adhering to their original programme, although he also gravely apprehended that the Russian masses might overpower the German defence, which was being constantly drained to help its ally. Alexeiev, however, decided on the whole to make the south-western theatre decisive, although he compromised to some extent by persevering in an attack by the central group starting much farther south. Baranovitchi, one of the two main links between Brest-Litovsk and Vilna, just north of the Prijpet marshes, was only a few miles behind the enemy's line. This was the immediate objective of an ill-prepared assault by Evert on July 2nd. His great numerical superiority was dashed to pieces against the German rock.

Brussilov, for his part, kept on attacking with terrible persistence until the end of September, although he met with no strategic success. He finally raised his score of prisoners to 450,000, and had made inevitable the break-up of the Austrian Empire. Yet the price paid by Russia, since June, in over a million men had broken the spirit of her army also. When winter came the number of deserters, most of whom lived quietly at home unmolested by the authorities, was estimated at the astonishing total of 1,000,000. This campaign did not cause the Revolution, for that was far more profoundly rooted in political and economic soil, but it ensured that, after the Revolution, the army would no longer fight for the Entente.

The failure to achieve decisive victory after so bright a dawn must be attributed primarily to the German reinforcements. With a rare courage, based on the exact calculation of risks, Falkenhayn transferred eastwards fifteen divisions from the west between June 4th and September 15th. As a price for this invaluable succour, he exacted the creation of unity of command under German direction for the whole eastern front. The Russian munition-supply gradually faded during the summer, partly owing to a real shortage, partly because of the incompetence of the railway administration. It has often been hinted that Stürmer, the hated German reactionary now established as Premier,[1] whose inclination towards the Central Powers was notorious, gave order to ensure that no sufficient supplies should reach Brussilov's southern armies. This charge, though quite credible, has not been established. In any event the human material was also failing. The men were becoming worn out; they were continually being driven to improvised attacks, where they had to tear down the barbed wire with their bare hands. One unit is said to have been launched seven times unsuccessfully at the same positions within a month. Moreover, the plain-bred moujik was very unhandy at mountain fighting, and the cavalry more useless than ever.

Yet the influence of the campaign upon the general

[1] In July he took over the portfolio of Foreign Affairs, on the dismissal of Sazonov, who had held it since the beginning of the war and had the confidence of the Allied ambassadors. Paléologue, the French representative, was so horrified at the change that he noted in his diary his first apprehensions that Russia might desert the Alliance.

situation was striking and diverse. Eighty-three divisions of the Central Powers had been actually engaged, including a Turkish corps sent by Enver into Galicia. By the close of the year their forces in the east had been increased by 535 battalions. Yet the Austrian menace in Trentino had been stopped dead: Rumania had been induced to take the plunge. Falkenhayn had been dismissed: and all these results were directly due to Brussilov's 'tap' of June 4th.

III

Although his position had been crumbling ever since the failure at Verdun became patent, the immediate occasion of Falkenhayn's fall was the Rumanian declaration of war on August 28th, when his resignation was forced by the Kaiser's decision to call Hindenburg into conference on the general situation of the war. The opposition of the Eastern Command had never been appeased, and had broken out with renewed vigour with the recrudescence of the Russian peril. Falkenhayn was accused of having lost his nerve, and of having brought Germany to the verge of defeat by cautious and half-hearted methods. It is perfectly true that after the failure at Ypres in 1914, he never expected decisive victory. His guiding principle was to avoid 'any overstraining of Germany's power either within or without'. If this was done, he believed that the 'war-will' of the Entente would be broken before that of the Central Powers, and that a satisfactory peace could be obtained. It was for that reason that he had pressed so strongly but unsuccessfully for the launching of unrestricted submarine warfare at the beginning of 1916. His successors (for Ludendorff was associated with Hindenburg in equal power and responsibility as First Quartermaster-General) commanded the reverential trust of the whole country in a quite unrivalled degree. The massive, religious, and kindly Hindenburg was adored almost as a god. His wooden statue was set up in the principal places of the German towns, and large sums were collected for war-charities by the nails which admirers were allowed for a fee to drive into the figure. He seemed the embodiment of the ideal expressed in Bismarck's famous phrase: 'We Germans fear God and nothing else in the world.' From this time forward he became, even more than before, a noble and comforting symbol of Germany's greatness. Ludendorff's devouring and restless activity now found a fresh scope: 'nil actum credens, dum quid superesset agendum.' It is he who presses for and takes decisions, who strives to bring the political and economic fabric of Germany, even the whole mass of the Central Alliance, within his controlling grasp.

One of the first-fruits of the new régime was the creation of unity of command in the person of the Kaiser, whose orders on the general course of operations, enunciated through the Chief-of-Staff, were to be binding on all his allies; although before important decisions were taken, the military chiefs of the respective countries had a right to be heard. Yet harmony between the two principal partners became increasingly difficult to maintain after the death of the aged Francis Joseph in December 1916. His reign of sixty-eight years began and ended with public calamity, and had been attended with so many domestic tragedies as to suggest his entanglement in a net of fate. His young successor Karl jibbed under the German bridle, was strongly influenced by his Bourbon wife, who had many connexions with the Entente, and desired above all immediate peace to save his crumbling heritage.

No less important for the further prosecution of the war was the adoption in Germany of the so-called 'Hindenburg programme', by which the output of munitions was to be enormously increased. It was made effective by the passing in November 1916 of an Auxiliary Services Law, which enabled the human resources of the country to be more fully exploited. Ludendorff pressed hard for a system of industrial conscription for all civilians between the ages of 15 and 60, but this he was never able fully to obtain, although the employment of women in munition factories was perhaps carried further in Germany than in any other country. They finally amounted to more than half the total number of workers.

The programme was expedited by the creation at the same time of a Supreme War Office (*Kriegs-Amt*), which centralized and directed all Germany's economic resources for the prosecution of the war. In each of the districts into which Prussia and the other States of the Reich were divided, there was established a departmental administration for the maintenance and supply of a particular army corps; and each of these administrations was, in fact, a local dictatorship under the central control of the new *Kriegs-Amt*. By the end of the year, under Ludendorff's impulsion, the efficiency and extent of German production had reached its maximum.

IV

The most immediate and pressing concern of the two chiefs on assuming power was the actual military situation of the Central Powers, which seemed to be most grievously jeopardized by the Rumanian declaration of war.

Rumanian egotism had based its action on the most careful, the most anxious calculation. The example of Italy had been an object lesson in the extreme difficulty of finding the right moment for intervention. Yet when fifteen months later Bratianu, the Premier, played his last card with the utmost deliberation, the moment had already gone by. The grasping hand had scarcely been stretched towards its prey before it was cut off, and the whole body received a series of catastrophic blows.

Opinion in the Entente had been long divided as to the value of Rumania as an ally. The Western Powers were becoming more and more anxious to obtain her intervention at almost any price. There was a traditional sympathy in France for the so-called 'Latin Sister' in the Balkans. Briand, still Premier, had always regarded the Salonika expedition, his own creation, with a particularly auspicious eye. He firmly believed that, in conjunction with a Rumanian invasion of Transylvania, it might deal a death-blow to the Danubian Empire. But in Russia very different views were held. The memory of 1877 had not been forgotten. Russia had most shabbily requited the aid of the Rumanian armies against the Turk in that year; for she had annexed Bessarabia and given her ally in exchange the undesired and barren Dobrudja. Rumania in return had become almost a vassal of Austria-Hungary, and for many years Bessarabia figured as her chief *terra irredenta*. Proud of her Roman origin, she could not figure in the Pan-Slav picture so dear to Russian imagination. There was therefore no tie, no sympathy, between the two countries. Moreover, expert Russian opinion, convinced of her military weakness, disliked and despised her extreme importunity of demand. Territorially Rumania demanded the Bukovina, the whole of Transylvania as far as the Theiss, and the Banat of Temesvar, a province north of the Danube principally inhabited by Serbs. The last-named claim was particularly distasteful, as a free hand was claimed to 'Rumanianize' the population. It was only the French insistence upon a speedy conclusion 'because the offensive on the Somme was not producing the desired results', which led to the reluctant assent of Russia.

Bratianu's military requirements were rejected as quite excessive. He had to cut down his original figure of 250,000 men to three divisions, whom the Russians promised to send into the Dobrudja as a defence against Bulgaria. The stipulations about munition-supply could not in fact be carried out.[1] Nor did Sarrail in Salonika fulfil

[1] This was the fault of the Russians. See Sir W. Robertson, *Soldiers and Statesmen 1914–18* (1926), vol. ii, p. 127. 'Rumania was badly, if not treacherously treated with respect to consignments of ammunition sent to her from Western Europe, which were deliberately side-tracked on Russian railways, and there delayed by orders, civilian not military, from Petrograd.' The Russians complained bitterly of the hostility shown to them by the Rumanian railway personnel; see Gen. B. Gourko, *Russia in 1914–17* (1918), who says that officers affirmed that 'there was a real manifestation of ill-will by the railway-men, who exhibited an actual pro-German tendency'.

his obligation to begin a general offensive a fortnight before the Rumanian declaration. The final date was precipitated by a Russian ultimatum, which actually threatened an invasion if Rumania did not take immediate action on the terms already concluded. A little more decision and less haggling would have served her turn far better, for German writers agree that if she had joined forces with the first tide of Brussilov's successes, Austria-Hungary would probably have been lost. But the need for more munitions, and the usual desire of an agricultural population to garner its harvest, kept her inactive till both the summer and the Galician offensive were far spent.

Even as it was, she entered the field pitiably equipped. The human material, 500,000 sturdy peasants, was fairly good in itself, but atrociously led. Eyewitnesses state that all through the campaign crowds of officers were strolling about Bucharest with painted faces, soliciting prostitutes or one another. They had no air force, their lack of telephone-equipment and its antiquated character moved the derision even of the Russians. German agents had just blown up the principal arsenal at the capital with 9,000,000 shells in it. But confidence was grounded on the belief that a sudden onslaught into Transylvania would shatter Austria-Hungary and compel the fulfilment of the Rumanian demands.

No country in Europe was worse fitted by nature for defence. Its configuration at that time resembled a high boot with a swollen foot. The whole of the western curve was bounded by the Carpathians, the Danube formed the rim of the sole, while the heel stuck out south-eastwards into the Dobrudja. On the east alone the frontier was secure, as it followed the Black Sea, and thence the Pruth, coterminously with Russian Bessarabia. Unfortunately, owing to the uneasy relations between the two countries, the rail-heads had been established at some distance from the frontier, so that speedy assistance, even if sincerely intended, could scarcely be sent. The whole of Wallachia, the largest and richest province, the district of the great oil-fields, lay sprawlingly open to a converging attack.

The Rumanian Government had hoped that Bulgaria would not declare war;[1] a vain illusion, in view of the events of 1913, when Bulgaria, at death grips with Serbia

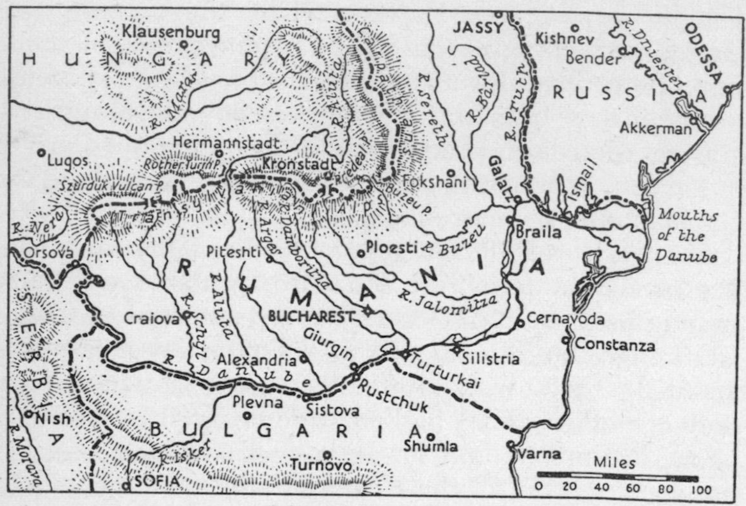

MAP 18. Rumania.

and Greece, was compelled to cede Silistria to her northern neighbour by actual armed intervention. Alternatively, it was expected that Sarrail's promised offensive would prevent any diversion of hostile troops to the Lower Danube.

Military prudence would have suggested an advance beyond the Dobrudja to the Balkans, in order to secure the dangerous back-door against a sudden irruption, before risking any decisive commitments in Transylvania. The character of the Rumanian intervention made this impossible, for the only appeal understood by the people was to free their brothers from the Hungarian yoke. Moreover, Transylvania was defended merely by a few posts of *gendarmerie*. Austria, in the hope of placating her neighbour, had built no fortresses there and few strategic rail-

[1] This notion seems to have been encouraged by Radoslavoff, the Bulgarian Premier, for his own ends.

ways. The advance, however, was of a most fumbling and hesitating character, partly because of the incompetence of the Staff, partly because of the frigidity of the Russians. Alexeiev washed his hands of the whole campaign. He had sent the minimum force agreed upon into the Dobrudja. That was enough; let the Rumanians play their own game of grab. Later on, he expressed his bitterness in these words: 'Such are my feelings, that if His Majesty ordered me to send fifteen wounded soldiers to Rumania, I would on no account send a sixteenth.'

Meanwhile Ludendorff was not losing a moment. While the Rumanians were vaunting the cheap successes of a military promenade which had penetrated fifty miles beyond their mountain frontier, the terrible Mackensen, who had remained in the Balkans since the conquest of Serbia, was hammering at the gates of Dobrudja with a mixed army of Germans, Bulgars, and Turks. As early as September 26th, Turturkai, the Danubian fortress, fell with 25,000 prisoners. The front crumbled and Mackensen pushed on towards the mouth of the Danube. It had been hoped that Bulgarians would refuse to fight against Russian soldiers, their traditional protectors, but with cynical levity Alexeiev had put in the forefront of the battle a division composed of Serb prisoners captured from the Austrian army.

Scarcely had the defensive front in the Dobrudja been reinforced before Falkenhayn, now in command of a Transylvanian army against the enemy whose advent had caused his fall, encircled the central group of invaders at Hermannstadt (September 27–9). The German Alpine Corps just failed to occupy the passes behind the retreating enemy, but even so the victory was decisive for compelling the abandonment of Transylvania. October found the Rumanians standing everywhere on a desperate defensive; on the 23rd Constanza, the chief Black Sea port, fell into Mackensen's hand, farther west he reached Cernavoda, where an immense girder-bridge carried the Bucharest railway over the thousand-yard-wide Danube. The defenders were thrust back another twenty-five miles into the desolate and railless region near the Danube mouth. The decisive act was now to begin.

It was essential that the passes should be forced before the end of November, before deep snow made them impracticable. The Rumanians fought gallantly, and the first week of that month found them still intact. Falkenhayn had no time to lose. Strategically it is clear that the farther north the mountain chain was pierced, the greater the catastrophe would be for the defenders. Averescu, the Rumanian Commander-in-Chief, therefore kept his principal reserves in this area. Falkenhayn fixed upon the Vulcan Pass about fifty miles north-east of Orsova for his principal effort. This was the shortest passage through the mountains; the Rumanian rail-head might be reached in one day's hard march. On the other hand, a success here would cut off only the detachments in the angle between the Danube and the Carpathians. Yet to get through somewhere and somehow speedily was of prime urgency. Falkenhayn justly prides himself on the passage of this defile (November 11) where the narrow road was cramped between a precipice and the Jiu torrent. Sixty thousand men with their full complement of artillery were speedily thrust into the Wallachian plain. It was now time for Mackensen to play his part. Most of his army had been withdrawn from the Dobrudja, and lay near the southern bank of the Danube over against Bucharest. In a thick fog the river was bridged and a surprise crossing effected (November 23). By December 1st the stage was set for the supreme battle. The Rumanian armies were standing in a great curve before Bucharest, assailed from the north, the west, and the south. Their situation was so dangerous that their enemies did not expect them to make a serious stand even to save the capital. But a gap still existed between Mackensen's left wing and Falkenhayn's army which was moving down the Arges. Averescu counter-attacked into this gap with a speed and energy of which he had appeared incapable.

Open warfare had brought again the same tactical danger which had led to the defeat of the Marne—von Kuhl, who had been Kluck's chief-of-staff at the latter battle, contrasts the firmness and daring of Falkenhayn's action with the timidity of Moltke. Thrusting out both his wings to north and south, Falkenhayn aimed at annihilating the forward-pressing Rumanian divisions by rear and flank attacks; and then at squeezing the northern group between his own left and Krafft's army on the upper Arges, and the southern between his right and Mackensen. The whole of his aim was not achieved. After a three-days' battle the Rumanian army was in full retirement, completely defeated, but still a fighting force, in spite of losing 70,000 prisoners. Bucharest was one of Brialmont's most famous ring-fortresses. Heavy artillery was in readiness to batter down its cupolas. Falkenhayn's patrols, however, were greeted not with fire but with a deputation from the Mayor, to state that the capital was an open town, entirely evacuated (December 6). The exhaustion of the troops and a torrential rainfall slackened the pursuit of the Central Powers. Their commander relates that even on the main metalled road horses were daily engulfed. The Rumanians, now at last powerfully reinforced by the Russian command (in fear for the safety of Odessa), escaped to the fortified line of the Sereth, which runs from theborders of Bukovina to the Danube. This was successfully held against all attacks. A large part of the Rumanian army was just saved. At the beginning of January 1917, according to Gourko, it could hold only thirty kilometres of front; but it was immensely improved in the next six months by the French general Berthelot. Three-quarters of the country had been lost, with all the fertile corn-bearing plains and the oil-fields, by far the most extensive in Europe. Happily the latter were to yield nothing to the enemy for several months, for Colonel Norton Griffiths, an English member of Parliament, went round in a car systematically destroying them. Sometimes he barely escaped from enemy patrols, and had often to face the not unnatural hostility of the population;

where time was lacking for him to set them on fire, they were put out of action by throwing obstructions down the pipes.

The Rumanian catastrophe completed the tale of unrelieved failure for the Entente in the Balkans. It contributed to the fall of the Asquith Ministry, for Lloyd George had foreseen the danger and had sent urgent warnings to the Premier early in September. Economically the Central Powers benefited greatly, but politically little; for serious quarrels ensued between Bulgaria and Turkey about the division of the Dobrudja. From a military standpoint, as Ludendorff confesses, it left the position weaker than before. The Eastern Front had been lengthened by 250 miles, and it now absorbed, as has been already shown, much larger forces than were needed six months previously.

V

The long-expected offensive of the Salonika army was postponed by every kind of difficulty, personal, political, and military. Sarrail was certainly a bold and able soldier,[1] but he everywhere enveloped himself in an atmosphere of distrust and dislike. Joffre never forgave the Government for creating so important a new command for a man whom he had dismissed from an army in France. When the Salonika force was placed under his general responsibility he inflicted such petty annoyances as he could upon Sarrail, and constantly complained of him to the Cabinet. Sarrail retaliated by numerous anonymous pamphlets attacking the method pursued by G.Q.G. in France, and aired his views continually in the Radical-Socialist press, even descending so low as the *Bonnet rouge*, edited by an adventurer named Almereyda in German pay.

The British Cabinet, which had been imbued with an extreme dislike of the whole expedition by Robertson, the Chief-of-Staff, naturally hesitated long before confiding their troops to a foreign commander who was believed to have screened a military incompetence by discreditable

[1] As he had shown in the first defence of Verdun in 1914.

political connexions. Nor were the reports from the spot encouraging. The Allied officers complained of Sarrail's arrogant manner and violent temper. British opinion was particularly offended by his luxurious life in Salonika, and the mistress with whom he openly lived. Consequently it was not until July 1916 that a limited authority as Commander-in-Chief in the field was accorded him by the governments whose contingents were assembled in that theatre.

The difficulties with Greece increased in a vicious circle. New interferences with Constantine's sovereignty were the logical result of the growing size of the expedition. The king therefore harboured an increasing ill will towards the Allies, which disposed him towards a more intimate connexion with Germany. The Entente, suspecting and sometimes obtaining proof of this, became still sharper and more peremptory. As the Greek army was still mobilized, its intentions were suspected, and fears were entertained that it was destined to act against the flanks and rear of the expedition, in conjunction with a Bulgar attack. Such fears seemed fully justified when a Greek garrison connived at the Bulgar occupation of Fort Rupel, a dominating frontier post. It is now known that this invasion had indeed been invited by Constantine. In retaliation, the British navy instituted a partial blockade, which forced the king to demobilize his army, though he evaded compliance with the Allied demands for a general election and a non-party government.[1] With the Greek army out of the way, the weightiest obstacle to an offensive was removed. Sarrail, however, was anxious to get Salonika entirely under his own control, and fomented a military rising of the partisans of Venizelos: its leaders on September 1st renounced allegiance to Constantine and declared Greece to be an ally of the Entente.

[1] Here again a legal justification for this interference with internal affairs has been adduced. The three protecting Powers guaranteed Greece in 1863 as an hereditary constitutional monarchy and were therefore entitled to see that the king acted constitutionally.

Now, Rumania, as we saw, had stipulated for a powerful diversion from Salonika at least a fortnight before her declaration of war. Joffre gave the order to start on August 10th. Sarrail can scarcely be blamed for non-compliance, for Robertson had instructed the British commander, Milne, to make no move until the mistrusted Rumanians had actually declared war.

In the interim the Bulgars themselves made the first move, advancing deeply into Greek territory in order to shorten their line. Some Greek detachments now obeyed Constantine's order to offer no resistance. A curious comedy was staged at Kavalla, where the garrison was disarmed and sent to Germany as the Kaiser's 'honoured guests', to quote the official language. Actually they were interned in a style scarcely distinguishable from captivity. Profiting by the humiliation which many Greeks felt at this incident, Sarrail carried through a Venizelist revolution at Salonika (August 30). He then finally launched his attack, the delay of which had been severely criticised in the French press by articles appearing with the connivance of the military censor. Its details need not concern us. The most notable feature was the fighting spirit shown by the reconstituted Serb army, which, in co-operation with the French, reconquered a little strip of its national territory, including the city of Monastir, the capital of Macedonia. The British had been assigned the Struma front together with the thankless task of holding the enemy, whose position on the mountain cliffs beyond Doiran proved impregnable throughout the campaign. The fighting had no effect either upon the Somme or the Rumanian campaigns, and attracted no reinforcements from Germany except a few detachments. But there is evidence to the effect that these Germans, who fought heroically and suffered cruelly, alone prevented a complete Bulgarian collapse. There is no reason to think that Sarrail's military direction was incompetent. Many of his troops were not of high quality, having indeed been sent to this subordinate theatre for that very reason. But as usual his personality created the maximum of personal friction. The worst impression was produced by the violent abuse which he showered upon his own French subordinate Cordonnier, for alleged lack of vigour, in the presence of numerous Allied officers. In spite of his powerful political protectors his days in command were numbered. Meanwhile the Allied relations with Greece had slipped still farther down the path of violence. Constantine had to bow before a naval demonstration outside Peiraeus on September 1st, which exacted the expulsion of the German agents (who had remained in constant communication with the Court at Athens), and an Allied control of railways and telegraphs. Venizelos found a hearty welcome in his native Crete, which as a young man he had stirred to insurrection against the Turks in 1897. After fomenting his separatist movement in the islands, he returned to Salonika. On the mainland, and particularly in Athens, the Venizelists were beaten and killed; a sporadic civil war had begun. The French suspected their allies of shielding Constantine: Russia and England for dynastic reasons inspired by their respective Courts, Italy because a Venizelist Greece, if it became a partner in victory, would lay claims to territory in Asia Minor already ear-marked for Italian ambitions.

They therefore shelved diplomatic methods by putting the negotiations in the hands of their Admiral Dartige du Fournet, Commander-in-Chief of Allied naval forces in the Mediterranean. This honourable and sensitive officer had now to carry out a series of orders which, as his account shows, he thought harsh and even unconscionable. The light craft of the Greek navy were seized. Demands were made for a surrender to the Entente of a quantity of war-material equivalent to that recently abandoned to the Bulgars. In conversation with a French deputy Constantine had agreed to the last proposal, but soon shifted his ground. Franco-British landing-parties were then (December 1) detailed to seize the key positions in Athens on the understanding that they would not be opposed. Greek troops, with a treachery natural to the weak convinced of the unjust constraint of the stronger, ambushed them and killed many. Shells had to be fired on the royal palace before our landing-parties could be extricated. The dethronement of Constantine was postponed until the United States had declared war; this hesitation was out of regard for the supposed susceptibility of America for the rights of small states. But a strict blockade was maintained over the Greek coast. In June 1917 Thessaly was occupied after some slight resistance, and the Greek troops found therein were made prisoners. The rear of the Salonika force was thus completely secured. A French commissioner arrived at Athens and, backed by a large force, declared, in the name of the protecting Powers, the deposition of Constantine. His second son Alexander, believed to be docile, was placed in his room (June 6, 1917). Venizelos returned triumphantly as Premier and Greece joined the Allies.

It is obvious that the treatment of Greece was entirely incompatible with the ordinary rights of neutrals, nor in the writer's opinion can it be justified by the special international position of the protecting Powers. There is no ground for imputing to the Entente a settled policy of coercing Greece into a declaration of war when their troops first landed. But the position was in fact an impossible one. If Constantine had been determined to uphold a real neutrality he should have dismissed Venizelos before the latter had made any kind of pledge. But, though autocratic and firmly convinced of his divine right (a trait which naturally increased his family sympathy with the Kaiser), he was shifty and evasive. He had that kind of weak obstinacy which digs itself in only at the eleventh hour, after a long show of apparent complaisance. To dismiss Venizelos and promise in the same breath 'a most benevolent neutrality' towards the Entente was totally inconsistent. The former action rendered him deeply suspect; the latter declaration led the Allies to think they had a right to ask for anything which they thought necessary. Any refusal was treated as showing a deliberate ill will founded on an understanding with the Central Powers and compliance was extorted by force or its threat. It is probable that the majority of Greeks in 1916 were neither pro-Ally nor pro-German but wanted to be left alone. Yet the course of the war proved that a small nation could only maintain neutrality (or its own ideas of neutrality), if such conduct was compatible with the vital interests of both the great alliances. If not, the maxim 'He that is not for us, is against us' was speedily applied.

XVIII

THE WAR IN THE NORTH SEA UNTIL JUTLAND

THE principal theatre of naval war presented a very singular contrast with its military counterpart in France. In the latter contact was close and incessant, fighting activity seldom quenched, many consecutive months consumed in the inexorable development of gigantic battles. In the North Sea, which is slightly larger in extent than the British Isles, as many months might elapse without an enemy's smoke appearing upon the waste of waters. In more than four years only three considerable cruiser actions occurred. Even in the one great general encounter, the battleships of the Grand Fleet, apart from the swift squadron detached with Beatty, were engaged for a bare half-hour. During this period their crews suffered the only casualties incurred throughout the war in battleship action against German gun-fire, two killed and four wounded. The total casualties of the Navy, of which perhaps three-quarters were in the North Sea, amounted to 39,812, or two-thirds those inflicted upon the British army on July 1st, 1916.[1] The maintenance of security at sea, of which the Grand Fleet bore the prime burden, was thus achieved with an extraordinary economy of life.

The passive policy adopted by the High Seas Fleet on the outbreak of war has been already described. It was illustrated and intensified by the enterprising incursion into the Heligoland Bight on August 28th of our light forces, with battle-cruiser support. The scheme was conceived and its execution aided by Commodore Keyes of the Harwich force, whom we shall constantly see originating deeds of daring and surprise. His submarines regularly on watch off Heligoland had reported the routine by

[1] 640,000 men served in the Navy during the war. The strength at the Armistice was 407,000. The total military casualties in France were about 2,750,000.

which the Germans relieved their protective cordon. The British destroyer flotillas under Commodore Tyrwhitt broke in at 8 a.m. from north of Heligoland, upon the morning watch of torpedo-boats, with the object of sweeping them westward away from their harbours. The enemy was surprised, as the vigilant expectancy of the first few days of war had been gradually relaxed; but managed to elude our flotilla with the loss of one boat sunk. The sound of guns could be plainly heard on the German coast. The battle-cruisers were lying in Jade harbour, and could not cross the bar before 1 p.m. owing to the state of the tide. This was an unforeseen piece of luck for the British enterprise. The enemy's light cruisers, on the other hand, came out singly as soon as each had raised steam. Their captains were ardent to engage and to avenge so insulting a penetration into these sealed and preserved waters. Such unsupported and isolated exits were a grave imprudence. The Commander-in-Chief, however, had no suspicion that Beatty was lurking only forty miles away from the British flotilla. Nor had wireless informed him that the visibility, which was good in harbour, was rapidly deteriorating in the Bight.

In all six light cruisers came out and made for positions north and west of the British to cut them off from home. From 10.30 onwards a confused and indecisive action was in progress, some twenty-five miles south-west of Heligoland. The two British light cruisers, *Arethusa* and *Fearless*, which led the destroyers, were hard pressed; the former indeed was practically crippled both in speed and armament: on the other hand, the *Mainz*, a most persistent and accurate enemy, which had brilliantly repelled a destroyer attack by shattering four assailants in succession, was finally put out of action by two torpedoes. British reinforcements arrived in the nick of time. First Commodore Goodenough with four light cruisers, who completed the destruction of the *Mainz*; then about 1 p.m., racing from the west and looming enormous in the gathering mist, Beatty's five battle-cruisers. The hardihood and swift decision of their admiral were thus dramatically justified by the first appearance of these monsters in battle. He had brought them straight to the call of distress through waters in which the enemy's submarines might be expected to be waiting. His squadron speedily dispatched two more light cruisers, the *Köln* and *Ariadne*, before turning back for fear of mines.[1] Thus the battle ended with good success. No British ship was lost, though the *Arethusa* was towed home with difficulty. All the four German ships sunk fought to the last with great determination. Every possible survivor was picked up by the victors, who ran considerable risks in accomplishing the rescue. The German losses amounted to 1,242; the British were no more than 75.

This defeat had for a time a serious effect upon German moral. The confidence of the navy in the defensive organization of the Bight was severely shaken. The crews of the light cruisers bitterly complained that they had been sent unsupported to so unequal a fight while the British battle-cruisers roamed unmolested through the Bight. The traditional prestige of the British navy seemed to be thoroughly justified by the first ordeal of battle. 'It was a considerable time before this psychological sequel to the fight was overcome.'[2]

The pessimistic impression made upon the High Command was even more important and lasting. It was apprehended that another similar attack might force the whole High Seas Fleet to engage piecemeal in a general action dictated by the enemy, which could not be broken off before the consummation of defeat. Accordingly the triple cordon of submarines and destroyers was withdrawn from the Bight, armed trawlers and the invisible sentinel of a great mine-field took its place. This measure deprived

[1] According to German reports the floating mines which were reported by British destroyers were really empty munition-boxes, which had been thrown overboard. The German submarines were all kept round Heligoland. Beatty was in much greater danger from British ones which had not been informed by the Admiralty that the battle-cruisers were out.

[2] *Der Krieg zur See, 1914–1918: Nordsee*, Band i, p. 216. The German Official History is very frank in making these admissions.

the fleet of any general or sudden access at will to the North Sea, but released a number of light craft for offensive excursions.[1]

The 'muzzling order' was more formally and rigidly enforced. The Commander-in-Chief was warned that the loss of ships must be avoided, and that all fleet sallies, all considerable enterprises, must be approved in advance by the Emperor.

In vain Tirpitz, whose opinion had not been sought, protested in the strongest prophetic terms: 'As time goes on our chance of success will grow worse, not better, as the English fleet receives a substantially greater increase by new building than we do, and keeps in full practice. In addition, the spirit of our men, which was admirable at the start, is bound to deteriorate if there are no prospects of a fight.' He was allowed to rage in complete neglect.

Meanwhile for different reasons the Grand Fleet was hanging uneasily back. The submarines were getting upon its nerves. Twice a U-boat was erroneously reported within the very sanctuary of Scapa. All the great ships in harbour instantly put to sea. In October the base was shifted round Scotland to Lough Swilly and even to Galway Bay; remote posts indeed from which to claim command over the North Sea. Even here a new peril overtook them. A large liner, the *Berlin*, fitted as a mine-carrier, evaded our patrols. Several times she avoided detection by the slenderest margin, before successfully laying her cargo off Tory Island on the northern Irish coast (October 22). Her quarry was not warships but merchantmen sailing on the main route from Liverpool to America. The good luck which had favoured her persistence attended also its consummation. The super-dreadnought *Audacious*,[2] proceeding peacefully with its

[1] Within little more than a month German submarines sank the armoured cruisers *Hawke*, *Cressy*, *Aboukir*, *Hogue*, and the light cruiser *Pathfinder*; and a Russian battleship and light cruiser in the Baltic. On the other hand, the German armoured cruiser *Yorck* was destroyed in the Jade mine-field when returning from bombarding Yarmouth, November 3.

[2] Launched 1912; displacement 23,000 tons; armament ten 13·5 guns.

squadron to battle practice on October 27th, struck one of these mines, and though taken in tow by the liner *Olympic*, snapped her line in the heavy weather and blew up.

In view of the desperate military situation in Flanders, and of Turkish neutrality yet hanging precariously in the balance, the Cabinet agreed to keep the loss secret. This reluctant decision was surprisingly justified. Although many passengers on the *Olympic* had seen and even photographed the sinking vessel, although the disaster was the subject of common gossip,[1] not even a rumour appears to have reached Germany for at least five weeks.

In general the enemy's system of naval intelligence was very imperfect as compared with the British. Our submarines kept a perpetual vigil in the Heligoland Bight, reporting the movements of ships and position of the mine-free channels. Our directional wireless stations were able by a combination of bearings to give the position of a ship sending messages, an advantage which the German Admiralty did not possess until much later. Finally, all unknown to the enemy, by a singular chance, the signal and cipher books of the German navy had fallen into our hands, together with a secret map of the North Sea divided into numbered squares. On August 27th the light cruiser *Magdeburg* had been lost in the Baltic. The body of a petty officer had been washed ashore with this precious freight. It was handed over by the Russians to the British Admiralty, which was thus able swiftly to decode all enemy orders until the cipher had been changed.

Had the enemy known this, it is probable that the ban against fleet enterprises would have been extended to the battle-cruiser squadron as well as to the battleships. As it was the long hours of winter darkness offered opportunities for a swift dash across to the English coast, which could be reached at dawn and bombarded safely before withdrawal. As the Grand Fleet was known to have been driven by the submarines far to the north, it was

[1] The writer finds from his diary that the news was brought to his mess at Chelmsford on 1 November by an officer who had been in London.

thought unlikely that the raiders could be intercepted before their return. Their objects were to lay mines round the coast, to shake the spirit of the civil population, and to cause an outcry for measures of coast-protection which would involve a dangerous strategic dispersion of our fleet.

Three times the battle-cruisers essayed this policy of 'tip and run' as it was popularly called in England, before meeting with defeat on January 24th, 1915. The squadron was fortunate in its commander Hipper, a grand sailor. This bluff, shrewd, unassuming Bavarian was intensely beloved by his men. They recognized the broad, human sympathy which underlay his strictness, and admired his outspoken independence towards superiors. No subordinate who did his duty was ever let down or forgotten by the Admiral. Hipper was a real executive seaman; he neither possessed nor desired any staff training. He despised long written orders and everything that the French called *paperasserie*. 'According to the regulations!' he once said to an anxious navigating officer in his flagship, 'You needn't worry about them; they're only for those who need them.' This 'great improvised leader', hardly ever set pen to paper, and consistently shunned both publicity and controversy. One sheet of paper contained his bald report to Scheer of the great deeds of the battle-cruisers at Jutland.[1]

His opponent Beatty has had perhaps the most meteoric, intriguing, and provocative career of any great leader of modern times. Completely undistinguished in his qualifying examinations, with singularly little sea-going experience, mainly conspicuous for land service in the Sudan and China, he had yet gained the unexampled promotion to Rear-Admiral at the age of 38. It is said that he was then junior in age to at least nine-tenths of the captains in the Navy List. Within four years he obtained the prize of the battle-cruiser squadron. He owed this great command to Churchill, who after choosing him as Naval Secretary had

[1] There is a pleasant life of Hipper by Capt. von Waldeyer-Hartz, translated into English (1933).

been deeply impressed by his untrammelled and vehement personality. It was indeed a personality towards which no one could feel indifference. After the Dogger Bank action we hear of a sailor clapping him on the back and calling out 'Good old David', of Admiral Pakenham reverently whispering to Churchill 'Nelson has come again'. On the other hand, detractors bitterly alleged that his advancement was principally due to social connexions, to skill at hunting and polo; that he was inexperienced, ignorant of tactics, incapable of controlling a fleet, profligate in welcoming a gambler's risk. All agree that he exulted in battle, and found complete self-realization in the exercise of command amidst the bursting of shells.

Hipper's first raid on Yarmouth (November 3) proved equally unsatisfactory to both sides. The British were taken by surprise, and the improvised arrangements for intercepting his return proved quite abortive. The German squadron, however, achieved practically nothing. It sank no ships, it did no military damage, the mine-field which it laid was observed and immediately swept, while on re-entry of the Jade the large cruiser *Yorck* struck a mine and was lost with half its crew.

The main interest to the historian in Hipper's next venture on December 16th lies not in what actually happened, but in what might so easily have happened. Early that morning the German strategic dispositions offered a better chance of inflicting a disastrous blow upon our naval superiority than on any other day in the war; while on returning the German squadron came within an ace of destruction. The enemy had for some time contemplated an attack on Hartlepool, and submarine reconnaissance had made it clear that the entrance was mine-free. On December 10th the publication of Spee's destruction showed that the British fleet in home waters was short of two battle-cruisers. The moment was therefore favourable for a raid. The preparations were on the grand scale. The High Seas Fleet of fourteen dreadnoughts and eight older battleships advanced towards the eastern edge of the Dogger Bank during the night of December 15th 16th to support Hipper's squadron, itself covered with light cruisers and destroyers, in its advance against the English coast.

The British Admiralty knew all about the proposed battle-cruiser operation, but was quite ignorant that the main German fleet was out. Consequently it sent Beatty with four battle-cruisers, and Warrender with six dreadnoughts of the 2nd battle squadron, to intercept Hipper's return, a force overwhelming for that purpose, but entirely insufficient to fight the High Seas Fleet.

Now it came about that the destroyers covering the British force and the screen of the High Seas Fleet came into contact in the darkness and engaged in a confused running fight between 5 and 6.30 a.m. Ingenohl, the German Commander-in-Chief, on receiving this news fell into serious alarm. He feared that a concentrated destroyer attack against him was imminent. He had already strained his muzzling order by bringing the fleet out beyond the limits of the Bight. If it was caught in such a position and suffered serious damage from torpedo, he might expect to be visited with the Kaiser's heaviest displeasure. Thus reasoning, he turned his fleet in the darkness, and, without informing Hipper, retired into the Bight.

His rendezvous had been only fifty miles from that assigned by the Admiralty to Warrender and Beatty. Had he remained cruising in the vicinity during the morning, it is probable that he would have gained touch with the two British squadrons. The superior speed of the latter might indeed have enabled them to evade him, but had they been brought to battle, they could hardly have escaped heavy defeat if not annihilation. The British margin of superiority in capital ships might thus have been practically obliterated at a stroke. Tirpitz indeed exaggerates in his bitter outburst: 'Ingenohl had the fate of Germany in the palm of his hand, I boil with inward emotion whenever I think of it.' Yet no other such opportunity was vouchsafed to the German fleet during the war.

Meanwhile this collision with the German screen had

naturally confused the appreciation of the situation by the British admirals, who hunted about for something to destroy until the news of the bombardment of the English coast brought them westward at full speed.

Hipper reached his objective about 8 o'clock, and, dividing his forces into two, sent part to attack Scarborough and Whitby, and appeared off Hartlepool with the remainder. The two Yorkshire ports were undefended and the enemy enjoyed an inglorious triumph in killing civilians at close range. Hartlepool was a legitimate objective, and the territorial gunners stood manfully to their three 6-inch guns. German accounts praise their practice, for they scored several serious hits on the *Blücher* and drove her off. The bombardment, however, wrought havoc in the town, and more than 500 civilians were its victims.

The Admiralty now, in correct anticipation, warned the two British squadrons to expect Hipper's return due east through the fifteen-mile gap known to exist in the minefields sown round the coast. About sixty miles from the coast dead in line with his route lay the south-west patch of the Dogger Bank, known to be impracticable for battle-cruisers in the stormy weather which had set in since dawn. Beatty therefore went to the north, and Warrender to the south, being thus separated by fifteen miles. Each kept his screen extended on either side of the Bank to sight the enemy if he made a detour either north or south.

With reason the hope was confident that Hipper must be brought to bay. The storm, however, proved his salvation. For his light cruisers and destroyers were labouring so heavily in the rough seas that, with the exception of one mine-layer, he sent them home before reaching the English coast. So it happened that they acted as long-distance scouts for him, some fifty miles ahead of his return.

They first fell in with Beatty, who lost touch with them, owing to confusion in his signals to our light cruisers.[1]

[1] The signalling in the battle-cruiser squadron does not seem to have been very efficient. A more glaring example of confusion will be noticed in the Dogger Bank Battle.

They then doubled south and ran straight into Warrender's squadron. With extreme presence of mind they made the British recognition signal which they had noticed when in contact with Beatty and disappeared into a thick squall before Warrender realized them as enemy. Thus they were able to warn Hipper of the battle squadron towards which he was steaming. He then turned north, and gave the patch a wide berth before resuming his direct course for home. He did not see Beatty. The British admiral, however, deserves no blame for his failure in this complicated game of hide-and-seek. Warrender's report led him to believe that the whole squadron was passing to the south. Consequently he steered to the east to bar their return, keeping obstinately to a fruitless chase on a divergent course until dusk. The last chance of catching Hipper was spoilt by the Admiralty, which did not order Keyes's submarines to proceed to Heligoland to molest his return until five hours after the eager commodore had first expected it. December 16th was a veritable day of dupes. The great chess-board of the North Sea had been elaborately filled with pieces, and either side had been distracted by pawns into making the wrong moves. The issue was humiliating for us. The enemy could at least boast of violating our coastal immunity, in the most spectacular way since the Dutch fleet sailed up the Medway. His more valuable though less-acclaimed success was the laying of a new mine-field of obscure limits north of Scarborough, which remained for many weeks a serious danger to shipping. The Admiralty naturally could not show how narrowly its dispositions had failed to bring the enemy to action, and public opinion was much exasperated by the unavenged insult.

Next time the enemy was brought to bay and heavily mauled, yet escaped almost certain annihilation through confusion in the British squadron. Hipper's intentions when he set out on the night of January 28th, 1915, were modest. His destination was the Dogger Bank, where he hoped to destroy British fishing-vessels, suspected of conveying information to our fleet, and perhaps any light forces in his way. He was not supported by the High Seas Fleet. As the Grand Fleet had been in the Bight only four days previously, it was expected now to be in harbour. The enemy still had no suspicion that we were deciphering his signals, and believed the intended enterprise to be entirely secret. The Admiralty, however, knew all about it. A great concentric movement against Hipper's rendezvous was put in train. Beatty came from the north and the Harwich forces from the south. The mistake of December 16th was not repeated, for the Grand Fleet put to sea and remained in discreet readiness some 150 miles behind Beatty. Day was scarcely breaking when the opposing screens fell in with each other at the expected place. At 8.50 the two battle-cruiser squadrons came into distant view. Beatty had five ships, including the newly commissioned *Tiger*, against Hipper's four, of which the oldest, *Blücher*, was scarcely fit to take her place in the line. She was slower and inferior both in armour and armament.[1]

Hipper, outnumbered and believing that a British battle-squadron was also in the offing, made off at once for home. With an envious alarm he saw the British squadron coming up behind him at the tremendous speed of 28 knots. Beatty was running on a parallel course south-west of his adversary, having gained the lee station in the hope that the north-east wind would confuse the German aim; for the dense smoke from their funnels drifting south-west would make our ships difficult to pick out clearly.

The *Lion* carrying Beatty's flag at the head of our line opened fire at more than 20,000 yards. The running battle was fought at a range and speed quite unprecedented. Beatty seldom closed to less than 17,000 yards, hoping thus to reap the advantage of his heavier armament. In this aim, however, his success was very partial. His order that

[1] She had taken the place of the *Von der Tann*, at that time in dock. The British squadron had a broadside of twenty-four 13·5-inch and sixteen 12-inch guns; against eight 12-inch, twenty 11-inch, and twelve 9-inch. The weight of British metal was superior by about 75 per cent.

each ship should take its corresponding enemy was not obeyed by the *Tiger*, next in line to the *Lion*. Both of these subsequently concentrated on the enemy's van, the flagship *Seydlitz*, leaving the *Moltke* next in line undisturbed. The shooting of the *Tiger*, newly commissioned with an unexperienced crew, was also very bad, and she probably never hit the mark at all. Practically throughout the battle all the German ships except the *Blücher* concentrated on the *Lion*, partly in the hope of knocking out the Admiral, but mainly because she alone was often distinguishable through the smoke clouds. Consequently the *Lion* received repeated hits, but her speed remained nearly unimpaired after fighting for ninety minutes. The *Blücher* had been badly smashed, and was being left astern. The *Seydlitz* narrowly escaped destruction from one of the *Lion's* shells. Piercing her deck it exploded close to the after turrets, wrecking both of them and killing 159 men. The cordite charges lying in the working chambers were set on fire and the flames leapt as high as the masts. The magazine was protected from explosion by a steel door closing the ammunition hoist. Otherwise the ship would have been instantly blown to pieces. Though presenting a fearful appearance with the fire wreathing for a long while about her stern, she had suffered no engine damage and kept her speed.

Just before 11 a.m., however, the whole course of the action was changed to our disadvantage. The *Lion* received a terrific blow, which smashed her feed-tank and damaged her engines beyond remedy. About the same time her look-out reported a submarine to starboard.[1] Beatty immediately signalled to his squadron to turn at right angles to the north, thus moving away from the enemy who was retreating south-east. The *Lion* now became unmanageable and fell out of the line. The signals made by the Admiral to 'Attack the enemy's rear' and

[1] No submarine was in fact present. The German official account suggests that the wake of a torpedo fired at extreme range by a German destroyer was responsible for the mistake. Beatty's action has been severely criticized on the ground that the proper procedure is to turn towards a submarine, and away from a destroyer.

'to keep closer to the enemy' were either misunderstood or not taken in by the rest of the squadron. There was moreover for some minutes uncertainty as to whether Beatty had given over the command. The next senior officer Admiral Moore had been appointed only a few days before, apparently against Beatty's desire. He was an ultra-cautious disciple of the Jellicoe school. Possibly he would have continued the pursuit if Beatty had at once relinquished the command without any further signal. But the garbled version which he had taken in was construed not as an incitement to attack but as a counsel of strict prudence. He conceived his instructions to read 'Attack the enemy's rear bearing north-east'. In that direction lay the unhappy *Blücher*, now fought to a standstill, but savagely defending herself against the light cruisers and destroyers, who sought to give her the *coup de grâce*. Accordingly he led the whole of the squadron to finish off the dying vessel, which fought to the last with the most glowing courage. Moore believed that his orders forbade him to proceed farther east into perilous waters (his position was now some 80 miles west of Heligoland) and made no motion of pursuit. When Beatty appeared in the destroyer to which he had transferred his anger and disappointment were great. He ordered a resumption, but Hipper had got clean away; for with a heavy heart he had followed the correct principle of abandoning the *Blücher* to her fate. The wounded *Lion*, taken in tow and surrounded by light cruisers and destroyers, made a most perilous return to Rosyth.

The victory was trumpeted abroad; its importance being exaggerated by the genuine though mistaken impression that two of Hipper's ships had fled in a practically sinking condition. Both Fisher and Beatty, however, were exceedingly sore over the wasted chance. The latter wrote to Keyes saying: 'We ought to have had all four.' The unfortunate Moore was speedily removed.

The Admiralty was convinced that the superiority of our battle-cruisers had been completely vindicated. The immense range at which the action was fought aroused extravagant belief in the superiority of our guns. The frightful effect of two hits upon the *Seydlitz* and the *Blücher* suggested a greater explosive power in our shells than they actually possessed. These two, owing to the steep angle of descent at long range, had penetrated the deck and found an exceptionally vulnerable target. But no British shell succeeded in riving the armour of a German battle-cruiser. The thinner plates of the *Lion*, on the other hand, were completely pierced by the smaller 11-inch enemy shells. Moreover, the German aim had been the more accurate, judged by the percentage of hits secured by either side.[1]

In Germany the accuracy of our Intelligence provoked profounder misgivings than the result of the action. To raid an enemy, who knew beforehand exactly what to expect, was to tempt Providence. Ingenohl, who had so exactly obeyed the muzzling policy which his professional instincts disapproved, was dismissed. Pohl, the Chief of the Naval Staff, reigned for a year uneasily and inefficiently in his stead. The great ships were most rigidly confined in harbour, and Germany's main naval hopes were transferred to the U-boats and Zeppelins. In January 1916 Pohl, a broken and dying man, suffered the unexampled humiliation of being ceremoniously informed by the Chief of the Operations Department that the Corps of Officers had lost all confidence in his leadership.

In his successor, Scheer, the German navy at last found a leader worthy of its high devotion and technical efficiency. A hard, strong, confident man with a happy admixture of daring and prudence, he at once began that more active and enterprising policy which was to lead on May 31st, 1916, to the one great fleet action of the war.

[1] This was mainly due to the system of director-firing of turrets already completed in practically all the modern German ships. The *Tiger* alone was thus fitted on the British side. It may be described as 'a device by which all the guns can be trained laid and fired simultaneously and accurately from one central position, generally on the foremast' (Filson Young, *With the Battle Cruisers* (1921)). Its effect was to make the salvoes more concentrated and deadly. The extreme efficiency of the German battle-cruisers at Jutland in utilizing this method will be noticed later.

XIX

JUTLAND[1]

I

THIS great battle was neither deliberately foreseen, nor was it the result of a purely chance collision. It was brought about naturally by the aggressive tactics of Scheer. The new German Commander, like his predecessors, hoped so to compel a strategic division of the Grand Fleet, as to catch it at a disadvantage; but unlike them he strove actively to achieve this end. As a result of the bombardment of Yarmouth and Lowestoft with his battle-cruisers on April 24th, the day on which the Irish Rebellion broke out in Dublin, the British Admiralty moved the 5th battle squadron of swift *Queen Elizabeths* from Scapa to reinforce Beatty at Rosyth. In May Scheer's mind was set upon a more ambitious enterprise. The surrender of his government to the *Sussex* note enabled him to recall a number of submarines from trade destruction to fleet duties. Sixteen of them were sent to lie off the Scottish harbours, Rosyth being particularly menaced. He then intended to bombard Sunderland, with the High Seas Fleet in close support and extensive Zeppelin reconnaissance. This port is so near the Firth of Forth that there seemed a good hope that Beatty, after toll had been taken of his fleet by the submarines as he put out, might be overwhelmed before help could reach him from Scapa. This plan, however, proved unrealizable as the weather continued unkind and one of the battle-cruisers, the *Seydlitz*, had been delayed in dock for repairs after striking a mine on April 24th. He was determined, however, to attempt something before his submarines returned from their stations on June 1st.[2] On May 30th therefore he sent Hipper

[1] The German name for the battle is Skagerack: it was fought over an enormous area but mostly some seventy miles west of the North Jutland coast.

[2] Submarines made an abortive attack on Beatty, leaving Rosyth, but otherwise, like the Zeppelins, played no part in the battle on either side.

out to show himself next day off the Norwegian coast, waging war against commerce as opportunity offered. The British Admiralty could not indeed now read their enemy's intentions so clearly as in the earlier days of the war, but it was known that an unusual activity animated the German ports. Accordingly Beatty received the order to make a sweep in the eastern area of the North Sea. The Grand Fleet, now increased to the majestic strength of twenty-four dreadnoughts and three battle-cruisers, steamed to the north of him out of visual touch at about the usual distance of seventy miles.

At 2 p.m. on May 31st Beatty had reached his prescribed limit and was about to turn north to close Jellicoe, when his light cruiser *Galatea*, screening his eastward flank, sighted smoke far to port. This was a Danish trader, which unwittingly became the magnet to draw the opposing battle-cruisers together. For Hipper, on his northerly course some forty-five miles eastward from Beatty, had also seen the same smoke and sent his cruiser *Elbing* to examine it.

The light forces on either side were thus drawn into collision, and the two admirals set their squadrons on converging courses. It was a piece of good fortune for Hipper that the meeting came so early. He had not an idea that the Grand Fleet was out, and might well have been lured into a fatal trap, if he had fallen in with Beatty an hour later with both squadrons running on parallel lines to the north.[1]

As soon as Beatty recognized his adversary, he made off at full speed in a south-easterly direction to intercept him from his base. The omens seemed very good. The High Seas Fleet had been reported by the British Admiralty to be still within the Jade at 11 a.m.[2] He had four fast battleships armed with 15-inch guns to reinforce his six battle-

[1] It is possible but improbable that he might have escaped notice altogether, as at this period of the day the visibility was unusually good for the North Sea.

[2] Our directional wireless had reported the German flagship as signalling from harbour at that hour. This, however, proved to be a successful attempt to mislead our Intelligence.

cruisers, themselves apparently more than a match for Hipper's less heavily-gunned five. Yet the results of the long running action which ensued were in Jellicoe's delicate phrase 'unpalatable', and fell scarcely short of disastrous. Beatty's exercise of command has been severely criticized for a failure to concentrate his forces, and for lack of tactical cohesion.

The position in which he had placed his four *Queen Elizabeths* on a bearing five miles north-west of the *Lion* was obviously ill adapted for a speedy intervention by that squadron against an enemy appearing from the expected direction, south or east. Further, its commander Evan Thomas held on his original course for ten minutes after Beatty had dashed off after his prey, and did not fire a gun until the battle-cruisers had been engaged for twenty minutes. This grievous misunderstanding was due to the usual inefficiency of the *Lion*'s signalling system.

Much to the astonishment and jubilation of the Germans, who feared the longer range of our guns, Beatty allowed the two squadrons to close within 16,000 yards before fire opened.[1] Then the first salvoes were fired by German guns. Incredible as it seems, the same mistake as at the Dogger Bank in arranging the distribution of fire against enemy vessels again occurred. Signals were missed by two of our ships with the result that the *Derfflinger*, the marksman of Hipper's squadron, was left out and 'free to engage our enemy with complete calm, as at gun practice' in the words of her first gunnery officer.

It is not surprising that in these circumstances the enemy had the mastery. One British ship, the *Indefatigable*, blew up within a quarter of an hour, and the *Lion* was only saved from a similar fate by the dying heroism of a marine, Major Harvey, who ordered the magazine doors to be closed in the nick of time, after his turret had been destroyed by a shell. The German gunners during this phase sent over their salvoes with deadly accuracy every

[1] The distance is stated to have been much over-estimated by the British gunnery officers. Our range-finders were very inferior to the German.

1a Earl Haig.

b General Hindenburg.

c Marshal Foch.

General Pershing.

2 German troops in Serbia, 1914.

3 German band playing in the main street of Lodz after its capture, 1914.

4 Gallipoli, 1915.

a A corner of the Anzac position.

b The old castle and village Sedd-el-Bahr.

5 Italian troops arriving in Salonika, 1916.

6a and b The Battle of the Somme was one of the greatest military disasters ever known. The mud was the 'worst enemy'.

7 8 inch Mark V howitzers in action on the Somme, 1916.

8 The sinking of the German battleship *Blucher*, 1915.

9 *HMS Lion* at the Battle of Jutland, 1916.

10 A seaplane being hoisted aboard *Ark Royal*.

11 German U-boats waged a relentless war against British shipping. U-42 (foreground) was commanded by U-boat ace Captain von Arnauld de la Perière, photographed in the Mediterranean with sister ship U-35.

12 British troops in Mesopotamia, 1917.

13 A balloon apron defending London against air attack.

14 A welcome at a British seaport for disembarking American troops.

15 The Krupp works at Essen.

a 12 inch naval shells.

b A heavy gun shop.

16 The entrance to the Bruges Canal at Zeebrugge showing *Thetis, Intrepid* and *Iphigenia* sunk in 1918 to prevent its use by U-boats. (See map 29).

17 The Western Front, 1918. British tanks going forward, German prisoners going back.

18 Officers address British troops.

19 No. 1 squadron (Fighter Command) with their SE5A aircraft on the Western Front, 1918.

20 General Allenby listens on the steps of the citadel in Jerusalem to the reading of the Proclamation of Occupation.

21 The historic dining-car in which the Armistice was signed on November 11th, 1918.

twenty seconds, while themselves almost immune from punishment. The advent of the *Queen Elizabeths* within extreme range relieved for a while Beatty's mauled squadron. Firing at 19,000 yards they made indeed few hits but threw their shells so rapidly and precisely all round Hipper's ships that the great fountains of water cast up obscured the aim of his gunners. Before long, however, our battle-cruisers received an even heavier blow. The *Queen Mary* had found her range and was doing great execution upon the *Von der Tann*, when at 4.26 she was caught simultaneously by two salvoes from the *Derfflinger* and *Seydlitz*. She blew up in the twinkling of an eye, and within thirty seconds nothing was left of her except fragments of debris cast upon the *Tiger*'s deck. Over her grave ascended 'a dark pillar of smoke rising stemlike till it spread hundreds of feet high in the likeness of a vast palm-tree'.[1] Beatty, who is said to have remarked to his flag-captain, 'Chatfield, there seems to be something wrong with our damned ships to-day', remained unflinching in pursuit. Meanwhile the destroyer flotillas, seeking an opening to launch torpedoes against the great combatants, were bickering furiously between the lines.

II

It was now 4.33, when Commodore Goodenough, who rendered invaluable service throughout the day as an accurate gatherer and swift transmitter of information, scouting in the light cruiser *Southampton* sighted the entire German High Seas Fleet in line ahead. Sixteen modern dreadnoughts and six older battleships were deployed in battle array. Scheer had first intended to steer north-west to cut off Beatty from his base, but upon hearing of the presence of the 5th battle squadron he ran straight to Hipper's assistance. This mighty apparition was entirely unexpected. Beatty, however, was in no serious danger. He was not within range, and the speed of the enemy, as

[1] Sir J. S. Corbett, *Naval Operations*, vol. iii (1923), p. 337. German eye-witnesses estimate the height of the cloud as over 700 metres (2,300 feet).

regulated by the pre-dreadnoughts, should not exceed 17 knots, whereas his squadron could do 28 and the *Queen Elizabeths* 25. He turned and ran to the north, sending the momentous discovery to Jellicoe by wireless. Hipper followed him within gun-fire. But the disengagement of the 5th battle squadron was not accomplished without great peril. For by yet another confusion of signals Evan Thomas did not at once take in the order of recall and held on his southerly course until he had passed Beatty's turning-point. His ships had to put about under heavy fire from the German van at long range, and for half an hour could not shake off their pursuers.[1] The enemy had the advantage of the eastern station, for the sun was beginning to pick out the silhouettes of the British ships, while the Germans lay in a gathering murk. This second stage of the battle was fitful and inconclusive. For while the 5th battle squadron was repeatedly hit and suffered considerable casualties[2] its fighting power was scarcely impaired; on the other hand, the *Seydlitz* was lightly struck in the bows by a torpedo.

Pursuers and pursued followed the long northerly course until 5.56, when at last Beatty made contact with Jellicoe. It was of little consequence that he had suffered heavy losses, for he had brought an entirely unsuspecting enemy almost under the guns of the overwhelming Grand Fleet.

III

For the last three hours Jellicoe had been steaming south with all speed. He had been fifteen miles short of his agreed position when Beatty first reported the enemy in sight, as he wished to economize the fuel of his destroyers for so long a cruise.[3] The Grand Fleet with its screen

[1] The leading German battleships of newest design worked up to 23 knots for a short time, or at least 2 more than had been credited to them. They had been specially keyed up for this premeditated enterprise, whereas the British ships, being constantly at sea, could never be relied upon to be in their best condition.

[2] About 100 killed and 50 wounded.

[3] Destroyers had several times stopped to examine merchantmen and the fleet had slackened speed in order to allow them to regain station.

spread before it in a great crescent was disposed in its usual cruising formation of divisions in line ahead. This may be described as six parallel columns of four ships; the distance between each column being 2,000 yards and between each ship in the column 500 yards. The *Iron Duke*, the fleet flagship, was the leading ship of the third column from the left.

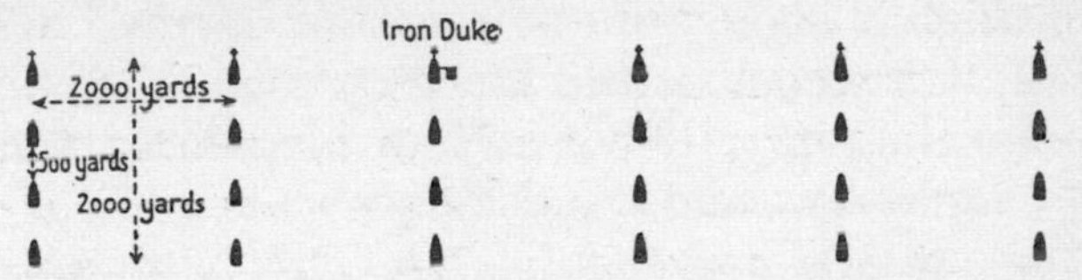

This formation was obviously unsuited for action since many of the ships must mask each other's fire, but was less vulnerable to torpedo attack than the long line of battle. It was therefore most desirable not to deploy prematurely, but absolutely necessary not to delay the deployment until too late. So to complete this manœuvre at the right moment and in the right way, it was essential for Jellicoe to know not only when to expect the enemy but also from what direction. After receiving the message from Goodenough that the High Seas Fleet had been sighted, he telegraphed to the Admiralty 'Fleet action imminent', thereby setting in motion a devouring activity in all dockyards and hospitals, and held on his course in eager expectation. It so happened that errors in plotting their respective positions had been made both by the *Iron Duke* and the *Lion*, so that when the latter ship came into visual contact just before 6 p.m., she was about eleven miles more to the west than had been expected. This must mean that Scheer's fleet, which was supposed to be approaching the British centre, would appear well to the south-west of the starboard division. The moment for deployment must be almost due if it had not already come. Before committing himself to a decision of such paramount importance as the direction in which to form line of battle, Jellicoe tried to get the specific information, which his own scouts were not able to provide. Twice he signalled urgently to Beatty

'Where is the enemy's battle-fleet?' But Beatty had himself lost sight of it. The precious minutes passed in the tensest anxiety, until at 6.14 Beatty signalled 'Have sighted the enemy's battle-fleet bearing S.S.W.' Thus the previous impression was definitely confirmed—Scheer was approaching the right flank of the Grand Fleet.

The object of deployment is to form a line of ships parallel to or slightly converging towards the enemy. Scheer's direction was such that the speediest method of deployment—turning the guide of each division simultaneously at right angles—was impracticable.[1]

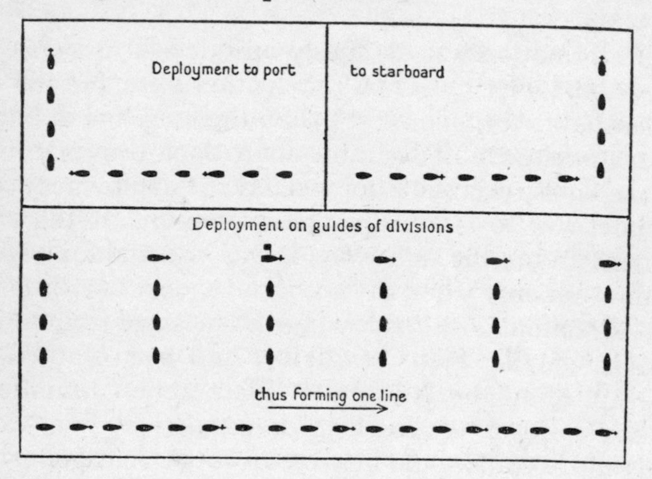

Consequently Jellicoe considered that only two alternatives were available,[2] to make the deployment on either his right or left wing. The time required was in either case eighteen minutes.

To form the battle-line to starboard would obviously bring the Grand Fleet closer to the enemy. In view of the late afternoon hour and of the ever-dwindling visibility

[1] This manœuvre took only four minutes for completion.

[2] A third deployment from the centre on the *Iron Duke* is not mentioned by Jellicoe as being present in his mind, and seems to be generally condemned by expert opinion as not offering any tactical advantage to compensate for its elaboration and slowness. It is, however, strongly supported by Churchill as the proper course for Jellicoe to have taken. *World Crisis, 1916–18* (1927), pt. i, p. 148.

such a plan might seem to offer the best chance of winning a decisive victory before darkness fell. Towards it Jellicoe's mind inclined at the first moment. But in his considered judgement, which is fully confirmed by German narratives,[1] the countervailing objections and dangers were insuperable. The starboard division, consisting of the oldest dreadnoughts, would have been for several minutes exposed without support to the concentrated fire of the enemy's van and to destroyer attack. Finally, the line thus formed would either be enveloped by the enemy, or compelled to turn away at comparatively low speed under easy range of his guns.[2]

On the other hand, deployment to port, though some 10,000 yards farther from the enemy, possessed decisive advantages. It could be completed without risk of serious interruption from shells. It would enable the battle to be fought at the desired range of at least 15,000 yards. This Jellicoe had always considered to be of capital importance. His guns were heavier, and he had an almost obsessing fear of the dangers to be expected from a massed attack by destroyers.[3] Further, as the enemy was coming up from the south-west, the line thus formed would 'cross his T', would interpose itself between the return route to the German harbours, and would compel Scheer to fight with the westward glow illuminating his battleships. Thus Jellicoe had good hope that even if the

[1] See, e.g., *Der Krieg zur See, 1914–1918: Nordsee*, Band v, p. 284: 'It must be allowed to the British Commander-in-Chief that such a decision in the circumstances would have brought his fleet into the very position desired by the German fleet' (welche der deutschen nur erwünscht sein konnte).

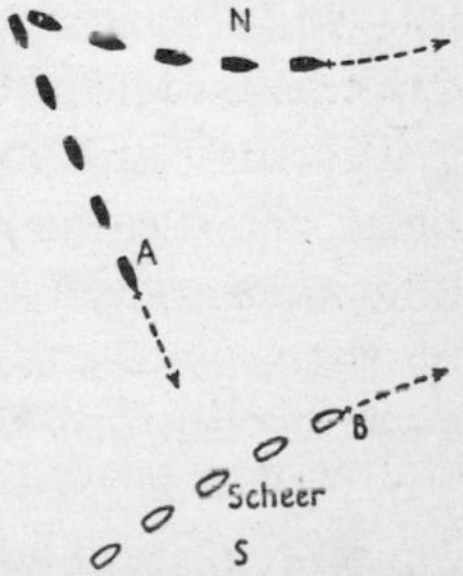

[2] It is clear that if Scheer got to *B* by the time that the leading British ship had reached *A*, the British 'T would be crossed', i.e. the leading ships would be subjected to enfilade fire from either side. This is traditionally the most dangerous tactical position possible in a fleet action.

[3] The German torpedo actually had an effective range of about 10,000 yards, and its track proved to be far more visible than had been feared

short span of daylight denied a decision that afternoon, it would be within his power to force Scheer far to the westward, and to stand next morning with annihilating prospects in the path of his return.

Tactically the deployment was hampered by the necessity for Beatty to pass right across the path of the battleships in order to take up his allotted station in the van. This passage both caused a good deal of bunching among the rear ships of the Grand Fleet, and also masked the fire of successive parts of the deploying line.

It was, moreover, most unfortunate that the *Queen Elizabeths*, also intended to operate on the van as an independent squadron, were behind Beatty and had not time to follow him across, but took station at the rear of the line of battleships. Thus all the advantages of their superior speed were squandered, and they played a negligible part in the main battle. Jellicoe has been often criticized for not improvising with them a harassing movement on the enemy's west flank. However, the rigid precise centralizing mind of the Commander-in-Chief was not apt in improvisation, admirably as it worked in coolly unfolding a preconceived plan.

Leaving this mighty line, some 15,000 yards in length, to straighten itself out on a south-easterly course, we must return to the fortunes of the approaching enemy.

IV

The latter stages of his advance had not been without dramatic incidents of sudden combat, both disturbing and gratifying. About 5.30 fighting developed between the light cruisers scouting on Hipper's east flank and the *Chester*, a similar British vessel. She was the forerunner of three *Invincibles*, a detached battle-cruiser squadron, coming hotfoot from the Cattegat to Beatty's succour. They had originally been sent to close the Baltic on first news of contact with the enemy. Emerging suddenly from a fitful mist, they wrecked one cruiser, the *Wiesbaden*, and damaged the remainder and put them to flight. This advent on so unsuspected a quarter, upon a flank believed to be free, caused grave concern. Were they the heralds of the Grand Fleet approaching against expectation from the north-east? The question remained unanswered for the present, as the *Invincibles* passed out of sight, and all remained quiet on the eastern wing. Soon afterwards, however, Hipper, now on an eastward course and in renewed battle-contact with Beatty, saw the flaming *Wiesbaden* the target of a concentrated fire. Her assailants were two old armoured cruisers *Warrior* and *Defence*, part of a squadron which for some unexplained reason Jellicoe had kept three miles in advance of his battleships. Their slowness made them useless as scouts; their armament left them an easy prey to battle-cruisers. The Germans could scarcely believe their eyes at the vision of these old ships so wantonly exposed. Four minutes at less than 6,000 yards sufficed to blow up the *Defence* and to batter the *Warrior* into helplessness[1] (6.20 p.m.). She also would have been sunk forthwith had not the *Warspite*, one of Evan Thomas's squadron, involuntarily protected her. The latter's steering-gear had been put out of control and she went round the *Warrior* in a wide circle, while all the enemy's battle van rained shells upon her. Fortunate beyond measure to escape destruction, she limped for good out of the fight.

On the balance of losses so far Scheer could show an overwhelming credit account. He had destroyed or put out of action three capital ships and two large armoured cruisers against a loss of one light cruiser.[2] Until the British deployment had begun he was quite ignorant of the proximity of the Grand Fleet, and was concerned only with the problem of whether the pursuit should be broken off owing to the late hour. Scarcely had his light forces informed him of more than twenty battleships moving south-east than great shells began to fall around his van

[1] This ship sank in the North Sea next day when being towed home. The tonnage of these cruisers was 14,600.

[2] Of destroyers the British had lost three, and the Germans two.

division (6.24). The whole horizon from north-west to north-east was terribly illuminated by the flash of a great crescent of invisible enemies towards which he was heading.

V

The fleet action therefore was opened for Scheer in most hazardous circumstances, demanding an instant decision.

To continue on the same course was to court destruction. He must disengage as soon as possible his battleships and the battle-cruisers at their head. Each ship was ordered to turn away independently to the south, a favourite manœuvre practised to perfection. It was a difficult moment. Fortunately for Scheer the smoke clouds and bad light allowed the Grand Fleet no more than intermittent targets. Yet the leading German battleship, the *König*, was so often hit that her end seemed near. Meanwhile Hipper's long-enduring squadron was powerfully assailed by Beatty, now well in station at the Grand Fleet's van. Still farther ahead were the *Invincibles* with 'Rear-Admiral Hood bringing his squadron into action in the most inspiring way, worthy of his great naval ancestors'.[1] At this stage the German battle-cruisers, a clearer mark than their opponents, suffered heavily for the first time. The *Derfflinger* was rocked by repeated blows, the *Lutzow* constrained to fall out of the line.

Yet these two contrived to inflict another instant catastrophe upon their leading and most hard-hitting adversary, the flagship *Invincible*, 'the mother of all battle-cruisers'. She too blew up and was riven asunder. Her two extremities stood straight up above the water for some minutes, a terrible seamark to her passing consorts (6.35). Within five minutes the whole German fleet, having completed its turn draped in smoke screens, was fading into complete invisibility on a south-westerly course. Jellicoe's battle had been broken off before it had been fairly opened. Faithful to those principles of caution which he had enunciated with the full approval of the Admiralty

[1] Quoted from Beatty's dispatch.

early in the war,[1] he declined to follow his enemy into waters probably infested with submarines and mines.[2] He lost touch, but continued to steam south, secure in the knowledge that his course barred the enemy's return. About 7 o'clock Goodenough, 'never in the way nor out of the way', signalled the surprising news that Scheer was in sight again steering east. His motive in thus returning to the very peril from which he had so recently fled has been much questioned. To the question put shortly after the battle 'What was in your mind?' he is said to have replied 'Nothing'; and often declared that had he used such a movement in peace-manœuvres he would have been relieved of his command forthwith. In his book he asserts that he feared to be brought to battle again before sundown on a retreating course and hoped by this manœuvre 'to surprise the enemy, to upset his plans for the rest of the day, and, if the blow fell heavily, to facilitate the breaking loose by night'. This explanation has appeared so incredible to British writers that his real intention has been commonly assumed to have been to make a passage direct back to his ports by escaping to the east astern of the Grand Fleet, the position of which he had mistaken. It is difficult, however, to disregard his own emphatic statement. Whatever his motives, he obviously fell into a hotter place than he had intended. He was running straight for the centre of the Grand Fleet now disposed in divisions in echelon (see diagram overleaf), and all firing furiously at his leading ships from 11,000 to 8,000 yards. Splendidly as the German ships bore up against the punishment, a few more minutes of such hammering would almost certainly have brought grave disaster.

[1] See *Jutland Despatches*, p. 601. The main portions of Jellicoe's memorandum of October 14, 1914, are quoted in Winston Churchill, *World Crisis 1916–18* (1927), pt. i, pp. 114–16. The British margin of superiority in dreadnoughts was then considerably smaller.

[2] Actually no submarine was present with either side. Mines he feared would be thrown overboard by the retreating fleet in its wake. These tactics were not used by the Germans, who carried no mines on their battle-fleet.

This, says the German official account, was 'the most critical moment of the whole battle', for Scheer's 'T' was completely crossed. The German fire was very wild, and only one British battleship, the *Colossus*, received a hit.

To extricate himself the German Commander again ordered each ship to turn about independently. To cover so perilous a manœuvre in the very jaws of the enemy he

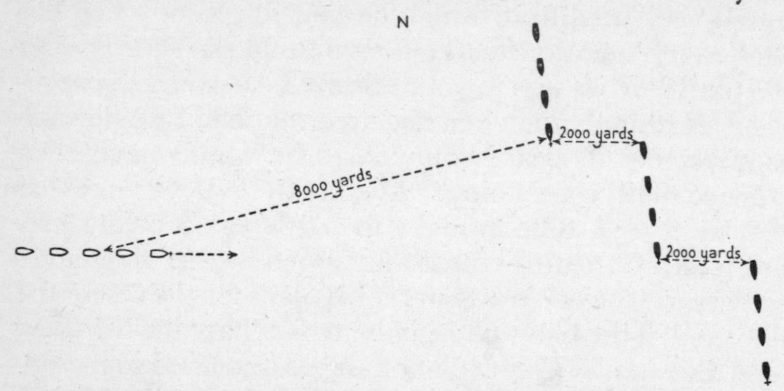

launched an attack by destroyers emitting a dense smoke screen (7.12). Now followed the famous exploit by which eleven destroyers firing fourteen torpedoes[1] forced twenty-seven battleships to turn away four points or forty-five degrees from the enemy. No battleship was hit, but the distance between the fleets was increased by about a mile. In thus flinching Jellicoe carried out his invariable routine movement, just as his opponent hoped and anticipated. This decision is counted by hostile critics as a capital error which deprived the Grand Fleet of garnering a great victory before night. It is generally admitted that the tracks of the torpedoes were plainly visible and their impact easily avoided. Consequently it is claimed that had the Grand Fleet held on, it would probably have suffered no loss; that in any case the risk of losing two or three ships ought to have been taken in order to keep close to the enemy.[2] In view of the acknowledged efficiency of the

[1] The number has been variously estimated. That given in the text is taken from the German official account.

[2] Against a fleet in line ahead, each ship 500 yards apart, the chances

hostile smoke screen and of the fading light, it is a bold assumption that the High Seas Fleet could not have escaped without irremediable damage from an enemy one mile nearer.

Still Scheer undoubtedly considered the need of deliverance to be so pressing as to demand a far more desperate expedient. A dramatic signal bade the battle-cruisers to 'charge the enemy; make straight for him'.[1] For five minutes the battered squadron gloriously fulfilled their mission until recalled. At that moment Hipper, who had left the disabled *Lutzow* in a destroyer, was about to board the *Moltke*, the least damaged of his ships. She could not stay for the Admiral, who was thus left as a spectator of the 'death ride' in his little craft. The battle-cruisers were half-crippled when they started—not one had shipped less than a thousand tons of water—and their escape from utter destruction must be put down to their marvellous strength of design. They emerged from the charge ruinous yet seaworthy. Three of the *Derfflinger's* four heavy turrets had been destroyed, with more than 150 men; the poisonous fumes spread so thickly that the survivors had to grope in gas-masks.

The turn-away of the battleships was not executed this time in such parade order. There was confusion and danger of collision as each tried to avoid the salvoes thundering at it. Still, it was accomplished without the loss of a ship. Within a few minutes the two main fleets had again lost touch.

Beatty now showed the greatest energy in searching out the enemy. Pushing far ahead of the Grand Fleet he begged Jellicoe at 7.50 to send his van division under Admiral Jerram to follow and to cut off the hostile battle-fleet. The signal was slowly taken in and the response was half-hearted. There was, however, not the least chance of

have been mathematically calculated as giving two hits to five torpedoes given accuracy of aim and favourable conditions. With divisions in echelon the chances of success must be materially less; while the visibility made the German attack difficult.

[1] 'Ran an den Feind, voll einsetzen.

this conjectural cutting off the High Seas Fleet being accomplished, as can be seen from the plan. At the most it might have been forced farther west. Nor could Jerram have pushed sufficiently far forward to have helped the

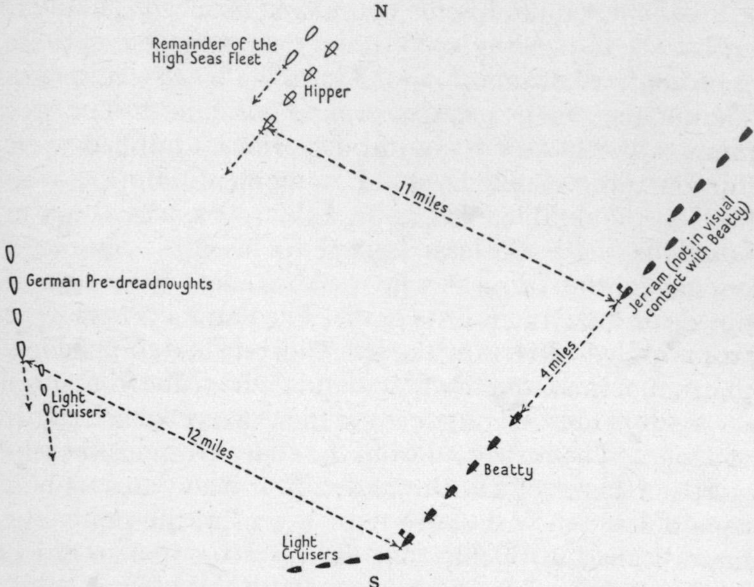

battle-cruisers, when they unexpectedly fell in again with Hipper about 8.25. Fixed in the western glow the enemy received a last hammering from invisible adversaries. The *Derfflinger* flamed fiercely in the twilight, the *Seydlitz* fell listing out of the line. The pre-dreadnoughts, however, proud of this first opportunity to show their antiquated metal, fired a few salvoes, which induced Beatty to withdraw into the gloom. His presence so far south had deeply disquieted Scheer, who altered course more to westward.

VI

Thus night descended upon the vast battle-field, merely postponing, as all believed, the inevitable event. The two fleets were then steering on roughly parallel courses, only six miles apart.

Jellicoe was determined to refuse a blind battle, where

numbers would play no advantage, which would degenerate into a crude hugger-mugger mêlée, in which the enemy's superior torpedo armament, his stronger searchlights, his wealth of star shells would be potent instruments of victory. He believed that Scheer's way home was barred. He held it for certain that his enemy would make for a harbour of refuge by dawn rather than face a renewed battle in the North Sea far from his base. Now there were known to be only three mine-free lanes of return: by the Frisian coast to the Ems, by Heligoland, or by Horns reef off the Jutland coast. By steering south Jellicoe was obviously well placed for closing the two former, which he considered the more likely routes to be taken, on the evidence of the course of the High Seas Fleet as last observed. Horns reef, however, was nearer, and might well be the goal. Against this event he guarded by detaching a minelayer to drop her load in the swept channel there, and placed his destroyers five miles astern of the fleet to prolong his line northwards. He thought with reason that an attempt by Scheer to break through in that direction must crash into the flotillas, and that the information would reach him betimes. So he held on south throughout the night in close cruising formation.

Scheer's general intention had been correctly divined. He was determined neither to be driven farther west, nor if possible to be brought to battle anywhere at dawn. At 9.10 he altered course direct for Horns reef in line of battle. He was steadfastly prepared to crash into the Grand Fleet, if and where he found it.[1] Such boldness deserved its reward. At 11.30 his leading battleships ran into our destroyers, and broke through safely after foiling a massed onslaught at close range. Less than three miles away two of our battleships saw and identified the enemy, illuminated by an explosion, but failed by astonishing

[1] Corbett, vol. iii, p. 395, seems mistaken in affirming that Scheer had received (from German wireless) Jellicoe's intercepted order stationing his destroyers astern in time to act upon it. German narratives agree in stating that he did not know what he was likely to meet when he struck the British line.

negligence to report to Jellicoe.[1] The Commander-in-Chief had, however, already received other evidence. The Admiralty had sent him an intercept of Scheer's order to steer south-south-east. Unfortunately the German position as given in it was manifestly incorrect. Relying also on certain misleading reports of the enemy's movements from his light cruisers, he therefore rejected entirely the authenticity of the information. He could scarcely have maintained this scepticism had the Admiralty deigned to send him the most definite news which it had received. Scheer had asked for an airship to reconnoitre Horns reef at daylight. By suppressing this vital fact the Admiralty must share with the two battleships the grievous responsibility for Jellicoe's persistence on the wrong course. Nothing less would have changed his determination, for he seems in Napoleon's phrase 'to have made a picture' of the enemy. Mere indications made no impression upon him. The firing in the north he interpreted as an attack of destroyers against destroyers. Nor was his confidence shaken by the intermittent rekindling of battle ever moving eastward through the late hours of the night. First the Germans destroyed the *Black Prince*, an armoured cruiser which had lost touch with the Grand Fleet and strayed tragically into the enemy's midst; then they brushed by the skirts of another flotilla, finally shedding an old battleship, the *Pommern*, to an eastward roaming division of destroyers in the first grey of dawn. Two light cruisers were Scheer's only other losses in the night. The failure of our destroyers had surprised even their enemies, who while paying high tribute to their bravery and persistence condemned their tactics as primitive. That night gave colour to the charges levelled against their training, as concentrated rather on the protection of our battleships than on attacking the enemy. By 3.30 a.m. the High Seas Fleet had reached waters of refuge by the Horns reef light.

[1] The two ships were the *Valiant* and *Malaya*. Their subsequent reports show how detailed their observation had been. The *Malaya* stated with great accuracy 'The leading ship . . . had two masts, two funnels, and a conspicuous crane (apparently *Westfalen* class)'.

VII

The desired dawn showed Jellicoe an empty sea. He held doggedly on his course until at 4.15 a.m. the receipt of an Admiralty intercept giving Scheer's position killed such dying hopes as the strengthening day had left. Not even the consolation of picking up wounded enemy stragglers was vouchsafed to him. The Grand Fleet had a melancholy home-coming. The Germans got their news out first, and faith in their announcement of victory was strengthened by the clumsy truthfulness of our *communiqué*. British officers interned in Holland have related that the Dutch spoke to them with the hushed and condescending kindness which might be shown to a son left bankrupt by the death of a reputedly wealthy father. Within a week, however, publication by the Germans of losses, until then kept secret,[1] swung the opinion of the world to a surprising degree against their claims.

In few battles of history has the palm of victory been so long and bitterly disputed. The German claims were entirely supported by purely material considerations. Against their own losses, they could set the destruction of nearly twice the tonnage and more than twice the personnel of their enemies.[2] In technique their superiority was clear. Whereas no German ship was sunk by the unaided effects of gun-fire, the British battle-cruisers had proved most tragically vulnerable. Two at least were destroyed by the flash of explosion in a turret passing straight down the ammunition hoist to the magazine. The German armour-piercing shells with their delayed-action fuses wrought greater havoc than our own heavier projectiles. Their ships were more heavily armoured, especially on the upper decks where many of our earlier dreadnoughts were devoid of protection against the

[1] The battle-cruiser *Lutzow* and the light cruiser *Rostock*. They had become unmanageable and had been sunk after the battle, out of sight of the British. In concealment the Germans followed the precedent of the *Audacious*, but without the same fortunate results.

[2] 115,025 tons against 61,180; casualties 6,945 against 2,058.

plunging shells in a long-range action, and better secured by their greater width against torpedoes, as the protective bulkheads were placed farther inside the ship. In range-finding, fire-direction, and the apparatus of night fighting[1] they had a definite advantage. All these lessons, so hardly learnt, were vigorously applied to the Grand Fleet after the battle.

If the cruiser action had stood alone, it would have been beyond dispute one of the severest defeats recorded in the annals of the British navy. It cannot, however, be separated from its sequel. The High Seas Fleet proved impotent in offensive power when confronted with its overmastering adversary. It registered only two hits upon one of Jellicoe's twenty-five battleships.[2] Its escape was brilliantly carried through, but it was a deliberate escape.

Within a month Scheer's report to the Kaiser frankly acknowledged that 'there can be no doubt that even the most successful result from a high sea battle will not compel England to make peace.... A victorious end to the war at not too distant a date can only be looked for by the crushing of English economic life through U-boat action against English commerce.' Jutland therefore while confirming the general thesis of German naval strategy gave it a definite bias towards submarine war. The High Seas Fleet did not remain passively in harbour as British propaganda falsely asserted. In August and October 1916 it made two bold and extensive sallies; even as late as April 1918 it issued as far as the Norwegian coast. Yet it gradually deteriorated in spirit, as more and more of the best officers and petty officers were taken for the U-boats; and from the mutiny in July 1917 it moved downhill on an inclined plane.

It is futile to blame Jellicoe for fighting a battle on the very principles which he had frankly laid down long

[1] e. g., the German searchlights and star shells were immensely superior to our own.

[2] During the same period four German battleships received in all twenty-five hits from heavy shells.

before, though it may be held that the rigid centralization of his control fettered the initiative of his subordinates beyond expectation. If he was wrong, the Admiralty must bear the responsibility for maintaining a commander whose mind had been so fully disclosed to it.

While the comparative failure at Jutland did nothing to impair British supremacy in the North Sea, it ruined all hope of opening the Baltic to Russia. Naval opinion in that country had always chafed at our policy of blockade, which it was pointed out was scarcely less injurious to Russia than to Germany; it had held that a great naval battle was long overdue.[1] Disappointment at the result was bitter and was intensified by the death of Lord Kitchener only a week later, when the *Hampshire*, carrying him to his Russian mission, struck a mine recently laid by a submarine in the stormy seas west of the Orkneys.

Thus Jutland may be reckoned among the many converging causes which brought the March Revolution of 1917 to birth.

VIII

The remainder of the war at sea entailed mere outpost actions. The two fleets were more and more hemmed in by ever-increasing barriers and counter-barriers of mines. The overmastering necessity of combating the deadly menace of the submarine deprived the Grand Fleet of an increasing number of light craft. The Navy accepted the direct responsibility for the safety of merchantmen by convoy with great reluctance, as is elsewhere related,[2] but the light cruisers and destroyers, detailed for this task, carried it through with unwearying devotion and astonishing success.

On the change in supreme command (November 1916) the mantle of Jellicoe fell upon Beatty, however unwilling. Only a month before his succession, the Admiralty had

[1] See the interesting remarks of the Russian naval attaché with the Grand Fleet, Com. von Schoultze, in *With the British Battle Fleet* (1925).

[2] See pp. 385–7.

decided that if Germany attacked Denmark we could give the latter hardly any assistance. In the face of submarine attacks it would be impossible for our battleships to secure the passage of an expeditionary force within 200 miles of the enemy's main base. The same recognition of the exceedingly narrow limits to which command of the sea had now shrunk was forced upon our naval command for the remainder of the war.

It is singularly ironic to hear the voice of Beatty himself informing a naval conference at Whitehall in January 1918 that 'it was in his opinion no longer desirable to provoke a fleet action even if the opportunity should occur'; that the German battle-cruiser squadron must now be considered definitely superior to our own, and that the new armour-piercing shells ordered after Jutland would not be ready till the summer of 1918. The sombre conclusion was drawn that if trade were to be adequately protected 'the correct strategy of the Grand Fleet is no longer to endeavour to bring the enemy to action at any cost, but rather to contain him in his bases until the general situation becomes more favourable to us'. And these words were written only a month after he had received the reinforcement of six most powerful American super-dreadnoughts.

The Navy in fact had become and remained the gigantic and indispensable instrument for pumping the blood of commerce into the arteries of the Entente, and for the slow strangulation of its enemies.

XX
MESOPOTAMIA
EGYPT AND PALESTINE, 1914–1917
I
MESOPOTAMIA

THE Mesopotamian campaign had the humblest origin of all the great 'side-shows' of the war, yet finally it yielded to scarcely any in magnitude,[1] and to none in calamities and horrors. The little expedition of a brigade originally dispatched by the Indian Government at the instance of the British Cabinet aimed simply at securing the Shatt-al-Arab, the name given to the united streams of the Tigris and Euphrates flowing into the Persian Gulf below Basra. We had for some years exercised a protectorate over the local rulers, the Sultans of Kuwait and Mohammerah. This influence it became the more vital to maintain when the Anglo-Persian oil pipe-line ran down to the river some thirty miles above its mouth. Our navy depended for its supplies on this great company, in which the Government had secured a controlling interest just before the war—an investment rivalling, for the enormous subsequent profit realized by its holder, our shares in the Suez Canal Company.

Adequately to protect the line through its long and wild journey into the Persian mountains would have been far beyond the military capacity of India in 1914. But it was believed that if the Turks could be driven out of Basra, where they were visibly planning an offensive against the head of the Gulf, the Arabs would be disposed in our favour, or at least be turned aside from any enterprise against us. They were in many cases restive under the cruel and inefficient government of the Turk, and might be expected, in accordance with their tradition of shifty time-serving, to incline towards the victors. Now British policy was not free from an unpleasing Machiavellism,

[1] Its ration-strength at the maximum was nearly half a million men.

for while the Arabs were urged to throw off Turkish allegiance, no pledge was given against their ultimate return to the vengeance of their ferocious masters. Doubtless, however, our action was regarded as a fair counter to

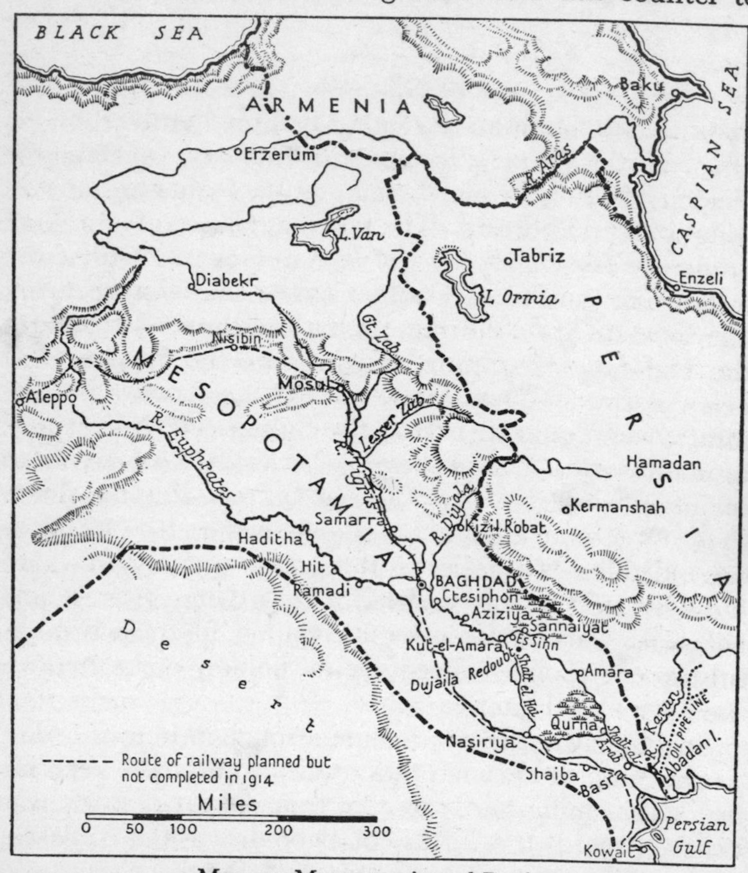

MAP 19. Mesopotamia and Persia.

Turko-German intrigues in India, for which Mesopotamia formed a useful base; and to the threat, afterwards fulfilled, of a *Jehad*—or 'Holy War'.[1] It had not, however, the advantage of success.

The occupation of Basra was effected almost by the sound of the trumpet. Two brigades of the Indian

[1] See General Barrow's appreciation: *Military Operations: Mesopotamia*, vol. i, pp. 86–7.

army,[1] with a few sloops-of-war, outmanœuvred the Turks into disorderly retreat, and reached their objective within three weeks of the opening of hostilities. The original aim of the expedition had, in fact, been accomplished. It would have been well indeed if a permanent halt had been made at the nearest points from which Basra could be securely defended. The Government of India was ill fitted both in organization and military resources to manage any considerable war outside its borders, as will become clear from this narrative. Expert military opinion before the war had recognized that no deadly blow could be dealt at Turkey by an advance up the rivers; in fact no plan for the invasion of Mesopotamia had ever been worked out. The climate is one of the most extreme in the world,[2] the country being mainly inundated during the less extreme heat and therefore in parts impassable, while almost every noxious disease is endemic. But *l'appétit vient en mangeant*; too often the capacity to advance is identified with the desirability of advancing. Already Sir Percy Cox, the greatest living authority on these regions, who had just resigned the Foreign Secretaryship to the Viceroy to become Political Officer to the expedition, was throwing the great weight of his authority in favour of an advance on Baghdad—scarcely any opposition, he thought, would be encountered, so sweeping were his deductions drawn from the rout of a vanguard of about 4,500 Turks.

One thing alone was quite certain. India, after the dispatch of another brigade,[3] had no more troops to send for some months. Every available man—military opinion thought more than was consistent with safety—had gone to France, Egypt, and East Africa.[4] The territorial divisions

[1] Each brigade contained one British and three Indian battalions.

[2] The extreme temperatures were about 122° and 20° Fahrenheit (each month showing a range of from 60 to 70 degrees).

[3] This completed the famous 6th division which, after performing prodigies under Gen. Townshend, finally surrendered at Kut, April 1916.

[4] During 1914 there were dispatched from India two cavalry divisions; three complete and two incomplete infantry divisions together with four infantry brigades.

which had partially replaced these were by no means fit, either in training or equipment, to take the field. Within the past few months a threat to Aden, trouble on the frontier, and disaffection in the Punjab, added to the anxieties of the Government. But if Baghdad was impracticable, could not the victorious force go a little farther, 'advancing by bounds' within the limits of the possible? Plausible arguments, both military and political, could always be advanced at every stage for occupying a little more territory, without clearly defining the end and the means.

Cromwell's maxim 'No man goes so far as he who knows not whither he is going' can be justly applied to the Mesopotamian adventure. There was a longish halt at Qurna, another fifty miles up the Tigris, at its junction with the old bed of the Euphrates, where Lord Hardinge the Viceroy visited the troops in February 1915, and returned with the optimism generally associated with the flying visits of such great potentates.

By the end of March enough additional infantry had been scraped together to form an incomplete corps, commanded by Sir John Nixon. It was terribly under-gunned, short of auxiliary troops and of medical stores, and almost entirely without aircraft. Nixon's instructions were to occupy the whole of the vilayet[1] of Basra and to prepare a scheme for advancing on Baghdad. Even the first of these steps implied an immediate advance of sixty or seventy miles up both Euphrates and Tigris, and occupation of Nasiriya and Amara, towns lying 100 miles apart from each other. It was calculated that the imminent assault on the Dardanelles would prevent the diversion of any Turkish reinforcements; and that a Russian advance in Armenia might facilitate the task.

Nixon had first to beat off a determined Turkish offensive, launched almost at the western gates of Basra and supported by hordes of Arabs. Its utter dispersal, after a hard three-days' battle (April 11–13), left his base secure. Meanwhile the Arabs to the east of the Shatt were proving

[1] The Turkish name for a province.

equally hostile to their deliverers; and, at the insistence of the Admiralty, a severe chastisement had to be inflicted upon some wreckers of the pipe-line, 100 miles up the Karun, before the road upstream could be securely taken.

Amara fell with absurd ease after a battle which, at least in retrospect, is singularly romantic. Townshend, a most flamboyant and dashing soldier, whose cheerful vanity endeared him to the troops in good times, launched his 6th division against the Turkish defences in a fleet of 'bellums', the native coracle, many of which were shielded with iron plates. The Turks fell into a wild panic, and were pursued relentlessly by a naval miscellany of sloops and launches. The little *Shaitan* with a crew of eight took 250 prisoners and routed great bodies of the enemy. Amara, a considerable Arab town, was actually occupied for a night by a tiny British party of forty-eight. Nasiriya was cracked with much greater difficulty, but fell into our hands by July 22nd. The success had been brilliant, the leaders and troops seemed invincible. Yet there were already evident signs of growing strain on the limited organization of the force. The miserably inadequate field-hospitals could scarcely deal with those afflicted by sun-stroke or disease;[1] the 450 wounded of Nasiriya suffered a foretaste of the indescribable horrors later to be associated with the evacuation of casualties after Ctesiphon. The improvised river-transport (on which alone the force depended) was being drawn out perilously thin. 'Beyond Amara our transport difficulties became greater than those of the Turk.'[2]

Sir John Nixon, however, cared for none of these things. His cheerful audacity never seems to have allowed him to see any cloud upon his horizon. Kut-el-Amara at once became as indispensable as any of his previous conquests. The ageing and harassed Commander-in-Chief in India, Sir Beauchamp Duff, was ill suited to stand up against

[1] The 1/14th Hants before going into action at Nasiriya had been reduced by these causes to 140 men.

[2] Sir A. Wilson, *Loyalties: Mesopotamia 1914 17* (1930), p. 49.

his robust arguments. The Government of India finally overbore the Secretary of State, Austen Chamberlain, whose cautious common sense was persuaded against his will. Moreover, both by Nixon and the Viceroy Kut was regarded as, though not formally avowed to be, the last stage towards Baghdad, whose occupation, Sir Percy Cox said, would be almost as important as that of Constantinople. Townshend staged another clever battle—he points out its Napoleonic quality in the amazing vein of naïve megalomania which runs through his book. The ground had been well reconnoitred by newly arrived aeroplanes; the Turks were cheated out of a powerful position astride the Tigris by a manœuvre which, if completely successful, would have destroyed them. But the mirage, even more baffling that day than usual, and lack of water for the cavalry, allowed two-thirds of their force[1] to escape in good order. Another 150 miles of river had been opened up, for they were fruitlessly pursued beyond Kut to Aziziya, about half-way from Kut to Baghdad (October 2).

The advance on Baghdad is perhaps the most remarkable example of an enormous military risk being taken, after full deliberation, for no definite or concrete military advantage.

The ultimate responsibility for this capital sin must lie with the British Cabinet, which sanctioned it, and indeed pressed it on a hesitating Viceroy. Had it not been for Nixon's distinctly expressed confidence, no such sanction could have been given. On the two most vital points he differed (and was proved wrong) from the considered opinion of his chief lieutenant. Townshend asserted that two divisions were necessary for the attack: Nixon told Chamberlain 'I am confident that I can beat Nur-ud-Din and occupy Baghdad without any addition to my present force' (October 8). Townshend estimated the enemy at 20,000; Nixon halved that number. Further, he stated

[1] British casualties 1,200, Turkish 3,000, out of totals of about 11,000 on each side.

that the transport difficulties, of which he had himself complained, had been overcome, which was incorrect.[1] Finally, he allowed provision for the treatment by the field-ambulances of no more than 400 wounded, and lightly assumed that, after any engagement, the majority could be directly housed in Baghdad. The Government of India was uneasy about the internal situation which 'was slowly deteriorating'; Afghanistan was wobbling; Persia, worked upon by the intrigues of the enterprising German emissary Wassmuss, was believed to be on the point of entering the war. Such were the political dangers which it was hoped to avert. At home the failure at Suvla, the imminent destruction of Serbia, and the collapse of the great offensive in France presented a picture of unrelieved gloom.

In London an Inter-departmental Committee sat on the problem, and the General Staff wrote a paper on it. Every argument was put. Probably on this evil day the Cabinet had subconsciously made up their minds in favour of the venture as soon as they had read the unqualified confidence of the soldier on the spot. Sanction was given on October 24th, though Kitchener dissented. Two divisions were to be sent as reinforcements 'as soon as possible'. No precise date for their arrival was given, though a period of two months had been suggested in the previous correspondence. The Government of India hoped to comb up two brigades in case of earlier emergency. So the little band of 12,000 veterans moved out on their last forward journey (November 20). Twenty thousand Turks were awaiting them at Ctesiphon, sixteen miles from Baghdad, in a prepared position known for months past to our Staff. A new Anatolian division of high value was among them, whose presence would have been reported to Townshend had not the aviator, who was bearing the information, been shot down and captured.

[1] Nixon's attitude is difficult to understand. The statement referred to was made on October 6. During the remainder of the month he constantly asked for more river-craft, but did not state his incapacity to move without receiving them.

On the field stood the desolate memorials of old glories, the broken arch and ruined wall of the palace of Chosroes, Justinian's great adversary.

The battle was fought with the greatest determination and ferocity. Townshend threw all his stakes upon the table, and kept no reserve in hand. The Turks, as at Kut, straddled the Tigris; their left was turned and shattered, but they made good a second line against every assault. At the close of this terrible day (November 22) the combatants were utterly exhausted: the British had lost 4,500 men and the Turks about 9,000. Fierce enemy counter-attacks next day were broken to pieces. So greatly did Nur-ud-Din fear this unconquerable remnant that he actually withdrew his whole force six miles behind the Diyala, his last line of refuge. But Townshend was in grievous straits: 40 per cent. of his infantry were casualties, and half his white officers. If he were pinned to the ground in such a state, annihilation was certain. So on the 24th he resolved to begin the retreat next day. Snapping back at its pursuers, the 6th division, very weary but almost intact, reached Kut on December 3rd. The opinions of eye-witnesses differ on the question whether exhaustion would have prevented further withdrawal before the enemy appeared in force three days later. But Townshend, who was very vain of his previous defence of Chitral on the Indian frontier in 1895, determined to stand. Weighty reasons justify his decision, for the Turks could not proceed far downstream with such an obstacle to bar their river traffic, and great stores had been accumulated in Kut which time would not have permitted Townshend to remove or burn.

In any case he was himself responsible for the failure of relief; for (i) he retained within the *enceinte* a population of 6,000 Arabs, useless and treacherous mouths; (ii) he took no steps systematically to search for food, or to reduce rations until nearly two months had elapsed; (iii) by the incorrect statement that he could hold out at the most for only two months, and by his constant, querulous, and almost hysterical appeals, he forced the hands of the relieving force to attack in January under conditions which invited disaster.

For the next five months this filthy little Arab mud-heap, 'the most insanitary place the British had occupied in Mesopotamia',[1] shared with Verdun the gaze of the world. After the bloody failure of an assault on Christmas Eve the siege slipped into a more or less passive blockade.

The relieving force, deficient in medical equipment and in boats, with only one effective aeroplane, without a single motor vehicle, with improvised and untrained staffs, hampered by the low moral inevitable from such patent disorganization,[2] and constantly exposed to cold and rain, was thrice heavily defeated in January, some twenty to thirty miles below Kut. Immediately afterwards Townshend, who had done nothing, by way of sortie, to assist the relieving forces, sent word that he could hold out for three more months.

The highest official posts in India were ransacked to find new commanders; the expedition was put under the direct control of the British War Office; reinforcements were poured in, only to stick helplessly for weeks in the Basra bottle-neck.[3] Fresh Turks, released by our evacuation of the Dardanelles, dribbled in sufficient numbers over the enormous road to help their best allies, rain, flood, and mud to bar the path.

There was the shadow of a Russian threat—for the Tsar's troops had captured Erzerum (February 15) and were roaming about in north-west Persia—but it grew no longer.

By far the most promising chance was flung away on March 8th when 20,000 troops had been collected at dawn by a wide flank march within two miles of the key of the final position of the Turkish right, the Dujaila redoubt, only seven miles from Kut. The enemy was utterly

[1] The words are those of Townshend's Senior Medical Officer.

[2] It may be noticed here that neither the Commander-in-Chief in India, nor any of his staff, ever visited Mesopotamia before the fall of Kut.

[3] As early as January 21 there were 10,000 men and 12 guns there, who might have turned the scale of battle. It must be remembered, however, that the floods made any enveloping movement almost impossible.

surprised, for there were only 200 within striking distance. The redoubt itself was empty, for Leachman, the famous political officer, had entered it in Arab disguise, and returned with the precious information. But, in spite of the remonstrances of his subordinates, Kemball, the commanding general, with a diseased pedantry, waited three hours in order to deploy his troops for the full-dress attack prescribed by his orders on the assumption that the positions were fully manned. In consequence the infantry were mown down in thousands on the naked desert, the cavalry did nothing, and Townshend, who could see the flashes of the guns, sat still.

Now, as happened every year with the melting of Armenian snows, the Tigris rose in high flood. For the first three weeks of April frontal attacks first on one bank then on the other were beaten back. Men were drowned and stifled in the mud; and their numbers were so much diminished that battalions had to be amalgamated, to the great detriment of moral.

Within the fortress starvation grew near, augmented by the refusal of many Indians on religious grounds to eat horse-flesh. It was found impossible to drop sufficient food from aeroplanes. An attempt instigated by Townshend to bribe the Turks with £2,000,000 to allow the garrison free on parole was refused. The Government who sanctioned it would have done well to remember the old Roman maxim 'Non cauponantes bellum sed belligerantes', for this huckstering was held in derision throughout enemy and neutral countries.

The unconditional surrender took place on April 29th after all guns and ammunition had been destroyed. Ten thousand combatants went into captivity; Townshend into an honourable and almost luxurious internment, the officers into endurable prison-camps. The men were herded like animals across the desert, flogged, kicked, raped, tortured, and murdered. Though the Germans gave them tokens of humanity and kindness almost wherever they met them, more than two-thirds of the British rank and file were dead before the war ended. Halil the Turkish commander had cynically promised that they would be 'the honoured guests of his government'. The relieving force had suffered 23,000 casualties. Mainly composed of young barely trained troops, it had nobly endured every kind of avoidable and unavoidable hardship and suffering. No troops—not even those before Passchendaele in 1917—were so sorely tried by their commanders and by physical conditions. The Anatolian Turk once again, as in Gallipoli, showed the rock-like solidarity of his defensive endurance.

II. EGYPT AND PALESTINE

Egypt, though not a British possession, was of vital importance to our Imperial strategy and sea-borne communications. Without control of the Suez Canal the transport of Indian and Australian troops would have been rendered very slow and hazardous. The volume of merchant shipping passing through became so great as the war progressed that vessels were moored for fifteen to twenty miles up the canal.[1] As it was feared that the Germans would try some enterprise against its safety, such as sinking vessels in the fairway, the canal was closed to enemy shipping and its banks were occupied by British troops. This was contrary to the convention which protected its neutrality and provided for free passage under all circumstances, and to which Great Britain had given her assent in 1904.

Turkey's declaration of war changed the international status of Egypt, which now became a British protectorate. The Khedive, a disreputable ruler, who had elected to stay in Constantinople after August 4th, was deposed and his uncle Hussein elevated to the rank of Sultan. The Egyptians, though sullen and mainly desirous of a German victory which might bring them independence, took these changes quietly, and showed no disposition to respond to the Turkish manifesto of a Holy War. No one, however, could calculate the effect of a hostile army appearing before Egypt.[2] This was an event which seemed probable, for it

[1] Lt.-Col. P. G. Elgood, *Egypt and the Army* (1924), p. 66.

[2] As a matter of fact the Egyptians showed no desire whatever to exchange

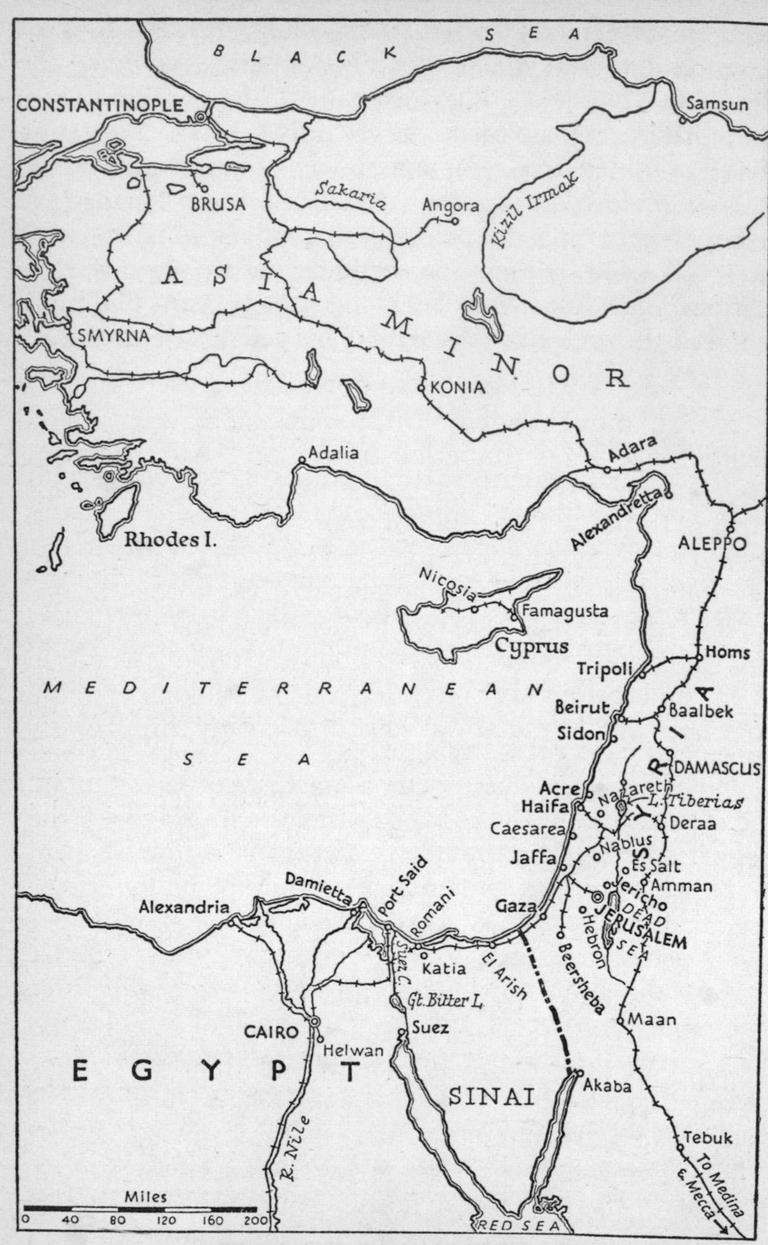

MAP 20. Egypt, Palestine and Syria

had been reported long before Turkey declared war that troops and supplies were being collected in south Palestine. Three divisions and a number of warships were available for defence. These were drawn up along the canal to await an attack, so that it was satirically said that instead of the army defending the canal, the canal defended the army. It was indeed a formidable obstacle, with a depth of 34 feet and a minimum width of 190. Its length of 100 miles would have made continuous defence impossible, but more than one-third was protected by lakes and inundations, on which the Allied warships rode. A light railway running close behind facilitated the transfer of troops. The enemy rejected the traditional path of so many conquerors, the northern road by the sea, for reasons of secrecy and security. About 20,000 men were admirably conveyed over the centre of the Sinai desert under the leadership of Djemal Pasha, and arrived in the neighbourhood of the canal at the end of January 1915. Their assault was unworthy of these preliminaries; very few of the pontoons or bridges (brought all the way from Germany) were used, only one platoon managed to cross the canal except as prisoners.

The Turks, however, were allowed, after losing 2,000 men, to make their way back unmolested. Maxwell, the British commander, though an admirable administrator, was a very cautious soldier, and was hampered by Kitchener's instructions that a reverse, which might endanger our prestige over the Moslem world, must be avoided.

Now, the ease with which so considerable a hostile force had been transported across the desert had falsified the views of our Intelligence, and, in consequence, the security of Egypt was held to demand the presence of large bodies of troops throughout 1915.[1] Kress von Kressenstein, the

British for Turkish masters. No disturbances or acts of sabotage were signalled during the battles for the canal; and the enemy seems strangely to have neglected his opportunities for propaganda.

[1] On July 9 there were 70,000 troops in Egypt exclusive of sick and wounded; by November the numbers had decreased to 60,000 of whom the majority were drafts, rising again to 100,000 by December 7.

ingenious Bavarian colonel who now commanded in Sinai, did his best to stimulate anxiety by sending continually little parties of raiders to drop mines in the canal or explosives on the lateral railway. But nothing except the tiniest of minor operations took place in the canal zone this year. An odd little war, however, broke out on the extreme western frontier of Egypt, which exercised the mind of Kitchener to an absurd degree. A roaming sect called the Senussi had been a thorn in the Italian side at Tripoli. They proved almost the only recruits to the Holy War, which excited their Sheikh the more, because he aspired to gain the spiritual rank recently forfeited by Hussein, the Shereef of Mecca, now in full revolt against Turkey. Prowling German submarines landed Turkish officers and modern weapons near the site of the ancient Cyrene, till constant provocation forced the unwilling Maxwell to take up the challenge in November 1915, and the elusive tribesmen evaded final defeat for the next eighteen months. Two curious episodes are worth remembering: first, the rescue of the starving crew of the *Tara*, who had been seized after the torpedoing of their vessel near shore; this was effected by the armoured cars of the Duke of Westminster, which sped to the rescue over the desert at forty miles an hour: secondly, the capture, in a cavalry mêlée, of Ja'far Pasha, a Mesopotamian Arab, sent by Turkey to organize the Senussian resistance, which he did admirably. He became a most loyal and hearty friend of Great Britain, fought against the Turk in Palestine, and has since been Prime Minister of Iraq.

By the end of 1915 an enormous host had been collected in Egypt.[1] Gallipoli had been evacuated; Salonika was demanding reinforcements; Townshend was crying out for the immediate relief of his beleaguered forces in Kut. The most extravagant estimates were made of the Turkish power. The Staff actually asserted that 300,000 Turks

[1] Fourteen complete divisions as well as numbers of drafts, probably nearly 300,000 men. The majority of these had been dispatched to other destinations by June.

might be launched against the canal in February 1916, now that German enterprise had extended the railway southwards to Beersheba on the edge of the desert. In point of fact the Turks never found it possible to feed adequately one-sixth of that number of combatants in their defensive lines in the south of Palestine the next year. Still, assuming this nervousness, a concentration in Egypt was admirably adapted for the 'Imperial Strategic reserve'.[1] At first a singular division of authority existed. Maxwell was responsible for governing Egypt and for the western frontier; Sir Archibald Murray[2] for the canal defences with the greater mass of the troops; whilst the War Office maintained direct control over the Levant base, to co-ordinate the transport and supply for the various expeditionary forces fed from the Delta. By March, however, Murray had succeeded to sole power.

The area immediately east of the canal had by now been converted into an immense fortified system, partly constructed by the forced labour of Egyptians. But with its completion the role of Murray's forces began gradually, almost imperceptibly, to change from that of defenders of Egypt to that of invaders of Palestine. It became increasingly clear that the Turks could not mass any great force against Egypt. Although they were known to have large reserves in Thrace, the heavy blow which they had suffered by the invasion of Armenia and capture of Erzerum by the Russians (February 15) was likely to swallow up any available reinforcements. At this very moment Murray was already proposing to sweep the frontier across the desert by establishing an 'active defence' round El Arish.[3] The advance kept pace with the progress of its two

[1] The expression of Sir W. Robertson, the new Chief of the Imperial General Staff. For his instructions to Murray, see *Military Operations: Palestine*, vol i, p. 100.

[2] He had also a power of supervision over Salonika until the autocratic Gen. Sarrail shook himself completely free.

[3] See his able paper quoted in *Military Operations: Palestine*, i. 170. El Arish, where there is abundant water, is about twenty-five miles south-west of the Palestine frontier.

indispensable auxiliaries, a railway and a pipe-line, conveying the water of the Nile. Our last purely defensive action was that fought at Romani some twenty miles east of the canal in August. Von Kressenstein made an imprudent attack with a mere 16,000 men, in the repulse of which he lost nearly half. His defeat delivered the desert into the power of the British. The Anzac mounted troops, thoroughly in their element, scoured the whole area.

The enemy was overthrown and dispersed in many minor engagements. El Arish fell on December 21st; and the Sinai Peninsula had been wholly cleared. A considerable army was standing before the gate of Syria. Murray, now affecting the proconsul rather than the soldier in the elaborate state of his head-quarters in Cairo, had every cause for satisfaction. The army was bound to its base by a triple chain, the railway, the pipe-line, and even an odd kind of road;[1] the desert, if not blossoming like the rose, pullulated with the vast semi-permanent paraphernalia of modern armies. The elaborate precautions taken for the success of the defence seemed to invite a change of plan towards an offensive.

It so happened that this opportunity or temptation coincided with the advent of Lloyd George to power, for the War Cabinet came into existence on December 9th, 1916. The new Premier had a position of uncontrolled and centralized power, only rivalled in modern English history by that held by Cromwell and Chatham. The military situation was dark. The enormous sacrifices of the Somme had apparently been brought to no effect by the winter mud. The German strategic reserve had overthrown the Rumanians. The arrogant peace-offer of the Central Powers sorely needed an Allied reply in the shape of some tangible success in order to prove that the enemy's assumption of a 'victorious defensive' was unjustified. It must not be supposed, however, that Lloyd George at this moment was seeking a decisive 'way round', or hoping to

[1] Consisting of pegged-down strips of wire-netting to make a surface practicable for motors.

win the war in Palestine. Murray was clearly informed that his 'primary mission remains unchanged, that is to say, it is the defence of Egypt'.[1] But he was urged to make his 'maximum possible effort during the winter'.[2] The main object was really political, to obtain such a success as 'would look well in the Gazette', as Dundas used to urge on Pitt. The fall of the Holy City would, it was thought, hearten our allies and impress the world. Any advance into southern Palestine might induce more Arabs to rebel against the Turk, and if pushed to the Hejaz railway, might prove decisive in favour of Hussein's independence.

Murray cautiously replied that he required two more divisions for a serious offensive, but though recognizing that no such reinforcement could reach him at present, undertook to do what he could.

The greatest naval power in the world elected by a curious paradox to take the narrow land-route into Palestine (although this involved a frontal attack upon Gaza) which Napoleon had been driven to use only because of the destruction of his fleet. The transference of the expedition by sea, even if practicable, would now have been beyond our powers in view of our already enormous and most perilous commitments.

At first all went well; the frontier was crossed and Rafah occupied after a brilliant little fight (January 9, 1917), in which 1,400 prisoners were captured for less than 500 casualties. By March the army was situated in a pleasant grassy land before Gaza. But Murray, far from receiving reinforcements, had been obliged to part with one of his divisions for the next campaign in France; and so he could no longer expect to capture Jerusalem, but merely to take his part in that converging onslaught against the Central Powers which was confidently expected to shatter them that spring. His army was tied by its communications to the neighbourhood of the coast. If therefore it was to deal

[1] Robertson to Murray, December 15, 1916, No. 26624.
[2] Ibid., December 12, 1916, No. 26289.

a blow, it must be against Gaza, the historic gate of entry into Palestine.

Murray had one great asset in his cavalry, which, composed mainly of Anzacs, was more numerous, better mounted, and far superior in quality to his enemy's, and had before it an admirable manœuvre ground. He could also rely on a flanking and rearward fire from the navy during the assault. On the other hand, surprise would be difficult, for the enemy's aircraft, mostly German machines well piloted, at the moment held superiority, and was able constantly to reconnoitre the position of our troops. The attack on Gaza was launched on March 26th. It had been admirably planned by Sir C. Dobell, who commanded the Palestine force. Murray had moved from Cairo to El Arish, which he called his advanced head-quarters, a mere fifty miles from the scene of action. The intention was for the cavalry, under Chetwode's command, to throw a wide net round the town from the east and north, with one infantry division lying ready to protect the eastern flank against enemy reinforcements. This done, another division (53rd) was to assault the ridge of Ali Muntar, protecting Gaza from the south, and having won that commanding eminence to rush the town. The Turkish garrison amounted to less than 4,000 men, but was concealed and protected, not only by the houses, but by the circumjacent olive-yards and bristling hedges of cactus.

A dense sea-fog at dawn somewhat hindered these sweeping movements over unfamiliar country, but by noon the cavalry cordon had been successfully drawn right across to the sea.

The 53rd division had a desperate day, its advance being delayed for hours by unco-ordinated staff work (for while Murray's enormous establishment at Cairo was the envy of soldiers and the butt of civilians, Dobell had been allowed barely half the normal number of staff officers for such a big command to plan his battle). Yet at nightfall they had finally driven the Turks through all the gardens and hedges into the town itself, and the morrow seemed to contain a certain promise of complete victory. For the Anzacs on their part had also broken widely into the northern suburbs.

Now, time lost in war is seldom retrieved. The reports of the progress of the 53rd division were naturally slow in reaching Head-quarters. The Turkish messages picked up in Cairo, decoded instantly (as we possessed the enemy's cipher), and telephoned to Rafah, were by some culpable muddle held up there for several hours. And so it came about that at this very hour of sunset, when the garrison was in utter despair, the mounted troops were withdrawn, and so a wide gap was left open, beyond anything the enemy could have hoped, for Turkish reinforcements. Chetwode was on the field and might have shown more vigour of personal investigation, but on the information before him the decision can be justified. He believed the infantry attack to have failed; there was little or no water for his horses; three Turkish divisions might attack him at dawn and drive him into the enclosed and hostile environs of Gaza, where his cavalry would be useless.

The retreat by night brought confusion. The whole of that hard-won ridge south of Gaza was abandoned by mistake, reoccupied at dawn, then recaptured by new Turkish troops. The British forces, exhausted and tormented by thirst, were withdrawn some six miles to the great ravine, the Wadi-Ghazze.

Murray's confidential report on the battle was more misleading than the *communiqués* commonly issued in London for general consumption. Even the official historian allows a note of discreet and muffled censure to creep into his narrative. Murray was hoist with his own petard. For Robertson, naturally believing him to have won a great victory, with casualties less than half of those inflicted (actually they were nearly double),[1] immediately ordered him to capture Jerusalem. Murray temporized, with a not unreasonable request for more heavy artillery,

[1] Murray estimated his casualties at 3,500 and the Turkish at least 8,000. The actual numbers were 4,000 to 2,450.

but could scarcely admit an inability to do anything. Consequently, within three weeks, he staged a second battle of Gaza in far more unfavourable circumstances. It is true that a French warship was available to bombard the coast; there were a few tanks and some gas shells (the last-named proving so ineffective that the Turks were in doubt whether they had been used). These were but straws in the balance against the necessity of attacking frontally a strong commanding prepared position, with insufficient artillery, and an infantry force little superior to its stubborn and confident defenders. The role of the cavalry was unambitiously restricted to forming a defensive right flank. The three infantry divisions were therefore set an impossible task, and spent the whole day in being slaughtered without avail on the southern slopes of the bare ridge of Ali Muntar. The repulse was complete, and our casualties more than threefold those of the Turk.[1] The first battle was a daring venture, robbed of success only by faults in execution. The second was quite unjustifiable. No urgent reasons, military or political, commanded an immediate attack. Time and patience, as events were to show, would make it easy to turn the Turkish flank by way of Beersheba. Though Murray acted under the orders of the Home Government, it is difficult to believe that those orders would have been given had the facts been put clearly before them. Though responsibility is divided, Murray must bear the heavier share for his lack of candour. His recall in June was just and wise; and the choice of Allenby as his successor even happier than the expectations of those who made it.

[1] 6,400 against 2,000.

XXI

ATTEMPTS TO NEGOTIATE PEACE

1916–1917

I

MODERN war resembles the infernal gods of Greece of whom it was written 'they are better at catching than at letting go'.[1] When the life of nations is so profoundly affected and transformed, when the vast sacrifices arouse the bitterest hatreds and demand the fulfilment of great expectations, the efforts of kings and statesmen, even if sincere, can avail little against the floods let loose. Inasmuch as war is not now waged for limited objects, nothing but absolute victory seems a justification for breaking it off; and until it has been gained a compromised peace is regarded as an unwarranted defeat by all the belligerents. It follows inevitably that the pacific influence of neutrals, never very great, was by this time, in the greatest of all wars, reduced almost to nothing. Each belligerent, confident of being in the right, regarded neutrality as a denial of moral principles, adopted merely for selfish interests.

The only great neutral Power, America, was particularly open to these shafts. The Central Powers pointed to the loans and ammunition which flowed across the Atlantic as a proof of her cautious malevolence. The Entente considered her hypocrisy to be patent because she had refused to protest against the violation of Belgium, and her honour to be compromised by her acceptance of the sinking of the *Lusitania* without an immediate declaration of war. President Wilson was widely accepted as the embodiment and director of this sordid ideal. No phrase was quoted with more contemptuous bitterness than his statement that the American people 'were too proud to fight'. Nevertheless the President, who had been anxiously

[1] οἱ κάτω θεοὶ λαβεῖν ἀμείνους εἰσὶν ἢ μεθιέναι. Euripides.

watching since the beginning for an opportunity, made two determined attempts to secure peace in 1916, one secret and one public.

The former was initiated by the dispatch of Colonel House to Europe in January 1916. The Colonel is perhaps the most remarkable unofficial diplomatist of modern times. He held no office. He was responsible only to the President and his own conscience, but it was recognized in every capital that he visited that his power far exceeded that of the resident ambassador. Wilson was a cold, secret, autocratic man; he gave his confidence to no other man. But to House he gave more than confidence. He not only handed him decisions and plans for criticism; he encouraged him also to analyse and mould his own unformed ideas. A comparison of the President's speeches with House's rough drafts shows the extraordinary extent of the man's influence. No one kept secrets better than House, and no man extracted so many out of war-time Europe. He combined great directness of speech with a peculiarly winning manner, and did his business best at meals or in the smoking-room.

His mission was to bring about, if possible, the armed mediation of America. The President believed that the war had now reached a deadlock, which might be prolonged indefinitely. So interminable a struggle would put the whole of civilization in danger. Wilson therefore regarded himself as a mediator on behalf of humanity. His sympathies, though restrained and qualified, had always been on the side of the Allies. He expected that his mediation would be rejected by the Central Powers, but hoped it would be accepted by the Entente. In that event America would throw in her lot with the latter and enforce a just peace. Consequently House's visit to Berlin did no more than explore the ground, and no indication was given as to the President's actual proposals. The attitude of England was regarded as decisive: she alone could exercise the required pressure on the other members of the Alliance, and House put more trust in his intimate friend Grey[1] than in any other European statesman. House laid his cards on the table before the War Committee. He gave, on behalf of the President, a virtual promise that, if the terms which he outlined were accepted by the Entente and rejected by the Central Powers, America would enter the war. The most important conditions were the restoration of Belgium and Serbia, the cession of Alsace-Lorraine to France and of Constantinople to Russia, with the formation of an independent Poland. Germany was to be compensated by colonial acquisitions. Competitive armaments were to be abolished, and guarantees secured against military aggression.

Grey communicated these terms to Briand through the French ambassador, but they were neither recommended to the Allies nor approved by the War Committee. The latter were still confident of a complete victory, which alone, in their opinion, could destroy 'Prussian militarism'. They were fortified in this view by the opposition of Page, the American ambassador in London, to the House plan. America it was thought would soon be compelled to join the Allies without conditions. Her military power was then rated very low. It seemed unjust that an overdue action, taken in her own interest, which could not affect the general situation materially for at least a year, should thus tie the hands of the Allies. They had borne the burden and heat of the day, and intended to remain free. Finally, Grey's personal view, characteristic of his chivalrous nature, was that Great Britain, whose sacrifice had as yet been comparatively small, could not honourably take the initiative in recommending peace to her Allies.

Germany would obviously have rejected the proposed conditions with scorn, for she was still hoping to control Belgium and to annex the mining districts of north-east France. The American proposal did not exactly lapse, as it was understood that the Allies could take it up again, though they were warned that America would not come

[1] House was allowed the use of the Foreign Office cipher, and is said to be the only foreigner who has been given this privilege.

into the war to save them from imminent defeat. Grey himself looked upon it more kindly, with the eye of disillusionment, in November 1916, and prepared a memorandum for his colleagues. Lansdowne at the same time prepared a Cabinet memorandum in favour of a peace of compromise, expressing much the same view as in his famous letter to the *Daily Telegraph* a year later, shortly to be described. But the overthrow of the Cabinet intervened. The increased willingness of some of his colleagues to negotiate was indeed one of Lloyd George's principal reasons for securing power. He became the public champion of the 'knock-out blow'.[1]

The stage therefore was not well set for Wilson's second attempt, though he spoke with the immense authority of a President just re-elected to a second period of office. Any faint chances of usefulness which it might still have possessed had already been destroyed by the publication, a week previously, of a peace offer by the Central Powers (December 12). The German Chancellor knew that a date was being considered by Wilson, but he got tired of waiting for it. The moment seemed propitious. The 'war-map', indeed, was better than ever, for Bucharest had just been taken; although, as we have seen, the military and economic situation had never been so bad. The German move therefore was intended to conciliate two opposing types of opinion. Moderate men like Helfferich, the Secretary of State, who originally suggested it, believed that publication would gather together and hearten all similar elements in enemy countries, and would stir up a demand which could not be denied. On the other hand the military and Pan-German party saw in it either an opportunity to divide their enemies and to secure a separate peace, or, in the more probable event of its rejection, the justification for immediately beginning an unrestricted submarine war. Speed and victory were inseparable. Only the U-boats could provide them both in certain combination.

[1] See pp. 392–4.

The wording of the note made it perfectly clear which party had won. Couched in terms of magnanimous yet threatening condescension, it emphasized 'the indestructible strength' of Germany and her allies in their victorious defensive. While proposing negotiations, it omitted to outline conditions even in the most general way. This had been contrary to the Austrian wish. As a matter of fact the war-aims of the two opposing groups were so unreconcilably opposed that any statement by the Central Powers would have been denounced by the Entente as unrepentant militarism. The only effective way of embarrassing their enemies would have been a simple, unqualified assurance that Belgium would be restored and compensated. Nothing would have been so well calculated to affect the whole of Liberal opinion in England.

The advance, then, was a very clumsy one, and it was summarily rejected by the Entente almost without discussion.

The President's move (December 18) was almost equally unwelcome to both belligerents—disclaiming any office of mediation, he proposed that 'soundings be taken'. He pointed out that their intentions, as stated by themselves, were virtually the same, and suggested that each side should publicly and authoritatively state the precise objects which the security of their peoples demanded. This, as we saw, was the very point which Germany was resolute in refusing. Hence any further negotiation could be regarded only as a waste of most precious time.

Public opinion in the Entente was exceedingly unfavourable. In spite of Wilson's disclaimer, most people believed in a connexion between two proposals launched within a week. The statement that the objects of both sides were virtually the same aroused, as House had predicted, the keenest indignation. The Foreign Office withheld publication for some hours in order to influence the London editors towards moderation of comment.

But the Allied statesmen had the courage of their convictions. They returned an answer to Wilson giving their war-aims in one of the most interesting and important diplomatic documents of the war. Their terms were stated to imply 'necessarily and first of all, the restoration of Belgium, Serbia, and Montenegro, with the compensation due to them; the evacuation of the invaded territories in France, in Russia, in Rumania, with just reparation; the reorganization of Europe guaranteed by a stable régime and based at once on respect for nationalities, and on the right to full security and liberty of economic development possessed by all peoples, small and great; and, at the same time, upon territorial conventions and international settlements such as to guarantee land and sea frontiers against unjustified attack; the restoration of provinces formerly torn from the Allies by force or against the wish of their inhabitants; the liberation of the Italians, as also of the Slavs, Rumanians, and Czechoslovaks from foreign domination; the setting free of the populations subject to the bloody tyranny of the Turks; and the turning out of Europe of the Ottoman Empire as decidedly foreign to Western Civilization.'

The manifesto is obviously inspired by an unshakable confidence in complete victory. Within the veil of idealistic language, it contains nearly all the principles embodied in the peace treaties. No direct specific reference is made to Alsace-Lorraine, doubtless in deference to English opinion, which would not have been prepared at that time to see its return to France stated as a *sine qua non* of peace. The independence of Poland is completely slurred over in order to conciliate Russia. The language dealing with the Austro-Hungarian Empire naturally suggests its complete disruption, though formally consistent with its reorganization as a federal state. Any reference to the German colonies is deliberately omitted. The Central Powers were confirmed in their belief that a 'war of annihilation' was being ruthlessly pursued against them, and the way was thus prepared for public opinion to welcome unrestricted submarine warfare. Wilson was not impressed by the note, which he described to House as 'bluff'. In fact it had the curious effect of improving American relations with Germany at the very moment when a rupture seemed imminent.

In the same note which communicated the decision of the German Government to begin the submarine blockade, Bernstorff, the ambassador at Washington, privately informed the President of the German peace terms. They included restoration of Belgium 'under special guarantees for the safety of Germany': restitution of occupied French territory 'under reservation of strategical and economic changes of the frontier and financial compensations'. France was to receive the small portion of upper Alsace still occupied by her troops. In the east Germany and Poland were to receive a frontier to protect them economically and strategically against Russia. Colonies were to be returned, German firms and individuals to be compensated for war damage, and the freedom of the seas to be established.

The result of these parleys proved that the two sides were poles apart.

II

A curious page of 'secret diplomacy' now followed, which might have been torn out of an eighteenth-century dynastic book. The young Emperor Karl had declared on his accession that he would bring peace to his subjects as speedily as possible. He lost no time about it. His brother-in-law, Prince Sixtus of Bourbon,[1] was serving in the Belgian army, owing to the good offices of Karl himself, who had chivalrously obtained permission for him to leave Austria at the outbreak of war. He had influential relationships in France and was encouraged to sound the French President. Karl informed his Foreign Minister, Czernin, of what was in train, knowing that the latter was passionately desirous of peace. He seems, however, to have acted with some duplicity. Czernin believed that the

[1] He was descended from the Parma Bourbons, who lost their Duchy in the reunion with Italy in 1859. As a Bourbon he was debarred by law from serving in the French army.

object of the negotiations was to secure a general peace for the Central Powers. But Karl was aiming at a separate peace for Austria, hoping thereby to preserve his empire practically intact.

The terms demanded by Poincaré were the restoration to France of Alsace-Lorraine with the frontier of 1814,[1] the restoration of Belgium and Serbia, the latter acquiring a port on the Adriatic, and the cession of Constantinople to Russia. Karl replied on March 20th, 1917, in an autograph letter to his brother-in-law, in which he promised 'to support, by all means and by the use of all my personal influence with our allies, the just French claims to Alsace-Lorraine'. His only reservation was on the question of Constantinople, whereon he suspended judgement until a legal government had been established in Russia.

So far the affair had been known only to Poincaré and Ribot, now Premier. Its progress was so promising that it was divulged first to Lloyd George, with whose long-cherished wish of detaching Austria it harmonized exactly. King Alfonso of Spain also joined in recommending the plan. But no definite step could be taken without bearding the lion in the way, Italy. This Power was a signatory to the Pact of London by which the great Entente Powers had pledged themselves never to conclude a separate peace.[2] It so happened that a meeting of British, French, and Italian statesmen was fixed on April 18th at Saint-Jean de Maurienne for the purpose of carving up Asia Minor between them. Sonnino, the astute and stubborn Italian Foreign Minister, held stoutly to the terms of the Treaty of London. He said frankly that Italy had entered the war to destroy Austria as a great Power, and could not be expected to support her. It was in vain that suggestions were made that Italy might exchange Somaliland or her

[1] This meant the inclusion of the Saar territory and Landau in France. France had just (February 1917) concluded a secret treaty with Russia, unknown to England, by which she was to receive this frontier, and an independent buffer-state was to be set up on the left bank of the Rhine.

[2] Russia was also a partner, but was not informed of the proposal. Presumably the provisional government was not thought trustworthy.

interest in Smyrna for a full satisfaction of her guaranteed claims on the Trentino, Tyrol, and Istria. Karl had been ready enough to barter German territory, but could not be induced to concede the Italian demands. Though ready to make a separate peace, he could not bring himself to declare war upon Germany and take Silesia in compensation, a suggestion which was apparently made by France.

Meanwhile Czernin, who had no idea of the extent to which his Emperor had committed himself in writing, was paving the way for an understanding with Germany. He arranged a meeting between the Kaiser and Karl, having primed the latter with a memorandum in which the position of the Central Powers was painted in the blackest colours. It asserted that another winter-campaign was absolutely impossible for Austria, who was at the end of her strength, and hinted that conditions in Germany were little better. As a conclusion it stated that peace must be procured before the autumn even at heavy sacrifices, or it might be anticipated that the monarchs would be swept away by a wave of revolution. Czernin's object was to induce Germany to cede Alsace-Lorraine, in which event Austria would hand over Galicia to a Polish kingdom controlled by Germany.[1] He hoped that Austria might obtain some compensation in Rumania. Czernin has stated that he never believed in the possibility of a separate peace, and his faithfulness to the Alliance has received testimonials from both Hindenburg and Ludendorff. But there is reason to believe that he would have been ready to conclude one if Germany had definitely refused to cede Alsace-Lorraine, and if the Entente had been ready to guarantee the integrity of the Austrian Empire.[2]

That Germany should ever give up these provinces except under the goad of a final defeat was unthinkable.

[1] Karl, on the other hand, had the effrontery at this meeting to press on the Kaiser the so-called 'Austro-Polish Solution', which meant that the Polish Kingdom set up by the Central Powers on November 5, 1916, should be united with Galicia under an Austrian archduke.

[2] See his memorandum of May 9 handed to Poincaré by Sixtus. The text is given in Mermeix, *Les Negociations secrètes* (1921), pp. 86–7.

They were the symbol of blood shed in common by all Germans to cement the Empire. 'The Reich', as Delbrück had said, 'would grow out of the Reichsland.'[1] At the moment the danger of defeat was receding. The attacks in the west were beaten off, Russia was quiescent, while the U-boats in April sank the unprecedented total of nearly a million tons of shipping.

The German Government therefore looked unfavourably on Prince Sixtus's activities. The Emperor Karl's compromising letters remained entirely secret until April 1918, when their existence and contents were revealed to the world by Clemenceau, the French Premier. Karl was reduced to the degrading expedient of denying their authenticity through Czernin's reluctant mouth; he had promised only to support the French claims 'if they were just, which they are not'. As his brother-in-law was exonerated, the world was asked to believe that Poincaré had been guilty of a fabrication. Karl was in the unfortunate position of a liar whom nobody believed. No doubt was felt in German military circles that he was false to the Alliance, and would get out of it if he could.

III

The Czernin memorandum, though abortive in its intended result, was not without an important sequel. Erzberger, a busy and ambitious leader of the Centre party of the Reichstag, himself a strong Catholic, was intimate with the ladies at the court of Karl's Empress, Zita. By some means he procured a copy of the memorandum, with which he was deeply impressed. He imparted a general summary of its contents to a secret meeting of his committee at Frankfurt: doubtless he acted from patriotic motives, though not unwilling to embarrass the Kaiser, who had always treated him with rudeness, and vulgarly recalled his humble origin by the nickname 'Postman'. He also probably knew that the views of the Crown Prince and

[1] This was the name officially given to the two provinces after their incorporation in the German Empire in 1871.

of Rupprecht of Bavaria coincided with his own. The former wrote a letter to his father in July in which he expressed himself in much the same terms as Czernin. Among the phrases were these 'If Germany does not obtain peace before the end of the year, the danger of a revolution will be imminent. . . . The hopes founded on the submarine warfare are groundless. . . . We must renounce all annexations even in the East, and start negotiations with our enemies.' In thus attacking the aims of the Supreme Command, Erzberger was influenced by what Hoffmann (Chief-of-Staff in the East) had told him of the effect of Russian propaganda upon German moral. He was also aware that the naval calculations upon the effect of the submarine campaign had been completely falsified. Any time-limit for British endurance had been abandoned and it was assumed that the war must last over the next winter. Finally, he knew that the Pope was contemplating mediation, and hoped to prepare his way. Consequently the Reichstag was induced to vote on July 19th, 1917, the celebrated Peace Resolution, which emphasized the defensive character of the war and called for a peace 'of understanding and the permanent reconciliation of the peoples without forcible acquisitions of territory and without political economic or financial measures of coercion'.[1] This phrase recalled one of Wilson's speeches (January 1917) in which he envisaged 'a peace without victory'. It resembled the peace 'without annexations and indemnities' of the Russian revolutionists, and the adoption of such similar terms by the Reichstag hastened the growing dissolution of the Russian army. Otherwise its results were far from fortunate for Germany. Erzberger and his friend desired the dismissal of Bethmann-Hollweg, but hoped to set up Bülow in his stead, whom they believed clever and powerful enough to conclude a speedy peace.

But the military party, even before the voting of the

[1] The resolution went on to condemn economic blockades; it demanded the 'freedom of the seas' and expressed a willingness to promote the organization of international law.

resolution, had put in an obscure Prussian bureaucrat named Michaelis. The new Chancellor contented himself with accepting the Peace Resolution 'as I understand it', thereby underlining its ambiguity of wording. Even Erzberger, its author, had confided to Prince Max of Baden that with it he expected to get Briey and Longwy at the Congress-table. And the Kaiser went so far as to deride it before a meeting of the party leaders; pretending to believe that they had asked for a 'guaranteed peace', he said 'Guarantee is a splendid word, it means taking money, raw materials, metals and oil from the enemy and putting them into our own pockets': 'the war,' he continued, 'would be over in two or three months, as all English ships had been driven from the sea. Germany would make a close agreement with France, and finally all Europe under my leadership would begin the real war against England—the Second Punic War.' This speech did the Kaiser enormous harm, and was one of the principal steps on his road to abdication. He had flattered himself at the time that he had avoided a step towards parliamentary control;[1] actually he became the prisoner of Ludendorff and henceforth counted for less and less. Though the Reichstag relapsed into insignificance, the union of the Centre, the Progressives and the 'Majority Socialists' against the Conservatives (who had still, however, the whole strength of the military and nobility behind them), was a portent of the changing order. 'The foundation-stone was laid ... of the middle-class German Republic.'[2]

Among Germany's enemies the resolution, preceded as it was by Erzberger's gloomy forebodings, was hailed with satisfaction as a proof of weakness. As Helfferich points out, the language of British and French ministers immediately became sharper and more confident.[3] A speech by

[1] One of the main reasons for his desire to get rid of Bethmann-Hollweg was that the latter was pressing for the immediate establishment of equal voting rights for all classes in Prussia, which would have resulted in the domination of the Socialists.

[2] Rosenberg, *Birth of the German Republic 1871–1918* (1931), p. 168.

[3] See K. Helfferich, *Der Weltkrieg* (1919), pp. 464–5.

Balfour set for the first time unqualified official approval on the French claim to Alsace-Lorraine.

IV

The papal move which immediately followed suffered in the Entente's eyes, like Wilson's December note, from the conviction, this time well grounded, that it had been prepared in consultation with the Central Powers. The Vatican was very well informed about the situation in Austria. Nothing could be a heavier blow to its diplomacy than the collapse in revolution of the only great Power in Europe still officially Catholic; for this might well involve in its fall the equally devout populations of southern Germany. The example of Russia showed how seriously the prolonged war was sapping the foundations of religion and authority. The Papal Nuncio Pacelli sounded Bethmann-Hollweg at the end of June, receiving private assurances that Belgium would be restored, and that the Alsatian question might be compromised 'by mutual rectifications of frontier'. The note, however, was not presented to the Powers until August 1st. It suggested methods by which the rule of law could take the place of force after the war. As a basis of peace it put forward the renunciation of indemnities and the restoration of occupied territory. Belgium was in particular to receive restitution 'with guarantees of her independence against every other Power'. With regard to the other disputed questions, no concrete proposals were made. They should be handled in a conciliatory spirit having regard to the desires of the populations concerned. A special word of ambiguous sympathy was given to Poland. The Vatican saw quite correctly that the only chance of peace was to bring Great Britain and Germany as closely into touch with each other as possible. It thought that the dispatch sent to our representative at the Vatican, Count de Salis, provided hope of a *rapprochement,* inasmuch as specific reference was made to Belgium alone.[1] In reality the Belgian question was regarded by

[1] 'Though the Central Powers have admitted their guilt in regard to

the British Government as only one among many questions; a careful reading of the whole text would have made this clear, for the Pope was asked to refer to the exhaustive Allied answer to Wilson of January 1917. De Salis himself was careful to point this out. The British Government did not really desire to carry matters any farther, partly no doubt because Italy had been promised (by the Treaty of London) that the Pope should take no part in a Peace Conference. But Cardinal Gasparri, the Papal Secretary of State, took a copy of this dispatch, which was in fact the only answer from Great Britain and France, and presented it hopefully to Michaelis in such a way as to suggest a definite advance towards negotiations.

In consequence, a Crown Council was held (September 10) to decide the German intentions with regard to Belgium. The German Admiralty wanted the Flemish coast, and Ludendorff wanted Liége, with a long military occupation of Belgium, but the Kaiser decided that these advantages must be given up in return for compensation elsewhere. The new Foreign Secretary, Kühlmann, who knew England well after spending several years in the London Embassy, was in favour of unconditional return, but refused to make any public announcement. When pressed to do so he replied: 'Who told you that I want to sell this particular horse? He is the finest animal in my stable.' He meant to use Belgium as a trump card after negotiations with the British Government had been begun; and in September he made abortive attempts to gain contact through the agency of the Spanish Minister in Brussels. And so the German reply to the Pope was an entirely featureless document, which merely referred His Holiness back to the discredited Peace Resolution. The Reichstag leaders must also share the responsibility for the omission of the declaration about Belgium. A Committee of Seven had been set up, with representatives from each of

Belgium, they have never definitely intimated that they intend either to restore her to her former state of entire independence, or to make good the damage she has suffered' (Balfour to de Salis, August 21, 1917).

the principal parties, to advise the Chancellor on questions of foreign policy. The answer was approved by the Committee in the form in which it was dispatched. Only the Social Democrats wished for the reference to Belgium. The omission was the more unwise as Asquith, now leader of the Opposition, had publicly challenged in the House of Commons the German Chancellor to make an unequivocal statement. Had he responded, the stock German argument that Europe was being turned into a rubbish-heap to gratify the French lust for Alsace-Lorraine would have sounded more plausible in English ears. Such a response would also have prepared the ground for the famous Lansdowne letter of November 29th,[1] which created a great sensation but had little effect. It was indeed surprising that an ex-Foreign Minister who had negotiated the Entente with France, who had joined with other Conservative leaders in pressing immediate British intervention upon the Government two days before the violation of Belgium had taken place, should now plead for a negotiated peace. But now, though he put the restoration of Belgium in the foremost place he proposed that the British Government should make it clear that the annihilation of Germany, or the forcible imposition upon her of any kind of government, was not desired; and that the freedom of the seas would be open to discussion. The core of the letter is composed of these sentences: 'We are not going to lose this war, but its prolongation will spell ruin for the civilized world. . . . What will be the value of the blessings of peace to nations so exhausted that they can scarcely stretch out an arm with which to grasp them? In my belief, if the war is to be brought to a close in time to avert a world-wide catastrophe, it will be brought to a close because on both sides the peoples of the countries involved realize that it has already lasted too long.' Lansdowne wrote as a disillusioned Conservative who saw the old order falling headlong into ruin. His words recall the prophetic

[1] It was published in the *Daily Telegraph*, having been refused by *The Times*.

remarks of Grey at the moment when war broke out: 'The lamps are going out all over Europe, we shall not see them lit again in our life-time'; and 'It is the greatest step towards Socialism that could possibly have been made. We shall have Labour Governments in every country after this.'[1]

Lansdowne was not the man to appeal successfully to the peoples over the heads of their rulers. It was easy to represent him as a worn-out aristocrat broken by the death of his son in battle. Attempts made in Germany by Solf, the Colonial Secretary, and Prince Max of Baden to exploit his letter fell on stony ground. The Russian armies had broken up, and an armistice was about to be concluded in the east. Italy was on her knees after the frightful blow of Caporetto. The air was beginning to be alive with rumours of a great spring offensive in the West, which would finish the war victoriously for the Central Powers.

But the distinguishing mark of this, as opposed to the preceding war-years, is that the filaments of negotiation, however secret and frail, are never out of the hands of statesmen. Apart from those already mentioned, attempts were made by Lancken, the Head of the Political Department in Brussels, to get into personal touch with Briand, and twice again by Austria, whose agents prolonged interviews with representatives of the Entente until the beginning of 1918.[2]

The fear lurking everywhere in the minds of the rulers was of revolution through war-weariness. As Czernin had put it, 'the bow was being strung too tight'. The signal of Russia was plain for the world to read. France herself had suffered her mutinies. A large part of the Italian army had been guilty of what Cadorna bluntly described as 'naked treason'. Even the German fleet had been the

[1] Visc. Grey, *Twenty-five Years 1892–1916* (1928), vol. ii, pp. 20, 234.

[2] For the Armand-Revertera negotiations authorized by French G.H.Q., see Mermeix, *Les Negociations secrètes*. Nothing authentic has been published on the conversations in Switzerland between the South African General Smuts, then a member of the War Cabinet, and Count Mensdorff, formerly Austrian ambassador in London.

scene of a serious outbreak (July–August 1917) which is described elsewhere.

The great International Socialist Conference at Stockholm in June 1917, for which German but not French or British delegates were given passports, showed by its proceedings how great had been the effect of the Russian Revolution among the working classes of neutral countries. The internationalism of Labour, which had received so heavy a blow at the beginning of the war, was raising its head again more powerfully than ever.

XXII

THE GREAT SUBMARINE CAMPAIGN AND THE ENTRY OF AMERICA INTO THE WAR

I

THE political and military situation at the end of 1916 has already been described. The reply of the Entente to Wilson's peace note naturally convinced the German Chancellor Bethmann-Hollweg that the two sides stood in absolute divergence, and that no prospect existed of ending the war by negotiation. At the same time General Head-quarters were equally clear that the war could not be won by military action alone. The Chancellor was categorically informed of this conviction.

It was inevitable that the naval and military authorities should again press with the utmost vehemence for the adoption of a ruthless submarine war, which the Chancellor had so energetically and successfully combated in February 1916. This time Bethmann-Hollweg surrendered, though with the deepest forebodings and searching of heart. The evidence given before the Committee of Inquiry after the war reveals in the fullest and most interesting way the arguments brought forward and the motives actuating those who were responsible for this most fatal decision.[1] Feeling in Germany had been whipped up to such a pitch of intensity that the decision was practically inevitable. Its consequences were bound to be a matter of speculation, and it was generally agreed that Germany was playing her last card. 'If', said Helfferich, the Secretary of State, 'it is not trumps, Germany is lost for centuries.' Moreover, it was urged that the decision could not possibly be postponed since the detailed memoranda brought forward insisted that barely sufficient time remained to bring England to her knees before the next

[1] See *Official German Documents relating to the World War*, vols. i and ii, published by the Carnegie Endowment for International Peace.

harvest. Consequently it would have been considered impossible to refrain in the hope of an imminent Russian revolution, though, curiously enough, such a possibility occupies a most fleeting and subservient place in the discussions.

The problems involved were of transcendent importance. First and foremost, could an unrestricted war upon commerce be expected to force Great Britain to make peace after a maximum period of six months? Secondly, would war with the United States result? Thirdly, if so what would be its consequences for Germany? The case of the German Admiralty was presented in a long and detailed memorandum, which sought to show statistically that a success was mathematically certain.[1] It reckoned that out of a British total of some 20,000,000 tons only 8,500,000 remained for cargo-space after deduction for military and other allied requirements. An outside figure of 2,000,000 might be added for neutral shipping. If the monthly sinkings were placed at the conservative figure of 600,000 tons, then after five months Great Britain would have lost 39 per cent. of her available total.[2] Moreover, owing to the failure of the American harvest in 1916 it was calculated that the proportion of wheat imported into Great Britain from that continent would drop from 92 to 64 per cent. of the total required. The remainder would have to come from the far-distant sources of India, Australia, and Argentine. Consequently the number of ships employed in the wheat trade during 1917 might be reckoned at least as double that of the preceding year. In addition it was anticipated that the submarines would almost entirely cut off the supplies of butter and fats from Denmark and

[1] This memorandum was afterwards criticized on the ground that it was almost entirely the work of financiers, and that no economist or representative of Germany's ocean trade had any share in it. Ballin, for example, Germany's greatest ship-owner, was not consulted.

[2] The percentage is reckoned on the assumption that owing to repairs, &c., the entire mercantile marine would never be capable of being employed at any given time. In fact about 100,000 tons of British shipping were damaged monthly by submarines. The average time for repairs was five months.

Holland, which normally amounted to at least 50 per cent. of the total British consumption. All these things taken in conjunction with the assumed impossibility of any serious remedial counter-measures appeared to the German Admiralty to furnish conclusive proof that Great Britain would be incapable of waging war after August 1st, 1917, as an extreme date. The claim was never officially made that she would be starved out by then, but that she would be forced to recognize her position as hopeless. It will be seen shortly how very nearly this prediction was fulfilled. The mistake of the German Admiralty did not lie in over-estimating the achievements of the submarines, for in fact the computed monthly average of destruction was (after February) consistently and sometimes greatly exceeded during the six-months' period. Moreover, the toll exacted of the U-boats was for some time lighter than was expected, and barely a quarter of the rate of new production. It lay in under-estimating the determination of the British people and the possibilities of protection, organization and adjustment which existed with regard to tonnage and supplies. Neither the Chancellor nor his principal economic adviser Helfferich was convinced of the infallibility of this statistical demonstration. In particular they agreed that no exact time-limit could reasonably be given for the destruction of the war-will of their principal adversary. Yet they could see no other possibility of achieving a reasonable peace. Bethmann-Hollweg had indeed for long nourished the secret conviction that Germany could expect no better issue than to end the war with undiminished territory. If the Entente had ever been so reduced as to offer peace on such terms he would certainly have done his best to gain acceptance. Yet in spite of this it was only the brutal insistence of the combined naval and military chiefs which forced him to consent to this desperate throw. An intimate friend has related that on the evening after the decision was taken he found the Chancellor in a state of utter collapse, declaring that he had signed the ruin of Germany. Only his extreme conscientiousness prevented him from a resignation which would have been welcomed by the protagonists of the plan; for he felt that to leave office at such a crisis would have seriously weakened the faith of the German people in the possibility of success.

II

As regards America, Bernstorff, who had served his country at Washington with great ability and candour, under tremendous difficulties, had consistently reported that she would declare war and that her resources were inexhaustible. The peril seemed to him so vast that he put Germany's only hope in the acceptance of a peace mediated by Wilson. This no doubt was impossible, given the state of public opinion at home, of which he was very imperfectly informed.

The risk of war was, however, fully accepted, when the decision was made to begin unrestricted war against commerce on February 1st. A faint hope was indeed entertained, and was encouraged by Gerard, the American ambassador at Berlin, that the President would confine himself to a diplomatic rupture. But in any event it was natural that neither the soldiers nor sailors attached any serious importance to the entry of the United States, since they pinned their faith to the five or six months' time-limit. Within that space it was manifestly impossible for a nation still so unprepared, still menaced with a war in Mexico, to weight the European balance appreciably against the Central Powers. For the Chancellor so easy and definite a forecast was impossible. Yet he also failed entirely to envisage the possibility of any great military effort. There would doubtless be a considerable increase in the number of American volunteers serving with the Allied armies.[1] Perhaps shipping might be found to transport at grave risk a contingent of 100,000 men to France. The American navy might be expected to send some cruisers and light craft to European waters. Such were the delusive

[1] Their number was estimated at about 28,000 at the beginning of 1917.

forecasts recorded in the memoranda and discussions of January 1917.[1]

On February 1st Germany proclaimed all the approaches to the British Isles, the western coast of France, and the Mediterranean to be in a state of blockade, and expressed her intention of sinking at sight any vessel of any description found within the prohibited waters.

Bernstorff immediately received his passports, but Wilson waited to declare war until 'an overt act' had taken place. At first it seemed as though he would not take the plunge. Congress was so unwilling as to refuse him power to arm merchantmen, which step he consequently took in virtue of his executive authority. In March, however, events moved rapidly. During that month five American vessels were sunk with loss of life. More important still, the British Admiralty decoded a cipher message from the German Foreign Office to Mexico offering an alliance, and engaging to restore Texas, New Mexico, and Arizona, which had been conquered by the United States in the middle of the nineteenth century. Mexico was further requested to get into touch with Japan in order to secure her adhesion as well. The publication of this imprudence turned the hearts of the southern and western states bitterly against Germany, to whom they had hitherto been indifferent or in some instances mildly favourable.

On April 2nd the President came to the Capitol and demanded war with Germany. With the grave and measured eloquence of which he was so consummate a master he said: 'To such a task we can dedicate our lives and our fortunes, everything that we are and everything that we have, with the pride of those who know that the day has come when America is privileged to spend her blood and her might for the principles that gave her birth

[1] The question of Holland and Denmark also entering the war was considered. That they would do so was considered possible rather than probable. Ludendorff engaged that he could transfer sufficient troops from Rumania to deal with them.

and happiness and the peace which she has treasured. God helping her, she can do no other.'

Thus the United States entered the war pledged to use 'force to the uttermost, force without stint or limit'.

III

For some months before February 1st, 1917, the British Government had been exceedingly uneasy at the depredations of the submarines. Though they had been moderately careful to spare American susceptibilities, their success in the autumn of 1916 had been startling. The average amount of tonnage sunk monthly from October to December had been over 300,000. The Mediterranean was continually infested, and a particular onslaught had also been directed against Norwegian ships,[1] principally engaged in bringing timber for pit-props, a vital import.[2] Jellicoe in October gave the serious warning that if such wastage continued Great Britain might be compelled in the summer of 1917 to conclude a peace very different from what she had a right to expect. Shortly afterwards he was transferred from the Grand Fleet to Whitehall as First Sea Lord, and was therefore responsible for anti-submarine policy during the critical year of 1917. In December a Shipping Controller was appointed to co-ordinate all the diverse conflicting claims upon tonnage, and to be responsible for new construction. The German memorandum had stated with approximate accuracy the state of British shipping. On paper the situation seemed fairly favourable. After two and a half years of war the total tonnage was only 5 per cent. less than at its outbreak. This, however, was far from representing the true facts. The immense deductions to be made for war services and for the Allies have already been noticed. The total included

[1] In the course of the war over 3,000 Norwegian sailors lost their lives through submarine and mine; and just over 50 per cent. of their mercantile marine was destroyed.

[2] About 40 million tons of coal were required for export, the large majority of which was absolutely necessary for France and Italy to continue the war. Home consumption was about 200 millions.

an important non-recurrent item, the million or so tons captured or seized in port from the enemy. Further, mercantile ship-building, partly from prior naval requirements, partly from lack of foresight, had declined during 1916 to the miserable figure of 539,000 tons. At the close of the year there were exceptionally few vessels on the stocks. Again, while the submarines became more powerful and their commanders more skilful, the mercantile marine was bound to decline in efficiency, for many of the best masters and officers had been transferred to the Navy or had been killed by the enemy. Finally, there was the haunting dread that the spirit of the British seamen might be crushed by the ceaseless and ever-increasing dangers, or at least that most neutral shipping would remain fearfully in port.[1] The enemy's redoubled onslaught was therefore awaited with very serious and justified apprehension.

The German Admiralty had now at least five times as many U-boats as in 1915.[2] They were naturally far more formidable; a few, the so-called cruisers, were armed with 6-inch guns instead of the old 12-pounder; the most modern had a cruising capacity of some 10,000 miles and could remain out for four months. The numbers actually at sea at a given moment ranged from 21 on February 1st to over 60 in June, when the short nights and long, bright days were so favourable to their marauding.

The task of defence was complicated by the habit now generally adopted by the enemy of using torpedoes. The guns carried by so many British merchantmen became practically useless against an invisible assailant.[3] Though every ship was given a route by the Admiralty, from which no deviation was allowed, though the western approaches

[1] During February–March 1917 neutral entrances and clearances were in fact little more than 25 per cent. of the previous year's total.

[2] The figure for 1915 was 24; for 1917 Scheer gives 134, Koch 120, Michelsen 111. The exact number was difficult to calculate as there were so many different kinds of U-boats some of which, e.g. mine-layers, were not generally suitable for the war against commerce. Jellicoe, *Crisis of the Naval War* (1920), pp. 35–8, gives a clear description of the various types.

[3] Thirty armed merchantmen were sunk off Queenstown in six weeks during the spring of 1917 without one of them having seen a submarine.

were divided into four distinct patrolled areas to prevent overcrowding, it was clear that these measures were mere palliatives, continually losing efficiency as the number of enemies increased. It was impossible to maintain an adequate force of patrolling destroyers, as two-fifths of the whole available number were permanently required for the protection of the Grand Fleet. During the spring of 1917 the maximum number allotted to the infested waters west and south of Ireland was 15, or about one for each submarine operating there. To root out the peril by an attack upon the fortified harbours of Germany was manifestly impossible. To destroy the lairs of Zeebrugge and Ostend whence many of the smaller craft issued, was left unattempted, except by unsuccessful bombardments from the sea, until more than a year had passed. Many junior officers chafed at the refusal of the Admiralty to sanction such an expedition. It was left to the Army to fling away 300,000 men in a forlorn hope of reaching them through the Flemish mud (August–November 1917).

Nor again was it yet possible to seal up the exits with mines. Mining had always been despised by the British navy as the weapon of the weaker power. For reasons of economy a cheap pattern had been selected before the war;[1] its explosive power was weak, and it frequently escaped from its moorings and floated on the surface. The submarine-commanders were reported to laugh at it. The supply, too, was exceedingly limited, and early in 1917 only 1,500 were available of a suitable anti-submarine type.

Broadly speaking, the British navy at this crisis was still relying on an expansion of the same methods of protection which had been evolved two years before. Many new ideas were being investigated but had not yet been brought to practical fruition. Necessity it is true was finally to prove the mother of invention, but she did not deliver her child until the last moment.

[1] The Russian pattern was much the best and had been adopted by Germany. Each mine, however, cost £200, which was supposed to be more than we could afford.

In April Admiral Sims, the American naval commander-in-chief, arrived in England, having been secretly dispatched before war was declared to consult with the British Admiralty. Sims on meeting Jellicoe heard with horror and astonishment of the extreme jeopardy into which the Allied cause had fallen. In the first ten days alone of that month 250,000 tons had been sunk. He has vividly recorded the dialogue that took place.[1] 'I was fairly astounded; for I had never imagined anything so terrible. I expressed my consternation to Admiral Jellicoe. "Yes," he said, as quietly as though he was discussing the weather and not the future of the British Empire, "it is impossible for us to go on with the war, if losses like this continue."

"What are you doing about it?" I asked.

"Everything that we can. We are increasing our anti-submarine forces in every possible way. . . . But the situation is very serious, and we shall need all the assistance we can get."

"It looks as though the Germans were winning the war," I remarked.

"They will win, unless we can stop these losses—and stop them soon," the Admiral replied.

"Is there no solution for the problem?" I asked.

"Absolutely none that we can see now," Jellicoe announced.'

By the end of the month the tonnage lost had risen to 875,000. Only six weeks' supply of corn remained within the country. In official circles November 1st was given as the uttermost limit of British endurance. Yet public opinion, at least in England, was cheerful, buoyed up by America's entry and the victory of Arras. There was scarcely a glimmer of suspicion[2] that this was the blackest

[1] W. S. Sims and B. J. Hendrick, *The Victory at Sea* (1920), pp. 6–7. This is by far the most attractive book written by any great protagonist during the war.

[2] The Government had ceased to publish the tonnage sunk, giving only the number of British vessels above and below 1,600 tons (ignoring Allied and neutral losses). It cleverly allowed the German lists to appear, thus

hour for the Entente. For now the peril seemed to the few who knew it to be without remedy; whereas in March and April 1918, though patent and pressing, it could be transformed by endurance into salvation.

IV

Painfully and by degrees the position was improved, until at the close of the year, though straitened and galling, it was no longer an imminent menace.

The measures taken had three main aims: first to protect the merchantman on its voyage from attack, secondly to deal offensive blows against the submarine, and lastly to provide more cargo-space and to increase production at home.

Protection was finally secured to an astonishing degree by the ancient and traditional method of convoy. It was in fact the only anti-submarine device which proved immediately and consistently successful. The story of its adoption is illuminating. The official hierarchy at the Admiralty fought against it with all the obstinacy of entrenched experts. Nor can it be denied that their formidable array of technical arguments had an extremely conclusive ring.

Figures were adduced to show that the required number of escorting warships was totally unprocurable. Indispensable time would be lost in organizing the convoys, so that the volume of imports must soon fall below the margin of existence. Losses would be greater with so imposing a target for the torpedo. The speed of each convoy would be reduced to that of the lamest duck. The discipline required would be unattainable. The masters had

inducing the public to think that they were wildly inaccurate. In reality they gave a considerably exaggerated picture of the tonnage put out of action during any given period. The amount of tonnage actually sunk was exaggerated by from 35 to 40 per cent. Submarine-commanders were apt (i) to exaggerate the size of vessels sunk, (ii) to claim as a loss a damaged ship, of which they had not time to observe the fate. On the other hand, Germany was often ignorant of losses caused by mines.

neither the skill nor the delicate instruments necessary for keeping station. There would be collisions and there would be straggling. A conference of masters at the Admiralty emphatically admitted their inefficiency in these respects and advised against the proposal. Even in the disastrous April days the experts continued to chant their reasoned *non possumus*, while confessing that the country was heading straight for disaster.

Lloyd George had been for months profoundly uneasy at this attitude. His own eager inquiring mind was naturally inclined towards experiment. He was reinforced by the views of junior naval officers, to whom he gave private and confidential access, and by one of Hankey's most prescient memoranda.[1] Moreover, in the western Channel the system was already operating with almost complete success to protect the coal trade with France. The Admiralty just saved its face by professing a tardy conversion on April 26th, but the credit for this life-bringing change belongs almost entirely to the Premier.

The ships for escort were found with the help of America, who sent eighteen destroyers to Queenstown within a month of her declaration of war,[2] and of Japan, who maintained fourteen of high efficiency in the Mediterranean. The escort kept the enemy at a distance and forced him to discharge his torpedoes at long range with uncertain aim. Twenty or thirty ships elaborately camouflaged with streaks and blotches of violently contrasting colours, all zigzagging in formation, presented an uncertain and bewildering target. These concentrations, moreover, proved much more difficult to find than single ships; for the same number of individuals dispersed over separate routes would have been visible over a much larger sea space. 'In theory [the convoy] should have been a

[1] See Hon. J. M. Kenworthy, *Sailors, Statesmen—and Others* (1933)—the author gives a verbatim report of his conversation with the Premier; and for the Hankey memorandum, Sir H. J. Newbolt, *Naval Operations*, vol. v (1931), ch. i.

[2] The total number of American destroyers in European waters rose to 79 in 1918.

bigger and more convenient target: in practice it was a will-o-the-wisp.'[1]

It was of course a long time before the system could be generally applied to Allied ships, and finally extended to neutrals.[2] But for the last quarter of 1917 the destruction of tonnage was little more than half that of April–June, and throughout 1918 the curve of decline though slow was steady.[3] No submarine ever succeeded in bagging a large proportion of any convoy. The only striking successes were won on two occasions by raids of light cruisers and destroyers in the North Sea. It is significant that the last great sortie of the High Seas Fleet in April 1918 was with the unfulfilled intention of intercepting a convoy off the Norwegian coast. The Navy triumphantly carried through a gigantic enterprise. By the time of the Armistice more than 88,000 vessels had been convoyed with a loss of 436.

The measures of offence devised against the submarine were manifold and ingenious. Though each one taken by itself proved a comparative failure, the cumulative effect was great. Annoyance and danger met the unseen enemy at every turn. Life in a submarine under the best conditions is harsh, cramped, and uncomfortable; the ever-increasing strain of war-risks gradually reduced the spirit and enterprise of the surviving commanders and crews, themselves the picked material of the German fleet. In all the enemy lost throughout the war 50 per cent. of his boats, about 180 out of 360.

The U-boat was detected and located by the hydrophone, a device for picking up the noise of its motors under water. It was assailed by depth-charges, 300-lb. bombs dropped by destroyers and motor-chasers to explode far

[1] *Naval Operations*, vol. v, p. 281.

[2] The credit for starting it so promptly after the decision had been taken must be mainly given to Capt. Henderson of the Admiralty staff, who had worked out all the details of the scheme when it was being rejected by his superiors.

[3] In April–June 2,050,000 tons were lost; in October–December 1,050,000 tons; the total lost in 1918 (January–November) was 2,666,942 tons.

beneath the surface; it was spotted and attacked by aircraft; it was stalked and torpedoed by Allied submarines. The supply of effective mines was now taken up in earnest. America embarked upon a gigantic programme for the speedy production of 100,000 in the autumn of 1917. The approaches to the German Bight and to the Belgian harbours were densely strewn.

In 1918 deadly girdles were laid across the chief defiles through which the U-boat had to pass in order to reach its main theatres of destruction. The Straits of Dover were completely obstructed by January. By July a net-barrage had been drawn across the Straits of Otranto. All through the summer and autumn the Americans with British assistance worked assiduously at the stupendous task of mining the stretch of 250 miles between Orkney and the Norwegian coast.[1] The unhappy enemy had to grope his way through a zone fifteen to thirty-five miles deep bristling with unseen death. It is said that members of a crew which safely emerged often went mad under the prolonged intensity of the strain.

Finally, in the spring of 1918 an attempt was made to seal up the Flemish lairs by the famous though mainly unsuccessful enterprises against Zeebrugge and Ostend, which will be separately described.

Many devices were employed to find more cargo-room, and use it more economically. All imports for the civilian population, beyond the bare necessities of life, were cut down with a ruthless hand; meat, sugar, and butter were strictly rationed. Every available article was brought to British ports by the short North Atlantic route. Neutrals were constrained by every kind of pressure to charter a larger proportion of their shipping for Allied service. In the spring of 1918 we actually requisitioned all Dutch vessels lying in British ports under threat of war. The impulse of America provoked declarations of war against

[1] The Americans laid 56,571 mines and the British 13,546. For a description of the work, see Adm. W. S. Sims, *The Victory at Sea*, ch. ix. The mines were of a peculiarly sensitive type, and were laid at varying depths.

Germany from the South American states, and from such remote regions as China and Siam. Everywhere the enemy's ships which had been lying in harbour since 1914 were seized, though their employment was generally delayed for months by the timely damage effected by their crews.

Great and increasing fleets of standard ships were rapidly laid down in British and American yards. Already by the end of May 1918 these combined sources gave the Allies for the first time a modest increase in tonnage over that available in the previous month. From that time forward new construction alone easily outsped the rate of destruction.

Such in bare outline were the ways and stages by which Great Britain and the Allied cause were saved from the extremity of danger.

Yet all would have been of no avail without the stolid and unwearying courage of the British seamen. 'In journeyings often, in perils of waters; in weariness and painfulness, in watchings often, in hunger and thirst, in fastings often, in cold and nakedness' they steadfastly pursued their calling. Of the mercantile marine there perished during the war more than 15,000 persons, or nearly three-quarters of the total death-roll of the Royal Navy.[1]

[1] Deaths in British merchant and fishing vessels 15,313: killed and died of wounds in the Royal Navy 22,811. The percentage of deaths to personnel was higher in the mercantile marine (about 5½ per cent. against 4 per cent. in the Royal Navy).

XXIII

CHANGES IN THE POLITICAL AND MILITARY DIRECTION OF THE ENTENTE

I

DECEMBER 1916 is one of the most crucial months of the war. It marks definitely the beginning of a new stage. In Austria-Hungary the young Emperor Karl was bending his energies towards the attainment of a speedy peace, which alone could secure the maintenance of the Hapsburg dynasty and of his impaired inheritance. The German Chancellor disclosed to the world the German offer of peace, described elsewhere.

In England the Coalition Government fell after a life of eighteen months. Its head, Asquith, had been Prime Minister for nearly nine years, a continuous period only thrice exceeded in British parliamentary history. Its success, regarded simply as a coalition, was mainly due to the great loyalty, open dealing, and conciliation which he had shown towards colleagues differing so widely from himself and from each other in outlook and opinion. But its defects as a war ministry were also widely believed to have been largely due to his equable presidency. Kitchener testified to the unshaken calm with which Asquith had faced the worst news. It was contended, however, that his judicial mind allowed too much latitude to debate, and that decisions were deferred until the hour of their usefulness had gone by. The Cabinet was too large and responsibility was too much divided. In the often quoted words of Lloyd George: 'You cannot conduct a war with a Sanhedrim.' In each of the two autumns since the Coalition was formed the Central Powers had destroyed a small nation which Great Britain as the principal pillar of the Entente was bound in honour to protect. It is true that it was not within our power directly to assist Rumania, but the warning note sounded early in September by Lloyd George does not appear to have been taken very seriously. At any rate the impression left upon the public was that the Government might appropriately be given as its motto the words 'Too late'. The recrudescence of the submarine menace, which many people believed to have been mastered, caused a general rise of prices and thereby called attention to the alarming decline in mercantile shipbuilding, and to the lack of any comprehensive plan for meeting the growing scarcity of food and other necessaries.

In the eyes of the public the Cabinet had lost much by the death of Lord Kitchener on June 5th. He was a weary man. The disasters of 1915 had stripped him of the awe and majesty which surrounded his earlier relations with his Cabinet colleagues. They had been embarrassed and annoyed when he returned from Gallipoli to the War Office. He could not throw off the habits of secrecy, which had been his garment during the long sojourn in the East, and felt lonely and ill at ease among civilians, whose judgement he distrusted but to whose arguments he could not extemporize a convincing reply. 'This is the first Christmas which I have spent at home for forty years,' he said to a friend who found him crouching over an enormous fire in the War Office on December 25th, 1914.

Yet his services to the Allied cause, as both friends and enemies admit, were literally incomparable. He alone could have created as by a magical wand those vast armies of devoted volunteers; the last division of which sailed from England on the very day of his death. He had now accomplished the task of expanding six battle-worthy divisions into seventy within twenty-two months. This is the most famous instance of his intuitive foresight piercing the future. Lloyd George in a noble simile compared such flashes to the beams of a great revolving lighthouse which shine the more intensely because of the intervening periods of gross darkness.

Happy in the opportunity of his death, he remains a figure of real heroic mould, preserving even to the last that rugged simplicity which is the hall-mark of true greatness.

Lloyd George, who succeeded him at the War Office (June 6, 1916), was constantly questioning the correctness of the whole conduct of the war on the part of the Allies. The Somme had confirmed him in his view that the soldiers had been given too free a hand, and that they had used it relentlessly, even to the breaking of the sword of the Allied armies against an impenetrable wall of enemies. He asserted that the division maintained between policy and strategy by the Coalition had practically placed the former in the hands of G.H.Q. He was therefore determined to secure greater concentration of power, greater secrecy, and greater dispatch in the British Cabinet. He set about his task with a characteristic mixture of subtlety and impetuosity. His interview with an American journalist, shortly before the Presidential election in November, had asserted the doctrine of the 'knock-out blow'. Its wisdom was doubted by Grey, and it provoked a rejoinder from Lord Lansdowne in the form of a Cabinet minute calling in question the capacity of the Entente to win the war, and suggesting the wisdom of opening peace-negotiations. This minute foreshadowed in secret those forebodings which he, Lansdowne, delivered to the public a year later in his famous letter to the *Daily Telegraph.*

Towards the end of November Lloyd George was brought into close touch with Carson, the most implacable and effective critic of Asquith's conduct of the war, and the Conservative leader Bonar Law. The meetings were arranged by an intermediary, Lord Beaverbrook, who enjoyed Bonar Law's absolute confidence. They agreed to demand that the Cabinet should be reconstructed in such a way as to place executive responsibility for the war practically in the hands of a small War Council of three or four members, of which Lloyd George was to be Chairman. The Prime Minister was not to be a member of this body. It was not, however, proposed to replace Asquith in that office, as he was known to exercise a paramount influence over almost all his colleagues, including the Conservatives, and retained great prestige in the

Commons owing to his unrivalled power of managing the House. The strength of Lloyd George and his associates lay mainly in the growing feeling of dissatisfaction in the country, which was now voiced by a sudden and vehement press campaign principally inspired by Beaverbrook. When the Conservative ministers learnt of what was afoot, they all showed hostility to Lloyd George's scheme, but demanded the resignation of the Prime Minister in order that the Government might be so reconstructed as to prosecute the war more effectively. Asquith, uneasy at this development, seemed at first inclined to agree with his adversary quickly and accepted Lloyd George's proposal (December 3). Under the arrangements then agreed upon Asquith would have been no mere *roi fainéant* or Mayor of the Palace, for 'The Prime Minister [is] to have supreme and effective control of war policy. The agenda of the War Committee will be submitted to him; its chairman will report to him daily; he can direct it to consider particular topics or proposals; and all its conclusions will be subject to his approval or veto. He can, of course, at his own discretion attend meetings of the Committee.'[1] Within two days, however, the Premier hardened his heart and went back upon his acceptance, determined by the arguments of Liberal colleagues who detested Lloyd George, and by the apparently unfounded belief that the latter was organizing the peremptory voice of the newspapers, and intended as soon as possible to seize the first place for himself. The crisis was instantly in full blast. The resignation of Lloyd George was followed by that of Asquith. Mistakenly confident in his indispensability as Premier the latter refused to serve under either Balfour or Bonar Law, whom the King sought as alternatives. He demanded with unpleasing arrogance: 'What is the proposal? That I who have held first place for eight years should be asked to take a

[1] Asquith to Lloyd George, December 4, 1916. The arrangement was confirmed by Lloyd George in letters to Asquith of December 4 and 5, 1916. The correspondence is quoted in Beaverbrook, *Politicians and the War* (1932), vol. ii, pp. 252 sqq., and in *War Memories of D. Lloyd George* (1933), vol. ii, pp. 987 sqq.

secondary position.' To his friends he predicted confidently of the dissidents: 'They will have to come in on my terms.' He was profoundly mistaken. Lloyd George formed a Cabinet, thanks to the abnegation of Bonar Law and the unexpected support of Balfour.[1] Though the Liberal ministers stood by Asquith, the Conservatives, in spite of a pledge to the contrary which several had given, became members of the new administration.

Thus the War Cabinet was set up. Its nucleus was the small committee of four or five dominated and inspired by Lloyd George and possessing almost dictatorial powers. Such was the flexibility of the British constitution that without any statutory change the new body included from time to time such great representatives of the Dominions as General Smuts from South Africa and Sir R. Borden from Canada. It proved undoubtedly the most effective instrument for waging war forged by any of the belligerents, except perhaps the popular autocracy conferred upon the President of a belligerent United States of America.

II

That the French Cabinet did not also fall was due to the personality of Briand. His extraordinary personal 'charm', his persuasiveness in smoothing an opposition into accepting an agreed formula, were unique. No one else could satisfy, and yet evade, the curiosity of the various commissions of the French Chamber; and these, we know, had exercised a continuous and harassing criticism of the Ministry which had no counterpart across the Channel. It is probably true that, in consequence of these gifts, Briand actually exercised his real power in considerable independence of the Chamber, as his opponents asserted.

The Ministry therefore survived, but at a double price. First it was reconstructed in a 'concentrated' form, sup-

[1] Balfour's action was the more surprising as he knew that Lloyd George had been urging Asquith to get rid of him from the Admiralty.

posed to be modelled on the new British War Cabinet, to which it bore a very faint resemblance. Second, and of capital importance, Joffre was compelled to resign. The Commander-in-Chief suffered from having been so long in office. As he expressed it himself, when relieving Foch of his army-group a few days before his own fall: 'Vous êtes limogé,[1] moi, je serai limogé; nous serons tous limogés.' Two years of the war of attrition had obscured the laurels of the Marne and had convinced most Frenchmen that some other method must be found of winning the war. The deputies grew more and more to distrust and dislike his operation officers, 'the young Turks', who constantly displayed an insolent disdain for politicians. Moreover, they believed that they had found the new Messiah in Nivelle. This general found himself famous after the model recovery of Douaumont. The perambulating deputies who flocked to Verdun found him courteous and forthcoming, ready to explain his plans with a confident lucidity which delighted them. His juniority proved an actual asset, for nothing was known against him. Foch could be set aside as worn out and excitable, Castelnau as a clerical reactionary, 'le capucin botté', Pétain as too harsh in manner, able to rebuff inquiries with an icy phrase of uncompromising rudeness.

Briand hoped, while elevating Nivelle to the chief command in France, to be able to retain the counsel of Joffre as titular Commander-in-Chief of all the armies of France. This he might have succeeded in doing, but for the new War Minister whom he had just appointed, Lyautey. This magnificent proconsul had been brought back very unwillingly from Morocco. He had pacified, and was civilizing, this turbulent province. Since the outbreak of war, the success of his administration, under the prestige of his name, had been such that he had been able to disregard the advice of the Government to retire to the coast when the majority of his troops had been withdrawn. On the

[1] Limoges is the head-quarters of an army-corps in the centre of France to which discredited generals were traditionally sent.

contrary, he had even enlarged French influence, particularly by holding great fairs in the principal towns, which excited the interest and admiration of the tribesmen, and inclined them towards peace.

Lyautey maintained that he was the constitutional head of the army, and would have no such intermediary as a 'reconstructed' Joffre between him and his undivided responsibility. The dignity of Marshal of France, in abeyance since the disaster of 1870, was thereupon revived, and Joffre was thus delicately hoisted into complete retirement. Lyautey had indeed no intention of being used as an imposing parliamentary figurehead to strengthen the Ministry, to which role he feared that he might be almost reduced by the encroachment made upon the powers of his office, since war began, both by the Chamber and G.Q.G. He obtained some satisfaction in both respects. In particular, he recovered the right of approving the appointments to the higher commands made by the Commander-in-Chief.

It was unfortunate for Nivelle that he was thus placed in a relation towards the Minister inferior to that which had been held by his predecessor, and had no authority over theatres of war other than France; his position with regard to the army was difficult enough. Even at the outbreak of war Joffre had been for three years its designated commander, and his authority had been incontestable. Nivelle, on the contrary, when thus exalted, was almost the junior army commander. His experience in high command had been confined to Verdun. In these circumstances he strove to impose a supremacy which he could not assume to exist naturally. He was to exemplify in a striking way the truth of the Greek proverb ἀρχὴ ἄνδρα δείξει : 'command will show the man'. All accounts agree that he became a changed man. He did not, it is true, lose confidence in himself or in his infallible receipt for victory, but he lost his serenity and grew anxious and fussy. His courtesy and accessibility, maintained indeed for his personal staff, were exchanged for an imperious and dictatorial manner towards his immediate lieutenants. The acute divisions which arose between him and them were to have an unhappy effect upon the fortunes of France in 1917.

III

We must now turn to the plans for that year, of which Nivelle was the principal and ardent exponent. It had already been settled before his elevation that the Central Powers should be attacked on every front by a strategically simultaneous offensive. This did not mean that the army of each Power would move on the same day, but that the interval between each attack would be too short to allow the enemy to transfer and retransfer his troops. The Franco-British effort had been timed to begin on February 1st. The principal blow, in the scheme prepared by Joffre, was to fall on an immense front from Loos to the Oise, with a subsidiary operation east of Rheims. The underlying idea was the same which had inspired the September battles of 1915: to cut off the great salient, now so heavily dented on its western front. British Head-quarters regarded this as a preliminary to a great summer attack in Belgium which should wrest the submarine bases from the enemy. The Admiralty urged it as vital and was prepared in certain conditions to co-operate.

It has been claimed that Joffre's plan would have consummated the enemy's defeat. It would certainly have caught him at a most awkward moment, when his definite preparations for retreating to the Hindenburg line had scarcely begun. But for various reasons the early date arranged would have been impracticable. None of the other allies were able to move till the late spring. The railways behind the British front were in such a state of chaos as to cause Haig serious anxiety until the end of March. Finally, the exceptional cold of the severest winter for twenty years would have made arduous and prolonged exertions almost impossible for the troops. For several nights at the beginning of February the thermometer fell below zero Fahrenheit.

Nivelle changed all this. He proposed that the British should extend their line south of the Somme, and confine their attacks to a smaller area on either side of Arras. The French share was correspondingly increased. Joffre had decided to leave untouched the great plateau stretching for thirty miles along the north bank of the Aisne, of which Laon is the centre and citadel. But Nivelle intended to place here the principal mass of his reserves, and to rive the whole German line apart by an overwhelming frontal attack. While his predecessor had envisaged a series of methodical bounds, each of which would carry the advance about three miles forward into the enemy's battery-positions, Nivelle spoke with astounding confidence of 'la percée en vingt-quatre heures', and then of a limitless pursuit. The motto of every commander must be 'violence, brutalité, rapidité', and with such a spirit he guaranteed to break the German front whenever he wished. Thus coldly described, his proposal sounds like a crude return to the insensate spirit of the offensive *à outrance* of August 1914. So indeed it really was.

But such was the magnetism of Nivelle's supreme confidence, such was the apparently flawless logical lucidity of his exposition, that it appears at first to have gained almost universal approval, except from that canny, dour, and unemotional pair, Pétain and Robertson. Lloyd George was enchanted with the new chief, who had inherited a perfect command of our language from his English mother. The Prime Minister had just been returning with renewed zeal to his earlier project of a great transference of troops from France to the Isonzo front to knock out Austria. Nivelle, however, converted him: 'Here at last,' he said, 'is a General whose plan I can understand.' He agreed to the French demand that his decisive attempt 'to destroy the principal mass of the enemy'[1] logically implied unity of command upon the

[1] Nivelle's words.

whole front, and secretly promised to ensure the subordination of Haig. This undertaking was concealed from both Haig and Robertson, who were justifiably astonished and infuriated when it was sprung on them at the Calais Conference (February 26), the sole ostensible reason for which had been to discuss the state of the French northern railways. In consequence of their objections the agreement was so far modified as to be confined to the proposed spring operations, and Haig was given the right to appeal to his Government, if, in his opinion, the orders received from G.Q.G. endangered the safety of his army. But even so, relations were still further strained between the two chiefs by the peremptory and inquisitorial 'directives' which were now sent to Haig, as if he were merely the recalcitrant commander of one of the French army-groups. The real spirit of comradeship which Joffre and Haig had been steadily fostering throughout the Somme battles was desperately endangered.

The omens therefore were already far from propitious, but a succession of more grievous blows was to strike the plan before it could be executed.

IV

German Head-quarters viewed the situation at the end of 1916 as profoundly depressing. For the first time signs of internal unrest were noticeable in Germany. The food shortage was becoming serious. Compulsory rationing had begun, but the food-stocks found in Rumania had fallen far below expectation, and it was clear that great hardships would be endured before the next harvest. The military revival of Russia, even though by now somewhat dimmed, made it impossible to reinforce the West to the required extent consistent with safety in the East.[1] Ludendorff placed on record his opinion that, if the war should be prolonged without the collapse of one of the Allies, the defeat of Germany was inevitable. At the same

[1] Seventeen divisions had actually been transferred before the Allied attacks began in April.

time Hindenburg told the Chancellor that 'the military position could hardly be worse than it is'. The effects of the Somme on German moral have already been indicated. At present nothing more than a strict defensive could be demanded of the troops. Local commanders were ordered to abstain even from minor undertakings, which they themselves were confident could be carried through.

But on the whole Somme sector even a successful defence was problematical. For the improvised lines in which the German soldier found himself at the advent of winter were both bad in themselves and lacking in depth. Renewed attacks on the Verdun model might well break clean through the last organized defences.

This possibility had long been exercising the mind of Ludendorff. Ever since September, he had been building the enormous system of well-sited fortifications at an average depth of some twenty-five miles in rear, called by the Germans the 'Siegfried', and by the Allies the 'Hindenburg' line. Droves of prisoners and of civilians were being ceaselessly employed at its construction. It was not yet completed but was expected to be ready by the end of March.

Ludendorff had no such tenacious objection to the abandonment of any territory in the West as had characterized Falkenhayn. But he realized that so considerable a retreat was bound to raise the spirits of his enemies and to depress his own people. It could be justified only by clear military necessity. The full plans of the Entente were not yet known when the Kaiser gave his consent to the retirement on February 5th, 1917. But the immense congestion of material behind the whole Somme front, and the beginning of British activity on the Ancre, left no doubt that the battle would be renewed there at the earliest possible hour.

The retirement was a master-stroke both in conception and execution. It ruined, as we shall see, the whole strategical conception of the Entente. It exchanged a bad, haphazard, bulging line for another well-sited, bristling with every device of the most up-to-date defensive art, and much shorter. It was calculated that thirteen fewer divisions were required as trench-garrison. The retirement could not be hurried: at least five weeks were required before the new works could be complete, and the same time was also necessary for those ruthless devastations by which Ludendorff hoped to turn the intermediate territory into an impracticable glacis.

The eyes of the Entente commanders were curiously blind. Though British G.H.Q. admitted the probability of the retirement before the end of February, and feared an attack in Flanders as its sequel, it was too busy with the preparations before Arras to interfere seriously. A constant series of successful little attacks on the Ancre racked the local enemy garrisons, but that was all. The French commander farther south, Franchet d'Espérey, entreated his chief to allow him to attack in force. Nivelle, misled by his 'Operations-branch', which scoffed at the idea of a German withdrawal, refused to allow him to act 'on so remote a hypothesis'. 'To retreat,' he said, 'is to renounce victory, of which no soldier is capable.'

On March 15th the last German posts were withdrawn and the Allies cautiously felt their way forward. A great desert was spread before them. Though a few towns like Noyon and Ham had been spared, practically every other building was in ruins.[1] Shell-craters had been blown in at all cross-roads, and the tall poplars, which line so many road-sides, had been felled as obstructions. The wells had been contaminated or poisoned. The cutting down of the apple-orchards caused the greatest indignation among plain homely folk everywhere.[2] History repeats itself in curious little ways. Two thousand three hundred years before, the Greek conscience had condemned as barbarous

[1] The few that were left were mined. Two French deputies were blown up in the Town Hall of Bapaume, and part of an English divisional staff suffered the same fate. Afterwards the higher commands were careful to bivouac.

[2] As a punitive measure British troops in India were accustomed to destroy the orchards of recalcitrant tribes on the NW. frontier.

the destruction of the Athenian olive-yards by the Spartans when they invaded Attica.

Prince Rupprecht had protested strongly to Ludendorff against the extreme rigour of these devastations, but had been forced to comply. An unknown fatalistic philosopher hoisted a great board across the main street of Péronne with the legend 'Nicht ärgern, nur wundern' ('Do not be angry, only wonder'). It expressed admirably the growing feelings of very many that the war had them in a grip of necessity, excluding all exercise of will.

V

While the Entente peoples were deluded into the belief that this retreat was the beginning of the end, and their soldiers skirmished briskly forward in the transient excitement of open warfare, there were great searchings of heart in responsible circles. Obviously no attack could be launched against the Hindenburg line. The offensive was reduced to two sectors, out of direct relation to each other strategically, Arras and the Chemin des Dames. The only object of the former could be to draw off the enemy's now strengthened reserves. But Nivelle was quite undismayed; he proposed to change nothing. He pointed to the 1,200,000 men and 7,000 guns concentrating on a front of forty miles. The break-through, he repeated, was certain: 'Laon in twenty-four hours and then the pursuit.' This confidence was not shared by Micheler, commanding the group of three attacking armies. He was at odds with his immediate lieutenant, Mangin, Nivelle's favourite, who, he alleged, disregarded all his orders. It was also notorious that the great chiefs, Pétain, Castelnau, and D'Espérey, were sceptical of success. They were convinced that Nivelle was making a most dangerous generalization from his limited experience at Verdun. An advance of three miles by a few picked divisions over a crater-field, against a dispirited enemy, offered no analogy to the proposal to take at a bound four fortified lines and ten miles of wooded hills.

These rumbles of discontent reached the ears of the Ministry, where Nivelle had lost his strongest support. Briand had fallen (March 17). His Cabinet had been destroyed by Lyautey, who roused the fury of the Chamber by refusing to give it, even in secret session, any technical details concerning aviation, on the ground that to do so 'would expose the national defence to the most perilous risks'.[1] Ribot became Premier in Briand's stead, an aged and respectable bourgeois, who had been first elected to the Chamber in 1878. But the ruling spirit was Painlevé, the new Minister of War. He had formed many acquaintances in the higher ranks of the army, as Minister of Inventions. He had resigned that post in December 1916 rather than consent to the passing over of Pétain, in whose judgement he had absolute confidence. He did not believe in Nivelle, whom he viewed as a gambler staking the last army of France. The statements of mobilized deputies and other emissaries from the army increased his anxiety. The responsibility either way was a terrible one, whether to stop the offensive or let it continue. He multiplied expedients, consulting the army-group commanders, and spending a day with Haig. On April 3rd Nivelle was cross-questioned at a Cabinet Council, but finally given leave to proceed. Even that was not the end. Messimy, Minister of War in 1914, now commanding a division under Micheler, handed to the Premier a note vibrating with a passionate and reasoned pessimism. It ended thus: 'Conclusion la plus urgente: donner toute de suite, sans perdre une heure, l'ordre d'attendre les beaux jours pour entamer les opérations offensives en France.' The last refuge of indecision was taken. A Council of War was held in the presence of the President of the Republic (April 6). Nivelle was on the defensive, cold and haughty. After his generals had again expressed their doubts he handed in his resignation. This caused general consternation. What would be the effect upon France, upon her allies and upon her enemies,

[1] He was fully justified. Among the deputies was one Turmel, afterwards convicted of having sold information to the enemy for 175,000 francs.

of discarding a commander, undefeated, untried, on the eve of a great battle? It was too late to draw back, as the other generals pointed out. The British had already started their bombardment at Arras; they could not be deserted. The enemy would feel that the initiative had been handed to him. He would probably seize the occasion to overthrow the Italians, already shrilly demanding reinforcements from the West. Finally, Nivelle promised in the most formal manner that if the prophesied success was wanting, the battle should be broken off in two days at latest: 'Under no circumstances', he asserted, 'will I engage upon another Somme.'

The unhappy Commander-in-Chief had therefore to wage a battle in whose issue, he knew well, no one had any confidence except Mangin, his own personal staff, and himself.

THE CONSEQUENCES OF NIVELLE

VI

The battle of Arras began on April 9th, a week before Nivelle's great effort. It was much the most successful stroke yet delivered by the British armies. Allenby, who directed it as commander of the 3rd army, was shortly afterwards to leave France to gather greater renown by his triumphs in Palestine. The German retreat and America's declaration of war had keyed up the troops to a high level of expectation. Painlevé, who visited our front just before, has recounted the vivid impression that he received of assured confidence in victory.

Allenby had, as an immediate tactical objective, the complete conquest of the heights of Vimy; as a strategical possibility the rupture of the switch line, now almost completed, by which the Hindenburg line linked itself with the old system north of Lens. To reach this an advance of about eight miles would be necessary. The initial point of attack and the force employed were little smaller than those on the Somme,[1] but there was no intention of

[1] 25,000 yards as against 27,000, 12 divisions against 14. Casualties for the first three days were 32,000 against 70,000.

maintaining the same continuous weight of pressure. Arras was a relatively short battle, and would have been broken off earlier but for the misfortune of the French.

The bombardment, contrary to Allenby's wish, followed the old model of a week's duration. It was heavier,[1] composed of far better shells (there was little complaint of 'prematures' and 'duds'), and better directed. A new kind of fuse, the famous '106', was now used for high-explosive shells. As it burst on graze, it cut wire more efficiently, did not make such deep craters, and had increased man-killing power. Another effective innovation had been found in the gas-projector, which lobbed large canisters of poison-gas into the enemy's trenches. According to Prince Rupprecht, the continuous wearing of gas-masks interfered greatly with his troops' efficiency, and so many horses were killed at the batteries that they could neither change their positions nor replenish their ammunition. The enemy had not been surprised, although, until the end of March, the character of the concentration observed by him had suggested rather fear of being attacked than any intention of attacking. Detailed information was then extracted from a Canadian prisoner, which left no doubt.[2] The German line was actually held by eight divisions, an unusually high figure. The British success exceeded Rupprecht's worst forebodings. He made the following entry in his diary that day: 'The further question arises. Is it of any use to pursue the war further under such conditions? Only if a peace with Russia is speedily concluded. If not . . . we must admit ourselves to be conquered. For if we delay longer, the peace-terms of our enemies will only grow harder.'[3]

The German VIth army contributed to its defeat by carrying out imperfectly the new defensive organization

[1] 88,000 tons as against 52,000 on the Somme.

[2] Kronprinz Rupprecht, *Mein Kriegstagebuch* (1929), vol. ii, p. 127.

[3] Ibid., p. 136. Ludendorff confirms this statement by saying that if the Russians had won only slight successes in April and May the war could not have been continued.

prescribed by Ludendorff, which was to prove so successful on the Chemin des Dames, and will be described in connexion with that battle. But the main cause of victory was the immense improvement in the tactical handling of the British troops. The town of Arras had been made a

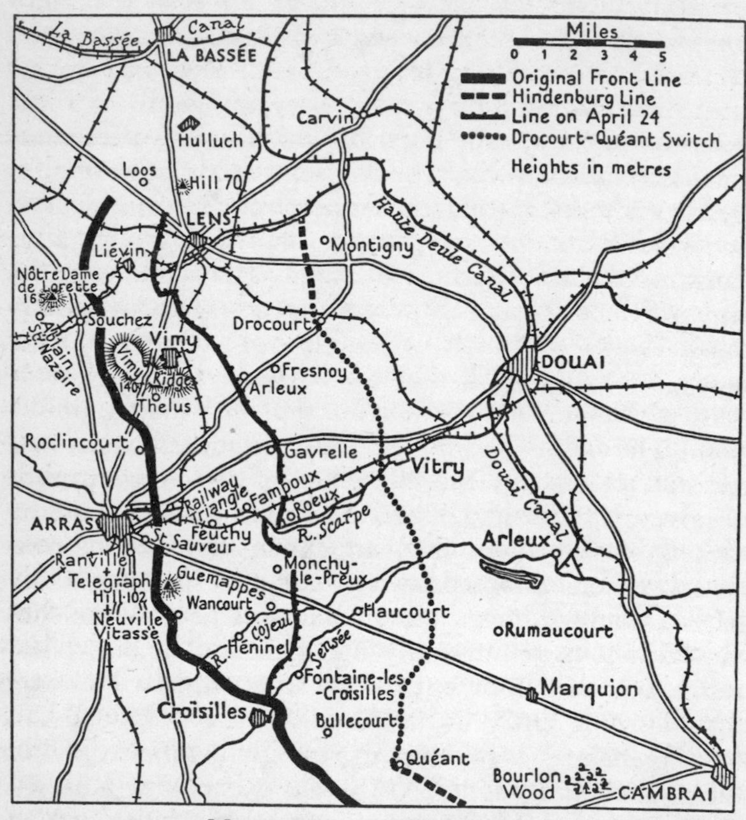

Map 21. Arras and Vimy ridge.

vast underground repository for reserves. Its cellars had been interconnected and lit with electricity. The troops emerged from them into the communication trenches. The approaches had been largely freed from congestion by the laying down of a large number of converging plank-roads. Thus fresh divisions were readily available to pass through the original attacking troops, and to continue the advance without interruption by the manœuvre known as 'leap-frogging'. On Easter Monday, April 9, the infantry progress fulfilled all reasonable expectation. Though held up in places by strong points, they overran a large number of batteries, taking 200 guns and 13,000 prisoners on the first day. In spite of continuous snow-storms, the creeping barrage and aeroplane liaison[1] worked admirably. The Canadians took the Vimy ridge, and due east of Arras the 4th division gained a footing in the enemy's last line at Fampoux. The way to the Hindenburg switch-line was open here on a narrow front. Experience showed that after a long bombardment, the state of the ground, and the probable readiness of enemy reserves, forbade an infantry advance of more than three or four miles at the utmost. The secret of further exploitation of such a tactical success had not yet been found. Only sixty tanks were available, a number little superior to that of September 1916—and they were still distributed in driblets to the infantry to help them to deal with strong points. Their role was to make uniform penetration easier, not to exploit it. Thus used, they were sometimes a curse rather than a blessing, as the troops bunched round them and suffered more heavily from the artillery fire which they inevitably drew. The only arm therefore which remained was that which Allenby adorned, the cavalry. Arras is the last battle in which mounted troops were used in a crater-field. To seize the flying opportunity, a whole corps had actually been brought into Arras on the night of the 8th, but only a few squadrons ever got ahead of the infantry on either side of the Scarpe, and one of them captured a battery. Farther south cavalry charges on the flanks of Monchy-le-Preux, a village on a commanding hill, which defied capture, were shattered in mud and against wire. Great mounds of dead horses remained for days to testify to their failure. It is probable, indeed, that the concentration of cavalry in an area so far forward actually impeded

[1] The losses of personnel in the Air Force during this month were the heaviest of the war, amounting to 316.

the infantry, as by the evening of the 9th they caused great congestion in and about Arras.

Very early on April 12th an interesting attempt was made to cut off the Germans in the southern sector of attack. It has been described as 'a miniature Cambrai'. At Bullecourt, where the Hindenburg line bends west to rejoin the old Arras front, an Australian division made a sudden irruption, preceded by eleven tanks, which were thus used for the first time, after Swinton's formula, as a substitute for artillery in the task of wire and trench destruction. The thrust bit deep, and went right through the defences with the ultimate object of joining Allenby's troops fighting round Wancourt on the Cojeul. But it was far too narrow. The deep galleries of the Hindenburg line disgorged unsuspected bodies of troops. The Australians taken in the flank and rear were badly cut up. This was the only occasion in the war when they lost any considerable number of prisoners.

The remaining stages of the battle brought unimportant gains and severe losses.[1] It was prolonged, entirely against Haig's original intention, until May 23rd to help the French, who were falling, as we shall see, into a state of utter calamity.

The capture of the Vimy heights had fully justified this offensive. As Colonel Boraston justly points out, their possession was of supreme importance in March 1918. The German assault on Arras (March 28, 1918) would certainly have been successful if that commanding point had still been in the enemy's hand; and Amiens could then scarcely have been saved. Haig had resolutely refused to omit the attack on Vimy from his programme, in spite of the reiterated opposition of Nivelle, who desired the battle-front to be extended farther south.

[1] Casualties for the whole battle up to May 3 are officially given as 84,000; those of the enemy are estimated at 75,000. Thirty-two German divisions had been engaged, or double the number of those engaged on the Somme for the same period.

VII

Nivelle's plan had been broadcast from mouth to mouth in the most reckless manner. Copies of his original memorandum were, according to Robertson's personal knowledge, handed to ten persons in London before the end of December 1916. The General himself held forth at length to a luncheon party of both sexes. By the beginning of February his intentions were said to be common talk in Allied and even in neutral countries. Worse still, the actual operations-orders were made out months in advance and freely issued to subordinate officers. As early as February 15th a German attack in Champagne captured a divisional order giving details of a great attack on the Aisne arranged for April. On March 3rd the original memorandum itself was captured, in a raid, from a Staff officer who happened to be touring the trenches and was caught. Most fatal of all, the whole detailed plan of the 5th French army,[1] with every unit and objective named, fell into the enemy's hands on April 6th. Nivelle knew at the time at least of the latest disclosure, but neither informed his Government nor thought it feasible to make any important change in the order of battle.

G.Q.G. had moved up from their remote station at Beauvais to Compiègne, little more than twenty miles behind the front. Pierrefeu has given one of his brilliant ironic sketches of the tension, now vibrating rather with foreboding than confidence, which prevailed in the beautiful *château* with its Napoleonic memories. All through the last week the signs of the weather were disastrous. Every morning the barometer was fixed at 'Stormy'. A cold rain fell in torrents. The attack, originally settled for the 12th, was inexorably postponed from day to day. These delays hampered the artillery preparation which had begun on the 5th and had been timed for a week; as the stock of shells could not be increased, it lacked concentration towards the close. Reports of its insufficiency on the

[1] On the right flank of attack immediately west of Rheims; see Gen. P. L. Palat, *La Grande Guerre sur le front occidental* (1917–1927), vol. xii, p. 214.

15th were sent from half the attacking divisions. The number of shells actually fired was about 11 millions, which sounds stupendous. But they were not only spread over thirty miles of front, but over the whole depth of the German defences. Moreover, the proportion of howitzers

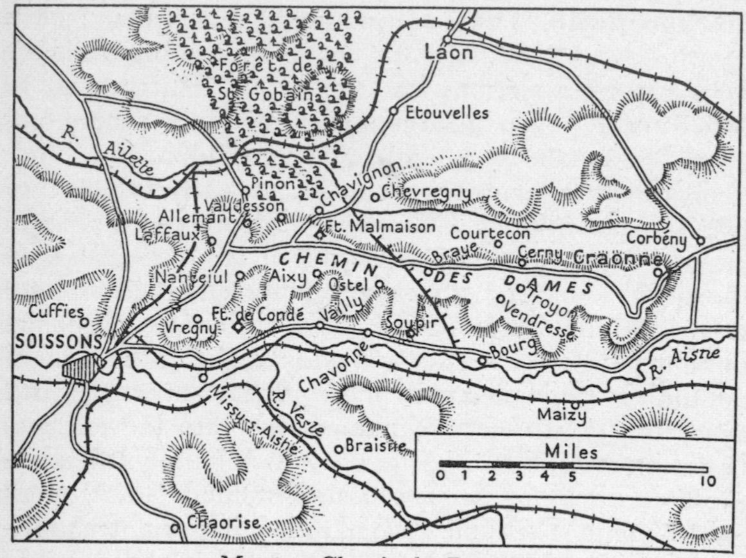

Map 22. Chemin des Dames.

was far too small. Plunging fire of extreme intensity alone could hope to deal with the ravines, caves, tunnels, and reverse-slopes with which the enemy's position was studded. Further, the French aircraft were almost impotent. With inconceivable folly, between 400 and 500 pilots had been sent to Le Bourget to pick up new machines; they took their own time to return and were not back until the second day of the attack.

The new German defensive organization had ground for which it was admirably adapted, and proved its great merit. It was not an entirely fresh system, but had been evolved out of the experience of the Somme. It was altogether more elastic in character. It aimed not at defending every foot of ground, but at creating zones beyond which the enemy could not pass. The front trenches were therefore lightly held as outposts. Behind them were generally three systems, to a total depth of about 8,000 yards, each complete in itself. Each again was divided into more or less self-contained sectors. The communication-trenches were furnished with numerous concrete machine-gun emplacements, and the whole sector broken up by strong points, each sharing the command of the intervening ground with its neighbour. The problem of providing both protection and rapid lateral movement for the garrison was solved by building tunnels, with their mouths parallel to the trench-line, so that they could be blocked up only by enfilade fire. One of these was one and a half miles long, and possessed a light railway. It was only thirty yards behind the front line, and had been completed without the knowledge of the French who were barely 200 yards away.

Finally, the greatest pains were taken in the organization of counter-attacks. Special 'storm troops' were held in readiness near the vital points, to be used with the utmost energy and speed at the right moment. Only small local tasks of restoring the line were, as a rule, to be entrusted to the supports of the trench-garrison; the 'counter-attack in depth' generally being launched when the assailants were trying to reorganize at the second position.

Such were the carefully worked out plans of the Germans. Nivelle's scheme, as his subordinates complained, treated the enemy as a mere abstraction. When his confidant and military secretary, Colonel d'Alenson, a gaunt and haggard fanatic, already dying of consumption, waved his hand casually over several fortified lines on the map saying 'On passe par là et par là', the officer who received his instructions muttered sombrely, 'Ou on ne passe pas'.

The schedule for the artillery-barrage arranged a uniform progress throughout the day of roughly one kilometre per hour, with periodic halts of ten minutes, as in a field exercise. 'After zero hour,' Nivelle said, 'the infantry will have no need of their watches, but the artillery will have to consult theirs most carefully.' The morning of the

16th arrived still in the grip of the belated winter, with interminable snow-showers.

The poor blacks, Mangin's speciality, employed in large quantities as usual for 'attack fodder', were so numbed that they could not fix bayonets or throw their grenades. They groped along miserably with their rifles under their arms, and soon fled in disorder. The great majority of French troops, in spite of the rumours which circulated later, seem to have fought with a devoted bravery. But the result was much the same everywhere. The second position had been reached in a few places, but the general failure was glaring. The German *communiqué*, which the French public was not allowed to read, proclaimed the defeat in high-sounding rhapsodical sentences, proportionate to the relief experienced. Nivelle would not admit it. He extended the battle to the chalk-hills east of Rheims and conquered the Moronvillers heights. In spite of his professed determination not to recommence 'a Somme battle', he renewed every few days partial attacks between Soissons and Rheims, until by the end of the month he could claim a general command of the Chemin des Dames. Justified alarm for the security of his own position led him to the most ignoble expedients. He threw over his Chief-of-Staff, who heard no word of his dismissal until his successor arrived to take over. He got rid of Mangin, the most ardent and faithful interpreter of his methods. Micheler was forearmed: on the news that Nivelle proposed to visit his head-quarters, he threw all the windows open and assembled his officers on the lawn. After the interview had proceeded for a while, Micheler's voice was heard declaiming: 'General, your intentions are infamous, cowardly, dastardly!' The Commander-in-Chief is said to have emerged staggering like a drunken man, and dared not proceed to the dismissal of his terrible subordinate. But he could not save himself. All and far more than all about the disaster was circulating at Paris. In sober truth the offensive compared rather favourably either with Joffre's efforts in 1915 or with the British opening on the Somme.

More than 20,000 prisoners and 150 guns had been taken at a cost of 118,000 casualties.[1] But such a result was not either what Nivelle promised or France expected. Painlevé had his way: Nivelle was 'limogé', and Pétain was made Commander-in-Chief. The latter had not merely to retrieve a defeat but to prevent the disintegration of the army.

VIII

Widespread mutinies were breaking out which, if not speedily repressed, would destroy the French power of resistance. It might be supposed that these disorders, which followed so closely after the Russian Revolution, were essentially political in character. It is true that the Russian brigades fighting in France had formed 'soldiers' councils' even before April 16th, had actually discussed the question whether they would take part in the attack, and, after suffering heavy losses, had broken up their discipline.[2]

It is also true that agitators and emissaries, some in German pay, but the majority of them socialists, anarchists, and pacificists, had for long been trying to seduce the French *poilus* from their allegiance. They haunted the railway stations, distributing seditious pamphlets and newspapers. Nivelle had made a detailed complaint to the Minister of the Interior in February, naming several of the ringleaders; Malvy, that sinister figure, who managed to hold this key position whatever ministry was in power, spoke of it as 'a stab in the back' and refused all satisfac-

[1] A great controversy has raged about those figures. These seem to be correct for the period April 16–30.

[2] These troops had been sent to France in 1916 at the urgent request of the French Government. They were of bad quality: one regiment signalized its arrival in France by murdering its colonel at Marseilles. Their favourite paper was for some time edited by Trotsky until he was expelled from France. They had finally to be reduced by a three-days' bombardment in the camp of La Courtine at Limoges, and were sent to Algeria, where they remained till long after the Armistice. Even their manifesto is not primarily political in character. It complained that they were sent to France to pay for munitions for Russia, were treated 'as things and not as men', and that their wounded, being useless for war, were inhumanly neglected.

tion. Some of the leaders no doubt were in such high positions of influence among the trades-unions that even Clemenceau did not venture to touch them. But Malvy was in close relation with Caillaux, who was widely believed to be planning to make himself master of France by a military *coup d'état*—and to conclude an alliance with Germany against England. Malvy probably therefore encouraged the 'defeatist' organizations with this object. His policy was certainly deliberate—as he gave 8,000 francs a month of government money to Almereyda, whose violent paper, *Le Bonnet rouge*, was also subsidized by the enemy.

All these subversive elements found their occasion and made the most of it in 1917, but the *poilu* as a rule broke into rebellion without accepting the programme of these instigators, and often by that kind of spontaneity of instinct, so common among great armies, particularly those composed of conscripts. The awful disillusionment of April, with all those obvious signs of vacillation and feebleness in the higher command which succeeded, brought to a head every kind of grievance and sense of injustice. One of the favourite cries was: 'We will go into the trenches but we will not attack.' The determination not to be led any longer to useless slaughter by incompetent commanders was the strongest of all motives. But there were many other causes for bitterness. The fighting man, living like an animal, was indignant with 'les embusqués'—the young munition-workers, living in luxury on 20 francs a day, remote from danger, hoping that the war would continue indefinitely. Leave was very irregular and seems not to have been granted at all since February 1st, the original date of the constantly postponed offensive. Thus, entirely cut off from home, the men fell ready victims to the wild stories which circulated to the effect that Paris was in revolution, and crowds were being shot down in the streets. It was this belief, rather than any deliberate intention to compel peace by a military *coup d'état*, which impelled so many of the mutinous formations to march on the capital.

All through May and June the troubles multiplied. Outbreaks were reported from sixteen of the French army corps. At one time it was reported that only two divisions were wholly trustworthy on the whole front between Soissons and Rheims. Though so many units refused to fight, there were two reassuring signs. Not a single officer was murdered, and very few suffered violence. Moreover, there were many examples of men who, in response to exhortations and appeals, returned to their duty. It is related that one regiment, encamped obstinately for three nights in a wood round which pickets of loyal troops had been set, was won over by a force of bearded territorials, whom somebody's happy imagination had sent to reason with them. As a French writer has truly said it was rather 'une grève professionnelle' than an outbreak of lawless violence. Yet the result would have been ruin for France if the 'strikers' had won, for the line could not have been held for lack of men.

Pétain was the ideal restorer of order and confidence. His marble calm was never shaken. Of all the great chiefs of the war, he understood the common man best. His massive simplicity, so sincere, so completely unselfconscious, above all his justice, made him a true soldier's friend. Within a month he had visited ninety divisions. The old soldiers were encouraged to speak their mind freely. The promises which he made to remedy their grievances were promptly kept. He even wrote an article on the causes of the war for the trench magazine. In a short time the politicians began to fear lest he should become too popular. The hand of severity was wisely restricted to a few ringleaders; only twenty-three in all were put to death. By the end of July the general spirit had remarkably improved. The enemy had never realized how low it had fallen, for the secret of the mutinies was kept with extraordinary success. But he knew that the French were fighting very feebly, and therefore he multiplied partial attacks on the Chemin des Dames, with many small successes.

Pétain was quite prepared to remain generally on the defensive. His answer to inquiries was always: 'We must wait for the Americans and the tanks.' The wastage in his army had been such that only one-third of the infantry consisted of men between 20 and 32. He confined his activity during the remainder of the year to two considerable local operations, one at Verdun, the other at the western angle of the Chemin des Dames. Both were prepared with the minutest care, with the utmost economy of infantry. In one army corps the artillery outnumbered them by 50 per cent. The specialization of the infantry itself was carried to greater lengths. The aim in 1917 was to make each platoon a self-supporting group, the sections being divided into riflemen, light machine-gunners, hand- and rifle-bombers, although to carry this fully into effect made too high a demand on the intelligence of the average soldier and on the time available for such intensive training. Both attacks, however, were completely successful. By the former in August the French recovered almost all their original line at Verdun. By the latter in October the German salient north-east of Soissons was completely cut off, their hold on the Aisne heights was turned, and they were compelled to fall back behind the Ailette, leaving the Chemin des Dames at last securely in French hands. More than 20,000 prisoners were taken at small cost.

Thus the main weight of the war fell for the first time on the British. The French were inactive, and the Russians rapidly crumbling into dissolution. Moreover, the submarine warfare had reached its zenith of destruction. Nearly a million tons of shipping had been sunk in April. The Entente was faced with the gravest crisis of the whole war. How the U-boats were gradually mastered has been told elsewhere. Lloyd George and Haig (although neither of them had great confidence in the other) faced the political and military situation with dauntless courage. French writers admit that the address of the former at the Paris Conference (May 4) put new life into the French ministers and confirmed their feeble knees. He insisted that the offensive must be continued and no respite allowed to the enemy. Ribot and Painlevé agreed, but, as we have seen, their army could play only a distinctly minor role. Haig and Robertson took up the military burden. The remainder of the year is a mere record of the most stubborn British persistence. Whether this persistence was wisely applied, or the campaign as a whole wisely conducted, may well be doubted, but no one can question the unstinted sacrifices made by the British for the good of the Alliance.

XXIV

THE RUSSIAN REVOLUTION

THERE is a saying of Aristotle in the *Politics*, often and deservedly quoted, that revolutions have small occasions but not small causes.

Russia by the end of 1916 was in such a condition that the smallest incident might light an unquenchable flame. The Imperial tyranny had now no friends (except those whose safety or interest was directly bound up with its continuance) and a multitude of enemies. Even with a popular government in power the situation would have been dark. An interminable prospect of war was ahead. The Russian armies were everywhere pinned down. Rumania had become an impotent and detested liability. The national pride had been cruelly wounded by the establishment of a puppet independence of Poland (November 5, 1916) under the direction of the two Germanic Powers. Yet from a purely military standpoint the coming year offered greater promise, for the stocks of munitions from the West transported over the Murmansk railway were calculated to suffice for all the needs of at least one more campaign.

The Tsar, however, was now even more than before in the hands of an obscure and corrupt camarilla, which typified what were known as 'the dark forces'[1] of reaction and superstition. Sazonov, the last minister whose name inspired any confidence either at home or abroad, had been dismissed from the Foreign Secretaryship in August.

The first blow was struck not by revolutionaries but by Conservatives from within the Imperial circle, including in their number a cousin of the Tsar, the Grand Duke Dmitri. These men killed the monk Rasputin in circum-

[1] This phrase comes from the secret manifesto of the Union of Towns and Zemstvos which said 'the government, now become the instrument of the dark forces, is driving Russia to her ruin and is shattering the Imperial throne. In this grave hour the country requires a government worthy of a great people. . . . There is not a day to lose.'

stances which recall the crudest 'Grand Guignol' melodrama (December 29th). The favourite was enticed to a luxurious apartment by the irresistible lure of a beautiful woman's presence, poisoned, shot, and thrown under the ice of the frozen Neva. The perpetrators hoped to terrify the Tsar into taking such remedial measures as would preserve the *ancien régime* in its essentials. But on the contrary, Nicholas hardened his heart, banished the murderers, and continued on his own way. Most singular stories are told how the Imperial couple spent many hours in séances trying to raise the spirit of Rasputin with the aid of Protopopov, Minister of the Interior, and Madame Viribova, the Tsarina's confidante, a mixture of courtier, *dévote*, and witch. It is not surprising that aristocratic gossip was openly suggesting the assassination or deposition of the Tsar. Both British and French ambassadors ventured upon formal remonstrances, which were turned aside with haughty frigidity. To Buchanan the Tsar said: 'My ministers are chosen by me alone; and it is for my people to deserve my confidence.'

Nicholas had indeed done everything in his power to destroy the long-suffering confidence of the loyal, liberal middle classes. The Duma was not allowed to meet, the Congress of the Union of the Towns and Zemstvos[1] was banned. The censorship of the press was more rigorously enforced by the secret police. At this ominous moment a great combined deputation arrived (January 29, 1917) from the three western Allies to concert final plans for victory. Amidst the last festivities of the Imperial Court, the French contrived, without the knowledge of their allies, to conclude a convention by which France was authorized to take the frontiers of 1814,[2] and to set up an independent Rhineland state, in return for allowing Russia a free hand on her western frontier. The foreigners

[1] The local committees of self-government in the rural areas.

[2] This included, besides Alsace-Lorraine, the Saar territory, and one or two isolated fortresses. The British Government expressly dissociated itself from this document when it was later published by the Bolsheviks.

seem to have departed without any suspicion that they had been assisting at the last prelude to revolution. Their impressions were on the whole favourable; though the greatest soldier, Castelnau, rated the army low, putting its ratio of efficiency as less than half that of the French, and the greatest statesman, Milner, was very much disturbed and anxious in mind. Paléologue, the French ambassador, relates that he had often wearily said: 'We are wasting time.'

The winter was now far spent, and the extreme cold had passed. Though supplies had been badly organized in the great towns, and long food-queues had been standing almost daily in the snow, there had been no serious riot or disturbance for about three months. It may be that the obscure revolutionaries who pullulated in the capital held their hand until the Duma had at last assembled at the end of February. At the beginning of March the problem of supplying Petrograd with food became more acute. The exceptionally heavy snow-falls of the winter had damaged or blocked many railway-engines and trucks, and had resulted in a great shortage of fuel. The goods traffic, therefore, for the first fortnight of the month was by order practically restricted to coal. As a result, hardly any wheaten flour was to be found in the capital, though there were considerable quantities of rye. This scarcity was increased by the bad arrangements for distribution, and by shop-keepers holding up their supplies for a higher price. Sporadic riots began on March 8th, with sacking of bakers' shops. Yet so little attention was directed towards them that Nicholas left that day for G.H.Q. Perhaps he would have achieved nothing had he stayed; still, in such a case, 'the presence of the master is the eye of the house'.

The bright, frosty weather favoured the fermentation in the streets, which for several days seemed less a revolt than a peaceful demonstration by vast numbers of bewildered folk, communicating to each other shocks of an intense excitement.

On the 11th, however, the Government set to work in

earnest to clear the streets. Police appeared in large quantities, some of whom directed fire upon the crowd from the house-tops. But the enormous garrison of the city, some 190,000 strong, including many units of the pampered Imperial Guard, not only refused to fire on the people, but began to go over to their side. The Volhynian regiment of the Guard was the first to kill its officers and to join the mob.

On the 12th a revolution was in full swing, accompanied by all the traditional and symbolic signs of popular victory. The Winter Palace was invaded, public buildings were burned, the prisons were entered—in particular the Russian Bastille, the notorious fortress of St. Peter and St. Paul—and their inmates released.

Twice within the last forty-eight hours Rodzianko, the President of the Duma, had telegraphed to the Tsar to the effect that a new government possessing the confidence of the country must be instantly formed. 'The final hour has come when the fate of the country and the dynasty must be decided.' The Duma itself ignored a decree for its prorogation issued on the 12th by the Premier, Golitzin, and established a temporary committee for preserving order, on which all parties except the extreme Right were represented. Petrograd was triumphant. The chances of the Tsar depended upon the reception of the news by the country and the army. The rest of Russia followed its capital, not with a resentful or divided voice, but with unanimous alacrity. Lockhart, the British Consul-General at Moscow, has described 'the compelling, almost infectious enthusiasm' with which the news was bloodlessly greeted.

It was the same in the army. 'The whole army was ready for a revolution. . . . Even the officers were wavering, and were as a body highly dissatisfied with the situation.'[1] Doubtless the views of the officers and of the rank and file on the possible consequences were, as the event proved, widely opposed. But no one thought of launching a military counter-blow to restore absolutism. All the troops

[1] Gen. A. A. Brussilov, *A Soldier's Notebook 1914–18* (1930), p. 300.

which the Tsar successively dispatched to Petrograd merely swelled the revolutionary tide as soon as they detrained. Except for the hireling police, who fought with a desperation inspired by the knowledge that they could expect no mercy, Nicholas had no defenders.

He himself could not reach the capital, for the peasants tore up the line before his train. On March 15th at Pskov he abdicated on behalf of himself and his son. His brother Michael, whom he nominated as his successor, was given no opportunity of taking up the bankrupt inheritance.

'Russia is a big country and can wage a war and manage a revolution at the same time', said Rodzianko to the British military attaché.[1] This was the great and capital delusion. The Russian Liberals firmly believed that when a Constituent Assembly had met to create a constitution, a regenerated Russia would prosecute the war with all the more resolution because the purifying breath of idealism had passed over the land. Deeply convinced of the justice of their struggle, they stood fast in fidelity to the Alliance. It was for this reason that the western democracies hailed the overthrow of Tsardom so rapturously. As a matter of fact, to argue thus was to beg the whole question. The Revolution and the war were not two separate problems to be settled concurrently. For the Revolution was itself pointed against the war, though not with the same direct and undivided aim with which it had struck down the autocracy.

This was made manifest from the beginning. The Provisional Government, mainly composed of Liberal members of the Duma with one 'Social Revolutionary', Kerensky, continued to reassure its allies, and to prepare the way for a bourgeois republic on a parliamentary basis. But side by side with it stood another self-constituted body, exercising an aggressive and irresponsible authority, the Council or Soviet[2] of Workmen and Soldiers'

[1] Maj-Gen. Sir A. Knox, *With the Russian Army 1914–17* (1921), vol. ii, p. 569.

[2] The word Soviet as here used does not imply adherence to the Bolshevik

representatives. It retained within its own hands the post offices, State bank, treasury, and railway stations of Petrograd.

Its primary aim was to destroy the existing system of discipline in the army. Order No. 1 published on March 17th enjoined that in all units elected representatives of the rank and file were to be chosen, who were to refuse to hand over any arms to their officers. Soldiers were placed completely under control of the Soviet in all political matters. Its representatives were sent to all the armies and to the fleets to ensure that these orders were put into general operation. The result was to divide the men from their officers; they often began to regard them as enemies, to depose and even kill them. Thus a demoralization was introduced which made it easy for further propaganda to be effective. The war was represented as an imperialistic struggle, waged only for the benefit of the class which had just been overthrown. The soldiers were told that it would be easy to obtain peace by adherence to the formula of 'No annexations or indemnities', which had been gradually becoming the stock formula of the International Socialists.[1] To attack would be to betray their own cause; their utmost duty would be to defend themselves against the enemy. The Germans were quick to see that the demoralization, which was obviously spreading in the Russian trenches, would grow by inaction; whereas to fight a defensive battle might prove the cement of discipline. Orders were therefore given not to attack at present on the eastern front. In many areas fraternization was allowed and even encouraged, for it was expected that the educated, intelligent German would be able by conversation still further to warp the war-will of his simple adversary.

party, as it was to do later. Similar Soviets had been set up during the ephemeral success of the 1905 revolution. It was therefore the natural revolutionary term.

[1] It appears to have been first adopted at the Zimmerwald International Socialist Conference in Switzerland in 1915, which included representatives of France, Italy, Russia, and Germany, as well as the neutral States.

The Russian soldier had received from the Revolution another incentive to desert. To the peasant revolution meant land. Every man feared that if he remained steadfast with the colours, he would be forestalled by his neighbour. Even before the March days over a million men had disappeared from the army, many of whom were living unmolested in their homes. Now the stream began to flow openly from front to rear. The army was reverting to its peasant origin.

While it was thus crumbling to pieces, the Provisional Government was wrestling with its enormous tasks in the capital. As usually happens, the men nominally in power were not those who had actually made the Revolution. Broadly speaking, the former meant by the Revolution a wide extension of those political principles of liberalism which they had formulated, when in constitutional opposition to the autocracy; or, like Kerensky, the Socialist Minister of Justice, burned with enthusiasm to create somehow a new brotherhood for all Russians. But the 'intellectual' revolutionary by vocation, the member of Secret Societies, the organizer of 1905, however he might interpret in detail the whole bible of Marx, held it as an elementary maxim that the only true revolution must be social and international.

Moreover, the grim army of exiles was returning to strengthen the hands and fix the views of the extremists. Stalin and Kamenev came from Siberia, Trotsky from America, suffering imprisonment *en route* at the hands of the British. But the master of them all came from Switzerland. Lenin, as he called himself,[1] was now forty-seven years old, and had been absent from Russia for ten years, when he had fled the country from fear of arrest for his share in the abortive revolution of 1905. He came of a family of revolutionaries, and his elder brother had been

[1] His real name was Vladimir Ulianov, the son of a school-inspector from the Middle Volga. He had for many years signed his articles in the press with the pseudonym M. Lenin. Singularly enough he came from the same village as Kerensky.

hanged in 1887 for complicity in a plot for the assassination of Alexander III. It was said of him by one of his earlier comrades that 'there is no other man who is absorbed by the revolution twenty-four hours a day . . . who, even when he sleeps, dreams of nothing but the revolution'. This extraordinary power of unwavering concentration was not merely applied to the idealization of Marxian materialism, but to thinking out all the appropriate means for achieving the desired practical end. The uniqueness of Lenin among revolutionaries lay in his brilliant combination of the roles of fanatic and staff officer. Bolshevism has often been compared to a new militant religion, and Lenin's closest parallel can probably be found among the great organizing captains of religion such as Mahomet, or (a more exact parallel) Ignatius Loyola. His accurate knowledge, his orderly method, his pitiless logic, helped to secure him ascendancy over his countrymen, among whom such qualities were rare. Though Lenin is revered by the followers of Marx all over the world as the greatest modern Internationalist, he had made little mark and few disciples during the many years of his prowls about western and central Europe. Yet, though he had lived in European Russia for less than two years out of the last twenty, he understood the Russian people, or at least how to use them, amazingly well. The German Staff, which allowed him to pass through their country in a sealed railway-carriage, thought of him indeed as a dangerous microbe, but had no idea of the infection which he would spread in Russia to their own ultimate detriment and danger.[1]

He came to give direction and coherence to the activities of the Petrograd Soviet. This body had not aimed at taking the Government into its own hands, but at forcing it by a kind of semi-official control to do what it wanted. The situation closely resembled that in Paris between

[1] Ludendorff and Hoffmann have both protested that, if they had known more of his character, they would not have let him through. He was regarded merely as one among a number of exiles who would serve as good living propaganda for destroying the war-will of Russia.

February and June 1848, when Lamartine and his bourgeois government were being continually harried and threatened by the extremists, who relied upon the workmen of the capital. From the moment that the war started, Lenin had described it as an imperialistic struggle in which the duty of Socialists everywhere must be to work for the defeat of their own country. Only through defeat would it be possible to overthrow the capitalistic governments. The autocracy had now been destroyed in Russia, but the character of the war remained unchanged. As the Provisional Government accepted the war as its own, it was denounced by Lenin as being in open treachery to the proletariat. Therefore it must be deposed. Then Russia would be able to give a lead to the world by starting the real revolution, the civil war of the proletariat against capitalism. To achieve success two things were necessary. First, the peasants must be united with the industrial workers by the expropriation of all landowners. Secondly, a dictatorial government must be set up, which alone could enable the proletariat to realize its own real will. Lenin had urged for many years that the workers could not carry out their own salvation. The intellectuals must stand at their head, not at their tail. This was the so-called Bolshevik[1] programme which was finally put upon its trial six months later.

Meanwhile Lenin was methodically and patiently preparing with the extremists, a considerable number of whom like Trotsky were Jews, for the decisive insurrection by which he intended to seize power. 'The death of a revolution', he constantly proclaimed, 'is the defensive.' But the Western Powers were striving by every means to hold the Provisional Government to the rigour of the Alliance.

[1] The word Bolshevik means 'majority'. It draws its origin from the majority programme of which Lenin secured the adoption in 1903 at a conference in London. Its opponents were known as Mensheviks and differed mainly in a greater readiness to co-operate with all Liberal elements in preparing a revolution, and in the belief that the revolutionaries ought to act 'from below' rather than 'from above', i.e. that they should force their programme upon the Government without themselves assuming power.

Miliukov, indeed, the Foreign Secretary, a former professor of history, was wholeheartedly striving to maintain complete continuity of foreign policy. He even hoped that the victorious Revolution would achieve the prime ideal of Tsardom by annexing Constantinople. So deputations of prominent Socialists were sent to Petrograd. The solid trades-unionists who came from England regarded their Russian comrades with uncomprehending amazement as a set of impractical lunatics. Socialist Cabinet ministers, Thomas from France, Henderson from England, arrived with instructions to override and if necessary supersede the existing ambassadors.

The position of the Provisional Government was really hopeless. The only way to have stabilized and closed the Revolution was through immediate peace. But it steadfastly refused to make the separate peace, which could probably have been secured by relinquishing Poland, and was quite unable to enforce peace by waging war.

It did indeed try heroically to create a great national outburst of democratic patriotism, such as had carried revolutionary France triumphantly through her extreme peril in 1792–3. In May the coalition was extended further to the Left by the inclusion of several 'Mensheviks', while the annexionist Miliukov was jettisoned. The burning and romantic Kerensky, who 'thanked God for all the idealists in the world', exchanged the Ministry of Justice for that of War. He became the animating soul of the Government. Modelling himself upon the great orators of the French Revolution, he toured round the front, haranguing vast bodies of men, talking individually to the discontented. His own exhausted body, his dead-white and drawn face, inspired conviction as he proclaimed his gospel of salvation through suffering and self-denial. But the effect of his eloquence was only fleeting, though he himself, not staying long enough to recognize its evanescence, grew strangely optimistic. Without the restoration of discipline, and in particular of the death penalty for desertion and cowardice, no army can fight. The commissaries who were sent round the armies, and even the new Commander-in-Chief himself, Brussilov, recognized that any such restoration was in fact quite impracticable. Even if death sentences were imposed, no firing squads could be found to put them into execution. A more dangerous state of active mutiny than already existed would be the only result.

With great difficulty a striking force of about 200,000 men was collected in Galicia to attack a front mainly held by Austrians. For the first time the infantry were supported by a number of guns superior to that disposed of by the enemy. It required the most circumstantial evidence from deserters to convince the opposing staff that an attack was either seriously intended or practicable.

On July 1st the Russians launched their last offensive of the war. On that same evening General Knox noted in his diary 'There will be no success'.

After a few spasmodic and quarter-hearted efforts, the last state of the Galician army was far worse than the first. Quantities of the most capable officers had sacrificed themselves in a vain attempt to encourage their men forward by example. The Germans had in readiness a counter-attack, timed to coincide with the Bolshevik rising in Petrograd, of which they were well informed. They cut through their disorganized opponents like a knife through butter. The Russians became a demoralized mob, and their retreat through Galicia was marked by most revolting outrages upon the population. Had troops been available, the advance might have been thrust forward to Odessa. As it was, a halt was called on the Galician boundary. Thus the Rumanian army, in far better heart and efficiency after its reorganization by the French General Berthelot, was still able to cling victoriously to its refuge on the banks of the Sereth.

Meanwhile the militant forces had shown their heads in Petrograd. As generally happens in the course of a revolution which it is impossible to stabilize, all the propertied classes tended to move towards the Right and the artisans and landless peasants to the Left. The Bolsheviks, under the instruction of Lenin, whose motto was 'Patiently explain', were growing daily in the Soviets, and preparing for a complete breach with the Mensheviks whom they contemptuously denounced as 'Compromisers'. The executive committees, however, were still mainly under Menshevik majorities. Therefore the Bolshevik masses in the capital, inspired by the workmen from the great factories, became increasingly eager to seize the power which they believed was ripe to fall into their hands. They were further encouraged by the numerous reports from the provinces of land-seizure by the peasants. The news of the 'Kerensky offensive' created strong nervous tension in the population. Hearts were distracted by the extreme poignancy of hope and fear. The spear-head of the insurrection was to be the 1st machine-gun regiment, which during its long residence in the capital had thrown in its lot completely with the extremists. Lenin and Trotsky endeavoured to prevent the blaze which their doctrines had kindled; for they regarded it as a prime principle of strategy that insurrection must be delayed until the moment when its success would automatically place an unchallenged dictatorship in their own hands. That time they rightly held had not yet come. Nevertheless they felt bound to join in the movement which they could not control, and appear to have done their best to give it the character rather of an armed demonstration than of an unequivocal rising. This was the easier as the leading men of the Soviets were exceedingly unwilling to have direct power thrust into their hands. 'Take the power, you son of a bitch, when it is given you', cried out a workman to one of them.

Consequently the July days wear a vague irresolute hue very different from the ruthlessness with which organized force was to be pushed home in November. Many of the troops in the capital declared themselves neutral. Even the ferocious sailors who marched in from Kronstadt, fed with the blood of their officers, showed little energy. The small bands of Cossacks who remained loyal to Kerensky kept, by well-timed sallies, the vast mobs in indecisive play, until the arrival of selected detachments from the front restored the authority of the Provisional Government. So half-hearted had been this great effervescence that the victims on both sides amounted to only 29 killed and 114 wounded. The victory of Kerensky in fact was not due primarily to force but to what Trotsky calls 'The Great Slander'. Lenin and his associates were denounced as German spies. The rumour, broadcast by the Government, ran like fire through the city. There were, it is true, many enemy agents in the capital, but neither Lenin nor Trotsky was among their number. Many believed and still more doubted. The chief Bolsheviks had their headquarters in the garish house which had belonged to a famous ballet-dancer, the rapacious idol of the young nobles of the *ancien régime*. Lenin slipped away into Finland, where he spent months in close hiding, but Trotsky and his associates were arrested and thrown into jail. No blood was shed in retribution, for Kerensky was a revolutionary of the emotional transitionary type, like the Girondin orators, who regarded eloquence as a substitute for decisive action. Nevertheless his régime, not through its own strength but by the discredit of its principal adversaries, enjoyed a transient flicker of deceptive revival. The German offensive coincided with the July days—the coincidence seemed too sinister to be accidental—and the Government purposely published details which showed up the demoralization of the Galician army in all its nakedness. Kerensky received almost dictatorial powers; Kornilov became Commander-in-Chief, a Cossack of peasant extraction, the hero of a legendary escape from an Austrian prison, a hearty fighting general, the last magnet to draw out the dying military spirit. He became the man of destiny for the counter-revolutionaries, who regarded Kerensky and most of his ministers as a noxious temporary makeshift. In the provinces landowners and professional men allied with the clergy in an attempt to recreate through fear a national revival directed against the Capital. Almost everywhere the more timid withdrew from membership of the Bolshevik party. Kerensky was determined neither to serve as the tool of counter-revolutionaries nor to permit a military rival. Both the Allied ambassadors and the workers of Petrograd noted with distaste how much he had altered for the worse from the simplicity of his earliest epiphany. Vanity, display, and the exaggeration of the outward and visible signs of power, coupled with a brusque tactlessness, began to be commonly imputed to him. At the great Moscow Congress in August, to which representatives of every branch of Russian life had been summoned, his manner of indispensable authority did not save him from many oblique criticisms.

Yet it is possible that the Bolsheviks might never have been given their second opportunity had the Germans kept quiet. Now, however, they struck at the most sensitive nerve of the capital. For two years the Russian line running through marshes and sandhills had warded off every direct assault upon the great city of Riga, while a firm grip was maintained upon the River Dvina to prevent envelopment from the south. Ludendorff had no troops available for a great blow at the Capital, for his strategic reserve had already been ear-marked for the Isonzo. But he calculated that even a limited stroke in this direction would suffice to shake the trembling weapons finally from palsied Russian hands. At the very least he would rescue a large German population, linked up to the Fatherland by the traditional ties of the old Hanseatic League; would provide his troops with spacious winter billets; and secure for the navy the use of the port and gulf of Riga.

Moreover, his mind was already turning to a decisive spring campaign in France, which would require a perfection of offensive organization tried out and matured by battle-experiment. Therefore the operation was entrusted to von Hutier, the chief apostle of the surprise attack. Bruchmüller, the incomparable conductor of the artillery orchestra, was provided as his assistant. The experiment proved highly successful, though the 'vile body' of Russian indiscipline was not a very searching test. Kornilov has been accused of treacherously abetting the breakthrough in order that Petrograd might be overwhelmed by a flood of indignant counter-revolution directed by himself as saviour. He had indeed, at the Moscow Congress, prophesied the loss of Riga, and had determined to use it for the benefit of Russia and himself. But there is no evidence which justifies the imputation of so base an action to the Commander-in-Chief. On the contrary, German accounts agree that the resistance which they encountered exceeded that on the Galician front in July, though the later operation was the more brilliantly planned; while the retreat was carried through without disorder. Meanwhile Kerensky, fearful of the effect of the loss of Riga upon the temper of the Capital, felt his own head loose on his shoulders, and was negotiating with Kornilov for the dispatch of a cavalry corps to Petrograd, and for the proclamation of martial law in the surrounding military district. The Bolsheviks were not in fact preparing another insurrection, but the Premier believed that they would take advantage of the general consternation to do so.

Kornilov, however, had no intention of using his force to bolster up such a man of straw. Surrounded at Headquarters by unintelligent military reactionaries, he convinced himself that the hour had struck for his dictatorship. He was to be the chosen instrument to save Russia. He determined to get the Capital within his grasp, and sent forward his most trusty troops, the so-called 'Savage Division', composed of Caucasians who could not speak Russian, of whom it was said 'these mountaineers do not mind whom they slaughter', under an equally 'trusty' commander.

Kornilov was naturally anxious to lull Kerensky's suspicions until these troops had reached their objective, but could find no better emissary than a half-witted royalist named Lvov, who naïvely tried to entrap Kerensky into a visit to Head-quarters to put himself under Kornilov's protection. Kerensky, now fully enlightened, paid the Commander-in-Chief with his own coin by tricking him in a famous conversation over the telephone—and so, at the very moment when the latter believed that the gates of Petrograd were open to his Caucasians, his rival, swinging to the left, deposed him and called upon the Soviets and the garrison to defend the sacred cause of revolution. Kerensky won a last victory. The organization of Kornilov's head-quarters was pitiable. The tide of his advancing army broke harmlessly and bloodlessly on the outer suburbs. The concerted movement planned by commanders on other fronts was a complete fiasco. Kerensky appointed himself Commander-in-Chief in Kornilov's room.

And now the Provisional Government found that it had been mortally wounded through its own victory. The extremists believed that it had acted in collusion with the leaders of the insurrection, the exceedingly lenient treatment of whom confirmed that view. The danger to Petrograd spread visibly like a thundercloud. The Germans, anxious to restore the spirit of their navy, lately cankered by mutiny, equipped an amphibious expedition, which seized the islands at the mouth of the Gulf of Riga. Thus the enemy stood over against the arsenals of Kronstadt and Helsingfors, whose sailors were the most ardent and ruthless instruments in Bolshevik hands. Mere naked danger drove men by fear to the Left, and the Petrograd Soviet passed into the hands of the extremists; Moscow followed its example almost at once. The Bolshevik leaders were liberated on bail. The Jew Braunstein, famous in history as Trotsky, was let loose for agitation and devouring propaganda, for which he had a genius seldom equalled. While Lenin was the intellectual begetter of the October Revolution, Trotsky was its tactical organizer. He has described these events in the finest work written by a revolutionary, full of a penetrating power of sardonic analysis.

The weary Kerensky was no match for this terrible pair,

no longer working in the shadows. He kept shuffling his ministers and could not abide in any one stay. Fits of feverish activity alternated with periods of almost cataleptic listlessness.

Unrest became uglier and more general as production grew feebler and distribution more irregular throughout the enormous land. Trotsky agrees that in many parts the so-called support of the Bolshevik programme dissolved itself into a simple determination to have 'Peace, Land, and Bread'. The Entente Powers had by now written off Russia, and scarcely concealed their contemptuous indifference to Kerensky. The Russian ambassador at Paris has recorded the harsh rating which he received from Poincaré, the President of the Republic, generally so cold and impassive, in his official interviews.

Ever since the middle of September Lenin had proclaimed that the hour was ripe, and believed that delay might be fatal if insurrection were delayed until the disintegration of the country had proceeded much farther towards chaos. Curiously enough it was the more emotional Trotsky, now President of the Petrograd Soviet, who counselled and obtained delay until support from the provinces had been more fully organized, and the support of the Petrograd garrison more carefully secured. Nearly all the men of this garrison now agreed to take their orders only from the military Revolutionary Committee of the Soviet, and not from the Government. It was therefore certain that, even if they did not actively assist the insurrection, they would not impede its vital moves. Revolution was not only in the thoughts but on the lips of the inhabitants, who moved about their daily tasks in a kind of waking fantasy. Three successive days, which had been confidently assigned by common rumour, passed without incident. The chosen date was November 7th,[1] on which the Congress of Russian Soviets was to meet at Petrograd. Trotsky and his fellow conspirators reaped the reward of their minute preparation. The post offices, telephone-

[1] October 25 old style: hence the name of 'October Revolution'.

exchanges, railway-stations, bridges, and banks were swooped upon with an almost bloodless speed. The Provisional Government was isolated in the vast Winter Palace, which its defenders were not numerous enough to fill. Amongst the faithful few was part of one of the Women's 'Battalions of Death', formed after March to shame the men into a continuance of the war. Kerensky fled to the army in an American motor-car before the cordon was completed. The Bolshevik cruiser *Aurora* steamed eagerly up the Neva from Kronstadt, and a few of its shells induced a speedy capitulation. The triumph of the Bolsheviks was easy and complete. It was carried through, said an observer, 'like a piece of music played from notes'. A far more bitter conflict endured for eight days in Moscow, where the fortified inner city of the Kremlin found resolute defenders who were finally betrayed from within.

The Congress of Soviets acting as provisional sovereign gave executive power to a Committee of Bolsheviks with Lenin as President. Each member held the title of Komissar, to which they gave world-wide notoriety. Decrees were passed to confiscate all land, except that held by poor peasants and Cossacks; to socialize all industry; and to begin immediate negotiations for peace.

Events were soon to show that the Bolsheviks did not indeed represent Russia; but that they were able to maintain that dictatorship which, as they declared, represented its real will. During November the long-delayed elections to the Constituent Assembly were held. While the industrial towns and much of the army returned Bolsheviks, the peasant vote secured a large majority of Social Revolutionaries. Lenin allowed it to assemble at Petrograd in January, where it was at once forcibly dissolved and its members dispersed or arrested. The alleged reasons can have convinced few. It was clear that parliamentary government was incompatible with the ruthless transforming absolutism of the new scientific Marxists, whose terrorism was already manifesting itself in wholesale butcheries.

XXV

THE CAMPAIGN IN FLANDERS, 1917

MESSINES AND PASSCHENDAELE

THE deterioration of the French army made it essential that the British should engage in a vigorous, and as far as possible an uninterrupted, summer campaign. The extreme danger of the submarine campaign dictated its direction against the Belgian ports, the closest and most infested 'nests of destruction'.[1] Yet it was impossible to break out coastwards from the Ypres salient until the right had been secured. South-west of the city the German defences were thrust forward on the Wytschaete–Messines ridge. The good observation gained therefrom enabled the British lines to be enfiladed, and even taken from the rear, for several miles to the north. The ridge extends for about eight miles, and is nowhere more than 200 feet high, but has, in places, an abrupt and dominating face towards the west. By the end of April the German command realized that an attack here was imminent; and if Rupprecht had had his way the position would have been evacuated. The Arras battle had taught him that commanding positions, where the defences can be easily picked up, were much more difficult to maintain against a superior artillery than inconspicuous lines carefully drawn in featureless country. Moreover, his guns were inconveniently crowded in forward positions round Messines, and he correctly anticipated that a large proportion would be disabled in the preliminary bombardment. Faced, however, by a unanimous protest from the local commanders, he lacked the strength of will to persist.

The battle of Messines proved in effect one of the most complete local victories of the war. It was the kind of victory that required immense and lengthy preparation. Its most essential and devastating feature, the mine-

[1] Actually the Germans relied much less on these ports than was believed at the time.

explosions, had been in train for eighteen months. The mines indeed would probably have been fired in July 1916 to divert attention from the Somme, had not the destruction of the great shell-dump at Audruicq rendered the enterprise inadvisable. The long delay seems to have lulled German suspicion, for the explosion of 500 tons of ammonal took them entirely by surprise. The perfect harmoniousness between preparation and performance which marked Messines is characteristic of its author, Sir Herbert Plumer, whom Haig justly called 'the most reliable of his army commanders'. Plumer had so much the appearance of the comic music-hall general that it was almost impossible to caricature him. His round face with its puffed-out rubicund cheeks and bulging eyes resembled, it was said, that of 'an elderly cupid'. But he had a remarkable gift of choosing and knowing men, of being exact in detail yet never hurried, and of inspiring the confidence which he felt. Both officers and men knew that they were better looked after in his army than elsewhere; his staff had rather the air of helpful collaborators than of imperious and inconsiderate dictators. Plumer made a point of seeing every division immediately it entered his area, and had the unaffected simplicity of direct approach which wins the soldier's heart.[1] His partnership with his Chief-of-Staff, Harington, whose steady diplomacy in 1921 was later to prevent war with Mustapha Kemal's advancing troops at Chanak, was so singularly fortunate as to be best described in Hindenburg's phrase of a 'happy marriage'.

The battle itself achieved in desired harmony the co-operation of all arms. The bombardment was of unprecedented length, seventeen days, and was directed by an air force which had almost undisputed mastery of the sky. As the objective was so strictly limited it mattered

[1] Orpen tells how, when he was painting a portrait of the general, his soldier-servant came and directed his master thus: ''Ere you just sit up proper—not all 'unched up the way you are. What would Her Ladyship say if I let you be painted that way?'

little if the ground was churned to pieces; while the nerves of the defenders were the more cruelly tried. At dawn on June 7th the nineteen mines were simultaneously exploded, blowing the top of the hill into the air and in places entirely altering its contour. The demoralization of the Germans was increased by the employment of two horrible new engines of war, the projection of boiling oil-cans and containers of gas into the hostile trenches. The British advance was in some places so rapid that tanks were unable to keep up with their allotted infantry. Success was complete, and the enemy was too much exhausted to make any effective counter-attack. This seems to have been the first considerable battle in which the British losses were less than those of the Germans.[1]

This action naturally confirmed the German Staff in its belief that the main campaign would now be launched in Belgium. Haig maintained a show of activity round Lens, but the densely populated mining area there was so unsuitable for a serious offensive that no deception was achieved. And, unhappily, a delay of seven weeks before the Flemish attack opened gave time for the new system of German defence to be completed.

The third battle of Ypres was, indeed, dogged by misfortune from the beginning. As originally planned in April it can be justified as a counsel of extremity to prevent our losing the war rather than to help in winning it. But even so, it is extraordinary that the Admiralty, before calling upon the Army to conduct a campaign in an area so far away from the enemy's main communications, in order to help the Navy, refused to sanction a blocking expedition, strongly urged by such bold and capable officers as Keyes. The plan when submitted to the War Cabinet aroused Mr. Lloyd George's strong distrust.

[1] The British casualties were 17,000 or just over 1,000 per division engaged, a proportion three times lighter than that of July 1, 1916. The Germans lost about 25,000, including 7,500 prisoners and 67 guns. These statistics do not make it clear whether the losses in the preliminary bombardment are included or not.

His *Memoirs* vividly relate how insistently he urged its dangers and difficulties on the Commander-in-Chief, both by word of mouth and by memoranda.

In any event by July, when Haig was irretrievably committing himself, the tardy adoption of the convoy system for merchantmen had taken away the immediate danger of England's being starved into submission. Again, an amphibious scheme for landing a force with tanks behind the German lines west of Ostend was never tried. If successful, it would have given a true strategical direction to the whole operation, unattainable by a mere frontal attack. The troops had been trained in a secret area in France, and everything was ready. The reasons for abandoning this plan have never been fully given. Apparently the risks were considered too great, as the enemy had at least an inkling of it, though it was expected rather to descend on the Dutch coast.[1] Further delay of at least a fortnight was caused by the insistence of the French upon their participation. It was not easy for them that summer to collect an army capable of sustained offensive action, though it is true that the force which fought on the British left under General Anthoine acquitted itself excellently. Finally, on the eve of the attack a Welsh sergeant deserted, taking with him valuable information which included the position of various head-quarters and the assembly-points of the tanks.

The preparations were of the most grandiose character. It was the last attempt to blast a way by the overwhelming concentration of mechanical force, without any vital element of surprise. The area chosen was particularly unsuitable for two reasons. In the first place the dead-level Flemish plain, extending rearwards for twenty miles, displayed all the British preparations as on a map. The

[1] For a detailed description of this scheme, see Adm. Sir R. Bacon, *The Dover Patrol 1915–1917* (1919), vol. i, ch. ix. Pontoons 560 feet long were to be pushed against the sea-wall by two monitors lashed together. About 14,000 troops were to be employed. Apparently Haig made the attempt conditional upon the occupation of Roulers by the main attack.

enemy airmen, who were bold and accomplished night-flyers, did great execution upon the dumps of ammunition and stores, on the railway-stations and the reserve hutments. After the battle had started and the guns moved up, they were pitiably exposed as targets, being stuck almost wheel to wheel in an open morass. Secondly, the ten-days' bombardment, during which some 65,000 tons of metal were discharged, destroyed all the surface drainage and created not merely the usual crater-field but an irremediable slough. British Head-quarters had been warned of such a result by the Belgians, but obstinately disregarded the local knowledge born of long experience. It is true that the weather was exceptionally unkind, for the August rainfall was more than twice the average,[1] but in any event the conditions would have made tanks practically useless, and seriously hampered the mobility of artillery.

The Germans adopted a system of elastic defence, which proved highly successful, and was copied in its essentials by the Entente in the following year, when it fell to their turn to be attacked. The credit for working this out is mainly due to Ludendorff, who was probably the best all-round tactician thrown up by the war, and who lost no opportunities of picking up the experience of regimental officers through personal interviews. The main object of a defensive battle was not to preserve every inch of ground intact, but to prevent a break-through, while inflicting the maximum amount of loss. Accordingly, the foremost resistance was organized as an outpost line, strong enough to repel patrols, but destined merely to disorganize an attack in force. There were no connected trenches but a series of strong points, each of which might hold anything from a platoon to a company, in mutual support with the aid of flanking fire from numbers of machine-guns.

Many of these posts were housed in small concrete structures, nicknamed, from their appearance, 'pill-boxes', which were both inconspicuous and solid enough

[1] 6·76 against 2·80 inches.

to resist direct hits from field-guns and field-howitzers. They often took advantage of the flooded country, being surrounded on three sides by water, with only one strip of solid earth communicating with a door in rear. Their capture by unaided infantry was, as may be imagined, exceedingly difficult; one desperate method was for bombers to crawl forward and throw their missiles through the machine-gun slit.

About a kilometre behind these outposts the battle-zone was organized in about three lines of trench. The garrisons of these supplied their own reserves for local counter-thrusts; and as far as possible one reserve division was kept behind each trench-division for counter-attack on a large scale, should the enemy break seriously into the battle-system. Nevertheless the German defences were tested to the uttermost, particularly in the latter half of this protracted struggle, which lasted for about a hundred days. Ludendorff speaks with admiration of the stubborn bravery of his opponents who 'charged our lines, time after time, like a mad bull'. During this phase the Germans suffered very heavily. There had not been time to furnish the new outpost-lines with pill-boxes on the same scale, so that much larger garrisons had to be maintained there in the inferior shelters of shell-holes. In consequence the numbers lost by shell-fire or as prisoners mounted up alarmingly. Moreover, the British staff-work grew much more efficient when the main burden of the attack was taken on by Plumer. The original execution had been entrusted almost entirely to Gough, the dashing favourite of the Commander-in-Chief, who had been promoted to command the 5th army at the exceptionally early age of 44. He had justified his promotion at the Somme, where he secured the biggest gains at the lightest cost. But he acquired the reputation of setting his troops impossible tasks and of being careless of their lives and comfort. He was unfairly blamed for the useless prolongation of the battle, for which Haig and Robertson were responsible, but he lost the confidence of the men, who dreaded being sent to the 5th army.

Passchendaele,[1] to use the familiar soldiers' name, was by no means as expensive as the Somme. It cost us about 300,000 men as against 400,000. Yet all the combatants engaged on either side regarded it as the culmination of horror. German writers have called it 'the supreme martyrdom of the war'. The rain was pitiless, the ubiquitous mud speedily engulfed man and beast if a step was taken astray from the narrow duckboards, upon which descended a perpetual storm of shells and gas. Some of the pictures in the Imperial War Museum preserve an aspect of the macabre grotesqueness of this blasted and mangled land. Long-distance gun-fire and the art of night-bombing had developed so much during the last year that reserves and resting troops were kept in a fever of perpetual apprehension. Men's nerves were badly frayed before they took part in the fighting, and had little chance of healing when they were withdrawn from it.

The British also suffered from the new mustard gas. Although seldom fatal, it inflicted painful burns and caused great blisters over all the body, which were long in healing. It possessed the insidious quality of remaining in the soil for days after its discharge, so that any chance resting-place might unexpectedly spread the poison. The German High Command hesitated much before using this invention. For while their chemists promised that the Entente could not produce it in less than a year, they also predicted that the capacity of their factories would be so great that practically unlimited quantities could be used with overwhelming effect against the original authors. It was, in fact, first employed against the Germans in July 1918 by the French.

Strategically nothing whatever had been effected. On the contrary, the enlarged salient, with its tip at Passchendaele, where an advance of about five miles had been

[1] See map 9, p. 102. This village was actually the farthest eastward point on the ridge beyond Ypres attained. Its capture on November 6 by the Canadians practically marked the close of the battle. The official title for this battle is "Third Ypres."

made, was even more unwieldy than the old All our gains here had to be voluntarily evacuated at a stroke next April, when the second great German thrust took the enemy forward beyond Bailleul.

Haig's official apologists cite as a justification the statements afterwards made by Ludendorff as to the great deterioration in the German soldier produced by this ordeal. But, as has been pointed out before, the conditions under which Ludendorff's book was written make him a suspect witness. Moreover, neither the contemporary diary of Rupprecht, nor the evidence of his Chief-of-Staff, von Kuhl, bears him out. Such an experience must undoubtedly lower the moral of any army which has undergone it, but there is no reason to believe that the Germans were more intensely or more permanently affected than the British. The latter were the heavier losers, and their casualties in officers were actually three times as high as the German.

Two serious consequences followed for the Allied cause. First, the reserves had been eaten up, which might have given to the bold stroke of Cambrai a success worthy of its conception. Secondly, it completed the distrust which had long been growing up in the mind of the Premier towards Haig and Robertson. It is generally supposed that the openness with which he displayed this feeling was due to the hope that the Commander-in-Chief might be induced to resign, as, indeed, he seriously thought of doing. It led Lloyd George to take up again, at the most inopportune moment, his favourite idea of winning the war in Palestine; and to keep in England until March 1918, 300,000 fit men, who should have been instantly available to stop the holes caused by the great German offensive of that fateful month.

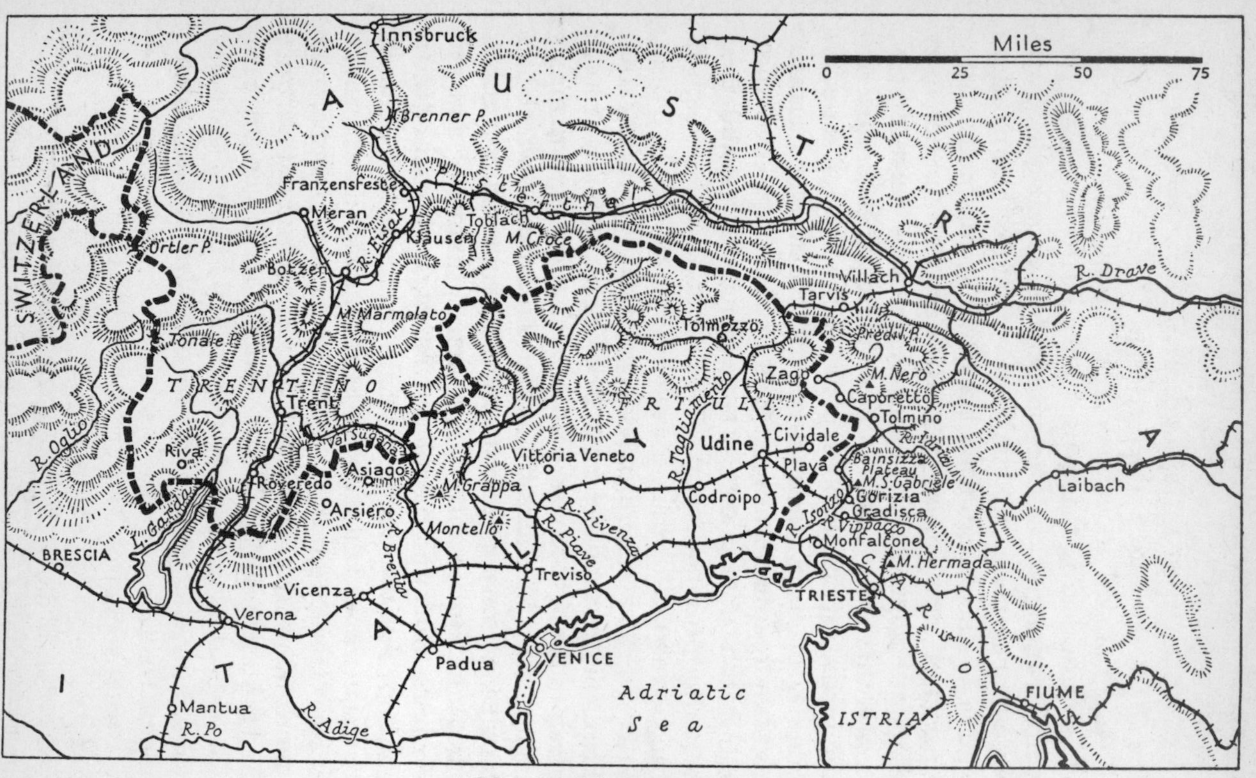

Map 23. The Italian Front

XXVI

THE ITALIAN CAMPAIGN TO CAPORETTO

I

THE Italians had done prudently in delaying their military action. In 1914, according to their Commander-in-Chief, the army was morally and materially unprepared for war, and could have offered no effective resistance to an Austrian attack; morally, because no country was more affected by a kind of easy-going anti-militarism, which had its roots in the individualism and volatility of the national character; materially, because the army had been meagrely fed in the annual budgets, and its technical equipment lagged far behind that of the great European armies.

Much was quietly done during the nine-months' interval to remedy the more glaring deficiencies, but even so Italy took the field terribly short of heavy guns, machine-guns, trench-mortars, and aeroplanes, and had to pay a grievous price for her neglect.

A striking force had been gradually collected by a process which was described as 'secret mobilization', and it was understood that the declaration of war would be immediately followed by preliminary operations of offence. It had been hoped that these, by effecting a surprise, would gain important success before the Austrians had reinforced their thin covering line. However, the denunciation of the Triple Alliance (May 3, 1915), and the publication by a French newspaper of the conclusion of the Treaty of London, gave the enemy three weeks' warning, of which he took clever advantage.

It was evident from the terms under which Italy entered the war that her action must be offensive. Not merely the calculation of politicians but the intense idealistic outburst of national emotion in those May days pointed the immediate way to the 'unredeemed' territories.

But the direction of attack was by no means easy to determine, since only a single direction could be chosen in view of the limited resources available. The frontier was almost everywhere drawn among the high mountains, except for a short space on the extreme east where the plain of Friuli touches Istria at the head of the Adriatic. Its total length was nearly 400 miles, stretching from north-west to south-east in a double curve like the letter S. Moreover this curved line strongly favoured Austria, whose boundaries in the Alpine regions stretched far down the southern slopes, with pillar upon pillar of ascending rock behind them, menacing the Italian plains. Hence it had been said that geography made it necessary for the two Powers to be 'either allies or enemies', and history has proved the truth of that saying.

On the extreme north-west no possible openings existed in the wall, but on either side of Lake Garda the Trentino, *Provincia Italianissima*, thrust a great prong down towards the Venetian plain. Here also the enemy's communications were good, for the double line from Innsbrück ran down over the Brenner pass, that traditional high road of the Imperialists into Italy, whose summit is only 4,000 feet above the sea. A very important side valley, the Pusterthal, with its railway, led to the Drave and secured connexion with Vienna and Hungary, while from Trent the Val Sugana pointed a side-door of irruption towards Venice.

Many strategists therefore favoured the chief advance here, both to remove the brooding menace of an Austrian descent, which if successful would cut the vital arteries of communication in rear of an army fighting in Friuli; and to release the inhabitants from alien rule. Trent was the chief magnet for Italian aspirations. Not many years before the inhabitants had put up in the square a great statue of Dante pointing prophetically south.

But the Supreme Command was opposed to this plan. It pointed out that the belt of mountain country to be conquered was immensely deep, that the area was studded with the most modern fortifications. Finally, a success here would be in a direction eccentric to co-operation with the Allies, and would completely isolate the Italian effort.

Farther east, on the other hand, any advance would converge towards the distant objectives of the Russians and Serbians on the lower Danube. Consequently the whole offensive effort of the Italians was concentrated for the next twenty-seven months on the short strip of sixty miles where the frontier leaves the Carnic Alps and turns sharply south, roughly following the course of the River Isonzo, which cleaves its way through the Julian Alps to the Adriatic. On the north of this sector the Italians threatened the great valleys of the Drave and Save (whose waters mingle with the Danube by Belgrade), and the key junctions of Villach and Laibach (Lubljana). By way of the coast they were within twenty-five miles of that coveted port Trieste, Austria's main outlet to the Mediterranean. This plan, so stubbornly pursued, originated with Cadorna, the Chief of the General Staff,[1] who probably had a unique knowledge of the whole frontier. He was 65 years of age, of an old noble Piedmontese family, with secular military traditions. With great theoretical and organizing ability he combined many of the defects of a Staff-College pedant. Autocratic and centralizing, he tended to make his orders over elaborate, too much based on rigid *a priori* conceptions, neglectful of the human element. As one of his subordinates caustically remarked: 'This is not manœuvre, it is algebra.' His own austere sense of duty, based on formulae of the most rigid conservatism, put him in little sympathy with the impressionable and mercurial Italian soldier. His notion of discipline was exacting and hierarchical in the extreme (he quotes with favour the old Piedmontese maxim, 'The superior is always right, especially when he is wrong');[2] he

[1] The King, Victor Emmanuel III, was the nominal Commander-in-Chief.

[2] 'Il superiore ha sempre ragione, specialmente quando ha torto.' The circular to commanders on May 19, 1915, dealing with discipline, begins with the words: 'The supreme command desires that in all times and in all

overworked his army and took no care to provide it with comforts, relaxation, or amusement in its rare periods of rest. But though part of this instrument broke in his hand at the shameful rout of Caporetto, it must be acknowledged that, during the two previous years, its capacity for reiterated attack was without even remote parallel in Italian military history.

II

When war broke out half the whole army of thirty-five divisions was concentrated on the Julian front, and the 350 miles of Alpine line were relegated to an active and enterprising defensive. These tactics were particularly successful in the Trentino, where a depth of several most valuable miles of mountain territory was won nearly everywhere. Thus the eastern armies could attack with a less imminent dread of being stabbed in the back if Austria were able to augment her forces. In June these were comparatively scanty, about twenty-one divisions, but mainly of high quality and united in a burning hatred of the Italians. Against Russia the Slavs fought languidly or even treacherously, but they were ardent against the Italians who were stretching out their hands towards Fiume and Dalmatia. Moreover, they had the advantage of nine months' fighting experience, while their adversaries had painfully to buy a familiarity with the technique of trench-warfare.

The Isonzo front invited attack only in comparison with the grim Alpine regions. The higher reaches of the river were surmounted by peaks 8,000 feet high. Even on the narrow strip of twenty miles by the sea, the eastern bank exhibited a naked and barren limestone plateau called the Carso, rising in places to over 1,000 feet to bar the road to Trieste. Almost everywhere trenches and dug-outs had to be hewn or drilled out of the rock with immense labour. The flying splinters dislodged by shells inflicted frightful wounds, and blinded far more men than in any other theatre of war.

places an iron discipline should reign throughout the army.' The remainder of the circular amplifies this remark in the severest manner.

The Austrians, generally speaking, based their defensive system on the east bank, but maintained two bridgeheads transformed by nature and art into great fortresses, Gorizia and Tolmino, the former shutting off access to the Carso from the north, and the latter twenty-five miles farther upstream. The curve of the river enabled these to fit in with the general configuration of the line without forming exposed salients. The stout defence of the southern buttress ruined the Italian strategy for fifteen months; the retention of Tolmino until October 1917 gave the Germans an open sally-port for their deadly thrust at Caporetto.

Thus it came about that the Italian strategy was confined to a monotonous series of bloody assaults against a line which they could never entirely penetrate. In twenty-seven months eleven distinct Isonzo battles were reckoned, most of which had their centre between Gorizia and the sea. Cadorna seemed more and more to be fascinated by the lure of Trieste, the nearest spectacular objective which might, he hoped, satisfy the ever-increasing restlessness of public opinion. But this concentration upon a purely national objective did much to turn the eyes of the Entente away from the campaign, and to strengthen its military leaders in their determination not to send Italy any assistance in men from the West. The Entente had expected far too great results from the Italian declaration of war; when these faded, a contemptuous indifference, equally unjustified, succeeded.

At the end of this offensive period the Italians had advanced less than half-way towards Trieste, at the cost of nearly a million casualties.

III

The one great pause in this continual hammering at the gates of Istria was due to Austrian initiative in the spring of 1916. Conrad's hatred of his new enemies was fanatical. It was noticed by his associates that he never uttered the name Italy without coupling with it the epithet 'perfidious'. In December he endeavoured to win over Falkenhayn to his grandiose scheme for utterly overthrowing the Italians by a swift stroke from the Trentino, which should reach the Po before their armies could be withdrawn from Friuli and the Carnic Alps. This having been done, a giant attack was to follow against the west, both on the existing front and by way of the Alps towards Lyons. Nine German divisions were demanded for the former operation.

Falkenhayn multiplied objections. To secure success in the Trentino twenty-five divisions were requisite, and could not possibly be collected. Italy in any event was so much in the grip of the Entente that, however heavily defeated, she would not go out of the war. Her exposed coasts and lack of raw material bound her irremediably to England. Moreover, Germany and Italy were not yet officially at war. The great commercial and financial interests of the two countries were still to delay its outbreak until August 1916. It suited Germany to keep another window open to the world, even if it was half closed by the suspension of diplomatic relationships. Moreover, the continual and important negotiations between the Central Powers and the Holy See were facilitated by this arrangement.

Falkenhayn had no objection to giving his allies limited and unostentatious help in their campaign (actually an Alpine division of German troops had been concentrated in the Trentino in May 1915); but he had no intention of diverting large forces thither until it was absolutely necessary. That necessity had not arisen, for he was set upon his attack at Verdun. This project he kept secret from his Austrian colleague, who retaliated by telling him nothing of the single-handed enterprise which he was none the less determined to carry through in the Trentino. For this Conrad collected sixteen divisions, six of them good fighters from the Galician front,[1] a gamble for which Brussilov cruelly punished him in June.

[1] When Falkenhayn finally heard of this project, he obtained a general assurance that the eastern front was not being unduly weakened. Conrad,

Throughout that winter for the first time in history the outposts of two great armies had faced one another on the Alpine peaks, with barbed wire across the glaciers, their needs marvellously supplied by aerial railways and other cunning engineering devices.

With a strangely optimistic assumption that the normal course of the weather would be altered to suit his plans, Conrad had completed his concentration by the beginning of April. Then the snows descended, and the troops even in the valleys were stuck for weeks with no possibility of movement. This delay gave Cadorna plenty of notice, for the Austrian concentration had been definitely known to his staff by March 22nd. He did not, however, believe that Conrad would be so imprudent as to venture an attack on a really grand scale; and the precautions which he took to reinforce the threatened sector seem to have been reasonably sufficient. For their failure he blames, with apparent justice, the commander of the 1st army, who had shown a consistently insubordinate spirit. He had always chafed at the subordinate role for which his forces had been cast; he had neglected to work out a defensive organization to the requisite depth; and the dispositions of his artillery and of part of his infantry still remained more suited for offence.

When therefore the attack opened on May 15th, 1916, supported by an artillery of crushing superiority,[1] the Austrians made alarming progress in the centre. Within a few days they were standing on the Plateau of 'The Seven Communes'[2] (that curious little fragment of German blood and speech which had remained, perhaps from the Middle Ages, as an outpost of Teutonism, far south of the watershed), and menaced the last hills which overlook the uttermost limits of the vital plain of Vicenza.

Cadorna now showed his best qualities of resolution and

however, knew of the risk which he was taking, and the intimation merely meant that he was determined to go on his own way.

[1] The Austrians had about 2,000 guns against 850, and in heavy calibres were more than three to one.

[2] Otherwise known as the Asiago Plateau.

technical capacity. He gave preliminary and contingent orders for the retreat of his Isonzo armies to the Piave, and brusquely refused the Prime Minister's suggestion of a council of war, threatening instant resignation should his responsibility be in any way impaired. At the same time he rapidly collected a large, new striking force to meet the heads of the Austrian columns if they debouched into the plain. He had, naturally, a far better network of roads and railways than his enemy in the high mountains.[1] By June 2nd nearly half a million men were duly concentrated in their new strategic positions. On this same day Cadorna could assure himself that they would not be required, for the attack which had been gradually losing vivacity was now definitely held.

The Italians are therefore justified in the claim that they were not saved by Brussilov's relief-offensive, which started two days later.

Thus ended Conrad's 'Strafe-Expedition' or punitive attack, on which such high hopes had been built. The heir to the throne, the Archduke Karl, had been brought down in titular command of the armies, and the soldiers had been advertised, quite in the Napoleonic style, of the abundance of good things which they would find in the rich Venetian plain. The Italians were even able to reconquer, though with hesitating steps, nearly half the ground from which they had been thrust.

The Austrian Staff hoped that at least the Italian losses,[2] the dislocation of their strategy, and the surrender of such important outworks in the Trentino, would combine to shatter their offensive intentions for the year. But Cadorna, again making skilful and rapid use of his railways and fleets of Fiat cars, overran the surprised enemy at the bridge-head of Gorizia in August, thus obtaining the first notable success of the war. The pursuit, however,

[1] The Austrian attack was served by only two railways, of which one was a single line. They had also to move round the arc of which Cadorna possessed the chord.

[2] 147,000 men with 294 guns. The Austrian losses were 80,000.

was feebly pushed and was held up indefinitely by the commanding hills which overlook the eastern suburbs of the city. The autumn was consumed in bloody grapplings on the Carso, which brought no signal advantage to either side, but lengthened the enemy's line and devoured so many of his reserves that Ludendorff's request for Austrian reinforcements against Rumania had to be refused.

IV

During the winter Italian hopes of assistance from their allies were doomed to disappointment. At a Conference in Rome (January 1917) Lloyd George, fresh in his supremacy, vigorously supported his old project of smashing Austria by a great advance on the Danube in which the Western Allies should participate. But the whole plan of coordinate offensives in every theatre had already been agreed upon by the Staffs at Chantilly a month before. The deceptive glamour of Nivelle's boundless hopes was beginning to have its effect. Consequently the French, with their eyes on the West, expressed the strongest objection to the diversion of ten divisions and 400 guns (the numbers suggested by Cadorna) and did not conceal their unwillingness to entrust their men to Italian command. In the light of future events it is clear that the dispatch of a substantial force to Italy would have been a prudent insurance. But the gradual decay of the Italian fighting spirit seems then to have been unsuspected by the responsible leaders themselves.

In effect, the only results of these discussions were the gradual dole of about 100 heavy guns, mainly British, and the working out of plans for improving the swift transport of troops between France and Italy. This latter measure proved invaluable when the Franco-British armies had to be hurried into Lombardy after Caporetto.

Cadorna was much piqued at the unceremonious shelving of his desires. After the Russian Revolution broke out, he professed again to fear an onslaught from the Trentino, but finally resumed his attacks in the middle of May, striking alternately north and south, winning ground but achieving little of solid value. It was of ominous significance that in this series of actions the attackers lost more prisoners than the defenders. In one sector three whole regiments delivered themselves up to a counter-attack without a blow. Cadorna protested to the Ministry against the contagion 'of the poisonous propaganda of the seditious parties'. But Orlando, then Minister of the Interior, played the same passive and blinkered role as his counterpart Malvy had done in France. Both apparently thought that measures of repression would be more dangerous than a closed official eye.

In August the Italian guns thundered offensively for the eleventh and last time on the Isonzo. This was the greatest of all the attacks staged, and was undertaken partly to rouse the nation from the pit of war-weariness into which it was rapidly falling.[1] The army was by now very 'patchy'. But it was still possible to assemble a great mass of offence. The Italian command had gone farther than those of other armies in creating special bodies of 'storm troops', who were obtained by denuding other units of their best elements. Prominent among them were the *arditi*, or 'men of daring', who had to pass exacting tests of courage and agility before admission, such as running through a machine-gun barrage in which wounds were actually inflicted!

The scale of the new operation was very great; fifty-two divisions and over 5,000 guns were concentrated between Tolmino and the sea.

Above Gorizia the Isonzo was crossed on a broad front, and the Austrians were thrust back six miles on the Bainsizza plateau, a tangle of low mountains, which form the outer bastions of Laibach. Fires and explosions marked the course of the enemy's retreat. The Austrians, as was afterwards confessed, were pushed to an extremity. But

[1] This condition will be described in the next chapter, dealing with the causes of Caporetto.

as happened so constantly in this war, the forward impulse died away just when the supreme effort was needed. Tired troops, even in victory, will not advance without the support of their guns. The roads on the plateau were scanty and bad, and the Italians never learnt the lesson of traffic-management. The new lines were precariously held. So the battle ended in the beginning of September. The new Italian positions were exceedingly awkward, for the Tolmino bridge-head outflanked them very sharply on the north. The troops who had been detailed to take it had failed, according to their army commander, to do their duty at all. The Italians had lost enormously, 165,000 men. The enemy had also been grievously shaken; the army commanders reported to the Chief-of-Staff, Arz, that their men could not stand up to another onslaught. It was therefore as a measure of desperate self-preservation that the decision was taken to make an attack which had results so astonishing and unforeseen even to its contrivers.

XXVII

CAPORETTO AND THE DEFENCE OF THE PIAVE

I

WHEN the Austrian Staff first decided upon an attack it was proposed to deal with the 'hereditary enemy' without German assistance, except that of some heavy artillery. It was hoped to induce Ludendorff to relieve a

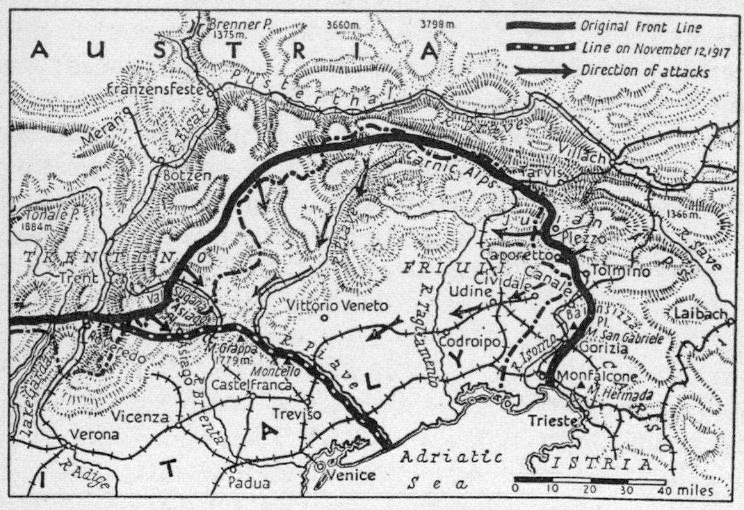

MAP 24. Caporetto.

sufficient number of Austrian divisions in the East. That, however, was far from Ludendorff's intention. He was not enthusiastic about attacking the Italians, and would have preferred to finish Rumania, after bringing off his hurricane *coup* at Riga. But if the general military position demanded it so peremptorily, he was determined, whether Karl asked for it or no, that a picked German force should do the lion's work. He rightly mistrusted the organizing power of his allies, and knew them to be incapable of using his own new method of rapidly penetrating an enemy's front by the careful co-operation of specialists of all arms. Consequently the Kaiser adroitly replied to Karl's request by intimating that German troops could not be kept indefinitely in the East by relieving an equivalent Austrian force, but offered his strategic reserve of seven divisions for an autumn blow at Italy, provided that they should be quickly returned to him.[1] A famous German general, Otto von Below, was put in charge of the mixed army destined to play the decisive part, and his chief staff officer, Krafft von Delmensingen, went at once to reconnoitre the chosen area. It was in the northern reaches of the Isonzo between Plezzo and Tolmino. At Plezzo a valley running in from the east gave some space for the concentration of troops, but the river had to be crossed at points where it was commanded by great mountains before success could be won. The opportunities of the Tolmino bridge-head for offence have been already exhibited. This was a very sensitive place for the whole Italian scheme of defence. The system of communications followed the valleys in Friuli from north to south. Consequently, if the prepared lines were overrun, the attackers would pour down into Cividale and Udine, cities of the plain, right in the rear of the forces still standing on the lower Isonzo.[2]

Though Krafft and some of the subordinate leaders nourished vaster hopes, the official plan aimed merely at hustling the Italians in confusion behind the Tagliamento. This river was more highly appraised for defence than it was worth, since the Austrians were unaware that the forts upon it had been dismantled of their heavy guns for service with the field-armies. Nor did they suspect the demoralization of the Italian units who were in front of them. Consequently the provision of cavalry, lorries, and so forth

[1] The exchange of letters between the two emperors is characteristic and interesting. The text will be found in Arz, *Zur Geschichte des Grossen Krieges 1914–1918* (1924), pp. 171–4. Karl's secret reason for deprecating German help was probably that he foresaw the dispatch of Franco-British contingents to Italy, which would make it more difficult for him to conclude a separate peace with the Entente.

[2] The rear Italian defences in Friuli faced east and west, and no systematic attempt had been made to bar the lower courses of the valleys.

was merely adapted to the scale of a limited objective. Von Below had at his disposal sixteen infantry divisions, of which seven were German, all experienced and rehearsed in mountain warfare. Though he had a slight superiority at the point of rupture, his actual strategic resources in men were less than those of his immediate antagonist, Capello, commanding the 2nd Italian army.[1]

The Italians had at least six weeks' warning of the impending blow, and forty-eight hours beforehand the detailed plans of the operation were delivered into their hands by two Rumanian officer-deserters.

The causes of their discomfiture were partly military and partly moral. The arrangements made by the 2nd army were so bad that they would probably have suffered a serious defeat however brave their resistance, but it was the refusal to fight which turned defeat into overwhelming rout.

Cadorna was an autocrat and a bully; such men are seldom well served, unless they have a remarkable capacity for themselves acquiring all the information needful to keep their subordinates efficient. He seems to have been often on bad terms with most of his army commanders, with the exception of the Duke of Aosta. Consequently his orders were seldom carried out if they conflicted with the views of the executant.

In the middle of September he issued orders for the whole Julian front to be defensively organized. The rear lines were to be strengthened, and the positions of both men and guns were to be arranged in greater depth to secure more elasticity. Capello, who was both obstinate and ill, took little or no pains to obey these instructions. He intended to strike into the flank of the Tolmino attack by a great counterblow from the Bainsizza and thus to stop it abruptly. On the actual sector of assault he placed

[1] The estimates of the exact figures vary slightly. Cadorna estimates the 2nd army at 353 battalions against 329, and 2,430 guns against 2,485. The German battalions were no doubt considerably stronger than the Italian. The superiority in the front line on October 24 was greater, 189 Italian battalions against 143 German-Austrian.

what must have been notoriously his worst troops. Northward from Tolmino there had been little fighting. The men were reputed to make bets on when 'they would declare war on Austria'. Among them were large numbers of munition-workers from Turin, who had been drafted into the ranks as a punishment for their revolutionary strike in August 1917. Certainly some among them were not merely unwilling to fight, but anxious to betray. It seems inconceivable that the High Command could have been ignorant of this serious infection. But the gulf between the Staff and the regimental officers was so great that apparently this was true.[1]

It must not be supposed that most of the men who broke had any intention of 'naked treachery', to use the harsh terms of Cadorna's uncensored dispatches. Some were simply terrified of the Germans, whom they held to be invincible; as it was said 'one glance at the *pickelhaube* coming over the hill was enough'. The majority were simply representing the intense war-weariness of the nation. Many of the symptoms were identical with those already analysed in the description of the French mutinies, others were peculiarly Italian. *Sacro egoismo* which aims at getting the desired objects as quickly and cheaply as possible is not a good basis for a cruel and stationary war. The men were always growling about 'the maximum of effort and the minimum of results'. It was obvious that the Allies cared little what happened to Italy, so long as she kept on

[1] The self-complacency of generals is often surprising. Neither Cadorna nor Capello in their published works blame themselves in the slightest for the moral condition of their men, or for being ignorant of it. On the eve of Caporetto, the former sent round staff officers to report on the spirit of the two corps at Plezzo and Tolmino, and these pronounced it excellent. Col. Calcagno's report of the 37th corps, which ran as follows, is truly comic: 'His Excellency (the Corps Commander) told me that yesterday he met a company on the march and having stopped them said: "I am your Corps Commander. We are going to be attacked by Austrians and Germans. Have no fear, boys. I have enough guns to smash them up as soon as they reach our lines." A corporal replied: "Sir, we shall not want all that artillery. We shall be enough for them with our machine-guns." His Excellency told me this as an indication of the spirit of the troops.'

fighting. 'You English are keeping it on', said a sergeant to G. M. Trevelyan.[1] The Revolution in Russia confirmed the opinion that the Government, the upper classes, and the Staff officers were conspiring with the Entente to sacrifice the workers. The cry 'This winter not one man in the trenches' had loud and wide reverberations. The proportion of illiterates in the army was very high, which gave an added importance to the breath of rumour. Moreover, the Vatican was opposed to the war, and subtly spread its opposition through the mouths and influence of many parish priests and some army chaplains. Its peace note of August 1917 had condemned 'the useless slaughter' and hinted that a compromise could be easily found on territorial questions with a little goodwill. As Italian territory was not invaded there could be no appeal to the most sacred source of patriotism, the defence of the soil. This was to come after Caporetto and to transfigure the nation most surprisingly.

Finally, the men themselves were callously neglected. They found none of the consolations for their dangers and suffering in the amusement canteens and other remedial provisions so amply provided for the British or German soldier. Their time in the rear was largely spent in grumbling, conspiring, and cursing their officers. Visits on leave to their families often excited a more burning resentment. The separation allowances were meagre and, unlike the wages of the munition-worker, showed no upward curve to overtake or overleap the increased cost of living.

Such in outline was the complicated malady which had conquered the 2nd army, and was beginning to ooze into the whole military structure in October 1917.

II

The attack, delayed by foul weather, took place on the morning of October 24th. The scene was swept by

[1] G. M. Trevelyan, *Scenes from Italy's War* (1919), ch. vii, gives a vivid and sympathetic analysis of the process of disintegration in the mind of the peasant soldier.

driving rain and snow on the heights, which were veiled in low cloud. These conditions affected the bombardment, which was of the short, concentrated type, perfected next March in France. Indescribable confusion rioted among the Italians when the infantry advanced. Their guns had made no attempt at counter-preparation. The heights being blinded, the machine-guns could make no use of their commanding positions, which overlooked the river crossings. The enemy round Plezzo were across almost unnoticed. The trench-garrisons for the most part either surrendered without a blow, or made off immediately, drawing the reserves with them in their flight. The corps commanders had been living in a fool's paradise. No arrangements had been made for mutual co-operation in the event of an attack about which they seem in their hearts to have been sceptical. When telephonic communication broke down, the head-quarters were left in a state of blank ignorance. The commander of the 27th corps was still unaware at 11 a.m. that the battle had started, though his men had covered several miles in full flight. By that evening the attacks from Plezzo and Tolmino had advanced ten or twelve miles, and had by encirclement annihilated two corps with many of their reserves. Next day Cadorna decided upon a general retreat to the Tagliamento, while he vainly tried to delay the enemy's advance southward through the hills towards Cividale in order to gain precious time for the escape of the 3rd army, still deeply involved in its trench system on the Carso. And the panic in the north grew with an irresistible contagion; the great masses of deserters pouring down the valleys swept away any reinforcements, both physically and morally.

German eyewitnesses have told of their astonishment at the way in which all the great pillars of the plain (precipitous mountains nearly 6,000 feet high) fell before the first patrols. In three days the entire hill-system had fallen. Cadorna himself left his head-quarters, Udine, only twenty hours before the enemy entered. The plains were encumbered with an immense multitude—400,000 soldiers were going home, with the determination that for them at least the war was ended. The reports of their behaviour are most curious. Having broken contact with the enemy, they were in no hurry: they stopped to eat, drink, and pillage. One observer notes their air of 'tranquil indifference', another that while they had all thrown away their rifles, they kept their gas-masks; nearly as many civilians were fleeing, more wildly, from the face of the enemy, blocking what remained of road space with their carts and household goods.[1]

It was clear to Cadorna that the question was not whether he could stand upon the Tagliamento, but whether he could preserve the vestige of an army to stand anywhere. He at least never lost his head, and conducted the retreat with fine calmness and skill. His difficulties were increased by the flooding of the Tagliamento, a capricious torrent, all the fords of which soon became impassable. 'Ira deorum in rem Romanam.'[2] All hope of safety depended upon the race for the lower Tagliamento, whither the Duke of Aosta was leading back the 300,000 men of the 3rd army, a well-knit fighting body, along a narrow corridor twenty miles wide, closely shepherded by the pursuing Boroevic. If Below's army could forestall them from the north at the crossing of the river, they would be hemmed in with the Adriatic barring their left flank. Light naval craft had indeed taken off some heavy guns at Monfalcone, but no large measure of succour could be expected from that quarter. How extreme the peril was may be judged by the fact that the 2nd army had begun to cross the Tagliamento before the 3rd had completed its withdrawal over the Isonzo.

German officers, notably Krafft, maintain that if Boroevic had allowed detachments of the German XIVth army to use some of the roads in his area, the catastrophe might have been completed. Such recriminations between rival

[1] E. Hemingway in the novel, *A Farewell to Arms* (1929), gives a wonderful description of the retreat.

[2] The words are from Tacitus.

staffs are common, and their substance is almost impossible to determine. Undoubtedly, if a few cavalry divisions and armoured cars had been available, the Italians would have been lost. Their own cavalry and aeroplanes did splendidly in stemming the enemy's advance-guards.

Though a premature order for bridge-demolition at Codroipo had left stranded 50,000 men and many heavy batteries, a remnant of the 2nd army which had come right back from the Bainsizza in tolerable trim, the remaining Italians were all behind the protection of the stream on November 1st. Here some reorganization was possible; units were sorted out; as the deserters crossed the bridges they were collected by military police, some were shot out of hand, and many more drafted back to the rear. The men began then to realize that they could not get peace by casting away their arms; they had merely abandoned an Italian province to the enemy.

But there was no continuing refuge on the Tagliamento. The flood had fallen, and high up on the river the enemy pushed some detachments across on the night of November 2nd–3rd.

Still the retreat to the Piave was orderly and methodical, except in the mountains, where several Italian units delayed too long in swinging back the extreme left and were caught. Fortunately for Cadorna, whose continual nightmare had been of a break-through in the Trentino, the enemy had not sufficient forces to bring this off. Conrad,[1] now in command there, had been sent two divisions from Friuli and was hammering away to the best of his limited strength, but his perseverance throughout November was rewarded with very small success.

III

The line of the Piave, so justly celebrated in Italian history, had been partially prepared by Cadorna's foresight

[1] He had been deposed from the position of Chief-of-Staff soon after Karl's accession, and was succeeded by the more pliable and pleasant-mannered Arz.

in 1916. It had two prime advantages. It covered Venice, although with only some fifteen miles to spare. Without the use of that port the Italian navy would have been thrown back 500 miles to Brindisi, and the Adriatic would have passed into Austrian mastery. Moreover, it is a very short river, so that the whole front had now been reduced by nearly two-thirds, a considerable compensation for enormous losses.

The lower reaches of the Piave wander through wide lagoons and marshes, being virtually unassailable; higher up it is a strong and unstable torrent, running in many channels through a deep, stony bed often a mile and a half wide. The whole river line to be guarded was less than fifty miles. Hereafter the defence curved westward to the Brenta, relying on the great hinge of Monte Grappa between the two streams, before it reached the comparative security of the old mountain positions. Cadorna had not failed to recognize the cardinal importance of the Grappa. Gun-emplacements, dug-outs, and cisterns for water had been providently prepared; without these it must have fallen to the repeated assaults prolonged against it until the close of the year.

To Cadorna also belongs the honour of having fixed upon the Piave as the *ne plus ultra* of Italian resistance, and of having rightly trusted in the army's power of recovery, although public opinion, both at home and abroad, anticipated a further retirement to the Adige, 'the best defensive line in Italy' as Napoleon had called it. Cadorna's last order, published on the morning of his dismissal, November 9th, ran: 'We have taken the inflexible decision to defend here the honour and life of Italy. Every soldier must know what is the cry and command issuing from the conscience of the whole Italian people: to die and not to yield.' The army nobly fulfilled this duty. The battle for the river was won before the Anglo-French contingents[1] had left their reserve positions. History can scarcely

[1] Six French and five British divisions under Foch and Plumer respectively had been hurried into Italy.

record a more wonderful transfiguration. The character of the rout is made abundantly clear by the official list of casualties. While 10,000 were killed and 30,000 wounded, the number of prisoners was 293,000 and of deserters 400,000. Yet this stricken army, apparently on the verge of dissolution, maintained for a month a steadfast and resolute front against great odds.[1]

The change of heart in the country was no less remarkable. The invasion in which so few believed had come, and was but precariously stayed, almost against hope, by the fragile barrier of a small stream. Nothing else could so concentrate and unify the will and emotions of the whole people. 'Are there in Italy other living waters—I will not think of them. . . . Forget all else for the moment and remember only that this water is for us the water of life, regenerative like that of baptism. . . . It runs beside the walls, and past the doors, and through the streets of all the cities of Italy; it runs past the threshold of all our dwellings; it safeguards from the destroyer all our altars and all our hearts.'[2] Thus D'Annunzio wrote, expressing and intensifying the inmost thoughts of his countrymen, as he had done also in May 1915. Orlando, the supine Home Secretary, transformed into Premier by a curious reshuffle, when the Cabinet, like the Commander-in-Chief, fell in the storm, was galvanized into an activity worthy of the crisis. Italy, he declared, would continue to fight, if the retreat had to be carried as far as Sicily. A vast work of reorganization was carried through during the winter; adequate attention was at last given to the welfare and comfort of the soldier. Caporetto had opened the eyes of the Entente to the essential unity of the whole western front from the North Sea to the Adriatic. They had speedily dispatched a large force of good troops under famous commanders. The soldiers of the two nations were the best

[1] According to Italian figures of uncertain authority on November 13, 423 Italian battalions and 3,500 guns were facing 736 with 7,000 guns. The inferiority of the Italians by the close of the battle was negligible. They lost 3,200 guns in the retreat.

[2] Quoted in J. Buchan, *History of the Great War* (1921), vol. iv, p. 62.

ambassadors of the common cause, hitherto so insincerely invoked and so wretchedly unrealized. Moreover, out of the Rapallo Conference between the heads of the three States arose the Supreme War Council, which was itself the fore-runner of true unity of command. Henceforward the Italian front was never denuded of a Franco-British contingent, though it was reduced in the spring crisis to five divisions; while, from July 1918 onwards, an Italian corps played a worthy part in the decisive victories in France.

XXVIII
CAMBRAI

THE battle which so dramatically concluded this weary year of deferred hope was the most original and interesting of the war, and had ultimately by far the most important consequences. In the first place it regained the seemingly lost art of surprise, and both sides hereafter clung desperately to this secret of decision.[1] Secondly, it signalized the correct tactical employment of the new arm, which till now had been so pitiably wasted contrary to the direct advice of its chief begetter, Swinton. The triumphant power of a massed onslaught of tanks, suddenly at a stroke without artillery assistance, to break clean through the strongest field fortifications, profoundly changed the character of trench-warfare. It was no longer possible to affix the label 'active' or 'quiet' to different parts of the front. Tired or inferior divisions could no longer be sent to a 'safe' area with any comfortable certainty that ample time would be available for their relief before an attack could be mounted. The mystery of the new tactics was indeed most improvidently revealed at a moment when, as Haig himself admits, the means at his disposal in November 1917 permitted no more than a gambler's blow. Yet fortune proved unusually forgiving. Labour shortage and the prior demands for other kinds of war-material made it impossible for the enemy to exploit this weapon for his own attacks in 1918.[2] Moreover, immediately after this battle the initiative passed to the Germans. The whole energy of their best minds was concentrated on a peace-compelling offensive with the old weapons. In consequence, no counter-measures against the tanks were

[1] See the memorandum of December 14, circulated by Prince Rupprecht's Staff, which contains the phrase 'Misslingt die Überraschung, so misslingt auch der Durchbruch', as the principal lesson to be learnt from Cambrai (Kronprinz Rupprecht, *Mein Kriegstagebuch* (1929), vol. iii, p. 193).

[2] See H. von Kuhl, *Weltkrieg* (1930), vol. ii, p. 235. In 1918 the Germans used 90 tanks, 75 of which were captured from their enemy, while only 15 were of home construction.

systematically thought out. When the wheel turned, and the opportunity of the Entente came, the German soldiers were just as helpless against these armoured masses on July 18th and August 8th, 1918, as they had been on November 20th, 1917. Had it not been so the war must have been prolonged over another season with incalculable results.

The tactical scheme of the battle originated in Swinton's imaginative insight into the proper use of the new arm, as Elles, the commander of the tank-corps, generously acknowledged in a telegram sent in the flush of initial triumph.[1] His staff officer Fuller, the well-known writer on war, had urged the enterprise on the Higher Command since the beginning of August, for he foresaw that tanks would be worse than useless in the Flemish morasses. It was, however delayed until any hope of a decision in the north had been abandoned. In consequence, when the belated day came on November 20th, the infantry available was for the most part war-worn, and few reserves were available or even drafts to replace battle casualties.

Fuller had envisaged a raid on a gigantic scale, which would destroy a whole section of the 'Hindenburg line', and capture its defenders after a surprise occupation of a few hours. Haig's dispatch envisages a far more ambitious but still definitely limited programme of rolling up a twenty-mile stretch of the German defences between Cambrai and Arras by a northward wheel, after penetration should be complete at the point of attack. According to him, the occupation of Cambrai was merely a subsidiary aim to secure a strong supporting place for the defensive right flank. There is, however, reason to believe that Byng, the commander of the 3rd army, which was engaged, hoped to rive the whole opposing front asunder by thrusting deeply beyond Cambrai to Valenciennes with a great irruption of cavalry. Such a success, even if not long maintained, would have created chaos in the enemy's chief lateral communications, and would perhaps have

[1] 'All ranks thank you. Your show.'—Elles.

forced him to retire between Lille and Rheims. The large bodies of cavalry available, though not used, the considerable force held in readiness by the French, and the course of events on the 20th itself, all suggest the more ambitious aim.

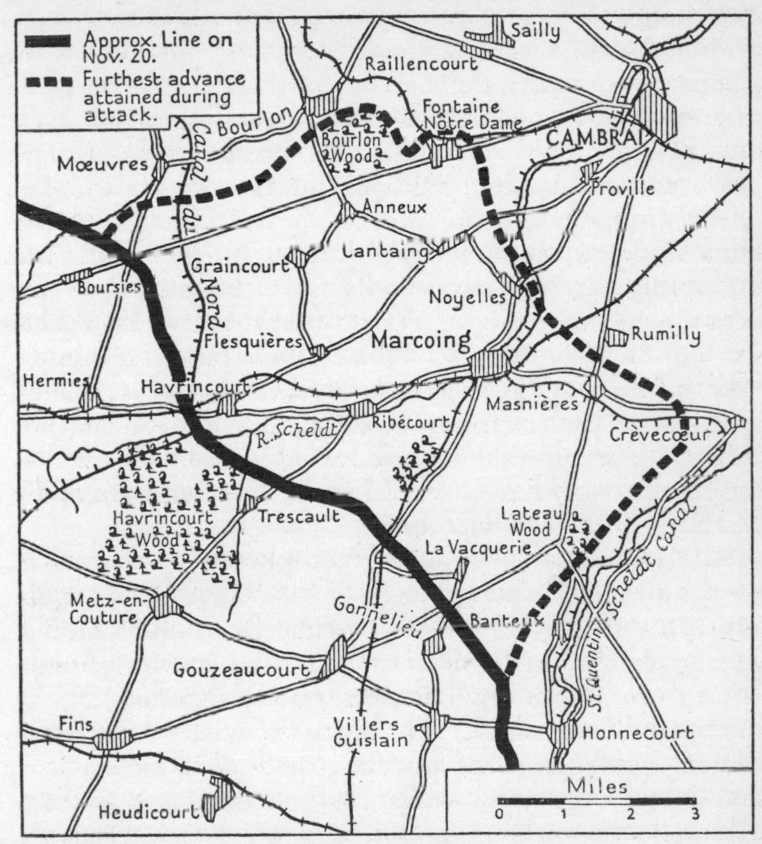

MAP 25. Cambrai.

The area selected for this experiment was highly favourable. The country round Cambrai is good, hard, rolling down-land, now yielding a rich harvest of corn. Since the German retreat the sector had been completely inactive, the ground was scarcely marked by shell-holes, the great wood of Havrincourt just behind our lines was still so undamaged as to afford an excellent lurking-place for the tanks.

The battle-field, unlike so many of the vast, featureless arenas of the war, was well defined and could be easily taken in at a single view. An observer looking north-eastward from British terrain would note that a section of the enemy's line, and his rearward communications, were confined within two artificial obstacles some 10,000 or 12,000 yards apart, the Canals de l'Escaut and du Nord respectively, from north to south. The attack was to be bounded by these two limits. Within this frame two features dominated the gentle undulations: the hill of Flesquières in the middle foreground, beyond which the land dips into a cup studded with villages, as far as Cambrai seven miles away, and secondly the wood-crowned ridge of Bourlon swelling on the north-east horizon like a great bastion flanking the city. Both of these played a decisive part in the coming struggle. For, as will be seen, if Flesquières had been overrun according to plan in the first few hours, Bourlon, that insurmountable rock of offence, would probably have been taken in the afternoon, and a fair field opened for victory.

The efficient secrecy of the complicated preparations merits all possible praise; no such utter surprise was again effected until the enemy overran the Chemin des Dames at a stroke on May 27th next year. The inevitable noise of the tank assembly was masked by accustoming the enemy to the drone of low-flying aeroplanes over his lines several nights before the landships, painted in the fantastic colour-stripes of the new camouflage, moved into position. Nearly 600 additional guns were slipped unsuspectingly into place; an unprecedented test of efficiency was demanded of the gunners, for they were denied any preliminary registration on their targets. And they passed this test with flying colours.[1]

The rank and file of the six attacking divisions knew

[1] The German artillery was never able completely to dispense with preliminary registration until May 27th, 1918 (Chemin des Dames). That the British could do it earlier must largely be attributed to the excellence of the work done by the survey-companies.

nothing of what was impending until forty-eight hours before the event. Even then the vital role of the tanks was hidden from them, so that prisoners captured on the 18th, though induced to disclose that an attack was impending, failed to alarm Rupprecht's Headquarters. It was expected that ample warning would as usual be given by a prolonged bombardment.

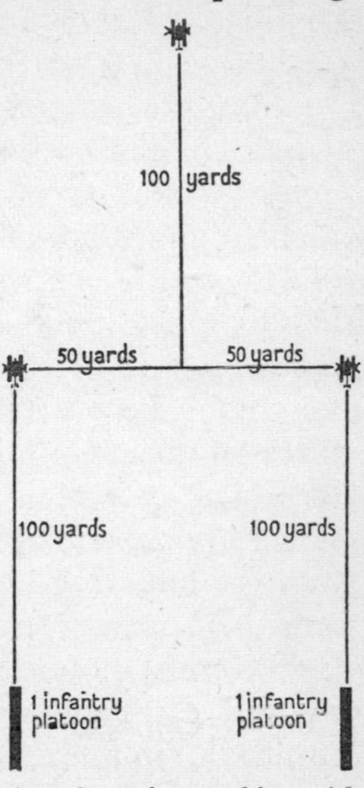

A tank section working with infantry.

At 6.20 a.m. on November 20th, the twilight limiting visibility to 200 yards, and all being quiet upon the scene of action, 381 tanks moved forward from their last assembly points, which had been indicated by broad white tapes and occupied during the night. As they passed the British trenches, the unsuspected barrage clanged out upon the astonished enemy.

Distributed over the whole front of attack, the four sections of each company moved in triangular formation, with two platoons of infantry in file a hundred yards behind. Each tank-company of twelve machines was supported by two infantry companies (of eight platoons). General Elles went into action, flying his flag on one of the leading machines in the true style of a 'land-admiral'. The wide belts of formidable wire were completely flattened out. As they entered the broad Hindenburg line great fascines of brushwood, protruding from the front of each machine, were dropped. On these improvised bridges they heaved themselves over the vast excavation. Scarcely a shot or shell was fired at the supporting infantry who swarmed in through the lanes, and occupied the system, 'mopping up', as the phrase went, by searching out, and if necessary bombing, all the dug-outs.

The overrunning of the front lines was everywhere a triumphant and almost bloodless progress. Battalions found themselves in undisputed possession of trenches deemed wellnigh impregnable at the cost of five or six casualties.

On the right progress was for a long time uninterrupted. The troops advanced through villages, still occupied by the French inhabitants who, released from their captivity, were sent back through our lines. But the intention of widening the flank of attack and of encircling Cambrai from the south-east was frustrated. The first tank which tried to cross the Scheldt Canal at Masnières, over a partially wrecked bridge, toppled over into the water. The enemy kept up a brisk machine-gun fire from the houses on the steep hill opposite, and gave time for their last trench position, the incomplete Masnières–Beaurevoir line, to be manned.

On the left wing also a fine advance was made. The enemy had been distracted by sham attacks farther north, where, amidst clouds of gas and smoke, dummy infantrymen were displayed on the parapet to simulate the act of assault. But in the centre the most famous of the attacking divisions, the 51st Highland Territorial, which the Germans rated as the most formidable in the British army, failed unaccountably before the hill of Flesquières. General Harper, its commander, who was adored by his men, had the defects of his excellent qualities. He had an old-fashioned disbelief in the tanks, and had openly shown his distrust of the new tactics at the conferences which preceded the attack. He insisted on his tanks going farther ahead of the infantry than elsewhere, touch was very imperfectly maintained, and so the German machine-gunners were given time to emerge. Also three batteries hidden in the orchards of the village, which stands back a few hundred yards from the crest of the hill, picked off the machines as they appeared on the skyline. When all but one gun had been silenced an officer, Lieut. Muller of the 108th regiment, single-handed, scored several final hits.

He earned the unique honour of being mentioned in Haig's dispatch, who wrote: 'The great bravery of this officer aroused the admiration of all ranks.' Even so, it is difficult to explain the lack of enterprise shown by the infantry, who continued throughout the day a futile frontal attack upon the isolated eminence. It is true that no general reserve was available, but a glance at the map, which shows that our troops in the afternoon were beyond Graincourt and Noyelles, suggests that there should have been little difficulty in pinching out the protruding salient.[1]

The inaction of the two cavalry divisions has never yet been intelligibly explained. They had been brought close up on the morning of the battle but, to the satirical derision of the foot-soldiers, stood all the day idle. One Canadian squadron alone roamed about in the dusk round Rumilly. Doubtless it was a grave risk to use cavalry in the west at all; yet if the risk was not to be taken on a favourable opportunity, why thrust them ostentatiously forward as the only 'reserve of exploitation'? The infantry were constantly pushed remorselessly on the forlornest of hopes. The cavalry were kept back for the impossible event of every detail of the schedule being performed with clock-like exactness. Haig's dispatch throws no light on this question; his silence is perhaps explained on the assumption that immediate orders from G.H.Q. were responsible for their inaction.

The failure to seize opportunity is the more striking since Haig himself emphasized its fleeting character. He staked practically everything on the first forty-eight hours, during which he calculated that no considerable reserves could reach the enemy. It was against his better judgement that he continued to fight this battle for another week until his superiority had completely crumbled away, and his

[1] Maj.-Gen. de Pree, who was Brigadier-General General Staff, to Byng, gives it as his opinion that 'a well-organized attack of infantry and tanks working from the north-west would probably have captured it any time' (*Journal of Royal Artillery*, vol. lv, No. 2, July 1928). The 51st division themselves had one brigade available as local reserve; it was not used at all on the 20th.

battle-weary men were faced with the extreme danger of a powerful counter-attack on either exposed flank.

The German commander, von der Marwitz, kept his head manfully and diverted his exiguous reserves correctly to the vital points. He had one stroke of luck, which his enemy could not have divined; for on November 18th a division from Russia, rested and freshly equipped, began to detrain at Cambrai. Several of its units were available to stop urgent gaps on the 20th. British eyewitnesses admired the vigour and initiative shown by isolated battalions, thrown piecemeal into the fray; they seemed in no way disheartened by the misfortune of their comrades. Still, der Marwitz had been very hard hit: two of his divisions had been destroyed. The British had taken 7,500 prisoners and 120 guns, and had lost less than 4,000 men. In some places the penetration was 7,000 yards deep—a 'record' since any continuous trench-lines had been dug on the Western Front.

Flesquières was evacuated that morning, and by the evening of the 21st Haig had to decide whether to continue a battle which he had hoped would be decisively won within forty-eight hours. He had either to go on or to go back, for his protruding salient, dangerous enough under any circumstances, was quite untenable while Bourlon remained in the enemy's hands. The tanks had all been put into the original attack; their battle casualties had not been severe, but many had suffered minor damage, and the strain on the crews, if used day by day, was terrible to the point of exhaustion. Moreover, the end of the campaigning season was at hand, and Haig had now only three reserve divisions. Yet, loath to acknowledge failure by a voluntary retirement, he pursued a limited battle. All British efforts were now concentrated on Bourlon. The wood could not be encircled from the north except by capturing Fontaine-Notre-Dame. For a week this sordid little village on the great highway from Bapaume was the constant scene of ferocious fighting. The tanks broke in repeatedly. The Germans installed machine-guns and 6-pounders in the top stories of the houses; their infantry showed much spirit, swarming over the tanks, shooting, and dropping strings of grenades tied together through the loop-holes. To the west a fluctuating struggle swayed in the wood, its dense undergrowth, further confused by the splintered trunks and branches, made progress a labour for pioneers, while its recesses harboured the gas freely flung upon it by both artilleries.

The British were therefore held in their awkward contorted salient as in a vice. They invited the encircling counter-attack which Rupprecht's Staff began to prepare with concentrated energy. It was on an ambitious scale—eleven divisions in all were to attack, southward from Bourlon, and westward from the Scheldt Canal. The local command had intended the two assaults to be simultaneous. Ludendorff, however, overrode this decision. According to Rupprecht he had been 'very nervous, telephoning on a thousand matters a day'. His intervention was based on the correct assumption that the attack from the east offered the better chances of success. He hoped to dent in the salient some four miles deep in the first three hours; after which the Bourlon attack was to cut off a demoralized enemy, whose reserves had all been engaged. At least 150,000 prisoners and an immense material would have been the trophies of such a victory.

In spite of warnings from the tired troops holding the eastern face of the salient, the British Higher Command was insistent in its belief that the main danger would come from Bourlon.

On November 30th at 7 o'clock a very short bombardment was followed by a massed attack of low-flying aeroplanes pouring machine-gun bullets on the weak and weary British divisions, who had attacked on November 20th and had been kept in the line without rest ever since. Meanwhile the German infantry in small parties trickled up the numerous little ravines on the western bank of the Scheldt Canal. All was confusion. The Germans pushed straight on into Gouzeaucourt, three miles behind the line.

They came so quickly that General de Lisle, commanding the 29th division, scarcely escaped in his pyjamas. One of their divisions, however, got out of hand and dispersed to loot the vast supply depot. This was the first occasion—there were to be many next year—on which the discipline of the pinched German soldier cracked before the sight of British abundance. An infuriated quartermaster, Captain Gee, performed the legendary feat of killing six pillagers with a loaded stick and escaped to win a V.C. Even here the advance was not stayed; the enemy pushed into the wood behind Gouzeaucourt, which was stiff with abandoned batteries and disabled tanks. A party of American Civil Engineers manfully assailed them with pick and shovel, thus coming to blows with the Germans before any of their comrades of their regular army. The Guards' division moving to counter-attack found a disorganization almost amounting to panic. Their calm, parade-like advance through the village and up the eastward slope was long remembered. The situation was restored to an uneasy equilibrium.

Meanwhile von Moser's unfortunate troops round Bourlon endeavoured to break out at eleven under an inadequate smoke cloud. The British were thoroughly prepared for them, and put up a magnificently sturdy resistance. The London Territorials (47th division) fought one of the best of their many distinguished fights. The enemy waves succeeded each other in futile attempts to surge down the bare slopes until the close of the day. Well-sited machine-guns took enormous toll of them: one company alone fired 100,000 rounds at close range. Thus Byng had escaped disaster, but had now perforce to straighten his line. He withdrew to a splayed but quite defensible semicircle, which in fact resisted all the most violent efforts of the enemy to cut it off on March 21st of the following year.

Thus at the close of this hurricane battle honours were about even. Each side had lost much the same quantity of prisoners and guns. The Germans, however, according to the testimony of their leaders, gained greatly in moral from the success of the first important offensive action carried out in the West since Verdun. They felt, as was indeed true, that the initiative was passing into their hands, and looked eagerly to the spring to impose decisively their victorious will.

A comparison of dates shows conclusively that Haig's claim to have diverted hostile reinforcements from Italy, and to have given the defenders of the Piave a fortnight's respite, is unfounded. The Austro-German staffs had already on November 10th decided to break off serious operations owing to the lateness of the season. This knowledge, however, was not available when the dispatch was written, and Haig must be allowed the credit of an attempt to help further an ally in adversity. The five fine divisions which had already been sent to Italy might well have consummated a great victory had they been available at Cambrai.

XXIX

PEACE IN THE EAST

THE peace proposal of the Bolsheviks was addressed to all countries. It called for an immediate armistice, and for a general settlement on the basis of the familiar formula 'without annexations or indemnities'. Lenin did not indeed expect that the Entente Governments would agree, but by broadcasting his terms he hoped to induce 'the more advanced' democracies of England and France to rise against their rulers. From this point of view therefore his manifesto was a move in the great game of creating universal civil war, out of which the new internationalist order should be born.

It was none the less essential that Russia should obtain an immediate, even if an 'indecent', peace from her own enemies now at her own gates. For without such a result Bolshevism would be speedily doomed. So while Lenin based some hopes on the subterranean activity of German and Austrian Socialists (which indeed bore a very meagre fruit in the strikes of January 1918) he was quite prepared to treat with the existing imperialists. It was obvious that Germany's attitude would be decisive. The war-weariness of her three lesser allies would certainly not decline a proffered chance of peace. The Germans hesitated before agreeing to a preliminary armistice. Nothing could have been more repellent to their stiff, hierarchical minds than intercourse with the Bolsheviks. Moreover, it might be expected that to treat with them officially would strengthen their precarious hold on the Russian people.

Germany, however, was in bitter need of an eastern peace and could not afford to be particular as to the instruments of its achievement. It was a 'bread peace', for without the foodstuffs from the Ukraine the civil population of the Central Powers would have been vanquished by famine before the harvest of 1918 could be gathered.[1]

[1] See the statistics given in Graf O. Czernin, *In the World War* (1919), pp. 251–7.

Moreover, it was the only condition of a decisive spring victory in the West. Ludendorff had providently given orders to transfer thither almost all his available divisions before the Peace Conference met. Hence he was able to agree without difficulty to the Bolshevik request, dictated by a last prick of compunction, that no more troops should be moved while the session continued.

There have been few stranger gatherings in history than that of Brest-Litovsk. The delegates of all the warring nations represented at the conference fed at the same table. Among the elegant diplomatists and the grimly correct staff officers of the Central Powers sat the unkempt, bearded peasants and workers of the Russian delegation. Their admirals and generals, who attended as mere technical advisers without a vote, were relegated to a lower room. Prince Ernest Hohenlohe, a connexion of the Imperial House, found himself next a murderess, Mme Byzenko, who had escaped from a life sentence in Siberia for shooting the Minister of War twelve years before. The Central Powers and their allies had much difficulty in agreeing upon their tactics. The faded, subtle, amiable Czernin had received an order from Karl under no circumstances to return without peace in his pocket, and was terrified lest too stiff an attitude might cause the rupture of the negotiations. Kühlmann, the German Secretary of State, on the other hand, while pliant and able to appear at least as conciliatory as he really was, a gift rare among Germans, intended that peace, if made, should fully represent the realities of the situation. The Turks and Bulgars were only anxious to tear off as much as possible from the Russian carcass. The reply finally approved to the Bolshevik invitation was adroit, if dishonest. The Central Powers declared that they would agree to a peace without annexations and indemnities which should 'safeguard the self-determination of peoples', if the Entente would signify their assent to the same within ten days. The Bulgars, who proclaimed their annexationist aims with a blunt crudeness, were only persuaded to concur with the worst grace by the assurance that this hypothetical 'principle with a time limit' would never be applied. In any case, as the Russians soon realized, to their horror, this phrase was held to be compatible with an immense diminution of their pre-war territory. Poland, Lithuania, and Courland had, under the prompting of their occupying masters, declared themselves, through their representatives, to be independent states. Their destiny therefore must be settled by the Central Powers to the exclusion of Russia. The Bolsheviks had indeed fallen into a trap set by themselves; for their own declaration of self-determination had been specifically held to extend to all nationalities forcibly annexed by any great Power before the outbreak of war. Even since they had seized power they had nominally recognized the independence of Finland and the Ukraine.

During the interval of waiting for an unexpected answer from the Entente, the heads of the delegations repaired for consultation to their respective capitals. When the conference reassembled on January 4th, the Russians were reinforced by the dominating and strident personality of Trotsky, who kept his nominal colleagues, as the Germans noticed, in a state of terrorized subjection. No more common meals, no more private intercourse, were permitted; the Bolsheviks kept themselves hermetically sealed within their lodgings. During the enormous debates which ensued, both sides still mouthed hypocritically the shibboleths of 'self-determination'. The Germans in fact intended to annex about two million Poles, whose absorption Ludendorff had urged on the reluctant Kaiser as necessary to secure the military integrity of East Prussia. Courland and Lithuania they hoped to unite with the Reich by a personal union. Austria, on the other hand, cherished the aspiration of attaching this new Poland to the Dual Monarchy. While no doubt these border populations would have preferred any fate to subjection by the Bolshevik tyranny, the Central Powers had no intention of genuinely consulting their freely expressed national desires. Meanwhile the Bolsheviks were forcibly flouting their own newly elected national assembly, and were sowing the seeds of a pitiless civil war in Finland and Ukraine.

Trotsky was an unrivalled propagandist. Day by day with passion and sublime assurance he poured out his rhetorical appeals to the proletariat of all countries. He even received several effusive messages from President Wilson. Finally Hoffmann, the German Chief-of-Staff, introduced a note of military realism. Russia, he quietly pointed out, was utterly defeated and at the mercy of her enemies. Her present rulers at that moment were engaged in destroying by violence and murder those very rights of nationalities which they invoked as their own sacrosanct shield. At his suggestion, the flank of the Bolsheviks was then pierced at a most sensitive point. Among the delegates at Brest were some young men claiming to represent the Ukraine as an independent state. Nothing could suit the Central Powers better than to detach these great granaries of the south from the Soviet, and to preserve them intact as a source of supply. So terms of a separate peace were arranged with the Ukrainians, whose country was being swept by a Bolshevik storm, and seemed likely to succumb. Yet so imperious was the call of hunger that Kühlmann and Czernin were ready to stir up bitter hatred in Poland by consenting to transfer its south-eastern districts of Lublin and Cholm to the infant state. Wholesale starvation in Vienna had in fact been most narrowly averted.[1]

Trotsky was left in a desperate position; but he maintained the courage of despair. After issuing an incitement to German soldiers to murder their officers, he played a final hand of bluff on February 10th. While refusing to sign the German terms he proclaimed a state of 'neither peace nor war', and the demobilization of the Russian

[1] See Graf O. Czernin, *In the World War* (1919), pp. 240–1. As it was, Austria had been compelled to entreat supplies from Germany. These were sent, and the obligation under which Austria was placed made it necessary for her to renounce any independence of action in dealing with the Russians.

armies. He calculated that it would be impossible again to set in motion the military machine; and that the Central Powers, remaining in possession of what they had won, would be glad to leave Russia alone. Such was indeed the desire of the politicians, but military logic, persuasively presented by Hoffmann, prevailed. The only object of an armistice was to make peace; if that were not made, the only alternative was renewed war. The Germans advanced inexorably through Livonia and Esthonia. No resistance was offered, for the disorganized rabble fled at their approach. Thousands of guns and vast quantities of supplies fell into their hands. They had been delivered by the Entente, and were soon to be used against their original owners in the West. The enemy was within 100 miles of Petrograd when Lenin finally prevailed over the opposition of the Central Bolshevik Committee. He had always been in favour of peace, however harsh the terms, provided that the deposition of the Bolsheviks was not one of them. To him it was infinitely more important to maintain the Russian Revolution than the integrity of Russia. The terms were indeed harsh. In addition to the territories formerly demanded, Finland, Livonia, and Esthonia were severed from Russia; and in Asia, Turkey acquired the Caucasus. The Germans were to remain in occupation of their present line of demarcation until the conclusion of a general peace. The Russian delegates ostentatiously refused the offer to discuss the treaty clause by clause, and so they signed *en bloc* to emphasize its dictated character as a 'peace of violence'. The character of this treaty has often been adduced as a precedent to justify the rigour of Versailles. But the Russians were entirely defenceless and were not induced to surrender their arms, while still capable of resistance, by promises which were afterwards broken. Moreover, the Germans hated and mistrusted the Bolsheviks, and would have given better terms to a more congenial government. In any case the new states which emerged in European Russia as a consequence of the treaty were recognized and

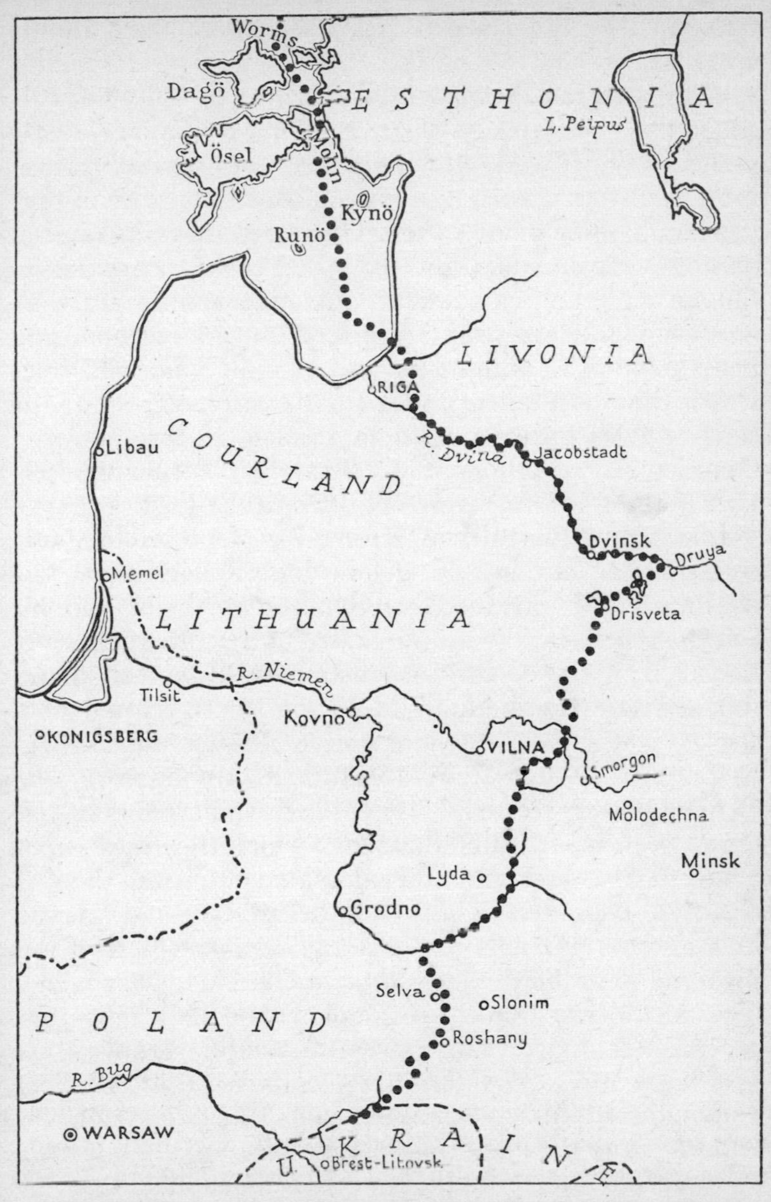

MAP 26. Terms of Brest-Litovsk. The dotted line gives the boundaries presented to Russia in the original draft of the treaty. By the treaty of 3 March, Russia further renounced the provinces of Livonia, Esthonia, and Finland.

welcomed by the Entente, presumably as just national creations.

German military responsibilities were little lessened by the so-called conclusion of peace. They dispatched an expedition to Finland, which rescued the 'Whites' from a most savage civil war, where even 'Boy Scouts' took part in a competition of atrocities. They purged the Ukraine of its Bolshevik invaders, and extended their occupation to Odessa and the Sea of Azov. Considerable forces were needed to squeeze supplies of food out of the hoarding peasants, and to administer and to police the vast areas which they had taken under their control. Even at the time of their bitterest need in France, in the following October, forty divisions (most of them, it is true, of miserably inferior quality) were detained in the East.

It was now the turn of Rumania. That unfortunate country was not indeed defenceless; for its army, re-equipped and retrained by General Berthelot and his clever French Staff, was as efficient as a Rumanian army is ever likely to be. But its defences could be turned and the inviolate fragment of Moldavia overwhelmed at a stroke. Nevertheless the alternative of peace was likely to be only less painful than the ordeal of conquest. The Central Powers viewed this enemy with a hatred and contempt even more bitter than that which they harboured against Italy. Her cold and calculated entry into the war was not likely to be forgiven because it had proved unsuccessful. Serious thoughts were entertained of dethroning King Ferdinand, but it was decided that such a blow at the monarchical principle would be a dangerous precedent for Conservative victors to adopt. He was, however, forced to meet Czernin, formerly Austrian Minister at Bucharest, and to hear such outspoken reproaches as seldom fall to the lot of sovereigns. The territorial clauses were comparatively mild and unimportant. Hungary took various strategic points on the eastern slope of the Transylvanian mountains, and the Bulgars acquired most of the Dobrudja. But from Russia Rumania was to acquire

Bessarabia, the fertile district between the Danube and the Pruth, and would therefore remain undiminished in extent. She was, however, destined for economic servitude; for she was cut off from the Black Sea, and merely given the use of Constanza as a free port. Her oil-wells were leased to Germany for a term of ninety years, and her agricultural products ear-marked for the Central Powers, who also gained a controlling interest in many of her principal companies. The far-reaching provisions of this treaty show both the powerful influence exercised by the German industrialists and the supreme confidence in ultimate victory felt and expressed by the soldiers in March 1918.

The Rumanians knew that, as they were making this separate peace, the provisions of the Treaty of Bucharest of August 1916 had ceased to have any binding force upon the Entente. And, with characteristic cunning, they again declared war on Germany a few hours before the conclusion of the armistice on November 11th. Their calculation served them well, for the territory of their state has been more than doubled. Rumania now possesses Transylvania with a frontier so generously drawn as to include at least 1,500,000 Magyars, together with Bessarabia. She is the most corrupt of the succession states, and does not fall short of any in her intolerance of minorities.

XXX

PREPARATION AND COUNTER-PREPARATION FOR THE GREAT ATTACK IN THE WEST

I

On November 11th, 1917, at Mons (a time and place surely chosen by the ironic Spirit of Hardy's *Dynasts*), Ludendorff, in consultation with his chief staff officers, decided in principle upon an attack in France for the ensuing spring.

This decision was, as the Quartermaster-General well knew, not merely a strategical one; it would determine not merely the issue of the campaign but of the war. For this reason Ludendorff has been reproached as the arch-gambler who staked the fate of his country upon one desperate throw. The responsibility is indeed his, and can be shared only in a subordinate degree by the so-called political rulers of Germany. Whereas in England and France, and even in Austria, the civilians had gradually curbed the soldiers with a stricter bridle, Ludendorff's tremendous, tireless, insatiable personality had completely cast into the shade not merely the Kaiser but the 'transient and embarrassed' succession of Chancellors. The ripe experience and the high character of Hertling, the aged Bavarian, who had now followed Michaelis, could not compensate for his lack of vigour. Germans bitterly contrasted his laboured orations, decked out with quotations from Saints Paul and Augustine, with the marvellous popular appeal of Lloyd George's eloquence and the laconic fire of Clemenceau. He merely accepted the blunt proposals dictatorially presented to his Government by Ludendorff.

Yet if the latter was a gambler, he considered every alternative and weighed every chance before making his throw.

The decisive offensive, in which he later told the Reichstag he was prepared to lose a million men, was, as he held, forced upon him by every consideration diplomatic, political, economic, and military. The general condition of the Alliance was such that peace must be unfailingly procured before the end of the next year. Contrary to Czernin's prediction, Austria was still struggling on. But she was on her last legs. Only the arrival of corn from Ukraine in the nick of time was to carry her through the winter. In 1918 she showed only one spark of offensive capacity in her futile June attack on the Italians. Turkey's man-power was rapidly collapsing, and what little remained was soon to be dissipated in wild Caucasian adventures. Bulgaria's war-weariness was patent and natural, for she had conquered all that she coveted and longed only to secure it. The American minister who remained in Sofia was pulling many influential persons towards the Entente by subtle strings. The crumbling alliance of our enemies could not therefore afford to wait on events.

In Germany itself signs of disintegration were scarcely visible on the surface. The people as a whole were facing the fourth war-winter with the same patient endurance, though the rigour of the blockade made food more and more difficult to obtain and less palatable, deprived the young of milk and fats, and enormously increased the deaths of infants and tuberculous persons. The whole country was growing out-at-elbows. Almost every article that could be bought was a dingy or repellent substitute for the original.[1] It is surprising, not that the Independent Socialists made some subterranean headway, but that visible unrest was not general. In January, it is true, great strikes broke out, which involved some 500,000 workmen, principally at Berlin. Their object was perhaps mainly political, to protest against the treatment of the Russians at Brest-Litovsk, but they collapsed speedily before the resolution of the authorities. Ludendorff, however, was so much disturbed that he sent a secret order to each army commander instructing him to keep two battalions ready for use against the civilian population.

If then a speedy end to the war was so imperatively

[1] A selection of these can still be seen at the Imperial War Museum.

necessary, could it be obtained by waiting in an attitude of defence? Clearly not. No responsible person now believed that the submarines could bring England to her knees. On the contrary it was tacitly admitted in all calculations of chances that the late summer would see a great army of Americans in France; though a year back German naval officers had contemptuously remarked that their only means of crossing the Atlantic was to swim or fly. It was impossible to suppose that the Entente would dissipate their enfeebled armies in disastrous attacks, when so puissant a reinforcement would build up an ever-increasing superiority.

There remained therefore but two alternatives; either so to use the favourable military moment as to display an attitude of conciliation, which would bring an acceptable peace, or to attack as soon as possible with the uttermost vehemence. The former course was pressed upon Ludendorff by Prince Max of Baden, and had the secret support both of the German and Bavarian Crown Princes. In particular it was urged that Germany should uncompromisingly renounce any pretensions direct or indirect upon the independence of Belgium. Such a declaration would undoubtedly have done much to divide at least British opinion, as giving real evidence of the desired 'change of heart' on the part of Germany's rulers, which had been so often laid down as a necessary preliminary of negotiations. But even apart from the soldiers, the statesmen could not bring themselves to give up what they believed to be their best bargaining counter. Even in July, when Kühlmann, the Secretary of State, had renounced all hope of ultimate victory, he excused himself from making any public statement on the subject.

While the voice of official Germany remained dumb on this subject, it would have been of small avail to start a 'peace offensive' against the Entente peoples over the heads of their rulers. The Governments of England and France were indeed deeply anxious, but they maintained an unwavering front against Germany. Broad hints of conciliation and of the revision of war-aims were thrown out to the allies of the Kaiser, in accordance with Lloyd George's policy of 'knocking down the props'. But the only detailed list of conditions, Wilson's famous Fourteen Points,[1] enunciated in January, was then scorned by the enemy as another proof, expressed in more general terms, of the old 'Vernichtungs-will' ('desire for annihilation') on the part of the Entente. If anything was lacking to harden the hearts of the Entente peoples to brave the uttermost perils, it was supplied by the harsh terms of the dictated treaty of Brest-Litovsk.

Thus Ludendorff considered his only alternative to be that of immediate battle. Though he dwells on the number of deserters living unmolested at home, or escaped to Holland, where a regular bureau for assisting them across the frontier had been established, he allows that the general spirit of the army was sound, and even that it was now raised to a pitch of enthusiasm long unknown at the prospect of the offensive. For the moment he had troops enough; with the divisions set free from the East he had a superiority of about 10 per cent. in men, but a much larger proportion of fresh divisions. His real danger would lie in the question of reinforcements. Though about a million fit men were engaged in the munitions industry, it was found impossible to 'comb out' more than 30,000. Such serious encroachments had been made on the capital of youth that very few new conscripts could be available in the field before the end of the year. Lack of man-power therefore made it imperative that 'the gambler's blow' should be as swift and terrible as possible.

Ludendorff himself approached his task in no boastful spirit. He told the Kaiser that 'it was the greatest military task ever imposed upon an army. I believe that I . . . am more than any one impressed by the immensity of the operation. . . . We must not imagine that this offensive will be like those in Galicia or Italy; it will be an immense struggle that will begin at one point, continue at another, and take a long time; it is difficult, but it will be victorious.'

[1] The text is given on pp. 574–576.

His aim, then, was by a series of terrific blows to break the enemy's continuous entrenched position in pieces; to make it impossible for them, through lack of reserves, to hold together in open warfare; to deal defeat to their separate armies; and, if not to reduce them to complete military impotence, at least so to break the war-will of their peoples as to make it impossible for them to await the long and doubtful process of rebuilding their shattered fortune with tardy American aid.

He proposed to accomplish the first act as follows. His attack was to be delivered on the British army, both because Great Britain was now the mainspring of the Alliance, and because he considered its soldiers less tactically skilful than the French.[1] It was long debated whether the blow should fall in Flanders on either side of Armentières, or farther south between Arras and La Fère. In favour of the former it was pointed out that the main British reserves were here crowded together in a small room with the sea at their back and on their left flank. Communication and distance made it difficult for the French to come quickly to their aid in force. Incidentally the ports on the Channel might fall; the Channel mouth, and that of the Thames, would be closed to traffic; long-range bombardments would annoy the Kentish coast. As against these advantages the time-factor was held decisive. The ground could not be ready before the middle of April; even then the oozy valleys of the Lys and Lawes might be impassable. The blow must fall sooner. So, while preparations for this attack (code name 'Saint George') went on, it was relegated to a *pis aller*, to be employed only in the event of ill success farther south. Here the harder

[1] See von Hindenburg, *Out of my Life* (1920), p. 330: 'The Englishman did not understand how to control rapid changes in the situation. His methods were too rigid. . . . These phenomena are due to the lack of appropriate training in peace-time. Even a war that lasts for years cannot wholly make good the effects of his inefficient preparation. But what the Englishman lacked in skill he made up, at any rate partially, by his obstinacy in sticking to his task and his objective.' To judge, however, from German reminiscences and novels, these criticisms were rather the view of the General Staff than of the rank and file.

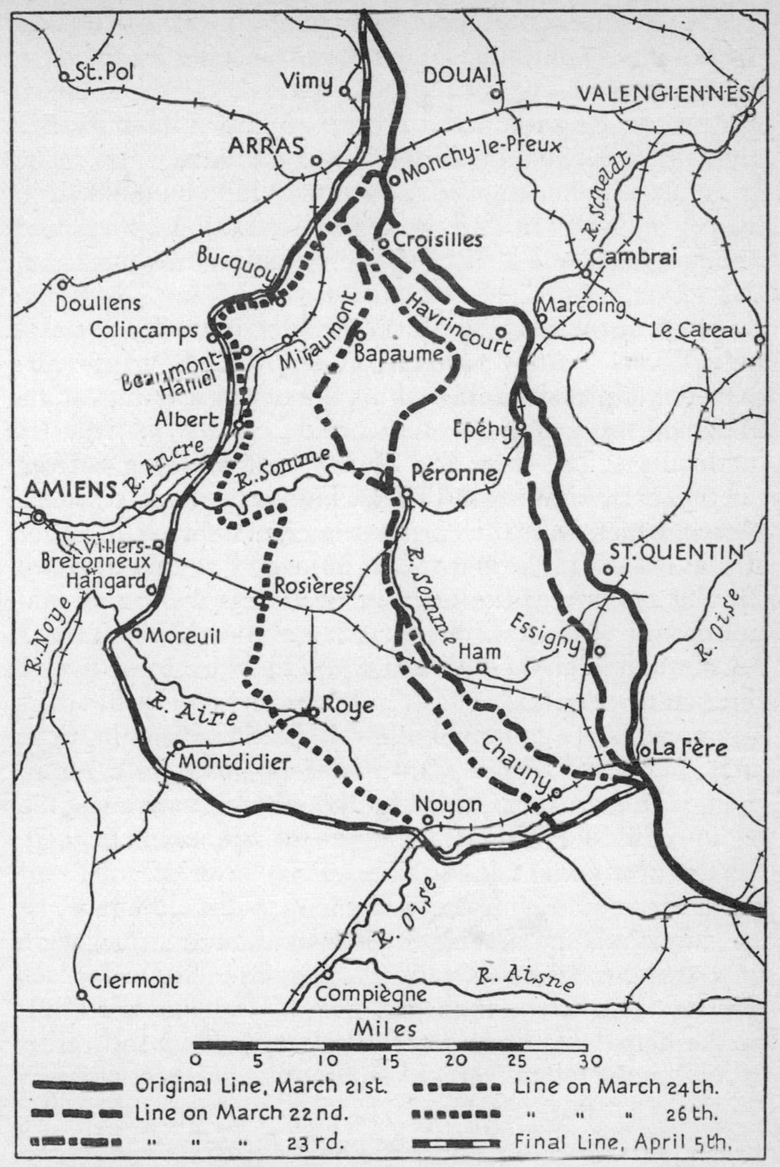

MAP 27. The British Front from Arras to Noyon (March 1918)

soil would normally allow great troop-movements after the beginning of March. The date was fixed for the 21st, as eight weeks' preparation was necessary, and the position in the East remained too obscure for Ludendorff to give his final definite orders until January 20th. The entire front to be attacked, now wholly held by the British, from Vimy to Barisis on the Oise near La Fère, measured about seventy miles. Behind the northern two-thirds lay the great crater-fields of the last two years, partially repaired and covered with good roads, but still a formidable obstacle. They might well delay the advent of really open warfare, at attaining which the new German training above all things aimed.

Moreover, the direction of the line, which ran from north-west to south-east, did not favour the main strategic object, which was a deep north-westerly thrust, in order to roll up the bulk of the British armies against the sea. Finally, mighty as the German resources were, they did not permit a simultaneous attack on the whole front. The northern limit on the 21st was to be Croisilles, some twelve miles south of Arras. The British would therefore have the advantage of an immovable flank, based on the bastions of Monchy and Vimy, with a well-fortified city between them. This area was indeed to be assailed as soon as the heavy artillery could be moved north, but, as will be seen, the delay of a week made the defence impregnable, and went far to ruin the whole German plan. Even so the operation was the vastest of the war. Three armies were to be employed with sixty-three divisions in line or in close reserve. The two on the right, the XVIIth and the IInd, the principal blade of attack, belonged to Rupprecht's group; on the left the famous von Hutier, the hero of Riga, commanded the XVIIIth, which was placed under the Crown Prince. This was done partly for political reasons, but mainly because, as Ludendorff confided to a friend, if all three armies depended upon the same group, the influence of General Head-quarters in directing the battle would be unduly diminished.

Hutier's role was at first to be merely defensive; his advance was to be limited to the Saint-Crozat Canal and the Somme, in order to form a resolute flank guard against the expected French counter-attacks from the south-west. A few days before the 21st he was encouraged, in the event of good success, to aim at the more ambitious objective of Péronne. The subordinate part cast for this brilliant general is very curious, and has never been adequately explained. A glance at the map will show that a north-westerly wheel by his army would have the double advantage of dividing the French and British armies, and of outflanking the Somme crater-field from the south. Ludendorff does not seem to have known how weak the opposition was; probably, like his enemies, he over-estimated the difficulties of crossing the Oise marshes which lay for nine miles in front of his left flank. Further, he was unaware of the completeness with which he had deluded the French Head-quarters, and thought that large reserves would be available round Compiègne to strike this army dangerously in flank if it made rapid progress.

Actually, as we shall see, Hutier ran through all organized opposition with embarrassing swiftness, but though he put the Allied armies for a few days into the imminent danger of disruption, it was already too late for German Head-quarters to use his success to any serious strategical advantage. This failure is the more surprising when Ludendorff tells us that he was primarily influenced by tactical considerations, 'first among them being the weakness of the enemy'. Yet, though the British forces south of Arras were much weaker than those in Flanders, he attacked the strongest portion of them with his own greatest strength, and persisted in the effort, even when its failure was manifest. Here he seems false to his own doctrine that 'a strategical plan which ignores the tactical factor is doomed to failure'. But apart from the choice of locality, the whole tactical framework was admirable, and was mainly due to Ludendorff's own inexhaustible mastery over detail. He relied on three principles, surprise, speed, and continuity of action. These three all dovetail into one another, and in their harmonious blending he found the solution of his great problem.

Surprise is obviously twofold. A man can be surprised when he is not expecting a blow at all. This Byng achieved at Cambrai, and Ludendorff on the Chemin des Dames in May 1918. Or again a blow may be expected, but the method of its delivery may be such that no effective parry is possible. This was the result obtained on March 21st. The British knew where and when the stroke would fall. But at the same time the lack of military unity still inherent in the Alliance enabled Ludendorff to obtain part of the effects of a complete strategic surprise. Until the last few days his reserves were massed far behind the front and in so central a position that they could be used no less readily against the French on either side of Rheims or even at Verdun. Pétain was so convinced that his army was the prospective victim that he made his own rearward arrangements accordingly, thereby making any battle-co-operation with Haig tardy and ineffective.

Ludendorff's initial success is chiefly due to the way in which he turned his best infantry, elaborately trained as storm troops, into specialists. The idea was not a new one; all the armies had been working at it in 1917, but no such degree of realization had yet been won. Small detachments, not in line, but working together in small groups, were practised in 'infiltration'. These picked men pushed through gaps in the outpost line (now nowhere continuous), taking advantage of such natural features as a valley or sunken road, limited by no fixed objective, ignoring strong points, which they could circumvent and which could be left to be encircled by those following behind. Their rate of progress was limited for the first few miles by their own barrage, which moved forward at a kilometre per hour. But their prime object was to keep the battle constantly alive and rolling. Composed in about equal proportions of riflemen and light machine-gunners, they had in the closest support under their local commands detachments of heavy machine-guns, light trench-mortars, and even field-guns, with a few pioneers and sappers. They were thus tiny mixed forces of all arms, light and mobile, infinitely different from the heavy waves of human beasts of burden such as had been broken on the Somme. The whole of the zone whence the attack was to be delivered was organized in immense depth; from the moment when the foremost infantry advanced, the answering tremor ran back through all the waiting masses from the battle-front. Most important of all, the foremost divisions were to control those next behind them. Thus it was hoped to anticipate the reinforcements which might be required against centres of resistance before the attack had been brought to a standstill. 'When once the cry for assistance has gone up, it is for that very reason already too late', wrote Ludendorff in one of his memoranda.

Such in general were the most original features of the plan which proposed to win, at the earliest moment, open warfare with its incalculable opportunities for rapid manœuvre.

II

We must now consider the position in the Entente countries, and see what steps were being taken to combat this enormous menace. The year had progressed towards its close into a climax of supreme disillusionment, Russia knocked out, Italy dangerously reeling, and the hope of Cambrai promptly extinguished.

Yet it is true that these disappointments and the returning shadow of the drawn German sword in the West produced a quickened criticism of the conduct of the war, but in no way a weakening of will. On the contrary the spirit of France had been strongly raised up. In Clemenceau, who became Premier in November, the country found the incarnation of that realistic spirit of impassioned yet stoical heroism which had made revolutionary France the wonder of the world. This tough fighter of 76, compact with energy, who had been in public life for nearly fifty years, who had witnessed the siege of Paris, who as Mayor of Montmartre had tried to intercede in the fratricidal savagery of the Commune, had at last come to his own. His time till now had mainly been spent in opposition; his nicknames 'The Tiger' and 'the Destroyer of Ministries' aptly suggest his qualities. Throughout the war his grimly outspoken criticisms had brought him into many conflicts with the censorship. He had ironically changed the name of his paper from *L'Homme libre* to *L'Homme enchaîné*. Now finally set in power, he enunciated and lived up to one simple policy of direction 'Je fais la guerre', a motto which he was to follow not less consistently throughout the course of the peace negotiations.

With a vigorous hand he sorted out the traitors, intriguers, and pacificists. Malvy, late Minister of the Interior, Caillaux, that sinister deputy, were thrown into prison, to be impeached next year for intelligence with the enemy.

The French were by now reaping the full advantage of one great war asset to set off against their cruel losses and their invaded territory. The fertility of their soil and the proverbial industry of its tillers rendered the country more nearly self-sufficient than any of the European belligerents. There was indeed a great lack of coal, but food, and fats in particular, were relatively plentiful. The crawling hours of discomfort spent in queues, the nerve-strain and physical deterioration which follow persistent under-nourishment, never loomed large in the French war-experience.

In England the economic situation, while in no way comparable to that of Germany, was yet far more straitened than that of France. But the curve of improvement was creeping up with a steady slowness since its lowest point in May 1917. The convoys were holding the submarines in check, and the drastic reorganization of shipping suggested by Chiozza Money had improved food-supply. Lord Rhondda, the Food Controller, to whom the civilian population owed an immense debt, gradually perfected a rationing system, mainly confined to meat, sugar, and butter, which worked more smoothly and fairly than any of its counterparts in other countries. In most industries, and notably in those connected with the prosecution of the war, wages had risen more rapidly than prices (the latter being officially controlled for nearly all articles of common consumption), and in many great towns and mining areas a flamboyancy of expenditure moved the anger or envy of soldiers on leave.

One great weapon by which Germany had hoped to break what was called 'the home front' had crumbled in her hands. The Zeppelin raids, which had been intermittent since 1915, came finally to an end in the autumn of 1917. Aeroplanes had gradually mastered the technique of destroying them by tracer bullets when they had been seized and held by the converging beams of searchlights, and several had been shot down in flames round the outskirts of London, their crews perishing miserably with them. Their last appearance over the Capital in November 1917 ended in complete catastrophe. A fleet of them, having shut off their engines in order to float over the objective unperceived, was caught by a fierce northerly wind, and driven down in various French localities, one actually making its forced descent in Algeria.

The casualties which they inflicted were singularly small,[1] and the military importance of their considerable damage to property was almost completely negligible. On the other hand, large numbers of trained gunners and pilots had to be kept at home away from service in France.[2] The transport of munitions was constantly stopped for some hours, as experience showed that it was safest to keep all trains within a threatened area motionless until 'all clear' was signalled. Finally, reports from munition factories were apt to show that efficiency and output showed a drop of about 60 per cent. on the day after a raid in the neighbourhood. The Zeppelins were therefore more effective in interfering with the war than in intimidating

[1] Fifty-two raids killed and wounded 1,806 people, of whom seventy were military.

[2] The largest number of German machines employed in a single raid was 41. More than 600 British aeroplanes were kept for Home Defence, of which 400 were of first-rate quality.

civilians. But the opposite effect was aimed at and achieved by the new mass attack by fleets of hostile aeroplanes.[1] Folkestone, Margate, and London were first bombed in broad daylight, then, as the defences grew more effective, by moonlight. For a week at the end of September, lighted by a brilliant hunter's moon, relays of enemy machines kept London under fire for several hours almost every night. If these visitations could have been continued for a full month, they might have caused complete moral collapse. As it was some sections of the population were reduced to panic, especially the poor aliens of the East End. The Tubes were packed solid with a shuddering crowd; while many less indigent people travelled westwards by train on clear evenings to camp out in fields round Slough or Reading. Though London had enjoyed a five-months' respite at the time of the Armistice, it was noticed that when the maroon proclaimed its signature, many people fled from the street into basements or stations, as at the sound of that official warning of a raid.[2]

Curiously enough Paris, though so much nearer the front, suffered less. German public opinion was particularly clamorous for the attacks on London, mainly because Great Britain alone of the belligerents had preserved her territory inviolate against invasion. Moreover, to reach Paris a pilot would have to fly over the defences of the zone behind the lines, every kilometre of it alive with guns and aeroplanes. Finally, a dummy Paris was constructed, where such prominent features as the Place de la Concorde were simulated by the side of a loop in the Marne similar to that of the Seine through the real Paris. This decoy, it was claimed, enticed away many would-be raiders. Paris, however, was to endure her own peculiar trial in 1918 in the shelling from the long-range gun. But neither in London nor in Paris did the fear of un-

[1] The German machines called Gothas were improved copies of the first English Handley-Page, which was sent over to France in charge of an inexperienced pilot. He landed it intact on the German aerodrome at Lille.

[2] Casualties from aeroplane raids amounted to 2,469, of whom 400 were military.

organized and helpless sections of the population embarrass the governments in prosecuting the war.

The growing distrust of British strategy in France, so long felt by the British Premier, was fanned to flame by the Italian disaster. Were these prodigal frontal attacks always to be followed by the autumnal destruction of another member of the Entente? After Serbia and Rumania, Italy? The event had been utterly unforeseen even in the best-informed quarters. Colonel Repington, reputed as one of the shrewdest critics in Europe, had written in *The Times*: 'General Cadorna will no doubt welcome this offensive.' It had seemed impossible either that the Germans could spare seven divisions from France, or that they could accomplish such great things with so small a spear. Lloyd George no longer refrained from attacking Haig (by implication) in public. He contrasted the British victories 'taking a few hundred of the enemies' soldiers, and wresting a ruined village from his cruel grip' with the enormous results of Caporetto. He personally insisted upon the dismissal of the Chief-of-Staff, Kiggell, and the Chief Intelligence Officer at G.H.Q., Charteris, and hoped that the Commander-in-Chief would resign. This, however, the latter was never prepared to do, unless he was convinced that an order given to him by a civilian minister would endanger the British army.

Having thus failed to gain the desired end by the method of pin-pricks, the Premier devised a plan both for securing greater unity of command, and for limiting the strategic independence of Haig. A Supreme War Council was set up, consisting of the Prime Ministers of each of the principal Allied Powers, each to be attended by another minister of Cabinet rank. This step merely regularized and made official the habit of intermittent Inter-Allied Conferences. Its importance lay in what it was intended to do. No British minister was as yet prepared to support a single commander-in-chief. The theoretical arguments against such a course were indeed unassailable, and the Nivelle experiment had been most unfortunate in practice. But the statesmen were to be aided by a technical military committee of four members. Lloyd George aimed at enlarging this body into a strategical executive, and here he received the warm support of Clemenceau, who foresaw that, with Foch as its agreed chairman, French influence would be paramount. Its first duty was to create and control an Inter-Allied general reserve of thirty divisions. Haig, however, wrecked this plan by refusing to contribute the British quota. He acted on the principle, which he was loyally to follow after accepting Foch as Generalissimo, 'I can deal with a man but not with a Committee'. He had only eight divisions in general reserve, under his own control, and he was asked to contribute seven to this experimental 'pool'. It is difficult to quarrel with his contention that he would have been robbed of any effective guarantee that his responsibility for the safety of his army could thus be maintained. It is true that his arrangement with Pétain for mutual succour worked very badly in the day of trial, and that the Committee might have sent him larger and readier help. This, however, reflects rather on Haig's ability as a negotiator than on the soundness of the principle upon which he based his decision.

The War Council paid polite lip-service to Lloyd George's scheme for knocking out Turkey, but emasculated it by the proviso that no troops were to be withdrawn from France for the purpose. Its importance in directing the war was never great, and became steadily less after the appointment of Foch as Generalissimo. Its principal usefulness lay in the co-ordination of Allied transport of munitions and supplies by a permanent body sitting at Versailles.

Though the plan in effect achieved scarcely any of Lloyd George's desires, it brought about the resignation of Robertson, whose dogged persistence in 'killing Germans' on the Western Front had created a complete incompatibility between two naturally disharmonious temperaments. He was succeeded by Sir Henry Wilson, the most lucid, supple, and ambitious of British generals, of whom a military colleague cruelly said that he got into a state of sexual excitement whenever he saw a politician.

Meanwhile the British army was preparing for the blow which as G.H.Q. correctly surmised was about to be directed against it. The question of man-power was a difficult one. Five divisions had gone to Italy. The losses of the past year—about 760,000 in France alone—had been only partially replaced, with the result that divisions had been reduced from twelve to nine battalions. This reduction seriously interfered with the existing organization of every division, and with the tactical handling of every brigade, while the breaking up of battalions was often bitterly resented by officers and men and tended to lower moral. Lloyd George, however, considered the West to be 'over-insured' as a defensive front, and Haig was not allowed to receive any of the 760,000 grouped in the different eastern theatres, or of the 300,000 'general service men' retained in England.[1]

He was also obliged by political pressure to take over some fourteen additional miles of line south of Saint-Quentin. This obviously diminished the British reserves, but proportionately increased those of the French. It proved in effect a blow to the Allied cause, but only because the French reserves were not available when and where they were required.

The British order of battle, as Ludendorff foresaw, was always strategically conditional on the amount of room available for retreat. Men must stand thickest in the cramped corridors of Flanders, where a recoil of twenty miles would be fatal. It was only south of Arras that so much ground could be yielded without endangering any vital centre. Moreover, it might be argued that here the

[1] It should be mentioned that in January 1918 the Admiralty still regarded it as not improbable that an invading force of 70,000 Germans could be transported across the North Sea (see Sir W. Robertson, *Soldiers and Statesmen 1914–18* (1926), vol. ii, p. 284). The actual decrease of the British army in France in March 1918 was 180,000 men, if compared with the same date in the previous year.

old crater-fields and the line of the Somme would impose powerful obstacles to an attack which was likely to diminish in impetus as it progressed in distance. Hence the British strength declined progressively towards the south, so that while Byng disposed of seventeen infantry divisions for a front of twenty-six miles, Gough on the right had only fourteen infantry and three cavalry divisions to protect forty-two miles. This extreme weakness, which was to prove so disastrous, was justified by G.H.Q. on the grounds that the Oise marshes would prevent an attack south of Saint-Quentin and that French reserves would be speedily available at need.[1] Haig was not convinced that the 5th army would be heavily engaged, in spite of Gough's confident assertions when he found that Hutier was commanding against him. In fact, the Secret Summary at G.H.Q. stated as late as March 16th: 'No serious attack is to be expected south of the Bapaume–Cambrai road.'

It is therefore clear that the violent abuse levelled against Gough after the virtual destruction of his army is undeserved. He was given an impossible task. Still, it was unfortunate that he should have been maintained in command of this army. His conduct of Passchendaele had destroyed the confidence of most regimental officers and the rank and file in the efficiency of his staff. It is well known that most units hailed with relief a transfer to Plumer. It is probable that Rawlinson, who was at the moment at Versailles, would have kept a firmer grip on the battle, and by co-ordinating the retirement of the various units more effectively, would have minimized an inevitable defeat. As no inquiry has ever been held into its causes, in spite of the promise made to Gough on his dismissal, such evidence as is yet available on many points is insufficient to allow the historian to dogmatize. For instance, we cannot be sure that everything possible was

[1] Haig certainly had a right to count on this. Elaborate arrangements had been made on paper with Pétain; see G. A. B. Dewar and J. H. Boraston, *Sir Douglas Haig's Command* (1922), vol. ii, pp. 40–1.

done to improve the rearward defences, which the French admittedly had handed over in a state of shocking neglect. There was much bitter contemporary criticism on this score. Gough defends himself in detail in his book.[1] But some of his justifying figures are very strange. It seems impossible that, out of at least 200,000 soldiers and 35,000 civilians, only 2,400 should have been available for digging trenches and other defence-work in the middle of February. Gough had won all his fame as an attacking general: he had not the temperament of the exact organizer of methodical retreat.

The system of defence employed was closely copied from the German methods elaborated at Passchendaele, and needs no detailed description. It consisted of an outpost line of mutually supporting posts and redoubts protected by continuous wire. Rather less than a third of the whole strength served as its garrison, with a number of field-guns in close support. Its object was to delay and disorganize an attack, until the battle-zone about a mile farther back could be fully manned and ready. The latter was a complicated system, from 2,000 to 4,000 yards deep, the various trenches being connected by diagonal switches to divert any partial break-through into blind alleys swept by enfilade fire. Upon this reef it was hoped that the German assault would break, as all such attacks of the Entente had broken. For while the front was everywhere reasonably complete, the rearward defences were generally mere scratches in the ground thinly guarded by wire.

The trench garrisons had all been in a state of vigilant expectation for at least a fortnight before Ludendorff struck. The enemy had made preparations for attack on so many sectors that he was at no great pains to conceal the visible signs. Round Saint-Quentin observers noticed mounds like great beehives, at intervals of 100 yards, running north and south for several miles. It was correctly conjectured that these were forward ammunition-dumps. The British Staff knew the day forty-eight hours

[1] Sir H. de la Poer Gough, *The Fifth Army* (1931), pp. 223 sqq.

beforehand. But they had no idea that so great a flood of strength was about to be unloosed. During the last six nights the great concentration marches of the enemy were being stealthily accomplished,[1] though Ludendorff, that grim realist, complains that the men would sing *en route*. Our aeroplanes had not yet perfected the technique of scouring roads at night by flying low and dropping lights.

German thoroughness and forethought had won the first victory of preparation, and was now to attempt the supreme hazard of decisive battle.

[1] In many cases troops were kept on the move till the last moment. One division marched thirty-two kilometres on the night of 20th–21st, taking part in the attack on the following morning.

XXXI

THE LAST GERMAN BID FOR VICTORY

I

For the next four months after March 21st, 1918, the enemy imposed his will by battle. He made five great attacks, in the first of which alone he used half his entire strength in the west. Thrice his tactics proved to be a master-key to unlock the great fortified system and to open the path to freedom of manœuvre. In extent of territory he won ten times more than the obliterated scraps wrested piecemeal by the Entente during the course of 1917. He advanced his line within forty miles of Paris. He took 225,000 prisoners and 2,500 guns, and inflicted nearly a million casualties. Yet this great achievement proved to be not merely a victory without a morrow, but one which had sown behind it the quick seeds of irremediable defeat. The initiative had scarcely dropped from Ludendorff's hand before Foch seized it, and in less than another four months Germany was thankfully accepting an armistice, scarcely distinguishable in its terms from a capitulation. The causes of this reversal of fortune—perhaps the swiftest and most dramatic in history—have, paradoxically enough, to be sought in the analysis of a series of striking successes. In fact, it was of momentous consequence for the Entente that the first blow was tactically so encouraging—had it been stopped dead, the Germans might in discouragement have reverted to defence. In that event their line, far shorter and straighter, and held by a far stronger and less exhausted garrison, would almost certainly have carried them in comparative safety through the campaigning season of the year. In 1919 it is improbable that defeat would have involved the terms dictated at Versailles, for a victory mainly achieved by American arms would have given President Wilson the power of imposing his 'Fourteen Points' in his own way.

II

On March 20th, 1918, Ludendorff, his preparations being now complete, anxiously interviewed his meteorological expert, for it was raining and the wind was unfavourable for gas. Partially reassured, he sent the signal to carry out the next day's programme.

At 4.30 next morning 6,000 guns started the bombardment in unison. The high-velocity guns attacked distant railway-stations; Saint-Pol, twenty-five miles away, received many hits. All the British batteries were drenched with gas; cross-roads and every tactical point in the whole trench system were subjected to an uninterrupted hail; trench-mortars aided in obliterating the wire and the redoubts of the outpost-line. All this terrific activity was completely blind. A dense, white mist blanketed the whole great battle-field. It was said to be the thickest of the whole winter, and visibility was restricted to twenty or forty yards. It had not lifted at all when the infantry came over about 9.45, nor did the sun pierce it until close on noon. Similar fogs preluded each of the cloudless days which followed. Much controversy has been expended over it. Some English writers affirm that without its aid the attack would have been shattered; and they are able to point to the great defeat of the 'Mars' onslaught before Arras on March 28th, where, under a clear sky, artillery and machine-guns wrecked the enemy's attempt with great slaughter as it reached our outposts. On the other hand, Ludendorff writes: 'Fog impeded and retarded our movements, and prevented our superior training and leadership from reaping its full reward. This was the predominant opinion, but a few thought it an advantage.' Gough, with a generous candour towards his opponents, expressed the opinion that 'On the whole the fog favoured our Fifth Army',[1] on the ground that, though the initial losses of the enemy in breaking through would have been

[1] W. S. Sparrow, *The Fifth Army in March 1918* (1920), letter from Gough quoted pp. 59–60. In Gough's own book, *The Fifth Army*, published eleven years later, he seems to have changed his opinion, see pp. 261–3.

greatly increased by clear weather, he would have been able to develop his success with greater rapidity. The writer's own opinion is that on the balance the fog favoured the attack. In the first place the bombardment was entirely upon fixed objects determined beforehand. For this no observation was necessary; the knowledge of ballistics and atmospherics had now reduced firing from the map to an exact science. Moreover, the fog made the gas hang about and increased its effectiveness beyond expectation.[1] The defence, on the other hand, could not fire at the moving targets of assembling troops, which could have been spotted only by our infantry or aeroplanes. Hence our counter-preparation was singularly weak.[2] The isolation of our advanced posts was absolute; many small bodies found themselves surrounded before they knew that any attack had begun. Telephonic communication had been almost completely destroyed by the bombardment, and runners found the greatest difficulty in finding their way to report-centres. The enemy, on the other hand, carried his own wires with him as he advanced. The German subordinate commanders had studied their trench-maps so minutely and so intelligently that the quickness of their infiltration seems hardly to have suffered. There is much remarkable evidence to this effect from survivors of the 5th army. In several places practically the whole day's advance had been achieved before the sky cleared at noon. For instance, Ronssoy in the north, three miles behind the line, had by then been lost; in the south the battle-zone had been penetrated between Essigny and Benay.

The results of the first day did not satisfy Ludendorff's expectation. Though he had laid down no fixed objectives, he had hoped to overrun the bulk of the British artillery, and so leave its infantry practically without support. But

[1] Kronprinz Rupprecht, *Mein Kriegstagebuch* (1929), vol. ii, p. 344.

[2] Ibid., p. 344. Constantly confirmed in German regimental histories. On parts of the 3rd army front, where it was sufficiently clear for aeroplanes to go up at once, the British barrage was effective and the enemy was held: see Jones, *War in the Air*, 1934, vol. iv, pp. 293–5.

the number of captured guns barely reached 150. Further, his converging assaults at the base of the Cambrai salient had failed to cut off the garrison of three divisions lodged therein.[1] But the strain on the thin British line made itself manifest during the night, when Gough withdrew his extreme right some seven miles behind the Crozat Canal. This was done precipitately, and many of the bridges remained passable by the enemy.

This wing remained in a state of dismal flux, and on the 22nd the enemy broke right through into open country north-west of Saint-Quentin. This catastrophe, reinforced by the false news that the Crozat Canal had been forced, induced Gough to order a general retirement behind the Somme on the 23rd. It proved a bad mistake. In the hurry and confusion of the evacuation enormous quantities of wounded, stores, and material were lost. Nor did the river prove effective as a barrier. The railway bridges, which the French were responsible for destroying, remained practically intact; the long drought had so diminished the stream that it was fordable at many points, and there was no prepared line on the left bank. Gough had indeed been sorely tried. Only one division from G.H.Q. reserve reached him on the 22nd, nor did any French help arrive till next morning, when a single regiment, with only thirty rounds of ammunition per man, was decanted out of lorries.

Meanwhile this swift sagging on the right increased the difficulties of the 3rd British army. Byng's left was indeed holding von Below in check by a most stubborn resistance, which never faltered throughout the battle and reduced its enemies to impotence. But the IInd German army, driving onwards north of Péronne, forced a dangerous gap between the two British armies, which is described in the official dispatch as 'critical'. It was a day of high hopes for Ludendorff. He believed that the whole British front was

[1] Very great importance was attached to its swift reduction, as the heavy guns employed there were necessary for the 'Mars' attack at Arras, which would have to be held up until they could be dispatched north.

on the point of disintegration. His original plan was enlarged. Von Below was still to thrust at Saint-Pol, with the object of rolling the northern armies against the Channel. Marwitz was to push straight on to Amiens. If that great railway-junction fell into his hands the French and British could no longer keep touch. Hutier was to make his principal effort south-west, smashing the French reinforcements piecemeal and threatening the approaches to Paris.[1] Pétain was still most miserly in his help. He could not shake off the nightmare belief that the enemy was on the point of dealing him an equally heavy blow between Soissons and Rheims; and would not draw seriously upon the reserves which he had placed to foil it. Nor were matters improved on the 24th when a French army-group became responsible for the whole line south of the Somme, Gough being placed under its orders. The French divisions on the right retreated continuously, edging away in a south-westerly direction. Meanwhile the 3rd army was being rapidly hustled across the old battle-fields of 1916, although Byng's cavalry, finding in retreat a brilliant scope for that usefulness continually denied them in attack, did just make it possible to maintain a cordon across the gaps, cutting down the advance-guards and keeping touch. It seemed as if a broad way must be opened to Amiens. That evening Haig and Pétain met at Dury. The British Commander came away with the conviction that he was to be left to his fate, while the French armies concentrated to cover Paris.[2] Throughout all this crisis Haig

[1] See Rupprecht's account of the orders (ibid., vol. ii, p. 351): even he was convinced that a strategic victory was on the point of achievement.

[2] This was certainly Pétain's intention, apparently acting upon instructions from his Government. Whether formal orders to this effect were given is disputed. For the evidence see G. A. B. Dewar and J. H. Boraston, *Sir Douglas Haig's Command* (1922), vol. ii, p. 115; Recouly, *La Bataille de Foch* (1920), p. 8. Gen. Mangin, *Comment finit la guerre* (1921), p. 171, professes to give an actual 'Directive' of Pétain dated March 24, which runs: 'Avant tout, maintenir solide l'armature des armées françaises. Ensuite, si possible, conserver la liaison avec les forces britanniques.' Poincaré, *Au service de la France*, vol. x (1933), p. 88, also states that Foch showed him the order of retreat given by Pétain. On the other hand P. Painlevé, *Comment j'ai nommé Foch et Pétain*

maintained a profound calm of spirit. His inherited Calvinism, so profoundly ingrained in his personality, gave him an unshaken inward conviction of victory. To ensure it, he determined to subordinate his own independence, and to bring about unity of command. He telegraphed to the War Minister, Lord Milner, and to the Chief of the Imperial General Staff, urging them to cross immediately. On the 26th at the little town of Doullens, with its memories of old French conquests in the great citadel on the hill built by Vauban, took place the famous conference which elevated Foch.[1] So uncertain was the outlook that tanks were stationed at the eastern exits, lest hostile cavalry might break in. Poincaré presided as representative of France. The tension between the two Commanders-in-Chief was manifest. When Haig came into the room Pétain whispered: 'There is a man who will be forced to see his army capitulate in the open field.' Pétain's address to the conference created a bad impression. His scheme for bringing up reserves suggested a deliberation which might be fatal. For it was agreed that Amiens must be protected at all costs. Foch, who was present, was unanimously appointed 'to co-ordinate the operations of the Allies on the whole Western Front'.[2] With his usual sly, searching cynicism Clemenceau turned to the new man of destiny saying: 'Maintenant vous êtes content.' Nor can it be doubted that this ardent, magnetic soldier welcomed the responsibility, though his first imminent task was to prevent a lost battle from becoming a por-

(1924), p. 293, professes to give Pétain's own words at the interview, in which the latter pointed out that the separation of the two armies would be the inevitable result of the methods of conducting the retreat, which were then in force. He denied, however, that he had given any orders to that effect.

[1] Clemenceau said to Milner on meeting him that day: 'C'est aujourd'hui une journée historique. Le sort de la guerre va se fixer' (Poincaré, vol. x, p. 89).

[2] His powers were more exactly defined on April 3rd, when it was agreed that full tactical freedom should be left to the commanders of the national armies, and that each should have a right of appeal to his Government, if he considered that the orders given him endangered the security of his army. The actual title of Commander-in-Chief was not given Foch until April 24th.

tentous disaster. Though his immediate orders against any further retreat proved impracticable, the new direction with its energy and confidence was soon to have its effect not only on the armies but among the population of the Allies.

Meanwhile crisis succeeded crisis in the battle. The 3rd army finally pinned itself securely to the upper Ancre on the 26th, but not before the enemy, flooding through a deep gap farther north, had threatened to turn it by occupying Colincamps. Here the Anzacs, just arrived from the north, drove them back with the aid of the new 'whippet' tanks, which thus received an auspicious baptism of fire. This action ended all serious anxiety north of the Somme. Rupprecht noted on that day that the German XVIIth army was completely exhausted. Yet Ludendorff would not desist—he still hoped to break down the strong pillar of Arras. On the 28th the 'Mars' attack was launched; it was a disastrous defeat. The 3rd army there was composed of some of our best troops, including the Guards. They were standing on carefully selected ground, having voluntarily retired from any weak spots or dangerous salients. The enemy, crippled by the losses among his storm troops, reverted to more primitive tactics. His men advanced with great resolution, but in some places shoulder to shoulder six lines deep. Artillery and machine-guns swept them away. At the close of the day eleven divisions had not made the slightest impression upon our battle-zone. Any faded hope of reaching Saint-Pol was completely extinguished.

But in the south a protracted battle was still swaying dangerously westward. On the 27th Montdidier, the principal detraining centre of the French reinforcements, was taken. Debeney put up a cry of despair to the commander of his group of armies: 'There is a gap of 15 kilometres between our two armies, in which there is nobody at all.' The enemy, however, had no cavalry to exploit the situation. Lack of fodder was so great that nearly all the fit horses had been attached for transport to the shock infantry divisions. Directly in the way to Amiens a singular scratch force was resisting heroically in the disused tumbled-down French trenches of 1914. Its organization stands to Gough's credit, and it became famous under the name of its second commander as 'Carey's force'. It was composed of 'details, stragglers, schools' personnel, tunnelling companies, Army troops companies, field-survey companies, and Canadian and American engineers'.[1]

But from the 28th the battle-flame burnt lower and lower. The problem of adding fresh fuel, to which Ludendorff had given such thought, proved insoluble. To vary the metaphor, by employing that constantly used by Foch, the circles in the pond, disturbed by the cast of a stone, grew smaller and smaller until they died away. The enemy was held at Villers-Bretonneux, about ten miles from Amiens, though he pushed so near the main railway-line to Paris as to make it practically useless. His trophies amounted to 70,000 prisoners and 1,100 guns, with stores innumerable (it is said that the British army lost two million bottles of whisky!). But the extent of his line had been increased by more than a third. It bulged out in a most repelling protuberance, with dangerously exposed flanks. Already on April 3rd the indomitable Foch was planning to batter it in and to free Amiens. Pershing had placed the Americans unreservedly at his disposal, writing generously: 'Everything that we have is at your disposal, to use as you like—we are here to be killed.' The day of recovery was not yet, but Foch was continually planning to be in readiness for its arrival; and, as we shall see, he economized the defence in men almost to breaking-point in order to build up a sufficient reserve. Ludendorff's first and greatest effort had proved a brilliant failure. He himself does little to analyse its causes, and contents himself with the candid admission: 'It was an established fact that the enemy's resistance was beyond our strength. We must not get drawn into a battle of exhaustion.' He himself contributed considerably towards it by stubbornly pinning

[1] Quoted from Haig's dispatch.

faith in a decisive effort by Below, until too late. The root-cause seems to have lain in difficulties of transport. It has been already shown how the imperative claims of the infantry for fit horses had robbed the cavalry of its effectiveness. Lorries and petrol were short, but there was a still greater scarcity of rubber, oil, and grease. Their own past deeds arose to make difficulties for the Germans: the desolated battle-fields of 1916, the devastations of the following year. Increasing congestion gave unrivalled opportunities to the Allied aircraft, of which they took full advantage. Already on the 23rd, when Humbert explained apologetically to Gough that, in place of troops, he had 'only the flag on his car', the French machines were in full blast of activity. On the previous night Pétain had given the order: 'Tout ce que vous avez d'aviation de bombardement sur l'Allemand.' In the later stages of the battle the pursuers were at least as exhausted as their enemies. It was often noticed that if the British lay down to rest, the Germans followed suit, too weary to fire a rifle.

That pillaging of British food and supply depots, with dispersal and drunkenness as its sequel, was a serious factor in stopping this advance seems, generally speaking, to be a legend. No doubt such excesses occurred in isolation, like the examples quoted from Rudolf Binding by Captain Liddell Hart.[1] Yet even in this particular instance Kuhl, after careful investigation, convinced himself that the troops in question were already in a state of such exhaustion as to be incapable of any forward movement. Ludendorff himself, who was quite ready if occasion arose to blame his own troops,[2] pointed out the feeble evidence for such charges in answering an obscure work by a Lutheran pastor, which brought them wholesale. On the other hand, both Ludendorff and Rupprecht admit that the progress of the VIth army next month in Flanders was in many

[1] *The Real War 1914–1918* (1930), pp. 427–9.

[2] See, for example, his account of August 8, vol. II, p. 683, and of the Lys, p. 608. Cf. also Reichsarchiv, *Schlachten des Weltkrieges*, Band 32, pp. 112 sqq., for accounts of drunkenness in Fismes, Soissons, and Braisne in May.

places seriously impeded by wild scenes of drunkenness. The young officers lost all authority over their troops.

The decline in German discipline was progressive. In March the Germans were foiled by the blockade[1] and the resistance of their opponents, which, though naturally unequal, was often heroic and enduring beyond words. The Kaiser told captured officers of the 9th division that if all the British had fought as they did he would have had no army left. Though the enemy had lost very heavily (he had in fact suffered about as many casualties as he had inflicted), Ludendorff now had 199 divisions in the West and he was prepared to go on. The second act began less than a week after the battle for Amiens had flickered out round Villers-Bretonneux, Hangard, and Moreuil.

III

In comparison with what Kuhl described as 'the ace of trumps' Ludendorff's new lead wears a very halting aspect. He attacked in Flanders because he hoped to shatter the British by another blow (they had now engaged 46 divisions out of 58), and because the sector had already been prepared for offence, the now diminished effort being coded, with an unconsciously humorous exactitude, as 'Georgette' instead of 'Saint George'. A moderate advance would give excellent tactical results. The only considerable coal-mines left for the French in northern France might be captured. Hazebrouck, with its junction of five railway-lines, might fall or be rendered useless. Finally, there loomed again, distantly but distinctly, the lure of the Channel ports. In short Ludendorff was not clear what he expected or hoped to do, nor what means he would be prepared to employ. There is something experimental in the whole affair.

The selected area presented a nice balance of features

[1] After the war the writer asked a friend who had been captured in this battle what were his first impressions. He replied at once that he was convinced that we had won the war, so astonishing was the contrast between the German and British equipment, transport, &c.

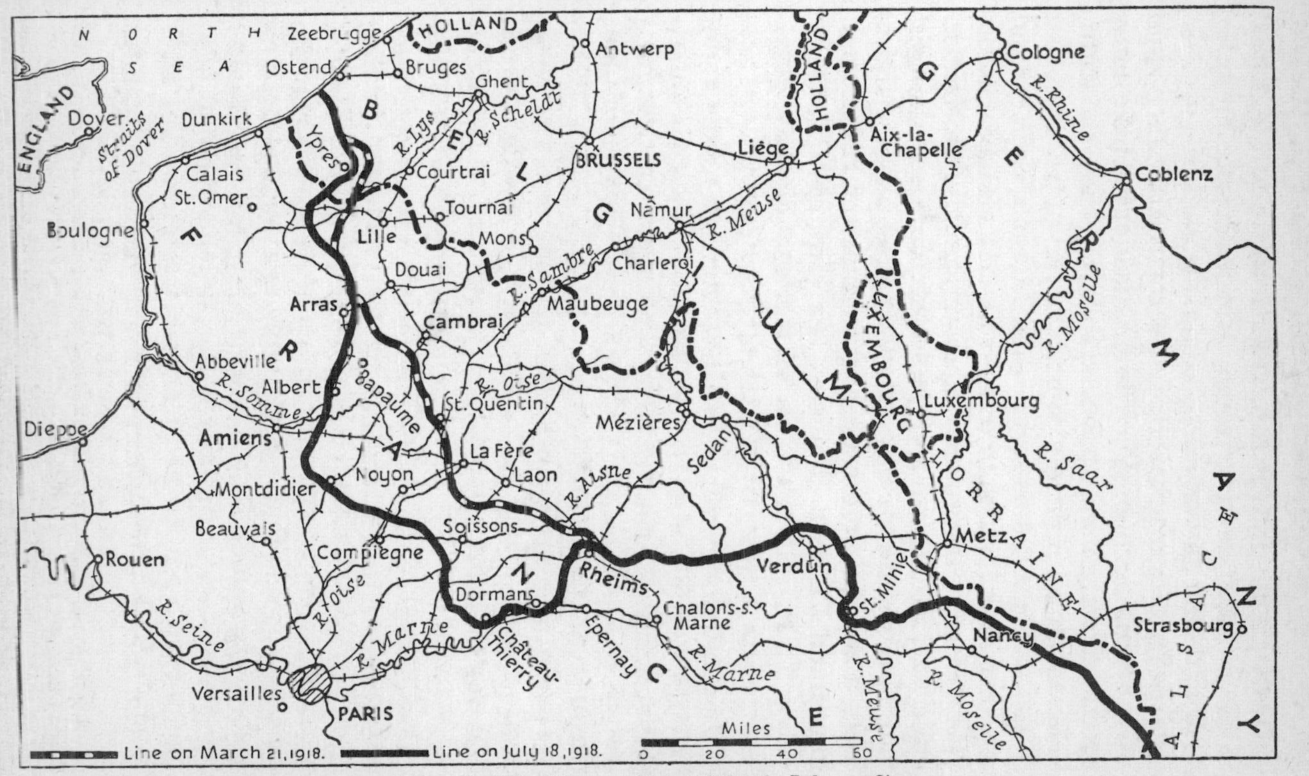

MAP 28. The Western Front (March–July 1918)

good and bad. Lille is the natural centre to which the railways in the north converge. Concentration would be swift and easy and could be completed with equal convenience and secrecy within the great city, only some nine miles behind the line. The communications of his enemy on the other hand were poor, especially towards the south whence help must mainly come.

The whole sector as far north as Messines had seen no serious fighting since the tragic fiasco at Festubert three years before. Consequently there were none of the sinister crater areas to be crossed, while the continued drought had hardened the spongy soil of the level plain. On the other hand, the landscape was perhaps the closest and blindest in the west. Flanders is a country of frequent villages, with outlying farms and cottages densely dotted between them; hedges, moats, and dikes cut up every few acres; while there is no lack of the more showy if not more formidable obstacles of rivers and canals. Such a country, as the event proved, was ideal for murderous delaying-actions by small bodies of resolute men, who understood machine-gun tactics.

The British front was held with extreme weakness, each division being strung out over some 7,500 yards, a good half mile more than that allotted to units of the 5th army on March 21st. But whereas Gough's men were fresh, almost the whole of Horne's 1st army was composed of divisions which had been cut to pieces during the last fortnight. Sometimes three-fourths of their effectives consisted of drafts just arrived. As a climax one Portuguese division, pending relief, was holding as a double front the sector just given up by the other. These troops were undoubtedly the worst of any nation in the West, and had always been regarded as practically worthless. The staff blunder which made one of them responsible for holding six important miles in an avowedly threatened area is one of the most grotesque of the war.

But the German army also was much less impressive both in number and quality. Tired divisions or mere trench-troops mainly took the place of the *corps d'élite*; several of them lacked 500 or 600 horses to complete their tale of transport. The artillery though powerful was not overwhelming, and Rupprecht complains that much time was lost in shifting it hither and thither over the battlefield to deal with stubborn centres of resistance.

Nevertheless the events of the first day were spectacular. The Portuguese towards the left of the attack rushed to the rear; some seized signallers' bicycles and were shot down in mistake for Germans by British reinforcements hurrying up the road from miles behind. In three hours the enemy had passed through this hole beyond the whole trench organization. Fortunately the breach was firmly closed on the left, and was shallower on the right. The 55th West Lancashire Territorial division,[1] ensconced in the strong keep of Givenchy, drove back repeated assaults, and when relieved five days later handed over this vital flank-bulwark intact. Their wonderful defence taught the double lesson of exact organization both of ground and men. The whole fortified village had been turned into a labyrinth of converging tunnels, while the garrison had so perfectly rehearsed their separate parts that the performance worked without a hitch on the day of trial. On the left King Edward's Horse held their ground indomitably in an epic struggle against immense odds.

Next day the battle was extended to the north beyond Armentières. Plumer was driven from Messines and Wytschaete, his model conquests of the year before.

By the 12th the British army was confronted with a crisis more intense than anything which it had faced since the day of Gheluvelt (October 31, 1914). The enemy had advanced more than half-way to Hazebrouck, eleven miles out of nineteen. One last obstacle lay before him, the forest of Nieppe, where in the earlier days of the war soldiers employed in wood-cutting had seen startled wild

[1] This division had been under a cloud for failing to stop the surprise counter-attack at Cambrai (November 30), supported by low-flying aeroplanes.

boars rushing through the undergrowth. Its fringe was lined, or rather dotted, with exhausted men; divisions and even brigades were mixed up with one another. No reinforcements could arrive at Hazebrouck until the evening, or reach the scene of action till late on the 13th. Those engaged had either just emerged from the ordeal of the last battle or were lads of eighteen, who had been sent out of England in defiance of pledges under the stress of imminent peril.[1] It is perhaps true that in the annals of an army, traditionally famous for dogged defence, no more unyielding and protracted resistance was ever opposed to greater odds. Most notable of all was the 4th Guards brigade, which defended more than two miles. Of the Grenadiers one company was entirely destroyed, fighting for four hours, a mile within the enemy's line, twice charging with the bayonet with a strength of less than twenty; another was reduced to six, and a third to twenty.[2]

What G.H.Q. thought of the situation may be judged by the fact that preliminary orders were given for the evacuation and even demolition of Calais, and that preparations were made for flooding the whole of the country west of Dunkirk, which, it is said, would have taken fifty years wholly to repair.

The best record of this great peril is Haig's General Order of the day, which in its moving simplicity and frankness holds a binding appeal:

'Many of us now are tired. To those I would say that victory will belong to the side which holds out the longest. . . . There is no other course open to us but to fight it out! Every position must be held to the last man: there must be no retirement. With

[1] The conscription law became operative at the age of 18, but soldiers were not to be sent out of the United Kingdom until their nineteenth birthday. This was the only time in the war when the fighting age-limit had to be lowered. These youths were reported to show extreme bravery and fierceness, but were quite unable to bear the prolonged strain of months in the lines of which older men were capable. Under the pressure of these defeats the conscription age in Great Britain was now raised to 50.

[2] The 29th and 31st divisions (in the latter of which the 4th Guards Brigade was included) were especially distinguished in the fighting.

our backs to the wall and believing in the justice of our cause, each one of us must fight on to the end. The safety of our Homes and the Freedom of mankind alike depend upon the conduct of each one of us at this critical moment.'

It may well be asked why the enemy did not exploit so fair a field, and why Foch allowed the British to come into such extreme strategical jeopardy.

If the Germans had shown as much cleverness and *élan* as on March 21st they would have reached Hazebrouck. But their powers of keeping a moving battle alive were now utterly inferior. As has been already stated, discipline was partially relaxed. The pillaging of Merville on the night of the 11th undoubtedly wasted at least twelve hours of invaluable time at the very core of the battle. Moreover, Ludendorff's control was weak and hesitating. He finally expended far more divisions (forty-six) than he had ever intended to use. But he doled them out too sparingly, was too easily discouraged by signs of tough resistance; he tapped at too many places with the idea of realizing somehow or other a big success.[1] It is clear that he had no conception of the extremity to which Haig had been reduced between the 11th and 13th; and he expected that the French were already coming up in strength. In point of fact no French troops came into the line here until the 19th. This long delay was due to Foch's deliberate act, and it caused by far the bitterest contention between him and Haig which occurred during the unity of command. Foch, as we have seen, was always planning the offensive, always scraping together reserves to strike at the Amiens salient. Ever since the first battle of Ypres he believed in the almost inexhaustible capacity of the British soldier for hanging-on. Reinforcements must be economized to the last degree. All units engaged must fight until complete exhaustion. His motto constantly repeated was: 'No

[1] His correspondence during the battle with the Chiefs-of-Staff of the IVth and VIth armies was captured by the French and has been published in *La Bataille de Flandres*, collected by Tournet and Berthenat. It is very instructive, both as showing his constant interference in tactical questions and his pessimistic nervousness.

reliefs during a battle.' He feared that if Haig received French troops at too early a stage he would put them into the line in place of his own, instead of using them for counter-attack.

Haig thought this both unfair and dangerous. If divisions were utterly cut to pieces, they might be permanently lost, as at that stage of the war it was difficult to find the cadre of officers and N.C.O.s necessary for their reconstruction. Ten in fact had to be reduced to skeletons at the beginning of May. Angry letters and interviews ensued. Haig went so far as to inform his Government through Milner that 'the arrangements made by the Generalissimo were insufficient to meet the military situation'. Admittedly Foch must be justified on results. He tried the British to the last ounce of their capacity, but the army emerged from the battle to fight its last marvellous campaign after no more than a hundred days' comparative inactivity.

The remainder of the battle, which continued with intermittent spurts of extreme violence until April 29th, seems to have given almost equal anxiety to both sides. We find Ludendorff constantly making querulous complaints of the strong resistance and, especially after Zeebrugge (23rd),[1] exceedingly nervous about the possibility of a landing on the coast; whilst at the beginning of May G.H.Q. reported to the British Cabinet that the retirement of our whole left wing was still possible, 'which, if hastily carried out and closely pressed by the enemy, might endanger our hold on the Channel ports'.

So far the struggle had been mainly confined to the Lys valley. Foiled before Hazebrouck, Ludendorff tried to force a decision by seizing the great pillars of the north, the only real hills in Flanders, running north-west from Bailleul towards Cassel, from which height the old saying gave a man the view of four kingdoms, France, England, Spain,[2] and Heaven. First, he threatened them from the south by taking Bailleul. Next, he tried to circumvent

[1] See Chapter XXXII, pp. 536–542. [2] i.e. the Spanish Netherlands.

them from the north by driving in the Belgians beyond Ypres, who counter-attacked in the most spirited fashion, taking 700 prisoners. Finally, the heaviest assaults were directed frontally against Mount Kemmel, the great outlier, which stands 500 feet above the plain. With characteristic thoroughness the principal role was cast for the Alpine corps, which, as Hindenburg says, had fought victoriously in the passes of Rumania, the mountains of Transylvania, of Serbia, Albania, and in the Alps of Upper Italy. The French lost it on April 25th. They were seized with panic following a violent discharge of a new gas, which is said to have penetrated their respirators. Their own historian, Palat, admits that it is difficult to be sure that there was any resistance.[1] This lapse did nothing to improve the relations between the two armies, at this time exceptionally bad. The French complained that they were constantly being hurried up to pull the chestnuts out of the fire for their incompetent allies. The countercharge of the British was that French promises of concerted attack seldom came off and never at the right time. The loss of Kemmel left a peculiar rankle as it had been handed over by tired to fresh troops.

The enemy, however, made but one effort to exploit this great tactical success, and on its failure turned at once to the defensive.

As far as the tactical position went the chief result had been to burden the German army with another salient embedded in a marsh. It became one of the most disagreeable bits of the line, raked by converging gun-fire and continually bombed. When the enemy evacuated it in September our men were amazed at the number of immense cemeteries which it contained.

But all these bulges and protuberances might have forwarded Ludendorff's plan, if his man-power had been improving, and that of his enemies declining; the time would then have come when not sufficient men were

[1] Gen. P. L. Palat, *La Grande Guerre sur le front occidental* (1917–27), vol. xiii, p. 223.

available to fill the ever-lengthening line. This disaster, however, was to befall the Germans, not the Allies.

At the moment the position of rival strengths was much the same on paper as on March 21st. The General Staff reckoned the German superiority at about 260,000. Their gross losses had been considerably larger than those of the British, in round numbers 350,000 against 305,000.[1] So far, the reinforcements received by either side were evenly balanced. But how different was the respective quality! The Allies saw arriving vigorous British divisions from Italy and Palestine, whose intervention in the battle was usually marked by immediate success, and the pick of American manhood, full of physical strength and self-confident eagerness to engage; whereas the German units now being combed out of the forces still kept in Russia were of pitiable quality; timid, spiritless, weary, middle-aged men, with a dull hatred of military life, and often vaguely infected with Bolshevism. Rupprecht tells an extraordinary story of the behaviour of one of these units on first coming under shell-fire. They threw up their hands and waved white flags in the direction of the invisible enemy. Such troops were fit for nothing but labour in the back areas.

Acute observers realized that the sands of Germany's opportunity were rapidly running out. Henceforth until the end of the war she received no addition of numbers except for four Austrian divisions, imperfectly trained and of low moral. The Americans on the other hand were now arriving at the rate of 250,000 a month, mainly carried by British shipping, in almost absolute security from the attacks of U-boats.

IV

Ludendorff would have preferred to continue his attacks in Flanders. Down to the very end of the time allotted to

[1] In net losses there was little to choose as the British prisoners and missing exceeded those of the enemy by 50,000. These were all dead loss, whereas it was calculated that 88 per cent. of the wounded became, later, available for service.

him, he cast his eyes most longingly towards the north. But he was convinced that his enemy there was too strong for him. In fact the whole front north of the Oise was now heavily defended. No local attacks towards Amiens had succeeded. The most ambitious of these, directed against Villers-Bretonneux (the final ridge from which the city is distantly visible) on April 24th had been heavily defeated by the Australians. It was also notable as the only occasion on which tank has ever fought tank, three or four machines on either side engaging in a brisk little action. If the whole northern front were defensively held for the present, a great mass of manœuvre could be directed against some weakly held point of the French line.[1]

The weakness inherent in Ludendorff's policy of a succession of isolated blows was double. The interval between each tended to become longer as the quality of the troops declined. Thus his enemy was allowed an increasing time for recovery from the last wound inflicted. Moreover, if one sector only was struck reserves could be sent thither more whole-heartedly than if fears were entertained simultaneously for several vital points. Ludendorff says that it was now beyond his strength to stage two separate battles at once. His method stands in a most unfavourable contrast with the sustained skill and magnetism by which Foch kept a many-headed offensive constantly nourished for nearly four months. About this time a Swiss military critic penetratingly described the German situation as 'brilliant but hopeless'. The attack which its director was about to launch added the last lustre to this treacherous glitter. The point selected was the Chemin des Dames, which had figured so often in the battle-pictures of the war. As we have seen, Pétain expected the great onslaught here in March, and indeed considerable preparations had been made. As it had been left in complete tranquillity it was supposed that German Head-quarters thought it impregnable. That, unfortunately, was also the belief of the

[1] At the beginning of May both sides maintained over 60 per cent of their total forces north of the Oise.

French. They held it very lightly, trusting that their numerous machine-gun posts would turn the steep ascent from the Ailette into a deadly glacis. So extreme was Foch's confidence that, wherever Ludendorff struck, it would not be here, that he persuaded Haig to send five completely crippled British divisions for a rest in these trenches in order that larger French forces could remain near Amiens to cement the junction between the two armies. The British Cabinet disliked this system of 'roulement', as it was called, believing that it would diminish the independence of our army, but G.H.Q. accepted it willingly on the strength of the French assurances.

Duchêne, the French army commander in this zone, was not responsible for the enormous front held by his divisions, for his strength had been ruthlessly cut down.[1] But, contrary to all recent experience, he insisted upon heavy garrisons in the forward zone, leaving scarcely any reserves for the rear lines to stem the tide.[2] Of a brutal and arrogant disposition (he too was nicknamed 'Tiger', without any of the half-complimentary nuance implied in Clemenceau's), he repressed all representations and initiative on the part of his subordinates. The British, for example, were forced, much against their inclination and habit, to take over every detail of the system left by their predecessors, which was handed over in a shocking state of neglect.

The weakness of the defence alone gave Ludendorff a prospect of good success, for the position was of enormous strength. The attack had first to cross the Ailette and its shell-ravaged swamps, then to climb 300 feet up the steep,

[1] Eleven divisions (including three of the British) were spun out over 92 kilometres, i.e. about 5¼ miles per division.

[2] There were no doubt weighty reasons for giving as little ground as possible in most of this area for (1) the plateau allows a defence to be co-ordinated more easily there than on the steep downward slopes towards the Aisne with their numerous spurs and shoulders; (2) if the defence was to be north of the river at all, it was obviously desirable to keep the bridges as far from fire as possible; (3) the Chemin des Dames had, next to Verdun, the greatest moral importance for French opinion. It was therefore worth while making unusual sacrifices to hold it.

bare slopes to the main position, and then, if successful there, to negotiate the crossing of the Aisne, some sixty yards wide, and seize the commanding south bank before any strong resistance could be organized. The surprise which was sprung upon the French was a triumph of German method, and may be compared in its classic perfection with the British preparations for August 8th.[1]

The whole area was subdivided by the Germans into sections under a number of 'security officers', whose agents supervised the civil population with the closest scrutiny and prevented military gossip in the canteens and soldiers' homes. No troops beyond the strength of a battalion were allowed to march by day. All bivouacs were surveyed by aircraft to prevent tell-tale traces being left. If such were revealed by photographs they were carefully raked over. Horses were fed and watered in relays. As the forward areas were approached, all tires were bound with bags of saw-dust and cloth wrapped round the axles to deaden noise. In the very foremost lines, the nightly 'frogs' chorus' in the Ailette marshes was found exceedingly helpful in allowing the pioneers to collect their great dumps of bridging material unheard.

The artillery concentration was as usual in the unrivalled hands of Colonel Bruchmüller, who made such excellent use of the broken wooded country between Laon and the front as to assemble unsuspected about 4,000 guns and a vast array of trench-mortars. As late as May 25th French Army Head-quarters were so completely deceived as to state that there was no evidence that the Germans had made any preparations which would enable them to attack at short notice. The only warning of the impending storm had come, curiously enough, from the inexperienced American Intelligence, which predicted the attack a fortnight before, but failed to win Foch's credence.

On the 26th the curtain of mystery was dramatically raised so as to allow the French to foresee the fate which it

[1] The details, which are of intense interest, will be found minutely given in the Reichsarchiv's series *Schlachten des Weltkrieges*, Band 32, pp. 12 sqq.

was now too late to prevent. A German under-officer and private were captured in a patrol-scuffle. The latter gave details of the attack, while the former denied that anything was in the wind. They were hurried down to Army Headquarters for further interrogation. The under-officer was threatened with the fate of a spy, if contrary to the laws of war he volunteered false information.[1] With death before his eyes he collapsed and gave a full account of the German plan. Nothing could be done except to warn the trench divisions of the unsuspected bolt which would fall on them within twelve hours, and to send preliminary orders to eight divisions to start at full speed from the northern reserves.

As dawn broke on the 27th the enemy came out on a forty-mile front. The feeble counter-preparation which the French gunners had put down since midnight had scarcely interfered with the storm-assembly. The German bombardment, on the other hand, had been of a frightful and minutely searching intensity.

On that day the enemy made the longest advance ever recorded since trenches were first dug in the West. His centre went forward thirteen miles, and by the evening German troops were in Fismes, having crossed three rivers, the Ailette, Aisne, and Vesle. As almost invariably happened, the progress on the flanks was less marked, so that another pocket was in process of formation.

Ludendorff was embarrassed by this flying start. He had designed the attack merely as a powerful diversion to draw away troops from the north while Rupprecht got his blow ready. He had meant only to reach the general line Soissons–Fismes and to halt there. But he could not resist the temptation to let the battle take its course. It was in full swing, its impetus was tremendous. It was breaking

[1] No prisoner is bound to give any information, beyond his name and rank, consequently he cannot be justified in telling his captors what is false except under threats. It must, however, be acknowledged that the Intelligence of all armies frequently resorted to 'third degree' methods to extort information from privates or N.C.O.s. Officers were generally cajoled, tricked, or made drunk in order to pick their brains.

into completely intact country, conquering great stretches of rich arable land and immense depots of every kind. When it entered Soissons the German wireless maliciously recounted that many new and unfinished houses were found, which proved how secure their enemy had felt against another flood of invasion. So the Crown Prince was fed with fresh troops. By May 30th the Germans were again upon the Marne after forty-five months, and were within thirty-seven miles of Paris. Securities, archives, and many inhabitants flowed away from the Capital.[1] The Generalissimo was bitterly criticized in the Chamber. But Clemenceau showed an iron resolution. 'I will fight before Paris, I will fight in Paris, I will fight behind Paris; we shall be victorious if the public authorities are equal to their task.' Wilson was requested to expedite with ever greater vigour the immediate dispatch of the waiting American masses.

In reality, as Ludendorff well knew, Paris was alarmed rather than threatened. By June 2nd he was definitely held within the very worst of the salients, which had been so unwelcome a result of all his offensives. Forty miles deep, it was served by only one railway which ran dangerously near its western face. It presented an impossible shape for defensive security. Yet it was obviously impracticable immediately to evacuate this trumpeted earnest of victory. Consequently the cherished northern plans must be yet further postponed. Hutier was now set in motion south of Noyon with the object of carrying the line forward through hills and woods to Compiègne and thence to Villers-Cotterets. This would not indeed wipe out the salient, but it would greatly broaden it, and would also involve a more real danger to Paris. For the roads in this region converge on the Capital, whereas their general direction in the Marne pocket is southwards.

This time surprise was completely lacking when Hutier opened on June 9th, and there was little disparity in

[1] See Poincaré, vol. x, pp. 218 sqq., for the elaborate measures taken to defend Paris and to evacuate the Government and the civil population.

numbers. In spite of this the French centre fought badly on the first day and was driven in six miles. Pétain for once lost his icy calm and rated its commander violently in the presence of other generals. This, however, was the limit of the German success. Mangin, who has been described as 'the incarnation of battle', comes again upon the scene, which he is now to occupy prominently until the final victory. Unavailingly sacrificed by Nivelle as his scapegoat, he had remained under a cloud. Now, restored to the command of an army, he organized with extraordinary speed the first deliberate counter-stroke of the year, powerfully supported by tanks. He struck the German flank and drove it back two miles, capturing prisoners and guns. It was not a very big affair, yet a very evil omen. Not less disturbing to the German Staff was the intervention of the Americans at Belleau Wood near Château-Thierry. In their first considerable action they attacked with the furious vigour which they invariably displayed. Though their opponents described their methods with justice as clumsy and amateur, these opponents found the greatest difficulty in warding off their continual assaults.

Thus the history of this campaign had repeated itself again. The outward and visible signs of victory made a brave showing in the newspapers; statistics of captured territory, prisoners, and guns[1] were truly impressive. Yet Ludendorff was more than ever entrapped in his own success. He had created a kind of triumphant mess, which had to be cleared up. He had made the pursuit of his real aim in the north more remote, and more contingent on success in the south, than ever. Most dangerous of all, he was still using up his best material, which was absolutely irreplaceable, at a rate which was quite out of relation with the sacrifices which he exacted of his enemies.[2] As a French writer impressively said of the Americans at Belleau

[1] Between May 27 and June 13 the numbers taken were about 70,000 and 830 respectively.

[2] In round figures the losses were Allies 172,000, Germans 130,000.

Wood, they were beginning a vast operation of transfusion of blood into the exhausted body of France. The Germans could not look for any such reviving and transforming specific.

V

A long month of suspense followed, the biggest pause since the spring, eloquent of the enemy's increasing perplexities. The foundations of Germany's trust and security were being heavily shaken. Austria's despairing offensive had been cast back behind the Piave with a tale of 150,000 casualties. The bitter recriminations which followed in the Hungarian Parliament witnessed to the growth of the separatist spirit. The disruptive elements were now receiving decisive support from the Entente; Polish, Czechoslovak, and Yugoslav emigrants, deserters, and rebels, had been recognized as *de facto* belligerents. The Czechs in particular were a thorn in the side of the Central Powers. A great body of ex-prisoners in Siberia were fighting their way eastward along the railway, taking with them in an armoured train an immense hoard of gold which they had seized from the Bolsheviks. Other regiments of deserters fought for the Allies in Italy at even more than the ordinary soldiers' risk, for the Austrians naturally shot any who fell into their hands.

Rupprecht, Prince Max of Baden, and other far-sighted persons had entirely lost any hope of victory, and implored the Chancellor to make peace, while the army still held its last great trump of the threatening military initiative. Kühlmann, the Secretary of State, knowing the feeling of the Reichstag, cautiously echoed these sentiments when he stated that in view of the great coalition arrayed against Germany a purely military decision could scarcely be expected. Ludendorff, who favoured peace propaganda only as an additional weapon for his coming offensive, not as a substitute for it, contrived Kühlmann's dismissal. In fact, however, it was the propaganda of the Entente which was eating away German confidence like some corrosive acid.

Northcliffe, the famous journalist, had been created Minister of Information. A subtle and intensive campaign against the moral of the enemy's troops was instituted. Balloons packed with subversive literature were floated over the lines. By every possible means the ordinary man was incited against his rulers. By a singular irony a German had forged the most deadly weapon against his countrymen: Prince Lichnowsky, German ambassador in London before the war (a man of stainless honour who had most faithfully served the best interests of his country), had written privately, for his own future justification, a memorandum in which he placed the blame for its outbreak principally upon his own Government, and particularly extolled the just and peace-ensuing character of Sir E. Grey. He lent a copy to a General Staff Officer, Captain von Beerfelde, who thought it his duty to have it published. No more sinister blow could be struck at the conscience and inner peace of the average German, who had profoundly believed in the justice of his cause, or at the endurance of the over-wrought soldier. Such was the effect of this and similar pamphlets that Ludendorff offered rewards for all brought in, and even threatened the death-penalty for any man found in unauthorized possession of them. The army was now beginning to go more rapidly down the inclined plane of indiscipline, helped by the first great influenza epidemic, which broke out in June and was far more severe among the Germans, owing to the poverty of their rations, than with the Entente.

As generally happens in modern armies, the contamination was creeping from the rear to the front. In the camps of the interior of the Reich, serious disturbances had already taken place, and these had not escaped the eye of our Intelligence. Soldiers were being systematically incited against their officers, who were reported to live in luxury and even to embezzle the funds of regimental canteens. The tendency of the German towards envy was exploited to the full. Agents of the Independent Socialists were busy distributing defeatist pamphlets at German railway-stations. The Reichstag itself had made a concession to the demands for milder discipline by abolishing the field-punishment, which consisted in tying a man for long periods to a fixed object.[1] Except on the extreme Right, a nervous depression was gaining ground among all parties and reflected the feeling in the country. The western population of Germany was at last being very sorely tried by air-raids. The Independent Air Force under Trenchard had been established round Nancy and bombed the Rhenish towns with assiduity both by day and night. The Allies were beginning to catch up, and were soon to outstrip, their enemies in the revolting competition for civilian slaughter. Paris since March 21st had been intermittently assailed by the famous long-range gun, which was ensconced in a quarry seventy-five miles away near Laon. The shell took more than five minutes to arrive, and hooters in Paris sounded the warning, as soon as the telephone announced the firing of the gun. Its most notorious holocaust was on Good Friday, when it killed seventy worshippers in a Parisian church. Its activities ceased for good in July, partly because it was itself constantly bombarded, partly because its bore wore out very rapidly. For political reasons the enemy, as defeat became more glaring, gave up attacks on great cities. In particular the employment of a new incendiary bomb against London was forbidden. On the other hand, if the war had lasted another week, British aeroplanes were under orders to drop giant bombs of a ton weight upon Berlin.

Meanwhile such minor fighting activity as took place must have disquieted Ludendorff. For it was the Allies who kept succeeding in small, neat, cheap attacks. In the Lys salient, and on the Somme, the Australians had obtained a superiority over the opposing garrison, which

[1] This punishment known as 'Field Punishment No. 1' was maintained in England until 1929, when the Labour Government abolished it. Contrary to the general belief at the time, it seems certain that British discipline during the latter part of the war was stricter than German. Rupprecht expressed his astonishment at the number of death-sentences carried out in the B.E.F. during 1917.

seemed to be under a kind of 'fascination'. They constantly advanced their outposts in broad daylight, little patrols bringing in scores of prisoners. On July 4th at Hamel, east of Amiens, aided by a few picked Americans, they co-operated with tanks in taking 1,500 prisoners at less loss to themselves. This little action was the true begetter of the great attacks in the following months, for it taught most important lessons. It proved that really systematic co-operation between tanks and infantry (every detail had been rehearsed beforehand) economizes men to a surprising degree. Each battalion attacked on a front of 1,000 yards, a space almost as wide as Ludendorff had allotted for the attacks of a division on March 21st. Moreover, an effective barrage just ahead of the tanks made it very difficult for the enemy to put these out of action (as at Flesquières) with his new anti-tank guns and heavy rifles.[1] Finally, on the western face of the Marne pocket, Mangin kept nibbling away at tactical points, the possession of which would greatly improve the French jumping-off line when the signal should be given for greater ventures. Foch indeed was straining at the leash of continued defence, and the chief fear of the cautious Pétain was lest the Generalissimo should break out too soon. Yet even he delivered himself of the prophecy: 'If at the end of June we have held firm, our position is excellent. In July we can resume the upper hand. Then victory is ours.'

Ludendorff, entangled in the net of his own partial successes, found no option but to go on where he had broken off. This he decided should be his last diversion. It should be on the greatest scale possible without denuding Rupprecht of his treasured reserves. It must on the contrary drag all the enemy's troops in haste towards the south. After that the British could receive a final defeat, and the Channel ports would fall with their retreat.

Ludendorff, with not unusual candour, described his immediate plan as clumsy, but could see no alternative.

[1] This weapon was so heavy (about 35 lb.) that it needed two men to fire it. The tanks inspired so much fear that it was seldom used.

Apart from its tactics, shortly to be considered, it had two fatal defects: it aroused extravagant hopes at home, and it became known to the enemy. It was described as the *Friedensturm*, the last great effort to impose peace. Neither the soldiers nor civilians thought of it as a diversion, but as the supreme ordeal. Hence, on its failure, the revulsion was terrible, and the remains of endurance were irremediably sapped. The German people felt that they had been unpardonably deceived. Hence also it was spoken of everywhere in terms of excited gossip, and was the common talk of Berlin and Brussels a fortnight before it was put to the test. Moreover, the actual preparations were obvious; on June 30th aeroplane photographs revealed them beyond doubt.

Thus the French had ample time to meet it, both on the ground threatened, and by concentration of reserves. Foch brought down ample forces from the north, boldly taking the risk that Rupprecht's blow would be delayed. Among them he requisitioned eight British divisions, which so much alarmed the Cabinet that General Smuts was sent over to make certain that Haig did not consider the danger to his weakened line too great. Ludendorff was preparing forty-seven divisions and 2,000 batteries[1] to strike between Château-Thierry and the Argonne. Except on either side of Rheims, a fortress scarcely to be taken by direct assault, the attack was practically continuous. Its object was to reach Épernay and Châlons, the fall of which would have caused the French front to collapse all round Verdun. In the confusion thus arising, German Head-quarters might have found other opportunities to seize. But the immediate object was not, as has often been stated, to prepare for an advance in force on Paris.

Where the enemy had to cross the Marne it seemed folly not to oppose him at an obstacle so formidable, though to do so meant keeping strong garrisons in the foremost line.

[1] This appears to have been the densest concentration of artillery employed in the war.

But where the country for many miles deep was a defensive web, as in Champagne, it was even more foolish to meet him on his chosen terms by packing the front lines with men. Pétain insisted that defence in depth should here be exploited to its uttermost, even though it meant voluntarily evacuating the great Moronvillers heights, so painfully won last year. Gouraud, most chivalrous of French generals, who felt any retreat like a personal stain, was in command. It is said to have taken seven days to persuade him to adopt this manœuvre. But as will be seen he made a triumphant success of it.

Nor were the French less fortunate in learning the exact details of the plan. As so often before, Alsatians came over with every scrap of information which they could collect. On the Marne front a reconnoitring officer, who had swum across contrary to orders, was taken with all his maps and papers. In Champagne twenty-seven prisoners taken on July the 14th proved so talkative and intelligent that Gouraud was able to piece together the whole time-table for the morrow. At that same midnight, the day of the French *Fête Nationale*, the many Parisians still abroad in the streets saw great flashes in the east and heard the distant rumble. They knew the great battle was beginning, but not that the sound came from their own guns forestalling the German preparation by two hours.

The battle of the next day falls into two halves locally divided by the *enceinte* of Rheims. East of the city the enemy met with a frightful defeat and was stopped dead. Gouraud had filled his evacuated lines with land mines and mustard gas. A few posts of devoted machine-gunners were left to promote confusion. The French artillery rained upon the advancing lines, which rapidly lost touch with their own barrage and were utterly unable to cross the three or four kilometres separating them from the main French resistance. They withered away and are believed to have suffered ten times the losses of the defenders.[1] No attempt was made to renew the struggle here.

[1] The French losses in Gouraud's army at the close of the day were about

On the Marne, however, between Château-Thierry and Dormans, things at first went very differently. The pioneers, as always, incomparable bridge-builders, threw numbers of bridges across, under cover of an intense gas-bombardment. The Germans soon had six divisions on the southern bank. Their performance was splendid. If one stands on the steep wooded hills which command the valley 400 feet above it, the feat of storming them against a fully prepared enemy seems almost impossible. Yet they not only achieved it but drove three miles beyond the summit, half-way to Épernay. This was their limit of advance. They were held by the Franco-Americans. They had got too far beyond the river to be properly supported by artillery from the northern bank, and it was impossible to get enough guns or even supplies across the river owing to the hail of bombs dropped on the bridges. Moreover, the supporting thrust towards Épernay on their left on the Ardre had been brought to naught in the difficult hill-country picturesquely called the Forest of the Mountain of Rheims. Here an Italian corps, the first to fight in the West, took a brave share in the defence. Already on the 17th, before the terrible counter-stroke had fallen upon his armies, Ludendorff had given the preliminary orders for withdrawing across the river, and breaking off the attack.

Thus the initiative passed, finally, out of the enemy's hand.

3,000. No exact figure has been given for the other side, but 30,000 is the general computation.

XXXII
ZEEBRUGGE AND OSTEND

THE possession of the Belgian coast by the Germans gave them advanced bases for destroyers and submarines 300 miles nearer their objectives than the Frisian river-mouths. From Zeebrugge to Dover is only sixty-two miles, and to Dunkirk less than forty. About two submarines a day issued forth to infest the Channel. Sixteen destroyers were generally in readiness. Except in high summer the hours of darkness were always long enough to give them a wide choice of enterprises, against which it was impossible to keep concentrated anything approaching an equality of force. The enemy might raid the drifters protecting the barrage, bombard Dunkirk or Dover, attack the great mass of shipping always anchored in the Downs, where the blockade examination took place, or go north against the mouth of the Thames and the coast towns of Essex and Suffolk. He could safely fire without warning on any ship encountered with the certainty that it must be hostile. Such raids were in fact much less frequent than the Commander of the Dover Patrol apprehended as possible, though they were well organized and dashingly executed. Once only were they caught and punished, when in April 1917 Commander Evans in the destroyer-leader *Broke* sank two enemy boats, one by ram and the other by torpedo.

Yet this imminent cloud of danger proved very exhausting to the Dover Patrol, and if the enemy had ever broken clean into the Straits he might have sunk thousands of soldiers in passing transports. It is therefore clear that large strategical issues were involved in an attack against the Belgian coast.

Until the end of 1917, however, the Admiralty always refused to sanction an expedition, partly because of the great risk, partly because it was considered only practicable in conjunction with an advance against Bruges by the Army. It must be remembered that Zeebrugge and Ostend are in no way natural harbours, but merely the exits of the two ship canals which branch out from the inland port of Bruges. As the Admiralty held that it could not provide for a permanent garrison of the two exits, while our army remained in its lines before Ypres, an expedition was continually postponed. As we have already seen, the great landing scheme of 1917 was conditional on a military advance of twelve miles to Roulers.

Still, it seems a feeble policy to refrain from doing anything because you cannot do everything that you desire. Clearly a surprise might enable demolition parties to blow up the lock-gates and the docks, and block ships to sink in the entrance, thus causing damage scarcely to be repaired by the labour of months under bombardment from sea and air. Such a scheme engaged no greater hazards than the assaults on immense field fortresses against which the army was daily unleashed without the advantage of surprise. So argued the daring Sir Roger Keyes when he took over the Dover Patrol in December 1917.

Definite leave for the attempt had indeed just been given by Jellicoe, who was on the point of retiring in favour of Sir R. Wemyss, and it was confirmed by the new Board of Admiralty. The blocking of fortified harbours is an ancient expedient with a picturesque history. Yet the only examples in the Great War are those now to be described. They came at a moment when German victories were daily announced in Flanders, when the fate of Calais and Boulogne hung in the balance. The vivid and terrible details of the midnight struggle, the publicity so unusually lavished upon romantic individual exploits, lifted up the hearts and sustained the feeble knees of the Allied peoples with a sovereign charm altogether out of proportion to the success which was erroneously believed to have been gained. It seemed as if the light of the unconquerable spirit of individual daring shone through the gloom of mass organization, where the man counted so much less than the machine.

Yet this enterprise itself demanded three months of the minutest and most elaborate preparation during which complete secrecy was preserved.[1] The volunteers who were demanded for an unspecified hazardous service were trained and rehearsed in a lonely area off the Thames mouth. In the dockyards many old ships were being curiously transformed.

Zeebrugge, against which the principal and more complicated attack was intended, has its canal entrance protected by a great mole, curving north-east from the shore just west of the harbour. It is about a mile and a half long, divided into three parts. A railway viaduct of 600 yards leads to the mole proper, a powerful mass of masonry 80 yards wide and 1,850 long, itself terminating in a narrow mole-head, crowned by a lighthouse. The mole-head was defended by a battery of light guns, which had an uninterrupted command over the approaches to the canal mouth. This area was a self-contained fort, separated from the mole by barbed wire and sand-bag barricades. There was also a standing garrison on the mole itself. The whole coast-line was studded with batteries, several of which, as the bombarding monitors had found to their cost, were effective up to a range of twenty-two miles.

Keyes had therefore two main problems. First, to bring his flotilla unseen within immediate striking distance of the objective; secondly, to prevent the defences of the mole from forbidding the passage of his block-ships into the canal mouth.

The approach was to be made in darkness; and to blind the illumination of search-lights and star-shells a special smoke cloud, which could be kindled without a betraying flame, was manufactured by Wing-Commander F. A.

[1] The remarkable capacity of the Press for reticence is illustrated by an incident. The two Mersey ferry-boats *Iris* and *Daffodil*, being almost unsinkable, were requisitioned for the expedition. The whole Press was circularized and asked to see that no mention of this was allowed to appear. Not only was it kept out of publication, but no rumour percolated through by way of private conversation, though a large number of persons must have seen the circular.

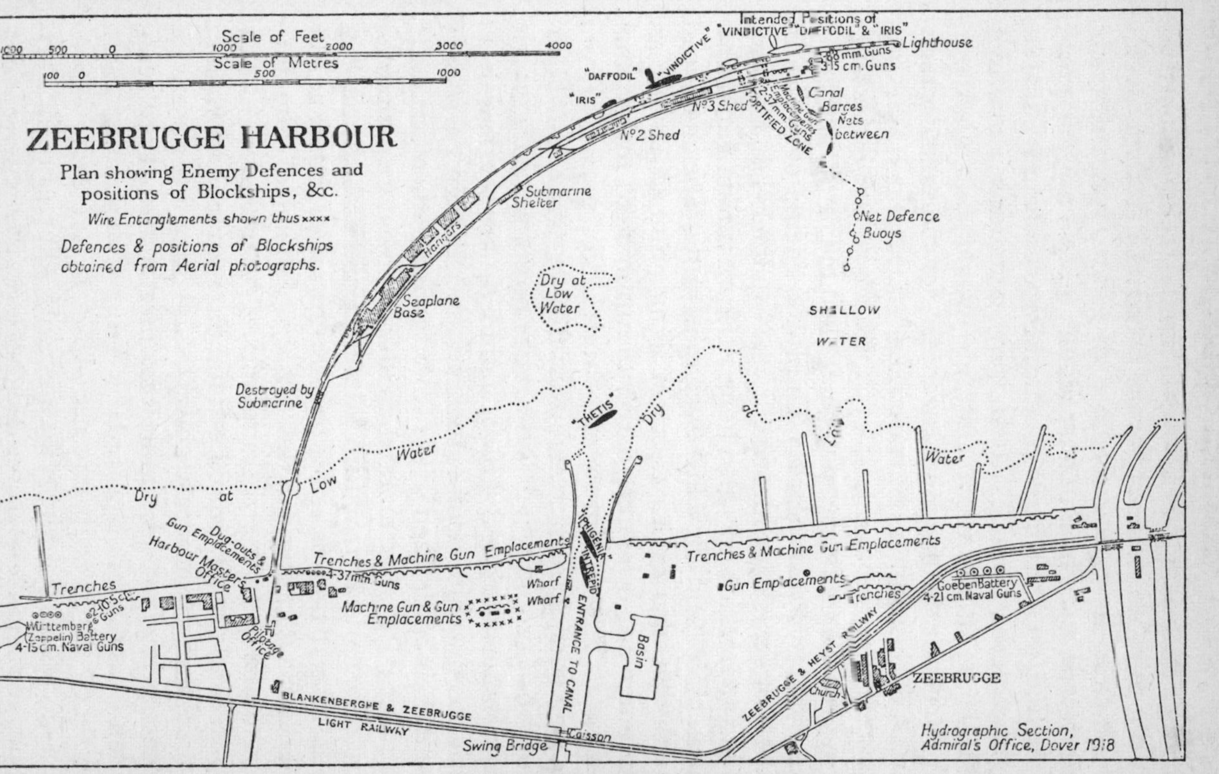

MAP 29. Plan of Zeebrugge

Brock, of the famous firework family. The task of the block-ships was to be lightened by a prior landing on the mole-head to subdue its battery. This diversion much narrowed the choice of available nights, for the great height of the mole made it almost impossible to get ashore except at high water. There were in fact only about five nights a month when the tide would be full about midnight without a moon. Finally, for the smoke-screen to be effective the wind must blow off the sea.

Twice in the first half of April Keyes led his flotilla towards Flanders, and was compelled to withdraw by unfavourable atmospherics. The third attempt, by one of those singular coincidences which rival the height of planning, started on the afternoon of April 22nd, the eve of Saint George. The battle began with the Saint's day at midnight. Keyes gave as his signal 'Saint George for England', and the mole is to-day surmounted by a statue of our patron warrior slaying the dragon.

A motley armada of light craft sailed from Dover, in all 116 vessels, of which the large majority were destroyers and motor-launches. Five ancient light cruisers had been prepared as block-ships, their masts had been cut away, and their holds filled with cement to make their removal, after sinking, the more difficult. Three were for Zeebrugge, two for Ostend. A larger cruiser, the *Vindictive*, was to serve both as a sally port for the mole landing party, and as a floating fortress for their support. She was crammed with picked companies of marines, and armed with the paraphernalia of trench warfare, howitzers, stokes-mortars, flame-throwers, and machine-guns. In company were eight monitors, mostly armed with 14-inch guns.

When the expedition was within twelve miles of the coast it divided for its two objectives.[1] For a preliminary hour the monitors bombarded the coastal batteries, as they had done several times previously about the same hour to allay suspicion. It was hoped that the hostile gun-

[1] Seventy-three ships attacking Zeebrugge; forty-three Ostend.

crews would take shelter in their dug-outs and be slow to realize what was afoot.

Just before the *Vindictive* reached the mole, the smoke-screen, lit by motor-launches, which had been a guardian pall, was driven back from the land by a sudden breeze from the south. Consequently she was seen coming along-side, and was raked by shells, and overran her mark on the outer side of the mole by several hundred yards.

The swell edged the ship away from the parapet so that at first instead of eighteen landing brows only two could be used. Even when the ferry-boat *Daffodil* pushed the *Vindictive* right up against the masonry the roll made landing extremely difficult as the brows bumped several feet up and down on top of the mole. Meanwhile the enemy's fire was very accurate and destructive, killing many of the gun-crews and working havoc among the marines. One shell killed or wounded fifty-six of the latter, as they were waiting their turn to rush forward. The detachment landed on the mole was cut off from the lighthouse battery by the barricade, which it vainly endeavoured to take in ferocious hand-to-hand fighting. Others moved along in the direction of the viaduct from which continuous machine-gun fire came. During this phase German attention was entirely focused upon the mole, where a landing on the grand scale was thought to be in progress.

At 12.20 a.m. two things happened almost together. The viaduct went up in a terrific detonation. It had been rammed by an old submarine filled with five tons of high explosive.[1] All telephonic connexion with the land was thus severed. At this moment the block-ships passed within hail of the lighthouse, and were instantly blasted by the mole-head battery. One sank before the canal entrance could be won but the remaining two, *Intrepid* and *Iphigenia*, were steered well within the piers and sunk diagonally across the fairway. Their crews were taken

[1] The submarine C 3 was steered right into its objective by Lieut. R. D. Sandford, who was rescued by his brother in a picket boat.

off by motor-launches which were flitting about everywhere with efficient heroism.

The *Vindictive*, riddled through her upper works, but protected by the mole against vital damage, lay alongside long enough to take off practically all those left alive on the quay. Only sixteen men were captured, and except for one destroyer, no ship was lost. Keyes himself had flown his flag in the destroyer *Warwick*, one of those engaged in guarding the harbour entrance.

It was confidently believed that at Zeebrugge complete success had been won. At Ostend, however, where there was no mole, and where no diversion had been planned, the two block-ships had been deceived in their direction by the shifting of an important buoy and stranded uselessly a mile east of the canal.

On May 10th the old *Vindictive* herself was transformed into a block-ship, and in spite of a blinding sea-fog was beached within the entrance. But unfortunately the angle at which she lay obstructed only one-third of the channel, though the Admiralty with calculated inaccuracy thought fit to inform the public that it was blocked.

The ingenuity of the enemy also permitted submarines to squeeze through the narrow gaps at Zeebrugge almost immediately in practically undiminished numbers. On the other hand, the bases were now too inconveniently restricted for destroyers, and the Dover Patrol was freed from one of its most serious cares.[1] The war ended without any further attempt upon our Channel defences. The Flemish coast with all its encircling armament was fated to fall before King Albert's attacks in October.

[1] For an authoritative summary of the consequences of these actions on the enemy's dispositions, see Sir J. H. Newbolt, *Naval Operations*, vol. v (1931), p. 275.

14 X 24'

7'5" x 9'3"

6"9

3"

3 A.

The Company endeavours to protect property of its patrons but will NOT be responsible for loss or damage to vehicles or contents. Lock valuables in your car trunk. CHARGES ARE FOR USE OF PARKING SPACE ONLY.

№ 22354

CHECK IN & OUT WITH CASHIER

XXXIII

FOCH'S COUNTER-STROKE AND THE GREAT REVERSAL OF FORTUNE

I

THE blow delivered against the German front between Soissons and Château-Thierry on July 18th deserves a special mention because, in the words of Talleyrand's hackneyed epigram, it was the beginning of the end. It ruined all the enemy's plans for further offence. It was the forerunner of the greatest and most decisive series of uninterrupted attacks in the history of warfare. It was not, judged by the standards of this bloody year, a very great affair. It was started with no more than twenty divisions. The losses which it inflicted, though serious, were not phenomenal.[1] But it was conclusive.

It was, moreover, the first visible triumph for the Generalissimo, whose tenure of command till then had appeared, to the uninstructed eye of the average citizen, as hardly distinguishable from uniform failure. Hence it was appropriate that the battle should itself exhibit to the world the real military unity of the Alliance, for French, British, Americans, and Italians all performed in it together as members of Foch's great military orchestra.[2]

No historian has failed to point out the extraordinary fact that twice in the war the Germans allowed their open right flank to be exposed to a disastrous surprise on almost the same ground. History has consecrated the Marne as the name given to both these Allied victories, but it is really round its less-known tributary, the Ourcq, that on both occasions the real decision lay. Twice, and twice on this same terrain, the miscalculation of the German Staff was the same: they under-estimated the strategic resources of their opponent.

[1] The German casualties, were about 100,000, including 35,000 prisoners. They also lost 650 guns.

[2] The metaphor is Foch's own.

Foch had indeed gone to the extremity of risk to collect his fighting force. He had left Haig in Flanders with no more than fifteen divisions to face the thirty-one of Rupprecht.[1] Even so, he agreed with Pétain that there were not enough men to form a real offensive front on the whole face of the southern salient. 'But,' he said, 'you must attack it all the same.' Pétain—the most cautious of any high commander in the war—was far from enthusiastic. By skilful and plausible procrastination he had prevented Foch from launching Mangin a few days before Ludendorff had shown his hand on the Marne. He still wished to postpone it when it actually came off, and on visiting Mangin while it was in progress made the chilly comment, 'This is all very fine, but would it not be better to break it off?' This attitude was due to his belief that the proper sequence was first to cut off the enemy struggling in the bottom of the pocket on either side of the Marne before proceeding to this larger hope.

Probably a further postponement for a few days would have given even completer success, though not for Pétain's reason. Ludendorff had already, as we have seen, decided to cut his losses, but by the 18th the programme of transferring masses of men and guns to Rupprecht had scarcely begun, so that the number of Germans crowded in the salient was still very large, and sufficient after the first day's surprise to prevent any major disaster.

The minor activities of Mangin had led Ludendorff to expect some kind of attack, and his suspicions had been quickened by information from a deserter on the 11th that it was imminent and would be accomplished by tanks.

When several days elapsed quietly, the weary trench-divisions, ravaged by influenza,[2] relaxed their vigilance. They had done little to improve their defences, which it

[1] For the coming offensive Rupprecht was to have forty-seven divisions and 1,200 batteries. It was to be on a front of thirty miles with Hazebrouck and Poperinghe as the immediate objects. H. von Kuhl, *Der Weltkrieg* (1930), vol. ii, p. 392.

[2] Company strengths never exceeded 65 and were in many cases between 30 and 40: Kuhl, vol. ii, p. 386.

must be remembered were very shallow and sketchy as they had been there for only six weeks.

The ground behind the French lent itself to secret assembly, especially to the north, where the great forest of Villers-Cotterets formed an impenetrable screen. As Mangin points out, batteries had been moved up and down so

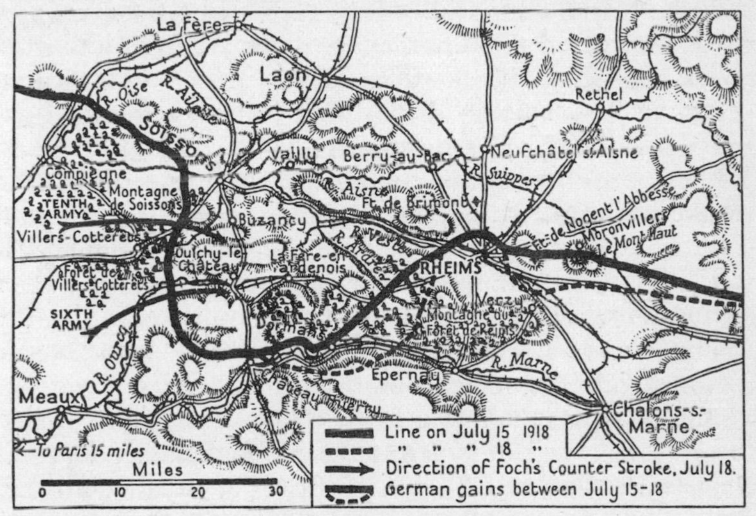

Map 30. Marne Pocket.

incessantly in this area that it was very difficult for new arrivals to be speedily located. 'Surprise', he had already written at the end of June, 'is perfectly possible', and he kept his word. This was the only occasion in the war on which the French used tanks on a scale, or with a success, comparable to that of the British.

The 18th July broke mistily after a furious thunderstorm throughout the night. Smoke clouds further concealed the unheralded onfall of 350 tanks, mostly of the light Rénault design capable of doing at least six miles an hour. Visibility at first was limited to fifty yards. The break-through for the first three or four miles was exceedingly rapid. Several of the trench-divisions were annihilated, the XVIIIth Bavarian for instance being reduced to 320 men. The French fought like men possessed. A friend of the writer, who was in an English division at their side, was amazed at their fanatical ardour. Before midday they were overlooking Soissons from the wooded hill which rises above its south-western suburbs. The railway-station became useless, and all reinforcements from the north had to be detrained several miles above the town. Though these holes had been stubbornly patched by the evening, the strategical position had been utterly altered in twelve hours. Ludendorff was actually discussing with Rupprecht at Tournai the dispositions of his Flemish offensive when the news came through. He ordered its postponement and the immediate dispatch of reserves to the threatened spot. It was clear that, even if a catastrophe could be averted, the salient was untenable. Its main railway line was useless, the great road from Soissons to Fère-en-Tardenois was under distant fire. Unless quantities of wounded and vast material were to be lost the withdrawal required to be carried out methodically by stages, on the assumption that the flanks held. The attacks soon spread to the south-west of Rheims, where fortunately for the enemy the Allies found it very difficult to advance up the Ardre. The German Staff managed the withdrawal most efficiently and their men fought stubbornly. The divisions south of the Marne were most adventurously placed, but made their escape on the night of the 18th. The French let them go so easily that it seems probable that the local commanders thought it a good riddance and did not intend to suffer any loss through interference with their flight.

By August 2nd the German armies, much harried and grievously fatigued, still remained substantially intact; they were out of an awkward trap and safely lodged behind the Vesle.

Though the Crown Prince now recognized the war as lost, and addressed a vigorous memorandum to his father to that effect, Ludendorff still deluded himself. One does not know whether more to admire or pity this indomitable man. At the beginning of August the following dialogue passed between him and the Kaiser's confidential aide-de-camp Niemann. 'Can I assure His Majesty that your Excellency will shorten the line? It appears to me that the positions in which our attacks have left us are awkward for defence and require too many troops.' 'Defence!' replied Ludendorff. 'I hope we shall soon have our attack on Amiens in full swing, when the men have pulled themselves together.' He actually began to prepare four minor offensives. This was, even for him, the last wintry gleam of optimism. In less than a week he had been thrown completely off his balance.

II

At this moment and for some time after the great battle had become general, no one, either soldier or statesman, supposed that the war would end in 1918. On the contrary the autumn campaign was conceived as a mere preliminary for next year's decision. The utmost expected was that the enemy, sorely vexed and harried, would be forced to retire to the Hindenburg line by the coming of winter. Enormous plans were being laid for the spring. Ten thousand light tanks were to break through on every part of the front, to raid the junctions and head-quarters far in the rear. The infantry, coming behind to secure possession, were to be supplied for mobile warfare, in practical independence of the railways, by 10,000 caterpillar tractors, each of which was to carry all the battle requisites of a platoon.[1]

But the soldiers, Foch and Haig above all, were swift to recognize that the widening cracks in the enemy's resistance gave unexpected opportunities for an immediate decision, if a supreme call were made upon the spirit and endurance of the troops. The Allies had indeed learnt much from the methods of their enemy in the last few months, and their attacks benefited thereby. The British had also forged the co-operation of infantry and tanks into

[1] See Winston Churchill, *World Crisis 1916–18* (1927), pt. 2, pp. 468 sqq. The original credit for this idea should apparently be given to Major S. Foot, see Stephen Foot, *Three Lives* (1934) pp. 214, 345 seq.

an offensive weapon of incomparable power and terror. Yet the increasing battle could never have been nourished and kept alive until it became and remained general, without the astonishing strength of mind and body which the exultation of certain victory imparted to the fighting men of all the Allied armies engaged. Moreover, now at last Foch could draw upon an ever-increasing reservoir of power in the great American army. The British, notwithstanding the partial quiescence of the last three months, had suffered most heavily in 1918. Yet it was the British who took the hardest part in this final contest, whose 'hammer blows', in Foch's own words, battered down the chief enemy defences at the vital and decisive spot.

III

The opening move was also made by Haig on August 8th east of Amiens. The place and motive are so obvious that it scarcely seems worth while to settle whether Foch or Haig was responsible for the selection. To free Amiens and the main line to Paris must necessarily be a preliminary for any wider move, just as the reduction of the Saint-Mihiel salient on the Meuse, and the freeing of the Paris–Nancy railway, must precede any offensive in Lorraine. The credit lies principally with Rawlinson and the 4th army Staff for the extreme efficiency and secrecy with which this model attack was mounted, while Foch ensured that any local success should be exploited by holding the French armies to the southward in readiness for a sympathetic advance.

The whole of the preparations were completed in three weeks, a remarkable achievement when it is remembered that only two railway-lines were available. Tanks to the number of 450 were assembled and 2,000 guns. The country is so open that it seemed difficult to suppose that complete surprise could be obtained, though the enemy's aircraft had been completely mastered. One essential point was to conceal the arrival of the Canadians, who, with the Australians on the spot, were cast for the principal role.

The Canadian corps was practically the only unit which had not been engaged in the defensive battles, so that its presence was certain to cause alarm to the enemy. Therefore two Canadian battalions (together with the corps wireless and hospitals) were ostentatiously placed near Kemmel, where their presence was duly noted by their opponents. No less than 38,000 air photographs were issued to the attacking troops to supplement their large-scale maps. The German defences were known to be weak, for Ludendorff's policy of keeping his trench-divisions in the line without relief made it impossible for them to have the energy to dig or to put up wire; so they remained in much the same primitive state as when they were first hurriedly constructed at the end of the great German advance, and every feature in them could be clearly picked out from the photographs.

The attack at dawn of August 8th broke out through a dense mist which was even more helpful to us than that of March 21st to our enemies, for it meant that the tanks were, in many instances, able to overrun the hostile batteries without a shot being aimed at them. In the centre, immediately south of the Somme, the Dominion troops had a triumphant day.[1] They opened the way at last for a real cavalry irruption. In conjunction with 'whippet' tanks they played havoc with the enemy's rear. Singular incidents were recorded. The Air Force captured an 11-inch gun by swooping down on its personnel. A divisional staff was surprised at a hasty lunch. A trainful of troops, a field hospital with a number of nurses, were taken. By nightfall the advance achieved was from seven to nine miles. Thirteen thousand prisoners and 400 guns fell into our hands.

In the next three days the whole front as far as the Oise began to flow back under French pressure.

[1] On the north of the Somme, where the 3rd British corps was engaged, progress was slower owing to the hilly ground, and to the fact that the enemy had himself been engaged in local attacks. The French on the right had also broken country before them and few supporting tanks; nor did they anywhere show great vigour.

There had been no intention on Haig's part to make a strategic breach, for the old German defences of 1916 offered a maze of shelter for a retreating enemy. But Ludendorff in the most frequently quoted passage of his *Memoirs* described August 8th as 'the black day of the German army'. The actual breach was not indeed much worse than at Cambrai, nor did it immediately threaten any vital point. Here, however, for the first time whole divisions had failed, and in many cases allowed themselves to be captured without resistance. Reinforcements were met with cries of 'Black Legs' and 'War Prolongers'.

General Head-quarters could no longer build on sound foundations. The war must be ended. A Crown Council was immediately called at Spa over which the Kaiser presided. The Crown Prince was present with the Chancellor, the new Secretary of State, von Hintze (a sailor turned diplomatist) and Hindenburg and Ludendorff: the proffered resignation of the latter had been refused. The protocol of its meetings makes it clear that the assembled company were all convinced that Germany could not win the war, but not that she had definitely lost it. The military opinion (Hindenburg's being, perhaps, the most confidently expressed) was that the troops could maintain themselves on French territory and 'gradually weaken the war-will of their opponents'.[1] Hence the position was not so desperate as to demand a direct proposal of peace to the Entente, but negotiations should be opened through the mediation of neutrals (the King of Spain and the Queen of Holland) as speedily as possible.

This, however, was not seriously done. The aged Chancellor Hertling seemed fascinated into inaction by the approach of ruin and tried to cheat himself out of realities by repeating to others what he knew to be untrue. He actually had the effrontery to tell the party leaders of the Reichstag on August 21st that General Head-quarters did not consider that the situation called for serious anxiety—'There is no ground for doubting our victory.'

[1] Quoted from the protocol of the Conference.

Hintze was scarcely less supine, and afterwards excused himself by falsely alleging that Ludendorff had desired peace-feelers 'only when the army has successfully completed its retreat to lines of security'. This procrastination lost Germany any chance of a severe but negotiated peace, which she might possibly have attained if Prince Max had become Chancellor as early as August, and had at once instituted responsible government, and also made a direct peace offer to the Entente in concert with his allies.

Meanwhile the war had to be carried on. It was perfectly clear that wide retreats must be ordered. The lines on which the army now stood were at least seventy miles longer than those of March, of awkward and dangerous shape, hastily and thinly fortified. The question to be settled was: 'Where is the retreat to end and how is it to be conducted?'

The Crown Prince advised as swift a retirement as possible to the Hindenburg line as far as the Oise, and hence to the 'Hunding' line north of Laon and the Upper Aisne; and to continue to hold the existing trenches south-eastward from Verdun to the Swiss frontier, except for cutting off the Saint-Mihiel salient. This, however, was far from Ludendorff's view. He was ready eventually to occupy these positions, but only at the close of the campaigning season. 'Not a foot's breadth of ground', he said, 'must be given up without stubborn fighting.' This resolve seems to show that, as so often in his book, he afterwards exaggerated in exile his impressions of coming disaster. For though there were exceedingly important reasons for such a fighting retreat, he obviously could not have undertaken it without preserving faith in the general quality of his troops. He now argued that a swift retreat would be the more dangerous manœuvre. It would allow no time for the destruction of railways and communications. The enemy might appear in strength in front of the new lines before they had been properly occupied and organized. If these were taken the last state of the army would be worse than the first. For, contrary to contemporary belief, which credited the Germans with an inexhaustible capacity for digging, the rearward defences were in a very rudimentary condition.[1] Above all, he could not bring himself to abandon the enormous quantity of every kind of war-material which had accumulated in the offensive zone. Foch himself said of his adversary at the beginning of September: 'The man could still get away if he did not worry about his luggage.'

The success of Ludendorff's plan obviously depended upon his ability to parry his enemies' thrusts and to retreat at his own pace. This he was unable to do, though his army never lost a certain cohesion until the first week of November.

IV

Foch's immediate plan was to give his enemy no rest, to keep on widening the battle (though not yet to make it general) by a series of connected punches at sensitive spots to which reserves must be sent; yet to make each punch sufficiently hard to compel a local retreat in its neighbourhood until a considerable part of the front was in a state of flux, very favourable for increasing captures of men and material. As far as the British army went, the credit for the successful development of the plan was due rather to Haig than Foch.

We have seen that the immediate result of August 8th was to shake the enemy's whole front between the Somme and the Oise into local dissolution. But the defences which the enemy was now manning were far stronger and deeper than those just carried at a bound. Both Foch and Haig wanted to get the Germans back to the Hindenburg line with all possible speed, but their conception of the method differed strongly. Foch urged the continuation of frontal attacks. All local opinion was against this; Monash, the

[1] These were (i) the 'Hermann-Stellung', running from Ostend behind the Upper Scheldt through Valenciennes to the Oise where it joined the 'Hunding', already described; (ii) the Antwerp–Meuse, running in front of Brussels and Namur and then east of the Meuse to Verdun; (iii) the 'Grenz (Frontier) Stellung', from Aix-la-Chapelle south to the Metz defences.

commander of the Australians, was 'emphatic' in his disapproval. Finally, the two leaders met on August 15th and for a time the contention was hot between them. Finally, Foch gave in and allowed the British plan to be adopted. This involved the turning of the defences round Roye by an attack north of the river in the direction of Bapaume by the British 3rd army. It was rightly surmised that the enemy in that quarter would prove quite incapable of parrying such a blow. The decision was of great importance, and it is possible to argue that had it been reversed the war might have dragged on beyond the year. Foch, who had a large generous nature—at least in dealing with his fellow soldiers—wrote of the British operations which followed that 'they were classic examples of the military art, perfectly conceived and perfectly executed'. Haig indeed had grown greatly in stature during the last few months, and was still growing. He was the first of any leader, military or civilian, to foresee the possibility of final victory as inherent in this autumn campaign. As early as August 22nd phrases in a letter to army commanders were to be abundantly justified in their prescience, 'Risks which a month ago would have been criminal to incur ought now to be incurred as a duty. . . . The situation is most favourable. Let each one of us act energetically and, without hesitation, push forward to our objective.'

These three months reveal Haig as a true strategist, as well as an unrivalled trainer and inspirer of troops.

So the battle of Amiens extended its flanks both south and north. First, the indomitable Mangin with his weary troops moved between Oise and Ailette, conquering those wooded hills (called locally 'la petite Suisse'), where Hutier had driven the French backwards towards Compiègne on June 9th. He kept the enemy in uncertainty by varying the hours of his attacks, one being successfully launched at the odd time of 6 p.m.

Then Byng struck on the 21st, placing his principal weight north of the Ancre, whence he was able to turn those hills of terrible memory, Thiepval and Pozières.

Though the enemy, copying Gouraud, withdrew from a deep forward zone, he was not able to stand. By the 23rd a great front of thirty-three miles from the southern suburbs of Arras to our junction with the French was lit up with battle. By the end of the month, all, and more than all, the tortured area so painfully nibbled in 1916 was in our hands. Bapaume had fallen. Above Péronne, at which point the river makes its sharp westward turn, the enemy was already across on the farther bank, having blown up all his bridges with praiseworthy completeness.

The victory was great and the trophies imposing, 34,000 prisoners and 270 guns. It was the more remarkable because the tank corps, depleted by its heavy losses in the earlier fighting, could supply only 100 machines. Moreover, the infantry were scarcely if at all superior in numbers,[1] and most of the divisions were not fresh but already in the line. But the battle-plan now was such that in many sectors the troops were attacking over ground which they knew intimately. This familiarity both economized men and promoted a smooth business-like progress; and a similar procedure was followed, wherever feasible, until the end of the war, which helped to keep the exhausted men in good heart and confidence. The credit can probably be given to Sir H. Lawrence, who had been Chief-of-Staff at G.H.Q. since the beginning of the year.

The enemy had now been hustled out of his great salient, and was standing on a line drawn roughly north to south from Arras to the Aisne. It was fifty miles shorter and economized some twenty-five divisions. Here he hoped to delay for a while and to make good the retreat to the Hindenburg line, if not at leisure, yet without enforced precipitancy. All such hopes were immediately foiled by two brilliant feats of arms.

The key to the upper Somme is Mont-Saint-Quentin,

[1] Actually twenty-three British fought thirty-five German divisions; the latter, however, were little more than skeletons, and were to go on diminishing. By the beginning of September twenty-two had been disbanded, reducing the total to 183.

the rounded hill just north of the town of Péronne, which it completely commands. It acts also as a strong bastion linking up the river line with the down-lands east of Bapaume. It is one of the few instances of the war where a tactical feature was really indispensable for the tenure of the surrounding zone. The enemy knew this well. The whole eminence had been turned into a great fortified keep, alive with machine-guns and garrisoned by a division of the Imperial Guard, which had orders to hold it at all costs. The proposals submitted by Monash, the Australian corps commander, for its capture led Rawlinson to exclaim: 'So you think that you are going to take Mont-Saint-Quentin with three battalions. What presumption! However I don't think I ought to stop you.' This great feat was in fact accomplished in a few hours on August 31st, while other Australian units crossed the stream and stormed Péronne in face of fierce resistance from the ancient ramparts by picked regiments who had volunteered to secure its defence. Thus the river line was lost and the enemy were again forced into an eastward move. No effective pursuit could be launched, as all the bridges had to be repaired. This was an arduous task, for the marshy bed is at least 1,000 yards wide, and in places the water flows in eight separate streams, each of which was surmounted by a now broken arch.

Meanwhile, far to the north, on September 2nd, an even more significant and ominous victory was won by Horne's 1st army. The Canadians, together with the Lowland Territorials (52nd) and Royal Naval Divisions, preceded by a great bombardment of nearly a million shells, and accompanied by tanks, broke clean through the famous Drocourt–Quéant 'switch line'. These elaborate fortifications had been completed for eighteen months and linked up the Hindenburg line near Bullecourt with the old German defences east of Arras. If they could be overrun at a stroke without a great concentration and with little loss, what bounds could be set to the progress of the attacking armies?

V

The tide of enemy retreat must now obviously flow back to the Hindenburg line without let or stay. The chances of a decision in the autumn, towards which every available man must be used, were daily growing less remote.

But there still remained one item in Foch's preliminary programme to be accomplished: the reduction of the Saint-Mihiel salient between Meuse and Moselle, to free the great line between Paris and Nancy. This had long been ear-marked for the first independent action of the Americans.

Their organization into a separate army had been long delayed. It was not brought about until the end of July, when the Allies could no longer plead the grim necessities of self-preservation for their dispersion in separate units between the French and British armies. With wise publicity the number of the punctual and increasing contingents of the last four months had been periodically broadcasted to the world. From Bordeaux to Brest the ports were swollen with their enormous establishments. At Saint-Nazaire alone their port-offices covered more than 2,000 acres. The towns of the Loire, Angers, Tours, and Orleans, were congested with their supply services. Yet they were very far from being a self-contained army. Infantry and machine-gunners were available in immensely disproportionate numbers, for in response to the Allied appeals these units had been given a constant priority of shipment. In many other arms their dependence was complete; they had no guns, no ammunition, no tanks, and very few aeroplanes (for the immense aviation programme in the United States was hung up by the prior necessity of manufacturing the standardized 'Liberty Engine' in sufficient numbers). As more than 60 per cent. of the troops had been safely borne across the Atlantic in British transports, it will be seen that the Allies could bring weighty reasons to support their desire that the Americans should continue indefinitely as auxiliaries of the Franco-British armies, stationed where the Generalissimo considered they could be most usefully directed to help their weary comrades.

Now, the American Commander-in-Chief, General Pershing, was the last man to yield to demands or entreaties, however flatteringly expressed.[1] Wilson had chosen well in sending out this dour, unmovable man immediately after the American declaration of war. He had been thrown back upon his profession with a singular intensity, for some years previously his wife and children had been burnt to death at his country-house. His own aim was to ensure that the great organization which he had helped to build from the start should come under his own undisputed control at the earliest moment. Rigidly Puritan in morals, censorious and unsympathetic towards Europeans, he had an absolute faith in the moral and physical superiority of the American. Yet his blunt directness, simplicity, lack of self-consciousness, and singleness of purpose were not unacceptable to the Allied military chiefs, who were further impressed by the austerity of the discipline which he maintained with an autocratic hand.

During August the main block of American fighting troops, some 550,000 in number, were concentrated on the Meuse. The Saint-Mihiel salient, which thrust a German prong right across the river, has been described earlier in this work.[2] As a defensive position it had no value, and much danger. At a time when every man was needed, it was folly to hold so contorted a line of more than fifty miles, when it could be straightened out at the base to something less than twenty. But since the spring of 1915 no attempt had been made against it, and the order for its evacuation was now delayed too long.

The original plan of assault was ambitious. Both faces

[1] He tells us of his attitude of calculated reserve when King George, on investing him with the G.C.B., pleaded for the continuance of as many American troops as possible with the British, saying that 'their presence had an excellent effect in stimulating the moral of his men' (J. J. Pershing, *My Experiences in the World War* (1931), p. 543).

[2] See pp. 93–4.

of the salient were to be driven in, the base-line overrun with all possible speed, and the advance carried, without limit of objective, to threaten both Metz and the Briey iron-basin, which lies north-west of the great fortress.

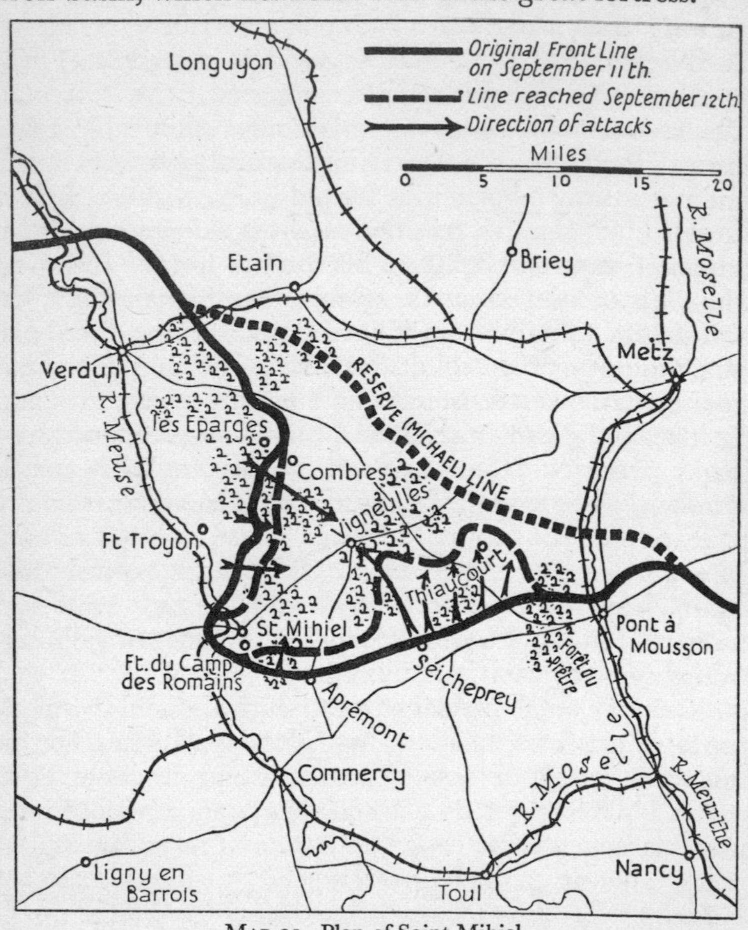

Map 31. Plan of Saint-Mihiel.

On August 27th, however, Haig, whose foresight already envisaged a great series of converging attacks from the sea to the Meuse, urged upon Foch that the main American effort should be diverted to the Argonne. The object of both attacks, indeed, was ultimately the same, to cut the great lateral railway, which alone provided cohesion and safety to all the German armies except the detachment in Alsace. And it was thought easier to reach Mézières than Metz (the strongest fortress in Europe); moreover, the great bulk of German forces were in the north and might thus have their rear directly cut by a swift advance down the Meuse. Finally, and this appealed strongly to Foch, it was hoped to induce the Americans, if transferred to the Argonne and Champagne, to act under French orders or at least direction. Foch eagerly pressed the new plan upon Pershing. His troops should go north immediately to fit into their allotted places in the French plan of attack timed to begin on September 15th. With less than his usual tact, he suggested that Saint-Mihiel, on which the American Staff were doting as on a first-born son, should be abandoned altogether. Pershing stood adamant on the unassailable ground that the Americans would fight only as the President had directed, as an independent army. He would limit Saint-Mihiel, he would even with grave reluctance abandon it; for Foch was constitutionally the sole judge of 'strategy'. But if he went to the Argonne it would be on his own terms.[1] Pétain, the conciliator, sided with the American,[2] and worked out ways and means. Finally, Foch, as was his wont, gave way handsomely and without recrimination.

It remained therefore to reduce the salient with all possible speed. The enemy was growing alarmed, for his garrison was weak and of poor quality. It included a ragged and dejected Austro-Hungarian division, and another composed mainly of Alsatians.

[1] Here is a part of the dialogue between them as reported by Pershing:
Foch: 'Do you wish to take part in the battle?'
Pershing: 'Most assuredly, but as an American army and in no other way.'
Foch: 'There will not be time.'
Pershing: 'If you will assign me a sector I will take it at once.'
Foch: 'Where would it be?'
Pershing: 'Wherever you say.'
(J. J. Pershing, *My Experiences in the World War* (1931), pp. 570–1.)

[2] Pétain was immensely taken with Pershing, who he used to say was the only man who could surprise him by the naïve unconventionality of his actions.

The word for evacuation was at last given, but the task was only beginning when the assault came early on September 12th. From the south and the west the Americans in overwhelming numbers broke through, while the French hammered at the tip. Within thirty hours the whole area had been cleared. The confusion of the enemy was very great, and there seems little doubt that, if the original plan had been carried out, the base line could have been secured. It is most improbable, however, that any great strategic result would have followed. The Germans still possessed considerable reserves within easy hail. There was no such concentration of heavy guns as would have been required to deal with the Metz forts. Finally, the complete break-down of the American transport in the Argonne suggests that they would not have been capable of organizing a continuous advance through the steep and narrow lanes leading eastward from the Meuse.

Yet as a limited operation the success, even in those victorious days, was striking Fifteen thousand prisoners and 450 guns had cost only 7,000 casualties. The American soldier had shown the greatest boldness and dash; in fact his chief defects arose from over-keenness, such as carelessness about liaison, overstepping of boundaries, overrunning the barrage. As further events were to show, in an army of such self-confident individualists, these defects could not easily be eradicated. Both Poincaré and Clemenceau came to congratulate the victors, the former also to visit his own country-house which had been left desolate within the liberated territory.

XXXIV

TOUT LE MONDE À LA BATAILLE[1]

I

THE stage was now set for the greatest of all battles. Events moved with an inexorable swiftness seldom recorded in history. Within three weeks Germany's two eastern confederates were utterly overthrown, and she herself received a blow recognized by her commanders as virtually mortal. The true relation between Germany and her allies became manifest. They were not her 'props', as Lloyd George used to affirm; for as long as she stood secure they stood also through her strength. But when her weakness was displayed, a mere push would overturn them. And with their submission the great fortress of 'Mittel-Europa' could be turned from the rear, so that the doom of Germany herself was certain. The Emperor Karl was expressing the feeling of all his allies when he said with pathetic *naïveté* that the 8th of August had caused far more alarm and despondency in Austria than the defeat of his own troops on the Piave in June, because the latter had been expected. His own despair was made manifest by a futile peace-manifesto on September 14th, independently of Germany, which the Entente neglected with a scornful satisfaction. Though neither Bulgaria nor Turkey had actually concluded an armistice before the supreme struggle began in the West (September 26), they had been so shattered that the issue was immediately certain. The story of Allenby's triumph in Palestine is told elsewhere. The collapse of Bulgaria was due to an utter listlessness and war-weariness which allowed an attack of no overwhelming strength[2] to develop into an overpowering blow.

We do not yet know in detail how the ground had been

[1] Foch's motto.

[2] The German estimate of fighting strength is: Allies 180,000, Bulgars 160,000 to 170,000.

prepared. But when the attack came on September 15th a pro-Entente ministry had for months been installed at Sofia. The British, aided by several divisions of Venezelist Greeks, were condemned as usual to advance up the bottle-neck of Doiran against a *cirque* of high mountains elaborately fortified, and were resolutely repulsed; but farther west the French and Serbs broke clean through. The ragged and half-starved Bulgars, many of whom had been almost continuously mobilized for the last six years, and had nothing left to fight for, ceased to offer even that delaying resistance for which the rugged and broken country was so ideally suited. The stiffening of German troops had been mainly removed—only three battalions, 100 guns, and some machine-gun detachments remained. These strove heroically to rekindle a fighting spirit by their devoted example, but with no success. The Bulgars marched stolidly back as they went forward, getting out of their way on the roads, sometimes even helping to push their transport out of the ditch, but completely unmoved by any appeal. The evil King Ferdinand abdicated and left the country to his popular son Boris, the present ruler (1934). The Serbian advance-guards, terrible avengers, were already invading the frontiers when a surrender at discretion was arranged on September 30th. Franchet d'Espérey, a happy choice to succeed Sarrail as Commander-in-Chief of this motley army of five nations,[1] had thus brought the campaign to a triumphant close in a swift fortnight. All communications were placed at the disposal of the Entente, whose armies occupied the country as a first stage towards Constantinople and the Danube. The Central Powers had to rake together the last remnants of their available strength to protect Hungary against the imminent threat of a winter invasion.

II

Meanwhile Haig with steadfast confidence was methodically working out the stages of approach to assaulting

[1] British, French, Italians, Serbs, and Greeks.

distance of the labyrinthine field fortress between Cambrai and Saint-Quentin.

His decision to attack caused the British War Cabinet great searchings of heart. They had often in the past been led, against their judgement, through his optimism, into sanctioning protracted siege-operations and thus assuming responsibility for the immense unrequited casualties which followed. Lloyd George has written of the sense of blood-guiltiness which oppressed him for the slaughter of Passchendaele, a battle which he had so greatly desired to avoid. Now, when the precious stream of reserves was rapidly dwindling,[1] it seemed to them highly dangerous to stake so much on an autumn decision, in which neither they nor the Chief of the Imperial General Staff believed. Therefore they sent, as they were perfectly entitled to do, a warning to Haig to the effect that heavy casualties incurred in an unsuccessful attack on the Hindenburg line would have grave effects on British public opinion. This time, however, the soldier had the truer judgement; he felt the unmistakable waft of victory, which had not yet been carried over to England. He came over to London, gained his point, and begged the Cabinet to send out everything which could increase the mobility of his army for the open warfare which he confidently foresaw.

In 1917 the Germans had fallen back to the Hindenburg line with a deliberate scientific precision. Now they were cruelly hustled. They could not find a resting-place in the strong outposts which guarded it, and by September 18th had been thrown back upon their last hope of a permanent refuge.

The supreme converging battle was now ready to start. Its two wings in Flanders and on the Meuse were 200 miles apart. The numbers engaged far exceeded those of the great opening-clashes of August and September 1914.

[1] The British casualties from August 8 to September 1 were about 115,000.

Foch's strategy, as has already been pointed out, was determined by the course of the German lateral railway of communication; and it was hoped that success in any of the projected attacks would force a general retirement to the Antwerp–Meuse line. An advance of ten miles in Flanders would secure its great northern junction, Lille. Forty miles east of the British was Aulnoye, where the line met those from Brussels and from Aix–Liége–Namur. A break-through at either of these points was not wholly incompatible with an orderly German retreat. But if the great Franco-American blow between Rheims and the Meuse were successful in driving forward twenty-five to thirty miles, and seizing Mézières and Sedan, the great mass of hostile forces, three-quarters of the whole, lying to the north of these places would be in the gravest danger. For they would be cut off from their route to Germany via Metz and Strasbourg, or by the Moselle Valley. They would be all compelled to squeeze through the junction of Namur, with only two lines of safety beyond; either by Liége to Aix-la-Chapelle, or by a dangerous southern curve, where the railway comes within fifteen miles of Sedan, to seek refuge through Luxembourg and Trèves. The effect therefore of the southern prong of 'Foch's Pincers' (to use the popular name for his strategy) might be catastrophic.

So this attack was timed, to be the opening of the closely connected series, for September 26th.

The American share had of necessity been hurriedly prepared to the point of precipitation. Only ten days had been allowed for the transfer northwards of half a million men fifty miles from Saint-Mihiel. Three-quarters of these had been carried in six nights by French lorries, but the bare concentration was accomplished only on the eve of the battle. It had not been possible to bring over in time the most experienced divisions who had been engaged at Saint-Mihiel. Consequently the new and far harder task was mainly allotted to comparatively raw troops, with the natural results. The Americans have

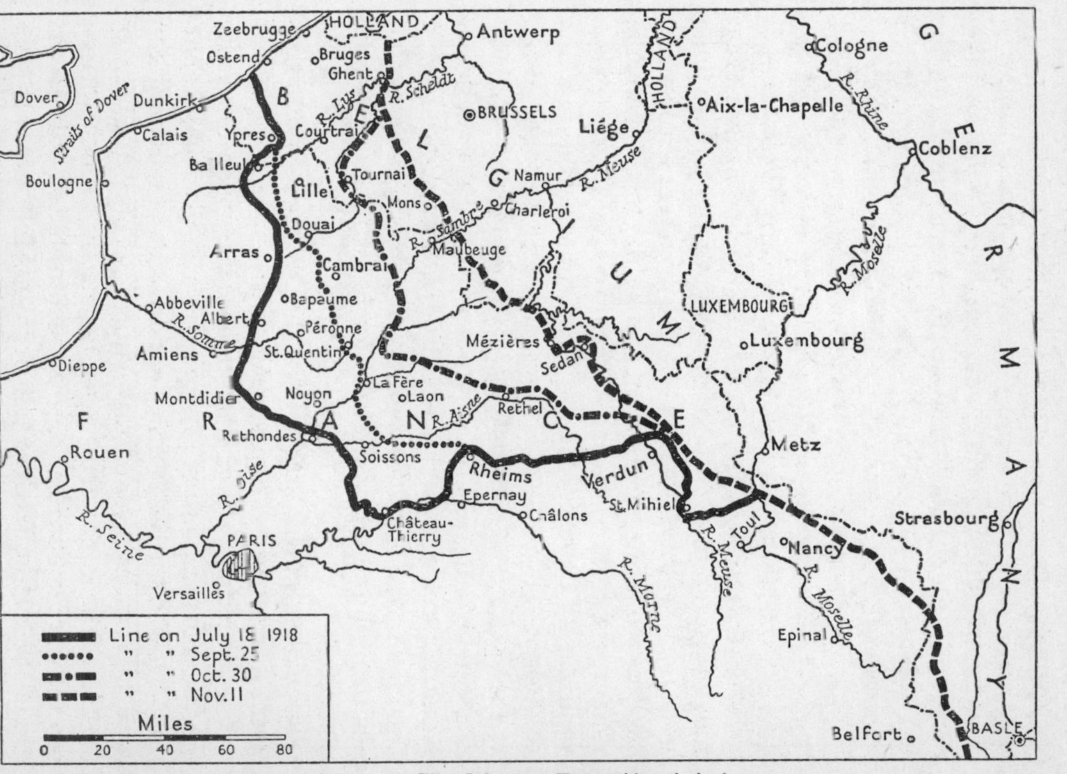

MAP 32. The Western Front (Armistice)

given to this, their greatest battle, which lasted almost continuously for forty-five days,[1] the name of the Argonne.

In reality most of the fighting took place between that hilly forest of pine-trees and the Meuse in comparatively

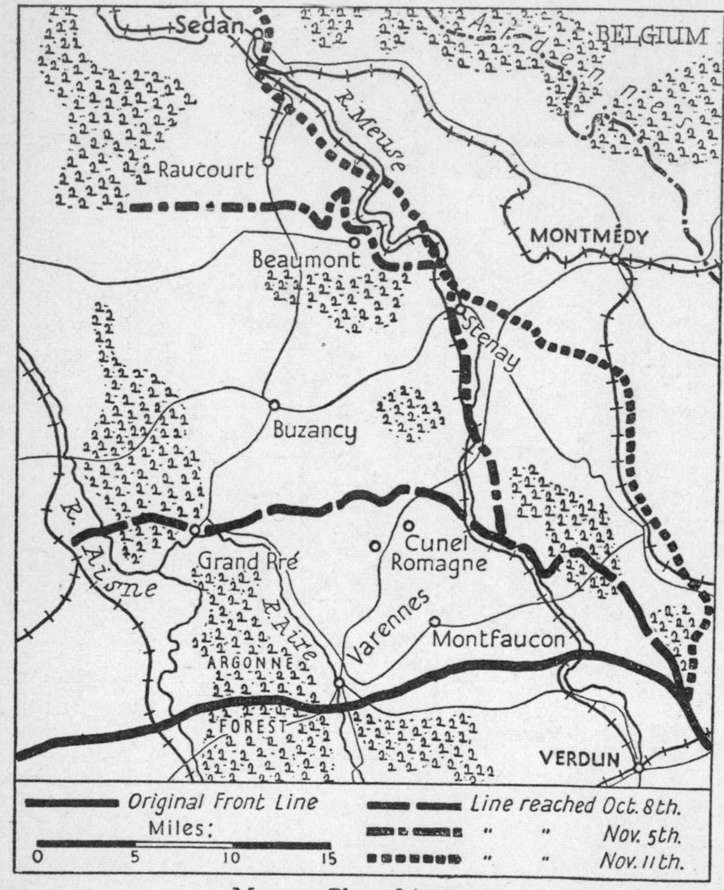

MAP 33. Plan of Argonne.

open country. The French similarly started their active front to the west of that obstacle with the object of pinching out an area so ideally fitted for economical defensive tactics.

The German Staff, not having thought so swift a transfer

[1] During this period their losses were 117,000.

possible, was badly surprised. Their five weak trench-divisions were assailed by a fourfold superiority. On the first day the Americans had good success, far outstripping the French on their left, and by the morning of the 27th had captured Montfaucon, seven miles from their start, the key of the enemy's second position, where the Crown Prince had his forward *poste de commandement* log-built on a commanding hill.

But neither here nor in Champagne could the attack maintain its forward impetus; in both sectors it fell back into the traditional struggle for a few hundred yards of mutilated ground.

The enemy had, of course, always been aware of the crucial importance of the area, and had multiplied his defensive organizations in depth. In Champagne there was one great continuous zone of obstacles for nine miles: in Argonne there were, besides intermediate defences, four prepared positions stretching back for fourteen miles on four successive ridges. His troops fought magnificently, and the machine-guns ensconced in the broken ground and frequent thickets took an enormous toll. But above all the Americans were hampered by their own haste of preparation, by the exiguity of their communications, and by their own dense numbers. The traffic congestion became fearful. It is said that 700 men were starved to death in the front-line trenches; many units, after receiving no rations for four days, returned to the rear to fetch them. Up and down traffic had been unwisely allowed on the same roads, and on one occasion an absolute block occurred for twelve hours. British and French officers were hurriedly sent to reorganize the whole system.[1]

By the beginning of October it was clear that the southern pincer was not working properly, to the bitter

[1] The Argonne front was reasonably served by three railway-lines, but there were only three south–north main roads, one for each corps, on a front of twenty-five miles. Far more troops were crowded into the area than its capacity could possibly allow.

disappointment of Foch, who complained of confusion and lack of energy. Had the advance proceeded according to plan, the enemy would have been left utterly without hope, for very great successes had been won to the northward.

The British were now standing in completed readiness before the Hindenburg line from Bullecourt to Saint-Quentin. Every detail of its construction, and of the system of communications leading thereto, was known to the attackers from a memorandum captured on August 8th. On the other hand, the enemy had effected a vast concentration. On the threatened front fifty-seven divisions were assembled, which, on paper at least, should be more than a match for the forty British and two American arrayed against them.[1]

Moreover, the position was for the most part covered by formidable water-lines, deep canal-trenches impassable by tanks. It seemed therefore as if the brutal frontal assault thus prescribed should, on all previous analogy, be doomed to failure. For the works were the most powerful ever yet constructed in the field, protected in advance by acres of the densest wire, arrayed in great overlapping chequers.[2] Consequently the attack could not be launched suddenly without preparation. The artillery had to be called upon for a prolonged work of devastating fury, which owed much of its scientific effectiveness to lessons learnt from our enemy.

The operation was divided into two parts. The bombardment for both began on the evening of September 26th, but whereas it was required for eight hours only in the north, it was prolonged for fifty-four in the Saint-Quentin sector. Altogether over 25,000 tons of

[1] The G.H.Q. order-of-battle-map of September 25 (reproduced in G. A. B. Dewar and J. H. Boraston, *Sir Douglas Haig's Command* (1922), vol. ii, p. 313; Churchill, *World Crisis 1916–18* (1927), pt. ii, p. 534) gives most vividly the relative denseness of forces on the whole Western Front.

[2] See the photographs and sketches in Maj.-Gen. Sir A. A. Montgomery, *The Story of the Fourth Army* (1919), pp. 148 sqq., which give a most exact panorama of the defences north of Saint-Quentin.

metal were discharged in a million shells. All battery-positions, all head-quarters, and all the entrances of the great tunnelled dug-outs were deluged with a continuous rain of mustard-gas, now at last produced without stint.

Early on the 27th the 1st and 3rd British armies crossed the Canal du Nord against a half-dazed resistance. Before nightfall they had securely conquered all the debatable land of the first Cambrai battle, including the much disputed hill of Bourlon, and were within three miles of the city.

Next day, while the guns were still thundering around Saint-Quentin, the focus of battle shifted momentarily to the north. A third new blow resounded in Flanders, where the whole Belgian army, commanded by its King, and supported by both British and French, overran at a stroke the crater-field torn to pieces during the four-months-struggle of the preceding year, taking Houthulst Forest and Passchendaele. The mud, however, was as usual a more effective hindrance than the weak reinforcements which the distracted German Staff could spare for this new menace, and the advance died down temporarily on October 2nd without having reached either Roulers or Menin. The spoils of victory were 11,000 men and 350 guns.

On the 29th the four-days' orchestra of battle reached its climax. The capture of the southern part of the Hindenburg line was the crowning glory of the much enduring British 4th army, which had fought victoriously ever since August 8th. Supported by the French below Saint-Quentin, it drove a great wedge through the last completed system of enemy defences.[1] The main laurels of the day were won by the North-Midlanders of the 46th territorial division. Their passage over the great canal at Bellenglise was a marvel of combined courage and organization. They crossed with life-belts, rafts, and portable bridges in the teeth of machine-gun fire. The steep

[1] A few miles east the Beaurevoir line was fully wired but dug to an average depth of one foot only.

northern bank had been sufficiently damaged by shell-fire to allow ramps of ascent. By the close of the day they had gone forward three and a half miles and had captured 4,200 prisoners and 70 guns with a loss of 800 men.

Farther north, however, success had been largely denied. Here the canal was carried under the high ground by a tunnel 6,000 yards long, and the whole area was honey-combed with a labyrinth of subterranean galleries and passages. The main task had been allotted to two American divisions, supported by, and under the orders of, the Australian corps. They met with many misfortunes. First, they had to advance 1,000 yards behind their barrage, because much of their proper jumping-off ground had been left in enemy occupation as a result of an unsuccessful attack overnight. Additional tanks had been allotted to them as compensation, but a number of these were destroyed by hostile fire, and twenty-one more were blown up by old British land-mines laid there last March. Nevertheless the Americans, though cruelly punished, thrust right through to their objective. Then, over-ardent and careless in their inexperience, they failed to clear the maze of dug-outs in their rear. The enemy emerged in strength and drew a cordon of fire between them and their Australian supports. Isolated bodies fought it out for hours, and nearly 2,000 were taken prisoners.

Thus, though a signal success, this great action did not fulfil the hope of driving the enemy in confusion through open country. The cavalry, 'whippets', and armoured cars which had been held in readiness were again denied their opportunity.

III

This same September day was rendered most memorable by Ludendorff's demand that a peace offer coupled with a demand for an armistice should be immediately made. He had arranged this move in conversation with Hindenburg the night before, on the reasonable ground that, even if the West held, Germany would be taken in the rear by the Bulgarian collapse.[1] On the 29th, however, under the accumulated blows of continual disaster, his iron nerve broke completely, if indeed he did not actually have a stroke of paralysis, as the evidence of some eye-witnesses suggests. He was obsessed by the terror of an immediate collapse of resistance in France, which events proved (and he himself fully realized a fortnight later) to be unfounded. He pictured Germany as utterly helpless and at the mercy of her enemies. His mind, however, was curiously confused. He apparently believed that, if President Wilson were approached with an offer to make peace on the basis of his 'Fourteen Points', he would insist upon Foch's concluding an armistice at once. He also assumed that the conditions of such an armistice would allow a slow methodical evacuation of France and Belgium. Thus the army would have the rest which it so bitterly needed, and would be able to fight again in secure positions on the German frontier, if the proposed conditions of peace proved unacceptable. It is obvious from his subsequent correspondence with Prince Max that he had never read the Fourteen Points, but merely thought them a vague collection of general principles, about which Germany could haggle until the military situation had been improved. His misconceptions were, indeed, most profound. Wilson was neither willing nor able to dictate policy to the Entente. Its military leaders had not the faintest intention of allowing an armistice on any terms except such as would render Germany incapable of further resistance. Finally, it was obvious to any one except Staff officers that, whatever might be the terms of the Armistice, its conclusion would be the equivalent of preliminaries of peace. After so frightful and prolonged a nervous strain, no

[1] Even if an invasion through Austria-Hungary were delayed for some months, it might be taken as certain that the Entente would gain control over Rumania, whose oil-wells were indispensable for the continuance of the war. The Air Force, it was calculated, would be crippled two months after the supplies of petrol ceased, and no supplies would be left for the civilian population.

soldier would start again when once the cease-fire had sounded.

He was, however, perfectly correct in supposing that if a peace offer were to be made, it could not be undertaken by the tottering Hertling, nor with the existing semi-autocratic constitution inherited from Bismarck. Hence at the very moment when the Centre party in the Reichstag had already intimated to the Chancellor that they could no longer support him, Ludendorff was planning the so-called 'revolution from above'. 'It has never happened that a dictator took such infinite pains to secure power to his antagonists as Ludendorff. . . . The parliamentarization of Germany was not fought for by the Reichstag; it was arranged by Ludendorff'.[1]

At the fateful meeting at Spa (September 29) the two great Captains, with the assistance of Hintze, persuaded the Kaiser, who remained 'unusually calm', to issue the proclamation which invited the German people to co-operate more effectively in the destinies of their country by the establishment of responsible government. Such a government, they insisted, must be formed within two days, or they declined to answer for the safety of the army. Frenzied telegrams arrived in Berlin from Head-quarters demanding the immediate publication of the peace offer, if a new Chancellor's nomination should be delayed.[2]

On October 2nd Ludendorff's emissary, Major von der

[1] A. Rosenberg: *Birth of the German Republic 1871–1918* (1931), p. 242.

[2] Ludendorff's state of mind is vividly depicted in a telegram to the German Foreign Office from its representative at Head-quarters on October 1: 'Ludendorff has just asked me . . . to transmit his urgent request to issue the peace proposal at once, and not to hold it back until the formation of the new government, which might be delayed. The troops still held their ground to-day, and we were in a respectable position, but the line might be broken at any moment and then our proposal would come at the most unfavourable time. He said he felt like a gambler, and that a division might fail him anywhere at any time.

'I get the impression that they have all lost their nerve here, and that, if things come to the worst, we can justify our action to the outside world by Bulgaria's behaviour'—Grünau.

Bussche, read a statement of the military situation to the party leaders of the Reichstag. He concluded that there was no longer any prospect of compelling the enemy to plead for peace. The two decisive factors were the tanks and the state of the German reserves. 'Every twenty-four hours can impair the situation and give the enemy an opportunity of clearly realizing German weakness.'

The Major did indeed assert that the army was strong enough to stand for months and to win local successes, and concluded with the brave words: 'Simultaneously with the offer of peace, a firm stand must be adopted by the nation, to give evidence that a firm will to carry on the war exists, if the enemy will grant us no peace, or a peace only under humiliating conditions.' Nevertheless the effect was terrific. 'The members were completely crushed. Ebert went white as death, and could not utter a word; Stresemann looked as if he had been struck. Seyda the Pole and Haase the Independent Socialist were present. Seyda came out first, his face beaming—Haase rushed up to Ledebour with the words, "Now we've got them".'[1] After this the new government formed next day (October 3) was doomed from the start to the hard road of virtual capitulation, for its supporters, the so-called Majority parties,[2] were determined to end the war on almost any terms.

The new Chancellor, Prince Max of Baden, was the 'transient embarrassed phantom' who presided over the last agonizing days of the Empire, a good man struggling with hopeless adversity. A pleasant, gracious aristocrat—he was the heir to the Grand Duchy—intelligent and sympathetic, he had long attracted the hopes of moderate men. His own liberalism was somewhat pompous and self-conscious, and not without a touch of amiable

[1] Max of Baden, *Memoirs*, English Translation, 1928, vol. ii, p. 12.

[2] These were the Centre, the Progressive party, and the Majority Socialists. The Extreme Right and Left were neither represented in, nor supported, the new government. The two most influential secretaries of State were Erzberger, author of the peace resolution of 1917, representing the Centre, and Scheidemann the Majority Socialist.

Pharisaism. He was fond of making speeches about 'ethical imperialism' and 'moral responsibility', and was known to favour a peace of conciliation. His humane efforts on behalf of prisoners of war had also, it was hoped, rendered him *persona grata* to the Entente statesmen; to the Entente peoples he was entirely unknown. But he was not a man of power or command. He took office most reluctantly, for he saw clearly that the change of régime, coupled with the demand for peace, would be hailed by the Entente as a death-bed repentance, as a mere uncovering of Germany's nakedness. He wrestled manfully with Hindenburg, who had come to Berlin, for at least a fortnight's delay to prepare the ground. He refused, quite correctly, to believe that the military situation was so desperate; if it were, the Supreme Command ought itself to raise the white flag in the field. But the Field-Marshal, as ever majestically calm and showing no signs of nervous strain, was insistent. It seems clear that in his heart he did not think so ill of the situation as Ludendorff, but could not bring himself to dispute the judgement of a colleague on whom he had leaned in the closest intimacy for more than four tremendous years.

Thus it came about that the first official act of the new Chancellor was to dispatch the following note:

'The German Government requests the President of the United States of America to take in hand the restoration of peace, to bring this request to the notice of all belligerent states, and to invite them to send plenipotentiaries for the initiation of negotiations. They accept as a basis for the peace-negotiations the programme laid down by the President in his message to Congress of 8th January 1918[1] and in his subsequent

[1] I. Open covenants of peace, openly arrived at, after which there shall be no private international understandings of any kind but diplomacy shall proceed always frankly and in the public view.

II. Absolute freedom of navigation upon the seas, outside territorial waters, alike in peace and in war, except as the seas may be closed in whole or in part by international action for the enforcement of international covenants.

III. The removal, so far as possible, of all economic barriers and the

announcements, particularly in his speech of 27th September 1918.

'To avoid further bloodshed, the German Government requests the President to arrange the immediate conclusion of an armistice on land, by sea, and in the air.'

establishment of an equality of trade conditions among all the nations consenting to the peace and associating themselves for its maintenance.

IV. Adequate guarantees given and taken that national armaments will be reduced to the lowest point consistent with domestic safety.

V. A free, open-minded, and absolutely impartial adjustment of all colonial claims, based upon a strict observance of the principle that in determining all such questions of sovereignty the interests of the populations concerned must have equal weight with the equitable claims of the government whose title is to be determined.

VI. The evacuation of all Russian territory and such a settlement of all questions affecting Russia as will secure the best and freest co-operation of the other nations of the world in obtaining for her an unhampered and unembarrassed opportunity for the independent determination of her own political development and national policy and assure her of a sincere welcome into the society of free nations under institutions of her own choosing; and, more than a welcome, assistance also of every kind that she may need and may herself desire. The treatment accorded Russia by her sister nations in the months to come will be the acid test of their goodwill, of their comprehension of her needs as distinguished from their own interests, and of their intelligent and unselfish sympathy.

VII. Belgium, the whole world will agree, must be evacuated and restored, without any attempt to limit the sovereignty which she enjoys in common with all other free nations. No other single act will serve as this will serve to restore confidence among the nations in the laws which they have themselves set and determined for the government of their relations with one another. Without this healing act the whole structure and validity of international law is forever impaired.

VIII. All French territory should be freed and the invaded portions restored, and the wrong done to France by Prussia in 1871 in the matter of Alsace-Lorraine, which has unsettled the peace of the world for nearly fifty years, should be righted, in order that peace may once more be made secure in the interest of all.

IX. A readjustment of the frontiers of Italy should be effected along clearly recognizable lines of nationality.

X. The peoples of Austria-Hungary, whose place among the nations we wish to see safeguarded and assured, should be accorded the freest opportunity of autonomous development.

XI. Rumania, Serbia, and Montenegro should be evacuated; occupied territories restored; Serbia accorded free and secure access to the sea; and the relations of the several Balkan states to one another determined by the friendly counsel along historically established lines of allegiance and nationality; and international guarantees of the political and economic independence and territorial integrity of the several Balkan states should be entered into.

XII. The Turkish portions of the present Ottoman Empire should be assured a secure sovereignty, but the other nationalities which are now under Turkish rule should be assured an undoubted security of life and an absolutely unmolested opportunity of autonomous development, and the Dardanelles should be permanently opened as a free passage to the ships and commerce of all nations under international guarantees.

XIII. An independent Polish state should be erected which should include the territories inhabited by indisputably Polish populations, which should be assured a free and secure access to the sea, and whose political and economic independence and territorial integrity should be guaranteed by international covenant.

XIV. A general association of nations must be formed under specific covenants for the purpose of affording mutual guarantees of political independence and territorial integrity to great and small states alike.

XXXV

THE NEGOTIATIONS

FOR the first time since the outbreak of war the minds of all the statesmen, soldiers, and peoples were fixed rather on its ending than on its continuance, though with a more agonized intensity in Central Europe than in the West.

It is a melancholy reflection that, while one fevered week sufficed to break the peace, five times that space of time was found necessary to arrange the terms of a suspension of hostilities. Within this period of the interchange of notes at least half a million men must have been killed or wounded;[1] for the battle raged continually in the West without ever reaching a decisive victory, and towards the end of October it flared up again in Italy.

The demand for an armistice did not take Wilson by surprise, though it was greeted almost unanimously in the American press as a 'manœuvre' or 'trap'. The President himself never wavered from his original standpoint: 'If the Germans are beaten they will accept any terms, if they are not beaten I do not wish to make terms with them.'[2]

Consequently, before committing either himself or the Associated Powers, he had to probe very closely into the intentions of Germany. Therefore, in his reply he asked two questions, and laid down one preliminary condition. He must be clear whether the German Government accepted the Fourteen Points, and would discuss only the practical details of their application; secondly, whether the Chancellor was speaking merely for the constituted authorities of the Empire who had so far conducted the

[1] There is no foundation for the statement which has been made that the negotiations were purposely protracted in order to intensify the existing military superiority of the Allies. A study of Col. House's *Intimate Papers* (edited by C. Seymour, vol. iv, 1926), the most authoritative account, makes this point quite clear.

[2] It must be emphasized that the first three Wilson notes (October 8, 14, and 23) were dispatched without any prior consultation with the Associated Powers.

war. The good faith of any discussion would manifestly depend upon the consent of the Central Powers immediately to withdraw their forces everywhere from the territory of the Entente Powers.

The tone of his reply, which was courteous and used no threatening language, came as a relief to the Chancellor, who had been prepared for all the points raised, and found no difficulty in making what he believed would be a satisfactory reply. The news from the front was also considered more cheering. It was clear that the great quadruple thrust of the Entente had failed to reach any of the vital arteries of German communication. Cambrai had been so desperately defended that, though the British had been within three miles of it on September 27th, they did not enter the city until October 9th. Farther south, indeed, they were standing in open and unravaged country, and advanced as far as Le Cateau in a new attack (October 8–10), but any immediate break-through was reported as unlikely. Their losses had in fact been very great, 140,000 in the last month. They were hampered in their communications by the thrice-devastated waste of the Somme in their rear, and by the efficiency of the German demolitions.

In Flanders, King Albert was held up before Roulers, which important junction he could not enter before October 14th. The comparative impotence of the Franco-Americans in the south was arousing the keenest disappointment. Foch sent a special communication to Pétain complaining of the lack of enterprise and determination which the insufficient results suggested. He was, however, wise enough to decline Clemenceau's proposal that President Wilson should be summoned to dismiss Pershing from his command. The Americans were now almost paralysed by lack of motor-transport. Ludendorff's confidant, von Haeften, went so far as to admit on October 8th that the request for an armistice 'had been from a military point of view unnecessary'.

On October 12th the Chancellor dispatched his second

note. In it he explicitly renounced any rights of negotiation on the principles of the Fourteen Points. Consequently it was left entirely to the enemies of the Central Powers to determine what they meant. This was fully realized by the German Government, which thereby reconciled itself to the loss of Alsace-Lorraine, and of 'indisputably' Polish areas. On the other hand, it was believed that some of the conditions, such as the freedom of the seas, the forbidding of economic barriers, and the impartial settlement of colonial questions, however interpreted, must prove favourable to Germany, and might lead to conflicts between Wilson and the Entente. The note further stated emphatically that 'the Government had been formed by negotiation, and in agreement, with the great majority of the Reichstag', and that the Chancellor spoke both for the German Government and the German People.

On this very day the last of the great submarine outrages on passenger-ships was perpetrated. The *Leinster*, a packet boat plying between England and Ireland, was sunk with the loss of more than 400 lives, amongst them being many well-known persons both British and American. For days the corpses were washed up on the beach to be identified by waiting relatives.

The tone of the President's next reply (October 14) reflected his anger; it was couched in a tone of sombre menace. He refused to consider any armistice while the German forces continued 'illegal and inhuman practices... acts of inhumanity, spoliation and desolation', which the Allied nations 'justly look upon with horror and with burning hearts'.[1]

[1] Besides the submarine outrages he specified the 'wanton destruction' by the German armies in their retreat in France. Though admittedly many acts of cruelty and pillage were committed by isolated troops, many of whom were deserters, the evidence does not suggest that the Supreme Command authorized anything which was not in accordance with military usage (unlike the orders given in 1917). The large towns in particular, where a stricter control was possible, were spared as far as was practicable. Rupprecht pathetically noted in his diary that the inhabitants of Lille spontaneously offered coffee to their retreating enemies.

If an armistice were to be practicable its terms must be left to the military commanders, and must be such as to provide absolutely satisfactory safeguards and guarantees for the maintenance of the present military superiority of the Entente Powers.

Finally, and with great impressiveness, he called attention to

'one of the terms of peace which the German Government has now accepted. . . . "The destruction of every arbitrary power anywhere that can separately, secretly, and of its single choice, disturb the peace of the world; or, if it cannot be presently destroyed, at the least its reduction to virtual impotency." The power which has hitherto controlled the German nation is of the sort here described. It is within the choice of the German nation to alter it. The President's words just quoted naturally constitute a condition precedent to peace, if peace is to come by the action of the German People themselves. The President feels bound to say that the whole process of peace will, in his judgement, depend upon the definiteness and satisfactory character of the guarantees which can be given in this fundamental matter. It is indispensable that the governments associated against Germany should know beyond a peradventure with whom they are dealing.'

This 'terrible note', as the Chancellor described it, was felt by all to mark the last turning of the ways. If it were accepted, Germany would end the war defenceless before her enemies, with her only hope in the intention and power of Wilson to conclude a just peace. Ludendorff had now swung round to demanding resistance *à outrance* rather than put his neck under so grievous a yoke. At a conference in Berlin he declared 'on his conscience that a break-through was unlikely'; that in four weeks the campaigning season would be over; and that, if provided with the reinforcements promised by the Minister of War, he could retire to the Meuse line, and start again in the spring.[1]

[1] Nothing can show more clearly both the ruthlessness and the blindness of Ludendorff than his proposal about Belgium. 'The territory under the Governor-General of Belgium must be made into a military base. We shall have to tell the Food-Commission not to send any more food into the

Despairing plans for a *levée en masse* were mooted. Max himself considered the question of breaking off the negotiations, and making a supreme appeal to the People. But Scheidemann truly expressed the popular feeling when he exclaimed 'Better a terrible end than terror without end'. The misery in Berlin was growing apace. Apart from the chronic semi-starvation, the supply of oil and coal was growing desperately short as the autumn drew on. An influenza epidemic was reaching its height. On October 15th, 1,722 people died of it in the Capital.

Moreover, the President's demand for the destruction of arbitrary power began to penetrate the popular mind. Though the abdication of the Kaiser was not yet openly demanded, the thought ran through countless distracted minds, 'If we get rid of him we shall get a decent peace'. Karl Liebknecht and the other leaders of the Extreme Left, now released from jail, eagerly fomented this feeling. The Government therefore concluded that only one road was practicable, and on October 20th replied submissively. They merely expressed the hope that no demand would be made 'incompatible with the honour of the German people or with paving the way to a peace of justice', and sought to convince Wilson that no arbitrary power now existed in Germany.

Three days later he replied, consenting to take up with the Entente the question of an armistice which must give unrestricted power to enforce the terms of peace. He again pointedly expressed his belief that responsible government had not been fully worked out, and that if he had to deal 'with military masters and monarchical autocrats' he must demand 'not negotiations but surrender'.

Wilson's doubts were indeed fully justified. The majority of the Reichstag, on which the new Government was based, was out of touch with its constituents. The

country . . . Belgium must be told that peace is still far off, and the horrors which are inseparable from war may befall Belgians once more *so that 1914 will be child's play compared to it.*' (Author's italics.) *Official Report of proceedings of War Cabinet*, October 25, 1918, quoted in Max of Baden, *Memoirs* (1928), vol. ii, pp. 191–2.

Chamber itself, of which the Chancellor was not a member, was so incredibly supine that during this period of supreme crisis it adjourned from October 5th to October 22nd, and again after a short sitting till November 9th. The decisive powers of the Bundesrat or Federal Council were unaltered. Its members were simply the delegates of the various German state-governments, and the preponderance of Prussia gave it a constitutional veto on any reform of the constitution. Martial law was still enforced independently of the civil power. The prerogatives of the Kaiser as Supreme War Lord were still untouched. All appointments had hitherto been, and were still being, made on his own personal unrestricted initiative. On the receipt of this note the Government felt obliged, with undignified and frantic haste, to pass a series of measures designed to bring all powers in the state under the control of the Reichstag. It also seized the opportunity to dismiss Ludendorff who, in a mistaken belief that he was representing the official view, had issued an order to the troops calling on them to resist to the last against the dishonourable capitulation proposed by Wilson. The fall of this tremendous personality passed almost unnoticed, as Hindenburg remained at his post. Groener, a railway expert, succeeded as First Quartermaster-General to apply his great organizing abilities to a hopeless task.

The front still held dourly in the West. The repeated blows of the Entente took more and more the form of beating the enemy back frontally upon his communications in Belgium. The whole of the Flemish coast had now gone, and all the enormous guns dug in on the dunes were left half-destroyed to be the wonder of sight-seers for many years after the war.

In their retreat the Germans, now almost everywhere in improvised lines, made use as far as possible of water-defences for delaying actions to check the tanks. In the last days of October, resting their right on the Dutch frontier, they were defending Tournai and Valenciennes. Farther south the French on the Oise were approaching

Guise, were well north of Laon, and standing on the upper Aisne by Rethel, but on the northern extremity of the Argonne they and the Americans were still struggling desperately to conquer the last portions of the last fortified line.

The decline in German man-power was now progressively steep. The Allies had a superiority of about 40 per cent. On October 31st only one fresh enemy division was in reserve. Half a million men remained on leave, the majority because they refused to return, but others because the congested railways could not bring them back. Nearly 300,000 prisoners had been lost since August 8th, and thirty-two divisions had been disbanded.

At this moment another broad road of invasion was being opened in the rear.[1] The general offensive of the Italian armies against Austria, which is related elsewhere, opened on October 24th.

Three days later the Emperor Karl wrote to the Kaiser expressing his 'irrevocable decision to issue within twenty-four hours a request for a separate peace and an immediate armistice'.[2] By the beginning of November it became necessary to deplete the West in order to form a Bavarian army of defence for the Tyrolese frontier.

The general collapse could not be delayed for many days.

[1] The French guns had already been heard on the Danube on October 19; for the first time, as Franchet d'Espérey grandiloquently reported, for 109 years.

[2] It should be remembered to the honour of the German Government that on this very day they chivalrously dispatched 12,000 tons of foodstuffs from their own scanty stores to the starving Austrians.

XXXVI

THE GERMAN REVOLUTION AND THE ARMISTICE

I

GERMANY was by now ripe for revolution, which meant the violent transfer of power by the masses to a republican government directed by the middle class on parliamentary lines. The Bismarckian system had kept the people in a tutelage which was popular only as long as it was successful. Even before the war the Socialist vote, most of which represented what would be called in England moderate radicalism, had risen to four and a quarter millions. The glitter of the Kaiser's flamboyant and self-advertising personality had long since been utterly dimmed. Already in May 1917 an official meeting had been held in the Ministry of War to whip up monarchical sentiment. The programme suggested was singularly German in its thoroughness and its complete lack of humour. Lectures were to be frequently delivered by teachers or 'other suitable persons such as wounded officers'. Articles, pictures, and films were to illustrate the devotion to duty, the simplicity of life,[1] the sacrifices of the Imperial Family. The Emperor was to be kept in the public eye by visiting factories, distributing decorations, and so forth. The historian of the republic truly remarks: 'Attempts to save a monarchy by such means prove that the monarchy is already dead.'[2] The whole régime was lost as soon as the

[1] Scheidemann quotes this passage about the stores found in the Palace after the Revolution. 'One could not imagine that after four years of war such colossal piles of food could still be found in store. Meat and poultry on ice, soups and sauces in big bottles, pure white flour in sacks piled up to the ceiling. Thousands of eggs, huge tins of lard, coffee, chocolate, jellies and preserves of every kind. Hundreds of blue sugar-loaves, stone-fruit, biscuits, &c. One was speechless. The value of the provisions amounted to several hundred thousand marks. We were told on good authority that these piles of stores were for the Kaiser's private household, and not for the Court.' (*Berliner Tageblatt*, November 20, 1918.)

[2] A. Rosenberg, *Birth of the German Republic 1871–1918* (1931), pp. 260–1. The full account of this meeting is well worth reading.

people woke up to realize that they had been brought by their autocrats almost without warning from secure expectation of victory to staring imminent defeat.

The moment of dissolution, however, was determined by two things: Wilson's denunciation of the monarchical autocrats with whom he would enter into no negotiations, and the mutiny of the fleet.

The only hope of saving the monarchical principle in Germany lay in the application during October of brutal and unrelenting pressure on the Kaiser to abdicate, and on the Crown Prince to renounce the throne in favour of his son. As the last-named was a child, a Regency would have been necessary for several years, during which a parliamentary régime might have been firmly established. Prince Max, however, both by birth and character was the last man for this task. Dynastic considerations, his own relationship with the Kaiser, and his amiable nature prevented him from exercising anything but the mildest indirect influence until it was too late. On October 29th William, alleging a number of false excuses, furtively left Berlin for General Head-quarters to seek the protection of the army, and declined the most pressing entreaties to return to the Capital. He still lived in his world of unreality, surrounded by a knot of 'Byzantine' courtiers.

On the day of his departure began the naval mutiny which set the spark of revolution flying across Germany. After orders had been given to abandon submarine warfare (October 20) Admiral von Scheer had intimated to the Chancellor that 'the fleet should once more be accorded complete freedom of action'. But beyond this cryptic remark the Government had no inkling of the great enterprise which the navy was about to launch in a supreme effort to help the army and to create a more favourable situation for the negotiation of an armistice. It was not intended as a 'death ride', a heroic gesture of unreasoning self-sacrifice, but was a well-designed and carefully prepared operation. Two cruiser squadrons were to make simultaneous raids on the Straits of Dover and the mouth of the Thames, in order to sever communications with France and throw the British army's supplies into confusion. It was supposed that the Grand Fleet would then steam south from Scapa. All the available submarines (now of course released from preying upon commerce) were to harry its course with torpedoes and mines; thus seriously crippled before a fleet action, it was to be engaged by the High Seas Fleet off the Dutch coast.

But as Thucydides wrote: 'It is the men who make the city, not the strong walls, or the ships.' The spirit of the fleet had long been deteriorating, particularly on the battleships. The partial mutiny of 1917 had been only a foretaste of what was now to come. Cooped up inactively in harbour, herded together with monotonous and insufficient food, deprived of their best junior officers and petty officers, who had been taken on submarine service, increasingly impatient of the precise discipline, and sometimes penetrated by the pacific propaganda of the Independent Socialists,[1] the sailors were in no mood for the heroism of a forlorn hope. Most of them regarded the armistice negotiations as equivalent to the end of the war, and were determined not to sacrifice their lives in what they believed to be a useless battle of prestige. When, therefore, the crews of two great ships refused to obey the order to put out to sea, and were imprisoned, the movement shortly became general, and by November 4th the great port of Kiel was in the hands of the mutineers.

Meanwhile both Turkey and Austria had accepted armistices with terms of pitiless rigour. In the West the military position was again most imminently perilous. On November 4th the British east of Valenciennes broke through their enemy between the Scheldt and the Sambre, taking 20,000 prisoners and 450 guns.[2] The much enduring German rearguards were for the first time thrown into

[1] The inquiry held into the mutiny seems to prove conclusively that political aims had comparatively little to do with its inception.

[2] An incident of this battle is worth recalling as a picturesque anachronism. The New Zealanders took the walled town of Le Quesnoy by escalade, mounting on ladders upon its ancient ramparts.

such great confusion that Haig described the enemy thereafter 'as capable neither of accepting nor refusing battle'.[1]

The advance of the Americans opened yet more sinister possibilities. Between November 1st and 7th they had gone forward twenty-four miles on either side of the Meuse, the French on their left keeping pace by the capture of Mézières and Charleville. The last exploit of the Americans was the curious race for Sedan, which scene of French humiliation lay just outside the zone of their armies. Spurred on by a kind of irrational sentimentality the 1st division swooped right across the boundary both of its left-handed neighbour and of a French division in order to obtain the coveted honour. The commander of the 1st American army, Liggett, however, sensibly allowed the French to have the right of entry.

Groener, who since his appointment had been straining every nerve to disengage the army in a rapid retreat to the Antwerp–Meuse line, now gave up the position as hopeless. On November 6th he told the Chancellor that 'we shall have to cross the lines with a white flag. . . . Even a week is too long to wait. It must be Saturday [November 9] at latest.'

This despair was not merely due to the events at the front, but to the swift spread of revolution at home. The mutineers at Kiel, some 40,000 armed men, were moving by warship, lorry, and rail, all carrying the red flag, over north-west Germany, setting up soldiers' and sailors' councils after the Russian fashion. By the 6th they already controlled Hamburg and Bremen. Next day Hanover, Brunswick, and even Cologne had fallen into their hands. On this day also the insurrection, born of the fear of invasion, had broken out independently at Munich, where the King of Bavaria was the first crowned head to be toppled unresistingly from his throne.

Nor was the revolution stayed by the news now published that Foch had been authorized to receive

[1] During the last week the total British casualties amounted to 9,100 as against 18,000 and 26,000 for the two preceding weeks.

representatives of the German Government and to communicate to them the terms of an armistice.

Berlin remained in tense expectation. The roads and railway-stations in the vicinity were picketed, and isolated bodies of sailors who arrived were successfully disarmed. But as the Kaiser stayed obstinately at Spa, evasively setting aside all remonstrances, it was clear that this thunderous calm could not continue. The Majority Socialists, who 'hated the Social Revolution like sin',[1] endeavoured to force the Chancellor's hand by demanding the immediate abdication of the Kaiser on pain of withdrawal of their representatives from the Cabinet. It was labour wasted. On November 9th the crowds came out into the streets, and the crack Jäger battalions, whose fidelity was deemed secure, fraternized with them instantly.

Meanwhile at Spa the Kaiser was playing his last and most poignant drama. The Socialist demand was curtly rejected on November 8th; and instead General Headquarters were ordered to prepare for civil war, 'an operation in the interior' as it was delicately described.

William as a young sovereign had told his troops at the swearing-in of recruits that they must be prepared to shoot down their fathers and brothers at his bidding. He now proposed to exact this last test of fidelity to the military oath. Even the faithful Hindenburg told him sorrowfully that the proposal was impracticable. Groener bluntly said: 'In a situation like this the military oath is a mere fiction.' Nay more, he told William plainly, that though the army would march back peacefully under its generals when the armistice was concluded, it would decline the leadership of its Supreme War Lord. 'It is no longer behind you.'

William had just reached the unconstitutional and unpractical decision of abdicating as Emperor but not as King of Prussia[2] when he was rung up for the last time on

[1] A saying of Ebert, the future President of the Reich, to Prince Max.

[2] By the Constitution of 1871 the office of Emperor was inseparably attached to that of King of Prussia.

the morning of November 9th by the Chancellor. An underling replied that the Kaiser was engaged in writing down the details of the act of abdication, which would take about half an hour. The receiver was then disconnected to avoid the further importunity of the Cabinet. Prince Max immediately announced in Berlin the Kaiser's unqualified renunciation[1] of the throne and handed over the Chancellorship to Ebert, the saddler's son, a staunch, imperturbable, upright man, who worthily filled later on the position of first President of the Reich. At 2 p.m. that day Scheidemann on his own initiative proclaimed the Republic from the steps of the Reichstag. Very early next morning the Kaiser fled in his car to the Dutch frontier, which he was allowed to cross after being detained six hours in the waiting-room of a small railway-station.

Hindenburg, that exemplar of duty, remained at his post to lead the army home.

While all these things were being done, the Armistice Commission had crossed the lines (November 7), had been received by Foch, and presented with the terms.

II

It is now necessary to go back a few weeks in order to trace the stages by which an agreement was reached between America and the Entente. The President had been careful not to commit his associates to an armistice, but had made it clear that, if an armistice were to be arranged as a result of his negotiations with Germany, it must be, so far as he was concerned, upon the basis of the Fourteen Points. The Allies had therefore to decide both whether the military position admitted an armistice, and whether they could agree to adopt the peace terms suggested. While their military experts were entrusted with a preliminary formulation of the armistice terms, the Supreme War Council met in Paris to consider the

[1] No reservations with regard to Prussia had been mentioned in the telephonic conversation.

political question. The great Allies were represented by their Prime Ministers, while Colonel House had come across the Atlantic as Wilson's plenipotentiary. 'I have given you no instructions', said the secret, lonely President to the one man whom he trusted without reserve, 'because I feel that you will know what to do.'

House, whose great merit as a diplomatist was his perfect mingling of frankness and conciliation, had a difficult task. An acute English observer wrote afterwards, 'it seemed for a time as if it would be utterly impossible to get the Allies to agree to an armistice based on the Fourteen Points'. This was natural. They had not been consulted as to their formulation, nor had they received any authoritative definition of their meaning. House therefore took care that they were interpreted point by point, and the commentary upon them, after much debate, was accepted as the official American version and was cabled to the President for his approval. To win his victory House had to go so far as to threaten that America might conclude a separate peace. Finally, it was agreed that the President could inform Germany that the Allies accepted the terms with two reservations,[1] which ran as follows:

'They must point out, that clause 2, relating to what is usually described as the Freedom of the Seas, is open to various interpretations, some of which they could not accept. They must, therefore, reserve to themselves complete freedom on this subject when they enter the Peace Conference.

'Further, in the conditions of peace laid down in his Message

[1] It has been much disputed whether the Fourteen Points applied also to Austria-Hungary. That Power never received a formal assurance from the Allies as was given to Germany that an armistice would be concluded on the basis of the Fourteen Points, and the demand for an armistice was at last unconditionally made from sheer military necessity. The points dealing with Austria-Hungary, on the other hand, were not excluded in the final answer to Germany, as Sonnino desired. But the French and British Prime Ministers seem to have assumed that, in making an armistice with Germany, the Fourteen Points applied only to questions which concerned that Power (see Col. House, *Intimate Papers* (1926), vol. iv, pp. 178–9). The author's own view is that a moral, but not a legal obligation was involved towards Austria-Hungary.

to Congress on 8th January 1918, the President declared that invaded territories must be restored as well as evacuated and made free. The Allied Governments feel that no doubt should be allowed to exist as to what this provision implies. By it they understand that compensation will be made by Germany for all damage done to the civilian population of the Allies and to their property by the aggression of Germany by land, by sea, and from the air.'

The first reservation was due to Lloyd George, who said with the utmost firmness: 'I could not accept the principle of the Freedom of the Seas. It has got associated in the public mind with the blockade. . . . The English people will not look at it. On this point the nation is absolutely solid. It 's no use for me to say that I can accept when I know that I am not speaking for the British nation.' Thus Lloyd George echoed the words of Castlereagh a century before. He did not go so far as his predecessor in refusing to discuss it at the Peace Conference, but as a matter of fact it was never discussed. The other reservation, which touched the pockets of all the Allies, was naturally made in common.

The only exceptions to the general agreement that the request for an armistice should be granted, were those of Poincaré and Pershing. The dour Lorrainer wished the bitterness of defeat to be brought home to the German people by the invasion and laying waste of their territory. His protest was most brusquely set aside by Clemenceau. Pershing, for his part, objected that the military position was now so favourable that the enemy could be compelled to a speedy capitulation in the field.

There was, however, much division of opinion between Foch and Haig as to the terms which should be offered. The latter, impressed by the weariness of the Franco-British armies, by their ever-increasing transport difficulties, and by the stoutness of the enemy's resistance, was of the opinion that the Germans would refuse any harsher conditions than the evacuation of the occupied territories and of Alsace-Lorraine, together with the restitution of rolling-stock taken from France and Belgium. Foch pointed out that if their withdrawal should be successfully accomplished, and the artillery and war-material brought back across their old frontier, the future defensive position of the German army, standing behind the Rhine, would be more favourable than at present.[1] His own terms involved complete evacuation, under pressure of a rigorous time-limit, the surrender of a large proportion of every kind of equipment, and the occupation of bridge-heads beyond the Rhine by the Allies. These terms would, in his opinion, be accepted; and he added, in the spirit of a true soldier, the servant of the state: 'We make war only for results. These terms will give us the desired results. That being so, no man has the right to cause another drop of blood to be shed.' With minor modifications his proposals were accepted by the Supreme Council, and were those set before the Germans. The naval terms, drawn up by the British Admiralty, involved the surrender not only of all the German submarines but of most of their 'super-dreadnought' battleships and battle-cruisers. Such conditions were considered by Foch and Clemenceau as unnecessarily severe and likely to court refusal. The former asked whether the war should be continued in order to suppress what he called 'the virtual influence' of battleships that never came out of their ports. Lloyd George retorted that if these had not existed Great Britain could have supplied far more men and supplies to the common cause. If they were left with power to strike, the British navy would have to remain fully mobilized, under the strain of war conditions, until peace was actually signed. He was ready to substitute internment in the ports of some neutral Power under surveillance, but would not go further. This proposal was accepted (November 4) after Austria had agreed without a murmur to the exceedingly harsh provisions of the armistice offered to her.

Finally, it was agreed on the proposal of Clemenceau,

[1] These were in fact the terms which the German Command had always hoped to obtain.

although against the desire of the British, to insert the words 'reparation for damages' into the armistice conditions, where they were obviously out of place. 'It would not be understood in France', he urged, 'if we did not make mention of the principle.' The cunning Klotz,[1] the French Finance Minister, insinuated that it would be prudent to put at the head of the financial section a clause running 'with the reservation that any future claims or demands on the part of the Allies remain unaffected'. Some French statesmen have not scrupled to declare that this casual insertion overrode the definition of reparations expressed in the note to Germany already quoted.

It was now possible for the President to inform Germany that the application for an armistice could be made (November 5).

III

Erzberger, the Secretary of State, undertook the hard task of presiding over the Armistice Commission. He had the reputation of a supple and intriguing politician, but in this extremity he showed both dignity and courage. Not many years afterwards he was murdered by so-called nationalists for this act of duty. On the evening of November 7th he and his fellow commissioners passed the lines in cars, with great white flags hoisted, and a trumpeter sounding, and were conveyed to Rethondes in the forest of Compiègne, where Foch held his travelling head-quarters in a railway-train.

Their demeanour was such that the Generalissimo telegraphed after the first meeting: 'They seem well disposed to accept our conditions.'

With Foch was associated Sir R. Wemyss, the British First Sea Lord, but no other of the Allies. When the two parties were facing one another at the table, Erzberger said that they had come to receive the Allied proposals. 'I have no proposals to make,' replied Foch. Another German member tried an alternative form of words: 'We

[1] He was some years later convicted of fraudulent bankruptcy.

ask the conditions of an armistice.' Foch replied as before: 'I have no conditions to make.' When the Germans read Wilson's note Foch said: 'Do you ask for an armistice, if so I will make known to you the conditions on which it may be obtained.' Thereupon the Germans formally requested it. The conditions were then read and it was intimated that they must be accepted or rejected within seventy-two hours. In vain the Germans begged that hostilities might be immediately suspended; every day's fighting, they urged, increased the peril of a triumphant Bolshevism sweeping over Europe. Foch answered with chilly common sense: 'That is a disease of the vanquished.' The terms were sent back to Spa by a courier who had the greatest difficulty in getting through the German line, where violent firing persisted. During the interval Erzberger tried valiantly to get some modifications. He pitifully explained that if 30,000 machine-guns were surrendered, there would not be enough left to fire upon the German people. Above all, he protested against the continuance of the blockade. Women and children, he pointed out, would be the chief sufferers. He tried to enlist the sympathy of the British admiral by using a favourite English word and asking: 'Is this fair?' He received the retort: 'Fair! Remember that you have sunk our ships without making any distinction of sex.' It was, however, promised that the Allies would undertake the provisioning of Germany.[1]

On the 10th at Spa the terms were being finally considered. The reports which poured in from all sides were desperate. All the crossings of the Rhine were now in the hands of mutineers. The contagion was spreading rapidly towards the front. At Liége, Namur, and Brussels mobs of frenzied soldiers were hoisting the red flag, pillaging and selling their weapons to the Belgians. When Rupprecht

[1] This promise was most imperfectly kept, until in the spring of 1919 Plumer, commanding the British army of occupation, telegraphed to the Supreme War Council that he could not answer for his troops unless adequate supplies were sent to Germany, so angered were they at the privations of the population.

saw these things he noted in his diary: 'We are utterly without defence and without honour. For the first time in my life I am ashamed to be a German.'

It was not known whether any government existed in Germany, or if so whether it had any power. Consequently the reply sent back by Hindenburg to Erzberger, after indicating various amendments to be sought, ended with the conclusive words: 'Even if you cannot obtain these points, you must sign nevertheless.' How are the mighty fallen and the weapons of war perished! From 2 till 5 in the morning of November 11th the delegates wrestled finally with Foch, and obtained some slight ameliorations. Erzberger read a statement to the effect that the Government would loyally do everything within its power, but that some of the clauses were unrealizable. He concluded with the poignant and prophetic words: 'A nation of seventy millions suffers but does not die'; to which Foch enigmatically replied: '*Très bien.*'

At 11 o'clock that morning the 'Cease fire' sounded over all the front, and the Allied troops stood fast on the line which they had gained. They had reconquered a third of Belgium and almost the whole of French territory.[1] Just before the hour British troops entered Mons, where they had fought their first battle on August 23rd, 1914.

The principal conditions of the Armistice were as follows:

i. *Military.* Evacuation of occupied territory including Alsace-Lorraine within fourteen days, and repatriation of the inhabitants. Evacuation of the left bank of the Rhine and of the bridge-heads of Mainz, Coblenz, and Cologne within thirty-one days, a neutral zone being established on the right bank; 5,000 guns, 25,000 machine-guns, and 1,700 aeroplanes to be handed to the Allies, together with 5,000 locomotives, 150,000 trucks, and 5,000 lorries. All Allied prisoners-of-war to be immediately returned without reciprocity.

ii. *Naval.* Surrender of all submarines. Internment in

[1] Since July 18 they had captured 385,500 prisoners and 6,615 guns, of which the British share was 188,700 and 2,840.

neutral or Allied ports of ten battleships, six battle-cruisers, eight light cruisers, and fifty destroyers. Free access to the Baltic with right of occupation of any forts. Immediate return of all Allied merchantmen in Germany's possession; no German merchantmen to be transferred to a neutral flag. The blockade to be continued.

iii. *Political.* The treaties of Brest-Litovsk and Bucharest to be renounced. All German troops to be withdrawn behind the pre-war frontier, and free access to be given to the Allies to enter the evacuated territory.

iv. *Financial.* Apart from reparations for damage, all valuables and securities which had been removed from the invaded regions to be immediately returned, and all gold taken from Russia or Rumania to be entrusted to the Allies for safeguard.

It is obvious that the German High Command would not have accepted such terms unless it had been reduced to the last extremity. In such a war of nations the power of resistance is broken as soon as the spirit of the country snaps under the strain. This had been recognized by the *poilus* of Verdun when they exclaimed: 'Pourvu que les civils y tiennent', and by Hindenburg himself when he said: 'The side which has the best nerves will win.' It is true that the German soldiers at the front were still fighting bravely, but within a few days the chaos of the rear would have deprived them of food and supplies, if it had not also infected them with the revolutionary spirit. It is also true that Foch had only one great card left to play, the attack in Lorraine on either side of Metz which had been timed for November 14th. In view of his overwhelming superiority in numbers this could not have failed of success, and the enemy's evacuation of the great fortress had already begun. Yet owing to the lack of cavalry Foch could not have pushed very far beyond Metz; but even this advance would have greatly increased the congestion of the railways at the junctions of Namur and Liége. It would probably have meant that great hordes of German soldiers would have crossed the Dutch frontier, but it would not have led to any great captures by the Allies. For between the sea and the Meuse the advance was on the point of coming to a standstill. It had outstripped the capacity of the railways for repair, and the devastations effected on the roads by the enemy had been most efficient. Further, the effect of delayed-action mines (some of which were timed to explode a month later) made the process of advance exceedingly hazardous. The march forward into Germany could not be undertaken by the British army until six days had elapsed after the Armistice, and then only with a third of its total strength. The greatest difficulty was actually found in providing adequate rations even for this fraction.[1]

It is therefore true, as both Foch and Haig subsequently acknowledged, that, if the revolution had not broken out, the bulk of the German army could have retired behind the Rhine. The Allies were in no condition to force a capitulation upon it as the sequel to the heavy and continuous defeats which they had inflicted. The Germans have every reason for pride in the steadfast constancy of their fighting troops. But even had it been possible, from a purely military point of view, to hold out until the following spring, the starving German army, deprived of petrol, vainly endeavouring to hold the western, the southern, and south-eastern frontiers against an encircling enemy, who would still have been increasing in numbers, would have reserved itself only for a worse fate.

The simple truth is that Germany ended the war because she had come to the end of her endurance, and it is doubtful whether any other country would have endured so long.

[1] Sir F. Maurice in *The Last Four Months* (1919), pp. 221–7, gives many interesting details of the Allied transport-difficulties.

XXXVII

THE LAST YEAR OF THE ITALIAN WAR AND THE END OF AUSTRIA-HUNGARY

I

THE Italian army was placed under the command of Diaz, a junior corps commander, a sensible, hardworking man who knew far more about the men than his predecessor, but himself of no great personality or commanding stature as a strategist. At least he fulfilled his principal task of maintaining the spirit and increasing the efficiency of his army. Except for two weeks of intense fighting in June and October 1918 the whole front maintained an almost unbroken calm.[1]

The Austrians, conscious of the progressive decay in their fighting power, would have been well content to remain on the defensive. As, however, Karl had refused to give any help to the spring offensive in France, except a few heavy batteries,[2] it was impossible to evade Hindenburg's demand for a vigorous effort on their own front.

In view of the fact that the opposing armies were approximately equal in numbers, Arz wished to postpone the operation as long as possible, and to keep it within modest limits. He intended to strike on either side of the Montello, the long guardian hill of the middle Piave, and simultaneously against Monte Grappa. If these converging blows were successful, the Italians might be driven back to the Adige with the minimum of effort. He felt convinced, however, that his resources were insufficient to compel peace through a decisive victory; moreover, he

[1] The writer's battalion, which was in Italy throughout the whole period and took part in both the June and October battles, lost in all twenty-three killed and 117 wounded. Its casualties for the two preceding years in France were about 600 and 800 respectively.

[2] These were very ill supplied with munitions and of little service. The Austrian War Office actually requested payment for these projectiles until they were informed that a counter-claim for German shells expended in Italy would weigh down the balance very heavily against them.

was far from master in his own house, the army commanders despising him as a mere 'court' adjutant, Karl's pleasant-spoken favourite.

With pitiable complaisance he allowed a plan to emerge which was simply a botched-up *cento* of the incompatible demands of his imperious captains. Conrad insisted on his old idea of a great drive from Asiago. That was accepted and the Grappa operation was to be worked in as a subsidiary. Boroevic declared: 'If Conrad attacks, I attack too'; and he was allotted an equal number of divisions for assaulting the whole line of the Piave. As if this was not enough, another general was flattered with the permission to use two divisions in a pet scheme against the Tonale Pass, near the Swiss frontier.

No attack in the whole war was so uselessly frittered and dispersed over so wide a front. Failure was made more certain by the weakness of the artillery preparation, in theory a slavish copy of the latest German model. Opposite the British the gas bombardment was so ineffective that they were astonished to learn from prisoners that it had been extensively used. The enemy had no advantage of surprise, for deserters with their usual regularity had revealed the plan and hour. Nevertheless the Austrian troops, in their last offensive battle, pressed bravely forward, and very hopeful messages streamed back to Headquarters during the first few hours. That evening, in Trent, Karl, Arz, and Conrad held a kind of Belshazzar's feast with the General Staff. As they were dining cheerfully the telephone rang. Conrad received the news that the attack on Tonale had completely failed. That was a small matter. A little later he was called up again to hear that the great main hope at Asiago had been shattered. The troops were everywhere back in their lines of departure. Forty thousand men had been lost, and not a single division was in a position to renew the fight. The diners were utterly cast down; a council of war was immediately held. As a forlorn hope it was decided to continue on the Piave where Boroevic had cut two deep slices into enemy territory, on the Montello and on the lower Piave. A few days sufficed to make failure here no less patent than farther west. The two bridge-heads were isolated and hemmed in. The stream came down in a summer flood, and washed away many of the bridges. To demands for reinforcements Arz replied that he had not a single fresh division. Boroevic retorted with justification, 'that is not the way to wage war', but he had to withdraw his troops speedily if he were to avoid a catastrophe. Fortunately for him the Italians felt their way forward with a caution scarcely distinguishable from timidity, and he got back to his old lines without major disaster. At least 150,000 of the best fighting men had been fruitlessly thrown away, and the Austrian army was permanently paralysed.[1]

II

The Italians, well content with their deliverance, proved exceedingly unresponsive to the demands of the Entente when the tide began to set so strongly in its favour in August.

Diaz had the support of his Government in refusing action unless he were reinforced by large numbers of Americans and supplied *gratis* with every kind of munition of war. The importunity of Imperiali, the Italian ambassador in London, so wearied Lord R. Cecil, then Foreign Secretary, that at the close of one interview he expressed himself more strongly than is usual between statesmen. Imperiali plaintively replied that 'he had never been so spoken to, even by the French!'

But after the collapse of Bulgaria the seeds of dissolution began to multiply with extreme rapidity in the body of the Dual Monarchy. The Hungarians turned alarmed and separatist eyes to their threatened Danube frontier They had already for months past treated Austria 'half as a foreigner, half as an enemy'. The Czechs and Southern

[1] How crushing this loss was may be gathered from the fact that, by October 1918, the whole available rifle strength against Italy had been reduced to a bare 300,000 men.

Slavs, now recognized as belligerents by the Entente, scenting the impending ruin, multiplied their disruptive activities. The contemptuous neglect with which the Entente had treated Karl's peace-note of September 14th made it obvious that his opponents confidently expected the 'ramshackle Empire' to commit suicide.

Its destruction was hastened by the despairing proclamation of October 16th, which transformed Austria into a federal state, granting full autonomy to the various nationalities. This death-bed manifesto was in itself grievously incomplete, for the iron resolution of the Magyars had assured that the integrity of all the lands historically belonging to the crown of Saint Stephen should be maintained. Thus the Rumanians, the Slovaks, and a great section of the Yugoslavs were to be abandoned to the hateful Hungarian yoke.

The Czechs, Poles, and Croats on their part mocked at so belated a concession; the confession of weakness only spurred them on to organize their own destinies with redoubled energy. The assurance of their coming 'nationality' was strengthened by Wilson's reply to the Emperor (October 15), in which he stated that he was 'no longer at liberty to accept a mere "autonomy" of these peoples as a basis of peace, but is obliged to insist that they, and not he, shall be the judge of what action on the part of the Austro-Hungarian Government will satisfy their aspirations'.

The body politic was thus writhing in its last throes when the Italians finally plucked up resolution to strike at its last instrument of unity, the army.

III

It had been said of the veteran Radetsky in 1848, when the Empire was riven with manifold revolution, that 'all Austria lies in your camp'. Though in 1918 there was no leader of the same compelling personality, the fighting army had yet wonderfully maintained its kernel of discipline. Its sacrifices had been most grievous, nearly two million dead and 1,800,000 prisoners. Desertion had further thinned its numbers; in Galicia alone it was reported that 40,000 desperate men were wandering about in great armed bands. And now, apart from scattered units in France, Albania, Serbia, and Ukraine, its whole surviving strength was waiting, without hope, deep in Italian soil. 'We are not heroes, we are beggars', cried out the poor men in the trenches in their tattered equipment, two-thirds of them without great-coats, half-starved, racked with influenza and malaria. Much as the Austrians fell behind their great ally in technical efficiency, it remains to the everlasting credit of their kindly and hard-working officers that this array of scarecrows and skeletons maintained for three days a strong and often desperate resistance to the utmost efforts of the whole Italian power.

Diaz had conceived his plan after the Bulgarian collapse. There is evidence that his Government feared lest the war should suddenly end before the army had moved, and that the results of such inaction would be to prejudice the Italian cause at the Peace Conference. In fact the attack came only just in time. Its intention was to break the enemy front in the region of the Grappa, thus isolating his right in the Trentino from the defenders of the Piave. The river line was then, in its turn, to be split in two by striking at the junction of two armies, always a sensitive point. In the event, the destruction of the enemy was achieved even beyond expectation, but not by this clean-cut strategy. The Austrians had massed their finest troops on the Grappa, and repeated assaults were beaten off without any important loss of ground. In consequence of this the crossing of the Piave proved to be decisive, for when the defences on the middle stream had been finally pierced, confusion and disarray ran with swiftness everywhere, converting the whole army within two days into a routed and hopeless mob.

Thus the first stage of the battle, which started on October 24th, the anniversary of Caporetto, answered not at all to Italian expectations. By the evening of the 26th the results were truly meagre; 25,000 men had fallen on the Grappa, and no lodgement had been made on the eastern bank of the Piave. The stream was in the usual flood, which always appeared to coincide with any fighting activity. A British division, the 7th, had indeed occupied for three days the great island of Papadopoli,[1] and three Italian detachments that of Caserta farther down-stream.

This, however, proved to be the end of the Austrian endurance. Next day the British and Italians broke through the river front, and thrusting cavalry and armoured cars far in advance, reached Vittorio Veneto, the enemy's Head-quarters, whence the battle was named, on October 30th. On the 27th Karl wrote to the German Emperor the despairing letter in which he expressed his irrevocable decision of immediately demanding a separate armistice without waiting for the result of the pending negotiations with Wilson. By so doing he vainly hoped to save the monarchical principle. But his Empire was beyond aid. Its component units were organizing themselves as independent states. The Hungarian Minister of War telegraphed to the Magyar units to lay down their arms. The military chancery at Vienna sent to the stricken and fugitive armies on October 31st the singular order to vote for or against the monarchy 'without compulsion from their officers'. But by now the barriers so long opposed between the disintegrating flood from the interior and the front had been completely swept away. Enormous fractions of the army fell daily into the enemy's hand, and the remainder melted away into groups of compatriots intent only on going home and helping to found their new nations. At every rail-head Magyars, Czechs, or Slavs fought for the trains to carry them away. 'Every man to his city and every man to his own country.' Unlike Russia, the Hapsburg Empire required no formal revolution to destroy

[1] Lord Cavan, who commanded the three British divisions left in Italy, had been given a new army of two British and two Italian divisions, which started the whole river-action by gaining a footing on the island during the night of October 23–4.

it, no months of gradual military disintegration to bring peace; this ancient and glorious monarchy simply fell to pieces like a machine which has been worked out.

The Austrian Staff, inefficient to the last, could not even conclude an armistice without bungling. The first emissary who crossed the lines on October 29th had no proper credentials. When these arrived it was noted with surprise that they were dated October 13th, a commission having been set up in Trent to study terms immediately after the dispatch of the first German peace-note. But its members were in no position to put up even a faint semblance of bargaining. It was useless for Arz, who had carefully kept himself in Vienna throughout these calamities, to enjoin that no humiliating conditions could be accepted. The Italian Command was naturally in no hurry, for every hour it was collecting most valuable booty and winning back territory. The Supreme War Council at Paris was studying the terms, and finally telegraphed them to Diaz on November 1st. 'We have left Karl his breeches and nothing else,' said Clemenceau cruelly.

Even now three days' delay was interposed while the Italian armies hunted the fugitives through the mountains and over the plains. By November 4th they had taken 500,000 prisoners and 7,000 guns.[1] They had entered Trent and Udine, and a naval expedition was landing at Trieste.

The most essential provision of this capitulation was for the free passage of Allied troops through Tyrol to attack Bavaria, which kindled the revolution in that country, and opened the back door of the mountains against Germany. The line of demarcation behind which the Austrians were to retire was drawn, not according to any military necessity, but in order to meet political claims; for it was to include, and did include, the territory promised to Italy by the Treaty of London. By it Istria and

[1] The writer's division (48th) took 25,000 prisoners and 600 guns, or about three men for every infantry soldier engaged in the advance. The total Italian casualties were about 37,000.

Dalmatia were left open to military occupation. The Austrian Admiralty hoped by a pitiable subterfuge to avoid the surrender of their fleet, which was on November 1st handed over to the hated Yugoslavs. The Italians, to whom the new colours were equally repulsive, torpedoed one of the great battleships in the interim, and placed their own crews aboard. This was the first of many disputes which envenomed the relations between Italy and the 'Succession State' for years after the war.

Within the territory of the defeated the transformation was rapid. Vienna would not keep Karl, and German-Austria, like the rest, created itself a republic.[1] The secret organization of the Czechs bore abundant fruit. The transfer of power was effected with astonishing smoothness and swiftness, and Professor Masaryk, the exiled head of the Nationalist movement, sat as President in the Palace of Prague, to which his father as imperial coachman had driven Francis Joseph.

[1] Hungary later on became a Regency, as it still is, and cannot be properly styled a Republic.

XXXVIII

THE OVERTHROW OF TURKEY

THE CONQUEST OF MESOPOTAMIA

I

'EXORIARE aliquis nostris ex ossibus ultor.' A worthy avenger of the great humiliation of Kut was not long in coming. The Turks themselves provided the opportunity. Despising the squandered and dispirited force, which for three months they had bloodily repulsed in the marshes, they detached an army corps to Persia to prey upon such parts of that unhappy and defenceless neutral as the Russians had not already devastated. So our expeditionary force was left at least twice as strong as its enemy, and was to increase yet more.

Robertson provided the man. The elderly relics of the Indian army were at last passed over by the elevation of a junior major-general in Mesopotamia. Sir Stanley Maude, who had won his fighting experience in France and Gallipoli, was a truly great soldier. Austere and exacting in his conception of duty, rigorous and minute in its performance, he had a concentrated devotion to his profession, not always associated with his nursing-mother the Brigade of Guards. 'His only holiday', it might be truly said, 'was to do his duty.'[1] A brother officer declared that he had never found so happy an admixture of strategical and tactical genius with capacity for staff work and the internal administration of an army. He had indeed a weakness for over-centralization and wore out both himself and others by his meticulous handling of unnecessary detail. Yet if this is a fault in modern war, it is certainly on the right side, for his methodical preparation, though sometimes verging on fussiness, led invariably to far-reaching victories. Modest and utterly unselfconscious, he had the essential kindliness so often found in dedicated lives, which was reflected in his gracious face, and earned him the constant

[1] Thucydides, i. 70; said of the Athenians.

affection of the men. Under his inspiration capable subordinates had every spur to give their best. His Inspector-General of Communications, MacMunn, entirely transformed the port of Basra,[1] and multiplied the rearward transportation system both by land and river. Complete organization was now always to precede action, for 'he that believeth shall not make haste'. When the attack began at the end of 1916 the British outnumbered the Turks by more than four to one; they were now lavishly supplied with the scientific equipment of modern war, while their enemies lay in the nakedness of increasing penury. The result could not be doubtful. Maude first ejected piecemeal the stubborn limpets who defended the maze of trenches on the right bank of the Tigris opposite Kut, and then by subtle feints achieved a crossing above the town. This success automatically forced the abandonment of the unconquered line at Sunnaiyat thirty miles farther down on the left bank.

The enemy was thus hustled into a hasty retreat on Baghdad. The armed river-craft, far outstripping the cavalry in enterprise and dash, converted it into a headlong rout. The Turks vainly tried to arrest their progress as they rounded the heads of the vast loops in which the Tigris flows. They caught up the retiring mainguard, which fell into such panic that thousands of men ran to the banks with upraised arms to surrender to four little vessels, a spectacle perhaps unique in war. The Turks lost three-quarters of their effectives before making a final stand for Baghdad, where the Diyala, a broad tributary, flows into the left bank near Ctesiphon arch, the scene of Townsend's Pyrrhic victory. The 6th North Lancashires made an epic crossing, a party of sixty men holding on to the farther bank for twenty-four hours without support.

The fabled city of the Caliphs fell to a conqueror for (it is said) the thirtieth time in history (March 1917). Distance gave enchantment to its blue and gold mosques and

[1] e.g. the time required for the turn-round of a ship in harbour was reduced from thirty days in 1916 to forty-eight hours in 1918.

minarets standing above laden orange-groves, but it was mainly a fetid and insanitary slum. To secure his conquest from attack or inundation Maude pushed farther up the three streams of Euphrates, Tigris, and Diyala and spent the burning summer in consolidation.[1]

The problems of civil administration were vigorously tackled by the great Political Officer, Sir Percy Cox. The Home Government, which had already staked out a claim to Mesopotamia by agreement with France,[2] desired to encourage Arab aspirations as far as possible without making any definite commitment. To this end a proclamation written in a kind of bastard biblical jargon had been prepared for the inhabitants, giving such delusive hopes to the Arabs as could subsequently be repudiated. At the same time Robertson with a soldier's realism urged the unwilling Maude to drill levies of this most treacherous people, writing that 'the Arab movement has been of distinct military advantage in the past and it would be unsound not to continue to encourage it'. These time-servers had all recognized the new conditions to the extent of killing, stripping, and mutilating Turkish as well as British stragglers. They were, however, far from welcoming a just and efficient government which interfered with their illicit activities. They viewed with great suspicion the blessings of the improvements in irrigation and agricultural production which were imposed upon them. Nor were they convinced of the permanent supremacy of their new masters. Enver was indeed during the summer of 1917 collecting a large force to drive the invaders out of Baghdad. But, as is related in the section on Palestine, this army had to be diverted thither in a futile attempt to stem Allenby's attack on Beersheba in September.

[1] The thermometer attained a daily height between 110° and 115° for months on end. The rainfall for the ten months March–December was 0·09 inches.

[2] The Sykes-Picot agreement of 1916 had arranged (i) an international zone in Palestine, (ii) a British zone in Basra and Baghdad, (iii) a French zone in Syria and Cilicia, (iv) an independent Arab state or federation between areas (ii) and (iii) itself divided into a British and a French sphere of influence.

After Maude died in November 1917 of cholera, his successor, Sir William Marshall, carried on his traditions worthily until the final victory. The triumph of the Bolsheviks and the peace concluded by them with Turkey (March 1918) caused great searchings of heart in London. It was anticipated that their armies in conjunction with the great masses of Austro-German prisoners interned in Turkestan and Siberia would sweep through Persia, invade Afghanistan, and force its ruler to depart from his faithful policy of neutrality and to attack India. Hence the Mesopotamian force threw out long but slender tentacles through Persia to the Caspian, where the immense oil-fields proved a powerful magnet.

The adventures of Dunsterville, the principal figure in these forlorn hopes, were very curious.[1] To achieve results by prestige rather than by power was the aim of these tiny columns. They tried vainly to co-operate with a faithless and rapacious crew of Tsarist Cossacks, called by the appropriate name of Partisans, whose brigandage intensified the bitter famine in southern Persia. In Hamadan and Kirmanshah hundreds died daily of starvation and all the main roads were littered with expiring victims.[2] Even cannibalism was added to the peak of horror. In Baku no less vain attempts were made to inspire Assyrian and Armenian levies to defend the town. The British had to trail back the seven hundred miles of the road to Baghdad, leaving a fleet of vessels to annoy the Bolsheviks on the Caspian, and bringing with them 50,000 Christian refugees in the last throes of exhaustion and terror, to be maintained at our cost in Mesopotamia.

Meanwhile the Turks, whose last reinforcements had been diverted by Enver to Armenia and the Caucasus, were being ever pushed back into the hills of the north. On the eve of the Armistice, after the destruction of their armies in Palestine, Marshall gained a crushing victory over the

[1] See *The Adventures of Dunsterforce*, by Maj.-Gen. L. C. Dunsterville (1920).

[2] See Sir Arnold Wilson, *Loyalties: Mesopotamia 1917–1920* (1931), pp. 32–4.

dispirited remnant south of Mosul, and occupied that city under his interpretation of the conditions of the Armistice. Including the immense throng of camp-followers from every part of Asia, he commanded nearly 500,000 men and by far the biggest river fleet in the world.[1] After the fall of Kut our widely flung forces were seldom opposed by more than 20,000 fighting Turks.

To this extent and by its converging direction over the great spaces of Asia it facilitated the stages of Allenby's advance to decisive triumph.

THE FINAL CAMPAIGN IN PALESTINE

II

The second battle of Gaza exasperated the War Cabinet. The army, of whose capacity they had received such optimistic reports, seemed destined to lie in spiritless inaction before the fortified gateway of Palestine. Lloyd George had already envisaged it as the principal instrument by which Turkey was to be driven out of the war, and was determined that it should be used offensively for this purpose. Accordingly Murray was recalled (June 1917), and Allenby brought in his stead from the 3rd army in France, where his laurels gained at Arras were yet fresh. It was an inspired choice. There were too many cavalry generals in the West, many of whom never comprehended the scientific and methodical elaboration of siege warfare. Allenby proved easily the best among them; indeed, it may be well held that his strategic handling of cavalry is unrivalled in British military history. He was thoroughly at home in an independent command, delighting in responsibility, but accessible and reasonable to his subordinates. Universally known as 'the Bull' from his enormous stature and heavy, determined face, he was a living personality to the troops amongst whom he constantly moved. He abandoned the Capuan splendours of remote Cairo and lived as a fighting

[1] The total number employed in this campaign between 1914 and 1918 was 889,702: the fleet in 1918 numbered 1,824 vessels with an establishment of 43,000 men.

general near the line. His presence infused energy and enterprise.

Lloyd George had told him on departure that he was expected to bring Jerusalem as a Christmas present to the British nation. So the summer and early autumn were consumed with the conception and preparation of a plan of offence.

It was impossible to make use of sea-power to effect a landing on the coast of Palestine. The rocky and turbulent coast denied access; even Jaffa, a so-called harbour, was merely an open roadstead. Moreover, even if the great hazard of isolated landings had been taken, the shipping crisis, now at its most dangerous height, forbade any increase in our sea-borne commitments.

The venture therefore must be by land. The Turkish position extended from Gaza to Beersheba, nearly twenty miles; the right flank resting upon the sea and the left scarcely less secure upon the tangled Judaean hills. It was not a continuous trench-line after the Western pattern, but consisted of three fortified areas connected by a chain of outposts. Gaza, the most elaborate, was separated by some eight miles from the central position of Sheria, which protected the narrow-gauge railway to Jaffa, the vital source of supply. Thence eastwards a lightly defended stretch of seven miles led to the strong point of Beersheba, the rail-head whence the attack on the canal had been organized.

At the time of Allenby's arrival the bulk of the British force was of necessity tied to the coastal strip, where alone the railway and pipe-line were available. But our new Commander had no intention of butting against the wall of Gaza. His plan was to seize Beersheba by a *coup de main*, to overrun the central defences by a flanking attack from the east, and then to entrap the garrison of Gaza by directing a mounted swarm towards the coast behind their backs.

The fulfilment of this scheme required time; and the utmost exertion was necessary to ensure its readiness by the end of October, when the advent of the rainy season was already imminent. Reinforcements of two divisions were drawn from Salonika and India, vast quantities of camels brought from Egypt with *fellaheen* drivers, whose conscription was an open violation of the British pledge that Egypt should bear no burden of the war. In order to deceive the enemy, whose aeroplanes held air-mastery until October, the bulk of troops was kept in the coastal area till the last possible moment, and the extension of the railway eastwards was similarly delayed. A famous ruse was played upon the enemy by a Colonel Meinertzhagen with singular success; after seeking contact with a Turkish patrol, he feigned a wound and dropped a wallet as he rode reeling away. Its ingeniously faked contents convinced the Turkish Staff that Allenby had reluctantly decided to concentrate upon Gaza; and their dispositions were taken accordingly. The Turks themselves were in the lengthy throes of organizing an offensive when the blow fell.

The collapse of Rumania and the staggering of revolutionary Russia had set free some of their best troops, which were being concentrated in Asia Minor under the inappropriate code-term of *Yilderim* or 'Lightning', with the famous Falkenhayn as commander. Enver wished to dispatch them against Baghdad, which had already fallen into British hands, but after long wrangling Falkenhayn secured them for Palestine. It was indeed obvious to the enemy that this southern flank must be firmly held, or his force in Mesopotamia would find its only route of supply cut if the British should advance to the Taurus. Moreover, it was hoped that the defeat of Allenby's army would enable the revolt in the Arabian desert to be crushed. Hussein, the wily Sheikh of Mecca, had already grievously humiliated Islam by besieging the sacred city. Sustained by monthly instalments of British gold, by warships in the Red Sea, and above all by the inscrutable genius of Colonel Lawrence, his irregulars harried the garrisons on the Hejaz railway for hundreds of miles. Lawrence, a young man of twenty-nine, who had spent some years excavating in the East after taking his degree at Oxford, exercised an astonishing ascendancy over the Arabs and scientifically organized their unrivalled endurance and mobility as guerrillas. The military importance of his exploits was not indeed great when weighed in the gigantic scale of the World War; but no other figure carried so mysterious a glamour of romance, enhanced as much by his aloofness and wilfulness as by the superb prose in which he has recounted his story.

The Turkish concentration, however, was too late even for defence. Its spear-head, the splendid 'German Asia Corps', a picked force of all arms amounting to some 6,500 men, was itself held up for two months till November 1st, 1917, at Haidar Pasha, the terminus on the eastern shore of the Bosporus, where it had the mortification of seeing the chief ammunition-dump blown up by British agents.

When the day of battle arrived (October 31) the Turks were outnumbered by nearly two to one in infantry, and ten to one in cavalry.[1] The unsuspected concentration against Beersheba proved overwhelming. It was captured, with its vital wells, on the first day, the *coup de grâce* being given by an Australian mounted brigade, who charged into the village from the east at sunset with drawn bayonets in their hand, as they had not yet been supplied with swords.

The enemy was now driven out of Gaza, which he held in strength, after a stiff fight, the attack being launched from the sand-dunes to avoid the dense cactus hedges and enclosed gardens of the southern suburbs, and supported by the fire of warships. Sheria also was outflanked from the east according to plan, and the whole of the prepared position had been lost. But the Turkish army as a whole, though cruelly mauled,[2] remained in being and reorganized itself on an insecure line some twenty miles farther

[1] The approximate numbers of fighting troops were—British: infantry 75,000, cavalry 17,000; Turks: 42,000 and 1,500.

[2] It lost 10,000 prisoners and 100 guns.

north. The mounted troops had indeed completed their coastward sweep, although just too late to close the net. They had been hampered by lack of water and by the omission (now remedied) to arm some units with the sword, which made it necessary to dismount for attacks which could have been speedily pressed home at the charge. Moreover, the Turkish rearguards bristled stubbornly with fight, and used their machine-guns cunningly.

The enemy was given no respite in his new positions. By November 16th he had lost the important junction where the railway from Jaffa to Jerusalem meets that running south to Beersheba.

The Turkish forces were thus split in two; half retired northwards along the coastal plain, half into the hills of Judaea, the immemorial defences of Jerusalem. The latter force precariously relied upon one metalled road running north to Nablus, and on any chance supplies that might be brought from Trans-Jordan by way of Jericho.

The weather until now had favoured Allenby, but the rainy season, which lasts until April, was overdue. Still, he boldly decided to press on against Jerusalem before Falkenhayn had time to marshal his reinforcements for a counter-stroke. Maintaining a defensive in the plains, where his left rested among the orange-groves of Jaffa, he swung his right wing east into the almost pathless mountains. The determination to avoid any fighting within range of possible damage to the Holy City caused him to aim at its surrender by cutting its communications with Nablus eight miles to the north. But the cavalry, entangled in a broken maze of hills and ravines, made slippery by the nightly rains, were never able to reach the road. Farther south his infantry clung desperately to the commanding height known as Nebi-Samweil, whence the city was in prospect some six miles away. Around the mosque which marked the tomb of the prophet Samuel a ferocious hand-to-hand struggle endured for days. Had it not been for the donkey-transport, providently organized before the

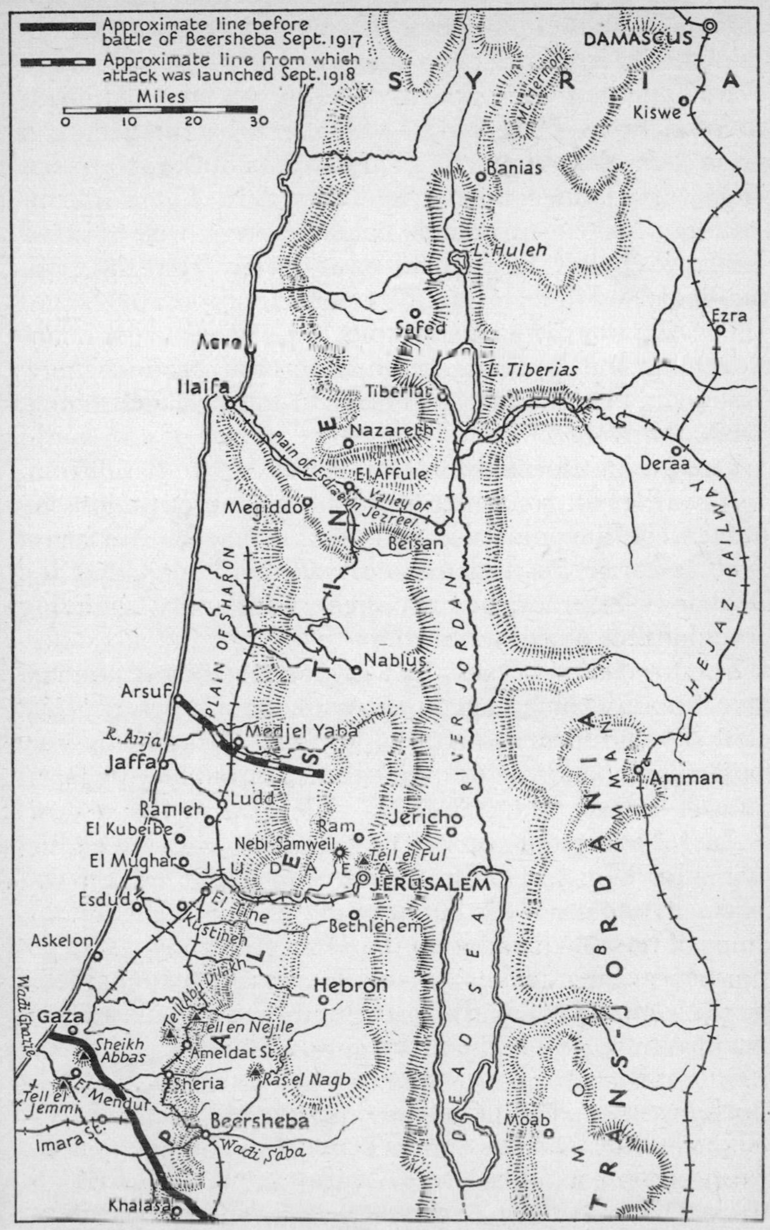

Map 34 Allenby's last campaign

campaign started, the British could never have maintained their precarious footing.

Allenby's army was now awkwardly placed, and invited a counter-attack. Its front was much lengthened, and curved from east to north. There were not enough troops to go round, and a gap five miles wide existed in the northern foot-hills. Fortunately Falkenhayn's well-directed efforts to exploit this gap failed, as the few Turkish troops available had to be brought by such circuitous routes that their sting was drawn before they arrived. Allenby's confidence in the spirit and endurance of his men was now justified. The assault was renewed round Nebi-Samweil, while the Holy City was threatened also from the south, where an unsuspected force appeared before Bethlehem.

The Turkish resistance suddenly collapsed; and they went while the going was still good, along the still intact Nablus road. So unsuspected was the climax that the Mayor of Jerusalem had the greatest difficulty in finding a responsible officer with whom to arrange the surrender. The official entry of Allenby was made on foot; its impressive humility being staged to provide the sharpest contrast with the flamboyant romanticism of the German Emperor, who twenty years before had ridden through a prepared breach in the wall.

The capture of Jerusalem was the only solid and enduring success of that lamentable year. Lloyd George was eager to exploit it further and urged upon Allenby the immediate task of knocking Turkey completely out of the war; promising reinforcements for that end from Mesopotamia and from France. He based his calculations on two assumptions, one of which was doubtful, while the other proved to be unfounded. The belief that Turkey could be induced by disaster in Palestine to make a separate peace, while German power remained unbroken in the West, was not shared by Allenby or by his advisers. Though the Turkish armies had been brought very low, and had lost an irreparable 25,000 men, they were far from the disintegrated condition which alone rendered possible the complete catastrophe of the following September.

The course of the war in France seemed indeed to favour Lloyd George's latter assumption: that the fortified trench system there was inexpugnable. The Allies, often in a superiority of five to three, had vainly battered for three years against the hostile wall. He was therefore confident that, with approximately equal numbers, they would be able to ward off the German assault already foreshadowed for the spring, while time could be found to open the back door into the house of the Central Powers by the subjugation of Turkey.

But before any effective steps had been taken to put this unhappy strategical plan to the test the events of March 21st fixed all eyes upon the death-struggle in France. Instead of receiving reinforcements from the West, Allenby was constrained during the next two months to send thither more than 60,000 of his best troops.[1] He was therefore reduced to an active defensive. And, being a man of great foresight and long plans, he looked forward to a date when he could deliver a decisive stroke by way of the coast. So his immediate endeavour was to alarm the Turks about their communications beyond the Jordan, and to pin down as large a force as possible in an area so eccentric from his true direction.

The threats of the Arabs against the Hejaz railway had grown more and more constant: they kept on settling upon some lonely bridge or culvert like destructive flies. Their bands, supported by British technical detachments, were raiding along the eastern shores of the Dead Sea. Allenby hoped to establish himself in the hills of Moab, and by cutting the railway at Amman to isolate completely the long-enduring Turkish garrison of Medina, which was still receiving sporadic supplies.

However, both the expeditions which he launched

[1] The excellent work done by Sir Charles Monro in expanding the military resources of India enabled Allenby to receive reinforcements from there without which his successes in 1918 would have been impossible.

beyond Jordan in the spring to attain this object were frustrated by the Turks, and the second came within a little of serious disaster, as the enemy defeated his flanking cavalry in the Jordan Valley, and nearly cut off its one road of retreat. But his main strategic object was accomplished, for from henceforward one-third of all the Turkish forces were retained east of the river.

Meanwhile Falkenhayn had been recalled and Liman von Sanders took his place (March 1, 1918). Liman with his long experience naturally understood the Turkish soldier better than his predecessor. Gallipoli had taught him that his great strength lay in defending trenches and fortified places, not in complicated battle manœuvres. He therefore cut down his reserves to a minimum, and held all important points as strongly as his feeble numbers permitted, retaining his incomparable Germans of the Asia Corps for the most vital services. But his lot was cast in a very evil ground. The army was melting away. Already in June he calculated that the number of deserters exceeded that of effectives. The troops were in rags; the summer heat scourged them with malaria and typhus. British propaganda showered upon them from the air, contrasting their miserable fate under their German masters with the well-fed happiness of prisoners, authenticated by photographs. The horses and baggage-animals either died or fell into such poor condition from lack of food that they could barely crawl a few hundred yards. Worst of all, Enver and the governing military clique in Constantinople had lost all interest in the Palestine front. Any available men were dispatched to adventures in the Caucasus and in Persia, where the peace of Brest-Litovsk had opened wide fields for Pan-Turanian dreams of empire. Enver even endeavoured to take away all the German detachments to hunt these shadows. Supplies for Palestine became smaller and smaller; coal and even wood became so scarce that the olive-yards and vine-yards had to be sacrificed to provide fuel for the engines. Having vainly threatened resignation, Liman was left to face the catastrophe, which he had constantly prophesied as impending.

The British, on the other hand, with a superb organization in the rear, were well clothed and well fed; except in the pestilential heat of the dust-choked Jordan Valley, 1,200 feet below sea-level, the summer brought no such epidemics as had devastated Gallipoli. The numbers of the army had been made up by Indian drafts, who were brigaded with British battalions to compensate for their lack of training. Everything was being secretly prepared for a master-stroke in September.

Allenby planned his 'knock-out blow' entirely on his own responsibility, for advice from home now breathed caution. A constant stream of deserters and spies gave him perfect knowledge of the numbers, disposition, and moral of the enemy. His own absolute air-mastery would make it possible both to conceal his preparations and to blind the enemy at the moment of decision.

He aimed therefore at a battle of annihilation. The astonishingly bold outlines of his scheme displayed complete confidence in the capacity and endurance of his troops. Its essence was secrecy in preparation and rapidity in execution. 'Time', he told his men, 'is the enemy, rather than the Turks.'

The Turkish communications depended entirely on Damascus. Only one railway ran south from that city as far as Deraa, where it forked. Its southern continuation was the Hejaz line, while its westward branch both fed the front and also served as a lateral communication, being prolonged across the plain of Esdraelon to the coast at Haifa.

Consequently it is clear that if the junction at Deraa were cut, no trains could run through to Damascus. Little importance was attached to south-bound traffic, as Syria had been so denuded of troops that no reinforcements could possibly arrive in time. The destruction of the railway at this point was entrusted to the Arabs. The enemy's rear would thus be dislocated and the eventual retreat of all his forces gravely compromised.

And Allenby counted upon even more than this; upon trapping the whole of the Turkish armies on this side Jordan long before they reached so distant a point. His intention was to open the wide coastal plain of Sharon to his cavalry by rolling up the enemy defences in this area towards the east. The disorganized Turks would thus be pinned against the hills, while a wide and effectual door was opened for the irruption of cavalry. Everything was staked upon this mass-ride of 15,000 men, who were to grasp securely the whole railway line in the valley of Jezreel between El Affule and Beisan within an outside limit of forty-eight hours. The retreating enemy would then emerge into their grasp from the northward exits of the Judaean hills, or would be forced to take the perilous passage across Jordan, up which stream other British forces would be advancing.

Such in outline was the plan, and its fulfilment was exact. Though Liman states that he anticipated an attack on the coast, he took no such steps to meet it as his depleted strength might perhaps just have allowed.[1] The British Staff, by an elaborate plan of deception, sought to turn his attention beyond Jordan. His eyes, moreover, were blinded by lack of air-reconnaissance; for only four enemy machines penetrated behind our front in September. The last hope of averting disaster was taken away when he refused the request of the local commander to withdraw his lines in the coastal sector.

Very early on the morning of September 19th overwhelming forces, accompanied, not preceded, by a hurricane bombardment, overran the weak and dispirited Turks, and shepherded the fugitives into the hills. The cavalry lost no time in exploiting the gap. Liman was cut off from all communication with the two army head-quarters west of Jordan by the furious bombing activity of the British air squadrons. He had, indeed, only one weak division in reserve, part of which was *en route* for Deraa, where the

[1] His rifle strength was about 30,000 as against 57,000 British. His cavalry was by now almost negligible.

Arabs had punctually performed their destructive part two days before. He did what little he could. He sent a detachment of head-quarters troops from Nazareth to guard the low but rocky pass by which the cavalry must emerge into the plain of Esdraelon. But they loitered by the way, and let the British through unopposed that night. Early on the 20th Nazareth itself was raided. Liman was almost caught in bed, but helped to organize a heroic resistance by the German clerks from the balconies and windows of the steep streets, and escaped safely to Tiberias. By sunset that day the whole valley-line from El Affule to Beisan[1] was picketed by cavalry waiting for their victims to emerge from the hills. Within the tangle of these hills utter confusion reigned; only the German detachment preserved its cohesion. By the evening of September 21st the destruction of the two Turkish armies west of Jordan had been completed. Their guns and transport were wrecked in the defile leading east from Nablus to the river. This was by far the most effective piece of ruinous pursuit from the air achieved anywhere during the war. The battle was appropriately called Megiddo, the modern version of 'the place which is called in the Hebrew tongue Armageddon', where John saw in a vision all the nations gathered together to battle.[2]

The fate of the IVth army beyond Jordan was even more grievous because more protracted. Pursued by the British into the desert of Moab, it essayed a dolorous march towards Damascus, and was cut to pieces by the relentless Arabs. The enemy was in no position to offer any effective resistance south of Damascus. The British advance was limited only by questions of transport and supply. The capture of Haifa enabled the Navy to turn this port into a base, from which trains could be run direct to Deraa.

Damascus fell into our hands on October 2nd, the

[1] The distance covered to reach this point was seventy miles in thirty-four hours. The division which performed this march lost only twenty-six horses.

[2] Revelation xvi. 16. All five continents were represented in this battle, America being included with the West Indian detachment.

motley collection of nearly 20,000 men who were huddled together there surrendering after a mere show of resistance. By now 75,000 prisoners had been taken at a total cost of some 5,600 casualties.

During the last month of the campaign political problems were more thorny than military. As the conquest extended itself, Feisal, son of Hussein and Commander-in-Chief of the Arab armies, was insistent that all areas should be handed over to his administration, in accordance with the original promise made by the British that a united Arab state should be created. This promise, however, was inconsistent with the secret Franco-British arrangement of 1916, known as the Sykes-Picot agreement, by which the two countries had marked out Syria and Palestine as their respective spheres of influence. Feisal knew of this, and was naturally determined to prejudge any final settlement by entering upon instant possession. Allenby had therefore to arrange a workable provisional compromise.[1] By the end of October the advance had been pushed a farther 200 miles north. Aleppo came into British possession at the moment when the Armistice was concluded with Turkey. With singular appropriateness Mustapha Kemal, the regenerator and ruler of post-war Turkey, had been left to keep alive the last dying flicker of resistance. The Ottoman Empire was without hope since the surrender of Bulgaria (September 30), which cut it off from Germany, and left the Thracian frontier at the mercy of the Entente. The disaster in Palestine did little more than throw into glaring relief the complete military impotence of Turkey.

Hence the terms of the Armistice were not dictated by Allenby, but by the Commander-in-Chief of the Mediterranean fleet (Sir S. Calthorpe), who dealt directly with the Government at Constantinople. The latter attempted to gain mitigated terms by bringing Townshend out of his luxurious captivity to act as an intermediary, a part which

[1] The final settlement by the statesmen at Versailles falls outside the scope of this work.

his vanity led him afterwards to invest with a grotesque importance. The conditions actually imposed amounted to complete surrender. The Dardanelles were opened, and Constantinople was speedily occupied by the forces of the Allies.

EPILOGUE

THE events of 1914–1918 have proved to demonstration that war between great states, equipped with all the resources of science, cannot now be regarded as 'an instrument of policy'. It becomes inevitably a struggle for existence, in which no limit can be placed on the expenditure of men and money, no objectives can be clearly defined and no peace by an agreed compromise attained.

Its object gradually became not merely to destroy the armed forces of the belligerents, vast beyond comparison as they became, but also to break the war-will of the peoples. Consequently in the latter stages of the war the desire to make intolerable the lives of all enemies, without distinction of age and sex, was limited only by the capacity of fulfilment. As was truly said, 'the side with the strongest nerves will win'. Except for the million Armenians massacred by the Turks, and half that number of Kazaks (a Turkish-speaking tribe of Central Asia) exterminated by order of the Tsarist Government, the number of civilians actually killed by weapons of war was comparatively small. But it is probable that the total of those who succumbed to privation, starvation, and the influenza plague was at least twice that of the ten millions who fell in battle[1].

The examples of Belgium, Luxembourg, Greece, and Persia showed that a defenceless neutrality was a mere invitation to the interested aggressor; while the repercussions of the conflict over the whole world brought into the camp of the Entente such remote and improbable allies as China, Liberia, and Brazil. To maintain a secure neutrality was to walk on the slenderest of tight-ropes.

Such a conception of war inevitably exalted the power of the state beyond all modern precedent by its destruction of the liberty of individuals, who for the most part demanded or welcomed the fetters into which they were cast.

[1] In India alone during 1918–1919 the population was diminished by 16 millions through the influenza plague.

It also paradoxically enough limited the power of the statesmen to direct the course of the war itself.

The dividing line between politics and strategy in history has always been blurred. It was often obliterated in the last war for the benefit of the soldier. The plea of necessity in a life and death struggle put forward by the General Staffs often overrode considerations of the highest political expediency. The invasion of Belgium was accepted by the German Government on the assurance of the soldiers that the French fortified area on the Meuse and Moselle could not be taken in time to allow of final victory in the West within the required six weeks. Similarly the Admiralty, supported by the massive insistence of Hindenburg and Ludendorff, forced the reluctant Chancellor to embark upon the fatal submarine campaign. 'How could I be justified', he pleaded afterwards to the Reichstag Committee, 'in refusing to the German people a victory promised as certain by the highest experts?'

Ministers were apt to find themselves at the mercy of the idols which they had created. In order to sustain public cheerfulness and confidence they had been obliged to use every art of publicity and advertisement to sustain the great military figures whose mistakes were suppressed and successes exaggerated. Universal service itself powerfully contributed to exalt the prestige of the military and to depress that of the civilian leaders. In Germany the Centre party of the Reichstag actually went so far as to pass a formal resolution calling upon the Chancellor to be guided principally in the conduct of the war by the views of the General Staff (October 1916). Hindenburg indeed was almost deified by the common voice of his countrymen. Even in France and Great Britain, where ministers held the reins with a far firmer hand, we have seen how great was their difficulty in controlling or dismissing generals in whom they had lost confidence earlier than the public. Nor could they rely upon support from their Parliaments except to a most limited degree, because it was too dangerous to allow such large bodies access to the vital facts.[1]

Moreover, the extremely technical character of modern war, the vastest and most complicated of all business enterprises, made it possible for soldiers to bury almost any project of which they disapproved under a statistical mass of plausible objections, the validity of which could not possibly be tested. Contrariwise, it was exceedingly difficult for statesmen to refuse assent to any operation proposed by their military commanders. For where a fortified line without vulnerable flanks could only be frontally attacked, strategy itself was reduced to massed tactics. If the responsible commander declared that his tactical preparations were calculated to ensure success, it appeared the height of presumption for a civilian to question such an assurance. Yet the results of failure might prove so disastrous in casualties and loss of moral as to create a political question of the gravest moment. Lloyd George has vividly recorded the intense reluctance and foreboding with which he sanctioned the desperate campaign of Passchendaele. Painlevé's Cabinet took every measure short of a counter-order, which would have involved Nivelle's resignation, to discourage the attack in the Chemin des Dames, which produced an even graver menace to France than they had foreseen in the widespread mutinies.

Less easily explicable was the violent hostility often aroused, particularly in the British military hierarchy, by the strenuous and beneficent efforts of ministers to improve the weapons at the disposal of the army. The indispensable instruments of victory so eagerly offered by civilian hands were angrily rebuffed. Lloyd George was regarded as a squandering megalomaniac when he insisted upon the great programme of machine-guns and shells which, when completed, was thankfully accepted by its

[1] The Commissions of the French Chamber of Deputies exercised a more important and inquisitive influence over the conduct of the war than the legislature of any other country.

bitterest opponents. The history of the tanks is a classic example of the dogged determination with which G.H.Q. fought against the most fruitful of all modern improvements in the art of war. Modern war is truly 'too serious a business to be entrusted to soldiers', yet it seems inevitable that they should play a part of dangerous preponderance.

A captious and jealous rigidity of outlook, a purblind psychology, were inevitably common, as a consequence of their narrow education, among many great captains. Though most of them (except the British) had been trained to handle vast armies they were unfitted to direct or determine the paramount political issues involved in the protracted wrestle of the nations, linked up with each other in jarring coalitions. The example of Germany shows clearly that the soldiers were most dangerous where their success in the field was the most splendid. Falkenhayn alone recognized that Germany must at all costs avoid 'over straining herself within and without'. With his fall went the last solid chance of a compromised peace, the only real victory for the Central Powers after the Marne, for which Bethmann-Hollweg impotently worked. The great pair, who succeeded to supreme control at General Headquarters, never realized that the military situation at a given moment was no indication of the peace terms, which Germany would be able to obtain. On the contrary they worked with noble devotion and disregard of self to force the destinies of the country into an unfitting military frame. They could not understand that no defeat, however frightful, except that of the British navy, would compel their principal enemies to accept 'a German peace' as long as the spirit of the population remained unbroken.

Consequently the achievement of Lloyd George and Clemenceau in lifting up the hearts of their peoples and sustaining their resolve was of incomparable value. Ludendorff himself has expressed a wistful and pathetic surprise at 'the iron will' of the two democracies, so despised by the pre-war prophets of autocratic efficiency. In strategical conceptions the two differed sharply. If they had been colleagues throughout they would never have agreed upon how or where the war was to be won. Clemenceau was a stubborn Westerner, Lloyd George a passionate Easterner. Yet probably the most convinced partisan of either's strategy would agree that their supreme importance lay in an unrivalled power of convincing their countrymen by example, precept, and the fire of the spirit that the war must and could be won somehow. 'Faith is the substance of things hoped for, the evidence of things not seen.' 'After every defeat', as it was written of the French revolutionaries, 'they prepared for an impossible but certain victory.'

Yet while the war could not be won by the fighting men alone, nothing in history is more astonishing than the endurance, patience, and good humour so generally shown by the great masses of hastily trained civilians from all the great countries engaged. In former campaigns, except during the comparatively rare incidents of battle, troops were generally withdrawn from the immediate contact of the enemy and immune from danger. In the Great War a large proportion of the total forces were continually standing over against each other in trenches sometimes a bare thirty yards apart. In dangerous sectors such as Ypres the normal wastage of a battalion acting as trench garrison would be at least twenty men a day. Men would live for long spells under conditions fouler and more horrible than the beasts that perish. Nor in the latter years did withdrawal even far behind the lines bring security and relaxation of spirit. If a billet was beyond the twenty-mile range of great guns, it was exposed to the more terrifying assaults of aircraft.

Moreover, the actual losses in battle far exceeded any proportion known to modern warfare. It had been calculated that no unit could maintain any fighting efficiency, if its casualties exceeded 50 per cent. In all the great battles, however, such a loss was often and greatly exceeded. Battalions would constantly emerge with one or two officers, and less than a hundred men, to be thrown after remaking within six weeks or two months into a no less consuming furnace. 'Many are the marvels', wrote the tragedian of ancient Greece, 'and nothing is more marvellous than man.'[1]

[1] πολλὰ τὰ δεινὰ κοὐδὲν ἀνθρώπου δεινότερον πέλει.—Sophocles, *Antigone*, 332.

APPENDIX I

CASUALTIES

THE total number of casualties suffered in the war will never be accurately known. Some countries, as Russia, Turkey, and Serbia, kept very imperfect statistical records. In France the total number of wounded has never been published. In Germany the lightly wounded remaining with their units were not included in the casualty lists. In order therefore to make an exact comparison with the British figures it would be necessary to add about 25 per cent. to the number of the German wounded. In many countries the proportion between missing and prisoners remains quite uncertain, owing to the revolutions, and changes in political boundaries which succeeded the war.

It is generally supposed that the total military and naval deaths amount to between ten and thirteen millions. One authority[1] reckons as follows:

Known Deaths . .	10,004,771
Presumed Deaths . .	2,991,800
	12,996,571

This total includes deaths from disease, as far as they were separately recorded from those of the civil population, as well as deaths in action.

Some detailed figures of the losses of the principal belligerents now follow.

I. BRITISH EMPIRE (*including* INDIA)

Total Enlistments 9,496,170. Total Deaths 947,023.
Total Wounded 2,121,906. Total Prisoners of War 191,652.

Grand Total 3,260,581[2]

Of this total the following proportion came from Great Britain and Ireland.

Total Enlistments 6,211,427. Total Deaths 744,702.
Total Wounded 1,693,262. Total Prisoners of War 170,389.

Grand Total 2,618,353

[1] E. L. Bogart, *Direct and Indirect Costs of the Great World War* (1920).
[2] *Hansard Parliamentary Debates*, May 5, 1921.

II. FRANCE[1] (*incomplete*)

Dead and Missing . .	1,385,300	(including 58,000 coloured troops)
Prisoners . . .	446,300	
Discharged owing to Wounds	447,000	
Total	2,831,600	

The total number of seriously wounded ('mutilés de guerre') is commonly given as about 2,000,000.

III. ITALY.

Dead . . .	460,000
Wounded . .	947,000
Prisoners . .	530,000
Total	1,937,000

IV. RUSSIA (*incomplete*)

Dead . . .	1,700,000
Wounded . .	4,950,000
Prisoners . .	2,500,000
Total	9,150,000

V. UNITED STATES

Dead (including died of disease in U.S.A.)	115,660
Wounded	205,690
Prisoners and Missing	4,526
Total	325,876

VI. GERMANY

Dead . . .	1,808,545
Wounded . .	4,247,143
Prisoners . .	617,922[2]
Total	6,673,610

VII. AUSTRIA-HUNGARY (*partly conjectural*)

Dead . . .	1,200,000
Wounded . .	3,620,000
Prisoners . .	2,200,000
Total	7,020,000

[1] These and subsequent figures are mainly taken from *Statistics of the Military Effort of the British Empire during the Great War* ([illegible])

[2] These are the official German figures but they are manifestly incorrect, as 774,000 Germans were taken prisoner in the West and nearly 150,000 in Russia, Palestine, and Africa.

VIII. Turkey (*very incomplete*)

Killed and Died	325,000
Wounded	400,000
Untabulated	1,565,000
Total	2,290,000

APPENDIX II

TABLE OF PRINCIPAL EVENTS

1914	Western Front.	Eastern Front (including Serbia).	Turkish Front.	Naval.	Political.
Aug. 1.	.. ..	War declared by Germany on Russia.			
2.	War declared by Germany on France. Luxembourg invaded.				
4.	Belgium invaded. War between Great Britain and Germany.				
10.	.. ..	.. ..	.. ..	*Goeben* and *Breslau* enter Dardanelles.	
14.	Battle of the Frontiers begins.				
17.	Last fort of Liége surrenders.				
23.	Mons.	.. ..	.. ..	.. ..	Japan declares war on Germany.
26.	Le Cateau.				
28.	.. ..	.. ..	.. ..	Heligoland.	
29.	Guise.				
30.	.. ..	Tannenberg. 1st Austrian invasion of Serbia defeated.			
Sept. 3.	.. ..	Lemberg.	.. ..	.. ..	Entente Treaty to make only a common peace.
6–11.	Marne.				
13–25.	Aisne.				
Oct. 9–19.	.. ..	1st battle of Warsaw.			
10.	Fall of Antwerp.				
19.	1st battle of Ypres begins.				
Nov. 1.	.. ..	2nd invasion of Serbia begins.	War with Turkey.	Coronel.	
9.	.. ..	.. ..	.. ..	*Emden* destroyed.	
11.	.. ..	2nd battle of Warsaw begins.			
18–25.	.. ..	Lodz.			
Dec. 6.	.. ..	Austrian rout in Serbia.			
8.	.. ..	.. ..	.. ..	Falkland Islands.	

1915		Western Front.	Italian Front.	Eastern Front (including Serbia).	Turkish Front.	Naval.	Political.
Jan.	2	.. ..	.. ..	.. ..	Turkish defeat in Armenia.		
	19.	.. ..	.. ..	.. ..	.. ..	. ..	1st Zeppelin Raid on England.
Feb.	4.	.. ..	.. ..	Winter battle in Masuria.			
	18.	.. ..	.. ..	.. ..	.. ..	1st German submarine campaign opens.	
March	1.	.. ..	.. ..	.. ..	.. ..	British blockade of Germany begins.	
	10.	Neuve Chapelle.					
	18.	.. ..	.. ..	.. ..	.. ..	Failure of attempt to force Dardanelles.	
	22.	.. ..	.. ..	Fall of Przemysl.			
April	22.	2nd battle of Ypres begins. First German gas attack.					
	25	.. ..	.. ..	.. ..	Landing on Gallipoli.	Treaty of London signed	
May	1	.. ..	.. ..	Gorlice and Russian retreat.			
	9.	Franco-British offensive in Flanders and Artois.					
	23	.. ..	Italy declares war on Austria.				
	26	.. ..	.. ..	.. ..	.. ..	.. ..	British Coalition Ministry formed.
June	22	.. ..	.. ..	Lemberg retaken by Austrians.			
Aug.	4.	.. ..	.. ..	Fall of Warsaw.			
	6.	.. ..	.. ..	.. ..	Landing at Suvla.		
Sept.	25.	Franco-British offensive. Champagne and Loos.					
	28.	.. ..	.. ..	.. ..	Battle of Kut.		
Oct.	2.	.. ..	.. ..	Russian retreat ended.			
	5	.. ..	.. ..	Allied landing at Salonika.			
	7	.. ..	.. ..	3rd Austrian invasion of Serbia.			
	12	.. ..	.. ..	Bulgaria declares war on Serbia.			
Nov.	24	.. ..	.. ..	.. ..	Ctesiphon.		
	28	.. ..	.. ..	Serbia conquered.			
Dec.	19	Haig appointed Commander-in-Chief.					
	20	.. ..	.. ..	.. ..	Suvla and Anzac evacuated.		

1916		Western Front.	Italian Front.	Eastern Front (including Rumania).	Turkish Front.	Naval.	Political.
Jan.	8.	.. ..	.. ..	.. ..	Helles evacuated.		
	16.	.. ..	.. ..	.. ..	Fall of Erzerum.		
Feb.	21.	Battle of Verdun begins.					
March	18.	.. ..	.. ..	Lake Narotch.			
April	29.	.. ..	.. ..	.. ..	Fall of Kut.		
May	14.	.. ..	Austrian attack in Trentino.				
	31.	.. ..	.. ..	.. ..	.. ..	Battle of Jutland.	
June	4.	.. ..	.. ..	Brussilov's offensive in Galicia beings.			
	5.	.. ..	.. ..	.. ..	.. ..	.. ..	Death of Kitchener.
July	1.	Battle of Somme begins.					
Aug.	8.	.. ..	Italians take Gorizia.				
	27.	.. ..	.. ..	Rumania declares war on Austria.	.. ..	.. ..	Hindenburg and Ludendorff become head of the German Staff.
Sept.	15.	First use of tanks.					
	24.	.. ..	.. ..	.. ..	.. ..	.. ..	Venizelos forms provisional government at Salonika.
Oct.	24.	Recapture of Douaumont.					
Nov.	13.	Battle of Ancre.					
Dec.	6.	.. ..	.. ..	Fall of Bucharest.	.. ..	.. ..	Lloyd George forms War Cabinet.
	12.	.. ..	.. ..	.. ..	.. ..	.. ..	German Peace note.
	18.	.. ..	.. ..	.. ..	.. ..	.. ..	American Peace note.

1917		Western Front.	Italian Front.	Eastern Front (including Rumania).	Turkish Front.	Naval.	Political.
Feb.	1.	.. ..	.. ..	.. ..	.. ..	Unrestricted submarine warfare begins.	U.S.A. breaks off diplomatic relationship with Germany.
March	11.	.. ..	.. ..	.. ..	Fall of Baghdad.		
	12.	.. ..	.. ..	.. ..	.. ..	.. ..	Russian Revolution begins.
	14.	German retreat to Hindenburg Line.					
	26.	.. ..	.. ..	.. ..	1st battle of Gaza.		
April	6.	.. ..	.. ..	.. ..	.. ..	.. ..	U.S.A. declares war on Germany.
	9.	Arras.					
	16.	French attack on Chemin des Dames defeated.					
June	7.	Messines.					
	11.	.. ..	.. ..	.. ..	.. ..	.. ..	Deposition of Constantine.
July	1.	.. ..	.. ..	Last Russian offensive in Galicia.			
	19.	.. ..	.. ..	.. ..	.. ..	.. ..	Peace Resolution in Reichstag.
	31.	3rd battle of Ypres begins.					
Aug.	1	.. ..	.. ..	.. ..	.. ..	.. ..	Papal Peace note.
	17	.. ..	Last Italian offensive on Isonzo.				
Sept	3	.. ..	.. ..	Fall of Riga.			
Oct.	24	.. ..	Italians routed at Caporetto.	.. ..	.. ..	.. ..	Bolsheviks seize power.
Nov.	7	.. ..	Italian stand on Piave.				
	9.	.. ..	.. ..	.. ..	.. ..	.. ..	Clemenceau becomes Premier.
	20.	Cambrai. First massed tank attack.					
	29.	.. ..	.. ..	.. ..	.. ..	.. ..	Lansdowne Peace letter.
Dec.	3	.. ..	.. ..	.. ..	Capture of Jerusalem.		
	17	.. ..	.. ..	Armistice between Central Powers and Russia.			

1918		Western Front.	Italian Front.	Eastern Front.	Turkish Front.	Naval.	Political.
March	3.	.. ..	.. ..	.. ..	.. ..	.. ..	Peace of Brest-Litovsk.
	21.	1st German attack against British in Picardy.					
	26.	.. ..	.. ..	.. ..	.. ..	.. ..	Foch appointed Commander-in-Chief of Allied Armies.
April	9.	2nd German attack in Flanders.					
	23.	.. ..	.. ..	.. ..	.. ..	Zeebrugge.	
May	9.	.. ..	.. ..	.. ..	.. ..	Ostend.	
	27.	3rd German attack on Chemin des Dames.					
June	15.	.. ..	Last Austrian attack against Italy defeated.				
July	15.	Last German attack on Marne.					
	18.	Foch's counterstroke on the Ourcq.					
Aug.	8.	Battle of Amiens begins.					
	14.	.. ..	.. ..	.. ..	.. ..	.. ..	German Crown Council at Spa.
Sept.	2.	Drocourt–Quéant line broken.					
	12.	American Victory at St. Mihiel.					
	14.	.. ..	.. ..	General attack on Bulgaria begins.			
	15.	.. ..	.. ..	.. ..	.. ..	.. ..	Austrian Peace move.
	18.	.. ..	.. ..	.. ..	Battle of Megiddo begins.		
	26.	General Allied attack.	.. ..	.. ..	.. ..	.. ..	Bulgarian Armistice.
	29.	Hindenburg line broken.					
Oct.	3.	.. ..	.. ..	.. ..	.. ..	.. ..	Prince Max of Baden Chancellor. 1st German Peace note.
	23.	.. ..	.. ..	.. ..	Final advance in Mesopotamia begins.		
	24.	.. ..	Italian attack begins.				
	29.	.. ..	.. ..	.. ..	.. ..	German mutiny begins.	
	30.	.. ..	.. ..	.. ..	.. ..	.. ..	Turkish Armistice.
Nov.	2.	Last General attack begins.	Austrians routed and dispersed.				
	3.	.. ..	.. ..	.. ..	.. ..	.. ..	Austrian Armistice.
	4.	.. ..	.. ..	.. ..	.. ..	.. ..	Revolution in Germany begins.
	9.	.. ..	.. ..	.. ..	.. ..	.. ..	Abdication of Kaiser. Republic proclaimed in Berlin.
	11.	British reach Mons.	.. ..	.. ..	.. ..	.. ..	German Armistice.
	21.	.. ..	.. ..	.. ..	.. ..	Surrender of German Battle Fleet.	

INDEX